FRENCH FOREIGN POLICY DURING THE ADMINISTRATION OF CARDINAL FLEURY
1726-1743

A STUDY IN DIPLOMACY AND COMMERCIAL DEVELOPMENT

BY

ARTHUR McCANDLESS WILSON

*Assistant Professor of Biography in
Dartmouth College*

GREENWOOD PRESS, PUBLISHERS
WESTPORT, CONNECTICUT

The Library of Congress has catalogued this publication as follows:

Library of Congress Cataloging in Publication Data

Wilson, Arthur McCandless, 1902–
    French foreign policy during the administration of
Cardinal Fleury, 1726-1743.

    Original ed. issued as vol. 40 of Harvard historical
studies series.
    Bibliography: p.
    1. France--Foreign relations. 2. Fleury, André
Hercule de, Cardinal, 1653-1743. 3. France--History
--Louis XV, 1715-1774. 4. France--Commerce--History.
I. Title. II. Series: Harvard historical studies,
v. 40.
DC133.5.W5 1972   327.44   70-138193
ISBN 0-8371-5333-6

Originally published in 1936
by Harvard University Press, Cambridge

Reprinted with the permission
of Harvard University Press

First Greenwood Reprinting 1972

Library of Congress Catalogue Card Number 70-138193

ISBN 0-8371-5333-6

Printed in the United States of America

To
MARY,
known as
MAZIE

PREFACE

PHASES of the diplomatic history of the administration of Cardinal Fleury have been treated by several very able and distinguished scholars, but as yet there is no treatment of the subject as a whole. The excellent work of Mgr. Baudrillart is confined to the history of Franco-Spanish relations, and Armstrong's competent life of Elisabeth Farnese is also limited by its subject. The extremely detailed and comprehensive study by Mr. J. F. Chance stops with the signature of the Preliminaries of Peace at Paris on May 31, 1727, while Goslinga's work covers in detail only the period dating from the election of Slingelandt as Grand Pensionary of Holland on July 17, 1727, and has never been continued beyond the Treaty of Seville (November 9, 1729). The remarkable study by Professor Vaucher traces the course of Anglo-French relations but does not extend over the whole period of Fleury's administration. The articles contributed to the *English Historical Review* by Professor Basil Williams analyze brilliantly the diplomatic situation of all Europe, but stop short with the second Treaty of Vienna (March 16, 1731). Readers of the following pages will be able to observe how frequently the writer has alluded to the excellent contributions of Sir Richard Lodge.

French relations with the German princes are treated incidentally, although thoroughly, in the excellent publications of Arneth, Droysen, Erdmannsdörffer and Rosenlehner. Mention should also be made of the article on Chauvelin by Driault, of Vandal's book on the mission of Villeneuve, of Pierre Boyé's study of the diplomacy of the War of the Polish Succession (a work strongly characterized by prejudice against Fleury) and of Sautai's volumes on the origins of the War of the Austrian Succession. Only one work, that by Abbé Verlaque, has been published which purports to be a biography of Fleury (1878); a brief examination of it is sufficient to indicate that its author would have been better advised to write lives of the saints.

In the following pages an attempt has been made to analyze the essentials of French foreign policy throughout the whole of Fleury's administration. It will not be difficult to observe that the study of this period has led the author to reject the interpretation of Fleury's ministry as presented by the ingenuous prejudice of Saint-Simon, the poesy of Michelet, or the prose of Henri Martin. Instead has been adopted that "revisionist" conception of the Cardinal and his ministry signalized by the late Émile Bourgeois in his excellent article on Fleury in the *Encyclopaedia of the Social Sciences*. In brief, it is submitted that the Cardinal's misleading and disarming show of simplicity has tempted historians, as it tempted his contemporaries, to underestimate the skill with which he conducted French affairs.

In addition, the writer has endeavoured to analyze the relationship between Fleury's diplomatic, commercial and naval policies, on the one hand, and the notable revival of French trade and navigation, on the other. For this purpose contemporary opinion, principally as represented in British economic and political pamphlets, has been utilized as much as possible, together with the findings of that growing school of historians who are interesting themselves in the economic history of the eighteenth century.

The writer's interest in this period was awakened during his residence at Oxford (for which he is indebted to the Rhodes Trust) by C. T. Atkinson, Esq., Fellow and Tutor of Exeter College, and by L. G. Wickham Legg, Esq., Fellow and Tutor of New College, and University Lecturer in Modern History. To his sense of obligation to them, already profound, these scholars have immeasurably added by meticulously reading this study in manuscript and by contributing numerous invaluable criticisms and suggestions. Sometimes, although very infrequently, he has had the temerity to disregard the suggestions of such eminent authorities, and has thereby assumed a grave responsibility, he is well aware; consequently he should state that the responsibility for the views expressed in this volume is entirely his own.

For the preparation and publication of this volume the writer is pre-eminently indebted to Professor William Leonard Langer of Harvard University, whose generous aid and encouragement have been freely bestowed; the stimulus gained from acquaintance with him and the inspiration of the example of his scholarship make the student's relationship with him an abidingly memorable experience.

The writer desires likewise to express his gratitude for the valuable suggestions made by Professor Frank Maloy Anderson of Dartmouth College, who read this study in manuscript and whose native kindliness and indulgence for a colleague led him to give unsparingly of his time. Professor Ernest John Knapton of Wheaton College read the volume in proof and contributed many useful suggestions, hereby gratefully acknowledged. To the judgment, devotion and efficiency of Mary Tolford Wilson the writer's obligation is simply incalculable.

ARTHUR M. WILSON

Hanover, N. H.,
January 15, 1936.

NOTE ON DATES

Two calendars were in use during this period. Most European countries used the still current Gregorian or New Style, which in the eighteenth century was eleven days in advance of the Julian or Old Style used in Great Britain until 1752. The British were also accustomed to begin their year on Lady Day, March 25. For example, January 25, 1730 in Paris was January 14, 1729/30 in London. In order to avoid confusion, references in this volume to correspondence and despatches emanating from Great Britain have been accompanied by a notation indicating that the Old Style calendar was used.

TABLE OF CONTENTS

FRENCH FOREIGN POLICY
DURING THE ADMINISTRATION
OF CARDINAL FLEURY
1726-1743

CHAPTER I

FRENCH FOREIGN POLICY, 1715–1726, AND THE RISE OF FLEURY TO POWER

THE administration of Cardinal Fleury extended from June 11, 1726 to January 29, 1743. No student of French history can fail to notice the striking amelioration of the diplomatic and economic status of the country during that time. In 1726 the kingdom was still exhausted by the wars of Louis XIV and shaken by the financial schemes of Law and the readjustments which their collapse entailed; abroad, its security was menaced by the hostile alliance of Austria and Spain, at the same time that France's own diplomatic freedom of action had been forfeited to her ally, Great Britain, because of the blunders which the Duke of Bourbon, Fleury's predecessor, had committed.

Yet, in the later years of the Cardinal's administration, France enjoyed the diplomatic leadership of Europe. She had thrown off her dependence upon Great Britain, had fought a successful war and had obtained the reversion of Lorraine. Economically, she was a more prosperous and powerful state than she had been in 1726, a fact of enormous importance in view of the sharply contested struggle for empire between the French and the British which was soon to break out anew, a struggle in which issues were decided which have permanently affected the political environment of a large portion of mankind.

When one contrasts the exhausted France of 1715, the year of the death of Louis XIV, or the yet unrecuperated France of 1726, with the France which fought the War of the Austrian Succession so hard and so well that Great Britain emerged from that contest "a defeated state," as Sir Richard Lodge has remarked, it is evident that beneath the surface of the diplomatic

3

shifts and changes of Fleury's administration a great and significant accumulation of national energy was taking place.[1]

As a matter of course, whatever Fleury was able to effect, whether in the field of domestic or of foreign affairs, was subject to the limitations imposed by the events of the years just preceding his administration. Indeed, it is notable that the Cardinal was able to accomplish so much while labouring under such serious initial handicaps. If, therefore, we aspire to judge the policy of Fleury in its entirety, we must survey not only the expansion of French commerce during these years and the policy of the Cardinal relative to it, but also the political and diplomatic conditions of Europe and France subsequent to the Utrecht settlement, which provided the soil in which Fleury's policy was rooted.

To the period of French hegemony which Louis XIV imposed upon Europe with ever diminishing success after 1685, succeeded a period when the aims of French policy were more modestly limited to the maintenance of the balance of power. The transition was not immediately effected by the treaties which concluded the War of the Spanish Succession; the surreptitious support which Louis XIV gave to the Jacobites in 1715 betrayed the will to make good the pledge he had given in 1701, when he recognized the son of James II as England's lawful king. It was the acquisition of power by the Duke of Orleans which implicitly marked the change; on September 2, 1715, he broke the will of Louis XIV, with the assistance of the *Parlement* of Paris, and made himself sole regent of France. Only the frail existence of the infant Louis XV stood between him and the succession to the throne, provided that the abnegation of the French crown sworn to by Philip V for himself and his heirs held good. The personal interest of the man who had temporarily become the sole director of French policy lay in making sure that the French succession would proceed in the manner determined by article VI of the Anglo-French Treaty of Utrecht (April 11, 1713). The endeavour of Louis XIV to efface the memory of a humiliating treaty by an

---

[1] Sir Richard Lodge: "English Neutrality in the War of the Polish Succession." *Transactions of the Royal Historical Society*, Fourth Series, XIV (1931), p. 171.

attempt to nullify it as far as possible is easily comprehensible. The obvious policy for the Regent to adopt, on the other hand, was not to evade, but faithfully to perform, France's obligations; not to overturn, but scrupulously to maintain, the European balance which the Treaties of Utrecht had set up. In order that no deviation from the treaties might undermine the settlement upon which the dynastic ambitions of the Regent were founded, it was plain that France, under the Regent's direction, would ultimately stand forth as a conservative power.[2] Nor is it surprising that, in pursuance of this policy, the Regent and his adviser, the Abbé Dubois, should seek support from the other powers most deeply concerned in the maintenance of the separation of the crowns of France and Spain.

Here the Regent's policy and that of the Maritime Powers met on common ground. For commercial and political reasons, England and the United Provinces had fought the War of the Spanish Succession to prevent Spain and France from uniting in what was tantamount to a personal union. In 1712, Bolingbroke flattered himself that he had found a solution to the problem. In return for extensive principalities in Italy, Philip V, moved by the persuasion of Louis XIV, would relinquish his claims to Spain, which would then devolve to the House of Savoy. The unexpected repudiation of this scheme by Philip V had necessitated the *pis aller* of permitting him to retain the Spanish crown on condition of his solemn renunciation of his claim to the French inheritance. But it remained extremely doubtful whether this undertaking was not *ab initio* invalid. As Torcy wrote to Bolingbroke on March 22, 1712:

The renunciation desired would be null and invalid by the fundamental laws of France, according to which laws the nearest prince to the crown is of necessity the heir. This law is considered as the work of Him who has established all monarchies, and we are persuaded in France that God only can abolish it. No renunciation therefore can destroy it; and if the king of

---

[2] The Regent at first showed hostility to Great Britain, as well as a disposition to support the Jacobite cause; the growing tension of French relations with Spain was principally what caused him to seek an alliance with the British (Basil Williams: *Stanhope* [Oxford, 1932], p. 190; Alfred Baudrillart: *Philippe V et la cour de France* [Paris, 1890-(1901), five vols.], II, p. 258; Louis Wiesener: *Le Régent, l'abbé Dubois et les anglais* [Paris, 1891-1899, three vols.], I, pp. 109, 121).

Spain should renounce it for the sake of peace, and in obedience to his grandfather, they would deceive themselves, who received it as a sufficient expedient to prevent the mischief we purpose to avoid.[3]

One of the principal causes for the profound dissatisfaction of the Whigs with the Treaty of Utrecht was the fact that the solution of the problem of the Spanish succession had really opened up the question of the succession in France, and the transparent eagerness of Philip V to claim his birthright gave the British ample warning of what they might expect if Louis XV should die.[4] Moreover, if Philip V should choose to repudiate his solemn engagements, and if the party in France opposed to his succession should not be encouraged, it was by no means certain that Great Britain could prevent a second time the union of the crowns of France and Spain. Her new dynasty could not count on the undivided allegiance of the people, nor did the diplomatic alignments which William III had fastened into a Whig tradition promise to be strong enough for this contingency. For, although treaties were signed with the Dutch in February, and with the Emperor on May 25, of 1716, it was extremely uncertain whether the United Provinces and the Emperor, exhausted by one great struggle, would have the will or the means for engaging in another.[5] Moreover, the alarming posture of affairs in the Baltic

[3] William Coxe: *Memoirs of Horatio, Lord Walpole* (Third edition, London, 1820, two vols.), I, p. 50, note; cf. Jean-Baptiste Colbert, marquis de Torcy: *Memoirs of the Marquis of Torcy* (London, 1757, two vols.), II, pp. 287-289. Torcy's real purpose was to persuade the British to recognize the accession of some other French prince to the Spanish throne in the event that Philip V should become king of France (Baudrillart: *Philippe V et la cour de France*, I, pp. 472-474); nevertheless, the British found this line of argument extremely disconcerting. The renunciation made by Philip V *was* valid, however, independently of the sanctions in the Treaties of Utrecht (Alfred Baudrillart: "Examen des droits de Philippe V et de ses descendants au trône de France, *en dehors des revendications d'Utrecht.*" *Revue d'histoire diplomatique*, III [1889], pp. 161-191, 354-384). But this opinion was by no means the one generally accepted at the time.

[4] Philip V, indeed, had intended to claim the regency in France upon the death of Louis XIV, but had been forestalled by Philip, Duke of Orleans; see Baudrillart: *Philippe V et la cour de France*, I, pp. 583-590, 679-680.

[5] For the negotiations with the United Provinces, see Williams: *Stanhope*, p. 209; and Wolfgang Michael: *Englische Geschichte im achtzehnten Jahrhundert*. I: *Die Anfänge des Hauses Hannover* (Second edition, Berlin, 1921), pp. 663-664. For the treaty of May 25, 1716, see Williams: *op. cit.*, pp. 210-211; and Michael: *op. cit.*, pp. 674-678; the text was printed by Johann Jacob Schmauss: *Corpus juris gentium academicum* (Leipzig, 1730, two vols. paged continuously), pp. 1612-1615.

countries made it necessary for the British to consolidate their position in the rest of Europe. Consequently, the Whig solution to the problem which the Tories had posed but not solved was that startling diplomatic revolution by which Stanhope (and the United Provinces) accepted the alliance proffered by the Regent and Dubois (January 4, 1717).[6]

From the point of view of France, the alliance with Great Britain was by no means to be condemned merely because it happened to coincide with the personal interests of the Regent. The exhaustion of the country made a continuation of peace imperative, and this could be brought about most effectively by an unadventuresome and unaggressive policy which was content to associate itself with that of other powers equally solicitous of averting conflict. The Utrecht settlement had been as favourable to France as the adverse fortunes of war could well have permitted; it was sound policy, therefore, to co-operate with powers interested in protracting peace in order to render nugatory the schemes of dissatisfied monarchs, who might easily be tempted to seek their profit in the subversion of European tranquillity.

Every general peace settlement is likely to leave its participants divided into two categories—the satisfied and the unsatisfied. At this period, the Emperor was numbered among the discontented because he persisted in regarding himself as the legitimate and dispossessed sovereign of Spain; until his death he maintained a Spanish council which deliberated upon the affairs of Spain and Italy; *Hispaniarum rex* figured among the list of his titles, and he regularly nominated grandees of Spain and knights of the Golden Fleece in defiance of the protests of Philip V. As Austrian Archduke, Charles had received the warm support of the Maritime Powers in his bid for the Spanish inheritance; with more than a little naïveté, he tenaciously resented their having grown cool in his behalf when the unexpected death of his brother, Joseph I, made him the inheritor of the Austrian Haps-

---

[6] For excellent discussions of the origin and conclusion of the Triple Alliance, see Williams: *Stanhope*, pp. 211-229; Michael: *Englische Geschichte im 18. Jahrhundert*, I, pp. 747-770; for text of treaty, see Schmauss: *Corpus juris gentium academicum*, pp. 1624-1631.

burg dominions, whereby, had he made good his Spanish claims, he would have enjoyed the power wielded by Charles V. This resentment revealed itself not so much in overt attacks upon the Utrecht settlement as in a policy of disobligingness which can best be described as being perversely inert.

More dangerous to the peace of Europe was the policy of Spain, the other major power discontented with the Utrecht settlement. One disturbing factor was the personal antagonism between the Emperor and Philip V, who solemnly listed among his titles those of Archduke of Austria, Duke of Brabant and Milan, King of the Two Sicilies and of Sardinia, and Count of Hapsburg, of Flanders and of the Tyrol. Peace between these two rulers was not signed until 1725, and then only under circumstances which afflicted the rest of Europe with sensations of panic.[7] In the second place, Spanish policy was essentially a dynastic one, conducted with very little regard for consistency by rulers who might fairly be regarded as diplomatic adventurers. In spite of Louis XIV's admonition to be a good Spaniard, Philip V always remained more than half a Frenchman, more preoccupied with the chances of his succeeding to the French throne than with the patient elaboration of a national Spanish policy. Moreover, Philip V, whose "robust health and delicate conscience obliged him to remarry," was ruled by his second wife, Elisabeth Farnese, whose absolute dominion over her husband was signalized in the diplomatic correspondence of the time by the almost invariable yet irregular reference to "Their Catholic Majesties," rather than to "His Catholic Majesty." The influence of Elisabeth Farnese was exerted in utilizing the resources of Spanish diplomacy for the aggrandizement of her family. With a characteristically Italian love of intrigue, untempered by any experience in the ways of diplomacy, she schemed with indefatigable pertinacity to secure establishments in Italy for her children, Don Carlos and Don Philip, whose succession to the Spanish throne

---

[7] As part of the European settlement envisaged by the Quadruple Alliance in 1718, and in return for being permitted to exchange Sardinia for Sicily, Charles VI had previously, on September 16, 1718, signed a formal renunciation of Spain and the Spanish Indies (Baudrillart: *Philippe V et la cour de France*, II, p. 300).

was rendered remote by the existence of elder step-brothers. Consequently, in no other country of western Europe was the policy of the government so purely dynastic, so little national. Ordinarily, even a dynastic policy coincides in some respects with the interests of the nation over which the dynast happens to rule; but such was not the case with Elisabeth Farnese because the dynasty in which she was most interested was not the national one.

For years the vagaries of this adventuress puzzled European statesmen, because they could never quite rid themselves of the assumption that a Spanish queen ought to be solicitous for the interests of Spain; their distress was increased by the notorious instability of Spanish policy, owing to the influence of the Queen, who had no patience with the slow jogtrot of diplomatic negotiation, and who tried one alignment after another in such vertiginous succession that Spanish policy became predictable only in the sense that statesmen learned to be prepared for anything. Finally, the danger to European tranquillity arising from the dynastic schemes of the Spanish King and Queen was the more grave because any project enlisted the support of the Spanish nation, if veneered with a seeming desire to regain the portions of Charles II's dominions which had been wrested from Spain in the War of the Spanish Succession. Spaniards resented the loss of the Netherlands and the Italian dominions, and found the British possession of Minorca and Gibraltar particularly galling. It was therefore easy for a dynastic policy to utilize the national dissatisfaction with the Utrecht settlement.

How easily the tranquillity of Europe might be disturbed by the restless and adventuresome policy of a discontented power is shown by the effects of the grandiose schemes of Alberoni, the able Parmesan envoy to the Spanish court, whose personal influence with Elisabeth Farnese was so great that he exercised undisputed ministerial authority in Spain after he had encompassed the downfall of Cardinal del Judice in May 1716. In 1716 Alberoni secretly gave subsidies to Goertz in aid of that complicated Jacobite intrigue by which the Swedish minister hoped to retaliate for George I's participation in the Northern

War.[8] In 1717, the same year as that in which the Triple Alliance was formed, Alberoni took advantage of the Emperor's preoccupation in the Turkish war in which he was then engaged, to send an expeditionary force to Sardinia.[9] In 1718 he meditated an alliance with Sweden and Russia, for the ultimate purpose of bringing about an invasion of Great Britain in the interest of the Jacobites; endeavoured to raise the Hungarians under the leadership of Rákóczy; sent out a fleet and army which occupied Sicily in July; and by means of Cellamare, the Spanish ambassador at Paris, encouraged the conspiracy against the Regent which was discovered in December of that year.[10]

By these schemes, undertaken in a time of nominal peace, Alberoni seriously endangered the general tranquillity. The members of the Triple Alliance, in their self-appointed function of *pompiers de l'Europe*, endeavoured to quench the flames and render the incendiary harmless. Their ultimate success was obtained as an indirect result of the death of Charles XII of Sweden (December 11, 1718), the effect of whose violent career upon his country had demonstrated that it is not always a virtue not to know when one is beaten. The events of the Northern War and the designs of Charles XII to assist the Pretender had constituted

[8] Max Immich: *Geschichte des europäischen Staatensystems von 1660 bis 1789* (Munich, 1905), p. 248, note; William Kirk Dickson: *The Jacobite Attempt of 1719: Letters of James Butler, Second Duke of Ormonde, Relating to Cardinal Alberoni's Project for the Invasion of Great Britain on Behalf of the Stuarts, and to the Landing of a Spanish Expedition in Scotland* [*Publications of the Scottish History Society*, XIX], (Edinburgh, 1895), p. xxii. As a result of this plotting, the British arrested Gyllenborg, the Swedish ambassador at London, on Feb. 9, 1717, while the Dutch arrested Goertz, at that moment accredited to the United Provinces on a special mission, on Feb. 22, 1717 (J. F. Chance: *George I and the Northern War* [London, 1909], pp. 180-182; Williams: *Stanhope*, pp. 246-247; Michael: *Englische Geschichte im 18. Jahrhundert*, I, pp. 737-743).

[9] It is now generally agreed, however, that Philip V forced Alberoni to this action before the latter was quite prepared to undertake it; cf. Williams: *Stanhope*, pp. 281-282.

[10] Vincent Bacallar y Sanna, marquis de Saint-Philippe: *Mémoires pour servir à l'histoire d'Espagne sous le règne de Philippe V* (Amsterdam, 1756, four vols.), III, pp. 240-241, 252-254, 333-340, 354-365. The account by Lémontey of Alberoni's connection with the Cellamare conspiracy and the Breton uprising of 1719 is still a good one (Pierre-Édouard Lémontey: *Histoire de la Régence et de la minorité de Louis XV jusqu'au ministère du cardinal de Fleury* [Paris, 1832, two vols.], chapter vii).

the most pressing of the several cogent reasons for Great Britain's alacrity in concluding the Triple Alliance. The death of the King of Sweden was a notable piece of ill luck for Alberoni, since it deprived him of the opportunity of encouraging diversions in the north. Freed from the domination of their late king, the Swedish nobility set up the oligarchical Constitution of 1720, which effectually crippled the power of the crown until the *coup d'état* of Gustavus III in 1772, and bought off their enemies as best they could, in a manner which relegated Sweden to the position of a subordinate power.[11]

Meanwhile, through the mediation of the British, who desired that the Emperor might be free to devote his attention to the defense of his Italian possessions, the successful course of the Turkish war, which, by reason of Prince Eugene's victory at Peterwardein and the capture of Belgrade, had reflected so much glory on the Austrian arms, was cut short by the Treaty of Pas-

[11] These treaties were: I. Treaty of Stockholm, November 20, 1719, between Sweden and the Electorate of Hanover, which ceded Bremen and Verden to Hanover (Jean Dumont, baron de Carelscroon: *Corps universel diplomatique du droit des gens; contenant un recueil des traitez d'alliance. . . .* [Amsterdam and The Hague, 1726-1731, eight vols.], VIII, part ii, pp. 14-17); II. Treaty of peace between Great Britain and Sweden, signed at Stockholm, February 1, 1720, by which Sweden recognized Great Britain's chosen dynasty in return for the latter's good offices in endeavouring to secure from the Czar a peace favourable to Sweden (*ibid.*, pp. 18-21); III. Treaty of peace between Prussia and Sweden, signed at Stockholm on February 1, 1720, by which Sweden ceded West Pomerania, including Stettin, Wollin and Usedom (*ibid.*, pp. 21-26); IV. Treaty of peace between Sweden and Denmark, signed at Stockholm on June 14, 1720, by which Denmark renounced her Swedish conquests in return for the recognition of her claims to Schleswig (*ibid.*, pp. 29-33). These claims to Schleswig were guaranteed to Denmark by Great Britain and, most unwillingly, by France, in their capacity of joint mediators (Chance: *George I and the Northern War*, chapters xxii-xxvi, *passim; British Diplomatic Instructions, 1689-1789.* I: *Sweden, 1689-1727* [Edited for the Royal Historical Society by J. F. Chance; Camden Third Series XXXII, London, 1922], p. xxx). Frequent mention of the French guarantee of Schleswig is made in the papers of Lord Polwarth, British ambassador to Denmark, who collaborated with Carteret in the conclusion of this treaty (*Historical Manuscripts Commission: Report on the Manuscripts of Lord Polwarth* [London, 1911-1931, three vols.], vols. II and III, *passim* [consult indices], but esp. II, pp. 547, 573; and III, p. 23). V. The peace between Sweden and Russia, signed at Nystad on August 30, 1721, by which Sweden ceded Livonia, Esthonia, Ingria, Carelia and a small portion of Finland (Dumont: *Corps universel diplomatique*, VIII, part ii, pp. 36-39). See also Otto Brandt: "Das Problem der 'Ruhe des Nordens' im 18. Jahrhundert." *Historische Zeitschrift*, CXL (1929), pp. 553-555.

sarowitz, July 21, 1718.[12] With the purpose of assisting the Emperor in Italy while retaining at the same time some control over his actions there, France and Great Britain agreed on a solution of the Italian difficulty in a preliminary convention dated July 18, 1718, to which the Emperor reluctantly acceded in the Treaty of London, August 2, 1718.[13] By this instrument it was agreed that the contracting powers should force Spain to accede to the treaty; that the Emperor should exchange Sardinia with Victor Amadeus II for Sicily;[14] that, following the extinction of the male line in the duchies of Parma, Piacenza and Tuscany, those duchies should be regarded as fiefs of the Empire, provided that the Emperor should issue Letters Expectative for their investiture to the eldest son of Elisabeth Farnese; in the meantime, six thousand Swiss soldiers, maintained by the mediating powers, were to garrison Leghorn, Porto Ferrajo, Parma and Piacenza.[15] Other points were to be settled in a congress under the mediation of Great Britain and France.

Almost at the same time, Admiral Byng made the prolonged resistance of Spain to an accession to the treaty impossible by

---

[12] Dumont: *Corps universel diplomatique*, VIII, part i, pp. 520-524; Michael: *Englische Geschichte im 18. Jahrhundert*, I, pp. 813-831; A. C. Wood: "The English Embassy at Constantinople, 1660-1762." *English Historical Review*, XL (1925), pp. 549-550.

[13] Schmauss: *Corpus juris gentium academicum*, pp. 1722-1740. Stanhope and Dubois had had to bring extreme pressure to bear upon the Regent and D'Huxelles to persuade them to engage in this scheme for coercing Spain (Williams: *Stanhope*, pp. 284-301; Michael: *Englische Geschichte im 18. Jahrhundert*, I, pp. 787-803). Since it was supposed that the States-General would accede to the treaty of August 2, 1718, it was called the Quadruple Alliance, and, in deference to usage, it will be referred to as such in these pages. In fact, the United Provinces were never a member of the alliance (Williams: *Stanhope*, pp. 449-450). Dutch failure to accede made little practical difference, because the first separate article of the treaty provided for its being carried out even without their accession.

[14] This exchange was most distasteful to Victor Amadeus (Saint-Philippe: *Mémoires*, III, pp. 291-293). Nevertheless, he acceded on November 8, 1718 (Schmauss: *Corpus juris gentium academicum*, pp. 1740-1742).

[15] Elisabeth Farnese was the niece of the last Dukes of Parma, Francesco and Anthony Farnese, who died without heirs in 1727 and 1731, respectively. As for Tuscany, the last of the Medici were Duke John Gaston, who died in 1737, and his elder sister, the dowager Electress Palatine; the next in line of succession was Elisabeth Farnese, whose grandmother, Margaret de Medici, had married Odoardo, Duke of Parma.

destroying the Spanish fleet off Cape Passaro on August 11, 1718.[16] Since Alberoni still remained defiant and continued to encourage the Cellamare intrigue in France and the Jacobite attempt upon Scotland, Great Britain and France declared war on Spain, on December 27, 1718 and January 9, 1719, respectively.[17] The war which ensued was distinguished by no event worthy of note, save the burning of the dock yard at Pasajes, but it was sufficient to disillusion the King and Queen of Spain as to the feasibility of their policy of setting Europe by the ears; on December 5, 1719, Alberoni was made the scapegoat and dismissed; and on January 26, 1720, Philip V signified his accession to the Quadruple Alliance.

The dismissal of Alberoni implied a radical change in the character of the relations between Philip V and the Regent. The dynastic ambitions of the King of Spain had hitherto nullified the diplomatic co-operation between Spain and France which ought to have existed, according to general expectations, from the fact that a Bourbon sat upon the Spanish throne. As a result of the pressure brought to bear upon Spain by the Quadruple Alliance, it became evident that the policy thus far adopted, first of covert antagonism and then of overt hostility, to the Regent, was not very practical. In consequence of this object lesson, the occasion was propitious for attempting to draw some benefit from the fact that the Spanish sovereign was a Bourbon, and Dubois

---

[16] For an account of the action in Byng's own words, see *Hist. MSS. Comm.: Report on the Manuscripts of Lord Polwarth*, I, pp. 587-589; cf. also Saint-Philippe: *Mémoires*, III, pp. 297-306. Lord Hervey declared in his memoirs that Byng's action was owing to the secret oral instructions of George I, who desired to facilitate his being invested with Bremen and Verden by securing the Emperor's gratitude (John Hervey, Baron Hervey: *Some Materials towards Memoirs of the Reign of King George II by John, Lord Hervey* [Edited by Romney Sedgwick; London, 1931, three vols., paged continuously], pp. 37-38; see also, *ibid.*, p. 51).

[17] It was really Elisabeth Farnese who forced Alberoni to maintain resistance to France and Great Britain (Émile Bourgeois: *La diplomatie secrète au XVIIIe siècle*. II. *Le secret des Farnèse. Philippe V et la politique d'Alberoni* [Paris, (1909)], pp. 330-335; Michael: *Englische Geschichte im 18. Jahrhundert*, II, pp. 144-148; Williams: *Stanhope*, pp. 318-319). For the Jacobite rising of 1719 and Alberoni's connection with it, see Saint-Philippe: *Mémoires*, III, pp. 354-365; Dickson: *The Jacobite Attempt of 1719*, esp. pp. xxvi-xxix, 219-221, 222-223; Williams: *Stanhope*, pp. 323-327.

and the Regent hastened to take advantage of this posture of affairs. The Treaty of Madrid, dated March 27, 1721, restored peace between the two Bourbon kingdoms, and a separate article, to be kept secret even from France's ally, Great Britain, bound the Regent to endeavour to secure permission from the impending congress for the admission of Spanish instead of Swiss troops into the garrison towns mentioned in the Treaty of London.[18] To mutual antagonism had succeeded co-operation quite in the character of the later Family Compacts, so famous in the diplomatic history of the eighteenth century, and this change was emphasized by the announcement, on September 14, 1721, of the betrothal of the Infanta to Louis XV. The reconciliation between the Regent and Philip V proceeded so auspiciously that on January 20, 1722, Don Luis, the heir to the Spanish throne, married the Regent's eldest daughter; later in the year was announced the engagement of Don Carlos, the elder son of Philip V and Elisabeth Farnese, to the Regent's second daughter.

However risky it might be for Great Britain to pave the way, by her own efforts, for a resumption of the close relations and diplomatic co-operation between France and Spain, nevertheless the new orientation of Spanish policy, insofar as it implied a sincere acceptance of the Utrecht settlement, was most satisfactory to Great Britain. On June 13, 1721, a treaty of alliance was concluded by Spain, France and Great Britain, for the purpose of guaranteeing the succession of Don Carlos in the Italian duchies, as provided for in the Treaty of London of August 2, 1718.[19] On the same day, through the good offices of the Regent, peace had been concluded between Spain and Great Britain, whereby the British trading privileges were confirmed and the British possession of Minorca and Gibraltar recognized, although in what later proved to be a very equivocal manner.[20] The

[18] For the text of this treaty, see Alejandro del Cantillo: *Tratados, convenios y declaraciones de paz y de comercio.* . . . (Madrid, 1843), pp. 194-198.

[19] Dumont: *Corps universel diplomatique*, VIII, part ii, pp. 34-36.

[20] Far from being the cat's-paw of Great Britain, the Regent had attempted to secure Spanish gratitude at the expense of the British in the matter of Gibraltar. In a manifesto published soon after the declaration of war against Spain in 1719, the Regent twice referred to George I's conditional offer to surrender Gibraltar, made in 1718, as if it had been an absolute promise (*The King of France's Declaration*

abrupt transition, indicated by these Madrid treaties of 1721, from war to alliance was necessitated by the fact that it was now the Emperor who was recalcitrant. The advantages allotted to him by the Treaty of London, which were the possession of Sicily and the evacuation of the Spanish troops, he had obtained almost without effort, thanks to the activity of France and Great Britain, who lived to regret that they had not devised some means of collecting their price from him upon delivery. For the Emperor and his ministers now brought their very considerable powers of chicanery to bear upon the problem of deferring as long as possible the arrangements for the succession of Don Carlos in the Italian duchies. The object of the Treaty of Madrid of June 13, 1721 was to present a united diplomatic front to the Emperor, while restraining the King and Queen of Spain from another attack on Italy. War was indeed prevented, but it was long before the Emperor could be brought even to the point of negotiation, and the affair was not settled to the satisfaction of Elisabeth Farnese until 1731. As early as 1722, the representatives of the several powers met at Cambrai to hold the congress stipulated by the Treaty of London; there they remained, in solemn *fainéance*, spinning out protocols concerning the precedence to be

of War against Spain, Dated January 9, N.S., With a Manifesto, containing the Reasons; and a Postscript of an Intercepted Letter from Cardinal Alberoni to the Prince de Cellamare. Printed by His Majesty's Order at Paris [London, 1719], pp. 29-30, 35). Consequently, the Regent attempted to persuade Great Britain to concede the point, and appeared willing to break up the alliance if refused (Williams: _Stanhope_, pp. 346-349). Stanhope was willing to give up Gibraltar, and introduced a motion in Parliament to that effect in 1720; the opposition to it was so pronounced that it had to be dropped (Stanhope to Sir Luke Schaub, Paris, March 28, 1720 [Philip Henry Stanhope, Lord Mahon: _History of England from the Peace of Utrecht to the Peace of Versailles, 1713-1783_ (Fifth edition, London, 1858, seven vols.), II, pp. 128-129]). As late as October 1, 1720, Stanhope favoured the surrender of Gibraltar in return for trading concessions (Stanhope to Secretary Craggs [Mahon: _op. cit._, II, appendix, pp. xcvii-cii]). In order to secure peace with Spain, George I was prevailed upon to write, under date of June 1, 1721, an autograph letter to Philip V, "promising you to make use of the first favourable Opportunity to regulate this Article, with the Consent of my Parliament" (_The Historical Register, Containing an Impartial Relation of all Transactions, Foreign and Domestick_ [London, 1717-1738, twenty-three vols.], XIV [_1729_], pp. 144-145). In reality, this formula adjourned the matter to the Greek kalends, although the Spanish sovereigns accepted it in good faith. British statesmen kept the existence of this letter secret from Parliament for several years; it was divulged in 1728, to their considerable annoyance; see Michael: _Englische Geschichte im 18. Jahrhundert_, II, pp. 266-282.

accorded to their several cooks and lackeys, until after the deaths of Cardinal Dubois and the Regent. Not until January 1724, did Charles VI sign the Letters Expectative which recognized the eventual succession of Don Carlos in the Italian duchies, and not until then did the congress proceed to its labours.

By the time of the deaths of Dubois (August 10, 1723) and the Regent (December 2, 1723), the Triple Alliance had already accomplished a great deal.

It transformed the contested and inconclusive Peace of Utrecht into a durable peace. It imparted solid authority to the Utrecht settlement, by sanctioning anew the order of the succession to the throne, as it had been regulated in France and England. From it France got general benefit, just as from it also the Duke of Orleans derived individual profit, as did George I and England.[21]

Had the Triple Alliance not existed, it might have been very easy to provoke a general war at the very moment when France needed beyond all else a continuation of peace. Even at this time, Europe had by no means settled comfortably in the bed of the Utrecht and the Northern settlements, which in several respects seemed rather too Procrustean. But it was no inconsiderable achievement for France and Great Britain to have brought to a congress under their mediation the representatives of Spain and the Emperor: so long as they stayed there, hostilities would be reduced to the marshalling of arguments instead of battalions, and to the expression of bad language in the studied politeness of diplomatic forms.

Much as the Triple Alliance of 1717 had profited Great Britain, since, as a result of it, she had secured the confirmation of her trading privileges in the Spanish colonies, the renewed recognition of her chosen dynasty, and the banishment of the Pretender beyond the Alps, it profited France perhaps even more. For France had used the assistance of Great Britain in order to convert Spain from an open enemy into a close friend. As far as Great Britain was concerned, the Triple Alliance came

[21] Wiesener: *Le Régent, l'abbé Dubois et les anglais*, I, p. 464; cf. Baudrillart: *Philippe V et la cour de France*, II, p. 538.

perilously close to overreaching itself. Under its auspices a branch of the Bourbons was to be established in Italy; moreover, not only had it firmly established the Regency in France, but, by doing so, it had also made evident to Philip V that his true policy was one of co-operation and intimate association with France. In 1723, although solid reasons of self-interest still united France and Great Britain, the position of the former was one of enormously greater prestige and independence than that which she had occupied at the time when the alliance was formed.

A comparison of the diplomatic position of France in 1716 and in 1723 easily demonstrates that such was the case. In the autumn of the former year, when the negotiations ending in the Triple Alliance were under way, France was governed by a regent whose authority did not pass without question either at home or in Spain; at that time the disputed succession to the French throne was a problem alarmingly imminent, threatening to bring in its train all the distraction and defenselessness usually consequent to civil disputes. Abroad, the British, alarmed at the Regent's tolerance of the Pretender, were endeavouring to build anew the Grand Alliance, until the exigencies of the Northern War and the blandishments of Dubois caused them to reverse their policy and seek alliance with France. In a word, the Regent in 1716 had had to cope with disaffection at home and diplomatic isolation abroad.

In the closing months of 1723 these perilous times had been long since past. Now, as first minister, the Duke of Orleans governed with undisputed authority.[22] To English hostility had succeeded alliance; by the united efforts of France and Great Britain, Spain had been pacified and the Emperor had been persuaded to renounce his pretensions to the Spanish throne. The dangerous question of the French succession had been temporarily shelved, and to the former hostility between Philip

---

[22] Louis XV attained his legal majority on February 16, 1723, on which day the Regent formally relinquished his power, although, in actual fact, he remained the governor of France. The coronation of Louis XV took place at Rheims on October 25, 1722. Dubois had been given the title of *premier ministre* on August 22, 1722, and had been a cardinal since July 7, 1721. The Duke of Orleans was *premier ministre* from August 10 to December 2, 1723.

V and the Duke of Orleans had succeeded more cordial relations. Far from being in diplomatic isolation, France in 1723 was on good terms with Great Britain, the United Provinces and Spain, and found her alliance eagerly courted by Russia.

Much as Dubois and the Regent had depended upon the alliance with Great Britain, they had taken care not to extend that dependence to the point of slavishness; the criticism that they sacrificed French diplomatic independence to the whims of Great Britain is untrue. The resistance which the Regent offered to coercing Spain by the formation of the Quadruple Alliance in 1718, and his bland undertaking to surrender to Spain Great Britain's Gibraltar, are illustrations of his independent attitude. Nevertheless, as in every other alliance, so in this, the price that had to be paid for the benefit and the prestige derived from the exercise of concerted action was the sacrifice, to a certain degree, of each member's freedom of choice in the elaboration of its own policy. The existence of the alliance with Great Britain, for example, made the conclusion of a French alliance with Russia very difficult, although Peter the Great had sought to conclude one in 1717 and likewise manifested in succeeding years his willingness to bring about a Russo-French alliance. France, however, was unwilling to contract such an alliance without including George I in the agreement. Otherwise, the resurgence of trouble in Lower Germany might involve her in the dilemma of being required to fulfill incompatible obligations. But it was exactly this question of the inclusion of Great Britain to which Peter the Great most strenuously objected because, in the first place, of his resentment against the King of Great Britain for having sent a hostile fleet to the Baltic in 1720; the British guarantee to Denmark of the possession of Schleswig was also a stumbling-block to agreement between Great Britain and Russia, for this engagement eternalized the dispossession of Peter the Great's son-in-law, the Duke of Holstein-Gottorp; finally, Peter the Great resented George I's having accepted the Emperor's appointment as co-administrator of the duchy of Mecklenburg, as a result of the dispute between its duke, Peter the Great's nephew, and the nobility of the duchy.[23] In this instance, the British alliance made a Franco-Russian alliance unlikely, so long as France chose to continue her diplomatic association with Great Britain.[24] But this fact does not constitute proof that the British alliance reduced France to a state of dependence upon Great Britain: the unending task of statesmen is to make a choice of the means at their disposal, whether it involves a shift in diplomatic alignments or a continuation of the ones already engaged upon. Had the Regent, however, conducted his policy in such a manner as to become so dependent upon the British that he lost all means of being able to modify or restrain English policy, his management of affairs would certainly have been worthy of censure. Piteous is the plight of a statesman who has so rebuffed or antagonized other powers that the mere withholding of his allies' accustomed support would leave his country in

[23] Consult Basil Williams: "The Foreign Policy of England under Walpole." *English Historical Review*, XV (1900), pp. 269-270. For the failure to conclude an alliance in 1717, see Chance: *George I and the Northern War*, pp. 220-222. The course of Franco-Russian negotiations between 1719 and 1724 was excellently summarized in the *Mémoire sur les négociations entre la France et le Czar de la Grande Russie Pierre I, fait en 1726 par m-r Le-Dran, premier commis des affaires étrangères* (*Sbornik Imperatorskago Russkago Istoricheskago Obshchestva* [Saint Petersburg, 1867-1916, 148 vols.], XL [1884], pp. i-lxxxii; XLIX [1885], pp. i-lxix; LII [1886] pp. i-xlvi). The most important instructions received by Campredon were from Dubois, dated October 14, 1722; only as a last resort was he to negotiate on the basis of not admitting Great Britain to the agreement (*Sbornik*, XLIX, pp. 175-177). See also *Recueil des instructions données aux ambassadeurs et ministres de France depuis les traités de Westphalie jusqu'à la Révolution française: Russie* (Edited by Alfred Rambaud; Paris, 1890, two vols.), I, pp. 247-250. The contention of M. Jean Dureng: *Le duc de Bourbon et l'Angleterre (1723-1726)* (Paris, [1912]), pp. 37-40, to the effect that Dubois was planning to conclude a Russian alliance and was drawing away from the British connection at the time of his death, seems overstated.

[24] Albert Vandal: *Louis XV et Elisabeth de Russie* (Paris, 1882), pp. 49-70; *British Diplomatic Instructions: Sweden, 1689-1727*, p. xxxii; precisely this point was made in the despatch of Hoym, Saxon-Polish envoy to France, to Augustus II, February 8, 1723 (Jules Flammermont: *Les correspondances des agents diplomatiques étrangers en France avant la Révolution* [Paris, 1896], p. 249). Townshend wrote to Stephen Poyntz, January 1/12, 1725/6: "The French have for some years past seen with pleasure the rising power and influence of the Muscovites in the Baltick, proposing to themselves greater advantages from a close union with them than they ever had from their former engagements with Sweden. And they never departed from this view till his Majesty drove them to the necessity of declaring whether they would place their confidence in him or in the Czar, and since in the Czarina. In the present state of affairs they wisely thought that point could bear no debate" (*British Diplomatic Instructions: Sweden, 1689-1727*, p. 201).

disastrous isolation: then indeed has the ally become the master. This *gaucherie* the Regent never committed. The method by which this state of affairs may be avoided is by cultivating the good will of some other power or powers so that the elaboration of alternative alignments may be undertaken if necessary. This method the Regent kept in mind. His successor lost sight of it.

The successor of the Duke of Orleans as *premier ministre* was Louis Henry, Duke of Bourbon, then thirty-one years of age. This man, the great-grandson of the great Condé, was endowed with a most unprepossessing exterior—lampoons referred to him as the one-eyed ruffian—joined to a very limited capacity. "He had just wit enough to know how he could make a show of his rank," wrote Duclos, the Academician who became historiographer of France; and the shrewd Barbier noted in his journal:

Our new first minister is not to the taste of anyone. It is known that he has no common sense, nor any experience in public affairs, which is melancholy in such a situation.[25]

The administration of the Duke of Bourbon quickly became unpopular because it soon manifested the disadvantages of entrusting affairs of state to an over-mighty subject; the French had been fortunate in being governed by the Duke of Orleans, but such was not the case with the Duke of Bourbon, and it is significant that no other prince of the blood was entrusted with ministerial power during the remainder of the *ancien régime*. The first disadvantage was owing to the fact that the abilities of the Duke were not equal to the position which his birth had secured. In the second place, the prestige of his rank permitted him to indulge his favourites with an impunity scarcely practicable on the part of an ordinary minister. His ministry came to be known as "the reign of the Marquise de Prie," whose elegant prostitution he rewarded with so much influence and so many favours that his administration soon fell into discredit.[26]

[25] Charles Pineau Duclos: *Mémoires secrets sur les règnes de Louis XIV et de Louis XV* (Paris, 1791, two vols.), II, p. 255; E. J. F. Barbier: *Journal historique et anecdotique du règne de Louis XV* (Edited by A. de la Villegille; Paris, 1847-1856, four vols., [La Société de l'histoire de France. *Publications*, No. 21]), I, p. 196.

[26] Duclos: *Mémoires secrets*, II, p. 282; Hervey: *Some Materials towards Memoirs*, p. 63.

No less distasteful to court opinion was the great influence of Pâris-Duverney, the most gifted of four brothers who, starting life as tavern factotums, had made their fortunes by becoming government contractors and had thus, through the mandates of an inscrutable destiny, risen to a position of influence and power. It was typical of the nature of Bourbon's administration that Pâris-Duverney was permitted to direct the economic and financial policies of the government from behind the scenes, for he was invested with no responsible office; it is regrettable that his praiseworthy efforts to effect reform, such as remedying the old abuse of the sale of offices, and endeavouring, by the *cinquantième*, to establish a precedent for taxing the goods of privileged and unprivileged alike, should have met with such intransigent public opposition. Nevertheless, it is true that, partly because of the resistance of the privileged classes to an attempted invasion of their immunities, partly because of the snobbishness with which the court nobility regarded a *parvenu* like Pâris-Duverney, the financial measures of Bourbon's administration contributed a great deal towards preparing public opinion to welcome his fall from power. Finally, the third disadvantage of the rule of the Duke of Bourbon, ascribable to his position as a prince of the blood, was the warping of French policy to suit his personal aspirations. His desire to strengthen his family's position by undermining the prospects of his greatest rival, the young Duke of Orleans, brought his administration into serious difficulties abroad. His conduct of foreign and dynastic affairs soon made it painfully apparent that the interests of the kingdom of France were not congruent with the personal aims of the Duke of Bourbon.

Had the Duke of Bourbon enjoyed the full confidence of the King's preceptor, Fleury, the latter's wisdom and influence might have prevented, or at least partially corrected, the blunders of the administration. No one enjoyed more fully than did Fleury the confidence of the King, and it was generally believed that the former Bishop of Fréjus might himself have become First Minister upon the death of the Duke of Orleans, had he so desired. For Fleury, at that time seventy years old, had proceeded by gradual steps to a public career of the highest rank, at a time of life when most men's thoughts for the future are bent more on securing immortality through the mercy of God than through efforts of their own.

Fleury's life had been a tranquil one, crowned with a moderate degree of success. Born in 1653 in Languedoc of an obscure noble family, he was educated in Paris from the age of six. Because of the interest of an uncle, who was a canon in the chapter of the cathedral of Montpellier, he became a canon there about 1670; by virtue of this position, he was a deputy of the second order at the famous Assembly of the Clergy in 1682. Meanwhile he received his license in theology at the Sorbonne in 1676 and was ordained in 1679. This same year, through the influence of Bossuet, he was appointed almoner of Maria Theresa, the queen of Louis XIV, and following her death was made almoner to the King in 1683. From 1685 to 1688 he travelled in Italy, and upon his return took up again the life at the court, for which he was temperamentally well suited. He was one of the most fashionable abbés of his day, with a reputation for wit and an aptitude for making and keeping friends; his ability to remain on intimate terms with both Bossuet and Fénelon throughout the course of their famous quarrel bespeaks a pretty tact. Yet his anticipated promotion to the episcopate was long deferred. The reason was that Louis XIV had taken a dislike to him, because, it is said, the King "had always detested gallantry and intrigue in priests" and suspected Fleury of hypocrisy.[27] Not until 1698 was he persuaded, by the intercession of Bossuet and the Cardinal of Noailles, to nominate Fleury to a bishopric, that of Fréjus. Fleury took up his residence there in 1701, and for fourteen years played with notable success the rôle of bishop resident in his diocese. But his bishopric was not entirely to his taste, and he is said by Voltaire to have signed himself in letters to his confidential friends, "Fleury, by the wrath of God, Bishop of Fréjus." [28]

[27] François-Joachim de Pierre, cardinal de Bernis: *Mémoires et lettres de François-Joachim de Pierre, cardinal de Bernis (1715-1758)* (Edited by Frédéric Masson; Paris, 1903, two vols.), I, pp. 44-48.
[28] Voltaire: *Précis du siècle de Louis XV*, chapter iii.

In 1715 he resigned his bishopric, inasmuch as Louis XIV had nominated him to be the preceptor of Louis XV.[29] Several reasons accounted for his nomination to this post. In the first place, Fleury's urbane reception of Victor Amadeus II during the latter's invasion of Provence in 1707 seems to have made a lasting impression on the ruler of Savoy; as a result his daughter Adelaide, who was the mother of Louis XV, is said to have requested the appointment of Fleury to be the preceptor of her son.[30] In the second place, Fleury was closely associated with the Villeroy family, and the recommendation in his behalf of Marshal Villeroy, whom Louis XIV selected to be the governor of Louis XV for the period of his minority, is thought to have had weight.[31] Finally, Fleury's anti-Jansenist prejudices served him well in the estimation of the old King who, in the closing years of his life, came more and more under the influence of the Jesuits, particularly of Le Tellier, the Jesuit Provincial of France; Le Tellier, it is said, recommended the appointment of Fleury to Louis XIV.[32] In these years the center of controversy was the alleged Jansenistic heterodoxy of a book which was being widely used in France and had been recommended by the Cardinal of Noailles himself. This work was Pasquier Quesnel's *Réflexions morales sur le Nouveau Testament*. In order, as he fondly hoped, to settle the controversy definitively, Louis XIV requested Clement XI to examine Quesnel's book and to issue a bull con-

[29] By a codicil of his will, dated August 23, 1715; reproduced by Jean Buvat: *Journal de la Régence (1715-1723)* (Edited by Émile Campardon; Paris, 1865, two vols.), I, pp. 42, 83. For an account of the events of Fleury's life, cf. "Éloge de M. le cardinal de Fleury," pronounced by Mairan, and printed in the *Histoire de l'Académie royale des sciences pour l'année 1743* (Paris, 1746), pp. 175-184; also the eulogy of Fleury pronounced by Fréret and printed in the *Histoire de l'Académie royale des inscriptions et belles-lettres*, XVI (Paris, 1751), pp. 356-366.

[30] V. Verlaque: *Histoire du cardinal de Fleury et de son administration* (Paris, 1878), p. 43.

[31] Bernis: *Mémoires . . . . du cardinal de Bernis*, I, pp. 47-48; Voltaire: *Précis du siècle de Louis XV*, chapter iii, says the same thing, as does the well-informed pamphlet *Memoirs of the Life and Administration of the late Andrew-Hercules de Fleury . . .* (London, 1743), pp. 4, 5, 7.

[32] Antoine Dorsanne: *Journal qui contient tout ce qui s'est passé à Rome et en France au sujet de la bulle Unigenitus, depuis 1711 jusqu'en octobre, 1728* (Second edition, Rome, 1753, two vols.), I, p. 220; cf. Georges Hardy: *Le cardinal de Fleury et le mouvement janséniste* (Paris, 1925), p. 10.

cerning it. The Pope obliged, on September 8, 1713, by issuing the bull *Unigenitus*, which condemned one hundred and one propositions contained in Quesnel's *Réflexions*. The Bishop of Fréjus was one of the French prelates who had challenged the orthodoxy of Quesnel's book. In 1711 he had written two letters to the Cardinal of Noailles, censuring it.[33] Since Louis XIV was naturally at some pains to choose for his great-grandson a preceptor whose theological views were in conformity to his own, Fleury's outspoken impugnment of Quesnel's orthodoxy and his unqualified acceptance of *Unigenitus* went far in prepossessing the King in his favour.

In 1717 Fleury was distinguished by being elected a member of the French Academy, on the principle that what was good enough for its patron was good enough for it.[34] In 1718 he distinguished himself by demanding the expulsion of the Abbé de Saint-Pierre from the Academy. Saint-Pierre published in that year his *Polysynodie*, which contained his arguments for government by councils rather than by ministers, and which incidentally contained some severe criticisms of Louis XIV; in his introduction he remarked:

So that it is matter of Astonishment, that with so imperfect a Form of Government, he did not commit more Faults than he did.

And in the course of his argument he burst forth as follows:

I wish to God, for the sake of his Honour and our Happiness, he had been employed during the whole course of his Reign, in making Trade to flourish, . . . in paving the Highways, ... in making Rivers navigable, and reforming the Laws, to lessen the number of Law-Suits; in altering the Methods of raising the Taxes, that the People might pay less, and the publick Treasury receive more; . . . in finding out Methods to dispose of Employs and Rewards with Justice, without any regard to Recommendations; in taking away the Sale of Places, Survivorships, and Sham-Com-

---

[33] Verlaque: *Histoire du cardinal de Fleury*, pp. 32-34. For a letter of a similar tenor from Fleury to Noailles, October 17, 1713, see Hardy: *Le cardinal de Fleury et le mouvement janséniste*, p. 10, note.

[34] Émile Gassier: *Les cinq cents Immortels: Histoire de l'Académie française, 1634-1906* (Paris, 1906), p. 89, note; *Les registres de l'Académie françoise, 1672-1793* (Paris, 1895-1906, four vols.), II, pp. 24, 29-30.

missions; . . . in improving our Manners, by rendring Virtue and other useful Qualifications more honoured and respected, by being more justly and regularly rewarded.[35]

This attack was very badly received by those who venerated the memory of Louis XIV, and Fleury led the counter-attack which ended in the expulsion of Saint-Pierre, in the course of which he emphasized that it was the duty of the Academy to praise French kings, living or dead.[36]

During these years Fleury was assiduous in his attendance upon the King. As the Mentor of his young Telemachus, he even composed for his edification something of a discourse on universal history, *à la Bossuet*. However, the educational regimen seems not to have been very severe; there are stories that Louis XV on one occasion was surprised during the lesson period while doing nothing more instructional than fixing curl papers in Fleury's hair, and that a marker in a book which the King and the preceptor were supposed to be studying rested at a certain page for six months on end.[37] Bernis accused Fleury of injuring the frail and timid Louis XV in the worst possible way, by inculcating in him a distrust of his own abilities. As Lacretelle remarked, Fleury taught the King to be governed.[38] Consequently, it is

---

[35] *A Discourse of the Danger of Governing by One Minister. In which is demonstrated, that the most advantageous Administration, both for the King and the People, consists in an Establishment of Many Councils; or, a Poly synody* (London, 1728), pp. xi, 50-51.

[36] Fleury's discourse was published in *Annales politiques de feu Monsieur Charles Irenée Castel, abbé de St. Pierre* (Geneva, 1767, two vols.), I, pp. vii-xv; and in *Les registres de l'Académie françoise*, II, pp. 48-50. For a discussion of the incident, see Louis de Rouvroy, duc de Saint-Simon: *Mémoires de Saint-Simon* (Edited by A. de Boislisle; Paris, 1879-1928, forty-one vols.), XXXIII, pp. 143-146; Charles Pineau Duclos: *Histoire de l'Académie françoise (Oeuvres complètes de Duclos* [Paris, 1820-1821, nine vols.]), VIII, pp. 393-395; "Éloge de l'abbé de Saint-Pierre." *Oeuvres . . . de d'Alembert* (Edited by J.-F. Bastien; Paris, 1805, eighteen vols.), XI, pp. 167-180; Édouard Goumy: *Étude sur la vie et les écrits de l'abbé de Saint-Pierre* (Paris, 1859), pp. 37-50; Albert Rouxel: *Chronique des élections à l'Académie française (1634-1841)* (Paris, 1886), pp. 89-90; Joseph Drouet: *L'abbé de Saint-Pierre: L'homme et l'oeuvre* (Paris, 1912), pp. 65-74.

[37] Bernis: *Mémoires . . . . du cardinal de Bernis*, I, pp. 48-49.

[38] Bernis: *Mémoires . . . . du cardinal de Bernis*, I, p. 60; J. C. D. de Lacretelle: *Histoire de France, pendant le dix-huitième siècle* (Fourth edition, Paris, 1819-1826, fourteen vols.), II, p. 267.

probable that Fleury gained more from their association than
did the King; for the strong attachment which Louis XV conceived for him had its obvious political uses. Dubois and the
Regent, for example, suspected Fleury of predisposing the King
against Dubois, which accounts for the embarrassing cordiality
with which they importuned Fleury to accept the archbishopric
of Rheims, in 1721. But he, fearing the Greeks bearing gifts,
politely refused.[39]

In general, Fleury was careful to keep in the background
during the Regency, but he did accept a position which he made
an important one, that of membership in the *conseil de conscience*. This council, which had been instituted by Louis XIV,
had to do with the appointment to benefices and with the general
secular administration of ecclesiastical affairs. In the early years
of the Regency it had been composed of men of Jansenist leanings, but had been dissolved on September 24, 1718, after it had
precipitated a conflict with Law. It was reorganized in 1720, and
was henceforth a body of very different spirit, although it performed the same functions as the preceding council. It now assisted the Regent in securing ecclesiastical peace by quietly
compelling acceptance of the bull *Unigenitus*, and Fleury became
the moving spirit of the council in its endeavours to stamp out
the tenacious tenets of Jansenist faith.[40]

In 1722, the arrest and exile of Marshal Villeroy, whose hauteur
and pretensions had involved him in a quarrel with the Regent,
left the field clear for Fleury to monopolize the King's affections.
In technical fulfilment of a private agreement between Villeroy
and himself, to the effect that if one were dismissed the other
would resign his charge, Fleury unexpectedly left the court a week
after Villeroy's arrest. The King was inconsolable; the Regent,
Dubois and their circle, in comic perturbation, racked their

[39] Saint-Simon: *Mémoires*, XXXVIII, pp. 239-251. In this year Fleury became
a member of the Academy of Sciences; in 1723, of the Academy of Inscriptions and
Belles-Lettres.

[40] Hardy: *Le cardinal de Fleury et le mouvement janséniste*, pp. 12-18; cf. Comte
Hélion de Luçay: *Des origines du pouvoir ministériel en France: Les secrétaires d'État
depuis leur institution jusqu'à la mort de Louis XV* (Paris, 1881), pp. 184-186, 225.

brains to think where Fleury might have gone, and when he was found, were so pressing for his return that they persuaded him to appear at the court again the very next morning, after a self-imposed exile lasting less than twenty-four hours. It had been a profitable day: to some extent, it had released him from his obligations to Villeroy, while at the same time it had remarkably enhanced his personal prestige.[41]

Had Fleury claimed the office of First Minister upon the death of the Duke of Orleans, he would indubitably have had to contend with the dissatisfaction and intrigues of the Duke of Bourbon. Whether Fleury realized this, and desired to give the Duke of Bourbon full opportunity either of governing well or of discrediting the rule of princes of the blood, or whether timidity prevented him from asserting his claims, certainly the administration of the Duke of Bourbon was, in the way of contrast, the best possible introduction to his own. In the meantime, Fleury assumed a position of greater public importance in Bourbon's government than he had occupied during the Regency: he tightened his hold on the administration of the ecclesiastical affairs of the kingdom, and, for the first time, became a member of the Council of State.[42] Now, too, he began a systematic although unostentatious study of foreign affairs.[43] For the moment, however, he still kept in the background, carefully contriving to avoid taking a stand which would compromise him in public opinion. He absented himself from the meeting of the Council when the decision to levy the *cinquantième* was taken, and only now and then made a rather ostentatious display of

[41] Saint-Simon: *Mémoires*, XLI, pp. 1-14; cf. Sir Luke Schaub to Lord Polwarth, August 11, 1722 (*Hist. MSS. Comm.: Report on the Manuscripts of Lord Polwarth*, III, p. 153).

[42] Hardy: *Le cardinal de Fleury et le mouvement janséniste*, pp. 12-36. Fleury told Horatio Walpole that he had been offered the post of First Minister when Dubois died (Walpole to Newcastle, May 3, 1724 [Dureng: *Le duc de Bourbon et l'Angleterre*, p. 122]).

[43] Dureng: *Le duc de Bourbon et l'Angleterre*, p. 123; Fleury's increasing participation in matters involving foreign affairs is illustrated by his letter to Philip V, August 7, 1725: if Ripperda should insist on precedence over the French ambassador at Vienna, it would result in an open rupture (Baudrillart: *Philippe V et la cour de France*, III, p. 204).

virtue by admonishing the Duke of Bourbon on the subject of Mme. de Prie and Pâris-Duverney.[44]

Fleury's abstention from interference in the direction of foreign policy, during the first months of Bourbon's administration, gave clear scope to the Duke, for better or for worse. In reality, the international situation did not warrant a modification of the foreign policy which the Regent had elaborated, that of alliance with Great Britain and friendship with Spain. Although hostilities between the Emperor and Spain were suspended, the issues between them had not been settled. A satisfactory settlement might be readily attained if joint mediation with Great Britain at the Congress of Cambrai were continued. This was, indeed, the policy of Bourbon and Morville (since August 1723, Secretary of State for Foreign Affairs). But, with reference to the maintenance of cordial relations with the Spanish sovereigns, the Duke of Bourbon's family ambitions brought about a serious deviation from the Regent's policy. Since the event which Bourbon most feared was the death of Louis XV and the consequent inheritance of the throne by his rival, the Duke of Orleans, it naturally occurred to him that the simplest method of nullifying the hopes of the Orleans family was to arrange the early marriage of Louis XV, the birth of whose hoped-for heirs would settle the succession question once for all.[45] But on this very point, the personal policy of the Regent had forestalled the family ambitions of the Duke of Bourbon, for arrangements had already been made for the betrothal of the Spanish Infanta to the French King. It was generally believed that the object of the Regent in arranging this match had been to postpone for as long as possible the marriage of Louis XV, thus increasing the risk that he would die without direct heirs, in which case the Orleans family would inherit the crown: for the Infanta had been born on March 30, 1718, and consequently it was rather sanguine to expect her to

[44] Claude Louis Hector, duc de Villars: *Mémoires du maréchal de Villars* (Edited by the Marquis de Vogüé; Paris, 1884-1904, six vols., [La Société de l'histoire de France. *Publications*, No. 72]), V, pp. 2-5.

[45] The Duke of Bourbon's fears were heightened by the marriage of the young Duke of Orleans to the daughter of the Margrave of Baden, July 13, 1724 (Paul de Raynal: *Le mariage d'un roi, 1721-1725* [Paris, 1887], p. 64).

bear an heir to France before 1734 or 1735. The Duke of Bourbon did not like to wait that long, and in this he was supported by the French public, which did not approve of the Regent's policy of long engagements.[46] But could the Infanta be sent back and another marriage arranged for Louis XV without hopelessly antagonizing her parents, the King and Queen of Spain, who, in other respects, were the Duke of Bourbon's most natural allies? That was the dilemma, made the more perplexing by the fact that Louis XV was a frail boy, who might be carried off by some slight indisposition at any moment.

The Duke of Bourbon's decision to repudiate the Infanta, and the way in which that decision was executed, formed the transcendent blunder of his administration, the repercussions of which were felt far into the administration of Cardinal Fleury. It was a blunder because it gratuitously insulted Philip V and Elisabeth Farnese, who promptly sought their revenge by allying themselves with the Emperor, thus leaving France in dangerous isolation. As a result, because France was helpless without British support, from 1725 on she became the unwilling handmaiden of English policy; not daring henceforth to do anything which the British might allege as a justification for the forfeiture of their support, France was placed in a position where she was forced to allow Great Britain alone to initiate all policy, and for some time the resources of French diplomacy were utilized more for the furtherance of British interests than of its own.[47] Fleury inherited this situation from his predecessor; so thoroughly had France been delivered into the hands of her ally that it was the work of years before the Cardinal, through patient and long-winded negotiation, was able to regain diplomatic equality.

Considering the restless ambition and the uncertain temper of the Queen of Spain, it might have been impossible in any event

---

[46] "Mémoire sur l'état de la France depuis la mort de Louis XIV jusqu'en 1726, fait le premier octobre, 1726" (Armand-Léon de Madaillan de Lesparre, marquis de Lassay: *Recueil de différentes choses* [Lausanne, 1756, four vols.], IV, p. 115).

[47] Bishop Atterbury remarked upon this consequence in a letter to the Pretender, Paris, June 25, 1725 (Lord Mahon: *History of England*, II, appendix, p. xxvi); cf. Basil Williams: "The Foreign Policy of England under Walpole." *E.H.R.*, XV, pp. 276, 669.

for France to retain for long the good will of the Spanish sovereigns. Nevertheless, it should have been the endeavour of French policy to conserve that good will for as long as possible, and, most of all, not to destroy it by French initiative. However, true policy was sacrificed for ambition by Bourbon, whose real purpose was to bring about a marriage between one of his sisters and Louis XV, as the events of 1724 were to make abundantly apparent. Two memorials, drawn up at the request of the Duke of Bourbon by La Marck, former French ambassador to Sweden, and dated April 20 and 30, 1724, set forth the advantages of sending back the Infanta and narrowed the alternative choice of a bride for Louis XV to one of the Duke of Bourbon's sisters or to a princess of Lorraine. The tone of the memorials indicated that the memorialist's real opinion was that trouble with Spain should be avoided at all costs and that, rather than send back the Infanta, it were better

> to concert secret measures with the King of Spain for his coming to France in the case of the death of the King [Louis XV], in order to avoid in this way having M. the Duke of Orleans for one's master.[48]

In other words, the personal interest of the Duke of Bourbon to prevent the accession of his rival to the throne was leading him into a policy which would either alienate Spain or which would encourage Philip V to repudiate his renunciation of the French inheritance. Either alternative was dangerous to the peace of Europe; neither was to the interest of France, save to this slight degree, that the modification of the arrangement for Louis XV's marriage might result in the birth of an heir to the throne earlier than could be anticipated from his marriage with the Infanta.

The Duke of Bourbon's dynastic policy constitutes an illustration of the harm which an over-mighty subject may do his country, if entrusted with the management of its affairs. Undeterred by the hesitancy and caution of La Marck's memorials, the Duke of Bourbon next broached the subject to his department of foreign affairs: a memorial written by the *premier commis*,

---

[48] Raynal: *Le mariage d'un roi, 1721-1725*, p. 68. For an *analyse* of La Marck's two memorials, see *ibid.*, pp. 65-68.

Antoine Pecquet the elder, dated June 20, 1724, recommended the sending back of the Infanta, provided that a close alliance with Great Britain, Prussia and Russia was first brought about. On October 29, 1724, the Council of State voted to send back the Infanta, but on the clear understanding that adequate precautions should be taken to prevent trouble with Spain; the decision was unanimous, but Fleury agreed to it only very reluctantly.[49] The next step was to choose a princess to be the bride of Louis XV, and the Duke of Bourbon reduced the choice to one of the two daughters of the Prince of Wales or to one of his own two sisters. This summary narrowing of the field was a cunning device designed to make the choice of one of his sisters seem inevitable; for it was dubious whether George I, who owed his crown to the fact that he was a Protestant and the Stuarts were not, would permit his grand-daughter to change her religion. The Duke of Bourbon permitted his real intentions to be seen in the council of November 6, 1724, when he openly advocated the choice of his sister, Mlle. de Vermandois. The members of the Council, desiring to curry favour with the *premier ministre*, all agreed to this proposition with the exception of Fleury, who had the courage to speak so vehemently against it that the Duke of Bourbon was fain to let his scheme for a family marriage drop once for all.[50]

In November 1724, therefore, there was still time to give up the project of repudiating the Infanta. Thus far the affair had been kept secret, and the objections which had been raised, the hesitating acquiescence which his advisers had manifested, ought to have shown the Duke of Bourbon that he was treading on dangerous ground. It had been the unanimous opinion of his councillors that the sending back of the Infanta would lead to trouble with Spain, only to be counterbalanced by the formation of an alliance with Prussia and Russia in addition to the one already existing with Great Britain and the United Provinces.

[49] Baudrillart: *Philippe V et la cour de France*, III, pp. 152-153; Raynal: *Le mariage d'un roi, 1721-1725*, pp. 69-70, 89-91.

[50] Villars: *Mémoires*, IV, p. 302; Raynal: *Le mariage d'un roi, 1721-1725*, pp. 101-104.

Morville had been endeavouring to conclude such an alliance, but the negotiations were difficult because the inclusion of Great Britain in the agreement was absolutely necessary in order to prevent France from incurring incompatible obligations. What Morville desired was one alliance system, not two; but the issues and ill will between the Czar and the King of Great Britain, on the one hand, and between the King of Prussia and George I, on the other, made the arrangement of an alliance between them slow work.[51] For this reason, the Duke of Bourbon ought not to have brought about the break with Spain until, at the very least, he was more nearly certain of being able to contract an alternative protective alignment.

Had the Duke of Bourbon attempted to use tact in dealing with the Spanish sovereigns, he might have been able to extricate himself from his difficulties amicably. La Marck had advised that Philip V should be sounded out, perhaps by Father Burmudez, his confessor,

in order that he should awaken scruples in the timid and devout mind of Philip V on the dangers for Louis XV of a prolonged celibacy and the necessity of promptly placing the morals of the young sovereign under the protection of marriage,

in the hope that Philip V might himself recall his daughter and release Louis XV from his obligations.[52] But this reasonable line of action was prevented by another item in the personal policy of the Duke of Bourbon, which caused him to act with singularly infelicitous duplicity. In this year Mme. de Prie conceived the idea of persuading the sovereigns of Spain to make her husband a Spanish grandee. The Duke of Bourbon fell in with this scheme, as the nomination would be of benefit to his offspring, who were nominally the children of M. de Prie. His desire to bring this business to a successful conclusion effectually prevented him from preparing the ground at San Ildefonso for the Infanta's return. To facilitate the granting of the grandeeship, he promised categorically, on August 19, 1724 and on February 13,

[51] Dureng: *Le duc de Bourbon et l'Angleterre*, pp. 207-235.
[52] Raynal: *Le mariage d'un roi, 1721-1725*, p. 66.

1725, that the formal ceremony of betrothal would take place as soon as the Infanta had completed her seventh year (March 31, 1725).[53] The sudden illness of Louis XV on February 20, 1725, so frightened the Duke of Bourbon that he lost his head entirely: he vowed that, if the King recovered, he would arrange his immediate marriage.[54] On March 9, 1725, the Abbé de Livry informed the King and Queen of Spain of the repudiation of the Infanta, an announcement which Elisabeth Farnese greeted with characteristic fury and bad language.[55]

The god of Misrule had most certainly presided over a policy as muddled as this. No attempt had been made to soften the blow to the pride of the Spanish sovereigns. The ground had not been prepared diplomatically either to conciliate Spain or, on the other hand, to conclude new alliances which would make it safe to brave Spanish resentment with impunity. Finally, to complete the awkwardness of the situation, Bourbon's precipitous action had got rid of one prospective bride before he knew where a satisfactory substitute was to be found. With his inveterate propensity for undertaking a project for which his diplomacy had not made adequate preliminary provision, a procedure by which he risked compromising his personal prestige and that of France as well, the Duke of Bourbon had counted on being able to arrange a marriage with one of the daughters of the Prince of Wales, after all. On January 19, 1725, the Count de Broglie, French ambassador to Great Britain, was instructed to negotiate this marriage proposal. On March 17, eight days after the sover-

---

[53] Baudrillart: *Philippe V et la cour de France*, III, pp. 50-51; Raynal: *Le mariage d'un roi, 1721-1725*, pp. 70-75. The Duke of Bourbon's promise of August 19, 1724 was addressed to Luis I of Spain; Philip V, having been under the impression that religious obligations demanded it, had abdicated on January 10, 1724 (Baudrillart: *op. cit.*, II, pp. 558-564); the act of abdication may be found in Saint-Philippe: *Mémoires*, IV, pp. 273-367. For the events of the reign of Luis I, which was terminated by death from smallpox on August 31, 1724, see *ibid.*, IV, pp. 164-199. After the death of Luis I, Philip V resumed the crown, in spite of his solemn abdication (Saint-Philippe: *op. cit.*, IV, pp. 199-203, 374-402; Baudrillart: *op. cit.*, III, pp. 80-93).

[54] Saint-Simon: *Mémoires*, XXXIV, p. 307; Duclos: *Mémoires secrets*, II, pp. 299-300.

[55] William Coxe: *Memoirs of the Kings of Spain of the House of Bourbon* (London, 1815, five vols.), III, pp. 112-113.

eigns of Spain had been informed of the repudiation of the Infanta, the Duke of Bourbon learned that George I had made a downright refusal of the offer of Louis XV.[56]

The Duke of Bourbon, having been thus rebuffed by George I, and being still desirous of accomplishing the marriage of Louis XV as quickly as possible, brought about the choice of a princess whose anticipated docility and gratefulness would reward him for having raised her so unexpectedly from the obscurity of exile. On March 31, 1725, the Council decided upon Maria Leszczynska, the daughter of the banished king of Poland, as the future queen of Louis XV. The King married his Cinderella princess, by proxy, at Strasburg on August 15, 1725; on September 5 she arrived at Fontainebleau.[57]

Aside from his veto of the proposal to marry Louis XV to Mlle. de Vermandois, itself a popular act, Fleury played a neutral part in the diverse negotiations which led ultimately to the marriage of the King with Maria Leszczynska.[58] Thus he contrived that the blame could not be laid upon him if the marriage ultimately decided upon was disliked by public opinion or was displeasing to the King.[59] His calculations were just: he maintained his great influence over Louis XV, failing which Fleury would never have been able to undertake the administration of affairs himself, and it proved to be a great advantage to him, both in his relations with the court of Spain and the court at Versailles, to be free from the odium which attached to the tortuous proceedings as a result of which Louis XV received his bride.

[56] Raynal: Le mariage d'un roi, 1721-1725, pp. 146-147; cf. Dureng: Le duc de Bourbon et l'Angleterre, pp. 246-249.

[57] Maria Leszczynska has been made the object of some excellent, sympathetic and somewhat sentimental treatment by French historians; see, for example, Comtesse d'Armaillé, née de Ségur: La reine Marie Leckzinska (Paris, 1870); Pierre de Nolhac: Études sur la cour de France. Louis XV et Marie Leczinska, d'après de nouveaux documents (Paris, [1928]); Casimir Stryienski: The Eighteenth Century (The National History of France, edited by Fr. Funck-Brentano, IV; New York, [1916]), chapter v.

[58] Saint-Philippe: Mémoires, IV, p. 217; Raynal: Le mariage d'un roi, 1721-1725, pp. 158-159, 179. Fleury was opposed to the English marriage, on the grounds of religion (Coxe: Memoirs of Horatio, Lord Walpole, I, pp. 165-172).

[59] Horatio Walpole to Lord Townshend, Paris, December 24, 1725 (Coxe: Memoirs of Horatio, Lord Walpole, I, p. 184).

While Fleury was content to remain in the background for the time being, nevertheless the relations between him and the Duke of Bourbon, which were daily becoming more antagonistic, were moving towards a crisis. Fleury had decisively interfered in the Duke of Bourbon's plan for marrying Louis XV to one of the Bourbon sisters; he strongly disapproved of the influence the Duke permitted Mme. de Prie and Pâris-Duverney to wield; he had deplored the manner in which the return of the Infanta had been accomplished; finally, he had always favoured unreserved acceptance of the bull *Unigenitus*, and disliked the Duke of Bourbon's toleration of Jansenist laxities.[60] In this silent struggle for power Fleury enjoyed the enormous advantage of possessing influence hitherto unrivalled over the young king. Louis XV refused to transact business with the Duke of Bourbon, except in the presence of Fleury, and it was on this issue that the decisive struggle took place.

The Duke of Bourbon hoped to utilize the influence of Louis XV's queen in order to undermine Fleury's power, an undertaking to which the Queen lent herself, out of gratitude to the author of her story-book rise, with perhaps more warm-heartedness than sagacity. On December 17, 1725, the Queen desired Louis XV to consent to transact business with the Duke of Bourbon alone. On the eighteenth, Fleury again went into voluntary retirement, as he had done in 1722. The coterie of the Duke of Bourbon rejoiced in their easy victory. In reality, it was a second *journée des dupes:* the King commanded the Duke of Bourbon to write to Fleury requesting his return.[61] In this trial of strength Fleury was unconditionally the victor. He never forgave the Queen for her share in the affair, and henceforth her influence in matters of state was in permanent eclipse. As for the Duke of Bourbon, his credit was irretrievably ruined; his favouritism had

---

[60] Dureng: *Le duc de Bourbon et l'Angleterre*, pp. 460-463.

[61] Upon returning from the hunt on the afternoon of Dec. 18, Louis XV was apprised of Fleury's departure; the Duke of Bourbon was ordered almost instantly to write to Fleury to return. Fleury complied, and was present at the King's *levée* on the morning of Dec. 19 (Saint-Simon: *Mémoires*, XXXIV, pp. 311-313: Duclos: *Mémoires secrets*, II, pp. 362-366; Lassay: *Recueil de différentes choses*, IV, pp. 121-122; Horatio Walpole to Lord Townshend, Dec. 24, 1725 [Coxe: *Memoirs of Horatio, Lord Walpole*, I, pp. 181-196]).

already cost him the support of court opinion, which was tending also to regard the marriage which he had arranged for the King as unsuitable to the dignity of France. Now it was evident that he could not rely upon the support of Louis XV; in short, Fleury was henceforth master of the situation, and the Duke of Bourbon retained office merely on sufferance.[62] As a corollary of this fact, it was safe to predict that when the conjuncture of foreign affairs would make it profitable to sacrifice the First Minister to the wrath of the Spanish sovereigns, Fleury would persuade the King to dismiss him.

But in December 1725, and the months immediately following, the time was not yet ripe. Great things had happened in Europe since the return of the Infanta, and their consequences were yet indeterminable. For the moment, the King and Queen of Spain were still confident that they could inflict condign punishment on France and the Duke of Bourbon, whose disgrace at that time, consequently, would have gratified without conciliating them. The means by which they proposed to dictate to Europe was the Alliance of Vienna, concluded on April 30, 1725.[63] Direct negotiation with the Emperor had been authorized by the Spanish sovereigns in November 1724, for the procrastination of the Congress of Cambrai, which was proving itself a monument of inconclusiveness, and the failure of the Marquis of Monteleone to persuade France and Great Britain of the advisability of permitting Don Carlos to reside in the Italian duchies to which he would ultimately succeed, had made Elisabeth Farnese very restive, and had convinced her that she had little to hope from the efforts of the mediating powers, France and Great Britain.[64]

[62] Fleury wrote to Victor Amadeus II, August 2, 1726: "il n'avoit tenu qu'à moi bien longtemps auparavant d'être chargé" with the government (*Recueil des instructions. . . . Savoie-Sardaigne et Mantoue* [Edited by Count Horric de Beaucaire; Paris, 1898-1899, two vols.], I, p. 354).

[63] For the treaty of peace between Charles VI and Philip V, April 30, 1725, see Dumont: *Corps universel diplomatique*, VIII, part ii, pp. 106-113; also Cantillo: *Tratados*, pp. 202-212. For the treaty of defensive alliance, April 30, 1725, see Dumont: *op. cit., loc. cit.*, pp. 113-114; and Cantillo: *op. cit.*, pp. 216-218. A treaty of commerce, drafted by Dumont himself, was also signed, May 1, 1725 (Dumont: *op. cit., loc. cit.*, pp. 114-118; Cantillo: *op. cit.*, pp. 218-228).

[64] For the Monteleone mission, see Saint-Philippe: *Mémoires*, IV, pp. 183-186; Gabriel Syveton: *Une cour et un aventurier au XVIIIe siècle: Le baron de Ripperda* (Paris, 1896), pp. 29-38; Baudrillart: *Philippe V et la cour de France*, III, pp. 118-130.

Baron Ripperda, a Dutch adventurer who had formerly been the diplomatic representative of the United Provinces at Madrid and who had subsequently become a naturalized Spaniard, was selected by the Spanish sovereigns to be their secret envoy. He was to endeavour to arrange an alliance with the Emperor based on the marriage of Don Carlos and Don Philip, the two sons of Elisabeth Farnese, with two of the Emperor's daughters.[65] The representatives of the Emperor responded to the advances of Ripperda with characteristic caution, and, had he not shown himself to be an infinitely obliging negotiator, no agreement could have been reached. As it was, the draft treaty of March 1, 1725, to which he consented, was of a nature to justify, under ordinary circumstances, his recall. In return for definite commercial concessions to the subjects of the Emperor and for subsidies in the event of war, Charles VI merely engaged to exert his good offices for the retrocession of Minorca and Gibraltar. In general, the Emperor refused to do more than to confirm the treaty of the Quadruple Alliance of August 2, 1718. This, it is true, constituted a recognition of the right of Don Carlos to the eventual succession in the duchies of Tuscany, Parma and Piacenza, but this bare confirmation did nothing to adjust the thorny question of the introduction of the neutral garrisons into the duchies, which the mediating powers at the Congress of Cambrai had been trying to negotiate, nor did it make any other provision with reference to the manner in which the succession of Don Carlos was to be made effective. By accepting Ripperda's draft treaty, therefore, the Spanish sovereigns were actually receding from their goal of settling Don Carlos in an Italian inheritance. This inconclusiveness would have been atoned for if the arrangements for the Austro-Spanish marriages had been definite; but, far from such being the case, the Austrian consent to Elisabeth Farnese's marriage proposals was couched in verbiage so cautious and so vague that it was practically worthless. The Spanish acceptance

[65] For Ripperda's early history, see Syveton: *Une cour et un aventurier*, pp. 60-66; an interesting but untrustworthy account is given in *Memoirs of the Duke de Ripperda* (London, 1740), pp. 1-68. In 1724 Ripperda was the director of the royal Spanish cloth manufactories (Saint-Philippe: *Mémoires*, IV, pp. 210-212). For the instructions to Ripperda, dated November 22, 1724, see Cantillo: *Tratados*, pp. 214-216.

of this draft treaty involved the exchange of concrete concessions for abstract promises; in ordinary times, the draft treaty would have seemed to constitute a clear demonstration of the fact that the number and gravity of the issues in dispute between Philip V and Charles VI were too great to permit of satisfactory settlement by direct negotiation.

Ripperda's draft treaty, however, had the fortune to arrive at Madrid at the moment when the Abbé de Livry was instructed to inform the King and Queen of Spain of the repudiation of the Infanta, and they, actuated by the desire to accomplish some notable discomfiture of the Duke of Bourbon, disregarded the unsatisfactory character of Ripperda's negotiation, and instructed him to close with the Emperor's representatives.[66]

The mere fact that Spain and the Emperor were undertaking to settle their differences by direct negotiation was disconcerting enough to the mediating powers. The effect was doubled by the fact that the information which they were able to gather of the nature of the Vienna treaties revealed such preponderant advantages accruing to the Emperor as could be compensated, they supposed, only by a secret agreement definitely stipulating the Austro-Spanish marriages.[67] By underestimating the length to which the Spanish sovereigns would go in an endeavour to flaunt their contempt of the Duke of Bourbon in the eyes of Europe, British and French statesmen overestimated the imminence of an Austro-Spanish marriage alliance. Consequently, although there was nothing in the divulged portions of the Vienna treaties

[66] Orendayn wrote Ripperda on March 9, 1725, the day on which the return of the Infanta had been announced to Philip V and Elisabeth Farnese, to conclude "a qualquiera precio" (Baudrillart: *Philippe V et la cour de France*, III, p. 175, note). Also at this time, Spain offered Great Britain the sole mediation at the Congress of Cambrai. This was merely a somewhat ingenuous attempt to break up the diplomatic union of Great Britain and France; moreover, it was not seriously intended, for at the moment the offer was made, Spain was endeavouring to conclude a treaty with Charles VI which would settle the business being mediated by the Congress without its being consulted. However, in later years the Parliamentary Opposition in Great Britain made much of the Ministry's having refused to act as sole mediator. For Spain's offer of the sole mediation, see Basil Williams: "The Foreign Policy of England under Walpole." *E.H.R.*, XV, pp. 490-491.

[67] The treaty of peace of April 30, 1725 and the treaty of commerce of May 1, 1725 were made public. Copies of them were printed in London in 1725. The defensive alliance of April 30, 1725 remained secret.

to which the mediating powers might not accede, and although Great Britain and the United Provinces were in fact invited to become members of the Vienna alliance, they suspiciously refused the honour. In order to protect themselves against this new and alarming combination, France, Great Britain and Prussia concluded the Alliance of Hanover on September 3, 1725, and devoted the ensuing months to busy endeavours to secure the accession to their combination of the United Provinces, Sweden, Denmark and various German princes.

In December 1725, Ripperda returned to Spain, after having negotiated the very secret offensive alliance of November 5, 1725, the existence of which was not known to historians until it was published by Cantillo in 1843.[68] This treaty, which had been called into being by the formation of the Alliance of Hanover, definitely provided for the marriage of two of the Archduchesses to Don Carlos and Don Philip; it stipulated, in addition, the immediate payment of subsidies by Spain, and envisaged a general war, as a result of which France was to be dismembered. Having arrived at Madrid, Ripperda was invested by his grateful sovereigns with a concentration of portfolios of which Il Duce would not have been ashamed. His treatment of the ambassadors of foreign powers was compounded of boasting and blustering, and served to heighten the apprehensions of the Hanover powers without intimidating them. In the early months of 1726 the affairs of Europe seemed hurrying to a crisis.

Yet the expected attack upon France and Gibraltar hung fire, and it began to be realized that Ripperda was finding difficulty in raising money sufficient for preparing Spain for war and for providing the stipulated subsidies to Austria. His difficulties were increased by the British government's sending Admiral Hosier to Carthagena to restrain the galleons from sailing home. As a consequence of this financial stringency, Ripperda was unable to forward any of the money promised to the Emperor, a matter which involved him in acrimonious discussions with Königsegg, the Austrian ambassador, whose influence with the

---

[68] Cantillo: *Tratados*, pp. 231-235; the Latin text is printed by Syveton: *Une cour et un aventurier*, pp. 283-284.

Spanish sovereigns was increasing by leaps and bounds. Under Ripperda's management Spanish economic and financial affairs were quickly reaching a state of chaos. When Philip V and Elisabeth Farnese discovered to their surprise that Charles VI did not regard Ripperda's retention in office as essential to the continuance of the Austrian alliance with Spain, although Ripperda had consistently endeavoured to persuade them that such was the case, they had no hesitation in divesting him of his offices (May 14, 1726).

The fall of Ripperda was the event which made timely the disgrace of the Duke of Bourbon, which occurred on June 11, 1726.[69] His dismissal, so long as Ripperda was in office, could have had little conciliating effect upon Spanish policy, whereas it might have compromised the dignity of France by seeming to be the result of French apprehensions of the hostility of Spain. This was a reason cogent enough to account for Fleury's having permitted him to retain office after his unsuccessful trial of strength with the former Bishop of Fréjus in December 1725; but there was another reason, equally cogent, for his dismissal, as soon as it could be accomplished with propriety. The Duke of Bourbon's participation in the direction of affairs made virtually impossible the solution of the complex situation in which the European powers were involved, other than by force. Bourbon could hardly have accomplished a peaceable reconciliation with Spain short of what would have been tantamount to a public confession of sins, a process not merely damaging to his own prestige but also compromising to the dignity of Louis XV, since it would reflect upon the manner in which his unpopular marriage had been made. The removal of the Duke of Bourbon made it possible for his successor to conciliate Spain and detach her from the Emperor without having to resort to war. This was the policy which Fleury pursued in the years following 1726. It was a policy requiring both skill and patience: on the one hand, he had to make a display of force sufficient to deter Spain from light-heartedly setting Europe in conflict; on the other hand, he

[69] Fleury did not learn of the disgrace of Ripperda until June 3 (Coxe: *Memoirs of Horatio, Lord Walpole*, I, p. 211).

had to restrain his eager British allies, particularly Lord Townshend, the most bellicose and anti-Imperial member of the British
government, from precipitating a war for the purpose of enforcing
peace. Yet this he was able to accomplish.

Fleury's task was a particularly difficult one because the exposed situation and economic exhaustion of France made the
prolongation of peace imperative, while the rashness of the Duke
of Bourbon in antagonizing Spain had bereft France of her
natural Continental ally and made her peculiarly dependent
upon her ally across the Channel. Gradually Fleury was able to
win back France's diplomatic equality at the same time that he
preserved European peace; slowly his policy accumulated the
prestige which only success can bring, until, some twelve years
after his accession to power, France once more enjoyed the diplomatic leadership of Europe, and Great Britain was suffering the
inconveniences of isolation.

CHAPTER II

THE COMMERCIAL, FINANCIAL AND NAVAL
POLICY OF CARDINAL FLEURY

"IF we can make commerce flourish, we shall have as many troops as we want; if we allow commerce to languish, we shall have fewer soldiers, and less money wherewith to pay for their keep." These words of the Abbé de Saint-Pierre are not the isolated expressions of a clever and original thinker thrown out several decades before their due time; they are the echo of opinion widely held in Britain, in France, in Austria, in Holland and in Spain at the time that they were written. If a statesman is to be judged by the success that attends his efforts to adapt his policy to public opinion, it follows that in the age of the Pragmatic Sanction and the disputed successions to Parma and Tuscany, Great Britain and Ireland, France and Lorraine, no less attention must be paid to the conceptions he formed of trade and commerce; and his place in history is to be fixed not merely by his diplomatic skill, but by the improvement he has effected in the economic status of the country. And that this is not merely the discovery of posterity is shown by the conduct of the princes of the time, whose ministers bear such names as Walpole, Patiño, and Fleury; and of these, by no means the least important and successful was the Cardinal whose administration of France extended from 1726 to 1743.

The war concluded by the Treaties of Utrecht was a struggle waged to determine who was to succeed to the Spanish trade quite as much as it was to decide who was to possess the Spanish crown.[1] This, as yet "the most businesslike" of English wars,

[1] Louis XIV wrote to Amelot on February 18, 1709: "Le principal objet de la guerre présente est celui du commerce des Indes et des richesses qu'elles produisent" (E. W. Dahlgren: *Les relations commerciales et maritimes entre la France et les côtes de l'océan Pacifique* (*Commencement du XVIIIe siècle*): I. *Le commerce de la mer du Sud jusqu'à la paix d'Utrecht* [Paris, 1909], p. 561). A Dutch diplomat, Bergeyck, wrote to Philip V from Paris, May 16, 1712: "L'offre de la sûreté contre l'union des

was followed by a very shrewd peace which made ample provision for British commercial expansion, however much the Whigs might inveigh against the "treason" of Bolingbroke. Besides having to cede Acadia and the Hudson's Bay region, the French were dispossessed of their monopoly of the supply of slaves to the Spanish colonies in America; this Asiento, now for the first time sanctioned by a public treaty, was guaranteed to the British for forty years, and they likewise secured that fruitful source of future contention, the privilege of sending an annual trading ship to Vera Cruz or Portobelo.[2] In view of the fact that the Archduke Charles had been the British candidate for the Spanish throne, and that his success would have been paid for by providing the English with valuable trading concessions in Spain and its possessions, a certain tenderness for Spanish susceptibilities had deterred the English from conquering portions of the

deux couronnes. . . . a été la base et le fondement sur lequel cette couronne [Great Britain] est entrée en négociations, parceque la crainte de l'union et *de la perte du commerce a esté le seul objet des deux puissances maritimes dans cette guerre"* (Georges Scelle: *La traite négrière aux Indes de Castille* [Paris, 1906, two vols.], II, p. 459). Cf. John Ker: *The Memoirs of John Ker, of Kersland, in North Britain, Esq.; Relating to Politicks, Trade, and History. . . . Containing his secret Transactions and Negotiations in Scotland, England, the Courts of Vienna, Hanover and other Foreign Parts. With an Account of the Rise and Progress of the Ostend Company in the Austrian Netherlands* (London, 1726, two vols.), I, part ii, p. 5: "and our being afraid to lose it [the trade to Spain], by its falling into the hands of the French, was what produced the War in the latter End of King William's Reign, . . . " For an amplification of this idea, see Sir J. R. Seeley: *The Growth of British Policy* (various editions), part v, chapter iii: "The Commercial State"; *idem: The Expansion of England* (various editions), lecture vii; *The Cambridge History of British Foreign Policy* (Sir A. W. Ward and G. P. Gooch, editors; Cambridge, 1922-1923, three vols.), I, pp. 42-44; Michael: *Englische Geschichte im 18. Jahrhundert*, I, pp. 222-224.

[2] For the evolution of the Asiento from a private trading agreement to an international contract, sanctioned by treaty obligations, see Georges Scelle: "The Slave Trade in the Spanish Colonies of America: The Asiento." *American Journal of International Law*, IV (1910), pp. 612-662. The Asiento was granted to the British by the Treaty of Madrid, March 26, 1713 (Dumont: *Corps universel diplomatique*, VIII, part i, pp. 330-337). The Anglo-Spanish commercial treaty, signed at Utrecht on December 9, 1713, confirmed the Asiento treaty as well as the treaties of 1667 and 1670 (*ibid.*, pp. 409-415). A supplementary Anglo-Spanish treaty of May 26, 1715, confirmed the Asiento and permitted the annual British trading ship to have a tonnage of six hundred and fifty for ten years, instead of five hundred (*A General Collection of Treatys of Peace and Commerce, Renunciations, Manifestos and other Publick Papers, relating to Peace and War* [London, 1732, four vols.], IV, pp. 449-456; also Cantillo: *Tratados*, pp. 171-174). The spelling of "Portobelo" is that recommended by Dominic Salandra: "Porto Bello, Puerto Bello, or Portobelo?" *Hispanic-American Historical Review*, XIV (1934), pp. 93-95.

Spanish West Indies; but, by the simple device of concluding a separate peace, they had prevented their Dutch allies from securing any acquisitions or privileges there.[3] Nearer home, Minorca and Gibraltar afforded bases both for the protection of British commercial interests in the Mediterranean and for the illicit dissemination of British wares in Andalusia.[4] Finally, the English, jointly with the Dutch, had exploited the Spanish Netherlands mercilessly ever since they had gained control there following the victory of Ramillies in 1706, and turned the country over to its new sovereign, the Emperor, only under conditions which made certain the continuance of that exploitation.[5]

---

[3] "In the last war we laid aside attacking the Spanish West Indies in complaisance to the Emperor. . . . " (Admiral Sir Herbert W. Richmond, editor: "The Land Forces of France—June 1738." *The Naval Miscellany*, vol. III [*Publications of the Navy Records Society*, vol. LXIII, London, 1928], p. 75). In his pamphlet on "The Conduct of the Allies," which he wrote in 1712, Swift made an allusion to this point (*The Works of Jonathan Swift* [Second edition, Edinburgh, 1824, nineteen vols.], IV, p. 328). During the early years of the War of the Spanish Succession, governors of British colonies were instructed to maintain friendly relations with the Spanish colonies and to endeavour to persuade them to declare for "Charles III"; for instances of this policy, see the *Calendar of State Papers, Colonial Series, America and West Indies, 1706-1708, June* (London, 1916), pp. 16-18, 28-29, 54, 95-98, 129-130, 138-140, 154-155, 168-169, 185-186, 217-218, 223-225, 279-280, 362-364. Moreover, privateers were forbidden to make prizes of Spanish ships or to attack the Spanish colonies ("Additional Instructions to Privateers, May 2, 1704" [*Calendar of State Papers, Colonial Series, America and West Indies, 1704-1705* (London, 1916), pp. 113-114]). After the battle of Almanza (April 25, 1707), this policy of encouraging the Spanish colonies to declare for "Charles III" met with very little success. For Anglo-Dutch contentions concerning matters of trade during the War of the Spanish Succession, see G. N. Clark: "War Trade and Trade War, 1701-1713." *Economic History Review*, I (1927-1928), pp. 273, 277-278. On British expectations of trading concessions in Spain as a result of the War of the Spanish Succession, see the separate article of the Treaty of Barcelona between Charles III of Spain and Queen Anne, July 10, 1707 (Frances Gardiner Davenport: *European Treaties bearing on the History of the United States and its Dependencies.* Volume III: (*1698-1715*). [Carnegie Institution of Washington, Publication No. 254; Washington (D. C.), 1934], pp. 123-132).

[4] [Thomas Gordon]: *Considerations Offered upon the Approaching Peace, and upon the Importance of Gibraltar to the British Empire* (Fourth edition, London, 1720), p. 18; *Gibraltar a Bulwark of Great Britain* (London, 1725), p. 28; *The Danverian History of the Affairs of Europe, for the Memorable Year 1731. With the present State of Gibraltar, and an Exact Description of it, and of the Spanish Works before it. Also of Dunkirk, and the late Transactions there* (London, 1732), p. 90; *National Prejudice, Opposed to the National Interest* (London, 1748), p. 34.

[5] The third Barrier Treaty (Antwerp, Nov. 15, 1715) declared (art. xxvi) that "no other Dutys of Importation or Exportation, than what are paid upon the present Foot" shall be paid by subjects of Great Britain or of the United Provinces

France, too, played for high stakes in the Spanish succession gamble. The policy of England's principal antagonist indicated that the consciousness of the value of trade had not died with Colbert. In 1700 was organized a central Council of Commerce, to which the Chambers of Commerce, organized in the following year in the principal trading and industrial cities of France, were ordered to send deputies.[6] Throughout the greater part of the eighteenth century the Council and Chambers of Commerce, whose activity was greatly admired by British mercantilists, exercised great influence in shaping official economic policy.[7] In

until the contracting parties "shall otherwise appoint by a Treaty of Commerce to be made as soon as possible" (*A General Collection of Treatys*, IV, pp. 20-21). The Maritime Powers, by their inertia, prevented a treaty of commerce from ever being completed. For the text of, and excellent comment upon, the third Barrier Treaty, see Heinrich von Srbik: *Österreichische Staatsverträge: Niederlande bis 1722 (Veröffentlichungen der Kommission für neuere Geschichte Österreichs*, X), (Vienna, 1912), pp. 430-500.

[6] F. A. Isambert, Decrusy and A. J. L. Jourdan: *Recueil général des anciennes lois françaises* (Paris, 1823(?)-1833, twenty-nine vols.), XX, pp. 363-365. This Council was displaced in 1716 by the Regent's Council of Commerce, which was part of his scheme to govern by notables, and was reconstituted in its original form in 1722 as the *bureau du commerce;* in this form it existed during the remainder of the *ancien régime.* Usually it met fortnightly and transacted a great deal of business, particularly in the first half of the century; see Pierre Bonnassieux: *Conseil de commerce et bureau du commerce (1700-1791). Inventaire analytique des procès verbaux* (Paris, 1900), pp. ix-xxxi. [The introduction was contributed by Eugène Lelong]. Chambers of Commerce were organized in 1700 at Bayonne, Bordeaux, La Rochelle, Lille, Lyon, Nantes, Rouen and Saint-Malo. Similar organizations already existed at Paris, Marseilles and Dunkirk.

[7] Paul Masson: *Histoire du commerce français dans le Levant au XVIIIe siècle* (Paris, 1911), pp. 8-9; Émile Levasseur: *Histoire des classes ouvrières et de l'industrie en France avant 1789* (Second edition, Paris, 1900-1901, two vols.), II, pp. 474-475. The members of the central Bureau of Commerce consisted of various *conseillers d'État*, one of whom was its president and functioned as a sort of director-general of commerce; four *intendants du commerce*, appointed from among the *maîtres de requêtes* of the *Parlement* of Paris; and the deputies from the municipal Chambers of Commerce, who, however, had no vote and gave their advice only upon invitation. The sessions were likewise attended by representatives of the tax farmers, the inspectors-general of commerce and manufactures, and various experts. For contemporary accounts of these institutions, see [Jean-François Melon]: *A Political Essay upon Commerce* (Translated by David Bindon; Dublin, 1738), pp. 200-204; *Encyclopédie méthodique* (Paris, 1782-1832, 155 vols.), under articles *Bureau du Commerce, Chambre de Commerce, Conseil de Commerce*, in the section devoted to *Commerce* (vols. LVI-LVIII [1783-1784]). An idea of the actual operation of this system may be derived from Joseph Fournier: *La Chambre de Commerce de Marseille et ses réprésentants permanents à Paris (1599-1875)* (Marseilles, 1920), pp. 28-37, 91-111. For British mercantilistic admiration, see Malachy Postlethwayt: *Great*

1701 a French company took over the Spanish Asiento, which had been previously carried on by the Portuguese; the French attempt to operate the Asiento proved unprofitable, however, partly because of the difficulty of carrying on trade in the time of war, partly because the frequent royal raids on the capital funds of the company discouraged adequate investment.[8] More lucrative had been the direct trade to the Pacific, which the Spaniards had permitted when it became impossible to supply adequately the western portions of Spanish America in the ordinary manner by way of Portobelo.[9] French interest in economic affairs during the period of the War of the Spanish Succession is shown also by Louis XIV's appointment of Mesnager, the deputy of the Chamber of Commerce of Rouen, to be one of the French plenipotentiaries at Utrecht. As a part of the peace settlement, Mesnager negotiated an Anglo-French commercial treaty which would probably have been of great value to France, and which

Britain's True System (London, 1757), pp. 247-249; *The Wisdom and Policy of the French in the Construction of their Great Offices, so as best to answer the Purposes of extending their Trade and Commerce, and enlarging their Foreign Settlements* (London, 1755), pp. 72-74; *A Miscellaneous Essay concerning the Courses pursued by Great Britain in the Affairs of her Colonies* (London, 1755), p. 47; [Edmund Burke]: *An Account of the European Settlements in America* (first published in 1757; Boston, 1835), pp. 190-191.

[8] Léon Vignols: "*L'asiento* français (1701-1713) et anglais (1713-1750) et le commerce franco-espagnol vers 1700 à 1730." *Revue d'histoire économique et sociale*, XVII (1929), pp. 423-424; Scelle: *La traite négrière aux Indes de Castille*, II, pp. 427-430, 432-435, 437. For the 1701 contract, see Adrien Dessalles: *Histoire générale des Antilles* (Paris, 1847-1848, five vols.), II, pp. 472-482; Davenport: *European Treaties*, III, pp. 51-74.

[9] Dahlgren: *Le commerce de la mer du Sud jusqu'à la paix d'Utrecht*, pp. 358-558, 582-618. This trade continued surreptitiously after the Treaty of Utrecht, in spite of French ordinances prohibiting it, dated 1712, 1716 and 1724. It was not of great importance, however, following the punitive expedition of Martinet to the South Seas in 1717 (Léon Vignols: "L'ancien concept monopole et la contrebande universelle: Le 'commerce interlope' français à la mer du Sud, au début du XVIIIe siècle, type de cette contrebande." *Revue d'histoire économique et sociale*, XIII [1925] pp. 239-299; E. W. Dahlgren: "L'expedition de Martinet et la fin du commerce français dans la mer du Sud." *Revue de l'histoire des colonies françaises*, I [1913], pp. 257-332). French ships sailing to the South Seas after 1720 were usually officially employed as Spanish register ships (E. W. Dahlgren: "Voyages français à destination de la mer du Sud avant Bougainville (1695-1749)." *Nouvelles archives des missions scientifiques*, XIV [1907], pp. 423-554). See also Henri Sée and Léon Vignols: "La fin du commerce interlope dans l'Amérique espagnole." *Revue d'histoire économique et sociale*, XIII (1925), pp. 300-313.

the House of Commons, suspecting such to be the case, refused to ratify.[10]

The emphasis on economic aims which had characterized the war likewise characterized the period of peace which ensued. The apparent ease with which England had financed large armies and poured out subsidies to her allies impressed all Europe. England's victory clinched the contention that trade was an essential instrument of national policy, and relegated the idea that commerce was incompatible with military power to the category of vulgar errors.[11] Consequently, the quarter-century of peace which followed the exhausting war was utilized by the countries of Europe not merely for passive recuperation, but rather for positive economic expansion: trade became the darling of the dynasts. Even in Spain, so long the victim of narrow bullionist theory, Uztariz and Ulloa agitated the necessity of encouraging Spanish manufactures and reviving Spanish navigation; there the Spanish Colbert, Don José Patiño, founded the Caracas Company (1728) and laboured diligently to build up the Spanish navy and merchant marine.[12] Even in Austria, Charles

[10] June 18, O. S., 1713; see Lord Mahon: *History of England*, I, pp. 35-37; William Cunningham: *The Growth of English Industry and Commerce in Modern Times; Part I. The Mercantile System* (Cambridge [England], 1903), pp. 461-463; G. N. Clark: *The Later Stuarts, 1660-1714* (Oxford, 1934), pp. 227-228. For the treaty (in part), see Davenport: *European Treaties*, III, pp. 215-222.

[11] "That the greatness of this Kingdom depends upon foreign trade, is acknowledged" (Sir Josiah Child: *A New Discourse of Trade* [Fifth edition, Glasgow, 1751], p. 114. This work was first published in 1668). Cf. Jerónimo Uztariz: *The Theory and Practice of Commerce and Maritime Affairs* (London, 1751, two vols.), I, pp. 360-361. "Si nous faisons fleurir le Commerce, nous aurons autant de Troupes que nous voudrons; si nous laissons périr le Commerce, nous aurons moins de gens de guerre, & moins d'argent pour les faire subsister" ([Charles Irenée Castel, l'abbé de Saint-Pierre]: *Les rêves d'un homme de bien, qui peuvent être réalisés; ou les vues utiles et pratiquables de M. l'abbé de Saint-Pierre, choisies dans ce grand nombre de projets singuliers, dont le bien public étoit le principe* [Paris, 1775], p. 197).

[12] Uztariz first published *The Theory and Practice of Commerce* in 1724 but most of the copies were destroyed; it was republished, without revision, in 1742. His first words are: "As no man of common understanding can be a stranger to the importance of commerce, it would be an idle thing to swell this treatise with the debate and illustration of so clear a point" (p. 1); the burden of his book is the necessity of "carrying on an active, instead of a passive trade, as well in respect to the merchants, as the shipping" (*op. cit.*, II, pp. 378-379, and *passim*); his arguments and schemes for reviving the Spanish navy, merchant marine and fisheries (*ibid.*, I, pp.

VI made Trieste and Fiume free ports (1718), founded in 1719 the Oriental Company for trade in the Turkish dominions, and granted the charter for the Ostend Company in 1723. How powerful this economic stimulus was throughout Europe is illustrated by Ulloa's assertion that nations owe their strength or decadence to commerce, and by Raynal's remark that for more than half a century the balance of power had depended more upon commerce than on war, a judgment which confirms the assertion of Dutot, written in 1741 or 1742, that if money is the sinews of war, the balance of power must follow that of commerce.[13] The degree to which statesmen and nations during this period modified their contempt for trade may be illustrated by the report, drawn up by leading Dutch merchants and submitted to the States General in 1751:

Now there is not a nation, but what, more or less, apply themselves to trade, and use their utmost endeavours to draw it into, and promote it in their native soil; nor is there one, but has in a greater or a less degree herein succeeded, to the manifest disadvantage of this republick.[14]

Great Britain was more fortunately circumstanced in this era than the other European nations. A long and painful period of national development had already made her a commercial state; the encouragement of trade was as palpably the national policy of the British in the eighteenth century as the Counter-Reforma-

342-430; II, pp. 1-51, 126-145). Ulloa likewise preached the necessity of converting the Spanish commerce from a passive into an active trade (Bernardo de Ulloa: *Rétablissement des manufactures et du commerce d'Espagne* [Amsterdam, 1753], part i, pp. 3, 125). This book, written in 1740, insisted that "it is less gold mines than commerce which enriches a state" (*ibid.*, pp. 10-11), and repeats the arguments of Uztariz for the revival of Spanish navigation and manufactures. For the history of the Caracas Company, see Roland Dennis Hussey: *The Caracas Company, 1728-1784: A Study in the History of Spanish Monopolistic Trade (Harvard Historical Studies*, vol. XXXVII), (Cambridge [Mass.], 1934).

[13] Ulloa: *Rétablissement des manufactures et du commerce d'Espagne*, part ii, p. 59; Guillaume-Thomas-François Raynal: *A Philosophical and Political History of the Settlements and Trade of the Europeans in the East and West Indies* (Second edition, London, 1776, five vols.), V, p. 462; Paul Harsin: "Une oeuvre inédite de l'économiste Dutot." *Annales de la Société scientifique de Bruxelles, Série D: Sciences économiques et techniques*, XLVII (Louvain, 1927), p. 161.

[14] *Proposals made by His late Highness the Prince of Orange, to their High Mightinesses the States General . . . for Redressing and Amending the Trade of the Republick* (London, 1751): reprinted by J. R. McCulloch: *A Select Collection of Scarce and Valuable Tracts on Commerce* (London, 1859), pp. 474-475; cf. *ibid.*, p. 439.

tion had been the national policy of Spain under Philip II. The prevailing sentiment that British wealth and power depended upon foreign trade was so deeply rooted that it became the undisputed postulate of the pamphleteers, their sole disagreement, the means by which it might be preserved and expanded:

> Trade once extinguish'd, Britain's sun
> Is gone out too; his race is run; . . . [15]

To persuade the public of one's solicitude for the trading interests of Great Britain was the prerequisite for securing a sympathetic hearing for one's views. Thus the "Gentleman of the Navy," while expatiating on the subject of Gibraltar, emphasized the importance of "our Commerce, which all must own to be the strength of Great Britain."[16] So, too, the leaders of the opposition against Walpole laboured to create the impression that the preservation of British trade was their first consideration: "Sir, We are a trading Nation; and whatever affects our Trade is our nearest Concern, and ought to be our principal Care."[17] And on this very same ground a pamphleteer defended Sir Robert Walpole for the measures taken during his period of power:

Peace was our Interest, because it always was, and will be the Nurse of Trade, it can't thrive without it, and I am sure, without Trade, this Nation can neither thrive nor subsist.[18]

Not only were the requisites for the expansion of national power clearly apprehended by the British people, but also "the spirit of the laws" encouraged the development of this national policy. The dynasty, which presided in a somewhat honorary and *ex officio* capacity over the destinies of Great Britain, was the choice of a Parliament itself responsive to the demands of

[15] The couplet is from Edward Young's *Imperium Pelagi: A Naval Lyric*, "Occasioned by His Majesty's Return from Hanover, September 1729, and the succeeding Peace."

[16] *Gibraltar a Bulwark of Great Britain* (1725), p. 24.

[17] [George Lyttelton]: *Considerations upon the present State of our Affairs, at Home and Abroad* (London, 1739), p. 3.

[18] *The Conduct of the Late Administration, with regard to Foreign Affairs, from 1722 to 1742, wherein that of the Right Honble the Earl of Orford (late Sir Robert Walpole) is Particularly Vindicated* (London, 1742), p. 61.

the trading interests. The Act of Settlement (1700) had exhausted human foresight in order to prevent dynastic ambitions
from conflicting with those of the British people. Even the existence of the Pretender favoured the uninterrupted development
of national policy. For the attempts of 1715 and 1719 made
clear that a restoration could be consummated only with foreign
assistance; since that was so, it was obvious that the restoration
endangered not merely the Hanoverian dynasty, the Church of
England, and the debt with which the Whigs had ingeniously
linked the fortunes of the reigning dynasty, but also involved
the surrender of some important trading privileges as a reward
to the power by whose aid the Pretender should be seated on his
father's throne. It was not for nothing that the trading interests
were predominantly Whig.

Moreover, Great Britain enjoyed a more favourable position
for the pursuit of trade than did her rivals. Besides the obvious
fact that her being an island made navigation and overseas commerce commonplace to a large percentage of her inhabitants, her
location made foreign invasions difficult and hazardous.[19] Consequently, Great Britain managed with a standing army which,
though a captious Parliamentary Opposition was fond of declaring
it to endanger the national liberties, seems remarkably small.[20]

[19] John Sinclair: *Thoughts on the Naval Strength of the British Empire* (London,
1782), pp. 4, 12, 22; cf. Montesquieu: *L'esprit des lois*, Book xix, chapter xxvii.
This sentiment was expressed in a ballad entitled "Tit for Tat: A Sea Kick for a
Land Cuff" (October 14, 1747 [Sir Charles Firth, editor: *Naval Songs and Ballads*
(*Publications of the Navy Records Society*, XXXIII, London, 1908), pp. 197-198]):

> While our salt water walls so begird us about,
> And our cruisers, and bruisers, keep good looking out,
> What force need old England to fear can offend her,
> From France, or from Spain, or a Popish Pretender?

[20] "But we have since seen eighteen thousand Men, a Number never attempted
before, voted necessary by Parliament during many Years of the most Profound
Peace" ([Hugh Hume, third Earl of Marchmont]: *A Serious Exhortation to the
Electors of Great Britain* [London, 1740], pp. 14-15). See Sir John W. Fortescue: *A
History of the British Army* (London, 1910-1930, thirteen vols.), II, pp. 15-18. The
following table of the number of troops voted annually by Parliament during these
years is compiled from *The History and Proceedings of the House of Commons from
the Restoration to the Present Time* (London, 1742-1744, fourteen vols.). In each
case, the total sum includes the number of invalids, the forces required to garrison
the Scottish Highlands, and all commissioned and non-commissioned officers.
These sums give the total of the British forces, whether employed in the colonies

A comparison of Great Britain with the United Provinces, also a maritime power, indicates how fortunate was the former because of her isolation. The motive of each in concluding the Grand Alliance (1701) had been the desire to safeguard commercial interests by opposing an overturn of the European balance; in addition, the safety of the British required European recognition of England's chosen dynasty, that of the Dutch, the erection of a satisfactory barrier against the encroachments of France. In the peace settlement both powers attained these aims, yet what an enormous advantage accrued to the British in comparison with their Dutch allies, quite apart from any exclusive concessions they had obtained by concluding a separate peace. Henceforth, British safety depended merely on retaining the mastery of the sea: Great Britain could neglect her army and still exact the consideration due to a first-class power. Indeed, national safety and commercial pre-eminence were maintained by identical means, her "floating castles." The fleets which in-

or at home, but do not include the contingents of foreign princes, paid for by subsidies. Not included in these figures are the eight thousand men kept on the Irish Establishment; the regiments were transferred from Ireland to England, and *vice versa*, as occasion required, so that the Army was really one, though on two establishments, as Sir Robert Walpole, in the days when he was in opposition, pointed out (Fortescue: *op. cit.*, II, p. 18). It should also be noted that during this period the Royal Regiment of Artillery was under the administration, and charged to the account, of the Office of Ordnance (Fortescue: *op. cit.*, II, pp. 48-49, 596).

Vol.	Page	Year	Total	Included Invalids
VI	225	1721	14,294	1,859
	268	1722	14,294	1,859
	291	1723	18,294	1,859
	322	1724	18,264	1,815
	333	1725	18,264	1,815
	357	1726	18,264	1,815
	383	1727	26,383	1,850
VII	21	1728	22,955	1,850
	40	1729	22,955	2,815 (?)
	55	1730	17,709	1,850
	Figures for 1731 omitted. Probably the same.			
	103	1732	17,709	1,815
	267	1733	17,709	1,815
VIII	70	1734	17,704	1,815
IX	52	1735	25,744	1,815
	131	1736	25,744	1,815
	239	1737	17,704	1,815
X	10	1738	17,704	1,815

timidated the Czarina and prevented the sailing of armies in support of the Pretender were the fleets which protected the trading liberties of Englishmen in the Baltic and at Cadiz. The manpower which in time of peace navigated British merchant-men was the manpower which in case of need protected her coasts and sailed her ships of the line. Nowhere else in Europe was the connection between trade and national defense so direct.

With the United Provinces this was not so. Great Britain had become almost invulnerable, but the Dutch remained merely mortal. For them the Barrier Treaty was an insurance policy, but one on which they had to pay a heavy premium. To remain a first-class power they would have needed both a large army and a formidable navy. Yet the necessities of their geographical position prevented them from having either. In this period, when the Dutch were losing their pre-eminence in commerce because of the competition of other nations previously negligent of trade, the financial strain occasioned by the necessity of pro-viding adequately for both military and naval defense, worsened by the cumbersomeness of the Dutch system of national supply and by the burden of the debt contracted in the War of the Spanish Succession, became painfully apparent.[21] Never certain of being able to defend themselves against invasion by land, they yet were forced by financial stringency to permit their navy to decay to such a degree that in 1745 Lord Chesterfield wrote that the Dutch had no other title but courtesy to the name of a maritime power.[22]

No less than the Dutch, the French were hampered in the race for commercial expansion by the exigencies of their location. While the long coast-line of France, with its adequate harbours, invited to overseas adventure, no French statesman dared forget the lengthy land frontier which had to be defended: the con-tingent gain of foreign trade would not compensate for the loss

---

[21] A. Goslinga: *Slingelandt's Efforts towards European Peace* (The Hague, 1915), pp. 41-43. The peace establishment in theory was 34,000 men, but it averaged in reality only 30,000, including the garrisons in the Barrier towns of the Austrian Netherlands (*ibid.*, pp. 9, 42).

[22] *The Letters of Philip Dormer Stanhope, Fourth Earl of Chesterfield* (Edited by Bonamy Dobrée; London, 1932, six vols.), III, p. 611.

of a province. As George Lyttelton, one of the secretaries of Stephen Poyntz at the Congress of Soissons, wrote to his father, in discussing French policy:

Much is given to future hopes, much obtained by future fears; and security is, upon many occasions, sought preferably to gain.[23]

While dynastic vagaries of foreign monarchs might annoy the British by threats of seizing Gibraltar or of cancellation of the Asiento, those potentates were scarcely able to endanger the metropolis itself; but France could be, and actually was, menaced with dismemberment by a powerful coalition.[24] Consequently, France's peace establishment had to be enormous in comparison with that of Great Britain, at the same time that French diplomacy had to make potential national defense a constant care.[25] For French statesmen the whole problem of governance was more complex than it was for the British. National security demanded the elaboration of a coherent policy in which, at most, economic desiderata were only a factor, while the indispensable attention paid by a French minister to diplomatic and military considerations might render unapparent his abiding consciousness of the value of encouraging trade. The British ministry could, on the other hand, afford to be "amateur."[26]

To combine economic recuperation with a due regard for the exigencies of national defense and the balance of power was the

[23] May 27, 1729 (*The Works of George Lord Lyttelton* [Third edition, London, 1776, three vols.], III, p. 244).

[24] By the tenth article of the Treaty of Vienna, Nov. 5, 1725 (Syveton: *Une cour et un aventurier*, pp. 147, 290-291; Cantillo: *Tratados*, pp 231-235).

[25] "The great Expence the French Court is at in training and supporting a numerous Land Army, a Multitude of Forts and Garisons, besides what is expended in common with us, renders it [a Navy of any Consideration] impracticable. Her Expences in the Land Service in Peace, being near equal to ours in War, notwithstanding the foreign Troops we support, and the Alliances we engage in; . . . " (*The State of the Nation Consider'd, in a Letter to a Member of Parliament* [Third edition, London, 1748], pp. 53-54). In 1730 the French army consisted of 156,916 regular troops, besides 79,802 militia, invalids and garrison troops (—Lemau de la Jaisse: *Carte générale de la monarchie françoise* [Paris, 1733]; compare R. Quarré de Verneuil: *L'armée en France depuis Charles VII jusqu'à la Révolution (1439-1789)* [Paris, 1880], pp. 229-236).

[26] *British Diplomatic Instructions, 1689-1789.* VI: *France, 1727-1744* (Edited for the Royal Historical Society by L. G. Wickham Legg; Camden Third Series XLIII, London, 1930), p. x.

policy which France required following the War of the Spanish Succession: her need was for competent but unadventuresome leadership. The unfortunate Mississippi Bubble had prevented the Regent from securing to France economic recuperation, and his successor, the Duke of Bourbon, was a blunderer; but Cardinal Fleury's personal predilections coincided exactly with the needs of his country. So strongly did Fleury's own pacific temperament characterize his administration that the peaceful nature of French policy became a European commonplace:

Peace is my dear delight—not FLEURY'S more.[27]

It will be observed later that the Cardinal's pacific attitude was a trifle deceptive, a pose sometimes adopted in order to entice his opponents into committing themselves to a policy which premised, quite erroneously, as the event was to prove, his timorousness and his determination to preserve peace at all costs.[28] But on the whole, although the Cardinal utilized the War of the Polish Succession (a war which had as much relation to Poland as some sermons have to their texts) as an instrument of national policy in order to attain his great diplomatic triumph, the reversion of Lorraine, and although public opinion forced him to bear a grudging part as the ally of Frederick II and the Emperor Charles VII in the early stages of the War of the Austrian Succession, he usually endeavoured to avoid war. Consequently the span of his administration came, in retrospect, to be regarded as the Antonine period of the eighteenth century. After the exhaustion incident to the War of the Spanish Succession, after the alarms and excursions of the Regency and the System, after the misrule

[27] Alexander Pope: *Imitations of Horace*, First Satire, book ii; in the Globe edition, p. 288, line 75.

[28] Frederick II wrote to Chambrier, his ambassador to Louis XV, on Nov. 19, 1740: "On connaît assez le langage du Cardinal ministre dans ces sortes de rencontres, qui affecte d'abord de grands sentiments de modération et de désintéressement, pour endormir les autres, les empêcher de prendre des mesures, et pour gagner du temps à préparer des matériaux à petit bruit, afin de frapper plus sûrement son coup avant qu'on s'y attende" (*Politische Correspondenz Friedrich's des Grossen* [Edited by J. G. Droysen, Max Duncker, Heinrich von Sybel and G. B. Volz; Berlin and Leipzig, 1879-   , forty-four vols.], I, p. 108).

of Mme. de Prie, France settled down to a period of recuperation during which she peacefully recruited her natural strength:

France is so much improved, it is not to be known to be the same country we passed through twenty years ago. Everything I see speaks in praise of Cardinal Fleury; the roads are all mended, and the greatest part of them paved as well as the streets of Paris, planted on both sides like the roads in Holland; and such good care taken against robbers, that you may cross the country with your purse in your hand . . . The French are more changed than their roads; instead of pale, yellow faces, wrapped up in blankets, as we saw them, the villages are all filled with fresh-coloured lusty peasants, in good cloth and clean linen. It is incredible the air of plenty and content that is over the whole country.[29]

Fleury's chosen field of activity was diplomacy, and it has been an almost universal fashion to assert that he neglected the economic, financial and maritime necessities of France. It is generally supposed, for example, that the commercial and maritime expansion of France owed little to his conscious guidance; that a policy of peace and economy was natural to him, and that consequently the resultant revival of French trade was a happy accident, so far as governmental policy was concerned; in short, that the Administration's policy was merely one of *dolce far niente*, and that no greater credit may be claimed for Fleury in the economic recuperation of France than this—that he prescribed no nostrums, and that he possessed an agreeable bedside manner.

The opinion hostile to Fleury on this score seems to be supported by the apparent paucity of evidence to the contrary under two important heads. In the first place, the very form of the French government precluded much discussion of public affairs, and makes it easy to suppose that commerce and navigation revived during a fit of governmental absent-mindedness. French statesmen did not hold their power, as their British colleagues did, on the sufferance of a suspicious public or by the votes of a parliamentary majority. There is no wealth of pamphlet litera-

---

[29] Lady Montagu to her husband, August 18, 1739 (*The Letters and Works of Lady Mary Wortley Montagu* [Edited by W. Moy Thomas; third edition, London, 1861, two vols.], II, pp. 42-43).

ture to overwhelm posterity with the conviction that the government cherished the interests of trade, no printed reports of parliamentary debates to attest the vigilance of ministers in extending and safeguarding commercial enterprise. In the second place, geography's inescapable logic fixed the character of French policy. In the mazes of the endless adventure, economic aspirations had to be co-ordinated closely with political guarantees. French diplomacy was forced to be political first, economic secondarily; from this arose the presumption that French diplomacy was oblivious of economic considerations, simply because their presence in negotiations was frequently overshadowed by political exigencies.

It might seem at first blush, for example, that the maintenance of the alliance with Great Britain, which was begun in 1717 and broke down in 1731, betokened a wanton and nonchalant disregard of France's commercial interests, particularly with regard to the Spanish trade. For by this alliance French statesmen were pledged to maintain the privileged British position in the Spanish Indies trade, which operated to their own disadvantage; moreover, since France traded with the Spanish colonies through the regular method of shipping goods on the galleons and flotillas, while the English did most of their trading there direct, it followed that Spain, when annoyed with the British, could easily hold French goods hostage in lieu of being able to penalize the real transgressors. But French statesmen by no means disregarded these facts; memorials submitted by the deputies of some of the Chambers of Commerce in 1728 emphasized these disadvantages of the connection with Great Britain, and the writings of Chauvelin, Secretary of State for Foreign Affairs from 1727 to 1737, and of Pecquet, *premier commis*, show that they were no less conscious of them:[30]

Since we know that commerce is the true and only means of extricating us from the state in which this kingdom is, means must be sought to make use of it. . . . Thus if our alliance with England and Holland seems to assure

[30] For the memorials mentioned above, see Léon Vignols: "*L'asiento* français (1701-1713) et anglais (1713-1750) et le commerce franco-espagnol vers 1700 à 1730." *Revue d'histoire économique et sociale*, XVII (1929), pp. 428-436.

peace, this peace can be maintained only at our expense, by the advantages which this alliance obliges us to preserve for England. . . [31]
One is more than ever convinced that commerce is the sole means of re-establishing the kingdom.[32]
The English have made it only too apparent that their design is entirely to ruin our commerce and to proceed to establish theirs on the débris.[33]

It is clear that French ministers were taking economic factors into consideration; what happened was that transcendent interests of state demanded the subordination of these elements in the interest of the whole. These memorialists, who enjoy the reputation of having been the most aggressive and anti-British members of the Ministry of Foreign Affairs at that time, arrived at the reluctant conclusion that the British alliance, with all its defects, was the only practicable one for the time being.

In fact Fleury's foreign policy was solicitous of the commercial interests of France. The chief source of friction within the Anglo-French alliance was caused by the conflicting commercial interests of the allies with reference to the Spanish trade. The English strategy in 1726 was to prevent the return of the galleons by sending Admiral Hosier with a strong squadron to Portobelo. Three things were accomplished by this project: Spain was deprived of the money so necessary for carrying on the war which the Austro-Spanish alliance of 1725 threatened; French merchants who were expecting their profits from their ventures on the galleons were distressed; and, finally, it afforded an excellent

---

[31] *Mémoire sur le parti à prendre pour une alliance* (Archives des Affaires Étrangères, *Mémoires et Documents: France*, vol. 494, ff. 171, 176). This memorial was written by Antoine Pecquet the younger in May, 1728; his office corresponded to that of the modern First Under-Secretary; the memorial bears approving annotations in the hand of Chauvelin.

[32] *Mémoire sur les partis à prendre*, dated March 19, 1729; it was written by Pecquet and annotated by Chauvelin (A. É., *Mém. et Doc., France*, vol. 494, f. 284).

[33] *Sur les instances que faisoient les Anglois pour faire déclarer la guerre à l'Espagne*, written by Chauvelin and dated June 1729 (A. É., *Mém. et Doc., France*, vol. 501, f. 35). Pecquet wrote a memorial entitled *Situation des affaires de l'Europe en 1726*, in which he said: "Mais l'état d'épuisement des finances du Royaume, le défaut total de marine, et l'impossibilité dans cette situation d'établir seule une considération suffisante dans l'Europe, n'ont pas permis de se détacher de l'Angleterre, quoyqu'il soit vray de dire, qu'à considerer le génie des Anglois, ils sont aussy incommodes amis que dangéreux ennemis" (A. É., *Mém. et Doc., France*, vol. 494, f. 43).

opportunity to extend the British illicit trade in Spanish America.[34] That the British anticipated French opposition to this scheme is shown by the fact that they despatched Hosier to his post before they even informed their ally what they had in mind, which annoyed Morville and the French Council of State exceedingly.[35] When, as a result, bankruptcies of French merchants occurred, Fleury's concern showed that he was sensitive to mercantile opinion, and he complained to Robinson, British *chargé d'affaires* during the temporary absence of Horatio Walpole, of the invidious situation in which the British action had placed his administration.[36] Fleury had been persuaded after the event to approve of the sending of Hosier, but that was before the fall of the Duke of Bourbon; in October 1726, when Fleury had the sole responsibility for the conduct of affairs, Horatio Walpole discovered that the project was not so much approved of as formerly. In November Walpole found that French merchants had memorialized the government, alleging that the British secretly intended to use Hosier's squadron in order to found new settlements in the Indies.[37] In March 1727, Walpole reported that he had never seen the Cardinal so "down and uneasy." It was claimed that Hosier's expedition had

given the English and Dutch interlopers opportunities to make vast advantages by their fraudulent commerce . . . while the French and other nations were entirely deprived of any benefit from the West Indies by the galleons being detained so long by force there, which was the chief reason of the scarcity of money, and the want of publick credit here. This, together with the uneasiness of the French merchants least their effects brought by the flota should be confiscated . . . created altogether a greater damp upon the Cardinal's mind than I ever saw. . . [38]

[34] "The continuance of Admiral Hosier's squadron in those seas has been of so great an advantage to our trade there, that never in so short a space of time have such quantitys of silver been brought hither from America" (Newcastle to H. Walpole, October 14, O. S., 1726 [J. F. Chance: *The Alliance of Hanover* (London, 1923), pp. 451-452]).

[35] Villars: *Mémoires*, V. p. 15; Chance: *Alliance of Hanover*, p. 351.

[36] Coxe: *Memoirs of Horatio, Lord Walpole*, I, pp. 253-256; cf. Chance: *Alliance of Hanover*, p. 447.

[37] Chance: *Alliance of Hanover*, pp. 351-352, 447, 457.

[38] H. Walpole to Newcastle, March 21 and 26, 1727 (Chance: *Alliance of Hanover*, p. 657).

When the tenseness of the diplomatic situation was temporarily relieved by the signature of the preliminary articles of peace at Paris on May 31, 1727, the stipulation that the galleons should be permitted to return and their "effects" distributed without extra tax was an important part of the agreement.[39]

The question of the Spanish trade cropped up again in 1729. Spain was pursuing an intentionally dilatory policy in the hope of breaking down the concert between Great Britain and France. To cope with this, the British Cabinet strongly urged war; this the French refused to undertake until the resources of negotiation had been exhausted, and their real reason for delaying was a tenderness for trade. According to Chauvelin, who discussed the situation in a series of memorials, one advantage might be gained from a war with Spain:

French merchants are put in a situation to recompense themselves for the loss which the injustice of Spain would cause them, and in that way commerce is supported, by putting them in a position to share the profits which it is unjust that the English alone should enjoy, and on account of which it would likewise be important to take measures to forestall them [the English] if possible.[40]

But, should such a course be adopted, care should be taken to prevent the British from securing too great advantages:

In fact, we ought never under any consideration to permit England, with all the advantages in trade which she already enjoys, to secure from these circumstances means of obtaining, through new establishments, the entire conquest of all the Indies, or at least of the whole trade of them, as one can not doubt the English have at all times desired.[41]

Chauvelin advised against a war with Spain. Was the best way of saving French goods from being confiscated that of declaring war on the power which had them in its possession?

Consequently it is clear that in the course in which the English propose to co-operate with us, they run no risk, at least for the present, and indeed find

[39] Article v (Alfred Francis Pribram: *Österreichische Staatsverträge: England bis 1748* [*Veröffentlichungen der Kommission für neuere Geschichte Österreichs*, III], [Innsbruck, 1907], pp. 457-464).

[40] *Sur les partis à prendre, 28 mai, 1729* (A. É., *Mém. et Doc., France*, vol. 501, f. 32).

[41] A. É., *Mém. et. Doc., France*, vol. 501, f. 29.

their advantage in it on account of the designs which they have always had on America, and that on the contrary Ruin is certain for us by the confiscation of the Galleons, which would be our first loss, and by the danger of events which, if they turned out unfortunately for us, could not do so by halves . . . One may truly say that we alone are the ones who have cause to complain of Spain, since the effects of the galleons are still held back contrary to the faith of treaties. How does it happen then that it should be the English who force us to participate in measures which suit their convenience? [42]

Representations should be made to the King of Great Britain

that it might appear strange that, in order to bring affairs to a conclusion, England should never propose anything except measures absolutely ruinous for us. . . . Can one resolve to destroy oneself for allies who propose to us the Ruin of all our merchants by the single measure to which they wish decisively to engage us? [43]

The desire to improve the conditions of commercial intercourse with Spain bore a significant part in Franco-Spanish relations during this period.[44] Brancas was instructed on the importance of this branch of trade (1728); Rottembourg carried with him, besides his regular instructions, which emphasized the value of the Spanish commerce to France, a special *Instruction sur le commerce maritime, la navigation et les privilèges des françois en Espagne* (1730).[45] The Treaty of the Escurial, better known as the First Family Compact (November 9, 1733), contained economic stipulations as important as its political ones. Article xii declared that the French should henceforth enjoy most-favoured-nation treatment, and that a commercial treaty should be concluded as soon as possible; article xiii stipulated for joint action in suppressing the illicit trade of the British in the Spanish Indies; and a separate article envisaged the repudiation of the treaty rights on which the British Asiento trade, with its "vessel of permission," was founded.[46] In 1739, when Spain was threatened

[42] A. É., *Mém. et Doc., France*, vol. 501, ff. 47, 35.

[43] Dated July 8, 1729 (A. É., *Mém. et Doc., France*, vol. 501, ff. 69, 65).

[44] Baudrillart: *Philippe V et la cour de France*, V, p. 451.

[45] *Recueil des instructions. . . . Espagne* (Edited by A. Morel-Fatio and H. Léonardon; Paris, 1894-1899, three vols.), III, pp. 160-161, 171, 177-178.

[46] Article xiii read in part: "Reconociendo su Majestad católica todos los abusos introducidos en el comercio contra la letra de los tratados, y principalmente por la nacion inglesa, á cuya estirpacion son igualmente interesadas las naciones española y francesa; ha determinado su dicha Majestad hacer poner todas las cosas en regla y segun la letra de los tratados" (Cantillo: *Tratados*, p. 281).

by the outbreak of war with Great Britain, she turned to France for a political alliance. The French ambassador, La Marck, had already been instructed to seek a commercial treaty, and in the negotiations which followed, Fleury made the conclusion of a treaty of commerce, which would regulate the taxes French merchants were required to pay in Spain and which would give a preference to French colonial coffee, the prerequisite of a political alliance.[47]

French diplomacy concerned itself with the betterment of trade in other countries besides Spain during this period. Campredon carried with him to Genoa, in addition to his regular instructions, a *Mémoire concernant le commerce maritime et la navigation des sujets du Roy*, signed by Maurepas.[48] Camilly was directed to study the commercial situation in Denmark, but without going so far as to suggest a commercial treaty; the instructions to Plélo, two years later, were more explicit:

The Dutch, especially, carry on a very useful direct commerce with Denmark, and those articles of northern origin, which it would be very desirable that His Majesty's subjects should themselves go to seek, are imported into France by the citizens of the Republic of Holland. . . . Nevertheless, it would be most fortunate if this state of affairs in matters of trade should be changed by the conclusion of a treaty which would be of utility to both nations respectively; . . . [49]

On August 23, 1742, a treaty of commerce between these two powers was concluded.[50] In Russia, La Chétardie was instructed to endeavour to improve trade relations between France and Russia, and particularly to secure the modification of the Russian tariff of 1724.[51] On April 25, 1741, a convention of commerce

[47] *Recueil des instructions.* . . . *Espagne,* III, pp. 201-202, 215; Baudrillart: *Philippe V et la cour de France,* IV, pp. 525, 531.

[48] Dated August 9, 1727 (*Receuil des instructions.* . . . *Florence, Modène, Gênes* [Edited by Édouard Driault; Paris, 1912], pp. 271-281).

[49] Instructions to Camilly, August 18, 1726 (*Recueil des instructions.* . . . *Danemark* [Edited by Auguste Geffroy; Paris, 1895], pp. 119-121); to Plélo, Nov. 6, 1728 (*ibid.,* pp. 139-140). However, Plélo was instructed not to take the initiative in suggesting such a treaty (*ibid.*).

[50] Printed by F. A. G. Wenck: *Codex juris gentium recentissimi, e tabulariorum exemplorumque fide dignorum monumentis compositus* (Leipzig, 1781-1795, three vols.), I, pp. 591-639.

[51] Dated July 1, 1739 (*Recueil des instructions.* . . . *Russie,* I, pp. 349-350).

with Sweden was signed.[52] With Portugal the French had long desired a commercial agreement which would place them on the same footing with Great Britain. France had agreed to mediate in the quarrel which broke out between Spain and Portugal in 1735 only on condition that a commercial treaty between France and Portugal would be signed; five years later the treaty was still pending, and Chavigny was instructed to endeavour to bring it to completion.[53] Finally, one of the greatest diplomatic triumphs of Fleury's administration was the renewing of the Capitulations with the Sublime Porte, which Villeneuve accomplished in 1740.[54] These instances of French diplomacy's being utilized for the purpose of improving France's commercial position cover the whole period of Fleury's administration. The years in which they fall are not exclusively those of any one of the three Secretaries of State for Foreign Affairs who assisted Fleury in the directing of French policy; the responsibility for the continuity of this policy may fairly be said to be his.

The interest in commercial development which French diplomacy reflects during these years is likewise seen in the domestic policy of the government. A token of this may be perceived in Fleury's establishment of the *conseil royal du commerce* in 1730, although this council met infrequently and was not of transcendent importance. The Cardinal himself wrote upon one occasion:

I interest myself too much in what concerns commerce not to do upon this occasion all which can contribute to sustain it and make it flourish for the nation's advantage.[55]

[52] Wenck: *Codex juris gentium*, II, pp. 5-7; J. B. G. de R. de Flassan: *Histoire générale et raisonnée de la diplomatie française* (Paris, 1809, six vols.), V, pp. 120-123.

[53] *Recueil des instructions. . . . Portugal* (Edited by the Vicomte de Caix de Saint-Aymour; Paris, 1886), p. 286; for the instructions to Chavigny, dated Feb. 12, 1740 (*ibid.*, p. 299). Similar instructions had been drawn up for D'Argenson in 1737, but he never proceeded on his mission (Flassan: *Histoire . . . . de la diplomatie française*, V, pp. 109-111).

[54] Printed by Wenck: *Codex juris gentium*, I, pp. 538-584. When Villeneuve was leaving France to proceed to Constantinople, Maurepas wrote to the Chamber of Commerce of Marseilles, August 11, 1728: "M. de Villeneufve doit avant son départ conférer avec vous sur l'état actuel du commerce du Levant et sur les moyens de l'augmenter et réformer les abus qui peuvent s'y être introduits" (François Charles-Roux: "Les Échelles de Syrie et de Palestine au dix-huitième siècle." *Revue d'histoire diplomatique*, XX [1906], p. 585).

[55] Émile Garnault: *Le commerce rochelais au XVIIIe siècle, d'après les documents composant les anciennes archives de la Chambre de Commerce de La Rochelle* (La

The most characteristic element in this policy was its stability and reliability, and the token of it was the fixing and maintaining of a definite monetary standard. Four days after the fall of the Duke of Bourbon, which occurred on June 11, 1726, a royal decree fixed the value of the gold mark at 740 livres 9 sols, and that of the mark in coined gold at 678 livres 15 sols. This involved a slight augmentation in the nominal value of the mark, which had a short time before been fixed at 637 livres 10 sols. This decree, at first ostensibly provisional in nature, was successively renewed until the decree of November 11, 1738 made it permanent.[56] Thus Fleury's government adopted a policy which was in accordance with the ideas of Cantillon and Dutot:

After what has just been seen, there is abundant occasion for astonishment that, against our own interest, there should have taken place in France such frequent alterations of our money. But if, on that topic, the past furnishes us occasion for astonishment, the present ought to win us over to eternal gratitude to the present Ministry. It is the first which has understood the necessity and the importance of not meddling with the monetary standards. It has been more than fifty years since they have been so long undisturbed in France as they have been the past ten . . . which ought to persuade the populace to bless this ministry and to desire that it continue.[57]

After 1726, it was possible for merchants who, like Magon de la Balue of Saint-Malo, had previously been "overwhelmed by the diminutions which have just taken place" (1724), to calculate with certainty on the value of the livre.[58]

Rochelle, 1888-1900, five vols.), III, pp. 43-44. This was written in reply to a letter of complaint from the Chamber of Commerce of La Rochelle, September 13, 1727, concerning the British illicit provisioning traffic at Martinique.

[56] Marcel Marion: *Histoire financière de la France depuis 1715* (Paris, 1914-1931, six vols.), I, p. 140. The livre, the value of which was not changed thereafter until 1785, was worth one franc two centimes of the pre-war currency.

[57] [C. de F. Dutot]: *Réflexions politiques sur les finances et le commerce* (The Hague, 1738, two vols.), II, pp. 127-128; see also *ibid.*, I, p. 6. Cantillon very much disapproved of changing the value of the coinage (Richard Cantillon: *Essai sur la nature du commerce en général* [Edited by Henry Higgs; London, 1931], pp. 293, 297).

[58] Henri Sée: "Le commerce de Saint-Malo au XVIIIe siècle, d'après les papiers des Magon." *Mémoires et documents pour servir à l'histoire du commerce et de l'industrie en France* (Edited by Julien Hayem; Paris, 1911-1929, twelve vols.), IX, pp. 50-51. Fleury's stabilization of the coinage was highly lauded by the anonymous author of *An Inquiry into the Revenue, Credit and Commerce of France* (Second edition, London, 1742), pp. 35-36; and by Dr. William Douglass: *A Discourse concerning the Currencies of the British Plantations in America* (Boston, 1740), reprinted

Besides fixing the monetary standard, Fleury's government showed by its interest in the improvement of the system of roads a desire to facilitate domestic trade. Before 1738 the system of the *corvée des grands chemins* was being applied in some of the generalities, and had resulted in that notable amelioration of the highways observed by Lady Mary Wortley Montagu in 1739. In a *Mémoire sur la conduite du travail des corvées*, sent to the several intendants in 1737 and presumably written by Orry, the Comptroller General, a solicitude for the betterment of trading communications manifested itself:

It is impossible to accomplish the complete mending of roads without *corvées;* but the more this aid is indispensable, the more it ought sparingly to be used; and as, by employing it wisely, it can be infinitely advantageous to trade, even so, if it is overworked, it can become onerous to the people and to the State.[59]

By an instruction addressed to the intendants on June 13, 1738, the system of the *corvée des grands chemins* was extended to include all France, a system which, although naturally unpopular with the peasants, resulted in those admirable roads which Arthur Young so highly esteemed.[60]

During the years of Fleury's administration, the government could count on an increase of the public interest in trade. Voltaire wrote in 1738 that "at present the principles of commerce are known by everyone."[61] The writings of the Abbé de Saint-Pierre frequently allude to the value of trade, and the translator of Melon's *Essai politique sur le commerce* concluded that the

and edited by Charles J. Bullock in *Economic Studies of the American Economic Association*, II (1897), pp. 297-299. M. Carré declares that this fixing of the valuation of money was one of the principal causes of French prosperity during the eighteenth century (H. Carré: *Le règne de Louis XV (1715-1774)* [Ernest Lavisse, editor: *Histoire de France depuis les origines jusqu'à la Révolution* (Paris, 1903-1911, nine vols. in eighteen parts), VIII, part ii], p. 95).

[59] E. J. M. Vignon: *Études historiques sur l'administration des voies publiques en France aux dix-septième et dix-huitième siècles* (Paris, 1862-1880, four vols.), III, p. 7; cf. *ibid.*, II, p. 98.

[60] Vignon: *Études historiques*, III, pp. 3-7 of the *pièces justificatives*.

[61] "Observations sur MM. Jean Lass, Melon, et Dutot; sur le commerce, le luxe, les monnaies et les impôts" (*Oeuvres de Voltaire* [Edited by A. J. Q. Beuchot; Paris, 1826-1840, seventy-two vols.], XXXVII, p. 529; see also, *ibid.*, p. 527).

appearance of such a book betokened that the temper of the French people was undergoing a change.[62] Melon strongly favoured the encouragement of navigation, the development of foreign trade and its release from import and export restrictions.[63] Commerce was the source of national power, and it was the function of governments to protect and foster it:

> Military Government did not make the Venetians great. Military Government doth not now support them. They are supported by their Polity and some remains of their Trade. . . . Their [the Muscovites'] Strength encreaseth, according to the Progress they make, in Polity and Commerce; and not, according as they enlarge their Territory, which hath always been immensely large.[64]

Dutot, in his *Réflexions politiques sur les finances et le commerce,* likewise emphasized the importance of trade.[65] He desired an increase of the navy with a corresponding decrease of the army: "He who is master of the sea is master of all."[66] There was a better way of making war than by armies:

> To utilize peace in order to procure for ourselves all the advantages of a large trade is to wage war on our enemies. Away, then, with those victories acquired by ruinous efforts! Let glory rest! . . . . . France, favoured by the advantages of her trade, will make neighbouring states realize that she is as capable of increasing her power by peace as by war.[67]

---

[62] *Les rêves d'un homme de bien,* pp. 208, 217, 246; Charles Irenée Castel, l'abbé de Saint-Pierre: *Annales politiques (1658-1740)* (Edited by Joseph Drouet; Paris, 1912), p. 26: "La source des grandes richesses d'un État, c'est le commerce." See also *ibid.,* pp. 291, 321; S. Siégler-Pascal: *Un contemporain égaré au XVIIIᵉ siècle: Les projets de l'abbé de Saint-Pierre, 1658-1743* (Paris, 1900), p. 146. Melon: *A Political Essay upon Commerce,* p. vi.

[63] [Jean-François Melon]: *Essai politique sur le commerce* (n.p., 1736), pp. 26-27, 130-131, 134, 143.

[64] Melon: *A Political Essay upon Commerce,* pp. 141-142.

[65] Dutot: *op. cit.,* II, pp. 394-400.

[66] *Ibid.,* II, p. 383.

[67] *Ibid.,* II, pp. 403-404. Richard Cantillon, who wrote between 1730 and 1734, although his book was not published until 1755, also emphasized the value of foreign trade: "I will conclude then by observing that the trade most essential to a State for the increase or decrease of its power is foreign trade, that the home trade is not of equally great importance politically. . . . and above all that care must always be taken to maintain the balance against the foreigner" (Cantillon: *Essai sur la nature du commerce en général,* p. 243); see also *ibid.,* pp. 163-167, 181, 191, 193. Cantillon declared that this desirable balance could be achieved most successfully by the encouragement of navigation (*ibid.,* pp. 170-171, 241).

But aside from fixing the monetary standard and introducing the *corvée* system, Fleury's government conspicuously refrained from that detailed regulation of commercial activity which had so strongly characterized the administration of his predecessors. Colbert was dead, and Colbertism was slowly dying. Mercantilist notions with reference to colonies and foreign commerce still prevailed, just as they did in Great Britain at that period, but the idea of making trade freer within the walls of France's mercantile empire was beginning to make headway. As early as 1701 a deputy from the Chamber of Commerce of Nantes had written:

The first thing which may be wished in favour of trade is liberty: it is too constrained at home and abroad; it is impossible for merchants to extend it on the present footing. That is the stumbling block. . . . Liberty is the soul and the element of trade . . . As soon as one sets limits to the ingenuity of merchants, one destroys trade.[68]

The same idea was expressed by Boisguillebert and, in the 1730's, by Melon and D'Argenson:[69]

The greatest and best known of maxims is that trade asks only liberty and protection.[70]
Trade in all commodities ought to be as free as the passage of air. . . .
Trade will never be led, as is supposed, by prohibitions and exclusive rights; inspections, acquittances, damages divert the peaceful trader from his undertakings.[71]

[68] *Mémoire du sieur des Casaux du Hallay, député de Nantes, sur l'état du commerce en général, remis au Conseil, le 4 mars, 1701* (A. M. de Boislisle: *Correspondance des contrôleurs généraux des finances avec les intendants des provinces* [Paris, 1874-1897, three vols.], II, p. 483). Cf. Eli F. Heckscher: *Mercantilism* (London, 1935, two vols.), I, pp. 213-214.

[69] For an *analyse* of the ideas of Boisguillebert, see Kingsley Martin: *French Liberal Thought in the Eighteenth Century* (London, 1929), pp. 59-61. The Abbé de Saint-Pierre likewise made frequent allusions to the desirability of liberating trade (Saint-Pierre: *Annales politiques (1658-1740)* [ed. Drouet], pp. 21, 356, 376; *Les rêves d'un homme de bien*, pp. 222-224; Siégler-Pascal: *Un contemporain égaré*, pp. 127-129).

[70] Melon: *Essai politique sur le commerce*, pp. 26-27.

[71] [This was written in March 1738]: René Louis de Voyer de Paulmy, marquis d'Argenson: *Journal et mémoires du marquis d'Argenson* (Edited by E. J. B. Rathery; Paris, 1859-1867, nine vols., [La Société de l'histoire de France. *Publications*, No. 34]), I, p. 375. Similar ideas were expressed in letters to Maurepas from the

Although economic opinion was not ready to commit itself in favour of international free trade, it was beginning definitely to oppose the extreme regulation of industry and commercial enterprise which Colbert had introduced. Governmental policy, too, was cautiously and tentatively turning the same way. An example of this may be seen in the King's instructions to the Governor and Intendant of San Domingo, under date of August 20, 1726:

. . . They ought always to hold for principle that trade sustains itself only in so far as it is free.[72]

Such evidence suggests that the commercial policy of the government may have been composed of something more than absent-mindedness. In short, it may fairly be argued that Cardinal Fleury's administration was not unmindful of the encouragement of trade.[73] The resources of diplomacy were put to work for the protection and extension of commercial activity abroad, while, at home, trade prospered as the result of the

Chamber of Commerce of Marseilles, July 25, 1723 and October 5, 1742 (Octave Teissier: *La Chambre de Commerce de Marseille* [Marseilles, 1892], pp. 123-124, 144). The anonymous memorialists of 1728 likewise complained of the noxious effects of internal customs duties and divers impositions of that nature (Henri Sée and Léon Vignols: "Mémoires sur le commerce rédigés en vue du congrès de Soissons (1728)." [Ministère de l'instruction publique et des beaux-arts: Comité des travaux historiques et scientifiques, section d'histoire moderne (depuis 1715) et contemporaine]: *Notices, inventaires & documents*, XII: *Études et documents divers* [Paris, 1926], pp. 14, 19-20).

[72] Médéric Louis Élie Moreau de Saint-Méry: *Loix et constitutions des colonies françoises de l'Amérique sous le Vent* (Paris, 1784-1790, six vols.), III, p. 186. A striking remark in similar vein is attributed to Maurepas (Jean Frédéric Phelippeaux, comte de Maurepas: *Mémoires du comte de Maurepas* [Edited by J. L. G. Soulavie; second edition, Paris, 1792, four vols.], III, p. 229), but it is difficult to distinguish in this compilation between what is authentic and what has been subjected to editorial improvement.

[73] The Prussian ambassador to France, Chambrier, wrote to Frederick II, June 17, 1740, that the British were becoming alarmed at the power of France "d'autant plus que celle-ci [l'Angleterre] est parfaitement instruite que le système de la France a beaucoup changé par rapport au commerce, depuis que le Cardinal est à la tête des affaires et qu'on tâche de l'augmenter tant qu'on peut, comme il l'est en effet de beaucoup, depuis une dizaine d'années, dans les villes de Bordeaux, de la Rochelle et autres maritimes de ce royaume, lesquelles se trouvent dans le département du comte de Maurepas . . ." (Flammermont: *Les correspondances des agents diplomatiques étrangers*, pp. 7-8).

government's improving the internal communications, fixing the value of the circulating medium and conducting public business with economy.

The allegation that the Cardinal and his ministers were negligent of the interests of trade is, at best, a hazardous one; and in reply to the further criticism which is frequently made that he failed to reform the financial structure of the monarchy there is no lack of countervailing arguments. For the universal resistance to Pâris-Duverney's project of the *cinquantième* was fresh before his eyes. This tax, which was to be levied in kind and was to fall on the goods of privileged and unprivileged alike, was announced on June 5, 1725. The first returns were to be made in 1726, but so great was the opposition that the government was unable to secure agents for its collection, while the unpopularity which it aroused contributed greatly to the discredit which enveloped the administration of the Duke of Bourbon. The resistance of the two privileged orders to this invasion of their immunities was inexpugnable; it was common sense on Fleury's part to drop the project when he came into sole power, and to avert a dangerous conflict between Church and State by accepting in its place an annual free gift from the clergy.[74] The opposition in 1726 was of that same selfish and unenlightened character with which Calonne attempted to deal in 1787; the prejudice against reasonable reform was as blind as that which defeated Walpole's excise scheme in 1733; but the tenacity and the strength of the opposition to fiscal reform was sufficient to demonstrate the danger of convulsing the kingdom by innovations. On the whole, the Cardinal's financial policy was nothing more stirring nor novel than simple economy; nevertheless, within the limitations of the existing fiscal system, Fleury's frugality and Orry's management worked wonders. Barbier wrote in March, 1737:

[74] For a history of the *cinquantième*, see Marion: *Histoire financière de la France*, I, pp. 130-137; cf. M. Henri Hauser's *analyse* of the thesis of a M. Cottier: *Le cinquantième, 1725-1727*, in *La Révolution française*, Nouvelle Série, No. 2 (1935), pp. 190-191.

The finances are in better condition than they have ever been, and it will be ever regrettable to lose the Cardinal.[75]

M. Marion observed that the short period of time which separated the War of the Polish Succession from that of the Austrian was the best in the financial history of the *ancien régime*.[76]

As far as Fleury's failure to accomplish financial reform is concerned, certainly it is true that there existed throughout the period of the *ancien régime* many crying abuses which sapped the vitality and the efficiency of the French monarchy. The existence of these abuses was a standing challenge to kings and ministers, and the eradication of them would have been most desirable. But did the reform of the fiscal system, which was so intimately and inextricably involved with the constitutional and social *status quo*, lie within the sphere of practical politics? Were not the privileged classes too strongly entrenched to permit the peaceful accomplishment of reform? The resistance to the imposition of the *cinquantième* was significant, and made it reasonable to conclude that a programme of fiscal readjustment would excite opposition which would, temporarily at least, impair the efficiency of the government and injure its prestige abroad. It is safe to say that it was precisely this which Fleury, to whom interest in the diplomatic position of France was fundamental, wished most to avoid. Consequently, the Cardinal ruled France in the spirit of an old man making the best of what is at hand, rather than with the zeal of a youthful enthusiast. By his too favourable treatment of the farmers-general, to whom he awarded on needlessly easy terms the farming of the indirect taxes, which under the Duke of Bourbon had been collected by officials in the employ of the State, he blundered and blundered badly.[77] But,

[75] Barbier: *Journal*, II, p. 145. Chambrier reported to Frederick II the excellent condition of French finances, June 27, 1740 (Flammermont: *Les correspondances des agents diplomatiques étrangers*, pp. 5-6).

[76] Marion: *Histoire financière de la France*, I, p. 161.

[77] The taxes were farmed in 1726 for eighty million livres; in 1732 the lease was renewed for eighty-four million livres annually; the lease for 1738 called for an annual payment of 83,083,000 livres, exclusive of 11,300,000 livres which the farmers-general paid for the tobacco monopoly and for the privilege of farming Lorraine

on the other hand, the attempts which he and Orry made to collect the *taille* in some *généralités* on the basis of a fairer imposition broke down as a result of the ignorant opposition of the peasants and the selfish resistance of the privileged orders.[78]

Fleury's generation was by no means blind to the existence of abuses or to the necessity of correcting them. To diagnose the causes of political distemper was relatively easy; it was done during Fleury's lifetime by such far-seeing and intelligent men as Vauban, Boisguillebert and Saint-Pierre.[79] But fiscal reform was not the sole problem of government which demanded attention from a *premier ministre* of France, as others had discovered before Fleury. What, for instance, can be more eloquent than the words of the man who criticized an Estates General for having brought about no other result than to make it clear to everyone that it is not enough to recognize evils if one has not the will to remedy them? This able and clairvoyant man attacked the institution of survivorships and the abuse of pensions, and on an extremely public and solemn occasion had this to say of the abuses inherent in the system of the sale of offices:

And thus, with evils accompanying and reinforcing one another, the venality of offices has brought about the multiplicity of them, which gives the finishing stroke to overwhelming the people by augmenting the burden imposed on them through the salaries allocated to all offices and by diminishing the

(Marion: *Histoire financière de la France*, I, pp. 143-144, 150-151, 152; cf. J.-J. Clamageran: *Histoire de l'impôt en France* [Paris, 1867-1876, three vols.], III, pp. 241-243, 261). Even though the lease of 1726 was granted at too low a figure, Marshal Villars, himself a member of the Council of State, favoured granting it at that figure because it was "indispensably necessary in order to re-establish the circulation which had totally ceased on account of the general indignation [*soulève-ment*] against M. the Duke, . . . " (Villars: *Mémoires*, V, p. 26).

[78] See Marion: *Histoire financière de la France*, I, pp. 162-164.

[79] Cf. Vauban's description of abuses in the imposition and collection of the *taille*, the indirect taxes, the provincial customs duties, the head tax and the exemption from taxation of privileged persons (Sebastien Le Prestre de Vauban: *Projet d'une dixme royale* [n.p., 1707], pp. 3, 24, 29-31, 38, 43, 80). Saint-Pierre decried the venality of offices (Saint-Pierre: *Annales politiques (1658-1740)* [ed. Drouet], p. 43; Drouet: *L'abbé de Saint-Pierre: L'homme et l'oeuvre*, pp. 171-172); inveighed against the inequality of tax impositions (Drouet: *op. cit.*, p. 185); argued in favour of the *taille tarifié* (*ibid.*, pp. 64-65); and was opposed to internal customs duties (Saint-Pierre: *op. cit.*, p. 22). For Boisguillebert, see Martin: *French Liberal Thought in the Eighteenth Century*, pp. 59-61; and especially Hazel Van Dyke Roberts: *Bois-guilbert: Economist of the Reign of Louis XIV* (New York, 1935), particularly cap. viii.

strength which is requisite for them to support such a burden, considering that, the more office holders exempted from dues and *tailles* there are, the fewer persons there remain to pay them; and (what is worth remembering), those who remain are each and every one poor, the rich having risen above the crowd by means of the money which offices provide.

Yet what was this man able to accomplish to remedy the abuses which he had so vehemently decried, when he became known to the world as Cardinal Richelieu?[80]

The administration of Cardinal Fleury is frequently criticized on still another ground. Besides the allegation that he was negligent of trade, which may be dismissed as untrue, and the stricture that he did not reform the financial structure of the French monarchy, which is certainly true although subject to extenuation, the criticism is often made that he neglected the French navy. This remark, upon analysis, usually reduces itself to the contention that the French navy during his administration was not increased to a point where it equalled that of the British. For, so far as expenditure is concerned, the Cardinal, far from neglecting the navy, allotted more money to it than his immediate predecessors had done. Following the death of Louis XIV, the new administration granted the navy eight million livres, of which a million and a half was earmarked for the galleys and two millions and a half for colonial expenses.[81] This sum was the usual one for the period of the Regency, with the exception of 1722, when the navy received 12,450,000 livres.[82] In 1724, the first year of the Duke of Bourbon's administration, the usual sum of 8,000,000 livres was allotted to the navy, and in 1725, 9,000,000 livres, of which 1,600,000 was to be used for refitting.[83] The allotment for 1726, 1727 and 1728 must have been more

[80] The quotation is from Richelieu's harangue to the King and Queen-Regent, as spokesman for the clergy, February 23, 1615 (*Mémoires du cardinal de Richelieu* [Edited by Count Horric de Beaucaire and Fr. Bruel; Paris, 1907-1929, nine vols., (La Société de l'histoire de France. *Publications*, No. 104)], I, p. 344); see also *ibid.*, pp. 351-358, 367-368.

[81] D. Neuville, editor: *État sommaire des Archives de la Marine antérieures à la Révolution* (Paris, 1898), p. 615; P. Levot: *Histoire de la ville et du port de Brest* (Brest and Paris, 1864-1866, three vols.), II, pp. 84-85.

[82] Luçay: *Des origines du pouvoir ministériel en France*, p. 541.

[83] Maurepas: *Mémoires*, IV, p. 208; Levot: *Histoire de Brest*, II, p. 87.

than nine millions annually, inasmuch as Maurepas, in the memorial which he submitted to the Royal Council of Commerce in 1730, stated that the navy's budget was reduced to that figure in 1728.[84] Nine millions seems to have been the customary allotment for the navy during the Cardinal's administration, except that in 1734 a total of 18,410,000 was granted and in 1739, 19,200,000.[85] These figures roughly indicate that the navy budget during Fleury's administration was low, yet was consistently higher than the sums allotted during the Regency. In years when there was danger of war, Fleury was by no means niggardly. The expenditure for the navy in 1739 was equivalent to £800,000 sterling, which surpassed the total British expenditure for *matériel* and personnel for each of the years 1730, 1731, 1732 and 1736.[86] The allotments to the navy were even higher in succeeding years: in 1740 the navy received 20,100,000 livres; in 1741, 26,100,000 and in 1742, twenty-seven millions.[87] These

[84] Maurepas: *Mémoires*, III, pp. 117-118.

[85] Luçay: *Des origines du pouvoir ministériel en France*, p. 541; these statistics cited from a contemporary manuscript, Fonds Fr. 11.145, *Bibliothèque nationale*. In 1739 the "ordinary" funds allocated annually to the navy amounted to 9,550,000 livres (E. de Chabannes La Palice: "Au seuil de la guerre de Succession d'Autriche, 1741-1744." *Revue maritime*, Nouvelle Série, No. 151 [July, 1932], p. 42).

[86] These calculations have been made on the supposition that the livre was equivalent to ten pence, and that, consequently, 19,200,000 livres was equal to £800,000 sterling. The following figures, compiled from Charles Whitworth: *A Collection of the Supplies, and Ways and Means, from the Revolution to the Present Time* (London, 1764), pp. 54-77, show Great Britain's total expenditure for the navy during this period:

1726	1,239,071- 7- 8	1735	1,027,436- 4-10
1727	1,485,561-14- 9	1736	789,201- 6- 5
1728	986,025-10- 5	1737	1,302,885-12- 5
1729	853,786-16- 5	1738	846,689- 2- 6
1730	732,034- 4- 4	1739	2,019,704- 8- 3
1731	688,885- 7- 5	1740	2,264,691-10-10
1732	731,498-19- 8	1741	2,268,756-17- 1
1733	1,242,670- 5- 9	1742	2,268,558-13- 5
1734	1,758,914- 9- 7		

[87] Clamageran: *Histoire de l'impôt en France*, III, p. 279. Clamageran cited as authority documents in the *Bibliothèque nationale*, Fonds Fr. 11145, and in the *Archives nationales*, *série* G7; the latter, which deal particularly with the years 1741 and 1742, he described as being "semi-official." According to another account, however, 9,550,000 livres were allotted annually to the navy during these years, with supplementary or "extraordinary" allotments of seven millions for 1740; eight

sums were expended upon the navy when Fleury was still alive, and during a period when a maritime war with Great Britain was only prospective. But in 1745, after Fleury was dead and while war with the British was in full career, only 19,300,000 livres were spent for the navy.[88]

The explanation of this anomalous fact is perhaps revealed in a memorial, written in the name of Maurepas in 1745, wherein complaint is made of the difficulty of getting the Comptroller General to apportion money for the fitting out of ships, inasmuch as such disbursements had, since 1715, been counted as extraordinary expenses.[89] If Maurepas had greater difficulty in securing funds after the death of the Cardinal than he did before, the personnel of the Ministry otherwise remaining unchanged, the inference follows that the Cardinal had used his influence to secure for

---

for 1741; six for 1742 and eight for 1743 (E. de Chabannes La Palice: "Au seuil de la guerre de Succession d'Autriche, 1741-1744." *Revue maritime*, Nouvelle Série, No. 151 [July, 1932], pp. 42-43; No. 152 [August, 1932], p. 200; No. 153 [Sept., 1932], pp. 342-348).

[88] Neuville: *État sommaire des Archives de la Marine*, p. 616, note 1. It should be remarked that these figures, for the authority of which Neuville cited documents in *série* G47 of the *Archives de la Marine*, do not agree with those cited (although without reference to authority) by Pierre Margry: "Une famille dans la marine au XVIIIe siècle (1692-1789)." *Revue maritime et coloniale*, LXVIII (1881), p. 102; according to Margry, the naval budget for these years, exclusive of sums allocated for the galleys and the colonies, was:

1744	27,059,847 livres	6 sols	4 deniers
1745	23,335,728	10	1
1746	28,594,782	16	2
1747	29,308,667	11	5
1748	26,349,839	6	4

This whole subject invites further research.

[89] "Les contrôleurs généraux des finances qui ont compté seulement sur les dépenses fixes et réglées et qui ont fait leurs arrangements en conséquence, ont regardé apparemment comme dépenses extraordinaires et non nécessaires les fonds qui ont été demandés pour les armements et prétendu le plus souvent n'être pas en état d'y pourvoir, la répartition des revenus du Roi étant faite sur un autre pied. C'est là ce qui a occasionné les difficultés que la Marine a toujours trouvées à obtenir des fonds pour armer. C'est ce qui la rend, en quelque sorte, dépendante des finances et qui est absolument contraire à l'ordre et à la bonne règle; c'est aussi ce qui a causé en partie l'épuisement où elle est tombée. . . . " (Neuville: *État sommaire des Archives de la Marine*, pp. 615-616, note).

the navy greater allotments than Orry, of his own initiative, had been willing to grant. When one considers in what leading-strings the jealous Cardinal kept his ministers, and contrasts with that fact the notorious lack of articulation of the several ministries following his death, the inference is strengthened.

However, the evidence on this point must be regarded as inconclusive. What is certain, on the other hand, is that more was expended upon the navy during Fleury's administration than had been spent during the Regency and the ministry of the Duke of Bourbon. Moreover, the navy, although small, was larger and in a more effective condition than it had been under the Regency. In 1719 there were only forty-nine vessels, of all rates, on the navy list, and of these almost all were unfit for service.[90] Twenty of the forty-nine belonged to the Toulon fleet, and of these only six were worth repairing.[91] In 1723 the arsenal at Toulon had not fitted out a vessel for several years; between 1717 and 1723 only two ships were constructed at Brest, a number insufficient to replace the superannuated vessels there. Construction increased to some extent under the Duke of Bourbon: the Count of Toulouse, Admiral of France, remarked in the course of a memorial to the King, dated November 20, 1724, that by the end of 1725 France would have thirty ships of the line.[92] Pursuant to his advice, in 1725 the effective was set at fifty-one ships of the line, and this number was raised to fifty-four in 1728; in 1730 the French navy counted fifty-one ships from the first to the sixth rate, besides fifteen freight ships.[93] Most of these vessels were not kept in active service, and had to be fitted out with rigging as the occasion arose, which explains

[90] Levot: *Histoire de Brest*, II, p. 85.

[91] V. Brun: *Guerres maritimes de la France: Port de Toulon, ses armements, son administration, depuis son origine jusqu'à nos jours* (Paris, 1861, two vols.), I, p. 173.

[92] Brun: *Port de Toulon*, I, p. 202. For the memorial by the Count of Toulouse, see Philippe le Valois, marquis de Villette: *Mémoires du marquis de Villette* (Edited by L. J. N. Monmerqué; Paris, 1844), p. lxvii.

[93] Neuville: *État sommaire des Archives de la Marine*, p. 615; Maurice Loir: *La marine française* (Paris, 1893), p. 83; Levot: *Histoire de Brest*, II, p. 87; [Alexandre] Lambert de Sainte Croix: *Essai sur l'histoire de l'administration de la marine de France, 1689-1792* (Paris, 1892), p. 159. Cf. Villars: *Mémoires*, V, p. 323; Baudrillart: *Philippe V et la cour de France*, IV, p. 95.

the British ambassador's information in 1735 that fifteen ships could not be fitted out at Brest and Rochefort in less than six weeks, "and to do that they must work night and day."[94]   In 1739 the British received information to the effect that the French navy was composed of forty-nine vessels from the first to the fourth rate, besides nine frigates and twelve smaller vessels.[95] An official French list computed that, in January 1740, France had forty-one ships of the line, that is to say, vessels larger than frigates; Great Britain at that time had one hundred and twenty.[96] In 1743 France had some forty to forty-five ships of the line and fifteen large frigates, all in a condition to put to sea.[97] Far from "allowing the French fleet almost to disappear," Fleury could count on respectable squadrons as the period of his administration drew to a close.

The navy which Fleury is supposed to have permitted almost to disappear was frequently engaged in active service during his administration. Whereas the Regency had failed even to fit out squadrons to keep the Mediterranean pirates under control, in 1727 eleven vessels were sent to Tunis and Algiers. In 1728 a squadron comprising twelve ships of various sizes overawed

[94] Waldegrave to Newcastle, Paris, June 1, 1735 (William Coxe: *Memoirs of the Life and Administration of Sir Robert Walpole, Earl of Orford* [London, 1798, three vols.], III, p. 257).

[95] Captain Lynslager to Robert Trevor, Amsterdam, June 14, 1739 (Trevor Papers, *Historical Manuscripts Commission, Report* XIV, Appendix Part IX [London, 1895], p. 33). Lower estimates are given by two contemporaneous British authors, but are probably understatements, inasmuch as the authors desired to commit Great Britain to war with France (Sir H. W. Richmond, editor: "The Land Forces of France— June 1738." *Publications of the Navy Records Society*, LXIII, p. 58; *An Inquiry into the Revenue, Credit and Commerce of France* [London, 1742], p. 52. Practically identical with the document edited by Sir H. W. Richmond is *The Present State of the Revenues and Forces, by Sea and Land, of France and Spain* [London, 1740]; cf., with reference to the French navy, p. 14: the French were thought to have twenty-five ships of the line, eighteen frigates and twelve old ships. The author of *An Inquiry* declared that the French had only twenty-eight ships of the line fit for service, besides twelve East-Indiamen convertible into men-of-war).

[96] Georges Lacour-Gayet: *La marine militaire de la France sous le règne de Louis XV* (Paris, 1902), p. 476.

[97] Ch. Chabaud-Arnault: "Études historiques sur la marine militaire de la France, XIII: La marine française pendant la guerre de la Succession d'Autriche." *Revue maritime et coloniale*, CX (1891), p. 377.

Tunis and bombarded Tripoli; in 1729 six frigates blockaded Tripoli; in 1730 six ships of the line were fitted out for a Mediterranean cruise, although they did not sail that year; in 1731 four ships of the line cruised in Mediterranean waters under the command of Duguay-Trouin; this operation was repeated in 1732 and in 1734 nine vessels were sent to Algiers. In 1737 the Marquis d'Antin commanded a squadron of five vessels which attacked the Moroccan port, Salé.[98] Year after year Maurepas sent out a small number of frigates to the Antilles, and these cruises in the Mediterranean and the Caribbean were consciously utilized to provide training for the personnel.[99] In 1733, during the troubles of the Polish succession, a squadron of eight ships of the line and five frigates was sent to the Baltic; in 1734, fifteen sail were fitted out at Brest; and in 1735, twenty.[100] This naval activity very much alarmed the British, who increased their own naval expenditure enormously during these years. Those who criticize the Cardinal for not permitting the navy to play a more important part in the War of the Polish Succession forget that the covert aim of the French Ministry in this contest was the acquisition of Lorraine, to the attainment of which naval demonstrations in the Baltic were almost irrelevant. In fact, if persisted in, they might have provoked the Maritime Powers to forsake their neutrality and form a dangerous coalition against France. In 1739 D'Antin appeared in Swedish waters, in command of a small squadron.[101] In 1740, following the outbreak of war between Great Britain and Spain, thirty-seven ships of

[98] Ch. Chabaud-Arnault: "Études historiques sur la marine militaire de la France, XII: La marine française sous la Régence et sous le ministère de Maurepas." *Revue maritime et coloniale*, CX (1891), pp. 68-71; Lacour-Gayet: *La marine militaire sous le règne de Louis XV*, pp. 108-111; Brun: *Port de Toulon*, I, pp. 244-246; for French policy with reference to Northern Africa during the administration of Cardinal Fleury, consult François Charles-Roux: *France et Afrique du Nord avant 1830: Les précurseurs de la conquête* (Paris, 1932), chapter vi, pp. 208-242.

[99] J. de Crisenoy: "Les écoles navales et les officiers de vaisseau depuis Richelieu jusqu'à nos jours." *Revue maritime et coloniale*, X (1864), p. 771.

[100] Lacour-Gayet: *La marine militaire de la France sous le règne de Louis XV*, pp. 112-113, 464-466; Pierre Loevenbruck: "La flotte française à Copenhague en 1733." *Revue maritime*, (July-Dec., 1926), pp. 156-171.

[101] R. C. Anderson: *Naval Wars in the Baltic during the Sailing-Ship Epoch, 1522-1850* (London, 1910), p. 214, note.

the line sailed from Brest and Toulon to cruise in the Caribbean. Not since the attempt of the Count of Toulouse in 1706 to assist in the reduction of Barcelona had France had at her disposal such naval resources.[102]

During this period, care was exercised in order that the *matériel* of the navy should not fall into dilapidation. Greater care was taken in the renovation of old ships, and more emphasis was placed on the accumulation of naval stores and timber for emergencies, a point of particular importance at a time when the government's exercise of its right of pre-emption (*mortelage*) was nevertheless insufficient to supply the navy adequately with timber because of the growing exhaustion of France's timber supply.[103] The ships that were built during this period were made to carry seventy-four guns, because experience had shown that this type combined economy with effectiveness; and naval

[102] W. L. Clowes: *The Royal Navy: A History* (London, 1897-1903, seven vols.), III, pp. 58-59; Lacour-Gayet: *La marine militaire de la France sous le règne de Louis XV*, pp. 127-128; Julian S. Corbett: *England in the Mediterranean, 1603-1713* (Second edition, London, 1917, two vols., continuous pagination), II, pp. 548-549. The French sank their Toulon fleet in 1707 in order to prevent its being burned by the Allies (*ibid.*, p. 554).

[103] Chabaud-Arnault: "Études historiques, XII: La marine française sous la Régence et sous le ministère de Maurepas." *Revue maritime et coloniale*, CX, pp. 53, 56, 57. The amount and quality of timber available for the navy declined during this period. French timber was said to have lost a good deal of its durable quality during the severe winter of 1709 ([Théodore de Blois]: *Histoire de Rochefort* [Paris, 1757], p. 207). The decline in supply was caused by the increased construction of merchant vessels, by the growing number of smelteries and sugar refineries, and by the newly-introduced custom of heating all the rooms in houses, including the vestibules (R. A. Ferchault de Réaumur: "Reflexions sur l'état des bois du royaume; et sur les précautions qu'on pourroit prendre pour en empêcher le dépérissement, & les mettre en valeur." *Mémoires de l'Académie royale des sciences pour l'année 1721*, pp. 284-300). Masts were secured from the Baltic, but the dwindling supply of native oak worried naval authorities (Brun: *Port de Toulon*, I, pp. 177-178, 235-239). Maurepas encouraged Buffon to make experiments to increase the durability and to facilitate the growth of timber (G. L. Leclerc, comte de Buffon: "Mémoire sur la conservation et le rétablissement des forests." *Mémoires de l'Académie royale des sciences pour l'année 1739*, p. 141). For evidence of French interest in this matter during these years, see Buffon: *art. cit.*, *loc. cit.*, pp. 140-156; Buffon: "Moyen facile d'augmenter la solidité, la force et la durée du bois." *Mémoires de l'Académie royale des sciences pour l'année 1738*, pp. 169-184; Buffon: "Mémoire sur la culture des forests." *Mémoires de l'Académie royale des sciences pour l'année 1742*, pp. 233-246; Marquis de Courtivron: "Discours sur la nécessité de perfectionner la métallurgie des forges, pour diminuer la consommation des bois." *Mémoires de l'Académie royale des sciences pour l'année 1747*, pp. 287-304.

engineers carefully proportioned their vessels to the weight of metal they carried.[104] The tradition of scientific craftsmanship in naval architecture was by no means impaired during this period. A second edition of Hoste's *L'art des armées navales* and *La théorie de la construction des vaisseaux* appeared in 1727. Duhamel du Monceau, the Academician who published the *Elémens de l'architecture navale* in 1752, was nominated Inspector General of the Navy in 1739, at the same time that the responsibility for the inspection of the two divisions of the French navy, that of the *Levant* as well as that of the *Ponant*, was centralized in one person. Pursuant to the advice of Duhamel du Monceau, a school in the theory of naval construction was begun at Paris in 1740; meanwhile, a French engineer, Blaise Ollivier, had been sent to spy out and compare Dutch and English methods of construction with French.[105] As a result of this emphasis on technical excellence, French men-of-war enjoyed the reputation of being more seaworthy than the British.[106]

Not only were high standards of ship construction maintained, but also the naval arsenals were improved. A masting machine and new forges were set up at Toulon; a wall was built around the arsenal at Rochefort, the entrance to the harbour at Bayonne was improved, and the construction of quays and jetties at Cherbourg between 1739 and 1742 made it into a respectable port.[107]

---

[104] Brun: *Port de Toulon*, I, p. 243; Chabaud-Arnault: "Études historiques, XII: La marine française sous la Régence et sous le ministère de Maurepas." *Revue maritime et coloniale*, CX, p. 56; R. G. Albion: *Forests and Sea Power; the Timber Problem of the Royal Navy, 1652-1862 (Harvard Economic Studies*, vol. XXIX), (Cambridge [Mass.], 1926), p. 80.

[105] Chabaud-Arnault: "Études historiques, XII: La marine française sous la Régence et sous le ministère de Maurepas." *Revue maritime et coloniale*, CX, p. 57; Alfred Doneaud: "La marine française du XVIIIᵉ siècle au point de vue de l'administration et des progrès scientifiques." *Revue maritime et coloniale*, XXI (1867), pp. 475-476; Count Marc de Germiny: "Les brigandages maritimes de l'Angleterre sous le règne de Louis XV." *Revue des questions historiques*, LXXXIII (1908), p. 482, note.

[106] Albion: *Forests and Sea Power*, pp. 78-79; Geoffrey Callender: *The Naval Side of British History* (London, 1924), p. 145.

[107] Chabaud-Arnault: "Études historiques, XII: La marine française sous la Régence et sous le ministère de Maurepas." *Revue maritime et coloniale*, CX, pp. 54-55; Alfred Doneaud: "La marine française et ses arsenaux." *Revue maritime et coloniale*, XXVIII (1870), pp. 682-686.

Complementary to the supply of the material needs of the navy was the provision for the supply of mariners in time of war. The system of registration of merchant mariners, with a view to wartime service in the royal navy, had been inaugurated by Seignelay, and operated much more efficiently than the British system of recruiting by press gangs.[108] The Regulation of May 10, 1728 renewed and improved this system; as a result, the recruiting of sailors during the War of the Austrian Succession was accomplished almost without difficulty.[109]

The fact really was that France had a navy second to none of the Continental powers, in the later years of Fleury's administration. The criticism, therefore, that the Cardinal neglected the navy must consequently be an elliptical remark by which the critics really intend to say that the French navy was not increased to a point where it equalled that of the British. True it was that the French navy was inferior in point of numbers, and it is difficult to see how it could have been otherwise without incurring ruinous expenses, so long as the political situation in Europe left France anything to fear from the aggression of her neighbours and forced her to maintain a large standing army. The importance of this fact was no secret to the British statesmen. On September 2, O. S., 1749, the Duke of Newcastle wrote to the Lord Chancellor, Hardwicke:

A naval force, tho' carried never so high, unsupported with even the *appearance* of a force upon the continent, will be of little use . . . France will outdo us at sea, when they have nothing to fear by land . . . I have always

---

[108] Difficulty was experienced by the British in impressing sailors in sufficient numbers after the outbreak of the war with Spain; a bill was introduced in 1740 to facilitate impressment (I. S. Leadam: *The History of England from the Accession of Anne to the Death of George II (1702-1760)* [London, 1909], pp. 364-365). An interesting pamphlet was written upon this topic (Thomas Robe: *Ways and Means to Man the Navy with not less than Fifteen Thousand able Sailors, upon any Emergency with less Expence to the Government; and in no wise Inconvenient to the Merchants, Traders, &c.*, [Third edition, London, 1740]). Jamaica merchants protested against the impressing of sailors in Admiral Hosier's squadron in 1726 (*Acts of the Privy Council of England, Colonial Series*, III [Hereford (England), 1910], p. 157; *idem*, VI ["The Unbound Papers"] [London, 1912], pp. 186, 190-191).

[109] [Théodore de Blois]: *Histoire de Rochefort*, p. 188; Chabaud-Arnault: "Études historiques, XII: La marine française sous la Régence et sous le ministère de Maurepas." *Revue maritime et coloniale*, CX, pp. 64-65.

maintained that our marine should protect our alliances upon the continent; and they, by diverting the expense of France, enable us to maintain our superiority at sea. . . . [110]

Over and above the fact that geographical and political exigencies necessitated the maintenance of a large standing army and militated against France's building a navy equal in size to that of Great Britain, several reasons combined to make French statesmen and naval experts regard with equanimity Great Britain's superiority in number of ships. As a result of the calculations based upon these reasons, it was possible for the French to rely upon waging a maritime war with Great Britain with a very considerable amount of success.

During the eighteenth century, the misconception that wars could be successfully fought without destroying the enemy forces was so deeply rooted that it was not until Suffren that any French admiral attempted to carry out in practice the idea that the enemy should be annihilated.[111] The prevalent conception of naval warfare, shared by generals and admirals alike, was negative and defensive, rather than aggressive and offensive. Because of the acceptance of this idea, the object of naval operations came to be the prevention of damage to one's own fleet rather than the infliction of loss upon that of the enemy. If one accepted such modest aims, it was possible to wage a war "successfully" while having at one's disposal naval forces considerably inferior in number to those of the enemy. The present-day emphasis on submarines as a weapon of defense illustrates the continuity of French policy in this respect, but with this difference, that naval experts of the eighteenth century seem to have presumed that results, really consequent only to aggressive

[110] Philip C. Yorke: *The Life and Correspondence of Philip Yorke, Earl of Hardwicke, Lord High Chancellor of Great Britain* (Cambridge [England], 1913, three vols.), II, p. 23.

[111] R. Castex: *Les idées militaires de la marine du XVIIIe siècle; De Ruyter à Suffren* (Paris, [1911]), pp. 27, 36, 43-45, 65, 111; A. T. Mahan: *Types of Naval Officers* (Boston, 1901), pp. 14-15. There likewise existed almost no conception of the "economy of forces" (Sir John W. Fortescue: "A Side Show of the Eighteenth Century." *Blackwood's Magazine*, CCXXXIII [Jan.-June, 1933], p. 343; Castex: *op. cit.*, p. 67).

warfare, could be achieved by tactics essentially defensive in character. The fact that French admirals almost invariably chose the leeward gauge in battle, in order to facilitate escape if they saw fit, and directed their fire at the enemy's rigging rather than his hull, was consistent with this essentially negative conception of the function of naval combat.[112] As late as 1763, a French naval expert was preaching the *advantage* of carrying on a naval campaign with forces inferior to those of the enemy:

At sea, the less numerous fleet, being able to maneuver with greater ease than a larger without becoming separated, can sometimes steal off under cover of night, or by the aid of a change of wind, and render pursuit useless by the enemy whom it beguiles, and whom it causes to carry on great expenditures and a campaign useless to its designs. Decisive actions at sea no longer exist, that is to say, on which entirely depend the close of the war. . . . [113]

What further tended to discount the British naval superiority in the minds of French naval authorities was an erroneous conception of the nature of sea power. That generation imperfectly realized the effect of naval strength as it manifests itself indirectly and unseen, an idea which the writings of Admiral Mahan have had the honour of rendering trite, and had no conception of

the noiseless, steady, exhausting pressure with which sea power acts, cutting off the resources of the enemy while maintaining its own, supporting war in scenes where it does not appear itself, or appears only in the background, and striking open blows at rare intervals. . . . [114]

The consequence was that naval engagements were regarded as being purely episodic, devoid of decisive results and interesting

[112] The writer on naval tactics, John Clerk, declared that the French "repeatedly" and "upon every occasion" "have made choice of, and earnestly courted a leeward position" (John Clerk: *An Essay on Naval Tactics, Systematical and Historical* [Third edition, Edinburgh, 1827], pp. 40-41); Clerk also commented "that the French have made it a rule to throw the whole effect of their shot more particularly into the rigging of their enemy" (*ibid.*, pp. 24, 140). This work was first published in 1782.

[113] Bigot de Morogues: *Tactique navale*, quoted by Castex: *Idées militaires de la marine du XVIIIe siècle*, p. 111.

[114] A. T. Mahan: *The Influence of Sea Power upon History, 1660-1783* (Boston, 1890), p. 209.

only as gratuitous exhibitions of strength.[115] The French were willing to concede that the British would probably be victorious in a major engagement, if they were given the opportunity; but, inasmuch as naval battles were thought to have no significance, at the same time that the fleets requisite to fight them were very expensive, the French did not propose to conduct their naval campaigns in that way.

As a consequence, expert French opinion calculated that France could contend with Great Britain in a maritime war on almost equal terms, in spite of the fact that England had many more ships of war.[116] The method proposed for accomplishing this was to prey on British commerce by means of privateers, cruisers and small squadrons, while scrupulously avoiding pitched naval battles. Modern naval theory teaches that it is extremely difficult to distress enemy commerce sufficiently to change the fortunes of war unless one also possesses the command of the sea. Such was not the doctrine of French naval experts in the time of Fleury; their policy of "the industrialisation of the navy," as it has been described by a recent author, was thought to be not only feasible but also quite as efficacious as the warfare waged by large fleets.[117] The doctrine had become fashionable through the influence of Pontchartrain, who had always urged that the most effective manner of carrying on naval warfare was to dis-

---

[115] Joannès Tramond: *Manuel d'histoire maritime de la France* (Paris, 1916), pp. 287-288, 471. "D'Estaing écriéra: 'Beaucoup plus de bruit que de besogne n'est que trop souvent le produit net des combats navaux (sic).' Vergennes, qui fut un grand diplomate et un piètre stratège, assurera: 'On a peu envie de renouveler des combats navals dont le succès ne laisse souvent que des pertes à regretter, que des dommages à réparer' " (Castex: *Idées militaires de la marine du XVIIIᵉ siècle*, p. 36); see also, *ibid.*, p. 152. Such was the doctrine of Guillaume Poncet de la Grave: *Précis historique de la marine royale de France (Ouvrage fait par ordre du Gouvernement)* (Paris, 1780, two vols.),—II, p. 210. The line of argument taken by Horatio Walpole in 1739, when endeavouring to persuade his countrymen against a war with Spain, suggests that the British themselves had no conception of the manner in which sea power functions: "And yet this is all our Fleet could do; it might preserve Gibraltar in case of a Siege, and in some little degree, but at a prodigious Expence, protect our Trade. But what could it do more?" ([Horatio Walpole]: *The Grand Question, whether War, or no War, with Spain, Impartially Consider'd* [London, 1739], p. 17).

[116] Cf. Castex: *Idées militaires de la marine du XVIIIᵉ siècle*, p. 20.

[117] "Les corsaires remplaçaient les amiraux" (René Jouan: *Histoire de la marine française. I. Des origines jusqu'à la Révolution* [Paris, 1932], p. 193).

tress enemy commerce.[118] This continued to be the orthodox doctrine in Fleury's time, as may be illustrated from the writings of the two leading naval experts of his day. In 1730 Duguay-Trouin advised against constructing ships of war carrying more than seventy-four guns:

He [Duguay-Trouin] asserts that this vessel of eighty guns would not be so useful, if we should have war with the English, as those of seventy–four, because, without priding ourselves upon fighting naval battles, which are infinitely costly to France and do not decide anything, and in which the English would most often have the superiority on account of the number of their vessels, it would be more useful for the service of the king and more ruinous for our enemies, to have forty to fifty ships in the port of Brest, from seventy–four to fifty cannon, with some small frigates to be sent off in squadrons, according to the information received of their undertakings and of their convoys, to sail after and surprise them; that this would be the means of distressing them on all sides and of ruining their commerce.[119]

Equally authoritative was the judgment of the Count of Toulouse, Louis XIV's legitimatized son, a man of considerable capacity joined with practical experience, who had commanded in the Battle of Malaga (1704) and was Grand Admiral of France until his death in 1737. In the memorial on naval affairs which he presented to the King in 1724, he summarized the opposing arguments for large concentrated fleets and for small detached squadrons. His own opinion was that both were useful and necessary, according to circumstances; but the significant thing to observe is that he took for granted that the purpose of both light squadrons and battle fleets was to facilitate preying upon the commerce of the enemy, and his argument was devoted solely, except in so far as considerations of coast defense were involved, to determining which would be the more effective for that purpose. It is notable that when he summarized the benefits to be derived from a large fleet, he remarked that a "naval army" produces "almost all the advantages" obtained from cruiser war-

[118] Castex: *Idées militaires de la marine du XVIIIᵉ siècle*, pp. 22-23, 30-33; Vice-Admiral Bourgois: "La guerre de course; la grande guerre et les torpilles." *Nouvelle revue*, XLI (July-August, 1886), p. 283.

[119] Mithon, intendant of the navy at Toulon, to Maurepas (Brun: *Port de Toulon*, I, p. 243). Maurepas replied that he agreed (*ibid.*, p. 244).

fare; moreover, his argument revealed his disposition to avoid pitched battles even should he have at his command a large and united fleet:

Divergent opinions have sometimes come into conflict on the most useful employment which can be made of war-ships; some have asserted that fleets were of great expense and little utility, because, they say, when a battle has been won, it is seldom that an immediate benefit is derived from it, and that it is not the case with sea-battles as it is with those fought on land, where a victory sometimes makes one master of a province or of some important place; that consequently it would be better to divide up the vessels into special squadrons, to cruise now in one place, now in another, depending upon the merchant fleets expected from distant countries or upon those which it is desirable to convoy, upon leaving France, in order to conduct them to places where it is to be presumed that they will be in safety from privateers. They add that at the same time these squadrons would protect one's own individual privateers, and would make it possible to capture sufficient prizes so that the damage which the enemy would receive would dispose him to desire peace more than would the loss of any sea-battle, of which the damage never appears to fall on individuals, and consequently does not give so much occasion for crying out and complaining; that besides these advantages, distant operations can not be undertaken when fleets, which absorb all available vessels, are fitted out.

Those who were of different opinion thought that a fleet produced almost all the advantages which the others asserted to be derived from these separate squadrons, of which I have just spoken, because the enemy can not disperse his forces when his isolated squadrons would be exposed to meeting the fleet, and that being on that account obliged to remain united, the sea remains free, as much for merchantmen as for the privateers who make war on the enemy, in which it has appeared that we have the advantage, the number of enemy prizes having always been much more considerable than those which they have taken from us. They add that the squadrons proposed by the others do not in any fashion place our coasts in safety against enemy descents, since they would be obliged to disappear as soon as the enemy's fleet should approach, instead of which a fleet prevents that of the enemy from being able to undertake anything of the sort. . . . To speak without prejudice, I believe that there are occasions in which fleets are not at all suitable, as there are also some in which they are absolutely indispensable, not only for the immediate use which may be derived from them, but also for the purpose of prestige; . . . . . [120]

The tenacity of the conception that the most efficacious naval strategy demanded cruiser warfare exclusively is illustrated by an anonymous *Mémoire sur les moyens de faire la guerre à l'Angleterre d'une manière qui soit avantageuse à la France, ou*

[120] Villette: *Mémoires*, pp. lxiii-lxvi.

pour prévenir que le roi d'Angleterre ne nous la déclare, dated October 28, 1734, which M. Lacour-Gayet has summarized:

> What he advised was a thorough-going policy of cruises on the several seas. . . . Cruises and not pitched battles; naval battles could compromise everything, and the most brilliant gained nothing, witness the victory of Tourville at Cape Béveziers [Beachy Head].[121]

A final example will indicate how widespread was the idea of confining naval warfare to preying upon the enemy's commerce, on the presumption that it was quite as practicable and effective as the warfare of naval battles and large fleets, and that consequently it rendered the latter otiose. A French author, writing during the War of the Austrian Succession, described the Spanish strategy in terms clearly applicable to the situation in France:

> Moreover, the value of the Spaniards' navy must not be judged by their armaments; if they do not equip to as considerable a degree as their condition would permit, or as other nations do, they utilize a method simple enough for waging war with advantage on maritime powers who carry on trade. To put large fleets into commission is to exchange, according to them, immense expenditures for very trifling advantages, however fortunate one might be. They believe that the slightest victory costs a great deal, and that the greatest is worth little; but that by confining themselves to cruising for enemy merchant vessels with privateers, they risk almost nothing and if ever they injure their enemies, injure them a great deal. Success has justified this wise conduct: Spanish privateers have inflicted inestimable losses on England, from whom they have taken more than six hundred ships since the beginning of the war.[122]

Dazzled by the exploits of famous corsairs like Jean Bart, Coëtlogon, Forbin and Duguay-Trouin, the French relied on privateering, supplemented by some assistance from cruisers and detached squadrons, to bring England to her knees should a maritime war break out.[123] And in the event, French and Span-

---

[121] Lacour-Gayet: *La marine militaire de la France sous le règne de Louis XV*, p. 123.

[122] *Histoire générale de la marine* (Paris, 1744-1748, three vols.), II, p. 36.

[123] D'Argenson: *Journal et mémoires*, I, p. 308, note; *ibid.*, III, p. 356. French privateers frequently enjoyed two advantages of which British privateers were deprived. It was sometimes possible to lease Crown ships for privateering operations, and these were often large and powerful vessels; in the second place, the *officiers bleus*, or non-noble naval officers, finding themselves discriminated against in the service, often found commands on privateers (J. K. Laughton: *Studies in Naval History* [London, 1887], pp. 256-257).

ish privateers did seriously distress British merchants, while the performance of the British navy fell far below expectations.[124] With confident anticipation that a war on trade would quickly make British merchants clamour for peace, French diplomats and naval authorities looked forward with equanimity to a war with Great Britain; as Broglie, the French ambassador to Great Britain, summed up the matter in a letter written to Fleury in 1731:

> I should think that when we shall be obliged to wage war with England we ought not to think of having fleets to combat theirs, even if we could; that it is much more to the purpose to have some squadrons at sea to support the largest number of privateers that can be got, having seen with my own eyes during the several years that I have been at London, that a captured vessel belonging to a merchant or to one of the English companies makes the nation cry out more than does the loss of ten battles.[125]

Inasmuch as the premier naval experts of the country were busily engaged in proving by false premises that France, with fewer ships than her antagonist, could successfully engage in a war with Great Britain, it is not surprising that Fleury should direct his policy in conformity to professional advice. Furthermore, the personal union of the Kingdom of Great Britain with the Electorate of Hanover tended to discount even further the British superiority at sea. In the event of war, France might anticipate little difficulty in threatening the Electorate, or even in occupying it. Hanover was a sort of hostage: should war break out, America might be won in Europe; at worst, the loss of colonies could be compensated for by the conquest and subsequent exchange of Hanover. This was notoriously the French policy in the Seven Years' War, until Pitt turned the tables.

[124] During the War of the Austrian Succession, the British made 3,434 prizes, of which 1,249 were Spanish and 2,185 were French. They lost 3,238, of which the Spaniards captured 1,360 and the French 1,878 (Robert Beatson: *Naval and Military Memoirs of Great Britain from 1727 to 1783* [London, 1804, six vols.], I, pp. 121-122, 414). For merchant discontent, see *A Short Account of the Late Application to Parliament Made by the Merchants of London upon the Neglect of their Trade* (Fourth edition, Dublin, 1742), pp. 3-6, and *passim*. Cf. C. Ernest Fayle: "Economic Pressure in the War of 1739-48." *Journal of the Royal United Service Institution*, LXVIII (Feb.-Nov., 1923), pp. 436-437.

[125] Quoted by Verlaque: *Histoire du cardinal de Fleury et de son administration*, p. 132.

But the discovery that Hanover was the Achilles-heel of British policy could hardly have escaped the notice of the French ministers in the negotiations between 1725 and 1731, when France and Great Britain were joined together in close co-operation.[126] Time after time, Newcastle, Townshend and Horatio Walpole emphasized the necessity of providing for the Electorate, and permitted the French ministers to see how apprehensive the British Government was lest some harm should befall the King's German dominions. That Fleury realized what advantages might be gained from a threat to Hanover is shown by the fact that the French utilized to this purpose the very first opportunity which offered. In September 1741, the approach of the army commanded by Maillebois forced George II to sign a convention of neutrality, and the incident demonstrated with what alacrity the Elector-King would tie the hands of his British ministers when the safety of Hanover was at stake. On the whole, the extent to which British interests were sacrificed for Electoral ones was undoubtedly overstated by the Parliamentary Opposition; but Chesterfield's grumble that "Hanover robbed us of the Benefit of being an Island, and was actually a Pledge for our good Behaviour on the Continent" had truth in it: Hanoverian necessities discounted some of Great Britain's naval power.[127]

These considerations suggest that it is unjust to fix upon Fleury the blame for a naval policy which does not square with modern

[126] Clear proof of French awareness of the vulnerability of Hanover is afforded by Chauvelin's admission in 1730, at a time when the French were endeavouring to persuade the British to undertake a joint campaign in Italy, of the force of the British contention that if eight thousand men were sent to Italy there would be no force left to defend Hanover (Chauvelin to Broglie, Fontainebleau, May 29, 1730 [A. É., *Corr. Pol., Angleterre*, vol. 370, f. 66]).

[127] [Philip Dormer Stanhope, Fourth Earl of Chesterfield, and Edmund Waller]: *The Case of the Hanover Forces in the Pay of Great Britain, impartially and freely examined: With some seasonable Reflections on the present Conjuncture of Affairs* (London, 1742), p. 13. George II talked some in 1737 of settling the Electorate upon the Duke of Cumberland; his motive was to spite the Prince of Wales, but the project was popular with British politicians, inasmuch as it would have eliminated the inconvenient complication of Hanoverian with British policy (Lord Hervey: *Some Materials towards Memoirs*, pp. 795-801, 855-857). Horatio Walpole wrote to Robert Trevor, January 29/February 9, 1737/8: "And indeed those Electoral considerations in which we have not the least concern do often prove inconvenient to us" (Trevor Papers, *Hist. MSS. Comm., Report* XIV, App. Part IX, p. 11).

conceptions of strategy. Limited by the exigencies of France's geographical location, counting with reason on being able to use Hanover as a pledge for British good behaviour on the Continent, and naturally accepting the conceptions of strategy, however misleading, entertained by the leading experts among his compatriots, he nevertheless supervised during his administration the development of a naval force larger and more effective than that under the Regency, a maritime strength considered by contemporaries as by no means so inferior to that of the British as modern strategists now know it to have been.

France, which had maintained peace with Great Britain during Fleury's administration, was to face the searching test of war soon after the Cardinal's death. What Fleury's administration had done for the country is shown by the fact that France was able to wage an important maritime and Continental war with a very considerable degree of success. For it should be remembered that, from the British point of view, the War of the Austrian Succession was a disappointing stalemate; that war, which they had begun in a spirit of confident anticipation, long bade fair to end in defeat, and was only ultimately retrieved, most opportunely and unexpectedly, by a peace which, French satirists declared, "passeth all understanding." During the progress of the war the British public became more and more discontented with the manner in which it was being conducted.

The Superiority of our Navy . . . answered . . . much worse than we conceived could possibly have happened. . . . This may truly be called the Nonsense of making War, . . .

wrote one pamphleteer;[128] and another, who maintained that ministers acted "by one eternal Solecism," also wrote:

The hanging half a dozen Sea Officers may possibly be a very meritorious Deed: And the obliging our Land Admirals to retire to their Country Seats, and direct the Navigation of their own Fish Ponds, the most becoming Act in the World.[129]

[128] *The State of the Nation, with a General Balance of the Publick Accounts* (Second edition, London, 1748), pp. 25, 43; see also *ibid.*, pp. 40, 42.
[129] *The State of the Nation Consider'd, in a Letter to a Member of Parliament* (Third edition, London, 1748), pp. 48, 19; see also *ibid.*, pp. 15, 39-40.

Likewise, as the war progressed, ministers became more and more disconsolate and defeatist. Chesterfield wrote to Robert Trevor on June 28, O.S., 1745: "Indeed, considering all the circumstances of the present situation of affairs, I see no salvation, but in getting out of it, *tant bien que mal*, by negotiation, . . . "; and on August 13/24 of the same year: "The situation of our affairs abroad, is in my opinion, the most melancholy and the most difficult one that I, or I believe anyone now alive remembers, ..."[130] Chesterfield and Henry Pelham were actually sorry that Cape Breton had been conquered, because it would make the negotiation of a peace more difficult.[131] George Lyttelton's letter to his father, upon hearing of the conclusion of the preliminaries, shows how profoundly glad the British were to have a cessation of hostilities:

I most heartily wish you joy of the happy and amazing event of the preliminaries being signed, at a time when even the most sanguine among us expected nothing but ruin from the continuance of the war, and almost despaired of a peace. . . . it has drawn us out of greater distresses and difficulties than can be conceived by those who do not know the interior of our affairs. . . . In short, *it is the Lord's doing, and it is marvellous in our eyes.* . . . Kiss my son for me; give him my blessing; and tell him, I now hope he will inherit Hagley, instead of some French marquis, or Highland laird, who I was afraid would have got it if the war had continued.[132]

Because the French threw away in a feckless peace the advantages won for them by the generalship of Maurice de Saxe, the real strength and vigour with which the French waged that war is sometimes forgotten.

[130] Trevor Papers, *Hist. MSS. Comm., Report* XIV, App. Part IX, pp. 116, 127. Edward Weston, Under Secretary of State for Foreign Affairs, wrote to Trevor on October 25/November 5, 1745: "Here is a strong party for abandoning the Continent entirely, and dying, if we must die, *se defendendo*. Where all this will end, God knows. But I doubt it must be little less than a miracle to save us. I write to you in confidence and can only return you sigh for sigh . . . " (*ibid.*, p. 132).

[131] Chesterfield to Trevor, August 13/24, 1745; Henry Pelham to Trevor, August 9/20, 1745; the same to the same, September 10/21, 1745 (Trevor Papers, *Hist. MSS. Comm., Report* XIV, App. Part IX, pp. 127, 129, 132). Bishop Sherlock wrote to Edward Weston, December 11/22, 1747: "By what I can observe the Military Sp[irit] abates very fast, among the higher ranks especially . . . " (Weston Papers, *Historical Manuscripts Commission, Report* X, Appendix Part I [London, 1885], p. 299).

[132] April 26, O. S., 1748 (Lyttelton: *Works*, III, pp. 326-327). At this time Lyttelton was one of the Lords of the Treasury.

Fleury's accomplishment is measured by the fact that he fostered and improved those reserves of strength which enabled France to engage with credit in a long and exhausting struggle with Great Britain. The record of a disastrous treaty (1763) and of the brilliant exploits of British soldiers and sailors under the directing genius of Pitt, written on the palimpsest of history, has tended to render somewhat illegible the account of Fleury's achievements. Yet it was he who presided over the economic recuperation of his country, whose diplomacy gave to France the commanding prestige consequent to the acquisition of Lorraine, and who fostered the prosperity and power of his nation during that period of peace which his diplomacy was skilful enough to prolong.

CHAPTER III

THE STATE OF EUROPE AND THE DIPLOMATIC
ORIENTATION OF FRANCE, 1726

THE downfall of the Duke of Bourbon was hilariously celebrated in the streets of Paris, and excited manifestations of
satisfaction equally profound, although more discreet, at the
courts of Vienna and Madrid.[1] It was confidently predicted
there that France would quickly become a member of the Vienna
alliance—an illustration of the apophthegm that prophecy is the
most gratuitous form of error. On the other hand, the British
statesmen were no less certain that Fleury would maintain the
French alliance with Great Britain, and they were more nearly in
the right.[2] Time was to show that Fleury's policy was essentially
the same as the Regent's had been: co-operation with Great
Britain and reconciliation with Spain; but much careful unravel-
ling of the tangle in which the Duke of Bourbon had involved
French diplomacy was requisite before France under Fleury once
more attained a position of such independence and prestige as
she had enjoyed under the Duke of Orleans.

Ostensibly, there was no First Minister appointed following
the disgrace of the Duke of Bourbon. But in the course of the
announcement which Louis XV made to his Council, to the
effect that the office of the *premier ministre* was henceforth to be
abolished, he stated that the Bishop of Fréjus would be present
at the transaction of all public business.[3] The fatigue of a few

---

[1] Barbier: *Journal*, I, p. 239; Chance: *Alliance of Hanover*, pp. 313-314.

[2] H. Walpole to Newcastle (very private), June 13, 1726 (Coxe: *Memoirs of Horatio, Lord Walpole*, I, pp. 223-239). British confidence in Fleury was built on the assurances of Horatio Walpole; he had visited the Bishop of Fréjus at Issy on the day of his self-inflicted exile in December, 1725, at a moment when the courtiers thought his influence was shattered. Fleury was grateful for this mark of esteem, and Walpole reaped great credit for it (*ibid.*, pp. 195-196).

[3] For this announcement, see Mathieu Marais: *Journal et mémoires de Mathieu Marais, avocat au Parlement de Paris, sur la Régence et le règne de Louis XV (1715-1737)* (Edited by M. de Lescure; Paris, 1863-1868, four vols.), III, pp. 423-424.

days' labour was sufficient to weaken Louis XV's resolution "to follow in everything the example of the late King, my great-grandfather." It is obvious that Louis XV never intended this very seriously, for immediately after the disgrace of the Duke of Bourbon and before the announcement made to his Council on June 15, the King had privately commanded his ministers "to do and dispatch all matters, that shall be told and directed by Bishop Fréjus, as much as if we should speak to him [them] ourselves."[4] It quickly became apparent that the project of following the example of Louis XIV was the thinnest of fictions; what was true was that Fleury wielded the power of a *premier ministre* at the same time that he refused the title. As Walpole had foreseen, Bishop Fréjus, "without the title of prime minister, will have the power in a more absolute manner than it was ever enjoyed by Cardinal Richelieu or Mazarin."[5]

Never did the King of France, not even Louis XIV, reign in a manner so absolute, so sure, so removed from all contradiction, nor has one embraced so fully and so despotically all the different parts of the government of the State and the court, down to the merest bagatelles.[6]

The first fruits of Fleury's administration were popular with the public. Mme. de Prie and the Pâris brothers were exiled.[7] The competent Le Blanc was restored to his former position of Secretary for War in the place of Breteuil, and Le Pelletier des

---

[4] The King's message to Morville, quoted by Walpole in his despatch of June 13, 1726 (Coxe: *Memoirs of Horatio, Lord Walpole*, I, p. 239). A similar message was delivered to the Queen (Villars: *Mémoires*, V, p. 23); cf. Marais: *Journal*, III, p. 427.

[5] Horatio Walpole's remark, despatch of June 13 (Coxe: *Memoirs of Horatio, Lord Walpole*, I, p. 237).

[6] Saint-Simon: *Mémoires*, XXXIV, p. 309. Saint-Simon, with his extreme snobbishness about birth and rank, was consequently critical of Fleury, whom he classed among "all those people . . . who, by the nothingness of their birth, and by their personal isolation were not [fit?] to take a great interest in the State which they governed" (*Mémoires*, XXXIV, p. 320). Duclos described the extent of Fleury's authority as follows: "Sans faste, avec un extérieur modeste, préférant le solide à l'ostentation du pouvoir, il en eut un plus absolu et moins contredit que Mazarin, avec ses intrigues, et Richelieu en coupant des têtes" (Duclos: *Mémoires secrets*, II, p. 375).

[7] Villars: *Mémoires*, V, pp. 23-24; Marais: *Journal*, III, pp. 425-430, 433-434, 437, 444, 447.

Forts succeeded Dodun as Comptroller General.[8] The personnel of the Ministry was strengthened also by making the Marshals d'Huxelles and Tallard members of the Council.[9] Moreover, in September 1726, just three months after he had attained a position of supreme power within the state, Fleury himself became a Cardinal. This move seems to have been inspired chiefly by a desire to avoid quarrels over precedence, for the marshals in the Council gave warning that their rank did not permit them to yield precedence to a retired bishop. On this account, Tallard and D'Huxelles did not take their seats at the Council until September 27, although they had worked informally with Fleury prior to that time.[10]

Thus, at the age of seventy-three, Fleury was invested with supreme and uncontested authority, after a career which had done little to reveal the ardent character of his ambition, or to foretell the jealous tenacity with which he would cling to power. His long administration lasted, for a period of almost seventeen years, to the day of his death (January 29, 1743), and in this span of years he accomplished notable things for the good of France. The manner in which Fleury's government fostered the financial recuperation of France and utilized the resources of diplomacy to further French commercial expansion has already been discussed. In foreign affairs his achievement was no less remarkable. By successive stages, he regained the diplomatic freedom of action of France, which his predecessor had com-

[8] Le Blanc died in 1728, and was succeeded by D'Angervilliers (Luçay: *Des origines du pouvoir ministériel en France*, p. 620). The British had not favoured his recall, because of his suspected relations with the Jacobites (Coxe: *Memoirs of Horatio, Lord Walpole*, I, pp. 233-235).

[9] These additions were necessary because the world had had a mean opinion of the Council in the time of the Duke of Bourbon, Horatio Walpole declared (Coxe: *Memoirs of Horatio, Lord Walpole*, I, p. 241). Both Marshals were "of the old court, which had indeed a most inveterate aversion to England, and the present happy establishment," but Fleury persuaded Walpole that D'Huxelles had changed his attitude and that Tallard would be submissive (*ibid.*, pp. 242-245).

[10] During the summer of 1726, Spain and the Emperor happened to have prior rights of nomination in the "promotion of the crowns." In order to persuade them to waive their turns in favour of France, Fleury naturally adopted a conciliatory attitude toward those powers, which greatly alarmed the British (Chance: *Alliance of Hanover*, pp. 328-331, 428, 434).

promised, and, as the result of a successful war waged with the Emperor, secured the valuable province of Lorraine. "After the peace of Vienna [1738], France became the arbitress of Europe."[11]

In spite of such solid accomplishments, it would be an exaggeration to maintain that Fleury's rule stirred the French imagination. It is true that the measures taken after the fall of the Duke of Bourbon were welcomed with "that sort of sober popularity which never fails to hail the return of good sense on the morrow of a prolonged fit of folly"; moreover, the frugality, the disinterestedness and the devotion to France and Louis XV which characterized Fleury throughout his administration were freely admitted by the memoir writers of the time.[12] Yet the virtues and the benefits of Fleury's administration wrung from them their approbation without exciting their enthusiasm, and their reluctant appreciation of his good qualities was tinctured with criticisms of his real or supposed weaknesses.[13]

In part, the failure of Fleury to arouse the enthusiasm of courtiers was due to temperamental differences. In a sense, Fleury's mode of governing was a glorification of the *bourgeois* manner. However sagacious his policy might be, his cautious methods remind one of a small French *rentier:* as Frederick the

---

[11] Frederick II: "The History of my own Times." *Posthumous Works of Frederic II. King of Prussia* (London, 1789, thirteen vols.), I, part i, p. 16.

[12] Charles Aubertin: *L'esprit public au XVIIIᵉ siècle* (Paris, 1873), p. 236. For commendations of Fleury, see Charles Jean François Hénault: *Mémoires du président Hénault* (Edited by François Rousseau; Paris, 1911), p. 162; D'Argenson: *Journal et mémoires*, III, p. 427; Saint-Simon: *Mémoires*, XXXIV, p. 314; Duclos: *Mémoires secrets*, II, pp. 371-374; François-Vincent Toussaint: *Anecdotes curieuses de la cour de France sous le règne de Louis XV* (Edited by Paul Fould; Paris, 1908), p. 212; Saint-Pierre: *Annales politiques (1658-1740)* (ed. Drouet), pp. 312, 317, 327-328; Bernis: *Mémoires . . . . du cardinal de Bernis*, I, p. 59; Frederick II: "History of my own Times." *Posthumous Works*, I, part ii, p. 3.

[13] Saint-Simon: *Mémoires*, XXXIV, pp. 315-326; Hénault: *Mémoires*, pp. 162-166; D'Argenson: *Journal et mémoires*, II, pp. 35-36; III, pp. 144-146; Toussaint: *Anecdotes curieuses*, pp. 212-214. "Ce fut toujours le malheur de Fleury d'avoir employé ses talents à réparer des fautes qu'il n'avait pas commises. Il eut plus de peine à défendre les intérêts français contre les intrigues de cour ou les entraînements de l'opinion publique, égarée par de fâcheuses traditions, que contre l'Europe. Il y réussit, pendant vingt ans, par des victoires obscures dont la France, loin de lui faire honneur, lui garda toujours rancune" (Émile Bourgeois: *Manuel historique de politique étrangère* [Paris, 1892-1926, four vols.], I, pp. 480-481); compare Flassan's high appreciation of Fleury (Flassan: *Histoire. . . . . de la diplomatie française*, V, pp. 166-170).

Great said of him, "His manner of governing was rather prudent than active . . . he was bold in his projects but timid in execution . . . " [14] Fleury's was a *money-saving* policy translated into the domain of politics. In his programme there was no room for the dramatic and little for the picturesque; by nature an investor rather than an *entrepreneur*, he administered France as if she were a trust fund. Consequently, as Lamartine remarked of the July Monarchy, France was bored. A song of the day characterized the administrations of the three Cardinals by saying that Richelieu bled the country, Mazarin purged it and Fleury put it on a diet.[15]

The administration of Cardinal Fleury might be characterized by a single observation: by detailing the events of any one month of his ministry, one would have the picture of more than sixteen years.[16]

Fleury's was not a policy calculated to cause a flutter in the breasts of the French aristocracy; his methods had none of the characteristic defects of the policy of a *grand seigneur*, and the courtly writers found difficulty in identifying this fact as a virtue. It is significant that the only diarist of the day who uniformly approved of the Cardinal's policy was the *bourgeois*, Barbier.[17]

Moreover, the jealous spirit with which Fleury guarded his power became somewhat oppressive. From his ministers he exacted absolute submissiveness. Indeed, they were more clerks than ministers, for his uneasy apprehensions of hostile intrigues,

[14] Frederick II: "History of my own Times." *Posthumous Works*, I, part i, pp. 12-13; compare *ibid.*, I, part ii, p. 3.

[15] Émile Raunié: *Chansonnier historique du XVIIIe siècle* (Paris, 1879-1884, ten vols.), VI, pp. 262-263.

[16] Duclos: *Mémoires secrets*, II, p. 377.

[17] Barbier: *Journal*, II, pp. 145, 189, 311. There is a characteristic exception to this rule in his comments (*ibid.*, I, pp. 249-250) on the reduction of annuity payments made by Le Pelletier des Forts in November, 1726; cf. Marion: *Histoire financière de la France*, I, pp. 147-148. Typical of Fleury's economy was his sending the four youngest daughters of Louis XV to the convent of Fontevrault in 1738; by doing so, he saved eight hundred thousand livres a year which would otherwise have had to be spent for the maintenance of their households at Versailles (Casimir Stryienski: *Mesdames de France, filles de Louis XV* [Fifth edition, Paris, 1911], pp. 9-12).

either on their part or on the part of those connected in some
way with their jurisdiction, caused him to encroach ceaselessly
upon their authority.[18] Beneath a mild and gentle exterior, the
Cardinal was suspicious and vindictive: he "very seldom forgave,
except where he could not punish," and he would tolerate no
rivals great or small.[19] Fleury's vigilance made him invulnerable,
either by an overt or a covert attack, for so great was his dominion over the King that Louis XV betrayed to him the names
of courtiers who were intriguing against his power.[20] His control
over ministers and courtiers alike was absolute. Bernis remarked
that Fleury was admirably qualified to disconcert intrigues because in his younger days he himself had been "fort expérimenté
dans cet art"; moreover, because of his great age, he possessed
an intimate knowledge of the life histories and connections of

[18] Chambrier wrote to Frederick II on December 31, 1742, only a month before
the death of the Cardinal: "As for the character of those who are at the helm of the
government of this kingdom, I have the honour to inform your Majesty that for the
present Cardinal Fleury is alone the master, and that the other ministers, who
are under his orders, have no power" (Maurice Sautai: *Les préliminaires de la
guerre de la Succession d'Autriche* [Paris, 1907], p. 468. Compare Frederick II:
"History of my own Times." *Posthumous Works*, I, part ii, p. 5). Horatio Walpole
gives similar testimony for the early part of Fleury's administration: at the moment
of Chauvelin's appointment as Secretary of State for Foreign Affairs (1727), Walpole
wrote to Newcastle that in a short time he would frame "some judgement about the
conduct and views of the new Secretary of State. In the mean time, the King may
be assured that Mr. Ch. will take care to persue strictly, as all the French ministers
are obliged to do, the Cardinal's sentiments and directions, well knowing that he is,
in a quiet way, as jealous of his authority as he is absolute and not to be shaken in
his power" (H. Walpole to Newcastle, Paris, August 19, 1727 [Br. Mus., *Add.
MS*. 32751, f. 253]).

[19] *Memoirs of the Life and Administration of the late Andrew-Hercules de Fleury*
. . . (London, 1743), p. 22; also *ibid.*, pp. 62, 99. Bernis remarked that gratitude
was not the Cardinal's favourite virtue (Bernis: *Mémoires . . . . du cardinal de
Bernis*, I, p. 52; see also *ibid.*, p. 56). The disgrace of Chauvelin on February 20,
1737, is an example of Fleury's treatment of rivals. On September 30, 1740, Antoine
Pecquet, *premier commis* in the Ministry of Foreign Affairs, was placed in the
Bastille; he was suspected of intriguing for Chauvelin's return ([Mouffle d'Anger-
ville]: *Vie privée de Louis XV* [London, 1781, four vols.], II, p. 41; Chambrier to
Frederick II, Oct. 2, 1740 [Flammermont: *Les correspondances des agents diplomatiques étrangers*, pp. 13-14]).

[20] First, in the case of the *conspiration des marmousets*, in November, 1730;
secondly, in the case of "the war of the myrmidons," in 1737 (D'Argenson: *Journal
et mémoires*, I, pp. 228-229; Duclos: *Mémoires secrets*, II, pp. 376-377; [Mouffle
d'Angerville]: *Vie privée de Louis XV*, II, pp. 42-44).

the *habitués* of the court.[21] This was an excellent qualification for rule, for, as Saint-Pierre declared, governing the court was one of the most difficult functions of the ministry.[22] Even the intellectual discussion of current topics was sufficient to excite the Cardinal's pervasive suspicions: the *Entresol*, a sort of debating society *à l'anglaise*, which had been founded by the Abbé de Saint-Pierre, became, in 1731, the object and the victim of his animosity.[23] It is not surprising, therefore, that the courtiers found the Cardinal's régime somewhat stifling.

To the absolute power which he cherished, Fleury clung passionately until the day of his death./ From the month of November 1742 to the end, he was incapable of sustained effort, yet he refused to relinquish his power.[24] The courtiers could not forgive him either his longevity or his deliberate manner of expiring. At length the suspense was over, and there is eloquence in D'Argenson's simple remark: "The Cardinal de Fleury died finally yesterday at noon."[25] A great deal of this impatience is

---

[21] Bernis: *Mémoires . . . . du cardinal de Bernis*, I, p. 53. Saint-Simon wrote that Fleury had the courtiers under such control that "not one of them, neither princes, nor *seigneurs*, nor ladies nor valets who were closest to the king, dared speak a single word to this prince on any subject whatsoever, were it only some bagatelle of entire unimportance" (Saint-Simon: *Mémoires*, XXXIV, p. 310).

[22] Saint-Pierre: *Annales politiques (1658-1740)* (ed. Drouet), p. 373.

[23] The primary source for the affairs of the *Entresol* is D'Argenson: *Journal et mémoires*, I, pp. 91-111, 203; VI, p. 168. Secondary accounts may be found in Paul Janet: "Une académie politique sous le cardinal de Fleury de 1724 à 1731." *Séances et travaux de l'Académie des sciences morales et politiques*, LXXIV (1865), pp. 107-126; Drouet: *L'abbé de Saint-Pierre: L'homme et l'oeuvre*, pp. 77-81; Goumy: *Étude sur la vie et les écrits de l'abbé de Saint-Pierre*, pp. 50-56; L. Lanier: "Le club de l'Entresol (1723-1731)." *Mémoires de l'Académie des sciences, des lettres et des arts d'Amiens*, Troisième Série, VI (1880), pp. 1-56.

[24] Barbier: *Journal*, II, pp. 339-340, 347-348; D'Argenson: *Journal et mémoires*, IV, pp. 44, 46, 49.

[25] D'Argenson: *Journal et mémoires*, IV, p. 49. This epigram circulated just after Fleury's death:

> Sans richesses et sans éclat,
> Se bornant au pouvoir suprême,
> Il n'a vécu que pour lui-même,
> Et meurt pour le bien de l'État.

(Charles-Philippe d'Albert, duc de Luynes: *Mémoires du duc de Luynes sur la cour de Louis XV (1735-1758)* [Edited by L. Dussieux and E. Soulié; Paris, 1860-1865, seventeen vols.], IV, p. 374). The extremely harsh judgment of Fleury made by

explained by the widespread desire that the King should take a greater part in governing: "*Le cardinal est mort, vive le roi,*" was the *mot* of Paris following Fleury's demise.[26]

The Cardinal might have generated much greater enthusiasm for his policies had he taken the trouble to elucidate his aims. But this was not his manner of proceeding: no man was more disregardful of public opinion than he, save when he chose in his negotiations with foreign powers to allege the pressure of French opinion as an excuse for his own immobility.[27] Nor could anyone be more secretive than he in the elaboration of his schemes. Even in his relations with his own diplomatic corps, to say nothing of the general public, the Cardinal did not attempt to explain the general aims and interconnections of French negotiations. It was characteristic of him that he gave steady diplomatic employment to men who neither understood nor approved of his policy.[28]

In fact, the Cardinal drew great advantage from the inscrutability in which he shrouded his aims, and it may fairly be said that the ingenuous gentleness and peacefulness which he permitted the world to assume to be his outstanding characteristics were, in a measure, part of a policy of systematic deception:

A minister of a foreign power said to me yesterday that France would lose, by the death of the Cardinal, an attractiveness of mildness and moderation

Félix Rocquain: *L'esprit révolutionnaire avant la Révolution, 1715-1789* (Paris, 1878), pp. 111-112, is the result of relying too heavily on the testimony of D'Argenson, who was very hostile to Fleury after the disgrace of Chauvelin (1737), and after the fiasco of D'Argenson's embassy to Portugal.

[26] "Chronique du règne de Louis XV, 1742-1743." *Revue rétrospective*, First Series, V (Paris, 1835), p. 229. The *Chronique* was the compilation of a police spy.

[27] For example, in 1727 and in 1729, when he refused to declare war against Spain, and in 1730, when he was unwilling to declare war against the Emperor in order to enforce the Treaty of Seville (Coxe: *Memoirs of Horatio, Lord Walpole*, I, pp. 254-257).

[28] Chavigny, for example, who was French envoy to the Imperial Diet from 1726 to 1731, and French minister plenipotentiary to Great Britain from 1731 to 1737, was bitterly opposed to what he conceived the Cardinal's policy to be (*Mémoire de M. Chavigny contenant quelques observations sur les anecdotes les plus importantes qu'il a recueillies dans les différentes négociations qui lui ont été confiées depuis 1712 jusques au mois de May 1738* [Archives des affaires étrangères: *Mémoires et Documents, France*, vol. 457, ff. 1-86]). He criticized the British alliance (*ibid.*, ff. 6-7); the Cardinal's policy with reference to Dunkirk (*ibid.*, f. 51); French policy in 1730 and 1731 (*ibid.*, ff. 43, 45); and in the succeeding document (A. É., *Mém. et Doc., France*, vol. 457, ff. 87 sqq.), opposed a *rapprochement* with Austria (ff. 90, 96, 105).

which had done more for France than was supposed; that in the midst of the greatest undertakings the Cardinal had always advanced pacific proposals and presented a pacific and moderate mask which had been worth to us more than two armies, and that is true.[29]

A great deal of Fleury's success in diplomacy is accountable to the fact that he gave the men with whom he negotiated the impression that he was more simple than he was. Thus, for example, he duped Horatio Walpole at the very time when the latter was making capital with his government of the influence which he presumed that he exerted over the Cardinal.[30] So too, according to Frederick the Great, he enticed Sinzendorff into believing that France would avoid war at all odds, a conviction which led the Emperor to interfere in the Polish election in a manner which resulted in the War of the Polish Succession.[31]

But the inconveniences which attended this subtle mode of procedure lay in the fact that it involved deceiving his own countrymen as well as foreigners. Some of the criticisms of Fleury's policy made by the memoir writers of his day would be serious indictments, were they based on fact. Besides being accused of negligence of trade and the navy, Fleury was also supposed to be the slave of the British during the whole time of his administration.[32] His critics did not consider that the previous mistakes of the Duke of Bourbon gave the Cardinal small choice during the first months of his administration; they had no means of knowing how fully Fleury and his government were aware of the disadvantages of the British connection. Nor had they means of knowing that the alliance began to show signs of fraying as early as 1727, following the appointment of Chauvelin as Secretary for Foreign Affairs, nor that Fleury did not regard it as having *de facto* existence after the second Treaty of Vienna

[29] D'Argenson: *Journal et mémoires*, III, p. 427.

[30] Paul Vaucher: *Robert Walpole et la politique de Fleury (1731-1742)* (Paris, 1924), pp. iv-v, 120-121, 292.

[31] Frederick II: "History of my own Times." *Posthumous Works*, I, part i, pp. 6-8. This was also Horatio Walpole's interpretation of how the Emperor became involved in that war (*The Grand Question, whether War, or no War, with Spain, Impartially Consider'd*, p. 12).

[32] Saint-Simon: *Mémoires*, XXXIV, pp. 310-312, 317; Hénault: *Mémoires*, pp. 164-165.

(1731).[33] So too, French opinion remained lukewarm concerning the War of the Polish Succession, because it was supposed to be a conflict waged merely in the interests of an exiled Polish king who happened to be the father-in-law of Louis XV.[34] Yet what was really happening was that the French government, under cover of an ostentatious pretence of disinterestedness which deluded its allies and deceived the Maritime Powers, was really playing for the acquisition of Lorraine. These examples sufficiently illustrate that Fleury's practice of deceiving his own countrymen resulted in false conceptions, the reiteration of which has been particularly injurious to his reputation; one is reminded of Sir Charles Grant Robertson's remark that "in politics unproved and reiterated assertion will in time become its own evidence."[35]

With a position at the head of the French government unshakeable and secure, Fleury could afford to indulge a pervasive cynicism which aimed at making every man his dupe. Characteristically, he exploited what he made to appear a genial *bonhomie*.[36] No fish was too small for his net: by flattering the diplomatic representatives of minor powers and making each believe that the Cardinal was his particular friend, he secured knowledge of important secrets; for these petty diplomats were frequently able to give him some inkling of what the representatives of the greater European powers were about.[37] It is characteristic of a certain type of man, of which Fleury was one, to proceed in a manner calculated to appease the jealousy of the

---

[33] Cf. Baudrillart: *Philippe V et la cour de France*, IV, pp. 81-84; Vaucher: *Robert Walpole et la politique de Fleury*, p. 46.

[34] "On commençoit à se dégoûter de l'affaire de Pologne et cette inconstance n'est malheureusement que trop à notre nation . . . " (*Mémoire de M. Chavigny contenant quelques observations sur les anecdotes les plus importantes qu'il a recueillies dans les différentes négociations qui lui ont été confiées depuis 1712 jusques au mois de May 1738* [A. É., *Mém. et Doc., France*, vol. 457, f. 60]).

[35] C. Grant Robertson: *England under the Hanoverians* (Sixth edition, London, 1923), p. 53.

[36] Thomas Robinson, who had been invited to a dinner party at which Fleury was present, wrote to Lord Carlisle, January 11, 1731: "He is a miracle of his age (being four score), a very good companion, and a great joker" (Carlisle Papers, *Historical Manuscripts Commission, Report* XV, Appendix Part VI [1897], p. 79).

[37] Flassan: *Histoire. . . . de la diplomatie française*, V, pp. 169-170.

gods and the envy of men by appearing to be buffeted by fate and circumstance, to soothe *amour propre* and put vigilance to sleep by sedulously cultivating in the people with whom one has to deal a comforting sense of personal superiority. Moreover, Fleury's methods, both in foreign and domestic affairs, were strongly characteristic of the resourcefulness and patience, the pliancy and persistency, of a churchman, whose stock in trade is the fundamental assumption of the depravity of man. To characterize Fleury's administration in the words of the *Aufklärung*:

With some good qualities for interior administration, the character of this minister in Europe was that of weakness and knavery; vices which he derived from the church in which he had been educated.[38]

By hiding disingenuousness under the appearance of candour and ambition under disinterestedness, by disarming distrust and inspiring confidence through his apparent sincerity, by seeking great aims through little expedients, Fleury attained very solid diplomatic success.

The posture of international affairs in 1726 called for an immediate exercise of those qualities, if peace was to be maintained, for France was still seriously threatened by the Alliance of Vienna, the fruit of the Duke's rushing in where the Cardinal feared to tread. Indeed, Fleury was confronted upon his accession to power with a diplomatic situation of more than ordinary complexity, which he seems to have approached with more than ordinary caution. A memorial written in 1728 by Antoine Pecquet and annotated by Chauvelin, indicates what was the point of departure of Fleury's government in analyzing the diplomatic situation:

The situation of this kingdom is such as is to be desired. The enlargement to which it has been brought, the reunion of all the parts of which it is composed, such as it is today, makes it apparent that any idea of conquests ought to be set aside.[39]

[38] Frederick II: "History of my own Times." *Posthumous Works*, I, part i, p. 14.
[39] *Mémoire sur le parti à prendre pour une alliance* (A. É., *Mém. et Doc., France*, vol. 494, f. 164); Pecquet also wrote *La situation des affaires de l'Europe en 1726*

In other words, France was to continue to play the part of a conservative power, as she had consistently done since the treaty settlement of Utrecht. It was not a question of imposing France's military hegemony over Europe: even had the Cardinal's pacific temperament not willingly forsworn such an ambitious policy, the financial exhaustion of the kingdom would have effectively precluded it. This voluntary abnegation of an aggressive policy was not, however, sufficient in itself to provide for the tranquillity of France and of Europe: there was still the problem of defense, always a peculiarly exigent one for France because of her geographical situation. Obviously, the defense of the country and the preservation of the balance of power required either an army strong enough in itself to triumph single-handed over any combination of aggressors, or else, by supplementing arms with diplomacy, the assistance of allies whose military and diplomatic resources would aid France in consolidating her security and in maintaining a conservative balance.

Since France in 1726 did not possess the financial resources sufficient to maintain an army large enough to guarantee her safety, the first conclusion to be drawn from an analysis of the diplomatic situation in that year was that some sort of alliance system was necessary. Indeed, it was particularly so; for mere neutrality at that moment promised to be particularly ineffectual and dangerous, since the Alliances of Hanover and Vienna were dividing Europe into two hostile camps which might gladly compose their common differences, if given the opportunity, at the expense of an isolated and friendless power.

The practical problem in 1726 was whether France should continue her connection with the Hanover alliance, of which she was already a member, or whether she should associate herself with the opposing combination. It would have been neither im-

(A. É., *Mém. et Doc., France*, vol. 494, ff. 38-102), in which he said (f. 43): "Mais l'état d'épuisement des finances du Royaume, le défaut total de marine, et l'impossibilité dans cette situation d'établir seule une considération suffisante dans l'Europe, n'ont pas permis de se détacher de l'Angleterre, . . . " Cf., in this general connection, Gaston Zeller: "La monarchie d'ancien régime et les frontières naturelles." *Revue d'histoire moderne*, VIII (1933), pp. 305-333.

possible nor fantastic for Fleury, who was reckoned a devout and even a bigoted Catholic, to direct French policy towards a *rapprochement* with the Catholic powers of Europe.[40] As has been mentioned, the courts of Vienna and San Ildefonso presumed that such would be the case, and the funds fell at London upon the news of Fleury's accession to power.[41] Instead, Fleury chose to continue the association of France with the Maritime Powers, pleading to the Emperor and Philip V, in extenuation, that "faith must be kept with all those with whom one is under engagements, even should they be Mohammedans and infidels."[42] Such a remark was, of course, merely a subterfuge: there were more fundamental reasons why the Cardinal chose not to incur the enmity of Great Britain by deserting the Alliance of Hanover and allying himself with the Emperor and Spain.

The first reason was the folly of placing any reliance on the stability of Spanish policy and support, so long as Elisabeth Farnese directed Spanish diplomacy. The unexpected tergiversations, as well as the tantrums, of "the Termagant of Spain" were becoming proverbial; no one could foresee in what breathless and perilous adventure the Queen of Spain would involve France if the Spanish consort were ever so fortunate as to be placed in a position where she could dictate French policy. The instability of Elisabeth Farnese's political friendships arose from the fact that she had no conception of the advisability of cementing one's alliances and promoting confidence by reasonably predictable and consistent conduct. A show of resistance frightened and intimidated her: instead of stiffening her resolution, it made her desire to woo the obdurate one. No temperamental contrast could be more extreme than that between Fleury and the Queen of Spain. In comparison with the Cardinal, who was always

---

[40] Bolingbroke wrote, probably to Lord Townshend, on Dec. 29, 1723: "Fréjus, beyond dispute, is in it [the Spanish faction] . . . his bigotry is very great, and his devotion to the Court of Rome" (Walter Sichel: *Bolingbroke and his Times* [London, 1901-1902, two vols.], II, p. 507).

[41] Chance: *Alliance of Hanover*, p. 312.

[42] Fleury to Victor Amadeus II, August 2, 1726 (*Recueil des instructions. . . . Savoie-Sardaigne et Mantoue*, I, p. 355).

patient and always conciliatory, who smoothed away difficulties and sought out compromises with a diplomat's love for the refinements of his art, Elisabeth Farnese seemed like a tyro confronting a complicated modern control board. She would pull a lever, not with the certainty which arises from masterful knowledge, but with the tentativeness which springs from experimental curiosity—and then she would pull another. What is more, she was a fair-weather friend; in times of adversity she had an incorrigible propensity for putting Spanish friendship up to auction. It was dangerous to depend upon her constancy; on the whole, she was likely to be more profitable and less exhausting as an enemy than as an ally. It was unfortunate for both the Spanish and the French monarchies that this was so; for the aims of the Spanish sovereigns, whether national, as in the desire to recover Minorca and Gibraltar and to suppress the abuses of illicit British trade in the Indies, or dynastic, as exemplified in the desire to establish a branch of the Bourbons in Italy, by no means traversed the interests of France. But the danger of being left in the lurch at a critical moment more than counterbalanced the profit to be extracted from a policy which relied implicitly on the constant collaboration and integration of family interests. Although Fleury was eager to cultivate good relations with the Spanish court, the vagaries of the Queen prevented a reconciliation in 1726, and always made the *premier ministre* cautious in his dealings with the Spanish monarchy.[43]

The second reason which determined Fleury to hold aloof from the Alliance of Vienna was his resolution not to guarantee the Pragmatic Sanction.[44] It is reasonable to conclude that France

[43] For Fleury's desire to cultivate good relations with the Spanish sovereigns, see the letter he wrote to Philip V in 1724 (undated), urging him to resume the throne (Alfred Baudrillart: "L'influence française en Espagne au temps de Louis Ier. Mission du maréchal de Tessé, 1724." *Revue des questions historiques*, LX [1896], pp. 544-545); also, Fleury's letter to Philip V, June 13, 1726 (Baudrillart: *Philippe V et la cour de France*, III, p. 256). Although Fleury did not assume the title of *premier ministre*, he indubitably exercised the power of that office: to allude to him by this title is justifiable, and provides a convenient variation of epithet.

[44] By an arrangement dated September 12, 1703, the Emperor Leopold and the Archdukes Joseph and Charles agreed that in default of male heirs, female heirs should succeed, those of Joseph to precede those of Charles (Gustav Turba: *Die pragmatische Sanktion. Authentische Texte samt Erläuterungen und Übersetzungen*

would have been required to recognize the succession rights of Maria Theresa, had Fleury desired to negotiate a treaty of alliance with the Emperor, for a solemn recognition by the several powers of Europe of the validity of the Pragmatic Sanction had by this time become one of the principal objects of the policy of Charles VI.[45] This had been the price which Spain had had to pay for the Alliance of Vienna, and a similar guarantee had been exacted from Prussia, Russia and the Wittelsbach Electors, upon the occasion of their respective accessions to the Alliance of Vienna in 1726.[46] But it is no less certain that it was a cardinal point in Fleury's policy, during the early years of his administration, to avoid guaranteeing the Pragmatic Sanction. That he eventually complied suggests that in these early years his dislike for doing so was determined by the small likelihood of securing an adequate *quid pro quo*. For the Cardinal very much exploited the presumption that France was a conservative and "satiated" power, which asked no favours of its neighbours

[Vienna, 1913], pp. 18-39). On April 19, 1713, Charles VI publicly promulgated the Pragmatic Sanction, which assigned the succession to his own daughters, in default of male heirs, and for the first time asserted the indivisibility of the Hapsburg dominions (Turba: *op. cit.*, pp. 48-53). At that time, Charles VI had no children. A son was born and died in 1716; Maria Theresa was born in 1717, Maria Sophia in 1718, and Maria Amalia in 1724. The Archduchess Maria Josepha, eldest daughter of Joseph I, was required to make a renunciation of her claims on the Hapsburg inheritance for herself and her heirs, on the occasion of her marriage to the Electoral Prince of Saxony, August 19, 1719 (Turba: *op. cit.*, pp. 54-72), and the same was required of her sister, Maria Amalia, when she married the Electoral Prince of Bavaria, September 25, 1722 (Gustav Turba: *Die pragmatische Sanktion, mit besonderer Rücksicht auf die Länder der Stephanskrone* [Vienna, 1906], p. 26).

[45] In 1720 Charles VI began taking steps to secure the recognition of the Pragmatic Sanction by the diets of the various portions of the Hapsburg dominions. Moravia, Bohemia and Silesia recognized it in 1720 (Turba: *Die pragmatische Sanktion. Authentische Texte*, pp. 94-121). Hungary recognized it in 1723 (*ibid.*, pp. 166-185). The Austrian Netherlands were the last Austrian possession to guarantee the Pragmatic Sanction, Dec. 6, 1724 (L.-P. Gachard: "Acceptation et publication aux Pays-Bas de la Pragmatique Sanction de l'Empereur Charles VI." *Études et notices historiques concernant l'histoire des Pays-Bas* [Brussels, 1890, three vols.], II, pp. 1-26). See also August Fournier: "Zur Entstehungsgeschichte der pragmatischen Sanktion Kaiser Karl's VI." *Historische Zeitschrift*, XXXVIII (1877), pp. 16-47.

[46] E.g., article xii of the treaty of peace between Spain and Austria, April 30, 1725; article ii of the Treaty of Wüsterhausen between Austria and Prussia, October 12, 1726 (Victor Loewe: *Preussens Staatsverträge aus der Regierungszeit König Friedrich Wilhelms I.* [Leipzig, 1913], pp. 311-321).

save the boon of living in peace, and that he himself was a peace-maker by temperament and design, ingenuous, sincere, perhaps a little naive. The advantage derived from the public consumption of this propaganda was that France under Fleury seemed to assume a detachment, a disinterestedness, which imparted to its policy a considerable degree of moral authority. The disadvantage was that Fleury dared not seek territorial acquisitions for France without straightway destroying the myth. Even in the negotiations leading up to the acquisition of the reversion of Lorraine, the Cardinal emphasized so strongly the necessity of securing some compensation for Stanislas Leszczynski, the dispossessed King of Poland, that he was able to make the extremely valuable advantages which France received from this transaction seem like a mere *pis aller*. In the early years of his ministry, when events were not yet ripe for selling France's guarantee profitably, Fleury turned a deaf ear to Sinzendorff, who "had let it be understood that the Emperor would pay well for the guarantee of the succession" (1730), and preferred to permit the Anglo-French alliance to be broken up in 1731, rather than give such a guarantee.[47] In a meeting of the Council of State on April 19, 1731, Fleury reiterated what he had said on a previous occasion to Sinzendorff and Königsegg, with reference to recognizing the Pragmatic Sanction, that *"si le roi avoit perdu trois batailles, il ne faudroit pas encore l'écouter."*[48]

But Fleury's eventual guarantee of the Pragmatic Sanction can not be explained solely by his instinct to drive a sharp bargain: political considerations figured conspicuously in that transaction, and it is significant that the guarantee was exchanged for a territorial gain which materially altered the relative strength of the French and Hapsburg monarchies.[49] The acquisition of

[47] Villars: *Mémoires*, V, p. 203.

[48] Villars: *Mémoires*, V, p. 314; quotation italicized in the original. Cf. Vaucher: *Robert Walpole et la politique de Fleury*, p. 55.

[49] In a sense, Francis, Duke of Lorraine, who was forced to exchange his duchy for that of Tuscany, was the victim of the transaction, and not the Emperor, who was merely the suzerain for Lorraine, as Louis XV was the suzerain for Francis's duchy of Bar (Francis paid homage to Louis XV for this duchy on February 1, 1730; see Villars: *Mémoires*, V, p. 209). But inasmuch as Francis was to become

Lorraine affected the balance of power in a manner very favourable to France, and came at a time when the Austrian ineffectiveness in the War of the Polish Succession indicated that Hapsburg strength was not proportionate to the considerable territories which composed the monarchy, nor equal to the ambitious policies of its ruler. Fleury did not guarantee the Austrian succession until it was evident that a perpetuation of the existing territorial status of the Hapsburg monarchy, which a recognition of the Pragmatic Sanction involved, was compatible with the safety of France. For, in strict logic, a French guarantee of Maria Theresa's succession implied a willingness to acquiesce in her inheriting the Austrian dominions as they existed at the moment when the guarantee was given.[50] Fleury could scarcely tamper with the territorial status of the dominions of Charles VI after France had guaranteed the eventual inheritance of those undivided dominions to the Emperor's daughter. Consequently, reasons of state demanded adequate adjustment of the relative strength of the French and Hapsburg monarchies before the guarantee should be made.[51]

An analysis of the policy of Charles VI, taken in conjunction with an estimate of the presumable strength of the Hapsburg

the husband of Maria Theresa and was quite likely at some time to be the Emperor, his lands would, in practice, be indistinguishable from those of the Hapsburgs. His revenues were considerable (the French farmed the indirect taxes in 1737 for 3,300,000 livres [Marion: *Histoire financière de la France*, I, p. 152]), and the strategical location of his duchy was of vast importance both to France and Austria (Hermann Stegemann: *The Struggle for the Rhine* [New York, 1927], pp. 194-200).

[50] For example, Great Britain, having guaranteed the Pragmatic Sanction in 1731, was conceivably under moral obligations to intervene in the War of the Polish Succession in order to prevent a dismemberment or diminution of Maria Theresa's eventual inheritance; Sir Richard Lodge thinks this to be the case ("English Neutrality in the War of the Polish Succession." *Transactions of the Royal Historical Society*, Fourth Series, XIV [1931], p. 155). On the other hand, Sir James Headlam-Morley (*Studies in Diplomatic History* [London, 1930], p. 111) thought the contrary.

[51] Sir Richard Lodge: "English Neutrality in the War of the Polish Succession." *Transactions of the Royal Historical Society*, Fourth Series, XIV, pp. 151, 154. Even when France did guarantee the Pragmatic Sanction, it was with the reservation that France's guarantee should not prejudice the prior rights of third parties (Albert, duc de Broglie: "Le cardinal de Fleury et la *Pragmatique Sanction*." *Revue historique*, XX [Sept.-Dec., 1882], pp. 257-281).

monarchy, indicates that Fleury was justified in the first years of his administration in exercising caution with reference to a guarantee of the territorial integrity of the Hapsburg lands. The period between the Treaties of Utrecht and the War of the Polish Succession was one of flux and diplomatic uncertainty, during which events did not clearly reveal the weakness and lack of cohesion of the Hapsburg monarchy. On the contrary, the campaigns of Prince Eugene against the Turks had been attended with the most gratifying success. Following his accession to the Quadruple Alliance in 1718, Charles VI held under his rule, over and above the territories and dignities which his immediate predecessors had possessed, the Netherlands, the Kingdom of the Two Sicilies, the duchies of Milan and Mantua, part of Bosnia and Servia including Belgrade, Western Wallachia (to the Aluta), and the Banat of Temesvar; it was natural to suppose that these extensive acquisitions of principalities, rich in themselves, had proportionately increased the strength of the Hapsburg monarchy.[52]

These extensive accretions of territory rendered the Emperor apparently more powerful without making him less ambitious. While on the one hand he persisted in his uncompromising opposition to the establishment of a branch of the Bourbons in Italy, on the other he endeavoured systematically to increase the Imperial power within the limits of the Empire. He seems to have attempted in Germany what was tantamount to a revolution by strengthening Imperial influence in a manner which had not been attempted since the Treaties of Westphalia. Saint-Saphorin, the British ambassador at Vienna, wrote to Lord Townshend on August 1, 1725:

This court disposes almost absolutely of the circles of Swabia, Franconia and of the Upper and Lower Rhine. . . . It is by means of the Aulic Council that the Emperor has been able to intimidate them so thoroughly, and put them under his domination. . . . as for the imperial cities, it is true that

[52] So thought contemporaries (Saint-Philippe: *Mémoires*, IV, p. 101, with reference to Charles VI's influence in Italy; John Ker: *Memoirs*, I, part ii, pp. 7-8). George Lyttelton wrote to his father on August 13, 1729: "The Emperor is too powerful already; . ." (Lyttelton: *Works*, III, p. 249).

they are, considering the present system of this court, protected from the Princes their neighbours much beyond what is just; but in exchange, the Emperor leaves to them, in relation to himself, only the shadow of their former liberty, and he rules them almost as despotically as he does his hereditary dominions.[53]

As part of this programme for the extension of Imperial power, the Emperor exploited religious differences within the Empire. This policy was inspired not so much by the profundity of his piety as by the desire to give scope for the play of the centralizing forces of which he disposed.[54] The period following the settlement of the War of the Spanish Succession witnessed in central Europe a recrudescence of Catholic zeal which the Emperor was able to utilize for political purposes. The conversion of the Electoral Prince of Saxony in October 1717 was a symptom of the renascence of Catholic activity, and the approach of what seemed to be a religious crisis in central Europe explains the alarm of the King of Prussia and the Elector of Hanover concerning the judicial murder of the Protestants at Thorn in 1724.[55]

The profit derived from playing off Catholic against Protestant was unmistakable:

At present, except in Lower Germany, where the Princes are too powerful to consider themselves obliged to submit to the yoke which the Emperor desires to impose on them, the Emperor exercises in the Empire a power almost as absolute as that which he exerts in his own States. He has been principally enabled to exercise this power to so great a degree by very ably making use of religious differences.[56]

[53] Dureng: *Le duc de Bourbon et l'Angleterre*, pp. 513-514.

[54] The importance of the rôle of the Aulic Council in strengthening the Imperial power is emphasized in the instructions (September 4, 1726) to Chavigny, French minister to the Imperial Diet from 1726 to 1731 (*Recueil des instructions. . . . Diète germanique* [Edited by Bertrand Auerbach; Paris, 1912], pp. lxxxv, 141-143).

[55] Bertrand Auerbach: *La France et le Saint Empire romain germanique depuis la paix de Westphalie jusqu'à la Révolution française* (Paris, 1912), pp. 273, 275, 281. For the Thorn "bloodbath" and the strength of Catholicism in central Europe, see J. G. Droysen: *Geschichte der preussischen Politik* (Leipzig, 1868-1886, five parts in fourteen vols.), Part IV, vol. ii, pp. 361-363; Basil Williams: "The Foreign Policy of England under Walpole." *E. H. R.*, XV, p. 672.

[56] Saint-Saphorin to Townshend, August 1, 1725 (Dureng: *Le duc de Bourbon et l'Angleterre*, p. 516). Chavigny's instructions (1726) make the same point (*Recueil des instructions. . . . Diète germanique*, pp. 138-139).

To the advantages gained by an exploitation of religious differences and by the increased transaction of Imperial business by
the Aulic Council were added those which resulted from intimi-
dation and corruption.[57] The policy of Charles VI was indubitably an invasive and aggressive one, and Chavigny reported in
1727 that the German situation was comparable, not to that
which had existed in the time of Louis XIV, but to that of the
period before the Treaties of Westphalia.[58]

When one considers the importance attached by French statesmen, from 1648 to the time when Thiers interpreted the Battle
of Sadowa as a national defeat for France, to the maintenance of
a disunited and particularistic Germany, it is not surprising that
Cardinal Fleury was reluctant to guarantee the succession of
Charles VI, unless compensation could at the same time be secured which would really diminish the Emperor's power to do
France mischief. This consideration was of particular validity
in 1726, because the aggression of Louis XIV had bankrupted
France's moral authority in Germany. Ordinarily France, in her
capacity as a guarantor of the Westphalian settlement, had been
able to thwart attempts to increase Hapsburg power within the
Empire. This was accomplished by furnishing moral or tangible
support to the princes opposed to the Emperor. Such had been
the case, for example, in the formation of the *Rheinbund* in 1658.
This right of intervention in German affairs was naturally regarded by the French as being of the utmost importance, especially at a time when the other guarantor of the Westphalian
settlement, Sweden, had become a second-class power.[59] But in

---

[57] Cf. Chavigny's despatch of October 28, 1726 (Jean Dureng: *Mission de
Théodore Chevignard de Chavigny en Allemagne, septembre 1726-octobre 1731* [Paris,
(1912)], p. 19); also, Saint-Saphorin to Townshend, August 1, 1725 (Dureng:
Le duc de Bourbon et l'Angleterre, pp. 514, 517); instructions to Chavigny, 1726
(*Recueil des instructions. . . . Diète germanique*, p. 140).

[58] Dureng: *Mission de Chavigny*, pp. 19-20. Saint-Saphorin wrote in similar
vein to Townshend, June 16, 1725 (Dureng: *Le duc de Bourbon et l'Angleterre*,
p. 296).

[59] Even in 1738, when Fleury was endeavouring to bring about a *rapprochement*
with the Emperor, the importance of France's function as a guarantor of the
Westphalian settlement and the necessity of maintaining a "juste milieu" in Germany were emphasized in the instructions to Malbran de la Noue (*Recueil des
instructions. . . . Diète germanique*, p. 181).

practice both the prestige and the effectiveness of French intervention depended upon the initiative of the German princes in
invoking French aid.[60] Since the War of the League of Augsburg
and the Treaty of Ryswick, however, the German princes had
on the whole shown themselves reluctant to invite French assistance. This was attributed by French statesmen themselves to
Louis XIV's insistence that the Catholic religion should be retained in the places restored by France to the Empire in compliance with the stipulations of the Treaty of Ryswick.[61] These
districts, which had been annexed to France as a result of the
awards of the Chambers of Reunion, had in some cases had
Catholicism forced upon them; that they were not permitted to
revert to their former religion was a derogation of the Westphalian treaties which greatly annoyed the Protestant German
princes. This stipulation, coupled with the general Protestant
disapprobation of the Revocation of the Edict of Nantes, highly
compromised French moral authority in Germany, and it remained a grievance in 1726, because the offending article had
been confirmed by the Treaty of Baden (1714).[62] French influence in the Imperial Diet had consequently sunk to a low level
under the Regency. Because of a dispute on a point of etiquette,
the French plenipotentiary, Gergy, lived in a diplomatic vacuum
during his residence at Ratisbon (1716–1720), and from 1721 to
1726 France was feebly represented there by an agent named

[60] "Mais il faut laisser naître cette disposition," said Gergy's instructions, May
22, 1716 (*Recueil des instructions. . . . Diète germanique*, p. 94).

[61] Article iv of the Treaty of Ryswick concluded: "religione tamen Catholica
Romana in locis sic restitutis in statu quo nunc est remanente." Cf. Auerbach:
La France et le Saint Empire romain germanique, pp. 252-253. The instructions to
Chavigny in 1726 (*Recueil des instructions. . . . Diète germanique*, p. 162) repeat
almost verbatim what was said of article iv of the Treaty of Ryswick in the instructions to Gergy (1716): "Il faut même avouer que si la clause de l'article 4ᵉ
du traité de Ryswick est un monument de la piété du feu Roi, le succès n'a pas ré-
pondu aux motifs qui l'ont fait agir, et que cette clause a été plus nuisible qu'avantageuse à la religion catholique." Cf. *Recueil des instructions . . . Diète germanique*,
p. 95.

[62] Chavigny's instructions insinuated that the confirmation of this article had
been a device of the Emperor, whose ministers negotiated the Treaty of Baden in
the name of the Empire, in order to perpetuate the dissension between France and
the German Protestant princes (*Recueil des instructions . . . Diète germanique*,
p. 164).

Groffey. In 1726 Fleury accredited Chavigny to the Diet in an attempt to build up once more a party in opposition to the Emperor.

Not only was Charles VI endeavouring to increase his power in Germany, but he was also attempting to improve the financial status of the Hapsburg monarchy by taking an active interest in commercial expansion. By the time of his death, the failure of some of these schemes and the relative unimportance of those which survived made clear that they had done little to strengthen the resources of Austria, but at the time of Fleury's accession to power they still showed great promise. As a result of the commercial treaty signed with the Turks at Passarowitz in 1718, which allowed to Austria consular jurisdiction and special privileges for a trading company in the Ottoman Empire, the "Imperial Oriental Company" was founded in 1719.[63] Chambers of Commerce were set up in Bohemia (1715), in Silesia and in the provinces of Austria Proper (*Inneroesterreich*) in 1716; and a central Chamber of Commerce (*Wiener Hauptkommerzkolleg*) was founded in 1718.[64] Care was given to the development of roads, especially those leading to the Adriatic sea ports, freedom of navigation on the Adriatic was proclaimed on June 2, 1717, and Trieste and Fiume were made free ports in 1719.[65] In the

---

[63] Josef Dullinger: "Die Handelskompagnien Oesterreichs nach dem Oriente und nach Ostinden in der ersten Hälfte des 18. Jahrhunderts." *Zeitschrift für Social- und Wirtschaftsgeschichte*, VII (1900), pp. 45-74; Heinrich von Srbik: *Der staatliche Exporthandel Österreichs von Leopold I. bis Maria Theresia* (Leipzig and Vienna, 1907), p. 293, note.

[64] Srbik: *Der staatliche Exporthandel*, pp. 292-303; A. F. Pribram: *Die böhmische Commerzcollegium und seine Thätigkeit (Beiträge zur Geschichte der deutschen Industrie in Böhmen*, VI [Prague, 1898]), pp. 27-35; Siegfried Tschierschky: *Die Wirtschaftspolitik des schlesischen Kommerzkollegs, 1716-1740* (Gotha, 1902), pp. 24-29.

[65] On the progress in the improvement of roads, see an official report printed by Franz Martin Mayer: "Zur Geschichte der österreichischen Handelspolitik unter Kaiser Karl VI." *Mittheilungen des Instituts für oesterreichische Geschichtsforschung*, XVIII (1897), pp. 129-145. On the establishment of free ports, see Gustav Lippert: "Die Entwicklung der österreichischen Handelsmarine." *Zeitschrift für Volkswirtschaft, Socialpolitik und Verwaltung*, X (1901), pp. 347-350; Ethbin H. von Costa: *Der Freihafen von Triest* (Vienna, 1838), pp. 34-40; Ernst Becher: *Die oesterreichische Seeverwaltung, 1850-1875* (Trieste, 1875), pp. 18-27. "Erst unter Karl VI. sind in grösserem Massstabe Handel und Industrie fördernde Institutionen in's Leben gerufen worden; erst unter Karl VI. wurde sich die Re-

same year, due to the necessity of providing naval defense for the Adriatic and the newly acquired island of Sicily, an arsenal was begun at Trieste.[66] By the time of the War of the Polish Succession the base at Trieste and the fleet depending upon it had become of sufficient importance to cause the French government to instruct the Chevalier d'Orleans, who commanded the French galley squadron, to campaign in the Adriatic, orders which were subsequently withdrawn because of the fear of British intervention.[67] At the time when Fleury came to power in France, it was quite possible that the Hapsburg monarchy would become a powerful competitor in the Levant trade and that Charles VI's "*ausgesprochene Mittelmeerpolitik*" would seriously alter the balance of power in the Mediterranean. Had France allied herself with Austria in 1726 she would indubitably have become involved in trouble with the Maritime Powers with reference to the Ostend Company, another enterprise of Charles VI, the diplomatic significance of which will be discussed later; she would also have been required to guarantee the undivided succession of a monarch whose ambitious policies both in Germany and in the Mediterranean gave legitimate cause for apprehension lest his House might even yet jeopardize the safety of the French monarchy.

The notorious instability of Spanish policy and the presumptive strength, coupled with the demonstrable ambition, of the Hapsburg monarchy were sufficient to deter Fleury from associating France in 1726 with the powers signatory to the Alliance of Vienna; by simple process of elimination, it followed that he must continue the alliance with Great Britain. The blundering

gierung über die Mittel und Wege klar, mit und auf denen die Hebung der österreichischen Industrie und des österreichischen Handels erfolgen konnte" (Pribram: *Die böhmische Commerzcollegium*, p. 11).

[66] Letters concerned with the entrance of Admiral George Forbes into the service of the Emperor in 1719 for the purpose of forming a navy in the Adriatic may be found in the Granard Manuscripts, *Historical Manuscripts Commission, Report* II, Appendix, (London, 1871), pp. 211, 212, 217.

[67] Cf. correspondence between Maurepas and Orleans in 1734 (Charles Gay: *Négociations relatives à l'établissement de la maison de Bourbon sur le trône des Deux-Siciles* [Paris, 1853], pp. 228-232, 293-294); Becher: *Die oesterreichische Seeverwaltung*, pp. 24-26.

policy of the Duke of Bourbon had made mere friendly neutrality impossible: France hungered for an alliance and consequently had to pay for it a famine price. The sacrifice of French freedom of action was the unenviable heritage which Fleury was forced to accept from his predecessor.

Yet alliance with Great Britain, subject to the qualification that it had temporarily become an unequal partnership because of the mistakes of the Duke of Bourbon, was as useful and rational as it had been under the Regency, even though it was never popular with the French public.[68] For both France and Great Britain were equally solicitous of maintaining the balance of power in Europe on the basis of the Treaties of Utrecht and of the Quadruple Alliance. Moreover, alliance with Great Britain offered the derivative advantages which come from diplomatic co-operation with a government whose aims are patent and whose policy is reasonably predictable. English policy, now become national in the sense in which Professor Seeley used the word, was devoted almost entirely to the expansion of British trade interests, the exclusion of the Pretender and, in order to accomplish and safeguard these aims, the preservation of the European balance. Since the accession of George I, the British government had fallen into the hands of the party whose interests were most closely identified with the maintenance of the Hanoverian dynasty, and the Whig party, although what Disraeli was pleased to call "our Venetian oligarchy" stood at the head of it, depended largely for its support on the merchant interests, who were not slow to realize their political power.[69]

[68] Dureng: *Le duc de Bourbon et l'Angleterre*, pp. 33-34 (an excellent summary of the character of the Anglo-French alliance).

[69] Delafaye wrote to Keene on Oct. 1, O. S., 1731: "These gentlemen [the merchants] upon this have assumed a quite different air from what I have formerly known. They used in times past to come Cap in Hand to the Office praying for Relief, now the second word is *You shall hear of it in another Place*, meaning in Parliament. All this must be endured, and now in our turn we must bow and cringe to them" (H. W. V. Temperley: "The Causes of the War of Jenkins' Ear (1739)." *Transactions of the Royal Historical Society*, Third Series, III [1909], p. 222). The Duke of Newcastle, Secretary of State for the Southern Department, was excessively deferential to public opinion (Temperley: *ibid.*, p. 201). A considerable literature is gathering about this colourful figure in British politics (Stebelton H. Nulle: *Thomas Pelham-Holles, Duke of Newcastle: His Early Political Career,*

Consequently, it was safe for Fleury to assume that so long as Walpole and Townshend, both of whom were sympathetic to the commercial interests of the electorate and desirous of maintaining the balance of power in Europe, remained in office, British policy might be expected to remain reasonably uniform and predictable.[70]

Although France was dependent upon the good will of Great Britain in 1726, there is no denying that the dependence was reciprocal. By opposing the Alliance of Hanover so overtly to the Alliance of Vienna, Townshend was risking war: consequently the building up of a powerful coalition had become necessary to the British. In retrospect, it seems probable that the British statesmen became too easily alarmed concerning the Alliance of Vienna. It is now known that the defensive alliance of April 30, 1725, as a counterbalance to which the Hanover alliance was formed, was a comparatively harmless document: Ripperda was subsequently able to negotiate the offensive alliance of November 5, 1725 (which did indeed endanger the interests of France and Great Britain), only because the Austrian ministers felt that the Emperor's position was endangered by the Alliance of Hanover.[71] Nevertheless, in the summer of 1725 the British were thoroughly alarmed by Ripperda's indiscreet bluster; they were certain that

1693-1724 [Philadelphia, 1931]; Donald G. Barnes: "The Duke of Newcastle, Ecclesiastical Minister, 1724-54." *Pacific Historical Review*, III [1934], pp. 164-191; Basil Williams: "The Duke of Newcastle and the Election of 1734." *English Historical Review*, XII [1897], pp. 448-488). For character sketches, see Yorke: *Life of the Earl of Hardwicke*, I, pp. 284-288; Tobias Smollett: *Humphry Clinker*, letters of June 2 and 5, from J. Melford to Sir Watkin Phillips; Princess Anna, consort of William IV of Orange, to G. O. Burmania, March, 1743 (P. Geyl: "Engelsche Correspondentie van Prins Willem IV en Prinses Anna (1734-1743)." *Bijdragen en Mededeelingen van het Historisch Genootschap*, XLV [1924], p. 138).

[70] The factiousness of the Opposition in Great Britain is probably explained by the fact that in fundamentals the views of Pulteney and his group were substantially the same as those of Walpole and Townshend. For an excellent characterization of the principal members of the Opposition, see Speaker Onslow's description (Onslow MSS., *Historical Manuscripts Commission, Report* XIV, Appendix Part IX, [London, 1895], pp. 465-473). Cf. C. B. Realey: *The Early Opposition to Sir Robert Walpole, 1720-1727* (Philadelphia, 1931), pp. 155-185. The first number of Pulteney's and Bolingbroke's joint journalistic venture, *The Craftsman*, appeared in this year, Dec. 5, 1726 (D. H. Stevens: *Party Politics and English Journalism, 1702-1742* [Chicago, 1916], pp. 125-128).

[71] Syveton: *Une cour et un aventurier*, pp. 139-141.

there existed a secret treaty, and were inclined to take it for granted that Spain and Austria were contemplating lending assistance to the Pretender.[72] Yet, although Lord Hervey, for example, considered the Alliance of Hanover necessary, he also thought that "the chief object of it was, I believe, a piece of flattery of Lord Townshend's to the late King, . . . ," and he declared that Sir Robert Walpole had always disapproved of that treaty.[73] In this disapproval were latent the germs of discord which finally caused Townshend's resignation in 1730; from 1725 on, Walpole began to concern himself more deeply in the conduct of foreign affairs. But in 1726 the die was cast, and, whatever might have been his private convictions concerning the utility of the Alliance of Hanover, Walpole always defended it in public.[74]

Although there was mutual dependence between Great Britain and France, it was not dependence of equal degree. The Alliance of Vienna had become to France a menace to her security, but to her ally it was, in the final analysis, no more than a threat to British prosperity. While France might actually suffer dismemberment as the result of an unsuccessful war, Great Britain, safe behind the ramparts of her "floating castles," could scarcely be struck a mortal blow. The consequence was that in order to keep English support, the French had to devote themselves to the attainment of ends which favoured the British more than themselves.

---

[72] Hervey: *Some Materials towards Memoirs*, pp. 53, 58.

[73] Hervey: *Some Materials towards Memoirs*, pp. 59, 82. Cf. Hervey's hostile and critical judgment of Townshend (*ibid.*, pp. 80-82).

[74] F. S. Oliver made the distinction that Walpole did not so much *disapprove* of the Treaty of Hanover as, rather, he disliked it (*The Endless Adventure* [New York, 1931-1934, three vols.], II, pp. 111-112). What was involved was the problem which has always confronted British statesmen in modern times: whether to take a part in Continental politics or, so far as possible, carry on in splendid isolation. Walpole's policy of non-intervention in the War of the Polish Succession and his remark to Queen Caroline: "Madam, there are fifty thousand men slain this year in Europe, and not one Englishman" (Hervey: *Some Materials towards Memoirs*, p. 361), show that he was an isolationist. On that ground, his policy has been severely criticized by Sir Richard Lodge ("English Neutrality in the War of the Polish Succession." *Transactions of the Royal Historical Society*, Fourth Series, XIV [1931], pp. 141-174).

These ends, as might readily be supposed, had mainly to do with preserving exclusive British trading privileges, of which the most highly prized was the Asiento. It was a most amusing paradox, although one readily explained, that the British should attach such importance to the exclusive legal right of supplying slaves to the Spanish West Indies when it was, ostensibly, not a profitable undertaking.[75] At the time when the Asiento treaty was concluded, the South Sea Company had foreseen, and had attempted to forestall, their probable losses, by securing the additional privilege of sending an annual "permission ship" to carry on a direct trade with the Spanish Indies. Various sorts of ingenious frauds were perpetrated in connection with the trade of the annual ship, yet even in this branch of the trade, if Adam Smith is to be believed, the company failed to make a large gain:

[75] Loss on the Asiento had been predicted, based on the experience of the Portuguese and the French (*The Assiento Contract Consider'd, as also, the Advantages and Decay of the Trade of Jamaica and the Plantations, with the Causes and Consequences thereof* [London, 1714], p. 7). In 1733 Spain offered the South Sea Company two *per cent.* on the returns of the galleons and flotillas, in exchange for a surrender of the privilege of sending the "permission ship." This was refused, but it caused the Company to cast up its accounts, whereby it appeared that a total profit of only £32,260-18-0 sterling had been made, which averaged £3,226 a year, including the profits made from the "permission ship" ([Adam Anderson]: *An Historical and Chronological Deduction of the Origin of Commerce, from the Earliest Accounts* [Dublin, 1790, six vols.], III, pp. 458-460, 468; the same figures are given by William Douglass: *A Summary Historical and Political, of the first Planting, progressive Improvements, and present State of the British Settlements in North America* [Boston, 1749-1753, two vols.], I, p. 75; and by David Macpherson: *Annals of Commerce, Manufactures, Fisheries and Navigation* [London, 1805, four vols.], III, pp. 194, 201). On the other hand, Professor A. S. Aiton states that the Shelburne papers in the Clements Library at the University of Michigan show that the South Sea Company exported its full quota of slaves and made large profits; there was "an average balance of £600,000 in the period immediately prior to 1739" (A. S. Aiton: "The Asiento Treaty as Reflected in the Papers of Lord Shelburne." *Hispanic-American Historical Review*, VIII [1928], p. 175). Professor Aiton, in correspondence with the author, points out that the average balance represents "the figure out of which, after deducting expenses, bad bills etc., a profit might be realized." He also writes: "The 'large profits' I referred to are, of course, shown by the secret books of the Company and were not made public at the time the Company was still existent. It is exceedingly doubtful that either Anderson or Macpherson had access to these account books. . . . The Company apparently deliberately issued statements of low profits and even losses to avoid paying the King of Spain his just due and to hide the extent of the illicit trade."

Of the ten voyages which this annual ship was allowed to make, they are said to have gained considerably by one, that of the Royal Caroline in 1731, and to have been losers, more or less, by almost all the rest.[76]

The explanation of these reduced profits is almost certainly to be attributed to the peculation of the employees of the South Sea Company; a considerable number of Englishmen enriched themselves by the Company's activities, even though its stockholders claimed that they themselves did not; and the fondness of the British public in general for the Asiento was because of the fact that under cover of its privileges was established a contraband trade of enormous proportions, which afforded an extremely valuable outlet for British manufactures.[77] Since, as a

[76] Adam Smith: *Wealth of Nations* (Eighth edition, London, 1796, three vols.), Book V, Chapter 1, part iii, article 1, p. 129. "It is thought, that the South-sea company cleared, altogether, about £70,000 by this voyage of the Royal-Caroline, almost the only prosperous voyage they ever made" (Macpherson: *Annals of Commerce*, III, p. 158). Only one "permission ship" was sent out between 1711 and 1718 (Elizabeth Donnan: "The Early Days of the South Sea Company, 1711-1718." *Journal of Economic and Business History*, II [1929-1930], p. 447). Only seven annual ships were sent out in the first fifteen years of the contract (James Hamilton St. John: *Anglo-Spanish Commercial Relations, 1700-1750* [State University of Iowa, manuscript thesis, 1927], p. 151). No annual ship was ever sent out after 1733 (James Houstoun: *Memoirs of the Life and Travels of James Houstoun, M.D.* [London, 1747], p. 190). The war periods of 1719-1721 and 1727-1729 prevented the annual ship from sailing, nor could it ever carry on its trade without a *cedula* from the King of Spain, which was frequently delayed on frivolous pretexts. The fraudulent overloading of the "permission ship" and its being provisioned by accompanying vessels, so that all its space might be utilized for the conveyance of goods, were noted by the Spanish travellers, Juan and Antonio de Ulloa (*Voyage historique en Amérique* [1735], I, p. 92; cited by Herman vander Linden: *Histoire de l'expansion coloniale des peuples européens*, I, pp. 239-447: *L'expansion coloniale de l'Espagne, jusqu'au début du XIXe siècle* [Brussels, 1907], p. 400, note). The testimony of two former employees of the South Sea Company, given to the Spaniards in 1729, enumerates the English abuses of their trading privileges under ten heads, among which were the false measurement of the capacity of the trading ship, the extra loading and fraudulent provisioning of it, and the surreptitious export of gold and silver from Spanish America, without paying a fifth of its value to the Crown (Vera Lee Brown: "The South Sea Company and Contraband Trade." *American Historical Review*, XXXI [1925-1926], pp. 662-678).

[77] Vera Lee Brown: "Contraband Trade: A Factor in the Decline of Spain's Empire in America." *Hispanic-American Historical Review*, VIII (1928), pp. 178-189; A. S. Aiton: "The Asiento Treaty as Reflected in the Papers of Lord Shelburne." *Hispanic-American Historical Review*, VIII (1928), pp. 174-175; Georges Scelle: "The Slave Trade in the Spanish Colonies of America: The Assiento." *American Journal of International Law*, IV (1910), p. 618; Vera Lee Brown: "The South Sea Company and Contraband Trade." *American Historical Review*, XXXI

result of the Asiento treaty, some Englishmen and some British ships had a legal right in the ports of Spanish America, it became very difficult to determine just who were carrying on an illegal commerce and who were trading legitimately. French or Dutch ships in Spanish ports were *ipso facto* subject to confiscation; that rule was easy to apply, and explains why the contraband trade of those nations in the Spanish Indies never reached the magnitude of that of the British, and also why they desired so ardently to secure a similar privilege, which might cast the mantle of legitimacy over their enterprises, as it did for the British.

Although the profits derived by the stockholders of the South Sea Company from carrying on the Asiento seem to have been meagre, the advantages to the British, as a nation, resulting from the illicit traffic for which the Asiento privileges were a cover, were inestimable. Anderson reproached the stockholders of the South Sea Company with consulting only their own private advantage in contemplating relinquishing the Asiento privileges for an equivalent:

there was a more important and extensive consideration to be duly weighed, viz. whether by the illicit and very profitable trade carried on by that company's supercargoes, factors, captains, and other servants, employed by them in the Spanish West Indies, and also under their wings, from Jamaica, &c. the nation was not a greater gainer, upon the whole, than they could be by the proposed equivalent, . . . [78]

Had the Spaniards required the same procedure for the distribution of slaves as was required for the distribution of goods in

[1925-1926], pp. 667-669, 671-676; Macpherson: *Annals of Commerce*, III, pp. 201-202; Anderson: *Origin of Commerce*, III, pp. 548-549: "although the South Sea Company might not be so great gainers, yet their factors, agents, &c. brought home great fortunes, frequently in a very short space of time; . ." Lord Hervey says that the directors of the company "cheated the Company by selling the goods of their own private trade first, and leaving those of the Company to be disposed of at any price that could be got for them after the best of the market was over." The Ministry thought it better to "permit a set of annual rascals to cheat the Company without being punished, in order to let England cheat Spain without being discovered" (Hervey: *Some Materials towards Memoirs*, pp. 185, 186).

[78] Anderson: *Origin of Commerce*, III, p. 468. Ulloa declared that the British carried on contraband trade to such a point that the legal commerce was nothing in comparison (Ulloa: *Rétablissement des manufactures et du commerce d'Espagne*, part ii, p. 25).

Spanish America, English contraband activities could not have been so extensive. But instead of bringing the slaves to one great central market, such as that of Vera Cruz or Portobelo, the negroes were taken in small numbers, and in vessels smaller and more numerous than the trans-Atlantic slave ships, to the several slave markets scattered throughout the Spanish dominions in America.[79] Thus the number of British vessels having legitimate business in Spanish waters was increased, as were, correspondingly, the opportunities for illicit trade. "By the Asiento it was hard to draw the line between the avowed English trade and the smuggling."[80] As Horatio Walpole wrote to Trevor, on July 21, O. S., 1738:

[79] A. S. Aiton: "The Asiento Treaty as Reflected in the Papers of Lord Shelburne." *Hispanic-American Historical Review*, VIII, pp. 174-175. There seems to be some doubt whether the British imported into the Spanish dominions their full annual quota of 4,800 slaves (Houstoun: *Memoirs*, p. 408; Vera Lee Brown: "The South Sea Company and Contraband Trade." *American Historical Review*, XXXI [1925-1926], p. 676). This system of distribution was especially beneficial to contraband traders in remote portions of South America, such as Buenos Aires, where the Spaniards sent ships of their own very irregularly and infrequently (Uztariz: *Theory and Practice of Commerce and Maritime Affairs*, I, pp. 421-422). Such a manner of distribution was doubtless employed in order to lessen the risk of loss for Spanish buyers. Jamaica was used as the clearing house of the slave trade; throughout this period, the Jamaica Assembly attempted to lay import and export taxes on the slaves intended for the Spanish market (*Journal of the Commissioners for Trade and Plantations, January 1722-3 to December 1728* [London, 1928], pp. 150-151, 154, 292, 332, 334; *ibid., January 1728-9 to December 1734* [London, 1928], pp. 306-310, 401, 402-403, 417, 418-419, 419-421, 425; *Acts of the Privy Council of England, Colonial Series*, III, pp. 159-167); cf. Frank Wesley Pitman: *The Development of the British West Indies, 1700-1763* (New Haven, 1917), pp. 84-85; Elizabeth Donnan: "The Early Days of the South Sea Company, 1711-1718." *Journal of Economic and Business History*, II, pp. 441-443. Jamaica planters also alleged that the South Sea Company sold the best slaves in the Spanish market, and left only inferior slaves for the Jamaican. Complaints were also numerous that the Company obstructed the private contraband trade from Jamaica (*The Assiento Contract Consider'd* [1714], pp. 2, 11-12, 47; *Some Observations on the Assiento Trade, As it has been exercised by the South-Sea Company* [London, 1728], *passim*, and esp. pp. 20-21; *The Importance of the British Plantations in America to this Kingdom* [1731], pp. 41-44, 53-54; *Considerations on the American Trade, Before and Since the Establishment of the South-Sea Company* [London, 1739], pp. 11, 18; *Journal of the Commissioners for Trade and Plantations, January 1734-5 to December 1741* [London, 1930], pp. 55-59). Consult on these matters, although for a slightly earlier period, Curtis Nettels: "England and the Spanish-American Trade, 1680-1715." *Journal of Modern History*, III (1931), pp. 1-33.

[80] H. W. V. Temperley: "The Relations of England with Spanish America, 1720-1744." *Annual Report of the American Historical Association for the Year 1911*, I, p. 234.

I trouble you at present for no other reason but to give you my notion of serving the Portuguese Colonies with Negroes, which I look upon as a very advantageous trade to those that can have an exclusive contract for that purpose, as what must necessarily afford opportunities of introducing with the negroes, or under colour of that trade the growth or manufacture of the country whose subjects shall have made such a contract; . . . the craft of the merchant joined with the interest of the Governor would steal an introduction of goods as well as blacks, . . . [81]

The British public, like Walpole, fully appreciated the advantages to be derived from an exclusive enjoyment of a trade like the Asiento, and watched over its perpetuation as well as its exclusiveness with a jealous vigilance. Inasmuch as the Alliance of Vienna seemed to threaten both, the continued alliance of France and Great Britain signified that French diplomacy had to exert itself, in its own despite, to safeguard for the British their trading status in the Spanish West Indies.

As a result of marketing their goods illicitly, British merchants enjoyed the benefit of all the economies which direct navigation, the elimination of middlemen, and the evasion of the payment of taxes afforded. French merchants, on the other hand, were forced to carry on their trade with the Spanish West Indies through the *Casa de Contratacion* at Cadiz; they were forced to employ Spanish commissioners, since no trading could be done in the Indies except in the name of Spanish subjects; and they found themselves hampered at every turn by all the bureaucratic and mercantilistic restrictions of a system whose regulations had been made sacred by prescription and hallowed by time. [82] The

[81] Trevor Papers, *Hist. MSS. Comm.*, *Report* XIV, Appendix Part IX, p. 20. The contraband trade in the Spanish American dominions was said to be worth two hundred thousand pounds sterling a year (*A Series of Wisdom and Policy, Manifested in a Review of our Foreign Negotiations and Transactions for several Years past* [London, 1735], pp. 49-50).

[82] There is no monograph which specifically deals with all the conditions of trade between Spain and the Indies from 1713 to the middle of the eighteenth century, but there are some excellent ones dealing with a slightly earlier period. An old but interesting and useful treatment is by José de Veitia Linaje (*The Spanish Rule of Trade to the West Indies: . . . Written in Spanish by D. Joseph de Veitia Linage, Knight of the Order of Santiago, and Treasurer and Commissioner of the India House. Made English by Capt. John Stevens* [London, 1702]). The original Spanish edition was published in 1671. The regulations affecting the Indies trade about 1700 are described by Dahlgren: *Le commerce de la mer du Sud jusqu'à la paix d'Utrecht*, chapters i and ii. Particularly noteworthy are the studies by

Cadiz trade was also made troublesome by being subject to variable and arbitrary taxation, in addition to the fixed charges, while its continuity depended at all times on the good will of the Spanish sovereigns and the vicissitudes of political events.[83] The ease, moreover, with which the Spanish government could impound the property of merchants who traded to the Indies through the *Casa de Contratacion* (and for the French there was no other legal way), tempted it to utilize its power for political purposes. In particular, since the goods of British merchants, because of their direct illicit trade, were not readily susceptible of Spanish control, French goods ran the risk of vicariously expiating British sins, so long as France was in alliance with Great Britain.[84]

The natural result was that the French merchants were forced to charge for their wares a price sufficient to cover their extra

Albert Girard: *Le commerce français à Séville et Cadix au temps des Habsbourg: Contribution à l'étude du commerce étranger en Espagne aux XVIe et XVIIe siècles* (Paris, 1932); and by C. H. Haring: *Trade and Navigation between Spain and the Indies in the Time of the Hapsburgs* (*Harvard Economic Series*, vol. XIX), (Cambridge [Mass.], 1918). The headquarters of the *Casa de Contratacion* were moved from Seville to Cadiz in 1717 (Albert Girard: *La rivalité commerciale et maritime entre Séville et Cadix jusqu'à la fin du XVIIIe siècle* [Paris, 1932], p. 80). Besides various harbour dues, brokerage and freight charges, foreign merchants had to pay a duty of fifteen *per cent.* on goods which they brought to Cadiz. On goods returning from the Indies they paid eight *per cent.;* on gold, silver and precious stones, six *per cent.;* there was besides a variable and arbitrary tax, called the indult (Henri Sée: "Esquisse de l'histoire du commerce français à Cadix et dans l'Amérique espagnole au XVIIIe siècle." *Revue d'histoire moderne*, III [1928], pp. 13-31).

[83] Cf. Henri Sée and Léon Vignols: "La fin du commerce interlope dans l'Amérique espagnole." *Revue d'histoire économique et sociale*, XIII (1925), pp. 308-313, wherein is published an anonymous memorial on trade, dated October 7, 1728. There were many frauds connected with the collection of customs at Cadiz, which tended to lessen the charges on foreign merchants (Uztariz: *Theory and Practice of Commerce and Maritime Affairs*, II, pp. 60-67); to remedy this, the indult was levied on goods brought from the Indies. In 1709 it was fixed at five *per cent.*, but in 1722 it was put at nine *per cent.* In 1727 it was twenty-three and three-fourths *per cent.*, and in 1738 it was thirteen *per cent.* on goods from Carthagena and twenty-one *per cent.* on goods from Mexico (Sée: "Esquisse de l'histoire du commerce français à Cadix." *Revue d'histoire moderne*, III, p. 18).

[84] Such were the apprehensions of a Nantes memorialist who wrote in 1726, when Admiral Hosier was blockading the galleons (Henri Sée and Léon Vignols: "L'envers de la diplomatie officielle de 1715 à 1730: La rivalité commerciale des puissances maritimes et les doléances des négociants français." *Revue belge de philologie et d'histoire*, V [1926], p. 474).

expenses and leave, besides, a margin sufficient to meet the arbitrary indult. It was claimed that the British were able to market their goods in the Spanish Indies at fifty-two *per cent.* of the total cost to a French merchant with the same wares. In other words, the British could and did undersell the merchants operating through the *Casa de Contratacion* forty *per cent.*, and while doing so they were still able to make a larger net profit than their competitors.[85] As a consequence, the high-priced goods at the fairs of Vera Cruz and Portobelo were difficult to dispose of. The flotilla sent to Vera Cruz in 1725 did not return until 1727, and the galleons sent to Carthagena and Portobelo in 1723 did not return until 1728.[86] To the uncertainty of eventual profits was added the disadvantage of receiving very slow returns on the capital invested in the trade to the Indies.[87] In proportion as it took longer to dispose of the goods at the fairs of Vera Cruz and Portobelo, the flotillas and galleons sailed less and less frequently, as it was obviously useless to replenish a market already overstocked.[88] Thus, the British enjoyed a continuous traffic, while

[85] This computation is made in one of the *Mémoires rédigés par des députés du commerce des grands ports pour le Congrès de Soissons* (Bib. Nat., Nouv. Acq. fr., 23,085); see Léon Vignols: *"L'asiento français* (1701-1713) et anglais (1713-1750) et le commerce franco-espagnol vers 1700 à 1730." *Revue d'histoire économique et sociale,* XVII (1929), pp. 430-431. Cf. Raynal: *A Philosophical and Political History of the Settlements and Trade of the Europeans in the East and West Indies,* III, p. 122. Private illicit traders enjoyed particular advantages: ". . . they can sell to the Inhabitants all such Commodities as they want, above a hundred *per Cent.* cheaper than they can have them from *Old Spain,* and above fifty *per Cent.* cheaper than they can have them from the Assient Ships, by reason that the People of our Plantations . . . are at no Charge of keeping Factors abroad, or paying Sailors at home, as the *South Sea* Company do" (*The Present State of the Revenues and Forces, by Sea and Land, of France and Spain,* pp. 25-26).
[86] The flotilla was sent out in 1720, 1723, 1725, 1729, 1732 and 1735; the galleons were sent out in 1721, 1723 and 1730. In 1735 the system of trading with Carthagena and Portobelo by the galleons was suspended; thereafter, trading was done by individual "register ships" (Hussey: *The Caracas Company, 1728-1784,* pp. 201-202); cf. Sée: "Esquisse de l'histoire du commerce français à Cadix." *Revue d'histoire moderne,* III, p. 16; also, Ulloa: *Rétablissement des manufactures et du commerce d'Espagne,* part ii, p. 95, note.
[87] Henri Sée: "Les armateurs de Saint-Malo au XVIIIe siècle." *Revue d'histoire économique et sociale,* XVII (1929), p. 32; Uztariz: *Theory and Practice of Commerce and Maritime Affairs,* I, p. 156.
[88] J.-B. Lemoyne to Delisle-Lemoyne, Cadix, Feb. 23, 1738: "Je ne fais pas de doute qu'il n'y ait pas de flotte cette année: la Nouvelle Espagne est trop remplie de marchandises; du moins les prix le font connaître'? (Henri Sée: "Les spéculations

the French had to make the best of a badly interrupted one. The French merchants naturally grumbled; one of them, Guillotou of Morlaix, wrote to his correspondent in Cadiz:

For a long time we have thought like you that the Company of the Asiento does great harm to commerce; war alone can deliver us and make commerce as flourishing as it was formerly.[89]

Yet, as has been mentioned, the French Ministry was fully aware of the harm which the illicit traffic of the British did to their own trade. Their connivance, and even their support of it, was the price they had to pay for an alliance which had become indispensable.

Because it was supposed that Spain contemplated giving the Ostend Company trading rights in the West Indies which would break down the exclusiveness of British trading privileges there, the British Government were particularly anxious to force the Emperor to withdraw the Company's charter.[90] There were other reasons, too, why the British were eager to get rid of the rival company. It was claimed that the India goods brought to Ostend were smuggled in great quantities into England.[91] The

---

d'un officier de finance à Cadix et dans l'Amérique espagnole (1734-1739)." *Mémoires et documents pour servir à l'histoire du commerce et de l'industrie en France*, XII [1929], p. 351).

[89] April 9, 1734 (Henri Sée: "Le commerce de Morlaix dans la première moitié du XVIIIᵉ siècle, d'après les papiers de Guillotou de Keréver." *Mémoires et documents pour servir à l'histoire du commerce et de l'industrie en France*, IX [1925], p. 179).

[90] "Such Alterations were made in the Commerce of Europe as must begin in the Ruine of our East and West India Trade, and end in that of all the other valuable Branches of our Commerce" ([Benjamin Hoadly, Bishop of Salisbury]: *An Enquiry into the Reasons of the Conduct of Great Britain, with Relation to the Present State of Affairs in Europe* [London, 1727], p. 29; also, pp. 72-74).

[91] Charles Forman: *Mr. Forman's Letter to the Right Honourable William Pulteney, Esq.: Shewing how Pernicious, the Imperial Company of Commerce and Navigation, lately established in the Austrian Netherlands, is likely to prove to Great Britain, as well as to Holland* (London, 1725), pp. 30-31, 64; *The Importance of the Ostend-Company Consider'd* (London, 1726), p. 33. Quantities of smuggled India goods were rowed up the Thames (Ad. Levae: "Récherches historiques sur le commerce des belges aux Indes pendant le XVIIᵉ et le XVIIIᵉ siècle." *Trésor national*, Première Série, III [Brussels, 1842], pp. 98-99). To prevent this, Parliament passed statutes forbidding boats of more than four oars to ply on the Thames (8 George I, cap. xvi, section 3; 11 George I, cap. xxix, section 4; 2 George II, cap. xxviii, section 6).

sluggishness of the sales of the British East India Company in March and September of the years 1724 and 1725 was attributed to this competition.[92] It was feared, too, that if the Emperor were permitted to establish the Company permanently, its success would strengthen the Catholic party in Europe, an apprehension not altogether chimerical in view of the support which the Emperor was giving to the Catholics in central Europe at that moment, and certainly an effective argument for a public fanatically anti-Catholic.[93] Not least, the British, with the memory of the Dunkirk privateers fresh in their minds, seem to have been seriously concerned over the incipient sea power of Ostend, which they apprehended might become another Dunkirk.[94] In short, the British objections to the Ostend Company, when dressed for popular consumption, were as follows:

I shall only add, that if this Company be not destroy'd, ours must be ruin'd; That if the reviving Trade, and Navigation of the Flemmings be not stiffled, our Commerce, and Maritime Power must dwindle, and decay: And that, the House of Austria become Mistress of Navigation, she will get Trade into her Power; and, by consequence, Riches; and, If I may say so, will have the World at her Beck; and then, the Liberties of Europe will soon be no more, and the Protestant Religion be destroy'd.[95]

[92] *The Importance of the Ostend-Company Consider'd,* p. 4; *A Letter to the Chairman of the East India Company by a Proprietor in the Company's Stock* (1727) (Gerald B. Hertz: "England and the Ostend Company." *English Historical Review,* XXII [1907], p. 267). These were the usual semi-annual sales to wholesale buyers.

[93] Hoadly: *Enquiry into the Reasons of the Conduct of Great Britain,* pp. 78-80.

[94] Hoadly: *Enquiry into the Reasons of the Conduct of Great Britain,* p. 76; *The Importance of the Ostend-Company Consider'd,* pp. 31, 43; Onslow Burrish: *Batavia Illustrata; Or, a View of the Policy, and Commerce, of the United Provinces: Particularly of Holland* (London, 1728), pp. 456-460; *The Treaty of Seville and the Measures that have been taken for the Four Last Years, Impartially Considered* (London, 1730), pp. 6, 8; *A Series of Wisdom and Policy, Manifested in a Review of our Foreign Negotiations and Transactions for several Years past* (London, 1735), p. 16. Not only was Ostend, like Dunkirk, very close to England, but also, which was more important, it was windward to the Straits of Dover for any easterly wind, which facilitated picking up prizes off the Downs. The argument for the demolition of Dunkirk had been that the French men-of-war would have no base nearer to England than Brest, while French privateers would have no base nearer than Saint-Malo; both ports, moreover, were leeward of the Straits of Dover (Sir Richard Steele: *The Importance of Dunkirk Consider'd* [London, 1713], pp. 26-30). Cf. a report with reference to Ostend as a naval base, endorsed as sent to Townshend at Hanover on July 30, O. S., 1725 (R. O., Treaty Papers 107) (Chance: *Alliance of Hanover,* pp. 7-8).

[95] *The Importance of the Ostend-Company Consider'd* (1726), p. 55.

The existence of the Ostend Company was a question of very considerable importance in an age of such fierce commercial competition as was the eighteenth century; for the Ostend venture was no mere "paper company," as Carlyle contemptuously and erroneously remarked.[96] Ever since the Spanish Netherlands had been turned over to the Emperor in 1715, the Deputy Governor, the Marquis of Prié, had granted authorizations to trade in the East Indies.[97] In December 1722, the Emperor decided upon chartering a privileged company; on July 20, 1723, the charter was issued.[98] Although the legal capital was fixed at six million florins, no more than four million five hundred thousand was ever called in, which was equivalent in English money to a capitalization of (approximately) £337,500.[99] Until the suspension of the Company in 1727, a total of fifteen ships

[96] "The Kaiser's Imperial Ostend East-India Company, which convulsed the Diplomatic mind for seven years to come, and made Europe lurch from side to side in a terrific Manner, proved a mere paper Company; never sent any ships, only produced Diplomacies, and 'had the honour to be' " (Thomas Carlyle: *History of Friedrich II of Prussia, called Frederick the Great* [London, 1869, seven vols.], I, pp. 353-354).

[97] The private profit which this unpopular governor received from these authorizations explained his antagonism to the setting up of the Ostend Company, the granting of whose charter was delayed on that account. For a good account of these early ventures (Marcel Aragon: "La Compagnie d'Ostende et le grand commerce en Belgique au début du XVIIIe siècle." *Annales des sciences politiques*, XVI [1901], pp. 219-233). Between 1718 and 1721 at least fifteen ships navigated between Ostend and the East (Hertz: "England and the Ostend Company." *English Historical Review*, XXII, p. 257).

[98] Michel Huisman: *La Belgique commerciale sous l'empereur Charles VI: La Compagnie d'Ostende* (Brussels, 1902), pp. 237-238. Charter printed by Dumont: *Corps universel diplomatique*, VIII, part ii, pp. 44-50; the protests of Spain, as well as those of the Dutch East and West India Companies, to the States-General (*ibid.*, pp. 78-85). The charter and other papers pertaining to the Ostend Company (Jean Rousset de Missy: *Recueil historique d'actes, négociations, mémoires, et traitez* [The Hague, 1728-1748, nineteen vols.], II, pp. 5-42, 77-109, 199-214).

[99] The capitalization was actually made in Dutch guilders, worth in English money 1s. 10 2/5d.; "the florins of Flanders and Brabant represented an imaginary value and were not coined." The florin was figured at one shilling sixpence (Hertz: "England and the Ostend Company." *English Historical Review*, XXII, p. 261, note). The calculations of equivalents which appear *supra* and in notes 101-103, *infra*, have been made on this basis. Hertz is wrong, however, in stating that all the capital was called in (*ibid.*; cf. Huisman: *La Compagnie d'Ostende*, p. 258; Louis Mertens: "La Compagnie d'Ostende." *Bulletin de la Société de géographie d'Anvers*, VI [1881-1882], p. 386).

sailed to China and Bengal.[100] The net profit on their cargoes amounted to 7,814,691 florins 5 sols 3 deniers or (approximately) £586,162-1-9.[101] By the end of 1730 the Company had declared dividends amounting to 6,180,000 florins, besides having capital invested in the Banks of Prussia and Poland, colonial factories, a merchant fleet, and goods to the value of 1,631,733 florins stored in their warehouses.[102] In 1725 the export and import duties on goods connected with the Ostend trade amounted to 2,012,988 florins 3 sols 10 deniers; and in 1726 to 1,985,315 florins 7 deniers.[103] The magnitude of these sums explains why the British and the Dutch became alarmed over the prosperity of their neighbouring rival.

The simple and natural desire to rid themselves of a prosperous competitor fully explains the attitude of the British and the Dutch, but it did not justify it. To do that, there was much furbishing of legal arguments on the part of the Dutch, mixed with hints of recourse to the *ultima ratio* of Kings and High Mightinesses.[104] The British did not argue legal refinements to

[100] Mertens: "La Compagnie d'Ostende." *Bulletin de la Société de géographie d'Anvers*, VI, pp. 414-415.

[101] This sum is reached as the result of the following arithmetical calculations: the net profit on the ships sent to China was 7,058,305 florins (Huisman: *La Compagnie d'Ostende*, p. 378); to this should be added the profit on the second expedition to Bengal, 362,328 florins (*ibid.*, p. 362), as well as that of the third expedition, 121,650 florins (*ibid.*, p. 370), and that of the fourth expedition, 907,590 florins (*ibid.*, p. 371). From this total should be subtracted the dead loss on the vessel which was shipwrecked, 635,181 florins 14 sols 9 deniers (*ibid.*, p. 282). According to the researches of another authority, however, the profit on these voyages was 8,198,340 florins (Mertens: "La Compagnie d'Ostende." *Bulletin de la Société de géographie d'Anvers*, VI, pp. 414-415).

[102] Huisman: *La Compagnie d'Ostende*, p. 471. The equivalents in sterling for the sums mentioned are £463,500, and £122,379-19-6, respectively.

[103] Huisman: *La Compagnie d'Ostende*, pp. 424-425. The equivalents in sterling are (approximately) £150,974-2-3½, and £143,898-12-6½, respectively.

[104] These legalistic contentions are well summarized by Huisman: *La Compagnie d'Ostende*, pp. 379-403. Huisman is sympathetic to the Belgian point of view, and stresses the argument of Patyn, Dumont and MacNeny, the leading Imperial writers on the subject, that it was not just to attempt to deny the *natural right* of the inhabitants of the Austrian Netherlands to engage in commerce. The Dutch argument was based on treaties: article vi of the Treaty of Münster (1648) limited in favour of the Dutch the trading rights of "Castilians" in the East Indies; the Dutch claimed that this clause had been intended to limit the trading rights there of *all* of the subjects of Philip IV. Inasmuch as this clause had been con-

such an extent, but maintained stoutly that the terms and intentions of the Grand Alliance (1701) forbade the Emperor from setting up in the Netherlands a rival to the Maritime Powers; in short,

That the Preservation of the Trade in the Indies, to the English and Dutch, upon the Foot they enjoyed it, and in the Manner it was carried on, to the Death of King Charles II of Spain, was one ground, and a main one, of the Grand Alliance; and that the Emperor's Pretensions to the Low-Countries were supported by the English and Dutch, upon this, amongst other Conditions, that the Emperor should reciprocally support their Trade to the Indies, on the Foot they had constantly enjoyed it.[105]

This frank contention, which rode so rough-shod over the Austrian argument of natural rights, smacked strongly of brutal *Realpolitik*, but there was a great deal of soundness in it; the Maritime Powers had some grounds for the display of injured feelings:

that instead of acknowledging the Services that have been done Him, at the Expence of so much Blood and Treasure, and repaying Them with acts of Friendship, he should endeavour to tear out their Bowels; is, it must be owned, extreamly supprizing, and a very great Reflection upon the Emperor's Gratitude and Equity.[106]

firmed by article xxvi of the third Barrier Treaty (Antwerp, November 15, 1715) the Dutch argued that the inhabitants of Flanders and Brabant were still excluded from the East India trade. The Austrians claimed that Philip IV had signed the Treaty of Münster in his capacity as King of Spain, but not in his capacity as Duke of Brabant; furthermore, that Charles VI inherited the Netherlands, not as the heir of Philip IV (and consequently was not bound by what Philip IV had agreed to), but as the heir of Charles the Bold and the Burgundian line. The Austrian arguments summarized and refuted (Burrish: *Batavia Illustrata* [1728], pp. 404-454; see also Hertz: "England and the Ostend Company." *English Historical Review*, XXII, pp. 271-273; Goslinga: *Slingelandt's Efforts towards European Peace*, appendix, pp. xiii-xxiv). Rousset: *Recueil historique*, II, pp. 43-76, prints the "Dissertatio de Jure" written by Westerveen, attorney for the Dutch East India Company; *ibid.*, III, pp. 24-135, the argument by Dumont: "La vérité du fait du droit et de l'intérêt," with an anonymous refutation.

[105] Hoadly: *Enquiry into the Reasons of the Conduct of Great Britain*, p. 68. This officially inspired pamphlet goes on to say: "Nay, it was likewise expressly stipulated, in this Grand Alliance, supposing it to end successfully; that the Spanish Netherlands should be (not the Property of the Emperor absolutely, and without any Conditions; but) a Barrier to the United Provinces" (*ibid.*, p. 69). Cf. Charles Forman: *Mr. Forman's Letter to the Right Honourable William Pulteney*, pp. 11, 13-14, 16.

[106] Burrish: *Batavia Illustrata* (1728), p. 394.

In supporting Great Britain in her opposition to the Ostend Company, France was also upholding a vital contention of the United Provinces, which tended to foster the improvement in her relations with the Dutch. Since the Peace of Utrecht, the French had made extraordinary efforts to overcome the very natural mistrust which the Dutch had conceived of them.[107] That this was also Fleury's policy in 1726 followed as a corollary of his determination to maintain close diplomatic relations with Great Britain. But other reasons, as well, inspired the French government with the desire to be on good terms with the United Provinces, and the instructions to La Baune (1728) emphasize this disposition, as those to his predecessors had done.[108]

Such was French policy, in spite of the fact that the exhaustion of the United Provinces and the consequent decay of their military and naval power were well known.[109] Financial strain had emphasized, besides, all the defects of a government which suffered from too much decentralization, and which had lost, by the death of William of Orange, the controlling hand of a strong-willed master. "Of all the constitutions formed by statesmen, or described by historians, none was more complicated and embarrassed than that of the seven united provinces."[110] Fearful of making enemies and of losing trade, the Dutch in the period following the Peace of Utrecht carried their customary caution

---

[107] Instructions to Chasteauneuf, August 13, 1713 (*Recueil des instructions.* . . . *Hollande* [Edited by Louis André and Émile Bourgeois; Paris, 1922-1924, three vols.], II, pp. 350-351; instructions to Morville, August 4, 1718 (*ibid.*, pp. 387-388); instructions to Fénelon, January 10, 1725 (*ibid.*, pp. 436-437).

[108] *Recueil des instructions.* . . . *Hollande*, II, pp. 471, 473, 498. These instructions were written by Fénelon; they have also been well edited by C. H. T. Bussemaker: "Een Memorie over de Republiek uit 1728." *Bijdragen en Mededeelingen van het Historisch Genootschap*, XXX (1909), pp. 96-197.

[109] E.g., Chambéry, *chargé d'affaires*, to Dubois, Oct. 10, 1721 (*Recueil des instructions.* . . . *Hollande*, II, p. 422); the same to the same, February 4, 1721: "Ils croient se réhabiliter en mettant six ou sept frégates en mer pendant l'été pour se faire voir à Lisbonne et à Cadix sous prétexte de favoriser leur commerce. Ils le projettent: mais, Monseigneur, ils n'en ont point le pouvoir" (*ibid.*, II, p. 423); Morville to Dubois, July 4 and Sept. 26, 1719 (*ibid.*, II, p. 376); instructions to Fénelon (*ibid.*, II, pp. 447-448).

[110] Coxe: *Memoirs of Horatio, Lord Walpole*, I, pp. 19-20. For the manner in which the foreign affairs of the United Provinces were conducted, see Goslinga: *Slingelandt's Efforts towards European Peace*, pp. 22-25.

to such a pitch that their foreign policy may be said to have reduced itself to merely an apotheosis of the *status quo:*

The experience of this disorder in which the Republic found itself as a result of having interfered too much in the general affairs of Europe, precipitated those members who had acquired the greatest influence since the peace into the contrary extreme of believing that their State could subsist tranquilly, while abstaining in the future from taking part in anything abroad. If they did not yet dare to adopt the maxim in its entirety publicly, they followed it in practice.[111]

The secret reason why the French were so eager to cultivate friendly relations with the United Provinces was not because they anticipated that Dutch diplomatic and military support, considering the decadence of the Dutch state, would be of preponderating value; it was rather that they hoped to utilize the inertness of the Dutch in such a manner as to disorganize the plans of the British. Frederick the Great's remark that the United Provinces followed after Great Britain "as a sloop follows the track of a ship of war, to which she is lashed," is, like so many epigrams, only partially true.[112] There were situations in which the sloop kept the ship from making way. For party reasons, the Whigs valued the maintenance of the friendship with the Dutch, and, for reasons connected with German politics, the continued good will of the United Provinces was desirable for the Kings of Great Britain in their capacity as Electors of Hanover.[113] Most important of all, the British, for commercial reasons, were hesitant about committing themselves to an aggressive policy which might result in war, so long as they were uncertain of carrying the Dutch with them.

The prime reason for the inertness of the Dutch was that they were afraid to engage in any action which might damage their trade. The French were well aware of this; the instructions to Fénelon, dated January 10, 1725, said on this point:

[111] Fénelon's instructions to La Baune, 1728 (*Recueil des instructions.* . . . *Hollande,* II, p. 483).
[112] Frederick II: "History of my own Times." *Posthumous Works,* I, part i, p. 25.
[113] Goslinga: *Slingelandt's Efforts towards European Peace,* pp. 54-55; *Recueil des instructions.* . . . *Hollande,* II, p. 494.

It ought also to be considered that whatever advantages it [the Republic] might find, in other respects, in the proposals which might be made to it of undertaking any engagement whatsoever, one would seek in vain to get it to approve of them, were they capable of inflicting the slightest injury to the welfare of its trade.[114]

It was for this reason that the Dutch had refused to co-operate with Great Britain in placing an embargo on the export of grain to Sweden in 1717, at the time of the arrest of Gyllenborg and Goertz.[115] It was for this reason, too, that they never ratified the Treaty of London of August 2, 1718, thus making the Quadruple Alliance a misnomer.[116] The pleasant consequence of such inaction was that the Dutch, as neutrals, picked up the trade which the British merchants lost. The irritation of the British is easy to imagine:

They have lain still, easing their Country of publick Burthens, whilst we have been encreasing ours; they have grown Rich by the Trade which we have lost, and, 'tis said, have even supplied our Enemies with the Materials of War, to fight against us.[117]

Even during the War of the Spanish Succession, Dutch and English ideas about the manner of carrying on trade in time of war had come into conflict.[118] British merchants, after their experience with Dutch neutral trade during the short war with Spain in 1719, to which the above quotation refers, were disposed to be opposed to intervention in a war on the Continent, unless

---

[114] *Recueil des instructions. . . . Hollande*, II, p. 444.

[115] Wiesener: *Le Régent, l'abbé Dubois et les anglais*, II, pp. 6-7; *The Cambridge Modern History*, VI: *The Eighteenth Century* (Cambridge, 1909), p. 28.

[116] Commented upon in the instructions to Fénelon, Jan. 10, 1725 (*Recueil des instructions. . . . Hollande*, II, pp. 443-444).

[117] [Thomas Gordon]: *Considerations Offered upon the Approaching Peace, and upon the Importance of Gibraltar to the British Empire* (London, 1720), p. 12. The British were so annoyed with the Dutch for carrying on trade with Spain that they even encouraged the Emperor to authorize Flemish privateers to prey on Dutch shipping (Michael: *Englische Geschichte im 18. Jahrhundert*, II, pp. 181, 186-189). Chesterfield and Waller referred to the Dutch as "A People that consider the Commotions of their Neighbours as so many Opportunities for them to enlarge their Trade, and increase their Wealth, as they have uniformly done, from the Treaty of Utrecht 'till now" (*The Case of the Hanover Forces in the Pay of Great Britain* [1742], p. 21).

[118] G. N. Clark: "War Trade and Trade War, 1701-1713." *Economic History Review*, I (1927-1928), pp. 262-280.

there was considerable likelihood that the Dutch would also intervene.[119] The British attitude towards Dutch practice in these matters was illustrated by a caricature, under date of October 8, 1739, which represented an Englishman fighting with a Spaniard while a Dutchman was busily engaged in picking the Englishman's pocket.[120] That the French realized that a large section of British opinion would be opposed to war unless the Dutch were also committed to belligerency is probably indicated by Pecquet's observation that the Dutch could become the regulators of British policy, inconstant and changeable as it was at the will of Parliament.[121]

Certainly the French action was in accordance with what such a calculation would dictate; for the Cardinal guaranteed the neutrality of the Austrian Netherlands almost as soon as the War of the Polish Succession broke out. By doing so, he secured Dutch neutrality, which was a source of extreme discomfiture to the British government. The British felt particularly aggrieved because this action had been taken without consulting them.[122] Every British scheme for mediation or intervention in the War of the Polish Succession was modified by the fear that the Dutch would not co-operate with them, and that Dutch trade would profit at British expense if Great Britain should decide to inter-

---

[119] Malachy Postlethwayt: *A Short State of the Progress of the French Trade and Navigation: Wherein is shewn, the great Foundation that France has laid, by dint of Commerce, to increase her maritime Strength to a Pitch equal, if not superior, to that of Great Britain, unless somehow checked by the Wisdom of His Majesty's Councils* (London, 1756), p. 75; cf. Sir Charles Wager to Lord Townshend, Jan. 1, O. S., 1726/7 (Townshend Papers, *Historical Manuscripts Commission, Report* XI, Appendix Part IV [London, 1887], pp. 116-117).

[120] Thomas Wright: *England under the House of Hanover; its History and Condition during the Reigns of the Three Georges, Illustrated from the Caricatures and Satires of the Day* (London, 1848-1849, two vols.), I, p. 169. The author of *Strenuous Motives for an Immediate War against Spain* (London, 1738), found it necessary to attempt to answer (pp. 8-9) the argument that the Dutch "will run away with all the Trade of Spain." Dutch trade increased conspicuously after the British declared war on Spain in 1739 (*Proposals made by His late Highness the Prince of Orange* [J. R. McCulloch: *A Select Collection of Scarce and Valuable Tracts on Commerce*, p. 444]).

[121] "Situation des affaires de l'Europe en 1726" (Dureng: *Le duc de Bourbon et l'Angleterre*, p. 337).

[122] Sir Richard Lodge: "The Maritime Powers in the Eighteenth Century." *History*, XV (1930-1931), p. 248.

vene in the conflict. Lord Hervey argued with that ardent inter-
ventionist, Queen Caroline, to this effect:

Could England engage in a war to regain Italy for the Emperor without
Holland?—No. Why?—Because, in the first place, it would in all probability
be ineffectual; and, in the next, because it must indisputably throw the trade
of all Europe into the hands of Holland, if Holland remained neuter.[123]

The same sentiment was being expressed in the House:

Mr. Willimot, the new City member, went so far as to say that he hoped this
House would pour down national vengeance upon the head of that man who
should advise his Prince to enter into this war without the Dutch, as by this
means we should exhaust our force and treasure, and in the meanwhile they
run away with all our trade.[124]

It is reasonable to infer that French statesmen, in the first
year of Fleury's administration, were aware of the principle that
British policy could be indirectly subjected to control by guaranteeing the security of the Dutch. The United Provinces could be
most readily confirmed in their congenial policy of doing nothing
if they were assured that France did not contemplate any aggression in the buffer territory of the Austrian Netherlands.
From 1715 to 1743 there is manifested a continuity and uni-
formity of French policy on this point which indicate that the
French were consciously utilizing this weapon from their diplomatic arsenal for the purpose of discomfiting and immobilizing
the British. In 1715 Chasteauneuf proposed to guarantee the
neutrality of the Austrian Netherlands, in order to prevent Dutch
accession to the Treaty of Westminster between Austria and
Great Britain.[125] By hastening to guarantee to the Dutch the
neutrality of the Austrian Netherlands in 1733, Fleury was able

---

[123] Hervey: *Some Materials towards Memoirs*, p. 352; cf. *ibid.*, pp. 412-413.

[124] Sir Thomas Robinson to [Lord Carlisle], Feb. 10, O. S., 1734/5 (Carlisle
Papers, *Historical Manuscripts Commission, Report* XV, Appendix Part VI, [Lon-
don, 1897], p. 149). Cf. Charles Howard to [Lord Carlisle], Jan. 31, O. S., [1734]
(*ibid.*, p. 128).

[125] For Chasteauneuf's proposal (*Recueil des instructions. . . . Hollande*, II,
pp. 331-332); also, René Dollot: *Les origines de la neutralité de la Belgique et le
système de la Barrière (1609-1830)* (Paris, 1902), pp. 412-417, 556-557. Chasteauneuf's proposal was for a general guarantee; Fleury's guarantee in 1733 was only
ad hoc.

to secure Dutch neutrality and throw British policy into confusion during the War of the Polish Succession. To what an extent the French relied upon this calculation in 1735 is shown by
a report submitted to Horatio Walpole by his gleaners of diplomatic small-talk, the Sicilian Abbés, then resident at Paris and
Versailles:

The French do not fear the effects of England, even though she should come
into a war, for they take for granted that if the Dutch being neutral England
enters into a war, they shall take their trade with Spain away and raise
disturbances at home, by giving it out that the interest of the House of
Hanover has caused a war which ruins the trade of the nation, whilst Holland who is the most exposed, has neither known this war to be just or necessary.[126]

Finally, inasmuch as this device had been so successful in 1733,
Fleury once more endeavoured to engage the Dutch to neutrality
during the War of the Austrian Succession by offering to respect
the territorial integrity of the Austrian Netherlands.[127] On this
occasion he was unsuccessful, but the incident illustrates the continuity of French policy in this respect.

The cultivation of good relations between France and the
United Provinces required the exercise of unlimited tact and patience. Fénelon was warned that "it is still true that the least
occasion for suspicion which might be given to the States General would destroy in a moment the work of several years."[128]

As to the States General, they found the Wounds that they had received in
the last War, so apt to throb and shoot upon any Change of politic Weather,
that one need not be surprised at their being apprehensive of every little
Storm.[129]

[126] Goslinga: *Slingelandt's Efforts towards European Peace*, p. 53. For the
Sicilian Abbés, see Chance: *Alliance of Hanover*, pp. 317 note, 743-744.

[127] Adolf Beer: "Holland und der österreichische Erbfolge-Krieg." *Archiv für
österreichische Geschichte*, XLVI (1871), pp. 308, 310, 315-316; Fleury and Amelot
told van Hoey, Dutch ambassador to France, that the British desired to engage
the Dutch in the war in order that their commerce might be destroyed (van
Hoey to Fagel, Feb. 22 and June 18, 1742 [*Lettres et négociations de Monsieur van
Hoey, ambassadeur à la cour de France. Pour servir à l'histoire de la vie du cardinal
de Fleury* (London, 1743), pp. 13, 27-28]).

[128] *Recueil des instructions. . . . Hollande*, II, p. 440.

[129] *Memoirs of the Life and Administration of the late Andrew-Hercules de Fleury*,
pp. 28-29.

The principal way by which Fleury and his predecessors lulled the fears and invited the confidence of the Dutch was by their constant assurances that the French had renounced the idea of any aggression in the Netherlands:

Nothing has contributed so much to give birth to these good feelings and to confirm them as the care which His Majesty has taken to convince this Republic, by all his acts and by the reiterated assurances which he has made, of the disinterestedness of his views and especially that he did not desire any aggrandizement in the direction of the Low Countries.[130]

So successful were the French in convincing the Dutch that it may be said that by 1726 the old Barrier policy of the Grand Alliance was turned inside out: the right to garrison Belgian towns, which had been secured for the purpose of erecting a barrier to French invasion, was now looked upon as a means of bringing the Emperor to fear

lest he be despoiled of the Low-Countries in a single campaign. The Republic, for its part, regarded those towns as the gates by which France was in a position to extend her hand to them and to protect them from all that the Emperor should propose to attempt against them.[131]

---

[130] Fénelon's instructions to La Baune, April 4, 1728 (*Recueil des instructions . . . Hollande*, II, p. 498).

[131] Fénelon's instructions to La Baune, April 4, 1728 (*Recueil des instructions . . . Hollande*, II, p. 498). The Grand Alliance (1701) had provided that, if the war should be successful, a barrier should be set up in the Netherlands for the benefit of the Dutch, which should take the form of the right to garrison certain key positions with Dutch troops. The towns were named and the general conditions laid down in the first Barrier Treaty (1709) (Roderick Geikie and Isabel A. Montgomery: *The Dutch Barrier, 1705-1719* [Cambridge, 1930], pp. 377-386). In 1713 the Tories negotiated the second Barrier Treaty, on terms much less favourable to the Dutch (text of the treaty published by Geikie and Montgomery: *The Dutch Barrier*, pp. 386-395). To the final or third Barrier Treaty, signed at Antwerp on November 15, 1715, the Dutch, the British and the Emperor were parties. The garrison towns were to be Furnes, Knocke, Dendermonde, Ypres, Warneton, Menin, Tournai, Mons, Binche and Namur. The Austrians also were to be permitted to have a garrison in Dendermonde. Twenty-one thousand troops were to be kept in the Netherlands, nine thousand of them Dutch, for whose pay and support the Emperor guaranteed payment from the revenues of the Austrian Netherlands (text in Geikie and Montgomery: *The Dutch Barrier*, pp. 395-415; see also, Henri Pirenne: *Histoire de Belgique* [Brussels, 1902-1932, seven vols.], V, pp. 121-130; Dollot: *Les origines de la neutralité de la Belgique et le système de la Barrière*, pp. 390-412; L.-P. Gachard: *Histoire de la Belgique au commencement du XVIIIe siècle* [Brussels, 1880], pp. 236-286). Subsequent territorial and financial modifications in favour of the Belgians were made by the convention of December 22, 1718; see the report of the events of his administration made by the Deputy-

Besides being willing to assist the Dutch in the suppression of
the Ostend Company and to assure them of the pacific intentions
of France, it was a part of the French policy with regard to the
United Provinces to pay close attention to the development of
the crisis in East Friesland which, by inflaming the irritation of
the Dutch against the Emperor, at the same time increased their
dependence upon France.[132] Another object of French policy

Governor of the Netherlands, the Marquis of Prié, to Charles VI, April 16, 1725
(L.-P. Gachard: *Collection de documents inédits concernant l'histoire de la Belgique*
[Brussels, 1833-1835, three vols.], III, pp. 492-500; also, Geikie and Montgomery:
The Dutch Barrier, pp. 364-368; Gachard: *Histoire de la Belgique*, pp. 471-484).
For good maps, showing the extent of Dutch territorial acquisitions in the Nether-
lands, as fixed by the treaty of 1715 and modified by the convention of 1718, see
those at the conclusion of the work by Edmond Willequet: "Histoire du système
de la Barrière dans les négociations antérieures à la paix d'Utrecht." *Annales des
Universités de Belgique*, VI-VII (*1847-1848*), (Brussels, 1850), pp. 188-363. A
good contemporary account of the condition of the Barrier towns may be found
in the report of an agent of the Landgrave of Hesse-Cassel (François-Michel
Janiçon: *État présent de la République des Provinces-Unies, et des païs qui en dépendent* [The Hague, 1729-1730, two vols.], II, pp. 469-504. The Barrier question
is summed up by Goslinga: *Slingelandt's Efforts towards European Peace*, pp. 61-66.
In practice, the system was of doubtful utility, and it was most certainly mutually
vexatious; for an account of the multifarious disputes over the exercise of religious
rights and rites, police administration, contraband trade activities, hunting and
fishing rights, taxes, the lodging of officers and the quartering of soldiers, the
upkeep of forts, etc., see Eugène Hubert: "Les garnisons de la Barrière dans les
Pays-Bas autrichiens (1715-1782)." *Mémoires couronnés et mémoires des savants
étrangers publiés par l'Académie royale des sciences, des lettres et des beaux-arts de
Belgique*, LIX (1901-1903), fasc. iv, *passim*. The Austrian government co-
operated very badly in keeping up the system, because they were indignant with
the Maritime Powers for continuing their economic exploitation of the Netherlands, and for refusing to conclude a commercial treaty. After the second Treaty
of Vienna (1731), representatives of Austria, Great Britain and the United Provinces met for a long time at Antwerp, for the purpose of concluding a commercial
treaty, but the sessions were finally adjourned without issue in 1739. The Barrier
system practically fell into desuetude after the Treaty of Aix-la-Chapelle (1748).
Fénelon mentions in his instructions to La Baune (1728) that many Dutch were
very discontented with the Barrier system, from which they had promised themselves such great benefits (*Recueil des instructions* . . . *Hollande*, II, pp. 496-497).
Tension between Dutch and Belgians was increased in July 1725, when the former
laid a higher tariff on imports into the United Provinces (Gachard: *Histoire de la
Belgique*, p. 506).

    [132] This question is well set forth in the instructions to Fénelon (1725) and
particularly well in the latter's instructions to La Baune in 1728 (*Recueil des
instructions* . . . *Hollande*, II, pp. 451-452, 501-509). Cf. Goslinga: *Slingelandt's
Efforts towards European Peace*, pp. 145-155. A detailed and purely factual account is given by Janiçon: *État présent de la République des Provinces-Unies et
des païs qui en dépendent*, II, pp. 505-532. An exhaustive account of these East-
Frisian disputes is given by Tileman Dothias Wiarda: *Ostfriesische Geschichte*
(Aurich, 1791-1798, nine vols.), particularly vols. VII (*1714-1734*) and VIII (*1734-

was to prevent the revival of the stadtholdership.[133] The French were apprehensive lest the setting up of a stadtholder would make the Dutch State stronger and more independent. French representatives, accordingly, were instructed to oppose the promotion of the Prince of Nassau as much as they could without letting their intentions be apparent; nor did they let opportunities pass for stirring up discord between Great Britain and the Province of Holland by insinuating that the British were sympathetic to the cause of the Prince of Nassau and hopeful of seeing him become ruler of the Dutch.[134] The final item in the

---

1758). The relative state papers covering the dispute from 1721 to 1730 may be found in Dumont: *Corps universel diplomatique*, VIII, part ii, pp. 163-212; and in Rousset: *Recueil historique*, IV, pp. 281-509. In 1611 the Dutch had secured the right of garrisoning Emden and Leer, places of great strategic importance to them. Their influence was subsequently increased by the granting of loans and by their mediation in the endemic disputes between the Princes and their Estates. In 1681, a Brandenburg garrison was also installed at Emden, and in 1694 the Emperor fixed the reversion of East Friesland upon the Elector of Brandenburg. In 1720 George Albert, who ruled from 1708 to 1734, received the Emperor's authorization to supervise the Estates of Emden in their administration of finances; the States refused his supervision, whereupon he set up new States and forbade the paying of taxes to the old, whose partisans were called "Renitents." In 1723 the Emperor appointed the Elector of Saxony and the Duke of Brunswick-Wolfen-büttel to enforce his decrees. At the time of Fleury's accession to power, civil war had broken out in East Friesland; the Dutch had thus far stayed neutral, but they were anxious to preserve their garrison rights in Emden, in order to perpetuate their influence and protect their investments there, and they bore a grudge against the Emperor for his interference in East Frisian affairs.

[133] The Prince of Nassau, who became William IV in 1747, was born posthumously in 1711. He was hereditary Stadtholder of Friesland and Groningen; the province of Gelderland elected him stadtholder in 1722. A powerful party in Overijssel also supported him, but he was vigorously opposed by the provinces of Holland and Zeeland, who were strongly republican, maritime and commercial. For reasons of protection, the more inland provinces favoured having a stadtholder. The Prince of Nassau married Anna, eldest daughter of George II, in 1734.

[134] Cf. instructions to Fénelon and to La Baune (*Recueil des instructions . . . Hollande*, II, pp. 457-459, 510-515). The British were well enough pleased at the match between Princess Anna and the Prince of Nassau, but they took extraordinary care not to give the couple any support in domestic Dutch politics, nor in any manner to awaken the fears of the party opposed to his promotion. For example, Princess Anna wrote to Queen Caroline, at the end of June or the beginning of July, 1735: "Horace [Walpole, then British ambassador at The Hague] a mille bonnes qualités et j'entre assez dans sa situation pour n'en avoir aucune rancune, mais vous jugerés de sa manière d'agir, quand vous sçaurés qu'il m'a dit luy-même, que son occupation devoit être de faire oublier tant qu'il pouroit le mariage du Prince et qu'il disoit journellement à son amy le Pensionnaire que l'on avoit fait le mariage, seulement parce que le nom plaisait en Angleterre, mais que cela ne

policy of France toward the United Provinces at the time of Fleury's accession to power was close attentiveness to the course taken by the mutual discontents of the United Provinces and the King of Prussia.[135]

The evidence of the preceding pages indicates that Fleury, upon his accession to power in 1726, regarded France as a "satiated" country which, although it had relinquished its ambitions to achieve and preserve military hegemony, still needed foreign alliances to safeguard its security and maintain the tranquillity of Europe. Although there were cogent reasons why Fleury would have avoided alliance with Spain and the Emperor in 1726, even had he been a free agent, the blunders of the Duke of Bourbon had, in reality, rendered impracticable an alliance with any group of powers save that of which Great Britain was the leader. As a consequence, France became temporarily an unequal partner in an alliance in which Great Britain took the initiative and forced the French to negotiate for objects more favourable to the British than to themselves. Partly as a corollary of the alliance with the British, but more especially because France was furthering in the United Provinces an independent policy of her own which might, if occasion offered, be of utility in disorganizing the schemes of the British and in assisting France to regain her diplomatic equality, the Cardinal determined on continuing the cultivation of the good relations between the United Provinces and France.

Toward the other European powers, French policy in 1726 was almost wholly governed by the fundamental premise of France's alliance with Great Britain. Such, for example, was

les gênoit en rien" (P. Geyl: "Engelsche Correspondentie van Prins Willem IV en Prinses Anna (1734-1743)." *Bijdragen en Mededeelingen van het Historisch Genootschap*, XLV [1924], p. 99).

[135] The Dutch were extremely disappointed that in the settlement following the War of the Spanish Succession Upper Gelderland was given to the King of Prussia, which deprived them of the acquisition of territory strategically located on both sides of the Meuse at the same time that it gave them a quarrelsome and troublesome neighbour. The King of Prussia also claimed the inheritance of some lands belonging to the family of Orange, and occupied them with his troops, a cause of dissension not settled until 1732 (*Recueil des instructions . . . Hollande*, II, pp. 498-501, 452-454).

the case with Prussia. Although it was true that France had entered a dual alliance with that State on September 14, 1716, and had also signed with Prussia and Russia the Treaty of Amsterdam (August 15, 1717), the relations between France and Prussia had remained most casual until the Alliance of Vienna had made desirable the membership of Prussia in a counteralliance.[136] In July of 1725 Rottembourg had been despatched on his third mission to Prussia, and on September 3 the King of Prussia had signed the Treaty of Hanover. Following that event, French policy regarding Prussia was confined to holding Frederick William I true to his alliance. By June 1726, it was already evident that he was manifesting "great inquietude and little firmness."[137] Fleury had ample reason to believe that he would be lost to the Hanover combination; when he was, by the Treaty of Wüsterhausen (October 12, 1726), Morville merely remarked that the King of Prussia would always be "an inconvenient and embarrassing ally, but he will come back some day to his first engagements."[138]

[136] The treaty of September 14, 1716, is printed in *Recueil des instructions . . . Prusse* (Edited by Albert Waddington; Paris, 1901), pp. lxii-lxviii; also by Loewe: *Preussens Staatsverträge*, pp. 149-158. Between 1721 and 1725 France had no accredited representative in Prussia; Rottembourg's secretary, Michel, took care of correspondence. As a result of the Treaty of Charlottenburg between Frederick William I and George I (October 10, 1723 [Loewe: *op. cit.*, pp. 278-284]), there was some correspondence between Ilgen and Rottembourg in 1724 having to do with the possible inclusion of France (*Recueil des instructions . . . Prusse*, p. 331). For the Treaty of Amsterdam, 1717 (Loewe: *op. cit.*, pp. 169-174; F. F. Martens: *Recueil des traités et conventions conclus par la Russie avec les puissances étrangères* [St. Petersburg, 1874-1909, fifteen vols.], V, pp. 157-168).

[137] Villars: *Mémoires*, V, p. 19. For other impressions early in 1726 that the King of Prussia was deserting the alliance (*ibid.*, pp. 1, 5-9, 10-12, 15-16).

[138] *Recueil des instructions . . . Prusse*, p. lxxii. The extraordinary character of Frederick William I, who esteemed *great men* and measured merit by the yard, as his son Frederick wrote to Voltaire on September 9, 1739, was well known by this time to French statesmen. Rottembourg described his actions and his personality in a series of despatches during 1726, those of February 19, April 30, May 14, August 13 and October 15 (Ernest Lavisse: *La jeunesse du Grand Frédéric* [Paris, 1891], pp. 80-81). Rottembourg and Du Bourgay, the British ambassador to Prussia, worked in close co-operation during these months to hold the King of Prussia true to his engagements. Du Bourgay wrote to Townshend, 20 to 30 April, 1726, that the King of Prussia was "a useless and unserviceable friend. For it is certain he will never be otherwise than a chargable ally, and one, against whose fickle humour human prudence can hardly guard" (Chance: *Alliance of Hanover*, p. 271).

As to Russia, the French in 1726, because of their alliance with Great Britain, had no policy, save that of self-defense against a power malevolently disposed. Both Dubois and Morville had been strongly inclined to a Russian alliance, but the formation of one, as has been explained, always broke down on the question of the inclusion of Great Britain, a point on which France insisted and to which Russia was obdurately opposed. As a result of Bonnac's mediation at Constantinople in 1724, whereby Russia and Turkey agreed to compose their differences at Persia's expense, Peter the Great permitted the French to hope that his gratitude would extend to the point of allying himself with France and Great Britain.[139] His death in February 1725 did not completely dissipate these hopes, for at first Catherine I manifested a desire to continue Russian policy in the direction it had taken during the last months of her husband's reign.[140] In part, the Czarina's good will for France was dispelled by the repeated snubs which the Duke of Bourbon administered to her schemes for the marriage of her daughter Elizabeth, but in greater measure it was the blandishments of Austria and the French connection with Great Britain which caused Catherine I to be hostilely disposed toward France.[141] For the Czarina attached importance, to even a greater degree than Peter the Great had done, to the restitution of Schleswig to her dispossessed son-in-law, the Duke of Holstein-Gottorp, and it was the British who were unalterably opposed to the restitution of Schleswig or to the giving up of any equivalent.[142]

---

[139] For Bonnac's mediation, see Charles Schefer: *Mémoire historique sur l'ambassade de France à Constantinople par le marquis de Bonnac, publié avec un précis de ses négociations à la Porte Ottomane* (Paris, 1894), pp. liii-lx, 145-147, 197-284; François Emmanuel Guignard, comte de Saint-Priest: *Mémoires sur l'ambassade de France en Turquie et sur le commerce des français dans le Levant* (Paris, 1877), pp. 121-123. For the prospect of a Russian alliance with France and Great Britain, see Dureng: *Le duc de Bourbon et l'Angleterre*, pp. 225-232; Chance: *Alliance of Hanover*, pp. 13-14, 42.

[140] Chance: *Alliance of Hanover*, pp. 23-24.

[141] Catherine I desired the marriage of Elizabeth to Louis XV or, failing that, to the Duke of Bourbon (Vandal: *Louis XV et Elisabeth de Russie*, pp. 80-103).

[142] Townshend to Poyntz, Hanover, Sept. 21/Oct. 2, 1725 (*British Diplomatic Instructions: Sweden, 1689-1727*, p. 196). Charles Frederick, Duke of Holstein-Gottorp, married Anna, daughter of Peter the Great and Catherine I, just before Peter's death, in 1725.

Not only had the British guaranteed the possession of Schleswig to the King of Denmark, but also the Hanoverian possession of the bishoprics of Bremen and Verden depended upon the sanctity of that guarantee. It had been the Danes, not the Hanoverians, who had conquered the bishoprics; and George I acquired them by a disguised purchase, a principal part of the bargain being Great Britain's guarantee of the Danish annexation of Schleswig. The final and definitive guarantee, which the Regent also gave, although very reluctantly, was embodied in the Treaty of Stockholm, June 14, 1720.[143] The Hanoverian possession of Bremen and Verden might be called in question, therefore, if the Danish possession of Schleswig were altered, especially since the Emperor had steadfastly refused to grant George I the investitures of them. Because of this connection between the bishoprics and Baltic affairs, Great Britain was uncommonly eager in 1726 to build up a coalition in the North which would hold Russia in check.

The French discovered that, because of the Schleswig difficulty, their negotiations with Russia had completely broken down. Morville wrote to Campredon on October 25, 1725, to continue

the policy you have adopted of avoiding occasions of explaining yourself on the subject of the co-operation of the king with the court where you are, in general affairs.[144]

On April 25, 1726, Campredon was recalled, on the pretext of desiring to instruct him by word of mouth on Baltic affairs.[145] When Fleury came to power, France was represented in Russia only by a *chargé d'affaires*, Magnan, who had been Campredon's secretary. His despatches were purely of an informational character, and Morville's instructions to him, in turn, indicate that the French court had temporarily given up all hope of influencing Russian policy.[146]

---

[143] Wiesener: *Le Régent, l'abbé Dubois et les anglais*, III, pp. 153-157. For British pressure on the Regent for his guarantee of Schleswig (Chance: *George I and the Northern War*, pp. 381-397).

[144] *Sbornik*, LXIV, p. 34.

[145] *Sbornik*, LXIV, pp. 344-346.

[146] Morville to Magnan, June 20, 1726 (*Sbornik*, LXIV, pp. 369-370; and *passim*). On August 6, 1726, Russia guaranteed the Pragmatic Sanction and en-

A third power with whom French relations were determined by the exigencies of the British and the necessities of the Alliance of Hanover was Sweden. Weak and divided as that country had become, nevertheless Stockholm was the scene of a fiercely contested diplomatic struggle between Great Britain and Russia. By securing Sweden's accession to the Treaty of Hanover, Great Britain hoped to retain a foothold in the Baltic, which otherwise might become closed to British sea power; at the same time, a Sweden hostile to Russia would force the Czarina to take thought of her own security and would prevent her from supporting very actively the grievances of her son-in-law, the Duke of Holstein-Gottorp. Such was the British aim, but it was by no means easy to attain, for there was a strong pro-Russian party in Swedish politics at that time. The Russophil proclivities of this group, which was opposed to the "Caps" under the leadership of Count Horn, were owing to the fact that their candidate for the succession to the Swedish throne was the same Duke of Holstein-Gottorp who had lost Schleswig and had become the son-in-law of Catherine I.[147] The triumph of this party would indubitably have compromised British policy in northern and central Europe most seriously. Already the Russians had won the first skirmish by concluding with Sweden the treaty of February 22, 1724, which engaged the two powers to secure the restitution of Schleswig.[148] To this treaty the Emperor was invited to accede,

tered into close alliance with Austria (Martens: *Recueil des traités et conventions conclus par la Russie*, I, pp. 32-44).

[147] A Swedish succession law of 1604 had provided that in case of the failure of male heirs, the crown should pass to the eldest unmarried daughter. On the death of Charles XII, his junior sister, Ulrica-Eleonora, had claimed the throne on the grounds that her own marriage to Frederick of Hesse-Cassel postdated that of her elder sister to Frederick IV, Duke of Holstein-Gottorp. This seems like rather tortured logic, but by this time (1726) the accomplished fact was recognized; however, since the King and Queen of Sweden had no direct heirs, there was a powerful Swedish party which desired the recognition of Charles-Frederick, Duke of Holstein-Gottorp, son-in-law of Catherine I and nephew of Charles XII and of Queen Eleonora, as heir-apparent to the Swedish throne (*Recueil des instructions . . . Suède* [Edited by A. Geffroy; Paris, 1885], p. lxxxix).

[148] Dureng: *Le duc de Bourbon et l'Angleterre*, p. 209; Chance: *Alliance of Hanover*, pp. 11-13. The British and Prussian desire in 1724 to secure the accession of France to their own alliance, made by the Treaty of Charlottenburg, October 10, 1723, as mentioned previously (see *supra*, note 136), was inspired by this treaty between Russia and Sweden.

and George I, when he heard of it, "began to be in pain for Bremen and Verden."[149] In opposition to this party, the British used all the resources of their own diplomacy and that of France in order to support the opponents of the Duke of Holstein and to secure Sweden's accession to the Alliance of Hanover.[150]

Under ordinary circumstances, it would have been to the best interests of France to avoid taking sides in Swedish politics. In consonance with her traditional policy, which favoured the support of Sweden, Poland and Turkey as client powers useful in checking the designs of the Hapsburgs, France desired a strong and united Sweden. But at this moment Sweden was so disrupted by faction and the outcome of the domestic struggle was so doubtful that the French would have preferred to permit their diplomatic relations with her to remain in abeyance. No French representative was resident at Stockholm between 1721, when Campredon left Sweden to take up his residence at St. Petersburg, and 1725, when Brancas was sent there. This lapse had been intentional, and would have been continued, if only French interests had been concerned, as the instructions to Brancas, under date of June 6, 1725, clearly stated:

The difficulty of conducting oneself under such circumstances in a manner which, while antagonizing no party, might contribute to conciliation, if that is possible, would perhaps have led the King to defer sending a minister to represent him at Stockholm, if the recent death of the Czar, and more still, the entreaties of the King of Great Britain had not finally determined His Majesty to take this resolution.[151]

The sending of Brancas to Sweden was a good example of French diplomacy's having to devote itself to the attainment of British aims, as a result of the Duke of Bourbon's *gaucherie*

---

[149] David Hume and Tobias Smollett: *The History of England from the Invasion of Julius Caesar to the Death of George the Second* (London, 1824, sixteen vols.), XIII, p. 67. This section was written by Smollett.

[150] How important the accession of Sweden to the Alliance of Hanover was considered by British ministers is illustrated by Townshend's letter to Stephen Poyntz, 14/25 October, 1725: "I shall conclude with telling you that the bringing about the accession of Sweden to this treaty is the most acceptable and most important service you can do the King at this juncture, and therefore I most heartily wish you success" (*British Diplomatic Instructions: Sweden, 1689-1727*, p. 198).

[151] *Recueil des instructions . . . Suède*, p. 305.

in the conduct of French affairs. Brancas was instructed to work in close co-operation with Stephen Poyntz, the British ambassador to Sweden. On the one hand, he was to endeavour to defeat the schemes of the party which favoured the claims of the Duke of Holstein; on the other, he was to attempt to avoid antagonizing that faction.[152] The surveillance of the British caused him to be more successful in the first part of this self-contradictory programme than in the second. French relations with Sweden had been temporarily determined when Fleury came to power; as in so many other instances, he had no free choice.

"The urgent solicitations of the British and the reflections which the general situation of Europe must have inspired" were likewise what determined Fleury's policy toward Denmark in 1726.[153] Since 1702, when Chamilly left Copenhagen as the result of a dispute over ambassadorial privileges, France had had no representative in Denmark; but in order to secure an agreement providing for the military assistance of the Danish King, Fleury was persuaded to send Count Camilly to Copenhagen, his instructions being dated August 18, 1726. Danish assistance, which was finally procured by the Convention of April 16, 1727, and for which France consented to foot the bill, was of direct utility to Great Britain as an added protection for her King's Hanoverian territories; for France it had only the distinctly indirect utility of bolstering up the Alliance of Hanover, which the mistakes of the Duke of Bourbon had rendered indispensably necessary.[154]

In Poland, the French policy was more independent of Great Britain and more devoted to ends purely French than it was in

---

[152] *Recueil des instructions . . . Suède*, pp. 313, 318-321.

[153] *Recueil des instructions . . . Danemark*, p. xlviii.

[154] For the rupture in 1702, see *Recueil des instructions . . . Danemark*, p. xlvi. For the Convention of April 16, 1727 (Chance: *Alliance of Hanover*, pp. 687-690). The Convention printed in Dumont: *Corps universel diplomatique*, VIII, part ii, pp. 144-146; Rousset: *Recueil historique*, IV, pp. 244-253. The only portion of Camilly's instructions which concerned purely French interests, as distinguished from the joint interests of Great Britain and France as allies, was with reference to the Danish intervention in aid of the Prince of East Friesland in the dispute concerning Emden (*Recueil des instructions . . . Danemark*, pp. 122-124).

the other countries of northern Europe. For example, the French made only mild representations to Augustus II with reference to the Thorn "Blood-bath": their reason being that France was herself a Catholic power; their fear, that the liberties of Poland would be jeopardized by a too willing intervention of foreign powers in Polish affairs; and their self-justification, that the infraction of the Treaty of Oliva, of which France was a guarantor, was not certain.[155] Moreover, although the father-in-law of Louis XV had been given to understand that the marriage of the French King to Maria Leszczynska definitely did not imply that France would support the claims of her father to the Polish throne, nevertheless his re-election became one of the secret and important objects of French policy. The Abbé de Livry was informed, in instructions dated April 30, 1726, that

King Stanislas is the one of all princes whom His Majesty would preferably raise to the throne of Poland.[156]

Consequently, France had reasons of her own for preventing Augustus II from joining the Alliance of Vienna, since, by doing so, he would doubtless purchase Austrian support for the election of his son to the throne of Poland following his own demise.[157] To forestall this, Livry was instructed to use all possible means to encourage opinion in Poland hostile to an alliance with the Emperor.[158]

Fleury's Polish policy was the same as that of his predecessor, and demonstrates that the French attitude towards the question of the Polish succession had been determined years before the death of Augustus II. In 1728 Michel de Villebois was sent on a secret mission to Poland to confer with Theodore Potocki on the general plan to follow when the death of Augustus II should

[155] Instructions to Livry, April 30, 1726 (*Recueil des instructions . . . Pologne* [Edited by Louis Farges; Paris, 1888, two vols.], I, pp. 304-311).

[156] *Recueil des instructions . . . Pologne*, I, p. 317.

[157] In the course of his reign (1697-1733), Augustus II initiated fourteen different negotiations for the purpose of making his dynasty hereditary in Poland; in each case he was willing to pay the price of a partial dismemberment of Poland (Félix Frankowski: "La dynastie de Saxe sur le trône de Pologne (1697-1815)." *Revue d'histoire diplomatique*, XLV [1931], p. 127).

[158] *Recueil des instructions . . . Pologne*, I, p. 314.

necessitate the election of a Polish king.[159] His instructions read, in part:

Since the recent indisposition of the Kind of Poland can have very disagreeable consequences, and since the King ought, for his own dignity as well as on account of the true esteem which he has for King Stanislas, to work to replace this prince on a throne from which the misfortunes of war have made him descend, His Majesty has deemed it necessary to take measures in advance to prepare for the success of the efforts which he proposes to make when the death of King Augustus shall take place.[160]

Although the French Government was clear as to the intent of its policy concerning Poland, there was in reality little that could be done for the attainment of its aims. Official relations could be had only with the Elector-King and his *entourage*, who were, of course, unalterably opposed to the candidature of Leszczynski, while, on the other hand, the weaving of a web of intrigue was dangerous "among a nation of whom it is not commonly believed that faithfulness in keeping secrets is the predominant virtue."[161] Stanislas Leszczynski himself advised not speaking prematurely in his interest, but merely letting those in whom he felt it safe to confide know that the King of France would gladly conduct himself in accordance with their advice when the proper time should arrive.[162]

---

[159] Instructions to Villebois (*Recueil des instructions . . . Pologne*, I, pp. 326-334). Potocki was Archbishop of Gnesne, and Primate of Poland from 1721 to 1738. As such, he was *ex officio* regent of Poland during the interregnum following the death of Augustus II. He was a relative of Stanislas Leszczynski, and the leader in Poland of the party favourable to his election. For excellent accounts of the Polish constitution, see R. H. Lord: *The Second Partition of Poland* (*Harvard Historical Studies*, XXIII), (Cambridge [Mass.], 1915), pp. 6-45; V. Olszewicz: "L'évolution de la constitution polonaise." *Revue des sciences politiques*, XXVI (1911), pp. 610-619; XXVII (1912), pp. 456-469; XXVIII (1912), pp. 58-68.

[160] *Recueil des instructions . . . Pologne*, I, p. 326. Chauvelin wrote to Villeneuve, French ambassador to the Porte, on Oct. 20, 1730: "Sa Majesté veut véritablement se tenir à portée, suivant le parti que les circonstances lui permettront de prendre lors de la vacance du trône de Pologne, de faire pour le roi Stanislas tout ce qui sera possible" (Albert Vandal: *Une ambassade française en Orient sous Louis XV: La mission du marquis de Villeneuve, 1728-1741* [Paris, 1887], p. 184). The instructions to Monti (May 5, 1729), spoke of "le rétablissement du roi Stanislas sur le trône de Pologne où Sa Majesté veut effectivement le replacer; . . ." (*Recueil des instructions . . . Pologne*, II, p. 10); cf. also *ibid.*, pp. 13-19.

[161] *Recueil des instructions . . . Pologne*, I, p. 303.

[162] *Recueil des instructions . . . Pologne*, I, p. 318.

Fleury's analysis of the diplomatic situation of Europe evidently suggested to him the advisability, as a general rule of action, of a more forward policy in the Holy Roman Empire. The well-founded reasons for French alarm at the growth of the Emperor's influence in Germany have already been discussed, yet since the year 1721 no French plenipotentiary had been present at Ratisbon.[163] More immediately, the pressing necessities of the international situation in 1726 demanded French and British co-operation in attempting to prevent the German princes from being won over by the Emperor to the Alliance of Vienna. Accordingly, Chavigny was accredited to the Diet, with instructions to maintain the closest relations with the British representative there, Isaac Leheup.[164] He was, besides, to cultivate good relations with the Elector of Bavaria, traditionally the friend of France. At the same time, he was to guard against being tempted to play too active a rôle, for as he himself remarked:

Germany, having been abandoned for more than thirty years, was a soil which had to be cleared before it could be seeded.[165]

As the French became more familiar with German politics, Fleury tended to develop a German policy independent of that of Great Britain. This slow divergence, which will be discussed in its place, was one of the means by which the Cardinal sought to regain French freedom of action.

At Constantinople, the political aims of French policy were wholly determined by the initiative of Great Britain. Although Bonnac had mediated brilliantly between the Russians and the Turks in 1724, and although his successor, Andrezel, also endeavoured to preserve peace between those two powers, Great Britain was eager to relieve the pressure in the Baltic by fomenting discord between Russia and the Porte, a policy to which

[163] Cf. Dureng: *Mission de Chavigny*, pp. 12-20.
[164] Chavigny's instructions, Sept. 4, 1726 (*Recueil des instructions . . . Diète germanique*, pp. 115-178); his particular orders to co-operate with Leheup (*ibid.*, p. 175). Leheup was brother-in-law to Horatio Walpole; see notices of him listed by D. B. Horn: *British Diplomatic Representatives, 1689-1789* (Edited for the Royal Historical Society, Camden Third Series XLVI, London, 1932), pp. 41, 45, 54, 58, 60, 62, 66, 68, 69, 142.
[165] Dureng: *Mission de Chavigny*, p. 12.

the Duke of Bourbon and Morville somewhat reluctantly acceded.[166] Both France and Great Britain were careful not to encourage Turkish hostility to the Emperor in the early months of 1726, but in September of that year, after news had been received of the Austro-Russian treaty of August 6, Fleury took the step of instructing Andrezel to hint at the necessity of an attack on both Russia and Austria.[167] But on the whole the French were too thoroughly convinced of the decay of the Ottoman power and of the feebleness of Ahmed III to presume that the Turks could be persuaded to play a very active part, and consequently the principal preoccupation of the French in relations with the Porte was the maintenance of France's commercial pre-eminence in the Levant.[168]

Finally, the Cardinal's immediate policy relating to the Kingdom of Sardinia was likewise conditioned by the insistence of the British and the needs of the Alliance of Hanover. The ease with which Victor Amadeus could attack the Emperor's Italian possessions always made him a valuable potential ally, while the international situation in 1726 made it necessary to secure his assistance at once. For this purpose Fleury commissioned a secret envoy, an agent named Anfossy, but Victor Amadeus knew only too well the value of his alliance, and set too high a price upon it.[169] None the less, the negotiations were of a nature to indicate that the alliance of Sardinia could be pur-

---

[166] Chance: *Alliance of Hanover*, pp. 213-215; A. C. Wood: "The English Embassy at Constantinople, 1660-1762." *English Historical Review*, XL (1925), p. 552.

[167] Chance: *Alliance of Hanover*, pp. 506-507. Charles VI attempted to make capital in the Empire of the allegation that the French and British were encouraging the Sultan to make war against him (Chance: *op. cit.*, pp. 215-218). The French denied this and seem to have told the truth, so far as the period before September 1726 is concerned (*Recueil des instructions . . . Diète germanique*, pp. 174-175).

[168] This statement presumes that French policy in 1726 was what it was on August 11, 1728, when Villeneuve's instructions were signed. For an analysis of these, see Vandal: *Une ambassade française*, pp. 73-75.

[169] Anfossy's instructions (*Recueil des instructions . . . Savoie-Sardaigne et Mantoue*, I, pp. 351-353). In a letter to Victor Amadeus, August 2, 1726, Fleury spoke "de l'envie extrême que le Roi a d'entrer avec elle [Votre Majesté] dans une liaison intime . . ." (*ibid.*, p. 356). On the failure of the negotiations at Turin (Chance: *Alliance of Hanover*, pp. 555-572).

chased whenever Fleury was willing to pay the high price asked for it, a conjuncture of affairs which came about in 1733.[170]

The intention of the preceding pages has been to deduce what were the elements of the Cardinal's policy at the beginning of his administration. Having premised his desire to prolong the tranquillity of France and of Europe and the consequent corollary that France needed an alliance to secure that aim, reasons for Fleury's choosing to maintain the connection with Great Britain in spite of his awareness of its disadvantages, and for refusing at that moment a close connection with Spain and the Emperor, have been adduced. On the whole, France's relations with foreign powers in 1726 were largely dependent upon the necessities of the Alliance of Hanover and the initiative of Great Britain, because the blunders of the Duke of Bourbon had temporarily rendered the British connection so necessary that the French dared not do anything which might justify the withdrawal of British support. While this was particularly the case with Prussia, Russia, Sweden, Denmark, Sardinia and Turkey, the outlines of a policy purely French were sharply defined in the relations with the United Provinces and the French attitude toward the question of Poland, and adumbrated in the relations of France with the Diet of the Empire and with some of the German princes.

The first thing which Fleury's government had to do was to continue, in association with Great Britain, the policy to which the Duke of Bourbon had committed it, of building up a coalition of diplomatic and military strength sufficient either to guarantee the security of France or, better still, to discourage the Alliance of Vienna from attempting an armed attack. The next most important thing was to prolong peace and establish it upon a firmer footing, while at the same time endeavouring to regain the diplomatic equality of France. Between these aims there

[170] Portugal has been left out of this account, because French relations with that country had been broken off in 1725 and were not resumed until 1740; the occasion was a dispute over precedence (*Recueil des instructions . . . Portugal*, pp. 268-269, 283-286).

was an intimate connection, for if the Cardinal should be able to find a means for pacifically reducing the European tension, he would to the same degree be able to decrease French dependence for security upon Great Britain.

Along these lines the Cardinal set to work; the Preliminaries of Peace, signed at Paris on May 31, 1727, were the token of his first notable success.

CHAPTER IV

THE FOREIGN POLICY OF CARDINAL FLEURY FROM HIS
ACCESSION TO POWER UNTIL THE PRELIMINARIES
OF PEACE AT PARIS, MAY 31, 1727

IN June 1726, affairs seemed to be hurrying towards a conflict
which promised to involve all the major European powers; a
year later the situation had very materially changed. The Preliminaries of Peace, which were signed at Paris on May 31, 1727,
in the negotiation of which Fleury played a leading part, signified
such a relaxation in the tension between the two hostile alliances
of Hanover and Vienna that it became reasonably predictable
that remaining difficulties could be satisfactorily adjusted without general recourse to the arbitrament of arms. Success had
crowned Fleury's insistence that the resources of diplomacy
should be exhausted before war be declared. His own prestige
was enhanced at the same time that this partial resolution of the
European diplomatic entanglement increased France's security
and correspondingly diminished her dependence upon Great
Britain.

An analysis of the vicissitudes of European diplomacy in the
months following Fleury's accession to undisputed power shows
that French policy was being constantly exerted along lines which
not only contributed to the conclusion of the Preliminaries of
Paris but also determined to a great extent the form which that
partial solution of Europe's difficulties took. Four immediate
aims inspired French policy: in the first place, to co-operate with
Great Britain in recruiting allies; secondly, to prolong the state
of peace by preventing Great Britain from hastily declaring war;
thirdly, to facilitate an eventual reconciliation with Spain by
being as tender as possible of her susceptibilities; and lastly, by
bringing pressure to bear upon the Emperor, to force him to
terms which would serve as a basis for re-establishing the tranquillity of Europe.

Although, for reasons previously explained, French policy at this time was subordinated to that of Great Britain, yet in some respects the very existence of such a programme as that indicated above represented a limited recovery of French diplomatic independence. On several occasions the French refused to recognize, as the British urged, that the *casus foederis* had taken place; their desire to deal as gently as possible with Spain frequently worried the British statesmen, and Fleury's insistence on bringing pressure to bear upon the Emperor differed from their proposal to deal first with Spain. Nevertheless, the specific issues at stake in the negotiations of that year were the suppression of the Ostend Company and the guarantee of the British possession of Minorca, Gibraltar and the Asiento, issues of far greater intrinsic interest to Great Britain than to her ally.

The first object of French policy, the obtaining of recruits to the Hanover alliance, had been determined upon during the administration of the Duke of Bourbon and this programme was continued under his successor. The sending of Anfossy on a secret mission to the King of Sardinia, of Chavigny to the Diet of the Empire, and of Camilly to Denmark has already been noticed. Perhaps the greatest importance was laid upon the accession of the United Provinces, which was long delayed because of the necessity of securing the consent of all the numerous Estates and municipalities which shared the sovereignty in that cumbersome government. The Dutch made the suppression of the Ostend Company a *sine qua non* of their accession, a point to which the French and British agreed readily enough.[1] The accession was finally made on August 9, 1726, but on terms which specifically excepted the United Provinces from any responsibility for the guarantee of the Treaties of Westphalia and Oliva, and which omitted any reference to the succession in Jülich and Berg.[2]

[1] Goslinga: *Slingelandt's Efforts towards European Peace*, pp. 88-92; Chance: *Alliance of Hanover*, pp. 113-114.

[2] Dumont: *Corps universel diplomatique*, VIII, part ii, pp. 133-135; Rousset: *Recueil historique*, II, pp. 166-179. For the history of this negotiation, see Chance: *Alliance of Hanover*, pp. 104-105, 120-122, 290-305, 377-380; Goslinga: *Slingelandt's Efforts towards European Peace*, pp. 92-98; *Recueil des instructions . . . Hollande*, II, pp. 429-431.

The accession of the United Provinces was by no means an unmixed gain for the Alliance of Hanover, for it was principally responsible for the defection of the King of Prussia. In general, relations between Prussia and the United Provinces at that time were none too cordial, because of the Prussian annexation of Upper Gelderland and the dispute over the inheritance to some of the lands which had belonged to the Orange family; in this particular case, Frederick William I was irritated because of the Dutch refusal to guarantee the Treaties of Westphalia and Oliva or to do more than to offer good offices in the affair of the Thorn Protestants, although he himself had absolutely refused to undertake any obligation in respect to the suppression of the Ostend Company. The known unwillingness of the Dutch to contribute towards increasing the possessions of a troublesome neighbour by guaranteeing to Frederick William the succession in Jülich and Berg filled up the cup of his discontent with the Hanover alliance.

For the succession in Jülich and Berg was dear to the heart of the King of Prussia.[3] Claims to the undivided inheritance of the last Duke of Cleves, who died in 1609, were disputed by the Hohenzollerns and the Neuburg Palatinate (Pfalz-Neuburg) line throughout the early part of the seventeenth century.[4] But because Philip William of Neuburg (*ob.* 1690) desired the influential support of the Great Elector for his candidacy for election to the Polish throne, a very important treaty (*Erbvergleich*) was concluded between them in 1666. The possession of Jülich, Berg and Ravenstein by the Neuburg line, as representing one of the sisters of the last Duke of Cleves, was solemnly recognized, with the provision that this inheritance was never to be split up. But in the event that the descendants of one of the contracting parties should fail, then the descendants of the other should

---

[3] "The acquisition of Jülich and Berg . . . is . . . the key to his [Frederick William's] policy, more especially to his relations with the Emperor" (C. T. Atkinson: *A History of Germany, 1715-1815* [London, 1908], p. 93). Cf. Bernhard Erdmannsdörffer: *Deutsche Geschichte vom westfälischen Frieden bis zum Regierungsantritt Friedrich's des Grossen, 1648-1740* (Berlin, 1892-1893, two vols.), II, p. 426.

[4] Henry IV was on the point of intervening in this dispute at the time of his assassination.

inherit all the lands comprised in the Cleves inheritance. Such an event, in view of the aptitude for legitimate paternity which the Great Elector and Philip William of Neuburg were manifesting, did not indeed appear very likely.[5] Nevertheless, in 1725, of the numerous Pfalz-Neuburg family only the Elector Charles Philip (1661-1742), who had succeeded to his inheritance in 1716, remained, and he had no issue save one daughter, who married Joseph of the Sulzbach-Palatinate line in 1717. There was no question as to the legality of the eventual succession of the Sulzbachs to the Neuburg lands and dignities *in the Palatinate* when the death of the Elector Charles Philip should occur. But there was doubt whether the Sulzbachs had a right to the succession in Jülich, Berg and Ravenstein, which they did in fact claim; first, by virtue of common descent from Anne, wife of Philip Lewis of Neuburg (1569-1614), the sister and co-heiress of John William, last Duke of Cleves; and secondly, by virtue of the marriage of Joseph of Sulzbach with Elizabeth, the only child of the Elector Charles Philip of Pfalz-Neuburg, in 1717. Frederick William I of Prussia, on the other hand, claimed that the eventual death of Charles Philip would extinguish the Neuburg line, that the treaty of 1666 applied only to male descendants, and that therefore he was the next legal heir of Jülich, Berg and Ravenstein.[6] To secure support for this claim became as important an aim to the King of Prussia as to secure recognition for the Pragmatic Sanction was to the Emperor.[7]

The most valuable concession to the King of Prussia in the Treaty of Hanover had been the fourth separate article, which was kept secret and in which France and Great Britain agreed

[5] The Great Elector was survived by two daughters and six sons; Philip William by six daughters and six sons. For the treaty of 1666 (Erdmannsdörffer: *Deutsche Geschichte*, I, p. 350; August Rosenlehner: *Kurfürst Karl Philipp von der Pfalz und die jülichsche Frage, 1725-1729* [Munich, 1906], pp. 1-3).

[6] For genealogical tables, see Atkinson: *History of Germany*, p. 707; *Cambridge Modern History*, XIII, tables 45 and 46; Erdmannsdörffer: *Deutsche Geschichte*, II, p. 425. For the Pfalz-Sulzbach claims, see Rosenlehner: *Kurfürst Karl Philipp von der Pfalz*, pp. 11-15; for the Prussian contention that the treaty of 1666 envisaged only male descendants (*ibid.*, pp. 9-11).

[7] The Emperor Charles VI also had a claim to the duchies of Jülich and Berg: his mother was a sister of Charles Philip. This claim was never pressed very seriously.

to prevent a sequestration of Jülich and Berg and to support the "just claims" of Frederick William I; in particular, they were to attempt to persuade all the interested parties to submit their claims to the arbitration of impartial powers.[8] But the Dutch were so opposed to the acquisition of those territories by Prussia that it was considered inadvisable, when their accession to the Alliance of Hanover was being negotiated, to communicate the secret article to them.[9] Early in 1726, the British and the French could foresee the defection of the King of Prussia, whose constancy to any alliance engagements, it may be said, was always impaired by his quick suspicions that the supposed finesse of his allies was taking advantage of him. In part, this reversal of policy was due to a lingering loyalty for his suzerain, in part to his alarm for the defense of his exposed frontiers, but most of all it was determined by the decision that more was to be gained with reference to the eventual acquisition of Jülich and Berg through co-operation with the Emperor than in opposition to him. The Treaty of Wüsterhausen (October 12, 1726) provided that the Emperor should persuade the Elector Palatine to agree to a compromise whereby Jülich should be inherited by the Sulzbachs, Berg and Ravenstein by Prussia. If this consent were not secured within six months, the whole treaty, which had been negotiated by Frederick William's friend, the Austrian General Seckendorf, would be considered null and void. The Emperor, as usual, had exacted Prussian recognition of the Pragmatic Sanction.[10]

On the whole, the Emperor gained more adherents among the German princes than did the French and the English, although time was to show that many of these accessions were ephemeral and of little importance. It is true that the Prince of mercenaries, the Landgrave of Hesse-Cassel, agreed to furnish twelve thousand

---

[8] Rosenlehner: *Kurfürst Karl Philipp von der Pfalz*, pp. 72-73. For the treaty (Loewe: *Preussens Staatsverträge*, pp. 287-293); the existence of the separate article about Jülich and Berg was first made known to historians by Leopold von Ranke: *Zwölf Bücher preussischer Geschichte* [Leipzig, 1874, three vols.], vol. II, book v, pp. 50-51).

[9] Chance: *Alliance of Hanover*, pp. 105-106.

[10] Treaty of Wüsterhausen (Loewe: *Preussens Staatsverträge*, pp. 314-322). For the detail of negotiations, see Chance: *Alliance of Hanover*, pp. 402-421.

troops and remained faithful to his engagements because Great
Britain was the highest bidder for his support.[11] But the Emperor, too, had money to offer now that the Spanish subsidies
were becoming available through the careful management of the
Spanish minister, Patiño. On July 19, 1726, the Duke of Bruns-
wick undertook, for a consideration, to keep up troops for the
use of the Emperor and to admit Imperial garrisons into his
territories, if requested.[12] The French regarded this as a great
blow,

considering his situation in the Empire, his being a Protestant and so near a
relation to His Majesty [George I],

and were inclined to think that the British had been negligent
on this point.[13] Their own success was no better. For the Emperor was able to gain almost all of the South German states,
even including Bavaria, always regarded as a special protégé of
France. On August 16 and 26, 1726, subsidy treaties for the
duration of two years were signed between the Emperor and the
Electors of the Palatinate and of Treves, respectively.[14] On September 1, Charles Albert, the young Elector of Bavaria and later
Emperor, who had succeeded his father on February 26, 1726,
signed a treaty of defensive alliance with the Emperor, to be of
two years' duration.[15] That it would be possible at some near
date to win him back to France, the Elector himself made clear
in a letter to Fleury dated September 3, 1726, in which he explained the impossibility of acceding to the Hanover alliance
when his Electorate was in such a defenseless position.[16] But,

---

[11] Chance: *Alliance of Hanover*, pp. 165-173.

[12] Chance: *Alliance of Hanover*, p. 389. One million fourty-four thousand florins
were paid over to the Emperor through a Genoa banking house in December
1726 (Syveton: *Une cour et un aventurier*, p. 236, note).

[13] Horatio Walpole to Townshend, Fontainebleau, Sept. 10, 1726 (*British Diplomatic Instructions: France, 1721-1727*, p. xxxi); Chance: *Alliance of Hanover*, p. 390.

[14] Rosenlehner: *Kurfürst Karl Philipp von der Pfalz*, pp. 144-147.

[15] For the negotiations with Bavaria before the death of Maximilian (Chance:
Alliance of Hanover, pp. 174-184); afterwards (*ibid.*, pp. 391-398).

[16] Maurice Sautai: *Les préliminaires de la guerre de la Succession d'Autriche*
(Paris, 1907), p. 437; see also his two letters to Louis XV, Sept. 4, 1726 (*ibid.*,
pp. 438-440). The official report of the Marquis of Maillebois, Sept. 20, 1726, on
the state of Bavaria, shows that it was in a comparatively defenseless state, and
unrecovered from the reckless expenditure of Maximilian (*ibid.*, pp. 430-437).

though at that moment the Hanover alliance was losing ground in Germany, the Duke of Würtemberg might readily have been gained had Fleury been willing to settle in his favour a dispute over the Montbéliard fiefs in Franche-Comté, which, however, the Cardinal refused to do in spite of the urgings of Horatio Walpole.[17] Furthermore, Chavigny and Leheup were able to make little impression on the Diet at Ratisbon; Leheup was expelled from Germany in March 1727, and although the Diet declared its neutrality in disputes inspired by the Ostend Company, this result was attained more by its inertia than by the activity of the British and French representatives.[18] Not until 1728 did Chavigny's influence make itself decisively felt.

By the beginning of 1727 the Hanover allies could rely upon the armed assistance of the United Provinces and Hesse-Cassel, but they had lost Prussia and had been unable to secure Sardinia. The Emperor had gained Russia (August 6, 1726) and Prussia, Brunswick-Wolfenbüttel, and the four Wittelsbach Electors, those of Bavaria, the Palatinate, Treves and Cologne.[19] To secure the accession of Sweden and Denmark became of greater importance than ever, for the one would be able to hinder the interference of Russia in Germany by threatening her with a flank attack, and the assistance of the other would be of great aid if trouble should break out in Lower Germany. After a severe diplomatic struggle, Sweden acceded to the Hanover alliance on March 25, 1727.[20] On April 16, a convention was signed with Denmark in which, in return for considerable subsidies, that power engaged

---

[17] Newcastle to H. Walpole, June 8, O. S., 1726 (*British Diplomatic Instructions: France, 1721-1727*, p. 167). The Montbéliard fiefs explained (Chance: *Alliance of Hanover*, p. 509, note); cf. instructions to Chavigny, 1726 (*Recueil des instructions . . . Diète germanique*, pp. 155-160).

[18] Dureng: *Mission de Chavigny*, pp. 33-48; Chance: *Alliance of Hanover*, pp. 508-523, 616-633.

[19] The Elector of Cologne acceded to the Treaty of Vienna on Sept. 1, 1726, the same day as that of the accession of Bavaria (Chance: *Alliance of Hanover*, p. 398).

[20] Chance: *Alliance of Hanover*, pp. 151-164, 249-261, 361-376, 538-554, 678-681. After the Preliminaries of Peace of May 31, 1727, Newcastle wrote to Horatio Walpole, May 28, O. S., 1727: "The alliance of Sweden must be allowed to have been of very great use to us in many respects, and especially in preventing the Czarina from sending her troops to the Emperor's assistance" (*British Diplomatic Instructions: France, 1721-1727*, p. 244).

to lend her military assistance to the allies of Hanover; unlike the Swedish agreement, however, the Danish convention was not an accession to the Hanover treaty. It was simply a separate military convention.[21]

In April and May of 1727, the British and French military experts, notably Marshal Berwick and Colonel Armstrong, were busily concerting plans for a military campaign.[22] In spite of the fact that Fleury and the British had not been so successful in recruiting allies as they might have wished, those which they had secured were valuable.[23] The result was that the Alliance of Hanover could count upon putting larger armies into the field than could their antagonists. Berwick figured the French army as totalling 229,438 men, and the Imperialist army as amounting to only 166,814, of which large contingents would have to be retained as garrisons in Naples, Sicily, Transylvania and Hungary.[24] Lord Hervey computed the total forces which the Alliance of Hanover could muster as being 375,000, including sixty thousand French militia; those of the Vienna alliance, 387,000, but of these many would be rendered inactive by the necessity of keeping up the garrisons.[25]

At the same time that this large force was being disposed for defense, it was the consistent policy of Fleury's government to prolong peace by preventing Great Britain from hastily declaring war. This was accomplished by refusing to mobilize on the frontiers large bodies of French troops whose presence might furnish temptations to engage in adventures, and also by being reluctant to admit that Spain's attack on Gibraltar constituted a *casus foederis*.[26] The policy of France was to wait for the

[21] Chance: *Alliance of Hanover*, pp. 278-282, 474-493, 682-690.

[22] Chance: *Alliance of Hanover*, pp. 708-725.

[23] Newcastle to H. Walpole, April 10, O. S., 1727 (*British Diplomatic Instructions: France, 1721-1727*, p. 236).

[24] Chance: *Alliance of Hanover*, p. 717. Another estimate gave the Emperor a total of 187,960 men (*ibid.*).

[25] Hervey: *Some Materials towards Memoirs*, pp. 64-65. Professor Basil Williams has calculated that the Emperor could muster only 212,250 troops for a war in Germany, while the Alliance of Hanover could muster 276,464 (Basil Williams: "The Foreign Policy of England under Walpole." *E. H. R.*, XV, p. 697).

[26] Fleury and Morville showed great reluctance about organizing a *corps de réserve* in the north of France, as they had previously agreed to do (Newcastle to

Alliance of Vienna to commit the first act of aggression. Great Britain, on the other hand, had immediate objects to gain by the use of force, such as the suppression of the Ostend Company, and were she given too readily the disposal of French armies, she might be tempted to force the issue by precipitating a Continental war of which France would bear the brunt.

The third immediate object of Fleury's policy in the months following his accession to power was to avoid as much as possible doing anything which would irretrievably antagonize the Spanish sovereigns, his design being to facilitate an eventual reconciliation between the Bourbon ruling families. The inadvisability of permitting French policy ever to become dependent on Spanish friendship, in view of the violent temper of Elisabeth Farnese, has already been discussed, but, on the other hand, Fleury could stop a good deal short of that point and still invest French policy with greater stability and popularity at home by restoring Franco-Spanish relations to a basis of ordinary comity. What Fleury desired at the moment was a personal, rather than a political, reconciliation, but Philip V would agree to this only if reached through the mediation of the Emperor and on condition that France would join the Vienna alliance.[27] As Fleury wrote to the King of Sardinia, the Queen of Spain was *"plus furieuse que jamais."* Nevertheless, a correspondence was carried on between Fleury and Bermudez, the confessor of Philip V, in the course of which Fleury hinted at the possibility of the Spanish King's becoming King of France if Louis XV should die. This promising correspondence was interrupted momentarily by the disgrace of Bermudez on September 29, 1726, because he had made the mistake of attempting to keep the contents of one of Fleury's letters secret from Elisabeth Farnese.[28] But it was resumed immediately, in an indirect way,

H. Walpole, Sept. 2, O. S., 1726; also, Newcastle to Robinson, secretary of the British embassy, Dec. 20, O. S., 1726 [*British Diplomatic Instructions: France, 1721-1727*, pp. 196, 215]). British insistence on the *casus foederis* (Newcastle to H. Walpole, March 4, O. S., 1726/7 [*British Diplomatic Instructions: France, 1721-1727*, pp. 225-226]).

[27] Baudrillart: *Philippe V et la cour de France*, III, pp. 259-260.

[28] His successor was Father Clarke, a Scot, a Jesuit and a Jacobite. Grimaldo, being suspected of the crime of being too favourably disposed to the British, was

through the correspondence of Aldobrandini and Massei, the Papal nuncios at Madrid and Paris. However much Fleury permitted his desire to secure a personal reconciliation between Philip V and Louis XV to be seen, it is also true that in all the letters which he addressed to the Spanish sovereigns or which he inspired the nuncio to write, this desire was coupled with a firm insistence that France would remain attached to Great Britain.[29]

The attempts of Fleury to secure a reconciliation with Spain were recognized by the British statesmen as being necessary in order to secure a partial resolution of European diplomatic difficulties. Nevertheless, although they blessed the Cardinal's efforts, they did it with reluctance, and only that they might be the better able to regulate the course of the reconcilement of the Bourbon monarchies.[30] Fleury, meanwhile, continued his policy of insinuating to Philip V that the succession to the French throne might some day be his. This, indeed, was very definitely the upshot of the negotiations centering about the mission of the Abbé de Montgon to Paris early in 1727, a negotiation the true aims of which were kept in the deepest secrecy. Montgon had been instructed by the Spanish sovereigns to endeavour to make the way clear for the succession of Philip V by sounding out the Cardinal, the Duke of Bourbon and other influential members of the French nobility. He was further instructed not to let Fleury know of his intrigues with the Duke of Bourbon, but Fleury outwitted him and managed to draw the whole business into his own hands, thus rendering Montgon superfluous.[31] With

disgraced on the same day as was Bermudez. Henceforth, foreign affairs were entirely in the hands of La Paz (Orendayn) (Baudrillart: *Philippe V et la cour de France*, III, pp. 265-266, 268-269).

[29] E.g., Fleury to Philip V, Dec. 24, 1726 (Baudrillart: *Philippe V et la cour de France*, III, p. 272).

[30] Newcastle to H. Walpole, June 8, O. S., 1726 (*British Diplomatic Instructions: France, 1721-1727*, p. 170).

[31] Montgon had been so impressed by the voluntary abdication of Philip V in 1724 that he had sought and received permission to become royal chaplain at San Ildefonso. His momentary political importance was owing to the fact that, although a Frenchman, he was permitted to remain in Spain after the return of the Infanta in 1725, and was almost the only Frenchman left there through whom any sort of connection could be maintained between the two countries (Baudrillart: *Philippe V et la cour de France*, III, pp. 235-238). For a summary of his negotiations (*ibid.*, pp. 276-312; Edward Armstrong: *Elisabeth Farnese* [London, 1892], pp. 211-214).

this for a lead, the Cardinal was able to persuade the King of Spain that he, Fleury, was very sympathetic to Philip V's ambitions to succeed Louis XV. An added proof of how thoroughly convinced Philip V became that he could count on Fleury's good will is shown by the fact that in the succeeding year, 1728, when a sudden illness of Louis XV gave cause for believing that the French throne might become vacant, Philip V signed documents appointing Fleury as Regent until such time as he might be able to reach France himself.[32] It is obvious that Fleury, by exciting the hopes of the King of Spain regarding the French succession, was playing fast and loose with his British allies, who of course were bitterly opposed to any such project's being mooted, to say nothing of its being consummated. The true object of the Montgon negotiations remained secret: had they been thoroughly known, Horatio Walpole would have had to revise his judgment of the Cardinal's candour.[33]

It is now clear that the Spanish sovereigns became more disposed to be reconciled with France because they began to suspect that they could not count entirely upon the support of the Emperor.[34] While they were digesting this unpleasant intelligence, together with the realization that France could not be detached from her ally, active hostilities between Spain and Great Britain had been begun by the opening of the trenches before Gibraltar on February 9/20. The siege was badly conducted, however, by the Count de las Torres, and the casualties of the British resulted principally from the explosion of their own guns.[35] As we have

[32] Baudrillart: *Philippe V et la cour de France*, III, pp. 463-464. The incident is treated at greater length by Alfred Baudrillart: "Les prétentions de Philippe V à la couronne de France." *Séances et travaux de l'Académie des sciences morales et politiques*, CXXVII (1887), pp. 723-743, 851-897.

[33] Walpole was of course aware of Montgon's presence at Paris and Versailles. He believed Montgon's own assurance that he was there only on private business (Chance: *Alliance of Hanover*, p. 659).

[34] Syveton: *Une cour et un aventurier*, p. 240. Consequently, even Elisabeth Farnese was forced to modify her resentment against Fleury for not acceding to the Vienna alliance; there was a somewhat amicable exchange of letters between them in the early months of 1727 (Baudrillart: *Philippe V et la cour de France*, III, pp. 314-318, 321, 323, 324-325, 329, 333).

[35] See the interesting "Journal of a Voyage from Leith to Newfoundland, Barcelona, etc., in 1726-1727," by Edward Burd, Jun., supercargo of the ship *Christian* of Leith (R. H. Hannay: "Gibraltar in 1727." *Scottish Historical Review*,

seen, Fleury steadfastly refused to recognize the siege of Gibraltar as a *casus foederis* which would oblige France to declare war on Spain. His firmness both with the Spanish sovereigns and with his British allies had the effect of rendering the former more malleable at the same time that he carefully avoided irretrievably antagonizing them.

Thus the fourth immediate object of French policy in the years 1726 and 1727 was brought into play. The greatest possible pressure was brought to bear upon the other principal member of the Vienna alliance, the Emperor, in an effort to cause him to weaken the solidarity of that alliance by his own initiative. So far as could be seen in December 1726, no definite arrangements concerning Austro-Spanish marriages or the disposition of Italy had been made. But this much was certain, that the commercial treaty of May 1, 1725, which had been made public, had granted extraordinary advantages to the Ostend Company and that consequently the abolition or suppression of that company would nullify at least one of the Emperor's reasons for maintaining his alliance with Spain. By focusing attention upon the Ostend Company, Fleury secured the tactical advantages derived from attacking a definite and concrete pretension of an antagonist. It was no less fortunate that by doing so he was pleasing his allies, easing the pressure on Spain, and ultimately facilitating the reconciliation of France with Spain by making Austria shoulder the onus of having been the first to impair the unity of the Vienna alliance. Accordingly, Fleury insisted in his interviews with Horatio Walpole that the suppression of the Ostend Company was of greater immediate importance than was war with Spain over the question of Gibraltar:

The more therefore the British urged war with Spain, the more they were helping to realise the Imperial wishes by making the galleons the sole cause of war and thrusting Ostend into the background.[36]

XVI [1918-1919], pp. 325-334, and especially p. 332); cf. *The Danverian History of the Affairs of Europe*, p. 89; also John Drinkwater: *A History of the late Siege of Gibraltar* (Third edition, London, 1786), pp. 18-22.

[36] Analysis of Morville's despatch to Broglie, Marly, March 9, 1727 (*British Diplomatic Instructions: France, 1721-1727*, pp. xxxvi-xxxvii).

On December 9, 1726, Fleury suggested to the Emperor, through the medium of Massei, the Papal nuncio at Paris, certain stipulations to serve as a basis for preliminaries of peace, and on December 31, the Emperor accepted them in principle, the chief point being that a European congress was to determine the legality of the Ostend Company, whose activities were to be suspended until judgment should be made.[37] The actual offers made by the Emperor at that time were rejected as being too vague and evasive. Soon thereafter, relations between Charles VI and Great Britain suddenly worsened, for George I, in his speech to Parliament on January 17, O. S., 1726/7, had declared:

I have likewise received Information from different Parts, on which I can entirely depend, that the placing the Pretender upon the Throne of this Kingdom is one of the Articles of the secret Engagements; . . . [38]

Since this was in fact untrue, the resultant irritation of the Austrian ministers can be conceived. The Imperial resident at London, Count Palm, was instructed to present a memorial to George I, in the course of which it was stated that

[37] The text of the Emperor's proposals (Rousset: *Recueil historique*, III, p. 386). Cf. Syveton: *Une cour et un aventurier*, p. 243; *British Diplomatic Instructions: France, 1721-1727*, pp. xxxv-xxxvi.

[38] *The Historical Register*, XII (*1727*), p. 62. The source of information upon which the King's ministers had depended was two Sicilian abbés, Platania and Carracciolo, who had been in very close touch with political affairs at the Spanish court in 1725 and 1726, but without having access to official papers. Consequently, they seem to have informed Walpole, in all good faith, that the Vienna alliance contemplated assistance to the Pretender, although this was really not the case. The Sicilian Abbés were disgraced by Elisabeth Farnese at the same time as Bermudez and Grimaldo; they subsequently settled in Paris. For bits of information about them, see Coxe: *Memoirs of Horatio, Lord Walpole*, I, pp. 250-253; Baudrillart: *Philippe V et la cour de France*, II, p. 397; *ibid.*, III, p. 131, note; Chance: *Alliance of Hanover*, pp. 317 note, 743-744. Even before this false information had been received, Newcastle wrote to Horatio Walpole, Nov. 15, O. S., 1725: "All these circumstances . . . leave no room to doubt that something in the spring will be attempted in favour of the Pretender. . . ." (Edward Armstrong's review of Syveton's *Une cour et un aventurier*, *E. H. R.*, XII [1897], p. 798). A translation of the misinformation transmitted by the Sicilian Abbés may be found in the Townshend Papers, *Hist. MSS. Comm.*, *Report* XI, Appendix Part IV, p. 119. This point has been of some confusion to historians; it was cleared up by Edward Armstrong (*loc. cit.*, *supra*), and by Gabriel Syveton: "Un traité secret de mariage et d'alliance entre les cours de Vienne et de Madrid en 1725." *Revue historique*, LIV (1894), pp. 82, 89.

his Sacred Imperial and Catholick Majesty has expressly commanded me, that I should declare to your Majesty, and to the whole Kingdom of *Great Britain*, how highly he thinks himself affronted thereby, solemnly affirming, upon his Imperial Word, that there exists no secret Article nor Convention whatsoever, which contains, or can tend to prove the least Tittle of what has been alledged.[39]

But insult was added to this giving of the lie-direct by Sinzendorff's instructions to Palm to have the memorial printed.[40] As the Houses of Parliament in their address to the King ably summarized the matter:

This audacious Manner of Appealing to the People against your Majesty, under the Pretext of applying to you for Redress and Reparation of supposed Injuries, and turning a *Memorial*, presented to your Majesty, into a Seditious *Libel*, is a Proceeding that creates in us the utmost Abhorrence and Detestation.[41]

Palm was expelled from London and Saint-Saphorin from Vienna; but, although the siege of Gibraltar and the Anglo-Austrian embroilment increased the European tension, for French diplomacy they had the advantage of forcing the entire negotiations into the hands of Fleury and the French ambassador to the Emperor, the Duke of Richelieu.[42]

Having rejected the Emperor's counter-proposals of December 31, 1726, the Hanover allies presented to Charles VI on March 26, 1727, a project comprising six articles, which provided for the suspension of the Ostend Company for ten years and stipulated the free return of the Spanish galleons and the Ostend ships then at sea.[43] To this the Emperor replied with a counter-project, dated April 13, which differed very little from his previous proposal, and seemed designed merely as an expedient to

---

[39] *The Historical Register*, XII (*1727*), pp. 146-148.

[40] Dated at Vienna, Feb. 20, 1727 (*The Historical Register*, XII [*1727*], pp. 149-151).

[41] *The Historical Register*, XII (*1727*), p. 155. "It was taken very ill that the Emperor should in this manner appeal as it were to the people against their King" (John, Viscount Percival, afterwards First Earl of Egmont: *Diary of Viscount Percival, afterwards First Earl of Egmont* [*Historical Manuscripts Commission;* London, 1920-1923, three vols.], III, p. 322).

[42] For an account of the expulsion of Palm, see Villars: *Mémoires*, V, pp. 52-53.

[43] Rousset: *Recueil historique*, III, pp. 388-390.

gain time.[44] Such, at least, was the Cardinal's interpretation of it, and accordingly he spoke very severely to the Imperial ambassador, Fonseca, while great preparations were made for war.[45] On May 9, an ultimatum was sent to the Emperor, which he was given thirty days to accept; he signified his acquiescence on May 21, and this ultimatum, with some slight verbal changes which were made in order to permit the Emperor to salve his *amour propre* by being able to say that he had not accepted the ultimatum word for word, became the Preliminaries of Peace, signed at Paris, May 31, 1727.[46] The Ostend Company was to be suspended for seven years (art. i); the status of possessions and trading privileges was to be that which had obtained prior to 1725; the Treaties of Utrecht, Baden and the Quadruple Alliance were confirmed (arts. ii and iii); the galleons and the Ostend ships were to be permitted an unmolested return (art. v); and a general congress was to meet at Aix-la-Chapelle within four months (art. viii).[47]

The Preliminaries of Paris were a very considerable diplomatic achievement, because they relaxed the European tension and established once for all the principle of the suspension, which was tantamount to the ultimate suppression, of the Ostend Company.[48] This was a cardinal point, on which European alignments hinged. Whatever wrigglings and tergiversations the members of the Alliance of Vienna might henceforth undertake in order to prevent the Preliminaries from being converted into a general peace, they could not escape the "pure, crude fact" that the Emperor, by recognizing the inexpediency of attempting

---

[44] Rousset: *Recueil historique*, III, pp. 390-394.

[45] Baudrillart: *Philippe V et la cour de France*, III, pp. 327-328.

[46] Morville, Horatio Walpole, Fonseca and Boreel, the latter the Dutch representative at Paris, were the signers of the original document. Because the Spaniards had no representative at Paris and the British none at Vienna, Bournonville signed for Spain at Vienna on June 17, 1727, at the same time exchanging copies with Horatio Walpole through the medium of the Duke of Richelieu (Rousset: *Recueil historique*, III, pp. 403-411). The text of the Preliminaries may be found in Rousset: *ibid.*, III, pp. 399-403; and in Pribram: *Österreichische Staatsverträge: England bis 1748*, pp. 457-464.

[47] The meeting place was subsequently changed to Soissons, to suit the convenience of Cardinal Fleury.

[48] Syveton: *Une cour et un aventurier*, pp. 248-249.

to carry on the Ostend Company in the face of the opposition of the Maritime Powers, had, to all practical purposes, compromised its claims to legitimacy as well.

In these negotiations, the interests of her allies had been the interests of France: for the moment, the object of the Cardinal was not that France should secure concessions but rather that peace should be prolonged. None the less, France profited from these negotiations in the improvement of her diplomatic position and in the enhancement of the personal prestige of the Cardinal. For the Preliminaries had been brought about by French diplomats working under Fleury's supervision. English policy had been able to express itself only through French lips, as no British envoy was accredited to Charles VI at the time, while the representations of Bruynincx, the envoy of the United Provinces to Vienna, commanded respect only in so far as they elicited the support of the Duke of Richelieu. By negotiation alone the Cardinal had gained for his allies all that they could reasonably expect to secure as the result of a successful war. As Fleury himself complacently summarized the situation in a letter to the Duke of Richelieu:

However, you see that these English, whom we were taunted with allowing to govern us and who were accused of desiring war at any price, have turned tractable and have done what we wished; they have approved of our not declaring war, although they had the right of demanding it from us; they have not declared it themselves and they have signed the preliminaries without reservation.[49]

The Cardinal's dislike of the use of force and his reliance on diplomatic action, so characteristic of his whole administration, received here for the first time their pragmatic justification. It was a justification which his prestige had sorely needed, for he had had to withstand the pressure of the British and the discontent of the Marshals in his own Council of State. Success in this instance stifled criticism and authorized him to continue

[49] L. F. A. du Plessis, le maréchal, duc de Richelieu: *Mémoires authentiques du maréchal de Richelieu (1725-1757)* (Edited by A. de Boislisle; Paris, 1918. [La Société de l'histoire de France. *Publications*, No. 120]), p. 26, letter dated June 4, 1727.

that policy of reliance on the efficacy of diplomacy which in general may be said to distinguish the entire period of his ministry.

By the Preliminaries of Paris, the first step was taken in regaining the diplomatic freedom of action of France. The protraction of peace increased French security and decreased her dependence upon Great Britain, while the ground had been prepared for the restoration of Franco-Spanish relations to the basis of ordinary comity. The task remaining was to convert the Preliminaries into a general and lasting peace.

CHAPTER V

THE APPOINTMENT OF CHAUVELIN AS SECRETARY OF STATE FOR FOREIGN AFFAIRS AND THE SPANISH RATIFICATION OF THE PRELIMINARIES OF PARIS, 1727-1728

BEFORE the signature of the Preliminaries of Peace at Paris on May 31, 1727, a general European war seemed possible. Already the British and Spanish governments were in open conflict, and the British ministers were constantly endeavouring to persuade Cardinal Fleury to take an active part in the war against Spain. Had he done so, a war against both the Vienna allies would have broken out; but, characteristically, Fleury postponed recourse to armed force until the resources of diplomacy should be exhausted. By negotiation with the Emperor and his ministers, he hoped to weaken the resistance of Austria and to make possible a general peace by detaching her from Spain. Fonseca's signature appended to the Preliminaries of May 31 indicated how feasible the Cardinal's programme had been.

Of course, this diplomatic victory added materially to the prestige of the Alliance of Hanover. That combination had held its ground *vis-à-vis* its antagonists, and had caused one of them to flinch. In several important respects, moreover, the Preliminaries predetermined in favour of the allies of Hanover the discussions of the impending congress. The Dutch and the British were gratified by the Emperor's suspension of the Ostend Company for seven years, while British interests were particularly safeguarded by the stipulation that no changes would be made in the territorial and commercial arrangements of treaties concluded prior to 1725. This constituted a guarantee of Minorca, Gibraltar and the peculiar trading privileges which the English enjoyed in the Spanish West Indies. A reluctant Spain was presented with an accomplished fact.

The Preliminaries of Paris may be said to constitute a landmark in diplomatic history, because they signalized an implicit change in the international alignments of Austria. The Emperor's decision to sacrifice the Ostend Company was merely the corollary of an antecedent decision that the results of the continued hostility of the Maritime Powers would more than counterbalance the gains that might accrue from the Company's activities. It should be remembered that, although the Emperor might attempt to utilize the Ostend Company as a lever with which to prize concessions from neighbouring powers, the maintenance of the Company's privileges was not an interest absolutely vital to the Hapsburg monarchy. The resistance of Charles VI to the suppression of the Company might have been greater had the gains of the Austrian government from its activities been more direct. The Company's charter, a model of its kind, had been drafted so as to minimize the amount of control which the government might have in its affairs: its capital was safe from government raids.[1] Moreover, useful as were the fees and customs charges which accrued from the Company's activities, these moneys were used for the support of the government of the Netherlands, and were not subject to being used as the Emperor pleased. This point was emphasized in the instructions to Kinsky and Fonseca, the Austrian representatives at the Congress of Soissons:

The Emperor has never made any pretensions to drawing treasure from the Austrian Netherlands; and his intention is merely to preserve them for the welfare of the common cause and to keep them in a state of defense, deemed necessary by the Barrier Treaty, without his being obliged for this purpose either to surcharge his faithful subjects or to employ the revenues of his other hereditary dominions.[2]

On the whole, this had been true. The possession of the Netherlands, at least under the conditions of restricted sovereignty permitted by the Barrier Treaty of 1715, seems never to have been highly prized by the Austrians. Prince Eugene told Stanhope in 1714 that

[1] Huisman: *La Compagnie d'Ostende*, pp. 255-257.
[2] February 1729 (Huisman: *La Compagnie d'Ostende*, p. 446).

the Netherlands were of little worth to the Emperor or the Empire; that they would always be a charge to the Emperor, and that, if he accepted them, it was rather for the good of his former allies than for his own.[3]

The finances of the Netherlands were handled separately from those of the Hapsburg monarchy as a whole. The government of the Netherlands was responsible for the support of its own military establishment, including the payment of the Dutch troops garrisoned in the towns of the Barrier, and it had had to accept the obligation for the payment of debts contracted during the reign of Charles II of Spain and during the joint occupation of the Dutch and the British between 1706 and 1715, while the Emperor, for his part, had had to confirm the long-established custom that the several provinces could not be taxed without the consent of their respective Estates.[4] From the most comprehensive point of view with regard to the diplomatic necessities of the Hapsburg monarchy as a whole, the perpetuation of the trading privileges of the Ostend Company was not a vital issue; in the face of the united and determined opposition of the Alliance of

[3] Stanhope to Townshend, Vienna, 13/24 November, 1714 (Lord Mahon: *History of England*, II, appendix, p. xlix); the Emperor will conclude the Barrier treaty because the Netherlands are the links uniting him to the Maritime Powers (same to the same, Vienna, Dec. 8, 1714 [*ibid.*, p. li]). Prince Eugene wanted to exchange the Netherlands for Bavaria, an interesting proposal, considering Joseph II's attempt to do the same thing (Williams: *Stanhope*, pp. 163-167).

[4] For a very clear analysis, supported by statistics, of the financial difficulties and obligations of the government of the Netherlands during the reign of Charles VI, see Charles Steur: "Précis historique de l'état politique, administratif et judiciaire, civil, religieux et militaire des Pays-Bas autrichiens, sous le règne de Charles VI." *Mémoires couronnés en 1828 par l'Académie royale des sciences et belles-lettres de Bruxelles* [in-4°], VII (1829), pp. 35-41, 46, 48-50, 204-210. Less satisfactory but still worth consulting is the study by Natalis Briavoinne: "Mémoire sur l'état de la population, des fabriques, des manufactures et du commerce dans les provinces des Pays-Bas, depuis Albert et Isabelle jusqu'à la fin du siècle dernier." *Mémoires couronnés par l'Académie royale des sciences et belles-lettres de Bruxelles* [in-4°], XIV, part ii (1841), pp. 83, 119-126. The government usually had a deficit of about a million florins (Steur: *op. cit.*, p. 46; cf. Briavoinne: *op. cit.*, p. 124). "The whole Revenue of the Spanish Netherlands has never been sufficient since the Pyrenean Treaty, to keep them in a tolerable Posture of Defence" ([Francis Hare]: *The Barrier Treaty Vindicated* [Third edition, London, 1713], p. 124). For the point that taxes might be levied only with the consent of the States (Pirenne: *Histoire de Belgique*, V, p. 129; Éd. Descamps: "La constitution internationale de la Belgique." *Bulletin de la classe des lettres et des sciences morales et politiques et de la classe des beaux-arts: Académie royale de Belgique, 1901*, pp. 151-152).

Hanover it was better to cede the point, to the certain disadvantage of a portion of the Emperor's dominions, than to risk the whole in a general war. The practical problem for the Emperor's ministers really resolved itself into a question of how he could be gracefully extricated from the predicament of having lent the Ostend Company his official support.

Nevertheless, the decision to sacrifice the Ostend Company fundamentally undermined, from the Austrian point of view, one of the reasons for the maintenance of the connection with Spain. What had enticed the Emperor to contract an alliance with Spain had been, in the first place, the hope of subsidies and, in the second place, the prospect of securing extensive trading privileges in Spain for the Ostend Company.[5] After May 31, 1727, the hope of receiving Spanish subsidies still remained, but the trade concessions which Austria had gained in the commercial treaty of May 1, 1725, henceforth became useless. By the Emperor's sacrificing the Ostend Company the common interests of Spain and Austria were greatly diminished: the action of France and the Maritime Powers had struck at the very foundations of the Alliance of Vienna, as Fleury had foreseen.

However, the desire to continue being the recipients of the Spanish subsidies made the Austrians regard the continuance of their alliance with Spain as very desirable for the time being. Prince Eugene instructed Königsegg to assure the Spanish sovereigns that Charles VI would neglect nothing to preserve the union and make it more binding.[6] Indeed, the Emperor's ministers found it difficult to see what grounds the Spaniards had for being dissatisfied with the Preliminaries, since it seemed to them that the Emperor had been the only one who had been called upon to make a real sacrifice.[7] For the moment, therefore, the diplomatic reorientation of Austria which the Preliminaries of May 31, 1727 rendered implicit, remained latent. Nevertheless, the sacrifice of the Ostend Company henceforth made pos-

---

[5] Syveton: *Une cour et un aventurier*, pp. 111-115.

[6] June 12, 1727 (Alfred Arneth: *Prinz Eugen von Savoyen* [Vienna, 1858, three vols.], III, p. 557).

[7] Arneth: *Prinz Eugen von Savoyen*, III, p. 226.

sible an eventual *rapprochement* between Austria and the Maritime Powers. The road to the second Treaty of Vienna (1731)
lay open.

In still another respect the Preliminaries of Paris may be said
to constitute a landmark in diplomatic history. Just as the decision to suspend the activity of the Ostend Company made
possible the ultimate *rapprochement* of Austria, Great Britain
and the United Provinces, to the exclusion of France, so too did
the weakening of Austro-Spanish solidarity make ultimately possible the First Family Compact between France and Spain
(1733). For the Spanish sovereigns were keenly aware that the
Emperor's having agreed to the Preliminaries forced their hands
and frustrated their cherished schemes. Philip V had desired to
regain Gibraltar and to modify the trade concessions which the
British enjoyed; his queen had hoped to force the marriage of
Don Carlos to an Archduchess by making Spain indispensable
to Austria. Both policies required for their consummation a
war, but the Emperor had forced peace upon them instead.[8]
The Spanish sovereigns did not immediately change their alliance system, because they did not relinquish all hope of fomenting a general war. Nevertheless they became more reserved with
their Austrian ally and more favourably disposed towards the
idea of regaining old friends.

Almost immediately after the signing of the Preliminaries
Elisabeth Farnese, at the moment the sole ruler of Spain because
of the indisposition of the King, modified her policy towards the
Emperor in a manner designed to make him feel the consequences
of her displeasure.[9] Subsidies had been necessary to bring over
the venal German princes to the side of the Vienna alliance, and
the finances of the Emperor had been too embarrassed to permit
him to manage this solely from his own resources. Ripperda had
promised magniloquently what he had been unable to perform,
but under Patiño matters improved, and the subsidies were paid

---

[8] Baudrillart: *Philippe V et la cour de France*, III, p. 339; Syveton: *Une cour
et un aventurier*, pp. 248-249.

[9] The Queen was made *gobernadora del Reyno* on June 8, 1727 (Baudrillart:
Philippe V et la cour de France, III, p. 338; Villars: *Mémoires*, V, p. 76).

in the later months of 1726 and the early months of 1727. But after the Preliminaries of Paris the supply was cut off; Jupiter became coy and trusted that Danaë would languish.[10] These ultimate implications of the Preliminaries of Paris were not, however, immediately apparent, and in the meanwhile there was much diplomatic drudgery to be done. For the European congress which was to endeavour to settle outstanding issues could not be convened until the King of Spain had ratified the Preliminaries. At first it seemed that the Spanish ratification could be secured without difficulty.[11] But in reality Elisabeth Farnese was not so docilely inclined as the rest of Europe hoped. Not only did she postpone the ratification of the Preliminaries, but she also refused to surrender the *Prince Frederick*, the "permission ship" belonging to the South Sea Company, which had been captured at Vera Cruz in retaliation for the blockade of the galleons by Admiral Hosier. The British insisted that the *Prince Frederick* be restored to them without equivalent, on the grounds that its seizure had been illegal, for the Asiento treaty of 1713 had provided that the Spanish government must give eighteen months' notice before it could legally confiscate South Sea Company property. Finally, she incensed the British by refusing to withdraw the Spanish troops from before Gibraltar, even though an armistice had been signed, on the plea that the British fleets had not been recalled from American or Spanish waters. Since the British made the recall of the fleets contingent

[10] By August 31, 1728, Spain had paid a *total* of only 1,950,000 florins, a sum 1,050,000 less than what she had agreed in 1725 to pay *annually* (Prince Eugene to Königsegg, Aug. 31, 1728 [Arneth: *Prinz Eugen von Savoyen*, III, p. 558]). Inasmuch as 1,044,000 florins were paid in December 1726 (Syveton: *Une cour et un aventurier*, p. 236, note), not more than 906,000 florins could have been paid subsequently. The Austrians, rather naïvely, ascribed the change solely to Patiño (Prince Eugene to Königsegg, Aug. 4, 1727 [Arneth: *Prinz Eugen von Savoyen*, III, p. 227]; the same to the same, Sept. 18, 1727 [*ibid.*, pp. 558-559]; the same to the same, Dec. 24, 1727 [*ibid.*, p. 229]; the same to the same, Aug. 31, 1728 [*ibid.*, pp. 228, 558-561]); cf. Adolf Beer: "Zur Geschichte der Politik Karl's VI." *Historische Zeitschrift*, Neue Folge, Band XIX (1886), p. 41.

[11] On June 19 La Paz told Königsegg that Philip V would ratify; he wrote to Aldobrandini, nuncio at Madrid, to the same effect, also on June 19. Orders were sent to suspend operations at Gibraltar and an armistice was signed there on June 23 (Syveton: *Une cour et un aventurier*, p. 248; Baudrillart: *Philippe V et la cour de France*, III, p. 340).

upon Spanish ratification of the Preliminaries, Anglo-Spanish negotiations solemnly proceeded to a condition of stalemate.

From the point of view of France, this was a most unsatisfactory state of affairs. The Cardinal had by now fairly committed himself to a policy of settling the affairs of Europe through the deliberations of a congress. The convening of that congress depended upon Spain's ratification of the Preliminaries of May 31, 1727; if Fleury had been unable to persuade Philip V to ratify, he would have found his whole diplomatic programme threatened with bankruptcy. Consequently it is not surprising to find that until March 6, 1728, when Spain at long last ratified the Preliminaries in the Convention of the Pardo, French policy was focused upon the solution of this problem.

In these negotiations, France was not yet in a position to take an independent line. In order to overcome the recalcitrance of Spain, the Cardinal needed the added authority derived from the diplomatic support of Great Britain as much as he had needed it in the negotiations prior to the conclusion of the Preliminaries. Alliance with Great Britain was still indispensable to France, while at the same time, it is true, the continuance of co-operation with France was heartily desired by the British ministers.[12] Although the British had occasion to observe during these negotiations that French policy was not so slavishly submissive to their suggestions as it had previously been, nevertheless, French policy was still forced to rely heavily upon British support. Conse-

---

[12] Evidence of the British desire to continue close co-operation with France after the conclusion of the Preliminaries (Chance: *Alliance of Hanover*, p. 735; Newcastle to H. Walpole, May 28, O. S., 1727 [*British Diplomatic Instructions: France, 1721-1727*, p. 244]). Fleury wrote to Horatio Walpole on June 26, 1727: "In regard to us, your excellency may assure his Britannic majesty, that we will not depart from that system; and that our reciprocal security consists in being firmly united" (Coxe: *Memoirs of Horatio, Lord Walpole*, I, p. 273). In this same letter Fleury advised Horatio Walpole to visit England for the purpose of confirming the political power of the Walpoles, inasmuch as George I had just died and it was by no means certain that George II would re-employ his father's ministers. Walpole took with him to England a letter from Fleury to George II which is thought to have been of weight in determining the new King to retain the services of the Walpoles (Hervey: *Some Materials towards Memoirs*, p. 31; Charles, comte de Baillon: *Lord Walpole à la cour de France, 1723-1730, d'après ses mémoires et sa correspondance* [Paris, 1868], pp. 285-295). The incident shows that Fleury fully desired to continue his alliance with Great Britain (Coxe: *op. cit.*, pp. 270-279)

quently, during these months, the Cardinal frequently found himself situated between the nether millstone of Spanish inertia and the upper of British impatience. Moreover, since French policy was interested most of all in the ratification of the Preliminaries, and since these Preliminaries guaranteed to Great Britain the possession of certain territories and privileges, the policy of France once more took on the complexion of appearing to concern itself with interests more particularly British than French. However, by the Convention of the Pardo the policy of the Cardinal received its second pragmatic justification, and in the meantime a series of significant incidents had occurred to warn the British that the implicit docility of the French could no longer be postulated.

This slight but significant change in French policy is illustrated by the nature of the secret instructions to Rottembourg, who was about to set out on an embassy to Spain.[13] His regular instructions, which were largely concerned with the restoration of the *Prince Frederick* to the South Sea Company, were read to Horatio Walpole, who highly approved of them. They were supplemented, however, by other instructions, kept secret from Walpole, in which it was stated that Louis XV demanded the restitution of the *Prince Frederick* only *"par principe de fidélité,"* and that there might be some middle course, as, for example, the surrendering the *Prince Frederick* to some neutral power, such as the United Provinces.[14] The instructions even accepted the idea of considering at the proposed congress the grant of

[13] Fleury was assisted in his negotiations by the formal reconciliation of France and Spain; on July 20, Elisabeth Farnese wrote to Fleury that Their Catholic Majesties consented to a public reconciliation. Announcements to this effect were addressed to all Spanish diplomatic agents in September 1727; in that month, Brancas was appointed ambassador to Spain, and Rottembourg was sent there immediately, as ambassador-extraordinary (Baudrillart: *Philippe V et la cour de France*, III, pp. 341-344). Rottembourg's instructions are dated Sept. 18, 1727 (*Recueil des instructions . . . Espagne*, III, pp. 123-139).

[14] *Recueil des instructions . . . Espagne*, III, pp. 132, 134. The British were violently opposed to putting the *Prince Frederick* in the possession of a third power. Any mediation or arbitration on this point, they felt, would *ipso facto* nullify their contention that a violation of their undoubted treaty rights had taken place, and would tend to call in question their privileged status in the Spanish Indies, which was what they most desired to avoid.

some compensation to Spain for having had to surrender Gibraltar.[15]

These instructions had been prepared by Germain-Louis Chauvelin, since August 17 and 19, 1727, Keeper of the Seals and Secretary of State for Foreign Affairs.[16] This able and aggressive minister had been brought to Fleury's attention through the influence of Marshal d'Huxelles and the support of the younger Pecquet, the *premier commis* in the Ministry for Foreign Affairs, and for some months previous to his appointment had exercised great, although secret, influence over the Cardinal.[17] It was he, according to Baudrillart, who had composed the letter to the Emperor which had accompanied the

---

[15] Baudrillart: *Philippe V et la cour de France*, III, p. 349; *Recueil des instructions . . . Espagne*, III, pp. 131 sqq.

[16] Chauvelin was born in 1685, and belonged to the *noblesse de robe*. For a genealogy of his family and a list of his offices, see François Alexandre Aubert de la Chesnaye-Desbois and M. Badier: *Dictionnaire de la noblesse* (Third edition, Paris, 1863-1876, nineteen vols.), V, pp. 528-537. In 1706 Chauvelin held conjointly the position of *conseiller au Grand Conseil* and *grand rapporteur au sceau* (The *Grand Conseil* was a "cour souveraine sans territoire fixe, qui connaissait de diverses causes, comme différends entre présidiaux, matières bénéficiales, etc." [Larousse: *Grand dictionnaire universel du XIXe siècle, sub art.* "Conseil"; see also Marcel Marion: *Dictionnaire des institutions de la France aux XVIIe et XVIIIe siècles* (Paris, 1923), *sub art.* "Grand Conseil"]; the *grand rapporteur au sceau* was attached to the Chancellery, and had principally to do with titles of nobility, naturalization papers, etc.). In 1711 Chauvelin became *maître des requêtes* (the *maîtres des requêtes* were members of the *Parlement* of Paris who were also attached to the Council of State; they received all petitions addressed to the King, and laid them before the proper authorities. To be eligible for appointment, one had to be thirty-one years of age [exception was made in the case of Chauvelin] and to have had six years of service in a superior court. There were eighty-eight *maîtres des requêtes* at this time). In 1715, Chauvelin became *avocat-général* in the *Parlement* of Paris (there were three of these, who represented the Crown in all legal actions appertaining to it or involving its rights). In 1718 Chauvelin purchased the office of *président à mortier* in the *Parlement* of Paris.

[17] Coxe: *Memoirs of Horatio, Lord Walpole*, I, pp. 292-295; Vaucher: *Robert Walpole et la politique de Fleury*, p. 27. Count Hoym, the Polish-Saxon representative at Paris, wrote to Augustus II on August 27, 1727: "Il [Chauvelin] s'étoit fort adonné depuis quelques tems à la cour & à s'instruire par le moyen de ses liaisons avec le maréchal d'Huxelle des matières publiques. Il y avoit déjà quelque tems aussi qu'il avoit été question de luy pour remplir le poste des affaires étrangères, mais cela étoit tombé alors" (Jérôme Pichon: *La vie de Charles-Henry, comte de Hoym, ambassadeur de Saxe-Pologne en France et célèbre amateur de livres, 1694-1736* [Paris, 1880, two vols.], II, p. 285). The Cardinal de Bissy also exerted his influence with Fleury in Chauvelin's favour (Hardy: *Le cardinal de Fleury et le mouvement janséniste*, p. 63).

ultimatum of May 2, 1727, and it is safe to conclude that the Cardinal had fixed upon him as the eventual successor to Morville some time before the actual change took place.[18] For Philip V, who disliked Morville because he had agreed with the Duke of Bourbon concerning the return of the Infanta, wrote to Fleury on May 17, 1727:

You will do very well to get rid of the Comte de Morville, for it is affirmed that he is entirely devoted to the English, and the sooner you can do it the better,

to which Fleury replied on June 9, 1727:

My resolution is taken to get rid of the Comte de Morville as soon as affairs shall have taken a firm and solid footing. . . . [19]

According to the reliable Hénault, who was well acquainted with the court and with all the persons involved, all the diplomatic policies of the government had been submitted to the judgment of Chauvelin for more than a year before his appointment to office, without Morville's realizing that this was the case.[20]

The moment of Chauvelin's appointment was determined by the posture of domestic affairs more than by the desire to effect an immediate change in the foreign policy of France. The question of the acceptance of the bull *Unigenitus* was emerging from the domain of theology into that of politics, and a conflict between the Crown and the *Parlement* of Paris was coming to a head over this very question. The interest which Fleury took in

[18] Baudrillart: *Philippe V et la cour de France*, III, pp. 332-333. Chauvelin had intrigued vigorously for advancement during the Regency, but without success: "Il voulait parvenir sous le régent; ce prince disait que tout lui parlait *Chauvelin;* les pierres même lui rappelaient ce nom ennuyeux. . . ." (D'Argenson: *Journal et mémoires*, I, p. 75).

[19] A. É., *Corr. Pol.: Espagne*, vol. 350, ff. 72, 93.

[20] Hénault: *Mémoires*, p. 301. Fleury is said to have disliked Morville because the latter, during the administration of the Duke of Bourbon, had helped to prevent Fleury's being made a cardinal at that time (Dorsanne: *Journal*, II, p. 385; Marais: *Journal*, III, p. 231). The Abbé de Montgon stated that the dismissal of Morville was rumoured for some time before it took place, the understanding being that Chauvelin would displace him. Montgon attempted to warn Morville, but he could not convince the latter of his danger (Charles Alexandre de Montgon: *Mémoires* [Lausanne, 1748-1753, eight vols.], V, pp. 46-50, 187-192).

enforcing conformity to the doctrine laid down in *Unigenitus* has already been observed; indeed, since almost all of Fleury's public participation in affairs prior to his accession to supreme power had been devoted to this end, it was natural that he should give it a large share of his attention after that event.[21] What the Cardinal particularly needed in his relations with the *Parlement* was the assistance of a law officer, that is to say, of a Keeper of the Seals, whose devotion to Fleury would equal, and whose aggressiveness and ability would surpass, that of D'Armenonville. The man who fulfilled these requirements was Chauvelin.[22]

The Cardinal's complete scheme had been to recall the Chancellor d'Aguesseau, who had been exiled in 1722, and thus to make capital of his popularity with the *Parlement* of Paris, while at the same time giving the seals to Chauvelin, whose *brusqueries* would suit Fleury's purpose more than would the congenital timidity of the Chancellor.[23] When D'Aguesseau was recalled, the Keeper of the Seals, D'Armenonville, took for granted that

[21] Hoym wrote to Augustus II on August 27, 1727: ". . . l'envie du Cardinal . . . de rendre la paix à l'Église en faisant triompher la Constitution, qui est l'objet dont il est le plus frappé, & qu'il faut toujours regarder comme le principal motif de toutes ses actions, est ce qui a opéré cet événement" (Pichon: *Vie de Hoym*, II, p. 282). See also Auguste Boullée: *Histoire de la vie et des ouvrages du chancelier d'Aguesseau* (Paris, 1835, two vols.), II, p. 36.

[22] Chauvelin enjoyed a great reputation for being an authority in public law, partly because of the fact that he owned a large collection of valuable manuscripts treating that subject (Philippe de Courcillon, marquis de Dangeau: *Journal* [Edited by L. Dussieux and E. Soulié; Paris, 1854-1860, nineteen vols.], XVII, p. 134; Saint-Simon: *Mémoires*, XXXII, pp. 66-67; Marais: *Journal*, I, p. 216; *ibid.*, III, pp. 228-231; D'Argenson: *Journal et mémoires*, I, pp. 76-77). Chauvelin's prestige with the *Parlement* was very high. On Fleury's need for an assistant of Chauvelin's stamp, see the comments by Hardy: *Le cardinal de Fleury et le mouvement janséniste*, p. 64. Horatio Walpole attributed Chauvelin's appointment as Keeper of the Seals to his intrigues in the *Parlement* and to his acquaintance among the men of the robe (H. Walpole to Newcastle, Paris, August 16, 1727 [Br. Mus., *Add. MS.* 32751, f. 246]).

[23] The duties of the Chancellor and the Keeper of the Seals were identical. The Chancellor was irremovable, but he could be exiled. In his absence or, more rarely (although it happened in this case), when present, his duties could be performed by the Keeper of the Seals, whose tenure of office depended solely upon the pleasure of the King, and who was consequently much more responsive to the wishes of the Crown. The appointment of Chauvelin was interpreted in the manner explained above by the Polish-Saxon envoy, Hoym, in a letter to Augustus II, Aug. 27, 1727 (Pichon: *Vie de Hoym*, II, pp. 281-282); cf. Boullée: *Histoire du chancelier d'Aguesseau*, II, p. 36.

the Chancellor would be permitted to resume the legal functions of his office. Thereupon D'Armenonville remarked generously that no one could acquit himself better in these functions than could D'Aguesseau, and accordingly resigned the seals in his favour on August 15, 1727. This precipitate action forced Fleury's hand; two days later Chauvelin was appointed to succeed D'Armenonville, although the slight to D'Aguesseau was very evident. On August 19 Morville, son of D'Armenonville and Secretary of State for Foreign Affairs, resigned his position, being very reasonably piqued that Fleury should accept his father's resignation with the tacit understanding that the seals should be given to D'Aguesseau, and should then give them to a third person. Chauvelin was then appointed to succeed Morville also, but it does not appear that Fleury had been eager for the immediate resignation of either Morville or his father.[24] Nevertheless, although the exact moment of Chauvelin's entrance into office may not have been precisely of Fleury's choosing, the Cardinal distinguished him with so many privileges and favours that it was inferred, as Hoym wrote his master, that the Cardinal had selected Chauvelin for his successor. Fleury heightened this impression when he said to Hoym, upon introducing him to Chauvelin, "You may regard him as my *alter ego.*"[25]

In the realm of foreign affairs, Chauvelin's appointment was an indication of Fleury's gradual progress towards the throwing off of diplomatic dependence upon Great Britain. The British feared that such was the case; from their point of view, Morville was entirely satisfactory and the very fact that a change was made at all was alarming.[26] Their concern was aggravated by

[24] Barbier: *Journal,* I, p. 259; Marais: *Journal,* III, p. 229; Villars: *Mémoires,* V, pp. 84-87.

[25] Hoym to Augustus II, Sept. 1, 1727 (Pichon: *Vie de Hoym,* II, pp. 287-288). It was the first time anyone had been Keeper of the Seals and Secretary of State for Foreign Affairs simultaneously. Chauvelin kept his office of *president à mortier;* he had the reversion of the Chancellorship, he was given precedence over marshals and dukes, and his wife was granted the right to a *tabouret* in the presence of the Queen (Marais: *Journal,* III, pp. 229-231; Barbier: *Journal,* I, p. 260; Villars: *Mémoires,* V, p. 88; Saint-Simon: *Mémoires,* VI, p. 321).

[26] Basil Williams: "The Foreign Policy of England under Walpole." *E. H. R.,* XVI, p. 311. Walpole thought very well of Morville and was convinced of his

the knowledge that Chauvelin was strongly supported by D'Huxelles and Pecquet, who were regarded as being hostile to the British connection.

The Cardinal tried very hard to reassure the British on this point, and succeeded temporarily in doing so. Horatio Walpole, although he regretted the resignation of the friendly Morville, and although he had been prejudiced against Chauvelin by him, was amply reassured by Fleury in a conference of August 18, 1727.[27] The Cardinal replied to Walpole's insinuations of Chauvelin's unsuitability:

> I am sensible M. de Chauvelin has many enemies, who envy him; but I have made a strict enquiry into his behaviour, and the facts alledged against him, and have no manner of reason to suspect his not being an honest man. Of his capacity nobody can doubt; and you will soon find, notwithstanding any airs the Marshal d'Huxelles may give himself, that M. de Chauvelin will be entirely devoted to my will and directions.[28]

This impression was confirmed by the first meeting which Walpole had with the new Keeper of the Seals, on August 25. Chauvelin, pointing to the Cardinal, said:

> Voilà, Monsieur, mes sentimens, mes intentions et mes vues, je n'en ai et asseurément je n'en aurai jamais d'autres que celles de Son Eminence.[29]

As a result, Walpole's fears were calmed, and he became persuaded that the bearing the new appointment would have on the Anglo-French alliance would not be unfavourable:

friendliness to the alliance with Great Britain (Letters to Townshend, Nov. 1, 1723, and to Newcastle, Sept. 28, 1726 [Baillon: *Lord Walpole à la cour de France*, pp. 48, 241]).

[27] On August 13, Morville had spoken to Walpole of Chauvelin; ". . . he immediately gave me his picture, by describing him as a person that had indeed great parts and application, and an insinuating way with him, but that he was known at the same time to be so false, so ambitious, so full of self-interest and intrigues, and so entirely void of any knowledge and experience in foreign affairs, that he thought it impossible for the Cardinal to trust a man of that character in such a station. . . ." (H. Walpole to Newcastle, August 16, 1727 [Br. Mus., *Add. MS.* 32751, ff. 242-243]).

[28] H. Walpole to Newcastle, August 19, 1727, quoting Fleury's own words (Br. Mus., *Add. MS.* 32751, f. 252).

[29] H. Walpole to Townshend, August 26, 1727 (Br. Mus., *Add. MS.* 32751, f. 294).

Therefore I think His M[ajesty] has no reason to be in the least uneasy at the various surmises and reasonings that may be made to the disadvantage of England on account of this change. [Such surmises are made only by those] ignorant of the true state of affairs here, which I am persuaded will still be carried on with the same spirit, and upon the same principles, but with greater vigour and dispatch, for Mr. Ch[auvelin] is certainly by the confession of his enemies a person of ready parts, of quick apprehension, and of great application in business. . . . [30]

Accordingly, the home Government, also, declared themselves satisfied with this appointment; Townshend wrote to Walpole on August 21, O. S., that, in the unhappy event that the Cardinal should die, his Britannic Majesty would have the consolation

of seeing the present measures steadily pursued by a successor in the ministry so well qualified as M. Chauvelin will be in all respects, after he has been some time under the Cardinal.[31]

The original apprehensions of the British concerning Chauvelin quickly returned. By May 1728, Walpole had had difficulties with him on three separate points. The first had to do with the fact that Rottembourg, with the consent of Benjamin Keene, had agreed on December 3, 1727, that the restitution of the *Prince Frederick* and a possible indemnity to Spain for the loss she had sustained from Hosier's blockading the galleons should be discussed at the impending congress. The British, who were extremely opposed to subjecting to European debate anything concerning their special privileges in the Spanish Indies, suspected Chauvelin of having instructed Rottembourg to make such an agreement. Their suspicions were increased by the fact that he was extremely reluctant to disavow Rottembourg on this point, and consented to do so only after Horatio Walpole had insisted upon it in conferences with the Cardinal.[32] In the

---

[30] *Ibid.*, Walpole also wrote in this same letter: ". . . and consequently in order to satisfy his own views and the character that is given of him, Mr. Chauvelin must be and act whatsoever the Cardinal will have him, and therefore notwithstanding all speculations about these changes the only question is, whether the Cardinal is changed or not, and I must own that I think him (and I never have yet been deceived in him) as firm as ever to the common cause and His Majesty's interests, ..." (Br. Mus., *Add. MS.* 32751, f. 296).

[31] Br. Mus., *Add. MS.* 32751, f. 350.

[32] Walpole poured out his suspicions of Chauvelin on this issue in a letter to Newcastle, Jan. 27, 1728 (Br. Mus., *Add. MS.* 32753, f. 540). For a discussion

second place, the British contended that the instructions to the
French plenipotentiaries at the Congress of Soissons were worded
so loosely that they seemed an attempt to make France play
the rôle of a mediator there, rather than to act as the ally of
Great Britain.[33] Finally, the British discovered that Chauvelin
was encouraging the Duke of Holstein-Gottorp to demand an
equivalent for Schleswig.[34] As has already been noticed, the
British desired to avoid a discussion of this at all costs, since it
might readily call into question George II's possession of Bremen
and Verden. It is significant, too, that the question of the demolition of the harbour of Dunkirk and the construction of new
waterways at Mardyck again became current almost as soon as
Chauvelin came to office.[35] Horatio Walpole naturally feared

of this incident, Baudrillart: *Philippe V et la cour de France*, III, pp. 380-383.
"It is still doubtful whether Rottembourg, in making the agreement of 3 December
had or had not authority from his own Court" (Sir Richard Lodge: "The Treaty
of Seville (1729)." *Transactions of the Royal Historical Society*, Fourth Series,
XVI [1933], p. 23).

[33] "The Garde des Sceaux having shewn me a rough draught of instructions
for the French Plenipotentiaries, I must own I was surprised to find them conceived in very loose and general terms, tending rather to prescribe them to good
offices than to tye them down to such a strict harmony and concert with their
allies as ought to be required in a common cause" (H. Walpole to Newcastle,
May 12, 1728 [Br. Mus., *Add. MS.* 32755, f. 416]). This was, in fact, precisely
the policy of Fleury and Chauvelin.

[34] Newcastle wrote on this subject to Horatio Walpole, May 14, O. S., 1728:
"But you will find that Mr. Chauvelin goes on in the same strain and appears
disposed, if it were in his power, to give such a turn to this matter as would be
not at all to his Majesty's satisfaction" (Br. Mus., *Add. MS.* 32755, f. 555).

[35] Basil Williams: "The Foreign Policy of England under Walpole." *E. H. R.*,
XVI, p. 311. British apprehensions lest the harbour of Dunkirk might be surreptitiously made practicable once more (*British Diplomatic Instructions: France,
1727-1744*, p. xvi; Townshend to H. Walpole, Aug. 17, O. S., 1727 [*ibid.*, p. 8];
"Instructions for John Armstrong appointed to go as Commissary to Dunkirk,
July 18, [O. S.] 1728" [*ibid.*, pp. 243-244]; similar instructions, March 6, O. S.,
1729/30, and October 12, O. S., 1730 [*ibid.*, pp. 244-248]). The Parliamentary Opposition very much exploited the Dunkirk question (*The Craftsman* [Collected edition,
London, 1731-1737, fourteen vols.], III, pp. 155-158 [July 20, 1728]; V, pp. 186-191
[Nov. 15, 1729]; VI, pp. 206-209 [June 20, 1730]; besides Bolingbroke's pamphlet,
which appeared anonymously: *The Case of Dunkirk Faithfully Stated and Impartially Considered* [London, 1730]). The Opposition finally managed to bring
about a debate on the state of Dunkirk, which gave rise to such brilliant oratory
on both sides that the anniversary of "Dunkirk Day" (February 27, 1730) was
long remembered in Parliamentary circles (Hervey: *Some Materials towards
Memoirs*, pp. 116-117; Charles Howard to Lord Carlisle, Feb. 27, O. S., 1729/30
[Carlisle Papers, *Hist. MSS. Comm., Report* XV, App. Part VI, pp. 68-69]; Thomas
Robinson to Lord Carlisle, Dunkirque, Jan. 11, 1731 [*ibid.*, p. 78]).

the man whom he suspected of endeavouring to nullify the famous friendship which had gained him such prestige with the Ministry at home. He never tired of ascribing all the vexations which the British met with in their negotiations with the French as emanating from Chauvelin alone. On January 6, 1728, he wrote to Newcastle: ". . . and I shall only observe, by the bye, that he is by no means an agreeable negociator to me . . . ," and on May 22, he wrote again:

I much apprehend that I shall have frequent disputes with M. Chauvelin; . . . but the joint opinion of the English and Dutch plenipotentiaries, with the credit I have with the Cardinal, will always, I flatter myself, turn the balance on my side, against the artifice of M. Chauvelin and of those that act underhand in concert with him.[36]

From Walpole the other members of the British Government took their cue; British despatches from 1728 until the end of Chauvelin's ministry express a profound distrust of him and a conviction that he alone was responsible for the decay of the Anglo-French alliance.[37]

The supposition that Chauvelin alone was responsible for the decline in Anglo-French cordiality was built on the assumption that Horatio Walpole could not be mistaken in the Cardinal. With a very natural reluctance to admit that he had played the dupe, Walpole convinced his colleagues that Fleury had weakly allowed Chauvelin to wheedle him into acceptance of an anti-British policy.[38] This view has contributed greatly to that in-

[36] Br. Mus., *Add. MS.* 32753, f. 551; *ibid.*, 32755, f. 531. Other instances of his distrust of Chauvelin may be found in his correspondence (Coxe: *Memoirs of Horatio, Lord Walpole*, I, p. 306; Coxe: *Memoirs of . . . Sir Robert Walpole*, III, pp. 2, 4, 5, 8, 10, 11, 31, 158, 200, 241, 331, 447).
[37] E.g., Sir Robert to H. Walpole, Aug. 28, O. S., 1730: "But one conclusion may be drawn from what we see, and every day feel, that, as far as monsieur Chauvelyn can influence, we are to expect but little, and depend upon lesse, from the friendship of France, or any prospect of a future confidence or good understanding betwixt us" (Coxe: *Memoirs . . . of Sir Robert Walpole*, III, p. 26). See also Newcastle to Horatio Walpole, Sept. 24/Oct. 5, 1736 (*ibid.*, p. 374); the scheme of Robert Trevor to bribe Chauvelin (*ibid.*, pp. 262-265); and the correspondence relating to the Pretender's letter to Chauvelin, given by him to Waldegrave by mistake (*ibid.*, pp. 397-448).
[38] Vaucher: *Robert Walpole et la politique de Fleury*, pp. 120-121. The Parliamentary Opposition made great sport of Walpole's friendship with the Cardinal;

terpretation of Fleury's character which makes him more obtuse than he really was and which declares that he had less control of Chauvelin and of foreign affairs than he really had. What seems to be a more reasonable interpretation is that Fleury's remark to Walpole that "M. de Chauvelin will be entirely devoted to my will and directions" was particularly significant—and true. For more than eight years the very closest co-operation characterized their relations, and French policy derived great benefits from this association of two temperaments so diverse. From 1727 on, an element of comedy entered into the method of French negotiations: Chauvelin's brusqueness gained the point in dispute, while Fleury's gentleness soothed ruffled feelings. Much was gained by this method, as is evidenced not only by the history of the relations of France with Great Britain from this time on, but also by the negotiations with Spain in 1729, prior to the Treaty of Seville, and by those with Austria which secured the reversion of Lorraine. As far as Great Britain was concerned, Fleury could work out through the instrumentality of Chauvelin a programme designed to recapture France's diplomatic freedom of action, while pretending that he himself was as great a friend of the British connection as ever. As Sir Richard Lodge has neatly described the situation, "Thus Chauvelin played the part of Jorkins to Fleury's Spenlow."[39]

The Regency had made customary the practice of dividing the labour required for the direction of foreign affairs between the *premier ministre* and the minister for that department. By this device the chief minister was saved the time and fatigue which the routine duties of a Minister of Foreign Affairs exacted. By 1726, the Secretary of State for Foreign Affairs had under his supervision and direction a rather elaborate and complex organization. At that time, the spade work of the Foreign Office was divided among three bureaus, each under the immediate direc-

e.g., *The Squire and the Cardinal: An Excellent New Ballad* (London, 1730). Lord Hervey makes a very harsh judgment of Horatio Walpole (Hervey: *Some Materials towards Memoirs*, pp. 284-285).

[39] *English Historical Review*, XL (1925), p. 441. Cf. Vaucher: *Robert Walpole et la politique de Fleury*, p. iv; Basil Williams: "The Foreign Policy of England under Walpole." *E. H. R.*, XVI, p. 311.

tion of a *premier commis* with three other *commis* under his orders.[40] In 1726, the younger Pecquet, who occupied the position his father had held, was in charge of the first bureau, which handled the drafting of despatches and other matters appertaining to French negotiations with Great Britain, the United Provinces, Switzerland, the Baltic kingdoms, North Germany and Lorraine.[41] The second bureau specialized in the affairs of the Empire, the Austrian Netherlands and South Germany; it also was responsible for the archives of the department, and its *premier commis*, Le Dran, distinguished himself for many years by composing numerous and voluminous summaries of divers French negotiations.[42] The third bureau was under the direction of La Porte du Theil, and had for its special province the affairs of Italy, Spain and Portugal.[43] Some slight changes in this organization were made during Fleury's administration. Be-

---

[40] There is no systematic account of the manner in which the work of the Ministry of Foreign Affairs was organized during this period. The book which most nearly performs that function is that by Camille Piccioni: *Les premiers commis des Affaires Étrangères au XVII* et au XVIII* siècles* (Paris, 1928). Inasmuch as the functioning of French policy appears not to have changed greatly from the time of Torcy to the Revolution, an excellent work which describes the mechanism of foreign policy in the time of Louis XIV is very useful (C.-G. Picavet: *La diplomatie française au temps de Louis XIV (1661-1715): Institutions, moeurs et coutumes* [Paris, 1930]). In 1784 Hennin, chief of one of the political departments of the Ministry of Foreign Affairs (the title of *premier commis* had been discontinued in 1776) drew up, in response to a request from Catherine II, a *Mémoire sur la manière dont le département des Affaires Étrangères est reglé en France;* this has been published by H. Doniol: "Le Ministère des Affaires Étrangères de France sous le comte de Vergennes." *Revue d'histoire diplomatique,* VII (1893), pp. 544-549. Besides this source, an excellent account of the Ministry of Foreign Affairs as it was organized in 1787 is given in the first chapter of the work by Frédéric Masson: *Le département des Affaires Étrangères pendant la Révolution, 1787-1804* (Paris, 1877). Considerable incidental information may also be gleaned from the book by Armand Baschet: *Histoire du dépôt des Archives des Affaires Étrangères* (Paris, 1875).

[41] For a brief biography of Pecquet, see Piccioni: *Les premiers commis,* pp. 206-212.

[42] Concerning Le Dran, see Piccioni: *Les premiers commis,* pp. 214-219; Baschet: *Histoire du dépôt des Archives,* pp. 179-190.

[43] La Porte du Theil very much favoured an alliance with Austria; he participated at Vienna in the negotiations dealing with the reversion of Lorraine to France. In 1745 D'Argenson, who disliked his Austrophil attitude, demoted him from the active work of the political bureaus and sent him to the Louvre to be archivist (Piccioni: *Les premiers commis,* pp. 24, 194-206; Baschet: *Histoire du dépôt des Archives,* p. 273).

ginning in 1727, Le Dran devoted all his time to the archives. The first bureau thereupon assumed responsibility for the preparation of business having to do with the affairs of the Empire, South Germany and the Austrian Netherlands, and the third bureau those pertaining to Austria; in 1737, a fourth *commis*, whose function was specialization in the affairs of Poland, was attached to Pecquet's bureau; in 1740, when Pecquet was disgraced, Le Dran became *premier commis* of the first bureau and still held that position at the time of Fleury's death.[44]

As may well be supposed, this group of *commis* played an important and devoted part in the transaction of the diplomatic business of the *ancien régime*.[45] They developed, besides, a very strong *esprit de corps*, which is readily explained by the facts that new *commis* were almost invariably recruited from families which already had members on the staff, that intermarriages within the families of this little group were common, and that the *premiers commis*, whose positions were desirable ones both from the point of view of perquisites and of prestige, were chosen from among the members of this staff. Only one traitor is known ever to have been numbered amongst them, a man named Bussy, who received large sums from the British for selling rather stale state secrets during Fleury's administration.[46]

Later in the century the organization of the Ministry of Foreign Affairs became even more complex, when a *bureau des fonds* was established; but in Fleury's day the financial affairs of the department were transacted, item by item, with the office of the general treasury of the kingdom.[47] Later in the century,

---

[44] Piccioni: *Les premiers commis*, p. 24.

[45] Cf. the high praise lavished upon them by Masson: *Le département des Affaires Étrangères pendant la Révolution*, pp. 10-11, 20, 33-34.

[46] Piccioni: *Les premiers commis*, pp. 233-238. Bussy first gave information to the British in 1728, when he was attached to the French embassy in Vienna. He was subsequently French minister to Great Britain from 1740 to 1744; in between times he was connected with the work of the political bureaus in the ministry at Versailles. There is frequent reference to "our friend" in the correspondence contained in the third volume of Coxe's *Memoirs of . . . Sir Robert Walpole;* see also, *sub nomine*, in the indices of Vaucher: *Robert Walpole et la politique de Fleury*, and *British Diplomatic Instructions: France, 1727-1744.*

[47] Masson: *Le département des Affaires Étrangères pendant la Révolution*, pp. 35-37. The *bureau des fonds* was created about 1755 (Piccioni: *Les premiers commis*, p. 38).

too, there was created a subordinate bureau of interpreters, and in 1767, a separate service for the ciphering and deciphering of despatches was instituted.[48] Since the days of the German enterprises of Louis XIV there had always been associated with the staff one or two "jurisconsults" who were authorities on German public law, and who, naturally enough, were usually Alsatians.[49]

The regular working hours of the staff were daily from nine in the morning until two in the afternoon, but representatives of each political bureau took turns in being on duty afternoons and evenings to receive and decipher despatches which arrived in odd hours. The *premiers commis* reported each day to the Minister of Foreign Affairs and either collaborated with him in the redaction of despatches or took them down at his dictation.[50] Such a regimentation of the work of the department organized it as efficiently, perhaps, as was possible, but the burden of labour on the Minister of Foreign Affairs was nevertheless severe. Especially was this the case when the Minister composed the drafts of many *mémoires* and despatches, as Chauvelin did.[51] By utilizing the energy of a Minister of Foreign Affairs whose function it was to transact the indispensable mechanical business of the ministry and to supervise the documentary crystallization of French policy, the Cardinal was able to direct French policy quickly and with a minimum of fatigue and expenditure of time in a series of oral decisions. The ultimate determination of

[48] Masson: *Le département des Affaires Étrangères pendant la Révolution*, pp. 42-43; Piccioni: *Les premiers commis*, p. 26. A *bureau géographique* was established in 1774 (Masson: *op. cit.*, p. 43). Later in the century, the Ministry of Foreign Affairs subsidized a staff of writers called the *rédacteurs d'ouvrages politiques;* of these, Rulhière, who wrote the *Histoire de l'anarchie de Pologne* was one (Masson: *op. cit.*, pp. 44-48).

[49] Piccioni: *Les premiers commis*, pp. 43-44; Masson: *Le département des Affaires Étrangères pendant la Révolution*, p. 25.

[50] Doniol: "Le Ministère des Affaires Étrangères de France sous le comte de Vergennes." *Revue d'histoire diplomatique*, VII, pp. 546-548. The offices of these bureaus in the Ministry of Foreign Affairs were situated in one of the wings forming the *cour des ministres;* they communicated with the office of the Minister of Foreign Affairs by a private staircase (Masson: *Le département des Affaires Étrangères pendant la Révolution*, p. 12).

[51] D'Argenson: *Journal et mémoires*, I, p. 187. The Minister of Foreign Affairs of course had his own secretarial staff, which was distinct from the permanent staff of the Foreign Office (Piccioni: *Les premiers commis*, pp. 23, 29-30).

French policy was made in Fleury's conversations with foreign
ambassadors, or in the sittings of the Council of State, or in his
conferences with Chauvelin, with whom he usually worked twice
a day. When foreign ambassadors came from Paris to transact
their business at Versailles (usually on Tuesdays), they customarily called on both Fleury and the Secretary of State for Foreign
Affairs. Naturally, as a result of this method of transacting
business, the documents in the archives bear greater evidence
of the activity of his ministers of foreign affairs than of his
own.[52] By this system Fleury husbanded his energy and, so
long as Chauvelin was the Minister of Foreign Affairs, conven-
iently combined actual unity of direction with an occasional show
of what seemed to be divided responsibility.

It is therefore reasonable to conclude that the appointment of
Chauvelin, from whose *brusquerie* Fleury drew great advantage,
was a part of the Cardinal's programme for regaining France's
diplomatic initiative. That programme continued to be the settling of the affairs of Europe on a firmer basis, which would have
the effect of rendering French dependence upon Great Britain
less necessary. In the winter of 1727-1728, as in the previous
period, Fleury carefully avoided downright action which might
have the effect of driving Spain and the Emperor into close co-
operation. Instead, he allowed ample time for the process of
mutual disenchantment to work, and persisted in relying on the
efficacy of negotiation, to the frequent disgust of the British,
who were eager to secure quick results and were willing to
achieve them, if necessary, sword in hand.[53]

[52] Rather rarely, *mémoires* in the hand of Duparc, Fleury's secretary, may be
found in the archives; sometimes, a *mémoire* minuted in the handwriting of Fleury
may be discovered. On the other hand, there are numerous *mémoires*, besides
numberless annotations, in the handwriting of Chauvelin, which is unfortunately
much easier to identify than to decipher. The preponderant number of papers in
the *fonds Mémoires et Documents* are written in a clear secretarial hand, evidently
copies made by the *commis;* these usually are minuted with an attribution of their
authorship. The French made extensive use of written memorials and summaries,
a method unknown to British diplomacy at that time. Nothing corresponding
to the volumes of *Mémoires et Documents* at the Quai d'Orsay is to be found in
the Newcastle Papers at the British Museum, which are the prime source for
British diplomatic negotiations of this period.

[53] For British pressure on the French to break off diplomatic relations with
Spain, see the letters of the Duke of Newcastle to H. Walpole, November 23 and
Dec. 14, O. S., 1727 (*British Diplomatic Instructions: France, 1727-1744,* pp. 12, 15).

As has already been observed, Rottembourg's secret instructions qualified that unhesitating support of British contentions which the instructions read to Horatio Walpole had contained. Fleury, who, it should be remembered, had not been altogether pleased with the British programme of naval blockades undertaken in 1726, strengthened these instructions by an autograph letter to Rottembourg, dated October 23, 1727, in which he expressed the view, which was anathema to the British, that Hosier's blockade had been an act of hostility which justified the Spaniards in claiming compensation, and suggested that the *Prince Frederick* should be handed over to the French or the Dutch, pending an adjustment of claims.[54] It is not surprising that Rottembourg, armed with instructions such as these, accepted, on December 3, Spanish proposals precisely to this effect. The outraged British promptly jumped to the conclusion that this was a result of Chauvelin's underhand work. Their pressure forced the Cardinal to disavow Rottembourg's agreement, and only on March 6 was the convention signed which guaranteed to British satisfaction Spain's performance of the stipulations of the Preliminaries of Paris.[55]

It is probable that Fleury, by showing his reluctance to declare war, encouraged the resistance of Elisabeth Farnese and accordingly increased unnecessarily the period of time between the conclusion of the Preliminaries (May 31, 1727) and Spain's ratification of them (March 6, 1728).[56] It is difficult to believe, however, considering the general set of the Cardinal's policy, that Fleury regarded this as an egregious blunder. For the Cardinal never showed signs of distress merely because time was consumed excessively in negotiations; throughout his whole ad-

[54] Baudrillart: *Philippe V et la cour de France*, III, pp. 361-363.

[55] The convention is printed in Baudrillart: *Philippe V et la cour de France*, III, pp. 403-405; also in Schmauss: *Corpus juris gentium academicum*, pp. 2096-2098. For a detailed account of the negotiations (Baudrillart: *op. cit.*, III, pp. 348-368, 378-405; Goslinga: *Slingelandt's Efforts towards European Peace*, pp. 138-209; Basil Williams: "The Foreign Policy of England under Walpole." *E. H. R.*, XVI, pp. 314-315).

[56] Baudrillart: *Philippe V et la cour de France*, III, p. 401, second note. Elisabeth Farnese finally consented to the ratification of the Preliminaries because she desired to earn the gratitude of France and Great Britain, in view of the apparently imminent death of Philip V.

ministration, his attitude, surprising enough in a man so old, was that time was on his side. An ultimatum with a thirty days' limit; an ambiguous period, neither war nor peace, extending for over three years between the signature of the preliminaries of a peace and the peace itself, were characteristic phenomena of his leisurely administration.[57] His negotiations were conducted on the postulate that his patience was more nearly inexhaustible than that of the persons with whom he dealt. Herein lay the great temperamental difference between the French minister and the British statesmen, especially Lord Townshend. The British ministers, responsible as they were to a critical Parliament, and lying, as they did, under the necessity of having something to show in return for their armaments and subsidies, desired to secure results quickly. France, on the other hand, had less to gain than the British by success in war and, because of her geographical situation, more to lose by defeat. Consequently the policy of France, under the management of Fleury, acted as a brake on her impatient ally. This action, or rather non-action, became more and more perceptible as the danger of a general war became less and less. In 1727, Great Britain had wanted France to declare war on Spain; Fleury had negotiated the Preliminaries of May 31, 1727, instead. In the next few months, the British desired the French to break off diplomatic relations with the Spanish monarchy; instead there had followed, in a very deliberate manner, the Convention of the Pardo.[58] Although in each case British interests were as effectively maintained and safeguarded as they could have been by the use of force, the ultimate result was to wear British patience thin. That was a risk worth taking; for by the Convention of the Pardo

---

[57] I. e.: I. The ultimatum of May 2, 1727; II. The period between October 5. 1735 and the third Treaty of Vienna, November 18, 1738.

[58] The Convention of the Pardo could have been signed in early February, had not the British, who were so eager for its conclusion, neglected to forward the proper credentials to Keene! This led to some appropriate remarks from Fleury and Chauvelin (*British Diplomatic Instructions: France, 1727-1744*, p. ix; Goslinga: *Slingelandt's Efforts towards European Peace*, pp. 206-207; Basil Williams: "The Foreign Policy of England under Walpole." *E. H. R.*, XVI, pp. 316-317).

the policy of Fleury achieved its second pragmatic justification: henceforth no impediment remained to the opening of the general congress.

CHAPTER VI

THE CONGRESS OF SOISSONS AND THE TREATY OF SEVILLE, 1728-1729

FOLLOWING the Convention of the Pardo, interest was transferred to the impending Congress. The Spaniards were armed with instructions designed to force the discussion, in open congress, of all of Spain's grievances against Great Britain.[1] To prevent this very thing, the British strongly supported the view that the object of the Congress was merely to register and sanction the stipulations of the Preliminaries of Paris of May 31, 1727; in a word, they desired the Congress to be as brief and as *fainéant* as possible, and to this end brought great pressure to bear upon the French.[2]

The Dutch, too, had their formula for the business which the Congress should discuss. According to an important memorial by Slingelandt, the Congress should welcome the opportunity of settling once for all the questions of the Emperor's succession and the establishment of the Spanish princes in Italy. But the British and the French quashed this, the principal one of "Slingelandt's Efforts towards European Peace," the former because they feared a general discussion of European problems at the Congress, and the latter because they opposed a guarantee of the Pragmatic Sanction.[3]

Even the Emperor was desirous of restricting the agenda and

---

[1] Baudrillart: *Philippe V et la cour de France*, III, pp. 423-424, 570-572.

[2] Newcastle to H. Walpole, March 14, O. S., 1727/8 (*British Diplomatic Instructions: France, 1727-1744*, pp. 19-20). The British were also fearful that the question of an equivalent for Schleswig might be raised (*ibid.*). Cf. the instructions to Horatio Walpole, William Stanhope and Stephen Poyntz, British plenipotentiaries to the Congress (*ibid.*, pp. 26-38).

[3] Memorial dated March 31, 1728; printed by Theod. Jorissen: *Historische Studien*, V. *Lord Chesterfield en de Republiek der Vereenigde Nederlanden* (Haarlem, 1894), pp. 266-271. Cf. Goslinga: *Slingelandt's Efforts towards European Peace*, pp. 220-222, 248-250.

the duration of the Congress as much as possible, for the Imperial power had much to lose if the German princes should be given a voice there and should make the Emperor's encroachments on their rights and privileges a subject of European discussion. Moreover, Imperial influence was losing ground in Germany in 1728. Prior to the Preliminaries of May 31, 1727, the Alliance of Hanover had not been particularly successful in securing German allies. But on December 6 of that year, Great Britain won over the Duke of Brunswick-Wolfenbüttel, and it was hoped that this alliance would be the nucleus of a general German Protestant League.[4] At the same time, France was beginning to regain her influence in Germany, a point which Chauvelin, as well as Fleury, considered very important.[5] On November 12, 1727, a secret treaty between France and Bavaria was concluded at Fontainebleau, in which Louis XV agreed to assist in raising Charles Albert to the imperial dignity when a vacancy should occur; subsidies were to be paid to the Elector when the treaty should come into effect, but that was not to be until his treaty with the Emperor should expire on September 1, 1730.[6] An extremely important qualification of this stipulation was made, however, by the second separate article: if the Elector of Bavaria should be able to sign a treaty "for the strengthening of the peace within the Empire" with the other Wittelsbach Electors on terms which France would suggest, then the Elector of Bavaria was to receive a million livres a year, dating from the signature of the joint treaty. Thus a powerful incentive was given Charles Albert for forming an Electoral

[4] Dumont: *Corps universel diplomatique*, VIII, part ii, pp. 148-149; Chance: *Alliance of Hanover*, pp. 727-728. The Duke had concluded a secret treaty with Würtemberg on July 24, 1727, to which the British ministers proposed that George II should accede in his capacity as Elector (Newcastle to H. Walpole, Feb. 27, O. S., 1727/8 [*British Diplomatic Instructions: France, 1727-1744*, pp. 16-18]).

[5] The "necessity of forming a party within the Empire" was discussed in a memorial written by Chauvelin and annotated in a hand which appears to be Fleury's, under date of December 31, 1728 (*Sur les mesures à prendre en conséquence de la situation actuelle des affaires de l'Europe* [A. É., *Mém. et Doc.*, France, vol. 494, ff. 230-241]). The same point was emphasized in another memorial by Chauvelin, dated January 18, 1729 (A. É., *Mém. et Doc.*, France, vol. 494, ff. 249-261).

[6] Printed by C. M. von Aretin: *Chronologisches Verzeichniss der bayerischen Staats-Verträge* (Passau, 1838), pp. 363-370.

Union inimical to the Emperor; it is not surprising to find, therefore, that through his initiative an "Electoral Union" of the Electors of Bavaria, the Palatinate, Treves and Cologne was formed on April 16, 1728.[7] The real purpose of this family agreement was to oppose the growth of Hapsburg power in the Empire, although this aim was disguised in the usual veiled phraseology which spoke unexceptionably of maintaining peace in the Empire on the basis of the Treaties of Westphalia. The Union was exactly in consonance with French policy, but it was brought about in such a manner that France appeared not to have figured in it, and thus escaped the reproach of having overtly fomented discord in the Empire. Even Chavigny was kept in the dark; it naturally occurred to him that France should join what appeared to him to be a heaven-sent combination, but, temporarily, Fleury and Chauvelin continued their policy of permitting the German princes to annoy the Emperor without France's overt interference.[8]

This posture of affairs weakened the Emperor's powers of resistance to the demands of the Hanover allies, as did also the situation in Russia. The accession of Russia to the Treaty of Vienna, in 1726, had been of considerable importance, but Russia was of little help or hindrance to anybody under the successor of Catherine I. The short reign of Peter II (May 1727-January 1730) was characterized by the rise to power of the reactionary party, headed by the Golitsuin and the Dolgoruki families, which was opposed to the influence of foreigners and the Europeanization of Russia. This party was able to overthrow Menchikov, who had himself got rid of Tolstoy, although they left the indispensable Vice-Chancellor Ostermann in the enjoyment of his office. The Duke of Holstein-Gottorp lost the support of Russia as a result of the death of Catherine I, which of course eased the tension in the north of Europe so far as Great Britain was concerned, and the dereliction of the Russian ship of state prevented

[7] Rosenlehner: *Kurfürst Karl Philipp von der Pfalz*, pp. 365-374.
[8] Chauvelin to Chavigny, Sept. 25, 1728 (Dureng: *Mission de Chavigny*, p. 79). Dureng wrote as if he were not aware of the second separate article of the Franco-Bavarian treaty (*ibid.*, pp. 75 sqq.).

the Emperor from deriving any utility from the treaty of 1726. The Polish-Saxon envoy, Le Fort, thus summed up the situation in Russia in his despatch of June 14, 1728, the very month, as it happened, in which the sessions of the Congress of Soissons began:

When I consider how this state is governed at present, the reign of the grandfather appears to me to be a dream. We live here in an indolence without parallel, and in a security so blind that the human mind can not conceive how a machine so large can sustain itself without either assistance or effort . . . [9]

The worsening of the diplomatic situation, so far as the Emperor was concerned, made the Austrians eager that German affairs should not be discussed at the Congress. But at the same time, the Emperor vented his resentment against the British and the Dutch by more openly supporting the East Frisian ruler against his rebellious Emden subjects, the so-called "Renitents," and by declaring the joint "conservatorship" of the Elector of Hanover and the Duke of Brunswick-Wolfenbüttel in Mecklenburg to be at an end; by Imperial decree the King of Prussia was henceforth to be associated with them in the supervision of the administration of that duchy.[10]

As was the case with the other powers admitted to the Congress, France also had very definite views concerning what should be the aims of her negotiation there. These views were concretely expressed by the Cardinal himself in the instructions

---

[9] *Sbornik*, V, p. 308.

[10] For developments in the East-Frisian crisis in 1728 (Goslinga: *Slingelandt's Efforts towards European Peace*, pp. 217-218). In Mecklenburg, Duke Charles Leopold, nephew-in-law of Peter the Great, had trouble with his nobility which ended in 1723 by the Emperor's releasing the Duke's subjects from their allegiance. As executors of the will of the German Diet, the Elector of Hanover and the Duke of Brunswick-Wolfenbüttel had occupied the duchy since 1719, but their commission expired upon the death of George I. The new decree of May 11, 1728, enraged George II because it emanated from the Aulic Council and not from the Imperial Diet; it may be said to have guaranteed trouble by associating Prussia with the former "conservators" on terms rather ambiguous, and seemed clearly to be a result of the Austro-Prussian entente (Goslinga: *op. cit.*, p. 242; Dureng: *Mission de Chavigny*, pp. 67-72; Dumont: *Corps universel diplomatique*, VIII, part ii, pp. 156-157; Rousset: *Recueil historique*, VII, pp. 19-25).

drawn up for the French plenipotentiaries, of whom he was one.[11] The chief thing to be done, the instructions declared, was to detach Spain from Austria and associate her with the Hanover powers. As usual, the Cardinal did not consider it practical for France to have no ally at all, but of the possible combinations which could be made, he regarded the one just mentioned as the only one feasible. The experience of the War of the Spanish Succession had shown that alliance with Spain alone was not sufficient. On the other hand, merely to hold fast to the alliance with the British and the Dutch, the Cardinal wrote significantly, would surely tighten up the Austro-Spanish alliance, break all the promises which had been made to Spain in order to persuade her to ratify the Preliminaries, and render more formidable the commercial and maritime power of Great Britain.

The alliance of France with Spain and Austria was a possible combination which was entirely compatible with keeping faith with Great Britain, he wrote, because at that moment France had executed almost all of her engagements with reference to the British; an alternative Bourbon-Hapsburg alliance, he thought, would be a very desirable thing, for it would dry up the source of European wars; but attractive as that idea was, he dismissed it in 1728 on the grounds that its stability at that time would really depend on the whim of Elisabeth Farnese.

The problem of France at the Congress, the Cardinal declared, was to make possible an alliance of France, Great Britain and Spain by bringing about the collapse of the Alliance of Vienna; to make this possible, France had to manage the reconciliation of Spain with Great Britain, being watchful, meanwhile, to prevent any unexpected recrudescence of the time-honoured com-

---

[11] "Cet écrit, où est discuté tout le système d'alliances qui convient à la France, est digne de la meilleure époque" (Baudrillart: *Philippe V et la cour de France*, III, p. 13). It may be found in A. É., *Mém. et Doc., France*, vol. 496, ff. 53-119. It is summarized by Baudrillart: *op. cit.*, III, pp. 408-413, and by Goslinga: *Slingelandt's Efforts towards European Peace*, pp. 224-229. In his excellent Presidential Address, Sir Richard Lodge discusses French policy at this juncture and sums it up by saying: "The Cardinal's extremely subtle policy was to gain Spain without breaking up the league of Hanover, and thus to leave Austria isolated and presumably impotent" (Sir Richard Lodge: "The Treaty of Seville (1729)." *Transactions of the Royal Historical Society*, Fourth Series, XVI [1933], p. 31).

bination of the Emperor with the Maritime Powers. This programme, though clearly conceived, was not an easy one to put into practice, especially because it envisaged France's playing the part of a mediator at the Congress, rather than that of a staunch ally of Great Britain, which she ostensibly was. Such a programme would obviously require of the French directors of policy an extreme resourcefulness and adaptiveness; its difficulty explains the chronic perplexity betrayed in the memorials by Chauvelin and others in the Ministry of Foreign Affairs during the succeeding months.

Two things were certain, according to Fleury's instructions: France's rôle ought to be that of a mediator rather than strictly that of an ally of Great Britain, and, in the second place, decision should be made concerning the detailed issues which the Congress was going to discuss, in such a way as to facilitate the attainment of the general aims which the Cardinal had pointed out.[12] Accordingly, the Cardinal's instructions advocated that the restitution of the *Prince Frederick* to the British should be made the occasion for proposing remedies for contraband trade. Without a doubt, the letter of the law was on the Spanish side in this dispute, and France ought to support Spain on this point without reserve, the more willingly because the British contraband trade was injurious to French merchants. Since, however, France was a guarantor of the legal commercial privileges accorded to the British, she could not endeavour to have those restricted, but she ought at least to demand a share in them.

It has already been asserted that Fleury's policy made itself solicitous for the commercial interests of France, and these instructions are an added proof of it. Moreover, in preparation for the Congress of Soissons, the deputies of the several Chambers of Commerce seem to have been requested to submit pro-

---

[12] Of course the Cardinal continued to reassure the British of his intentions to maintain the alliance with them as close as ever. He wrote to George II from Compiègne on June 16, 1728: "Le Roy mon Maitre m'a ordonné d'expliquer si clairement Sa ferme Resolution de ne jamais Se departir de l'Alliance qu'il a contracté avec Votre Ma^te, que les Alliés de Vienne ont perdu toute Esperance de nous desunir, et n'osent Seulement en temoigner la moindre Pensée" (Weston Papers, *Hist. MSS. Comm.*, *Report* X, App. Part I, p. 202).

posals for the improvement of trade, for the purpose of instructing and assisting the French plenipotentiaries.[13] The solicitude
for the interests of trade on the part of the French government
at this time is shown also by Chauvelin's letters to Rottembourg
with reference to the excessive indult of twenty-three and three-
fourths *per cent.* which the Spanish sovereigns had charged in
December 1727, on goods returning from the Indies. On January
27, 1728, he wrote that if such things kept up French merchants
would prefer to suspend their Cadiz trade. What this really
meant he made clear in his letter of March 2, in which he said:

It is greatly to the interest of the King of France to tolerate a direct commerce to the Indies. He has forbidden it, under pain of the most severe
penalties, in order to be agreeable to the King of Spain, who draws immense
revenues from the obligation of our subjects to make use of the galleons and
the flotilla. If the King of Spain makes this trade too hard for the French or
breaks faith with treaties, we shall do as the British and the Dutch, who
have never deprived themselves of an illicit trade with the Indies.[14]

And in a letter of July 6, 1728, he remarked, with good reason,
that such conduct, far from serving to detach France from Great
Britain, only served to draw more tightly the French connection
with the British.[15]

Besides indicating his interest in the promotion of French
trade, Fleury's instructions for the use of the French plenipotentiaries at the Congress of Soissons discussed the questions of
Gibraltar and of the establishing of Don Carlos in Italy. As to
the first, since it would be very easy to antagonize Spain, who
insisted upon its restitution, or Great Britain, who refused to
give it up, the French should endeavour to be non-committal.

[13] Some of these memorials have been published by Henri Sée and Léon Vignols:
"Mémoires sur le commerce rédigés en vue du congrès de Soissons (1728)." [Mi-
nistère de l'instruction publique et des beaux-arts: Comité des travaux historiques
et scientifiques, section d'histoire moderne (depuis 1715) et contemporaine]:
Notices, inventaires & documents, XII: *Études et documents divers* (1926), pp. 1-33.
Low profits on French goods legally sold in Spanish America, because of the competition from goods illicitly imported, and the facility with which the British illicitly sold goods in conjunction with the legal distribution of slaves are commented
upon; the remedy lay in depriving the British of their Asiento privileges (*op. cit.*,
pp. 8, 10-11).
[14] Baudrillart: *Philippe V et la cour de France*, III, p. 578.
[15] This letter addressed to Brancas (Baudrillart: *Philippe V et la cour de France*,
III, pp. 578-579).

With reference to the second, also, the French should take no steps until it could be seen that the alliance between Austria and Spain had completely broken down.

These instructions show, in Fleury's own words, that he proposed to act the part of a mediator and a good friend to all the powers represented in the Congress, and that, by doing so, he would be less the devoted friend of Great Britain than that power desired him to be. In this projected policy he would be aided by the fact that France had no immediate grievance to settle, as had Spain, Great Britain and Austria, involving such questions as Gibraltar, the *Prince Frederick* and the Ostend Company. The logic of events cast France in the rôle of mediator; to play it successfully, her policy would need to be one of adaptation, rather than of initiative. In spite of the difficulties inherent in such a policy, Fleury observed in the instructions which he composed that it was not particularly to the interests of France to bring the Congress to an early conclusion; its protraction would give the Spaniards opportunity to air their grievances against the British, and would likewise allow added time for the Austro-Spanish alliance completely to collapse.[16]

The French were aided in the accomplishment of this difficult programme by the fact that the Congress of Soissons turned out to be something very different from a congress: after a few preliminary sessions, the really important negotiations were carried on wherever the Cardinal happened to be, and only the junior diplomats were left to mark time at Soissons.[17] It is difficult to explain why the representatives of the several powers fell in so readily with a procedure of such obvious advantage to French

[16] This was precisely the policy also advocated by the *premier commis* Pecquet, in a memorial dated May, 1728 (A. É., *Mém. et Doc., France*, vol. 494, ff. 153-161). Horatio Walpole wrote to Newcastle from Paris, April 9, 1728, that he feared "that the Marshall d'Huxelles and his friends, and amongst them Mr. Chauvelin, may be of opinion of having the Congress continued and spinned out, . . ." (Br. Mus., *Add. MS.* 32755, f. 146).

[17] For example, Stephen Poyntz, the junior of the British plenipotentiaries, remained at Soissons. Slingelandt wrote to the Dutch representatives that "Soissons sera pendant le cours de cette négociation partout où sera le Cardinal et les principaux négotiateurs" (Goslinga: *Slingelandt's Efforts towards European Peace*, p. 248).

policy. As a result of it, the Cardinal and not the Congress became the sole clearing house of negotiation; the threads of the several negotiations were held in his hands, and he was permitted to transact in separate and secret conferences what otherwise would have been discussed in general congress. And to this advantage was added the further one, that the Cardinal was playing the game on his home field, so to speak, and had the assistance of Chauvelin, whereas the representatives of foreign powers were at the disadvantage of having continually to consult, through the medium of tedious correspondence, the wishes of their superiors in the capitals at home.[18]

What may be said to be the first period of activity of the so-called Congress of Soissons lasted from its opening, on June 18, 1728, until August of that year. This period was characterized by the sparring of the several powers represented at the Congress in an endeavour to secure special concessions from unwary opponents and ended in mutual lack of success and deadlock.

As was expected, the Spaniards immediately vented their complaints about Gibraltar; but what was more important was the endeavour of the Austrian Chancellor, Sinzendorff (who was the Emperor's principal delegate), to manoeuvre Fleury into a position where he would become the butt of Elisabeth Farnese's resentment. Some months previously, the Spanish court had asked the Emperor to explain his intentions regarding the marriage of Maria Theresa and the introduction of garrisons into the Italian duchies.[19] The Emperor had temporized by promising to have these matters discussed at the Congress, his secret presumption being that Fleury would show himself squarely opposed to the marriage of Don Carlos with Maria Theresa and to the introduction of Spanish garrisons into the duchies. But Fleury was too astute: he spoke rather favourably of the proposed marriage, although he refused to put his remarks in writing, and

[18] The importance of this has been emphasized by Sir Richard Lodge, who remarks as well that "there can be no doubt that in 1728-9 he [Fleury] was the most important personage in Europe" (Sir Richard Lodge: "The Treaty of Seville (1729)." *Transactions of the Royal Historical Society*, Fourth Series, XVI [1933], p. 25).

[19] Syveton: *Une cour et un aventurier*, pp. 256-259.

as for the Spanish garrisons, he blandly acknowledged, to Sinzen-dorff's confusion, that France and Great Britain had already consented in principle to that point by the Treaty of Madrid (1721).[20] What was more, Fleury, having foreseen that some attempt might be made to draw France into alliance with Austria and Spain, and having already come to the conclusion that such a policy would be impracticable, scotched the efforts of Bournon-ville and Sinzendorff to draw France into the Alliance of Vienna.[21] The Spaniards were more cast down than were the Austrians by this refusal. Consequently, in an effort to satisfy them and to detach them from the Emperor, the Cardinal made the rather astonishing offer of France's aid in driving the Austrians out of Italy and settling the Spanish princes there.[22] This idea has been ascribed to Chauvelin, whose notions on the Italian *équilibre* were the most characteristic of his statecraft and were to come into greater prominence in 1730.[23] But the Spaniards knew well that such schemes could be accomplished only by war, and they were so sure that Fleury would avoid war at all costs that they treated the proposal very coldly.

By August 1728, therefore, the various negotiations at the French court had reached a deadlock. In Germany, the King of Great Britain was toying with the idea of allying himself as Elector of Hanover, and consenting to be allied as King of Great Britain, with the newly-formed "Electoral Union" of Wittelsbach princes; his ministers were alarmed at the rumoured efforts of Charles VI and the King of Prussia to detach Denmark from the Alliance of Hanover, and were convinced, doubtless by the un-favourable turn which affairs in Mecklenburg were taking, that

The Emperor has for some time exercised a despotick power in the Empire, not inferior to that which was assumed by Ferdinand the 2nd which occa-sioned the long and destructive war that was ended by the Treaty of West-phalia.[24]

[20] Baudrillart: *Philippe V et la cour de France*, III, pp. 435-436.
[21] Similar attempts had been made earlier in 1728 (Baudrillart: *Philippe V et la cour de France*, III, pp. 424-426, 432-434).
[22] Baudrillart: *Philippe V et la cour de France*, III, pp. 436-440.
[23] Vaucher: *Robert Walpole et la politique de Fleury*, p. 28.
[24] Townshend to the plenipotentiaries, August 5, O. S., 1728 (*British Diplomatic Instructions: France, 1727-1744*, p. 40); for the effort to detach Denmark (New-castle to the plenipotentiaries, July 26, O. S., 1728 [*ibid.*, p. 38]).

But the Austrians themselves, having been unsuccessful in laying traps for the Cardinal, now became eager to bring the Congress to a close in order to prevent German affairs from being brought before it. Such action was all the more necessary for the Austrians because the Cardinal was now considering linking France overtly with that "Electoral Union" of the Wittelsbachs which his diplomacy had secretly inspired.[25]

Accordingly, Sinzendorff brought forward his project for a "provisional" treaty, which inaugurated the second period in the existence of the Congress of Soissons. This second period may be said to have endured until March 1729, when Spain finally showed some signs of life after a winter during which she had permitted her diplomacy to remain completely dormant. During this period the Cardinal was subjected to severe pressure from the British who, as usual, wanted tangible results quickly, while at the same time the final and irretrievable decay of the Austro-Spanish alliance was silently going on.

The Cardinal would have preferred a definitive to a provisional treaty; the former he thought could be secured and the peace of Europe consequently placed upon a solid basis, if Great Britain would give up Gibraltar. Nothing short of this would satisfy Spain, but, inasmuch as the French were unable to secure British consent to the surrender of Gibraltar, a "provisional" treaty was draughted and communicated to the several powers on August 21.[26] It merely extended the suspension of the Ostend Company for an undetermined number of years, and referred the really difficult questions, such as British contraband trade in the Spanish Indies and an eventual equivalent for the Duke of Holstein-Gottorp, to commissioners especially appointed for the purpose.[27]

---

[25] Cf. *supra*, pp. 193-194. This action was taken with the knowledge and approval of the British (Newcastle to the plenipotentiaries, July 26, O. S., 1728; Townshend to the same, Sept. 12, O. S., 1728 [*British Diplomatic Instructions: France, 1727-1744*, pp. 39, 41]).

[26] For French pressure to surrender Gibraltar, see *British Diplomatic Instructions: France, 1727-1744*, p. xi, note. Fleury, in an indirect way, secured the support of Slingelandt on this point (Goslinga: *Slingelandt's Efforts towards European Peace*, pp. 258-259, 262-268).

[27] Summarized by Baudrillart: *Philippe V et la cour de France*, III, p. 442; Goslinga: *Slingelandt's Efforts towards European Peace*, pp. 281-282.

The several plenipotentiaries had agreed amicably on the articles of this proposal except on one significant point: Chauvelin had desired that the question of commercial privileges should be examined by a commission representing all the contracting parties, which meant that the French and the Dutch would have something to say about British contraband trade in the Indies. This was hotly opposed by the British plenipotentiaries, and the Cardinal was obliged to yield the point in their favour.[28]

The Spanish reply of September 6 to the terms which this provisional treaty set forth was tantamount to a refusal, and at the same time the principal Spanish delegate, Bournonville, was recalled on the pretext of his sovereigns' desire to confer with him in person.[29] Since Spain refused her collaboration, the next device tried was to fix the terms of a treaty which would be satisfactory to the Emperor, if not to Spain. In this, Fleury's real object was, as always, to detach the Emperor from Spain.[30] Sinzendorff fell into this trap, and on September 29 sent to Vienna the project of a treaty, based substantially on those *Idées Générales*, as they had been called, which were discussed in August.[31] These Charles VI rejected, with a great show of refusing to sign any agreements without the cognizance of his ally Spain, his real

[28] Hop to Slingelandt, August 14, 1728 (Goslinga: *Slingelandt's Efforts towards European Peace*, p. 280).

[29] Baudrillart: *Philippe V et la cour de France*, III, p. 445. All through this period, Spain continued to irritate the French either by charging heavy indults or by impounding French goods; Fleury wrote a sharp letter to Brancas about this on Oct. 4, 1728 (*ibid.*, p. 450). George Lyttelton wrote to his father on October 16, 1729 (*Works*, III, p. 280): "though they [the trading part of this nation] are at present protected by good fleets, and much encouraged by the court, they are still very full of complaints: they are terribly exasperated against the court of Spain, for their frequent infractions of treaties of commerce, in detaining the effects of the galleons, and demanding extravagant indults of the proprietors; . . . ."

[30] Chauvelin to Broglie, French ambassador to Great Britain, Sept. 26, 1728 (Baudrillart: *Philippe V et la cour de France*, III, pp. 447-448).

[31] However, this change was made from the preceding project of August: the wording was altered so as to make the Dutch, indirectly, guarantors of the Quadruple Alliance, which they had not previously ratified. The Emperor attached great importance to this because the Quadruple Alliance called for neutral garrisons in the Italian duchies (C. Höfler: *Der Congress von Soissons, nach den Instructionen des kaiserlichen Cabinetes und den Berichten des kaiserl. Botschafters Stefan Grafen Kinsky*. Band I: *Die Instructionen und Berichte des Jahres 1729 enthaltend* [*Fontes rerum Austriacarum*, zweite Abtheilung, Band XXXII], [Vienna, 1871], pp. 112, 244, 289, 338-339).

reason being that no compensation was offered to him for the suppression of the Ostend Company; Sinzendorff was recalled, and for the moment the Vienna allies seemed to be united almost as closely, and to be as difficult to detach from each other, as they had ever been.

The breakdown of this attempt subjected the Cardinal to severe pressure from the British ministers, who were apprehensive, as usual, of what Parliament would say.[32] It was a particularly anxious period, for no word came officially from the Spanish court between September 1728 and March 1729. This delay on the part of Spain was chiefly due to intentional procrastination, but there had also been distractions which diverted attention from the affairs of the Congress. In November 1728, Philip V had become so excited at the prospect of becoming King of France, assuming that Louis XV would not recover from the smallpox which he contracted during that month, that he had forsaken those symptoms of mania which had characterized his conduct all through that year.[33] Nothing came of his schemes, which had merely the immediate effect of delaying the Spanish reply to the proposals of the other powers; but, in the long run, the incident served to show how preposterous it was for Spain, with a French monarch, to attempt to conduct a policy antagonistic to France. Another diversion had been the journey to the Portuguese border for the purpose of exchanging princesses there.[34] Not until February 1729, did the Spanish court become settled (at Seville), and not until then did Philip V manifest any

---

[32] The concern of the cabinet is proved by the entries in the journal of the Lord Chancellor (Lord King: "Notes of Domestic and Foreign Affairs during the last Years of the Reign of George I and the early Part of the Reign of George II," *Life of John Locke* [London, 1830, two vols.], II [separate pagination], pp. 68-71). Pulteney and Bolingbroke, meanwhile, were trying to excite public dissatisfaction with the Government's foreign policy (*The Craftsman* [collected edition], III, p. 246 [Oct. 5, 1728]; IV, pp. 1-9 [Nov. 23, 1728]; IV, pp. 30-40 [Dec. 14, 1728]; IV, pp. 47-51 [Dec. 21, 1728]; IV, pp. 57-87 [Jan. 4, 1728/9]).

[33] Baudrillart: *Philippe V et la cour de France*, III, pp. 415, 455-478.

[34] A Portuguese princess married Don Ferdinand, Prince of Asturias; she was exchanged for the Infanta, the princess whom the Duke of Bourbon had sent back to Spain in 1725, who now married the Prince of Brazil. The Spanish court subsequently settled in Seville in order to make it more difficult for Philip V to abdicate, which he constantly had the impulse to do.

disposition to resume the interrupted negotiations of the preceding year.

Meanwhile, the British were bringing the strongest possible pressure to bear upon France to take action against Spain. George II said in his speech to Parliament on January 21, O. S., 1728/9:

It is with no small Concern, that I am again obliged to speak to my Parliament in this State of Uncertainty, nor am I insensible of the Burthens which my Subjects bear, and that in our present Circumstances some may be induced to think, that an actual War is preferrable to such a doubtful and imperfect Peace.[35]

And he added, significantly, that "the Exchange is very easy to be made at any Time." British alarm was increased by Patiño's extensive prepaiations for an expeditionary force, which was ostensibly destined for the siege of Oran, although the British had information that it was secretly intended for an attack on Jamaica.[36] The pamphlet warfare continued, with the Opposition emphasizing the Spanish depredations in the Indies and making great sport of the provisional treaty, and the war fever mounted dangerously high.[37]

[35] *The Historical Register*, XIV (1729), p. 75. For British pressure on France (Baudrillart: *Philippe V et la cour de France*, III, pp. 495-497; Villars: *Mémoires*, V, pp. 164, 165).

[36] Basil Williams: "The Foreign Policy of England under Walpole." *E. H. R.*, XVI, p. 322. Keene had written to the Duke of Newcastle, Madrid, August 23, 1728: "Ever since I returned to this country, I observed with the greatest concern, the progress Patiño was making towards a powerful marine, and I have repeated it in most of the dispatches I have had the honour to write" (Coxe: *Memoirs of the Kings of Spain*, III, p. 284).

[37] Two important pamphlets were inspired by the Government at this time: [Benjamin Hoadly]: *A Defence of the Enquiry into the Reasons of the Conduct of Great Britain* (London, 1729); and *Observations on the Conduct of Great-Britain, with Regard to Negociations and other Transactions Abroad* (London, 1729), which particularly defended the provisional treaty (*ibid.*, pp. 40-54). An uninspired (double meaning intended) pamphlet which appeared at that time also defended the administration: *The Conduct of Queen Elizabeth, Towards the Neighbouring Nations; and particularly Spain; Compared with that of James I. In View of the late and present Behaviour of Great Britain. By Palaeophilus Anglicanus* (London, 1729). An Opposition pamphlet of the time was *Some Considerations on the National Debts* (London, 1729); another attacked the Observator for pointing out how the contraband trade was really conducted in Spanish waters: "His chief Design is to prove that our West-India Merchants in general, and those of Jamaica in particular, are no better than a vile Combination of Smuglers, Pyrates and

Spain's protracted silence and the clamorous impatience of the British forced the Cardinal, at last, to make honestly intended overtures to Vienna, although these subsequently came to nothing because Elisabeth Farnese herself finally broke the spell.[38] In March 1729, she had received from the Emperor a polite but really explicit refusal to marry Maria Theresa to Don Carlos.[39] This information was all that was necessary to determine the Queen of Spain to have done with the Austrian alliance; Spain now turned to the Hanover league for support in establishing the Spanish princes in Italy.

This change of attitude did not crystallize into an accomplished fact until November 9, 1729, when the Treaty of Seville was signed. Nevertheless, the change was implicit from March of that year, and this point may be taken as the beginning of the third stage of the negotiations covering the period between the opening of the Congress of Soissons and the conclusion of the Treaty of Seville. La Paz wrote to Fleury on March 29, 1729, making the continuance of negotiations dependent upon the consent of France and Great Britain to the introduction of Spanish garrisons into the Italian duchies.[40] By itself, this communication was unsatisfactory, for it gave no guarantee with reference to the settlement of trade grievances. Fleury, at the moment, was very irritated at the impounding of French "effects," and his first reply to the Spanish overtures was not very conciliatory.[41] However, by June 13 the principle that France and Great Britain would assist in obtaining Spanish garrisons

---

Thieves, who make it their Business to plunder the Spaniards, and carry on an illicit Trade, contrary to Treaties; . . . ." (*Some Farther Remarks on a late Pamphlet, intitled, Observations on the Conduct of Great Britain;* . . [London, 1729], p. 25).

[38] Baudrillart: *Philippe V et la cour de France,* III, p. 499.

[39] The treaty of November 9, 1725, had provided that Don Carlos and Don Philip should marry two of the Emperor's daughters. In the autumn of 1728 Charles VI's third and youngest daughter died. This event had precipitated mutual explanations.

[40] Baudrillart: *Philippe V et la cour de France,* III, pp. 501-503.

[41] Goslinga: *Slingelandt's Efforts towards European Peace,* p. 339; Baudrillart: *Philippe V et la cour de France,* III, p. 498. This irritation continued throughout the summer (Kinsky and Fonseca to Charles VI, July 6, 1729; the same to the same, Sept. 4, 1729 [Höfler: *Der Congress von Soissons,* I, pp. 25, 207]).

for the Italian duchies, provided satisfaction was made on other points, was established.[42] In July, the Spanish sovereigns gave the Emperor one last chance to preserve the Alliance of Vienna by asking him to consent to the introduction of the Spanish garrisons of his own free will.[43] His refusal signified the disruption of the Alliance of Vienna, and on July 30 the sovereigns of Spain submitted draft articles which at last showed a sincere disposition to effect a definite settlement.[44]

Up to the last moment, the British had threatened belligerent demonstrations against Spain, but the Spanish proposals of July 30, 1729 furnished the basis for a satisfactory accommodation and rendered unnecessary the sailing of the combined Anglo-Dutch fleet which was riding in the Downs.[45] These Spanish proposals caused the British to accept the principle for which Fleury had striven since September 1728, of making a treaty with only one of the Vienna powers, instead of holding out for a general settlement.[46] The temporary worsening of Great Britain's diplomatic position at that moment encouraged Brit-

[42] Baudrillart: *Philippe V et la cour de France*, III, p. 519.

[43] Königsegg wrote to Fonseca in June 1729, that "le tout consiste à voir comment on pourra contenter la Reine sur le point des Garnisons Espagnols en Toscane et Parme surquoy elle insiste inflexiblement" (Höfler: *Der Congress von Soissons*, I, p. 35).

[44] Baudrillart: *Philippe V et la cour de France*, III, pp. 525-529.

[45] Townshend and Chesterfield were the British statesmen who had desired the union of the fleets; according to Goslinga, they well knew that it would tend to clog action against Spain. Their object was to force the French and British governments to bring pressure to bear on the Emperor, instead (Goslinga: *Slingelandt's Efforts towards European Peace*, pp. 344-350). The combined fleets enumerated (Thomas Lediard: *The Naval History of England in all its Branches, from the Norman Conquest in the Year 1066 to the Conclusion of 1734* [London, 1735, two vols., continuous pagination], p. 913). The wags made great sport of *The Pacifick Fleet:*

So our wrath was provoked, and our rage was so great,
That a fleet was equipped, those proud Spaniards to beat,
And we sent for Dutch help in a violent heat.

(Sir Charles Firth, editor: *Naval Songs and Ballads.* [*Publications of the Navy Records Society*, XXXIII], pp. 170-171).

[46] Sir Richard Lodge points out that it was dangerous ground for the British to accept a treaty with only one of the Vienna powers, in lieu of a general settlement. Besides the other reasons, mentioned *infra*, Sir Richard thinks that their object in doing so was mainly because George II and Townshend thought it would be just as well to give Charles VI a lesson (Sir Richard Lodge: "The Treaty of Seville (1729)." *Transactions of the Royal Historical Society*, Fourth Series, XVI [1933], pp. 37-38).

ish ministers to adopt this policy, for they were distracted by
the Hanoverian quarrel of their King with Frederick William I,
whose agents had been a little over-zealous in their recruiting of
tall grenadiers in Hanoverian territory.[47] In consequence, earlier
British plans for a punitive expedition against Spain had to be
sacrificed to considerations for the safety of the Electorate.

French policy, on the contrary, had increased its influence
and prestige in Germany during that year, for the Elector Palatine, who had concluded in 1726 a treaty with Charles VI
which mutually guaranteed their successions, became alarmed
at the Emperor's concurrent negotiations with Prussia, which
meant that he was playing a double game with reference to the
Jülich-Berg inheritance.[48] Consequently, the Elector Palatine
concluded with Louis XV the Treaty of Marly (February 15,
1729), whereby the latter guaranteed the inheritance of Jülich
and Berg to the Sulzbach line. In return, the Electors of Bavaria
and the Palatinate agreed to remain neutral in the event of war
between France and the Empire, as well as to endeavour to persuade the Electors of Treves and Cologne to accede to the
treaty.[49] Thus, after a year's delay, the French brought about
a direct connection between their country and the Electoral
Union.[50]

Not only was the diplomatic situation taking a turn for the
better, but also at this time the dangerous question of the French
succession was laid to rest on September 4, 1729, by the Queen
of France's "being brought to bed of a Dolphin," as Horatio

---

[47] The recruiting incident occurred in June (Heinrich Schilling: *Der Zwist
Preussens und Hannovers, 1729-1730* [Halle, 1912], pp. 25-30); the greatest danger
of war was in August (*ibid.*, pp. 51-60); the crisis was settled, in principle, by a
convention of Sept. 6, 1729 (*ibid.*, pp. 100-101).

[48] The Austro-Prussian treaty of Wüsterhausen, Oct. 12, 1726, which had
marked Prussia's defection from the Alliance of Hanover, failed of ratification;
another treaty, which was ratified, was signed on Dec. 23, 1728. The Emperor
guaranteed Berg and Ravenstein to Prussia and Frederick William I guaranteed
the Pragmatic Sanction (Loewe: *Preussens Staatsverträge*, pp. 360-373).

[49] A detailed exposition of these negotiations may be found in Rosenlehner:
Kurfürst Karl Philipp von der Pfalz, pp. 385-468.

[50] In this year the French were eager for George II, as Elector of Hanover, to
join the Wittelsbach "Electoral Union," as then France could count on the disposition of five Electoral votes out of a total of nine. Chavigny went on a special
mission to Hanover for this purpose (Dureng: *Mission de Chavigny*, pp. 83-96).

Walpole somewhat inaccurately described it.[51] All things were tending towards a solution of the immediate diplomatic problem by means of an accommodation with Spain. On September 9 the plenipotentiaries of Great Britain, the United Provinces and France concerted their terms, which were discussed in the French Council of State on September 11, and on September 18 William Stanhope, soon to be rewarded with the title of Lord Harrington, was sent to Seville to expedite the signature of the treaty, which occurred on November 9.[52]

The most important stipulation of the Treaty of Seville was that Spanish garrisons should be introduced into Leghorn, Porto Ferrajo, Parma and Piacenza. British pretensions were safeguarded by articles which indirectly and implicitly guaranteed their possession of Gibraltar and their trading privileges in the Spanish Indies.[53] The British would have been better pleased had they been able to obtain from Spain a categorical confirmation of their rights, but here, significantly enough, the support of their French allies failed them.[54] Finally, commissioners appointed by the British and Spanish governments were to adjudi-

[51] *British Diplomatic Instructions: France, 1727-1744*, p. xvii. George Lyttelton wrote to his father, Sept. 8, 1729: "Sunday by four o'clock we had the good news of a dauphin, and since that time I have thought myself in Bedlam. . . . The king is as proud of what he has done, as if he had gained a kingdom, and tells every body that he sees, *qu'il sçaura bien faire des fils tant qu'il voudra*. . . . It is very late; and I have not slept this three nights for the squibs and crackers, and other noises that the people make in the streets; . . . ." (*Works*, III, pp. 258-259).

[52] Villars: *Mémoires*, V, pp. 194-195, 197; Baudrillart: *Philippe V et la cour de France*, III, pp. 532-535. The treaty is published by Dumont: *Corps universel diplomatique*, VIII, part ii, pp. 158-160; also by Guillaume de Lamberty: *Mémoires pour servir à l'histoire du XVIII siècle* [The Hague, 1724-1740, fourteen vols.], X, supplement, pp. 189-194.

[53] Articles ii and iii, and the first two separate articles.

[54] The British pretext for a specific confirmation of their privileges was that a state of war had existed between Spain and Great Britain in 1727, and that consequently all former treaties would have to be formally and specifically guaranteed in the new treaty; since war had not been *declared* in 1727 this view seems a dubious one. Chauvelin, in September 1729, had drawn up articles for the proposed treaty which dealt with the British rights in vague and ambiguous terms which greatly alarmed the British plenipotentiaries. Horatio Walpole managed to persuade the Cardinal to accept a different wording (Coxe: *Memoirs of Horatio, Lord Walpole*, I, pp. 299-303). Walpole claimed that the resignation of D'Huxelles from the Council of State was really caused by Fleury's having given in on this point (*ibid.*, pp. 303-304).

cate claims arising from the activities of Spanish *guarda costas* and British illicit traders in the Indies.[55]

The Treaty of Seville marks another important milestone in the history of French diplomacy during the administration of Cardinal Fleury. Through an extended and anxious period, he had restrained his allies from breaking the peace of Europe and had utilized every expedient in order to attain his ends, and to a lesser extent those of his allies, without being reduced to the necessity of engaging in armed conflict. Those ends had been to break up definitively the Alliance of Vienna of 1725, to associate Spain with the Hanover powers, and to prevent a revival of the Grand Alliance by thrusting Austria into the outer darkness of diplomatic isolation. The treaty of November 9, 1729 made it perfectly obvious that the alliance between Spain and the Emperor was broken off completely; no longer would France's security be jeopardized by the danger of a joint invasion on two frontiers. Even should it be impossible, at some future date, to prevent the *rapprochement* of the Emperor and the Maritime Powers, such a realignment, disturbing as it might be, would not be so dangerous for France as had been the situation in which the Duke of Bourbon had involved her in 1725, when she was exposed both to the schemes of the Emperor and the fury of the Termagant of Spain.

Although the negotiations during this period had brought about no modification of the trading privileges which the British abused so profitably, in other respects the increasing security of France permitted the French statesmen to take a more independent line with their British allies, whose support was becoming less indispensable day by day. This independence was increased, rather fortuitously, by the birth of the heir to the throne, the existence of whom, by assuring the orderly succession to the

---

[55] In this year the Parliamentary Opposition began to exploit Spanish "outrages"; it was a favourite theme from then until 1739. Cf. [Nicholas Amhurst]: *A Letter to Caleb d'Anvers, Esq.: Occasioned by the Depredations committed by the Spaniards in the West Indies* (London, 1729). Amhurst was the hack writer who edited the *Craftsman* for Bolingbroke and Pulteney: see *sub nomine* in *Dictionary of National Biography*.

French throne, increased the stability of Fleury's administration and of his foreign policy.

The diplomatic aims of the French statesmen during this anxious period had been clearly conceived; France had managed, on the whole, to play the part of a mediator and to thread her way, by means of a rather subtle policy, to a haven of substantial success. But, although the directors of French policy had perspicuously envisaged the ends to be achieved, they had often betrayed chronic perplexity concerning their choice of means. This uncertainty was clearly reflected in a series of *mémoires* composed by Chauvelin, which tend to cause one to conclude that the ultimate success of the French was assisted as much by good fortune as by skill. On December 31, 1728, he tried to determine what course to follow with Spain, since it was evident that no definitive treaty would result from the negotiations of the Congress of Soissons, but he was able to form no conclusion.[56] The same inability to formulate a conclusion was true of a second memorial by him, dated the same day; he mentioned the necessity of forming a party within the Empire favourable to France, and of keeping Sweden, Denmark and the King of Sardinia in good humour, but, far from being able to propose anything definite, he contented himself with saying:

It will be necessary to observe what resolution Vienna will take in relation to Spain and wait until then to come to a decision.[57]

On January 18, 1729, he advised concluding a treaty with Spain by which, in case of war, Don Carlos would receive the Two Sicilies and the King of Sardinia the Milanese.[58] This he thought was practicable, although he confessed he did not know the state of the relations between Austria and Spain at the moment, beyond feeling reasonably certain that their co-operation was not

[56] A. É., *Mém. et Doc., France*, vol. 494, ff. 212-229. There is no ascription to an author noted on this *mémoire*, but M. Vaucher believes it to have been written by Chauvelin (Vaucher: *Robert Walpole et la politique de Fleury*, p. 29); it was annotated by a hand which appears to be that of Fleury.
[57] *Sur les mésures à prendre en conséquence de la situation actuelle des affaires de l'Europe* (A. É., *Mém. et Doc., France*, vol. 494, f. 241).
[58] A. É., *Mém. et Doc., France*, vol. 494, ff. 249-261.

smooth. The war which would probably result would no less probably be successful:

We shall gain thereby a considerable diminution of the Austrian power, which is certainly equivalent to our personal aggrandizement, since we shall become more important as a result of it.[59]

But in a memorial dated March 19, 1729, written by Pecquet and annotated by Chauvelin, the attitude of hesitation and procrastination was resumed.[60] His memorial showed the results of the British pressure to declare war on Spain. But supposing, he declared, that such a war should take place, England would thereby be able to extend her commerce and her maritime supremacy. Such a war,

while exhausting us can produce utility only for a nation whom she [France] has always rightly regarded as her rival in relation to trade.[61]

If war did come, the French should put some warships of their own into action, and not leave to the British all the advantages to be derived from a successful naval campaign.[62] In the meanwhile, the French should avoid doing anything at all, a policy which would be at once inconvenient for Great Britain and safe for France.

Succeeding memorials struck this same note of caution and uncertainty. One dated April 15, 1729, of which Chauvelin was the author, feared lest the Queen of Spain "should ask us to undertake engagements which we could not well adopt," and advised, instead, that negotiations be opened with the Emperor.[63] Another, dated April 28, again summarized the reasons why the British wanted to force action; but, although Chauvelin admitted the desirability of doing something, he advised that it was best

---

[59] A. É., *Mém. et Doc., France*, vol. 494, f. 259. This is characteristic Chauvelin doctrine. He also speaks in this *mémoire* of the necessity, in case of war, of detaching an army corps for the protection of Hanover, which shows how aware the French were of its vulnerability.

[60] *Mémoire sur les partis à prendre* (A. É., *Mém. et Doc., France*, vol. 494, ff. 277-289).

[61] A. É., *Mém. et Doc., France*, vol. 494, f. 282.

[62] A. É., *Mém. et Doc., France*, vol. 494, f. 285.

[63] A. É., *Mém. et Doc., France*, vol. 494, ff. 290-302.

merely to watch the trend of events.[64] Likewise, in a memorial dated April 29, 1729, he complained that the British wanted to take action without having first concerted definite plans. It is evident that he was very apprehensive lest Great Britain should involve France in disastrous adventures; he concluded, lamely, that something should be done, although he obviously had no plan of his own to offer.[65]

On May 28, 1729, Chauvelin contemplated a war against Spain, which should, he thought, be a maritime war in which the French should participate; but in a memorial dated merely June 1729, he manifested extreme distrust of the British.[66] His irritation with them reached its highest pitch in a memorial dated July 8, 1729, in which he remarked:

No article [of our alliance] gives to any one of the allies such a superiority as the English seem to arrogate to themselves.[67]

He emphasized how ruinous for the French would be a war against Spain, although "the English, on the contrary, would become by it the sole trading people of Europe."[68] And he concluded his memorial in these words:

At the same time nothing is more indispensably necessary than not to permit the English any longer to flatter themselves with the expectation of gaining us over to everything they wish.[69]

These memorials show clearly enough that France's policy had been one of patient obstruction, a policy which, in spite of its passiveness, was none the less accompanied by perplexity and anxiety, and a concomitant irritation with the exacting attitude of a masterful ally. But, though the Anglo-French alliance was

---

[64] *Mémoire sur les partis à prendre en conséquence des instances de l'Espagne et des Anglois* (A. É., *Mém. et Doc., France*, vol. 501, ff. 1-11).

[65] A. É., *Mém. et Doc., France*, vol. 501, ff. 12-22.

[66] A. É., *Mém. et Doc., France*, vol. 501, ff. 23-34, esp. ff. 29, 32. Memorial dated June 1729 (*Sur les instances que faisaient les Anglois pour faire déclarer la guerre à l'Espagne* [A. É., *Mém. et Doc., France*, vol. 501, ff. 34-60]). "Si une fois les Anglois nous font faire le premier pas pour lequel ils nous sollicitent, ils seront en état de nous mener dans la suite à tout ce qu'ils voudront" (*ibid.*, f. 39).

[67] A. É., *Mém. et Doc., France*, vol. 501, f. 66.

[68] A. É., *Mém. et Doc., France*, vol. 501, f. 74.

[69] A. É., *Mém. et Doc., France*, vol. 501, f. 74.

wearing thin, the period of the Congress of Soissons, like an old-fashioned melodrama, "came out all right in the end." It is only upon reflection that one suspects that (like many a piece on the boards) the *dénouement* resulted as much from the happy ministrations of beneficent fortune as from the stern logic of inner necessity.

Yet the diplomatic problems of Europe were by no means entirely solved by the signature of the Treaty of Seville. The introduction of Spanish garrisons into the Italian duchies involved a breach of the Treaty of London of August 2, 1718, and on that point it was to be expected that the Emperor would have something to say. How would it be possible for the allies to gain his consent without either declaring war upon him or else recognizing his Pragmatic Sanction? This was the dilemma which confronted the French statesmen in the ensuing months.

CHAPTER VII

THE SECOND TREATY OF VIENNA, 1731, AND THE DIPLOMATIC ISOLATION OF FRANCE

ALTHOUGH the Treaty of Seville marked the definite disruption of the Austro-Spanish alliance, it by no means solved the diplomatic problems of France and Great Britain. As Chauvelin had foreseen, Elisabeth Farnese was clamorous for the immediate introduction of the Spanish garrisons into the Italian duchies.[1] According to the treaty, four months was allowed in which to secure the consent of the Emperor and the Grand Duke of Tuscany; then, if this consent should not be forthcoming, force was to be used. In any event, the garrisons were to be introduced not later than May 9, six months from the signature of the Treaty of Seville. But the Emperor, for his part, took refuge in strict legality and refused to consent to this infraction of the Quadruple Alliance.[2] It was clear from the beginning that his consent would have to be either bought or forced.[3]

It was only with reluctance that the allies squarely faced this fact. The British took the disingenuous attitude that the substitution of Spanish for Swiss garrisons was a matter of very little consequence, to which the Emperor could have no reasonable objection.[4] Inasmuch as the Emperor continued to express

---

[1] Baudrillart: *Philippe V et la cour de France*, III, pp. 547-549.

[2] This was the Emperor's attitude throughout; see the *Mémoire instructif* to Kinsky and Fonseca, Aug. 31, 1729 (Höfler: *Der Congress von Soissons*, I, pp. 182-190). Also Villars: *Mémoires*, V, p. 199.

[3] In December 1729, six thousand Imperial troops were moved into Tuscany (Villars: *Mémoires*, V, p. 201). Later there was further concentration of Imperial troops in Italy (*ibid.*, V, pp. 202, 204-205, 210, 212, 215-216).

[4] Townshend to Horatio Walpole and Stephen Poyntz, Dec. 2, O. S., 1729 (*British Diplomatic Instructions: France, 1727-1744*, p. 61). What reason had the Emperor to object to the substitution of the worst troops in Europe (the Spanish) for the best (the Swiss), asked the anonymous author of *Some Observations on the Present State of Affairs* (London, 1731), p. 22. The juridical question was very

his opposition to the Treaty of Seville in no uncertain terms, it became necessary to continue the subsidies to German princes for the purpose of defending the Electorate of Hanover, which gave the Opposition an opportunity to ask

what Advantage we may expect to reap from the Situation of our Country, as an Island.[5]

It was altogether likely that the Emperor's consent could be purchased by a recognition of the Pragmatic Sanction, for prior to the Treaty of Seville he had offered very considerable concessions to France and the Maritime Powers in return for such a guarantee. But France was entirely opposed to such a recognition, especially as a guarantee of the inheritance of the Emperor's undivided dominions to his successor would preclude, in strict logic, any attack on those dominions during his life time.[6]

ably argued in a pro-Administration pamphlet (*The Pretensions of Don Carlos Considered: With a View to the Treaty of Seville, and the Nature of Feudal Tenures* (London, 1730). The Parliamentary Opposition complained that the Treaty of Seville was really an offensive treaty against the Emperor (*The Observations on the Treaty of Seville Examined* [London, 1730], pp. 14-17). Another effective Opposition pamphlet was that attributed to Pulteney (*A Short View of the State of Affairs, with Relation to Great Britain, for four Years past; with some Remarks on the Treaty lately Published* [London, 1730]).

[5] *The Observations on the Treaty of Seville Examined*, p. 9. The same sentiment was expressed in *The Case of the Hessian Forces, in the Pay of Great-Britain, Impartially and Freely Examin'd; With some Reflections on the present Conjuncture of Affairs* (London, n.d.), pp. 11, 35. There was also strong mercantilist feeling against sending money out of the country to pay foreign troops (*ibid.*, p. 22). The Ministerial writers denied that any favouritism was being shown Hanover ([Sir Robert Walpole]: *Observations upon the Treaty between the Crowns of Great-Britain, France, and Spain, Concluded at Seville. . . .* [London, 1729], pp. 23-24; *The Treaty of Seville, and the Measures that have been taken for the Four Last Years, Impartially Considered* [London, 1730], pp. 28-29; *Considerations on the Present State of Affairs in Europe, and particularly with Regard to the Number of Forces in the Pay of Great-Britain* [London, 1730], pp. 49-50; *A Defence of the Measures of the Present Administration* [London, 1731], pp. 23-24). Lord Hervey wrote a skilful pamphlet in defense of the policy of Walpole's government ([Lord Hervey]: *Observations on the Writings of the Craftsman* [London, 1730]). A pamphlet sympathetic to the administration, but not well informed, which appeared at this time is that by Thomas English: *The Crisis; or, Impartial Judgment upon Publick Affairs* (Second edition, London, 1731).

[6] For the Emperor's offers with reference to the Pragmatic Sanction, see the Imperial Rescript to Fonseca and Kinsky, dated Aug. 31, 1729 (Höfler: *Der Congress von Soissons*, I, pp. 117-130). They were decisively refused on Nov. 3, 1728 (*ibid.*, pp. 324-328, 350-351). For France's opposition to guaranteeing the Pragmatic Sanction (Horatio Walpole to Stephen Poyntz, Nov. 4, 1729 [Coxe: *Memoirs of . . . Sir Robert Walpole*, II, p. 662]).

Nor were the British in favour of guaranteeing the Pragmatic Sanction at that moment; Lord Townshend's influence still counted for a great deal, and it was feared that recognition would increase the Emperor's power in the Empire at the same time that it would disoblige the court of Spain.[7]

Nevertheless, both French and British were willing to make a slight concession by offering to guarantee the undivided inheritance of the Emperor's *Italian* dominions in return for his consent to the introduction of the Spanish garrisons. Such a guarantee would have the added advantage of nullifying the plans which Elisabeth Farnese might be cherishing for a further change in the Italian balance over and beyond the succession of Don Carlos in Parma, Piacenza and Tuscany. This ingenious scheme suggested itself independently, first to the British, and then to the French. With some confusion, the two allies discovered that they were mutually detected in separate negotiations with Vienna; however, on May 26, 1730, Fleury proposed this solution to the Austrian representatives in the name of all the allies. The Emperor refused it in July.[8]

Although neither France nor Great Britain desired to recognize the Pragmatic Sanction, they were not, on the other hand, willing to adopt forcible measures. The result was that each tried to retain the good will of Spain by throwing the responsibility for inaction on the other. Throughout the year the French complained that the British were not willing to provide their fair share of soldiers and subsidies; the British, on the other hand, were annoyed at Chauvelin's favourite project of attacking the Austrian Netherlands, which could have little coercive effect on

[7] Townshend to H. Walpole and Poyntz, Dec. 2, O. S., 1729 (*British Diplomatic Instructions: France, 1727-1744*, p. 60). Townshend was greatly in favour of George II's joining the Wittelsbach "Electoral Union," to which the Walpoles were opposed (H. Walpole to Poyntz, Nov. 4, 1729 [Coxe: *Memoirs of . . . Sir Robert Walpole*, II, pp. 659-660, 663-664]).

[8] Newcastle wrote to Harrington and Poyntz of this scheme, March 24, O. S., 1730 (Coxe: *Memoirs of . . . Sir Robert Walpole*, II, p. 682). For Fleury's communication to the Austrian plenipotentiaries of the project of May 26, see Fonseca and Kinsky to Charles VI, June 1, 1730 (Höfler: *Der Congress von Soissons*, II: *Die Instructionen und Berichte der kaiserlichen Botschafter in Paris vom 2. Jänner 1730, bis zum 6. März 1732* [*Fontes rerum Austriacarum*, zweite Abtheilung, Band XXXVIII], [Vienna, 1876], pp. 188-193).

the Emperor as far as the Italian situation was concerned and was designed, it was thought, merely to throw the onus for refusing a definite plan of action upon the shoulders of the British and the Dutch.[9] March 9, the last day allowed by the Treaty of Seville for securing the amicable consent of the Emperor and the Grand Duke of Tuscany, came and went with those potentates emphatic in their refusal and with the allies entirely undecided on what measures to pursue. Conferences were held to such purpose that the Spanish ambassador at last asserted: "You only desire to trifle with us and make us lose the campaign."[10] On May 5 the allies adopted, in principle, the British suggestion that an attack on Sicily would be best, but May 9, the extreme limit fixed by the Treaty of Seville for the introduction of the Spanish garrisons, passed by without definite plans formulated.[11]

In a conference held on May 11, the Dutch and British representatives admitted that they did not believe that the garrisons could be introduced without a general war.[12] This gave the French reason for saying, and this was a point on which they insisted for the rest of the year, that no offensive action should be taken until a general treaty of *equilibrium* (it would be called "war aims" now) should first be worked out. For this point of view they had the justification of the sixth separate and secret article of the Treaty of Seville, which provided that if recourse to arms should be necessary, a treaty should be made to regulate the establishment of a just equilibrium in Europe.[13] The British

[9] Vaucher: *Robert Walpole et la politique de Fleury*, p. 33. British opposition to a campaign in Flanders (Newcastle to Harrington and Poyntz, March 24, O. S., 1730 [Coxe: *Memoirs of . . Sir Robert Walpole*, II, p. 680]; same to the same, April 14, O. S., 1730 [*British Diplomatic Instructions: France, 1727-1744*, pp. 75-76]).

[10] April 20, 1730 (Villars: *Mémoires*, V, p. 232).

[11] Newcastle to Harrington and Poyntz, April 23, O. S., 1730 (*British Diplomatic Instructions: France, 1727-1744*, pp. 76-77). These futile negotiations are set forth in Baudrillart: *Philippe V et la cour de France*, IV, pp. 21-36; Villars: *Mémoires*, V, *passim*.

[12] Villars: *Mémoires*, V, pp. 237-239; Baudrillart: *Philippe V et la cour de France*, IV, pp. 36-37.

[13] Cantillo: *Tratados*, p. 254.

were disgusted at the French insistence on this point, which they attributed to the chicanery of Chauvelin:

But the ingenious monsieur Chauvelin is fond of this word *equilibre*, without any vast views of conquests for France, or settling a new partition or ballance of power in Europe; but as, being subject to so many senses and interpretations, and made a previous condition to all action, may serve, if he pleases, to prevent any action at all; while at the same time he talks loudly to the Spanyards of his resolution to act with vigour, when an honourable plan can be fixed for that purpose.[14]

While the general trend of the negotiations makes it seem probable that the Cardinal was glad of this excuse for inaction, it seems no less probable that Walpole did Chauvelin less than justice on this point. To regulate the Italian balance so as to increase French and diminish Austrian influence in the Italian peninsula was a fundamental part of his policy, for which careful preparation had to be made, especially since Elisabeth Farnese desired "nothing less than the conquest of all Italy for her children," as Horatio Walpole himself admitted.[15] At all events, discussions on the general treaty, and especially the accession to it of the new King of Sardinia, were protracted to such an extent that it became impractical, in that deliberate age, to contemplate any military measures for the remainder of that year.[16]

During the course of these debates, a very considerable rearrangement of offices took place in the British Cabinet. Relations between Sir Robert Walpole and his brother-in-law, Lord

[14] H. Walpole to Sir Robert, Aug. 2, 1730 (Coxe: *Memoirs of . . . Sir Robert Walpole*, III, p. 11).

[15] Coxe: *Memoirs of . . . Sir Robert Walpole*, III, p. 10. For Chauvelin's Italian policy (Édouard Driault: "Chauvelin, 1733-1737: Son rôle dans l'histoire de la réunion de la Lorraine à la France." *Revue d'histoire diplomatique*, VII [1893], pp. 33-34). Chavigny, who was a strong supporter of Chauvelin's ideas, reflected his chief's policy when, in a memorial composed in May 1738, he wrote that "notre intérêt véritable seroit d'établir en Italie un équilibre qui pût assurer avec son repos celuy de toute la Chrétienneté" (*Mémoire de M. Chavigny contenant quelques observations sur les anecdotes les plus importantes qu'il a recueillies dans les différentes négociations qui lui ont été confiées depuis 1712 jusques au mois de May 1738* [A. É., *Mém. et Doc., France*, vol. 457, f. 54]).

[16] On September 3, 1730, Victor Amadeus abdicated in favour of his son, Charles Emmanuel. For French and British desire to include Sardinia in a general treaty (Coxe: *Memoirs of . . . Sir Robert Walpole*, III, p. 16; *British Diplomatic Instructions: France, 1727-1744*, pp. 81, 85, 87, 88-89, 94).

Townshend, became very strained in November 1729, and early
in 1730 Townshend made known his intention to resign as soon
as Parliament should rise, an intention which he made good on
May 15.[17] Lord Harrington, formerly William Stanhope, cousin
of the late Lord Stanhope and of Lord Chesterfield, took Townshend's place as Secretary of State; Horatio Walpole resigned as
ambassador to France in order to become cofferer of the royal
household.[18] Lord Waldegrave was transferred from Vienna to
Paris, where he had formerly been *chargé d'affaires* under Horatio
Walpole, and Thomas Robinson (later Lord Grantham) became
ambassador at Vienna. The results of these changes were that
Walpole secured a cabinet more docile to his will in foreign
affairs, and that British policy, because of Walpole's management, became less Hanoverian and more sympathetic to a *rapprochement* with the Emperor.[19] For, although Walpole had
stoutly defended in public Townshend's German policy, he knew
well enough how unpopular were the Hanoverian connection and
the German subsidies. He knew, too, that if Spain were not
satisfied in the matter of the Italian duchies, she might repudiate
the Treaty of Seville and thereby jeopardize both the interests
of British traders and the life of his own ministry. In order to
obviate this, Sir Robert turned to the idea of guaranteeing the
Pragmatic Sanction in its entirety, in return for the total suppression of the Ostend Company and the Emperor's consent to
the introduction of the Spanish garrisons. By adopting this
policy, he took the initiative in destroying what remained of
the cordiality of the Anglo-French alliance, and accepted the

[17] Horatio Walpole wrote of the impending resignation to Stephen Poyntz so
early as Jan. 21, O. S., 1729/1730 (Coxe: *Memoirs of . . . Sir Robert Walpole*, II,
p. 667).

[18] The office was a sinecure; in reality, Walpole was kept on hand as an adviser in foreign affairs. Besides, he sincerely desired to retire from Paris because
of his declining credit at the French court (Horatio Walpole to Sir Robert, July
23, 1730 [Coxe: *Memoirs of . . . Sir Robert Walpole*, III, p. 8]).

[19] Lord Townshend made a great show of his zeal for the protection of Hanoverian interests: "His lordship has represented us, as giving up Hanover quite"
(Newcastle to Harrington, March 24, O. S., 1729/30 [Coxe: *Memoirs of . . . Sir
Robert Walpole*, II, p. 678]). "Hanover is lord Townshend's great merit, and we
have been all represented as wanting *zeal*" (the same to the same, April 23, O. S.,
1730 [*ibid.*, p. 689]).

responsibility of obtaining for Hanover by negotiation what Townshend had promised to secure by the use of force.[20]

Sir Robert's decision was prompted by the fact that the British were really eager to effect the establishment of the Spanish garrisons.[21] Consequently they were very really annoyed at what they regarded as the evasions and the procrastination of the French. In recommending his change of policy, Sir Robert Walpole wrote:

If there was the least prospect of their [the French] acting a better part another year, the inconveniencies of this year's delay would be more tolerable.—But I take it for granted, that the same or some other difficulties in another shape, will arise another year.[22]

A study of the situation in 1730 makes one feel confident that the French attitude was not entirely inspired by the spirit of chicane, as the British supposed. It is manifest that the French interests were being safeguarded merely by the postponement of recourse to force and the protraction of peace, and that, consequently, Fleury and Chauvelin were not particularly disposed to force the issue. But transcending this programme of simple obstruction was the further need of making adequate diplomatic preparation for the waging and the *settlement* of that general war which the British themselves admitted would break out if force were brought to bear upon the Emperor. To the British way of thinking, the introduction of the Spanish garrisons was simply an item of necessary business, which should be accomplished as quickly as possible; they had no conception of it as part of a co-ordinated and articulated policy, as Chauvelin re-

[20] The letter of Horatio Walpole to Sir Robert on Sept. 1, 1730, shows that the latter had determined on this change of policy by that time (Coxe: *Memoirs of . . . Sir Robert Walpole*, III, p. 27). Harrington's instructions to Robinson to negotiate the treaty are dated September 14, O. S., 1730 (*ibid.*, III, pp. 33-39). Waldegrave was informed by Newcastle that the negotiation was going on, on Nov. 30, O. S., 1730 (*British Diplomatic Instructions: France, 1727-1744*, pp. 92-93). The Government-inspired pamphlet *Considerations on the Present State of Affairs in Europe* (1730) twice hints that the British Government intended guaranteeing the Pragmatic Sanction (pp. 37, 46).

[21] Cf. Newcastle's despatches to H. Walpole, Poyntz and Waldegrave for this year (*British Diplomatic Instructions: France, 1727-1744*, pp. 71 sqq.).

[22] Undated (Coxe: *Memoirs of . . . Sir Robert Walpole*, III, p. 23).

garded it, and consequently they regarded Chauvelin's talk of the *équilibre* as pure sham.

But if the British had little insight into the diplomatic difficulties of the French, these latter erred in their understanding of the Parliamentary necessities of the former. During this period, when the diplomatic situation in Europe was so unsettled, the British had to pay subsidies to allies and maintain fleets on a war footing. This state of affairs, if continued too long, would endanger the Ministry and impair the popularity of the dynasty; already the Opposition was making the best of its opportunities, and there was a very real necessity for the British government to settle European affairs definitively. For the French, on the other hand, the army expenses during this period of uncertainty hardly differed from the ordinary expenditure in times of complete peace; France's security perpetually demanded the maintenance of a large standing army. It may be doubted, therefore, whether Fleury felt the financial urgency of making a European settlement quickly, as did the British, or had an adequate realization of the problems which beset a minister responsible to a captious House.

At all events, Sir Robert Walpole came to the decision in 1730, that the British connection with France had outlived its utility:

But one conclusion may be drawn from what we see, and every day feel, that, as far as monsieur Chauvelyn can influence, we are to expect but little, and depend upon lesse, from the friendship of France, or any prospect of a future confidence or good understanding betwixt us.[23]

The resultant change in British foreign policy seems a simple and natural one because of our knowledge that it was successfully accomplished. In reality, it was an extremely risky thing to do, because it was by no means certain that an agreement could be reached with the Emperor on Hanoverian issues, such as the investitures of Bremen and Verden, and compensation to George II for his expenses incurred as "conservator" of Mecklenburg. Horatio Walpole was totally opposed to this new departure in British policy, because, if it failed, Great Britain would be placed

---

[23] Sir Robert to Horatio Walpole, Aug. 28, O. S., 1730 (Coxe: *Memoirs of . . . Sir Robert Walpole*, III, p. 26).

in a very real and humiliating dependence upon France.[24] On this point Lord Chesterfield wrote to Harrington on December 26, 1730:

> I heartily wish this Affair may succeed, for if it does not I think we shall be in a very bad condition; . . . And if the Emp[r] is obstinate enough to reduce us to return to France, after this Jealousy, we shall be oblig'd to give them fatall pledges of our future fidelity.[25]

Sir Robert was really making a rather desperate gamble; even if he won and thereby placed France in diplomatic isolation at the same time that Spain was satisfied, he was voluntarily relinquishing British control of French policy and consequently was facilitating the ultimate conclusion of a Bourbon family compact; if he lost, there would be nothing left but to renew the French connection on France's own terms, or else consent to remain in a condition of awkward and inconvenient diplomatic isolation.

However, by the first of January, 1731, the die had been cast. The urgency of closing with the Emperor was increased in January by the fact that the French got wind of the negotiations, as also by the fact that the Spanish ambassador to France, the Marquis of Castelar, solemnly announced Spain's repudiation of the Treaty of Seville (January 28).[26] But, in spite of British impatience, the Imperial court proceeded with its usual deliberation, and, finally, a conclusion could be reached only at the cost of a complete postponement of all of the Hanoverian pretensions.[27]

[24] See his letters to Sir Robert, July 23, August 16 (two), Sept. 1 and 10, 1730 (Coxe: *Memoirs of . . . Sir Robert Walpole*, III, pp. 7, 15-20, 20-21, 27-28, 30-31).

[25] Weston Papers, *Hist. MSS. Comm.*, *Report* X, App. Part I, p. 245. See also his letters to the same, Dec. 19, 1730; Jan. 16, 1731; Feb. 14, 16, 1731 (*ibid.*, pp. 244-248). Also, his letters to the same, dated Sept. 19, 1730 and Feb. 27, 1731 (Coxe: *Memoirs of . . . Sir Robert Walpole*, III, pp. 32-33, 94).

[26] This event happened so *mal à propos* for the British that they ascribed it to the influence of Chauvelin (*British Diplomatic Instructions: France, 1727-1744*, p. 97).

[27] As Robinson pompously phrased it in his letter to Chesterfield, April 7, 1731: "I as boldly suspended his majesty's electoral affairs for the sake of Europe" (Coxe: *Memoirs of . . . Sir Robert Walpole*, III, p. 114); Harrington's instructions for him to do so (*ibid.*, pp. 83-87); see his letters to Harrington of Jan. 16 and March 18, 1731, recounting the trouble he experienced with the Austrians in trying to negotiate Hanoverian points (*ibid.*, pp. 48-77, 94-98).

This sacrifice constituted an example of the great influence which Sir Robert Walpole was able to exert over his King and Queen; it also illustrates the inconsistency of the policy of what Mr. Wickham Legg has called "the amateur, pacific and essentially opportunist ministry of Britain."[28] For, ever since 1717, the British had emphasized to their French allies the necessity of protecting the interests of the Electorate. For that purpose the French had been forced to pay out subsidies to the Danes, and the Swedes had been invited to join the Alliance of Hanover. The Hanoverian quarrels of George I had prevented the formation of a triple alliance of Russia, France and Great Britain, and the necessity of providing for the protection of Hanover had fixed the character of the plans for military action which had been concerted in 1727. It had been the interests of Hanover which had caused the British to be so opposed to discussing an equivalent for the Duke of Holstein-Gottorp at the Congress of Soissons; the Mecklenburg question, still pending in 1731, had caused the British to be extremely solicitous for protection against the designs of Austria and Prussia, a fact which had gone far to fix the character of Fleury's and Chauvelin's policy with reference to Germany. In 1729, George II, as the result of his quarrel with Frederick William I about the recruiting of soldiers, had been in a panic for the safety of Hanover, and the British statesmen had called on France for military assistance.[29] In order to safeguard his Electoral interests George II, both as Elector and as King of Great Britain, had contemplated allying himself with the Wittelsbach "Electoral Union" in 1730, and throughout this whole period he had regarded himself as particularly aggrieved because of the Emperor's steadfast refusal to grant him the investiture of the bishoprics of Bremen and Verden.

---

[28] *British Diplomatic Instructions: France, 1727-1744*, p. x. Droysen, as Sir A. W. Ward noted, alluded to this negotiation as an illustration of "the 'parliamentary' style of foreign policy characteristic of Walpole—a policy which provides for the day and the morrow, and leaves the day after to take care of itself" (*Cambridge History of British Foreign Policy*, I, p. 83).

[29] Townshend to the plenipotentiaries, Göhrde, August 23, 1729 (*British Diplomatic Instructions: France, 1727-1744*, p. 59).

The answer to the question whether the French ministers ought not to have foreseen and guarded against the separate negotiations of the British may be found in a consideration of this question of Hanover. While it was certain that the Emperor would consent to the introduction of the Spanish garrisons in return for a general guarantee of the Pragmatic Sanction, his previous policy gave the French every reason to suppose that he would not, in addition, give satisfaction to the Hanoverians on their several points of difference with him; and having heard for several years the constant reiteration of the British that the Emperor was exercising "despotick power" in Germany, they had still less reason to believe that the British would give their valuable guarantee without securing a settlement of the Hanoverian pretensions of their King. This was an *impasse* which could safely be counted upon, to all appearances; but, with an inconsistency worthy of Elisabeth Farnese herself, the British took the initiative in breaking up a long-standing alliance with France, and concluded, instead, a treaty in which the Hanoverian claims were entirely disregarded.[30]

There is no doubt that Fleury and Chauvelin were taken by surprise, and most disagreeably so, by this sudden turn of affairs, which left France in uncomfortable isolation until, in 1733, advantage was taken of the opening of the question of the Polish succession. Essentially the French policy in 1730 had been similar to that of the preceding years of Fleury's administration. It had been characterized by a stubborn repugnance to have recourse to arms, an unabated faith in the efficacy of negotiation, and a continued progress towards the goal of regaining French diplomatic equality. This policy apparently had been so successful that it seemed no European settlement could be made without the participation of France: indeed, in a negative sort of way, the French monarchy had become something of an arbiter of European relations, a fact which shows how greatly the diplo-

---

[30] It is surprising that no account of this sacrifice of Hanoverian interests is taken by Sir A. W. Ward: *Great Britain and Hanover* (Oxford, 1899). It is noticed and commented upon by Sir Richard Lodge: *Great Britain and Prussia in the Eighteenth Century* (Oxford, 1923), p. 23.

matic status of France had changed since Fleury had taken charge of affairs. The growing independence of France had naturally been a source of irritation to the British, and Franco-British relations had become progressively less cordial. For example, the question of Dunkirk had come very much to the fore, and there had been some acrimonious discussion, later amicably settled, about the ownership of Santa Lucia.[31] The French, who had customarily received permission to recruit for their Irish regiments in Ireland, had been irritated by the refusal of that permission in November of 1730.[32] But in spite of this growing friction between allies, the diplomatic situation did not seem to be favourable to any new and unexpected alignment: little was to be feared from the discontent of the Queen of Spain, for, as Horatio Walpole remarked:

By what I can learn matters seem to be upon too desperate and angry terms between the emperour and the king of Spain, to expect a reconciliation in that quarter.[33]

Consequently, were only a common diplomatic front against Spain maintained, that power might very possibly be as disobliging as it dared to be, but could scarcely be dangerously so. As for Great Britain, a reconciliation with the Emperor had

[31] For Dunkirk negotiations during this year (Coxe: *Memoirs of . . . Sir Robert Walpole*, III, pp. 2, 6, 14-15, 19-20, 24, 26, 29-30). A history of the dispute over Santa Lucia during 1722-1723 may be found in the *Calendar of State Papers, Colonial Series: America and West Indies, 1722-1723* (London, 1934), pp. xliii-xlv, 14-15, 59-60, 201-205, 231-234, 428-429. An account of the whole controversy is given by Malachy Postlethwayt: *The Universal Dictionary of Trade and Commerce* (Second edition, London, 1757, two vols.), I, pp. 378-379, with copies of Newcastle's letter to Henry Worseley, Governor of Barbados, Nov. 30, 1730, and Louis XV's to Champigny, Governor of Martinique, Dec. 26, 1730, containing orders to evacuate the island, inasmuch as it had been neutralized. The Opposition had tried to embarrass the Government by making Santa Lucia the subject of a debate (Coxe: *op. cit.*, II, pp. 670-671, 673, 676; Leadam: *History of England (1702-1760)*, p. 339). Numerous references to Santa Lucia for the years 1729 and 1730 may be found in the *Journal of the Commissioners for Trade and Plantations, January 1728-9 to December 1734, passim, v. sub* index.

[32] Lord King: "Notes of Domestic and Foreign Affairs." *Life of John Locke*, II (separate pagination), pp. 115-118. *The Craftsman Extraordinary*, Wednesday, November 18, 1730, endeavoured to arouse public opinion against the Ministry for permitting these Irish enlistments.

[33] Horatio to Sir Robert Walpole, Aug. 2, 1730 (Coxe: *Memoirs of . . . Sir Robert Walpole*, III, p. 12).

every appearance of being improbable because the Hanoverian issues seemed insuperable. Perhaps, too, Fleury and Chauvelin had relied to some extent on the sincerity of the British insistence

that the first and unalterable maxim and principle, upon which His Majesty will always regulate his sentiments and his actions, is that which the Cardinal himself laid down as a foundation, of preserving inviolably a strict and indissoluble union and harmony among the Allys; which has hitherto been the means of conducting our affairs, with so much honour and success, to the prosperous condition in which they are at present, and of making so great a progress towards the establishing of an universal and durable peace and tranquillity. . . . [34]

Moreover, Horatio Walpole had asserted categorically that the resignation of Lord Townshend would make no difference in the foreign policy of Great Britain.[35] Finally, granted that the Emperor would be willing to countenance the Spanish garrisons in the Italian duchies in return for a general guarantee of the Pragmatic Sanction, what reason had the French to suppose that the Emperor would consent to the satisfaction of Hanoverian pretensions at the instance of Great Britain alone, when the united efforts of France and Great Britain had not been able to move him? And what reason had they to suppose that the British would permit themselves to accept anything short of a satisfaction of those claims? In short, it seems that Fleury and Chauvelin had reasonable justification for their presumption that no measures would be taken for the settlement of Europe without their participation.

By December 30, 1730, the French were aware of the British negotiation with the Emperor.[36] In order to counteract its ef-

[34] Townshend to H. Walpole and Poyntz, Dec. 2, O. S., 1729 (*British Diplomatic Instructions: France, 1727-1744*, pp. 61-62).
[35] Horatio to Sir Robert Walpole, July 7 and Aug. 2, 1730 (Coxe: *Memoirs of . . . Sir Robert Walpole*, III, pp. 6, 14).
[36] The British negotiation became public as the result of a news-letter purporting to come from The Hague, published in the *Craftsman* on Jan. 16, 1731, for which indiscretion the Government prosecuted its publisher, R. Francklin. This letter is not printed in the collected edition of the *Craftsman*, but is alluded to in the next issue, January 23, 1731, No. 238. The British Government consequently made a virtue of informing the French of their separate negotiation (Newcastle to Waldegrave, Jan. 23, O. S., 1730/1 [*British Diplomatic Instructions: France, 1727-1744*, pp. 95-97]).

fects, they themselves opened a negotiation with him on the basis of guaranteeing the Pragmatic Sanction, which, apparently, they were willing to do in exchange for Luxemburg.[37] At the same time, they endeavoured to interest the Spaniards by offering to conclude an agreement which was a distinct adumbration of the later First Family Compact.[38] But although Philip V and Elisabeth Farnese were greatly annoyed by the Imperial occupation of Parma and Piacenza, which took place in January 1731, following the death of Anthony Farnese, they were too well convinced that Fleury would stop short of forcible measures to be much interested in the French offers.[39] Consequently, both the negotiations with Austria and with Spain broke down; the British had the field clear for their own diplomacy, and on March 16, 1731, the second Treaty of Vienna was signed.[40]

This Treaty of Vienna provided for the introduction of six thousand Spanish troops into Porto Ferrajo, Leghorn, Parma and Piacenza; the establishment of Leghorn as a free port; the permanent suppression of the Ostend Company and the general guarantee of the Emperor's succession, with the proviso that no Archduchess should be married to a Bourbon or Brandenburg prince.[41] It is noteworthy that, although the primary object of

[37] Villars: *Mémoires*, V, pp. 299-300, 308, 310.
[38] Villars: *Mémoires*, V, pp. 306-307; Baudrillart: *Philippe V et la cour de France*, IV, pp. 68, 78-79, 94-95.
[39] The Austrian troops occupied the duchies to protect the rights of Anthony Farnese's unborn child, since the widowed Duchess of Parma declared that she was pregnant. This assertion taxed the credulity of Europe. Some months later, after an examination in which the midwives representative of five different nations participated, the Duchess was fain to confess that her hopes had been deceived.
[40] For the treaty, see Pribram: *Österreichische Staatsverträge: England bis 1748*, pp. 491-514.
[41] The States General acceded to this treaty on Feb. 20, 1732 (Pribram: *Österreichische Staatsverträge: England bis 1748*, pp. 541-548). Great Britain and the United Provinces agreed by this treaty to conclude a new commercial treaty which would regulate tariffs in the Austrian Netherlands, but they eventually managed to evade this stipulation; for the Congress of Antwerp, where this matter was discussed, see Gachard: *Histoire de la Belgique*, pp. 506-522. Newcastle instructed Waldegrave on March 26, O. S., 1731, to communicate the treaty to the French (Coxe: *Memoirs of . . . Sir Robert Walpole*, III, p. 109). The provision with reference to a Brandenburg marriage was probably an effect of George II's resentment against Prussia. In 1730 negotiations for a double marriage had broken down, under circumstances which increased the mutual dislike of George II and Frederick William I (Wilhelm Oncken: "Sir Charles Hotham und Friedrich Wilhelm I. im Jahre 1730." *Forschungen zur brandenburgischen und preussischen Geschichte*, VII [1894], pp. 377-407; VIII [1895], pp. 487-522; IX [1896], pp. 23-53).

the British in concluding this treaty had been to satisfy the Spaniards in the matter of the garrisons, these negotiations had been kept secret from them, the presumption being that they would be glad enough to accede to the treaty, once it had been settled.[42] Chauvelin presumed, in a manner which seems to be wholly without reason, that Spain would refuse the benefits which the Treaty of Vienna accorded her; consequently, Spain's treaty with Great Britain and Austria, also signed at Vienna on July 22, 1731, surprised him no less than the treaty of March 16 had done. The isolation of France was complete.[43]

The French isolation, although naturally very disagreeable for Fleury and Chauvelin, was not one positively dangerous to the interests of the country. For some time, it is true, Fleury feared, or affected to fear, that the British had contracted obligations to coerce the French into a recognition of the Pragmatic Sanction. This was really not the case; the British assured the Cardinal that no such undertaking was in view, and were able to persuade the French that they told the truth.[44] What happened in 1731 was that the British demonstrated to the French that Europe could get along without them. In view of the fact that the British policy indirectly facilitated the First Family Compact, it is open to doubt whether the lesson was worth giving; but at the moment, although this demonstration did not endanger French security, it was a mortifying blow to French pride. After a period of consistent obstruction, by means of which Fleury was gradually regaining France's diplomatic freedom of action and was making the combinations of Europe depend upon French concurrence, France suddenly found herself isolated. In a certain sense, she had regained her freedom of action, but scarcely

[42] The Spanish sovereigns were not aware of the negotiation before the first days of February 1731 (Baudrillart: *Philippe V et la cour de France*, IV, p. 75).
[43] Pribram: *Österreichische Staatsverträge: England bis 1748*, pp. 517-526. French negotiations with Spain from March 16 to July 22, 1731 (Baudrillart: *Philippe V et la cour de France*, IV, pp. 83-104). On July 25 the King of Spain and the Grand Duke of Tuscany signed a treaty which recognized Don Carlos as the heir to Tuscany. The Spanish garrisons were transported, with the escort of a British squadron, and were admitted to Tuscany in October.
[44] Under-secretary Delafaye to Waldegrave, August 16, O. S., 1731; Newcastle to Waldegrave, same date (Coxe: *Memoirs of . . . Sir Robert Walpole*, III, pp. 118, 120-121).

in a form which she could have desired. As a French memorial, under date of August 3, 1731, stated the matter:

For a long time, and with justification, we have been annoyed at having always to depend upon the views of others; today, in truth, we can depend only on ourselves, but it is precisely the manner in which we have arrived at this liberty which demands on our part the most serious reflection, as well as resolutions from which nothing can deflect us.[45]

The British excused their separate negotiation with the Emperor by trying to minimize its significance. Newcastle made the extraordinary statement that the British failure to divulge the secret to their French allies was only an "omission of form";

that the King was persuaded that whenever this transaction should come to be known, both France and Spain would be satisfied with it, and for that reason, His Majesty did agree to the keeping of the secret which had been demanded of him; . . . [and that, consequently], His Majesty hopes that the same union and concert will subsist among the other Allies [i.e., all except Spain, who had just declared her repudiation of the Treaty of Seville] that has hitherto done, . . . [46]

A month later Newcastle wrote that the declaration the Cardinal had so often made that he could never guarantee the Pragmatic Sanction was the reason why the British had not divulged the secret of their negotiation to him.[47] This statement explained but it did not excuse. The British might really have communicated their design to the Cardinal from the beginning, had they believed that Chauvelin could be trusted with the secret.[48]

However much the British endeavoured to palliate their defection, it is certainly true that thereafter the Anglo-French alliance existed in name only, at least so far as the French were concerned. The Cardinal responded to Waldegrave's communication of the treaty by the simple but devastating remark that it was a breach of the Treaty of Hanover, which had forbidden secret and separate negotiations of just such a character. Chau-

---

[45] Baudrillart: *Philippe V et la cour de France*, IV, pp. 105-106.

[46] Newcastle to Waldegrave, Jan. 26, O. S., 1730/1 (*British Diplomatic Instructions: France, 1727-1744*, pp. 98, 100).

[47] Newcastle to Waldegrave, Feb. 23, O. S., 1730/1 (*British Diplomatic Instructions: France, 1727-1744*, pp. 103-104).

[48] Delafaye to Waldegrave, Aug. 16, O. S., 1731 (Coxe: *Memoirs of . . . Sir Robert Walpole*, III, p. 120).

velin wrote to Rottembourg on June 18, 1731: "We desire nothing which binds us, directly or indirectly, with people who have failed us so explicitly."[49] The instructions, written by Pecquet and corrected by Chauvelin, which were given to Chavigny, who was being sent to England as minister plenipotentiary, ran in part as follows (December 16, 1731):

There is no further occasion for negotiation between His Majesty and the King of England; and their reciprocal interests are separated by a distance so considerable that it is no longer a question of deliberating together upon the affairs of Europe.[50]

Chavigny was merely to play a passive rôle and to cultivate good relations with the Parliamentary Opposition.[51]

In adjusting itself to the fact of its isolation, French policy had a choice of alternatives, one of which was particularly favoured by Chauvelin and Pecquet. This was to increase France's army and navy, and to take the initiative in building up a group of powers in opposition to that formed by the second Treaty of Vienna. This policy was attempted to a certain extent in the north of Europe, at least sufficiently to alarm the British.[52] Opposed to this policy was that of the Cardinal, which was the one adopted. Fleury disapproved of the expenditure of the money which would be required to subsidize allies and to bring

---

[49] Baudrillart: *Philippe V et la cour de France*, IV, p. 98. Fleury's remark to Waldegrave on the Treaty of Vienna (Vaucher: *Robert Walpole et la politique de Fleury*, p. 44).

[50] Vaucher: *Robert Walpole et la politique de Fleury*, p. 59.

[51] Vaucher: *Robert Walpole et la politique de Fleury*, pp. 60-61. Since January 1731, when the French were aware of the separate negotiation, Broglie had been closely associated with the Parliamentary Opposition. The British ministers were very surprised and displeased to find that Fleury justified him against their complaints (*ibid.*, p. 47). Chauvelin's instructions that Chavigny was to be a "meer spectator" very much upset the British (Newcastle to Waldegrave, Dec. 9, O. S., 1731 [*British Diplomatic Instructions: France, 1727-1744*, pp. 107-108]). Sir Thomas Robinson wrote to Lord Carlisle from Paris, June 29, 1731: "I find the French in general are much discontented at our late behaviour. . . ." (Carlisle Papers, *Hist. MSS. Comm., Report* XV, App. Part VI, p. 82).

[52] For French attempts in 1731 to cultivate relations with Sweden and Denmark hostile to Great Britain (Newcastle to Waldegrave, Dec. 9, O. S., 1731 [*British Diplomatic Instructions: France, 1727-1744*, pp. 106-107]; also Harrington to Edward Finch, March 5, 1731; the same to the same, June 1; the same to the same, Oct. 1; the same to the same, Nov. 2, 1731, all Old Style [*British Diplomatic Instructions: Sweden, 1727-1789*, pp. 19, 20, 23, 23-25]).

France's own military power to a point where it could engage
in war with a revived "Grand Alliance" with any reasonable
expectation of success. His project was, instead, to wait until
the affairs of Europe so changed that foreign powers, of their
own accord, once more sought the alliance of France. His exact
views are known from the annotations on an anonymous memorial dated May 14, 1731. The writer advocated the exercise
of patience, and Fleury annotated:

You know that these are my sentiments; it is melancholy but unavoidable.
. . . We have in our favour only accidental events, such as the death or
abdication of some one of the potentates among our enemies . . . [We must
await] the benefit which time will bring . . . the single advantage which
we have left.[53]

While, on the whole, French foreign policy in 1731 and 1732
was regulated by these unheroic sentiments, it was nevertheless
not reduced to that state of absolute passivity which Fleury's
remark seemed to recommend. In this period Fleury and
Chauvelin did what they could to organize a combination whose
common and unifying principle should be hostility to the Emperor's Pragmatic Sanction. The most important element in
such a programme was to secure a family alliance with the
Bourbons in Spain. That this was long delayed was not the
fault of the French; France constantly endeavoured to conclude
such an alliance from the time when she first learned of the
separate negotiations which the British were carrying on with
the Emperor (January 1731) until, in November 1733, it at long
last became an accomplished fact.[54] During this period the
French negotiators found to their chagrin that they could make
no headway, until Elisabeth Farnese once more became discontented with the Emperor. Even then it was impossible to conclude an alliance because of her conviction that France would
never fight so long as the Cardinal was at the head of affairs.
Only when France gave conclusive proof to the contrary, by

[53] Vaucher: *Robert Walpole et la politique de Fleury*, p. 48. The contrasting
views of Fleury and Chauvelin at this time (*ibid.*, pp. 52-58).
[54] For these negotiations, see Baudrillart: *Philippe V et la cour de France*, IV,
pp. 118-153.

declaring war on the Emperor, was it possible to bring about an alliance with Spain.[55]

In consonance with this policy of combining powers whose common interest was the nullification of the Pragmatic Sanction, the French tried very hard to build up an alliance system in Germany. The Treaty of Vienna in 1731 had been as hard a blow to French interests there as it had been elsewhere. Now, for the first time, the Emperor felt it safe to attempt to secure the guarantee of the Empire for the Pragmatic Sanction.[56] Busy negotiations to that effect were carried on through the summer, one of the effects of which was to seduce the Elector of Cologne from that Electoral Union on which France had counted so heavily. On October 18, 1731, the Pragmatic Sanction was presented to the consideration of the Diet, an event which significantly synchronized with Chavigny's recall.[57] On January 11, 1732, it was passed by the Electoral College by a vote of six to three, the Electors of Bavaria, Saxony and the Palatinate being the dissidents.[58] Following that event Augustus II became outspokenly hostile to the Emperor, and France, whose policy now became that of preventing the election of a King of the Romans, endeavoured to make use of the antagonism of the Elector-King and to increase its effectiveness by sponsoring a Bavarian-Saxon accord. This had been the goal of Chavigny's efforts in the months just preceding his recall, and the negotiation was continued in 1732, through the Marquis de Monti, French ambassador to the Elector-King. Progress was slow, however, and

[55] Austro-Spanish relations again became strained after June 24, 1732, when the Senate of Tuscany paid homage to Don Carlos before he had received the Imperial investiture.

[56] Hans von Zwiedineck-Südenhorst: "Die Anerkennung der pragmatischen Sanction Karls VI. durch das deutsche Reich." *Mittheilungen des Instituts für oesterreichische Geschichtsforschung*, XVI (1895), p. 288. At that moment, too, Austria could count on the support of Prussia in the Diet (Sir Richard Lodge: *Great Britain and Prussia in the Eighteenth Century*, p. 24 and note).

[57] Zwiedineck-Südenhorst: "Die Anerkennung der pragmatischen Sanction Karls VI. durch das deutsche Reich." *Mittheilungen des Instituts für oesterreichische Geschichtsforschung*, XVI, pp. 301-302; Dureng: *Mission de Chavigny*, pp. 125-129.

[58] Zwiedineck-Südenhorst: "Die Anerkennung der pragmatischen Sanction Karls VI. durch das deutsche Reich." *Mittheilungen des Instituts für oesterreichische Geschichtsforschung*, XVI, pp. 315-316; Albrecht Philipp: *August der Starke und die pragmatische Sanktion* (Leipzig, 1908), p. 135.

the accord which was finally reached was neither very valuable nor trustworthy. Bavaria and Saxony regarded each other with distrust, for the Elector of one and the Electoral Prince of the other had each married a daughter of the late Emperor Joseph I, and were suspicious of each other's designs on the Hapsburg inheritance. Moreover, Augustus II desired very much to have his son succeed him as King of Poland, and he suspected, quite rightly, that the French cherished secret hopes for the election of Stanislas Leszczynski instead. As a result, the French were forced to dissemble their plans for the father-in-law of Louis XV, in the hope that the solution would suggest itself to Augustus II of voluntarily relinquishing his aspirations to set up a dynasty in Poland in exchange for French support of his claims for a share in the Hapsburg inheritance. On May 25, 1732, a subsidy treaty was concluded between France and Saxony, and on July 4, 1732, Augustus II and Charles Albert of Bavaria signed a treaty of "friendship." The results of this promising negotiation, however, were quickly dissipated in the crisis which followed the death of Augustus II on February 1, 1733.[59]

Strangely enough, negotiations for an alliance between Russia and France were carried on in 1732. Chauvelin welcomed the overtures which Münnich made to Magnan, the French *chargé d'affaires* at St. Petersburg; to win Russia from the Emperor would of course weaken the prestige of the latter and consequently would go far in spoiling his plans for the election of a King of the Romans. Such an alliance would also tend to nullify the Treaty of Copenhagen, signed by Austria, Russia and Denmark on May 26, 1732, which Chauvelin thought, quite erroneously, contained a secret article to the effect that no foreign prince nor a relative of one might be elected to the Polish throne, a stipulation which would exclude Leszczynski.[60] The Franco-

[59] For these negotiations, see Philipp: *August der Starke und die pragmatische Sanktion*, pp. 119-120, 134, 136; Dureng: *Mission de Chavigny*, pp. 121, 125; Sautai: *Les préliminaires de la guerre de la Succession d'Autriche*, pp. 39-40; Rudolf Beyrich: *Kursachsen und die polnische Thronfolge, 1733-1736* (Leipzig, 1913), pp. 2-3.

[60] This treaty, which merely attempted to settle the Schleswig question by offering monetary compensation to the Duke of Holstein-Gottorp (which he refused), signalized Russia's withdrawal of her support of his territorial claims; see Martens: *Recueil des traités et conventions conclus par la Russie*, I, pp. 48-63.

Russian *pourparlers* in 1732 in reality never offered very bright prospects of amounting to anything serious, except for a brief moment in September, when Chauvelin, accordingly, gave Magnan authorization to conclude.[61] From the very beginning, the negotiation was kept secret from Ostermann, and consequently there was never much hope of coming to a definite conclusion since he, devoted as he was to the Austrian alliance, would be sure to oppose a treaty with France.[62] Besides, the Russians wanted France to guarantee Courland to Biren, the favourite of the Czarina, to which Chauvelin was opposed because it would prejudice the chances of a French candidate's being elected King of Poland.[63] The Russians, on the other hand, did not show the slightest disposition to meet French views with reference to the Pragmatic Sanction and the election of a King of the Romans. It is easy to see that these negotiations were hardly of a serious character; by December 1732, they had become almost extinct.[64] In January 1733, they flared up momentarily, but the real opposition of French and Russian interests was brought into prominent relief in the months following the death of Augustus II, for the French desired Russian neutrality and insisted on the freedom of the Polish election, since they knew full well that under such circumstances Stanislas Leszczynski would become King of Poland.[65] Far from there being any longer a question of an

[61] Münnich's overtures to Magnan (Magnan to Chauvelin, April 26, 1732 [*Sbornik*, LXXXI, pp. 320-321]); Chauvelin's replies, May 22 and June 5 (*ibid.*, pp. 333-336, 336-337, 341-342). For Chauvelin's suspicions about the Treaty of Copenhagen, see his letters to Magnan, Oct. 26, 1732, Feb. 9 and March 2, 1733 (*Sbornik*, LXXXI, pp. 473-475, 533, 541). For Chauvelin's hopes that Magnan might be able to conclude, see his letters of August 28, October 16, 26, 30, 1732 (*ibid.*, pp. 422-424, 468-472, 473-475, 475-476). During this year French negotiations in Turkey flagged, probably because the French did not want to prejudice their negotiation with Russia (Vandal: *Une ambassade française*, p. 191). The British were probably aware of this negotiation; there is a catalogue of Chauvelin's and Magnan's despatches for this year in the Weston Papers, *Hist. MSS. Comm.*, *Report* X, App. Part I, p. 203.
[62] Chauvelin to Magnan, July 24, Sept. 18, Dec. 4, 1732 (*Sbornik*, LXXXI, pp. 396-400, 449-451, 498-499).
[63] Chauvelin to Magnan, Aug. 3, Oct. 2, 1732 (*Sbornik*, LXXXI, pp. 414, 460-462).
[64] Chauvelin to Magnan, Nov. 30, 1732; Jan. 8, 1733 (*Sbornik*, LXXXI, pp. 490-491, 521-523).
[65] Chauvelin to Magnan, Jan. 12, 22, 1733 (*Sbornik*, LXXXI, pp. 524-525, 526-527). His letters to Magnan on April 13 and Oct. 16, 1732, constitute added

alliance between France and Russia, Magnan was instructed on May 3 merely to assume the attitude of an observer, and a month later he was directed to ask for his passports.[66] He left the court of Russia on the fifth of July.[67]

It may readily be seen that neither the German nor the Russian negotiations in 1732 were of transcendent importance. Though potentially very important, the same was true of the Franco-Spanish negotiations in that year. Finally, the French overtures for an alliance with the King of Sardinia, begun in June of 1732, also remained in a state of suspense. The diplomatic combination of 1733 which Chauvelin was able to form with what seemed to be such astonishing celerity was already in preparation in 1732, but in that year it remained both secret and inchoate, dependent as it was, for its final elaboration, on the accident of events.

This period was, indeed, one of *détente* throughout Europe; a precious moment when the British ministers were able to triumph over their Parliamentary adversaries and to inspire a pamphlet vaingloriously entitled *The Natural Probability of a Lasting Peace in Europe*.[68] In France itself, matters of domestic interest supplanted those of foreign. On April 1, 1732, through Fleury's initiative, Chauvelin was made his adjunct or co-minister, with authority to carry on independently the business of the realm in

proofs of the French determination to secure the election of Leszczynski (*ibid.*, pp. 319, 471). On Feb. 9, 1733 he wrote to Magnan: "Nous ne voulons pas encore déclarer publiquement nos desseins pour le roi Stanislas" (*ibid.*, p. 533).

[66] Chauvelin to Magnan, May 3, June 3-4, 1733 (*Sbornik*, LXXXI, pp. 628-629, 651-652).

[67] *Sbornik*, LXXXI, p. 670.

[68] In this period the British ministry took advantage of their improved position in matters of foreign policy to inspire a furious counter-attack in the pamphlet warfare of the day (*Some Observations on the Present State of Affairs* [London, 1731]; [Sir William Yonge]: *Sedition and Defamation Display'd* [London, 1731]. This pamphlet caused a duel between Lord Hervey and Pulteney. There also appeared an anonymous pamphlet by Lord Hervey: *A Letter to the Craftsman on the Game of Chess* [London, 1733]). The British ministers during this period were very irritated with Chavigny, who cultivated close relations with the Opposition (Newcastle to Waldegrave, March 3, O. S., 1731/2, and May 18, O. S., 1732 [*British Diplomatic Instructions: France, 1727-1744*, pp. 108-109, 109-110]; Horatio Walpole to Baron Gedda, Swedish ambassador at Paris, May?, 1733 [Coxe: *Memoirs of . . . Sir Robert Walpole*, III, pp. 137-141]).

the event of the absence of the Cardinal.[69] The obvious significance of this appointment was that it was a designation of Chauvelin as Fleury's successor. In part it may have been caused by a desire to disoblige the British, but more particularly it was designed to strengthen the government in its conflict with the *Parlement* of Paris. In several recent instances, parish priests who had accepted the *Constitution*, that is to say, who had subscribed to the bull *Unigenitus*, had refused to administer the last sacraments to Jansenists. This procedure was approved by Fleury, but the *Parlement* of Paris, which was Jansenist in temper, allowed suit to be brought on the plea *appel comme d'abus*. All through the year 1732 there was friction on this issue between Court and *Parlement*. Since the most opposition came from the younger members of the *Parlement*, those who principally comprised the *chambres des requêtes* and the *chambres des enquêtes*, the government conceived the idea of permitting only the *Grand'Chambre* to have jurisdiction in ecclesiastical cases, which was decreed by the royal Declaration of August 18, 1732.[70] As a result, the *Parlement* went on strike. Not even

[69] See Appendix I, *infra*.

[70] For this declaration, see Isambert: *Recueil général des anciennes lois françaises*, XXI, pp. 374-378. The declaration also provided that all royal acts "shall be inviolably observed from the day of their publication"; article ii restricted the right of the *Parlement* to make remonstrances, and article iv restricted the liberty of the several chambers of the *Parlement* to meet together. The *appel comme d'abus* was a very old legal institution, on which the *Parlements* had founded their justification for resisting the encroachments of the spiritual on the temporal power. There were six grounds of appeal which the *Parlements* accepted as sufficient to authorize the transference of a case from an ecclesiastical to a secular court; in practice, these six became capable of extension to almost any case involving ecclesiastical disputes. It was on account of this that it was so important for Fleury to keep the *Parlement* in a good humour. See *La grande encyclopédie*: article *appel comme d'abus*. The *Grand'Chambre*, composed of a first president, nine *presidents à mortier*, twenty lay and twelve clerical counsellors, was disposed to be much more docile than were the younger and more irresponsible members of the other chambers. In 1731 the government had been annoyed by the political effect of the miracles of a Jansenist "saint," the Deacon Pâris, because his posthumous thaumaturgic powers seemed to attest the soundness of Jansenist doctrine. The credulous flocked to his grave in the cemetery St. Médard: this was the era of the "*convulsionnaires*." The cemetery was closed by royal ordinance on Jan. 27, 1732. See Barbier: *Journal*, I, pp. 371-373, 393-396; D'Argenson: *Journal et mémoires*, I, p. 83 note; Saint-Pierre: *Annales politiques (1658-1740)* (ed. Drouet), pp. 335-338; Rocquain: *L'esprit révolutionnaire*, pp. 61-75; J. B. Perkins: *France under Louis XV* (Boston, 1897, two vols.), I, pp. 107-111.

a *lit de justice* at Versailles on September 3, and the subsequent exiling of 139 members, could quiet the resistance of the *Parlement*. The Cardinal stopped short of carrying matters to the extreme position later taken by the Chancellor Maupeou; consequently, his only choice was to surrender as gracefully as possible. On December 4, 1732, it was announced that "His Majesty is pleased to wish that the Declaration of August 18 last should remain in suspense"; subsequently the government was glad to utilize the Polish crisis as a source of distraction from constitutional issues.[71] Certainly, as far as Jansenism was concerned, the Polish succession was assuredly the worst misfortune which the Jansenist party experienced during the ministry of Fleury; from foreign war was born domestic tranquillity.[72]

The period from the conclusion of the second Treaty of Vienna in March 1731, until the opening of the question of the Polish succession two years later, marked the nadir of Fleury's fortunes. Until that time his policy had been rewarded by substantial although not sensational success. His manoeuvres had been largely instrumental in causing the collapse of the Austro-Spanish alliance, and he had regained the diplomatic equality of France which his predecessor had forfeited. Consequently, when France was suddenly thrust into diplomatic isolation in 1731 as the result of Great Britain's having taken the unexpected course of destroying the cordiality of the Franco-British alliance, she was nevertheless not put in peril by this unwelcome turn of affairs. It was perfectly safe for Fleury to make the

[71] In a *Mémoire pour le Conseil du Roy par M. le garde des sceaux Chauvelin*, dated April 28, 1733, Chauvelin wrote: "L'on sent que la guerre en soy est un grand engagement, mais si elle est convenable, ... si elle est utile pour faire diversion à l'esprit de liberté qui s'établit dans une nation dont il faut que la vivacité soit occupée d'un côté ou d'autre, ..." etc. An annotation in an unknown hand stated: "M. le Président Chauvelin a en vue les affaires du Parlement de Paris de l'année précédente, 1732" (A. É., *Mém. et Doc., France*, vol. 503, ff. 124-125).

[72] Hardy: *Le cardinal de Fleury et le mouvement janséniste*, p. 317. For particulars on this series of incidents, see Villars: *Mémoires*, V, pp. 342-347, 349-350, 355-361, 370. When the question of the Polish succession arose, Saint-Pierre wrote in his *Annales politiques:* "A quelque chose malheur est bon. Cette grande affaire nous donne du calme sur la petite affaire des jansénistes et de la Constitution . . ." (Saint-Pierre: *Annales politiques (1658-1740)* [ed. Drouet], p. 345).

characteristic choice of waiting to see what time would bring forth, instead of challenging the new combination which Great Britain had formed. In the meantime, France had not yet utilized one potent weapon in her diplomatic arsenal: she had not yet guaranteed the Emperor's Pragmatic Sanction. For two years French ministers had the daily mortification of observing that French prestige was at a discount. But time, as usual, was on Fleury's side. The death of Augustus II on February 1, 1733 gave scope to the formation of European diplomatic realignments; advantage was taken of this fortuitous event to such purpose that in a few short months France, through Fleury's skill, became "the arbiter of Europe" and Great Britain experienced all the discomforts of diplomatic isolation.

CHAPTER VIII

FRENCH POLICY DURING THE WAR OF THE POLISH SUCCESSION

THE events leading up to the War of the Polish Succession can be narrated in short compass. As has already been mentioned, the determination to assist the King's father-in-law in his candidacy for election to the Polish throne had consistently been a principle of French policy ever since the marriage of Louis XV, a principle no less subscribed to by the government of Fleury than by that of his predecessor, the Duke of Bourbon.[1] This secret determination was well known to the British, dating from the time when they had been on good terms with the French. Indeed, they had even encouraged it. The instructions to Woodward, the British resident at Warsaw, under date of November 2, 1728, had gone so far as to prescribe his support for the eventual election of Stanislas, and, according to Chavigny, Lord Townshend had promised that Great Britain would not oppose the election of Leszczynski when a vacancy in Poland should occur.[2] These commitments help to explain the embarrassments of the British government concerning the question of intervening in the crisis and war which resulted from the death of Augustus II.

The first thing which the French government did to facilitate the election of Leszczynski was to send campaign money to their

[1] Cf. *supra*, pp. 144-146.

[2] Vaucher: *Robert Walpole et la politique de Fleury*, p. 85, note; Chavigny, writing in 1738, declared that before 1731 British ministers had suggested to the French that the latter were not adequately preparing the ground for the contingency of the Polish vacancy, and had offered their close co-operation for that purpose (*Mémoire de M. Chavigny contenant quelques observations sur les anecdotes les plus importantes qu'il a recueillies dans les différentes négociations qui lui ont été confiées depuis 1712 jusques au mois de May 1738* [A. É., Mém. et Doc., France, vol. 457, f. 52]).

ambassador in Poland, the Marquis de Monti.[3] The second was to take steps to prevent foreign influence from interfering with the free choice of the Poles. This resolution was not so much inspired by a deeply rooted respect for Polish institutions as it was the result of a conviction that, in this particular case, the French candidate would readily be elected if the Poles were not subjected to outside pressure.[4] In opposition to this policy was the one immediately manifested by the court of Vienna. By March 1, 1733, the French knew that Charles VI was already moving troops into Silesia.[5] It was evident that the Emperor contemplated intimidating the Polish Diet; meanwhile, the French schemes for diverting Saxon ambitions from Poland and focussing them upon a future division of the Hapsburg inheritance died with Augustus II. From the first, it was clear that the new Elector of Saxony had set his heart on the Polish crown.[6]

The French reply to the military activity of the Austrians in Silesia was the royal Declaration of March 17, 1733, which as-

---

[3] By March 1, one million six hundred thousand livres had been sent to Monti; by April 12, 1733, three million more, with *carte blanche* for as much as he needed (Villars: *Mémoires*, V, pp. 391, 396-397).

[4] Cf. Chauvelin's displeasure at what he thought were the secret articles of the Treaty of Copenhagen (*supra*, pp. 234-236).

[5] Villars: *Mémoires*, V, p. 390. Throughout February 1733, the French minister at Vienna warned Chauvelin that the invariable design of the court of Vienna was to employ artifice, money and force in opposing the election of Leszczynski (Bussy to Chauvelin, February 7, 11, 14, 21, 25, 1733 [A. É., *Corr. Pol., Autriche*, vol. 175, ff. 53, 58, 73, 88, 94]). A serious attempt had been made by Austria, Russia and Prussia in 1732 to come to an agreement concerning the Polish succession. By the so-called Löwenwolde Punctation of September 13, 1732, later modified by the Löwenwolde Declaration of December 13, 1732, it was provided that the contracting powers should give their support to a Portuguese prince, and that, on the extinction of the ruling house in Courland, Russia and Austria should aid in the election of a Prussian prince to rule there. Both Charles VI and the Czarina, however, refused their ratifications, which so annoyed Frederick William I that he took no active part at all in the Polish crisis of 1733 (Droysen: *Geschichte der preussischen Politik*, IV, vol. iii, pp. 174, 179; Martens: *Recueil des traités et conventions conclus par la Russie*, I, pp. 311-324; cf. also the editorial comment in *ibid.*, pp. 63-66).

[6] Cf. *supra*, pp. 233-234. The day following the death of Augustus II, the new Elector wrote to influential Poles soliciting their support (Pierre Boyé: *Un roi de Pologne et la couronne ducale de Lorraine: Stanislas Leszczynski et le troisième traité de Vienne* [Paris, 1898], pp. 120-121). Negotiations to secure the Emperor's support had been decided upon at once (Beyrich: *Kursachsen und die polnische Thronfolge*, p. 11).

serted that Louis XV would not tolerate any interference with the free choice of the Polish nation. The rather contemptuous reply of the Emperor, who "had not judged these ill-founded insinuations worthy of his attention," declared that Charles VI had a right to move his troops wherever he pleased within the limits of his own dominions.[7] Fleury and Chauvelin rather naturally manifested resentment at this reply, and in the Council of State on May 20 the principle was established that war would be declared on the Emperor. That it was not declared for some months Villars attributed to the fecklessness of the Cardinal, but it should be remembered that as late as July 23, Chauvelin, who is usually regarded as the member of the French government most eager for war, advised in the Council of State against it, on the grounds that France had not yet been able to secure allies.[8]

The British were opposed to war, but they were also by now opposed to the election of Leszczynski.[9] They hoped that the

[7] For the French Declaration, see Rousset: *Recueil historique*, IX, p. 185; for the Emperor's reply, see *ibid*., pp. 186-187. Also Pierre Massuet: *Histoire de la guerre présente* (Amsterdam, 1735), pp. 5-6.

[8] Villars: *Mémoires*, V, pp. 407, 420. A good deal of rhetoric has been expended in admiration of the statesmanship of Chauvelin during this crisis (Boyé: *Stanislas Leszczynski et le troisième traité de Vienne*, pp. 99-100; Driault: "Chauvelin, 1733-1737." *Revue d'histoire diplomatique*, VII, p. 36); however, in a *Mémoire pour le Conseil du Roy par M. le garde des sceaux Chauvelin*, dated April 28, 1733, Chauvelin considered what ought to be French policy toward Great Britain in the event that France declared war on the Emperor. He remarked that the French might either attack Great Britain or secure her neutrality; that the latter was easier but, on the other hand, Great Britain might eventually intervene in the war notwithstanding, and, besides, her neutrality could be gained only by France's guaranteeing the neutrality of the Austrian Netherlands. Chauvelin regarded this as disadvantageous, because it would merely serve to warn the Emperor where the French would attack, i.e., on the Rhine (A. É., *Mém. et Doc., France*, vol. 503, ff. 121-122). By this argument, Chauvelin showed himself willing to brave the intervention of the Maritime Powers, and revealed not the slightest conception of the advantages to be gained from guaranteeing the neutrality of the Austrian Netherlands. Yet this guarantee (which was an integral part of Fleury's policy) was absolutely crucial in serving to keep the war localized and in preventing the intervention of the Maritime Powers. Further comment is superfluous.

[9] Vaucher: *Robert Walpole et la politique de Fleury*, p. 69. The Opposition twitted the Ministry on their sometime support of Leszczynski; Pulteney said in the House that "we gave orders to our Ministers abroad to act in concert with theirs for the election of Stanislaus to the throne"; however, Sir Robert Walpole, in reply, denied this (Sir Thomas Robinson to [Lord Carlisle], Feb. 10, O. S., 1734/5 [Carlisle Papers, *Hist. MSS. Comm., Report* XV, Appendix Part VI, pp. 149-150]).

danger of war had been averted when the Emperor, after Robinson had informed him that the British disapproved of the use of force in Poland, promised that his troops would not cross the border, and even began to withdraw some of them from Silesia.[10] However, this action was the merest subterfuge: on July 16, a treaty had been signed between the Emperor and the Elector of Saxony, whereby the latter's guarantee of the Pragmatic Sanction was given in return for the promise of Austrian support in the Polish election.[11] As a result, the Imperial troops which were withdrawn from Silesia were replaced by Saxon ones, which not only further irritated the French but also made it very difficult for the British to defend the Emperor's policy, as they had hitherto done. As an anonymous but well-informed biographer of Fleury stated the matter:

There was something so visibly wrong in this Proceeding, that Powers not immediately interested in it could not be brought to approve, much less to support it.[12]

On August 22, Stanislas Leszczynski started for Warsaw, and arrived there on September 8. His election took place on September 12, and was succeeded by the usual scission on the following day. The Russians under Lacy had entered Lithuania late in August and were marching on Warsaw. Leszczynski left Warsaw on September 22, and took asylum at Dantzig on Oc-

[10] Vaucher: *Robert Walpole et la politique de Fleury*, p. 72. See also Newcastle's letter to Waldegrave, July 23, O. S., 1733, and Harrington's letter to the same, July 30, O. S., 1733 (*British Diplomatic Instructions: France, 1727-1744*, pp. 119-122).

[11] Beyrich: *Kursachsen und die polnische Thronfolge*, p. 31. This was converted into a triple alliance on August 19, when Russia acceded to it; her price was the promise to invest the Czarina's favourite, Biren, with Courland when the then reigning family should become extinct; this was performed in 1737. For the treaty see Martens: *Recueil des traités et conventions conclus par la Russie*, I, pp. 63-69.

[12] *Memoirs of the Life and Administration of the late Andrew-Hercules de Fleury*, p. 35; cf. Vaucher: *Robert Walpole et la politique de Fleury*, p. 73; and *British Diplomatic Instructions: France, 1727-1744*, p. xxii. Lord Harrington wrote to Robinson, British ambassador at Vienna, on August 21, O. S., 1733: "I must not conceal from You, that this Conduct on the Part of the Emperor, can not but put his Majesty, and the rest of that Prince's Allies under very great Difficulties" (Weston Papers, *Hist. MSS. Comm., Report* X, App. Part I, p. 204).

tober 2. On October 5, the Elector of Saxony was declared King of Poland, and on October 10 France declared war.[13]

While these events were occurring in eastern Europe, Chauvelin was busily engaged in forming a coalition, the object of which was to fight the Emperor in Italy. On September 26, 1733, an offensive and defensive alliance between France and Sardinia was concluded at Turin, to the chagrined surprise of the British, who had been very poorly served by their eccentric ambassador at Turin, Lord Essex.[14] By this treaty Louis XV had had to promise all of the Milanese to Charles Emmanuel, as well as to undertake to provide subsidies and a French army of forty thousand men. Moreover, both parties regarded it as essential that Spain should likewise guarantee to Sardinia the whole of the Milanese as the latter's share in the spoils.

Chauvelin's schemes for ejecting the Emperor from Italy ultimately split upon this rock. Both Spain and Sardinia laid claim to Mantua, the strategic importance of which was such that whoever possessed it would always have it in his power to permit the Austrians re-entrance into Italy. Each would have preferred to see the campaign a military failure rather than to permit the other to secure possession of such an important fortress. As a result of this deep-seated suspicion, Spain and Sardinia could never be brought to be allies throughout the course of the War of the Polish Succession; each was the ally of France, but the third side of the triangle was never sketched in. This was the source of infinite difficulty to the French and both explains and justifies the moves they later made to secure a separate peace.

[13] For these events, see Boyé: *Stanislas Leszczynski et le troisième traité de Vienne*, pp. 138-164. Austria and Russia justified their mobilizations by claiming that they were protecting the liberty of the election: Russia by virtue of a treaty with Poland concluded in 1717; Austria by virtue of an old mutual agreement between Poland and Hungary, the Hungarian share of which Austria claimed she had a right to exercise (Claude de Rulhière: *Histoire de l'anarchie de Pologne et du démembrement de cette République* [Paris, 1807, four vols.], I, pp. 153-154). Austrian troops did not actually cross the frontier during this crisis.

[14] The provisions of the treaty are given by Baudrillart: *Philippe V et la cour de France*, IV, pp. 183-184; for its negotiation, see *ibid.*, pp. 145, 165-169, 175, 182-184; also Arneth: *Prinz Eugen von Savoyen*, III, pp. 377-381; and Villars: *Mémoires*, V, pp. 344-426, *passim*. For a characterization of Lord Essex, see the delightful article by Basil Williams: "The Foreign Office of the first two Georges." *Blackwood's Magazine*, CLXXXI (Jan.-June, 1907), pp. 92-105.

In 1733 these difficulties had not yet emerged, and Chauvelin and Rottembourg redoubled their efforts to conclude a treaty with Spain, now that the King of Sardinia had been secured. The Spanish sovereigns had constantly asserted that they would declare war once they were sure that the French really intended to fight. On November 7, 1733, was signed the First Family Compact, otherwise known as the Treaty of the Escurial, a treaty which was known to the British almost immediately and which worried them infinitely, although it remained a secret to historians for over a century.[15] In his despatch of February 5, O. S., 1733/4, Newcastle mentioned to Waldegrave his fears of the treaty,

> which, as you will see by the enclos'd copy of it, not only threatens the liberties of Europe in general by having for its foundation the aggrandisement of the House of Bourbon, but is particularly level'd at His Majesty and his dominions.[16]

On the whole, the French diplomatic programme was a very successful one, even though it remained impossible to conclude a treaty between Sardinia and Spain. For, supplementary to the other negotiations mentioned above, Fénelon, throughout the summer of 1733, was treating with the States General on the basis that if the Dutch would undertake to be neutral, the French would promise not to carry the war into the Austrian Netherlands. Significantly enough, the French did not start their war against the Emperor until it was apparent that an agreement could be reached with the Dutch. The action of the United

---

[15] Printed by Cantillo: *Tratados*, pp. 277-281, who was the first to publish it (1843). Its significance was considerably over-stated in the article by Sir J. R. Seeley: "The House of Bourbon." *English Historical Review*, I (1886), pp. 86-104. The mutual distrust of Fleury and Elisabeth Farnese prevented the Compact from being as dangerous in reality as on paper it seemed to be. Lord Hervey says that in 1733 Sir Robert Walpole drew up a plan whereby Charles VI was to give the younger Archduchess to Don Carlos, with Naples and Sicily as dowry, Spain to guarantee the territorial integrity of all the rest of the Emperor's Italian possessions. This was suggested to Montijo and Kinsky, Spanish and Austrian ambassadors at London. Montijo received full powers to conclude, but Kinsky did not receive the Emperor's consent until October 9; the Spanish ambassador said that it was then too late (Hervey: *Some Materials towards Memoirs*, pp. 228-229).

[16] *British Diplomatic Instructions: France, 1727-1744*, p. 126.

Provinces was taken without consulting the British, which displeased the latter heartily, and had the effect of paralyzing the projects of mediation or intervention which the British were meditating.[17] What the declaration of Dutch neutrality did to British policy may be gathered from the words of Sir Robert Walpole himself:

Great Britain can neither with safety nor prudence enter into this war but in conjunction with the States. Lett us admitt that it is a common cause betwixt us; as they are more nearly and more immediately concern'd, it will be expected that they should go hand in hand with us, and unite in our common defence. I will not enter into the consideration of the advantages [disadvantages?] and prejudices that must attend our being ingaged in a war against France and Spain, and the Dutch continuing in a state of neutrality; they are too evident, and we must conclude it is what this nation cannot, will not bear.[18]

The final link in the French negotiations of 1733 was forged by the conclusion of the secret treaty with Bavaria, November 15, 1733, which increased the amount of the French subsidies to Bavaria, and in other respects renewed the treaty of November 12, 1727. The fruits of this alliance were shown on February 26, 1734, when the Emperor appealed to the Diet to declare war on France. For the Electors of Bavaria, Cologne and the Palatinate refused to furnish their contingents, although the other Electors granted the Emperor's request and declared war.[19]

---

[17] For the Convention of Neutrality, signed on Nov. 24 and ratified on Dec. 23, 1733, see Rousset: *Recueil historique*, IX, pp. 461-463. A Resolution of the States of August 26, 1733 (mentioned in the Convention) had signified the desire of the United Provinces to secure a neutrality agreement. The Duke of Newcastle wrote to Lord Lonsdale on July 21, O. S., 1733: "Five of the seven provinces have agreed to a neutrality for Flanders, . . This resolution they have taken without communicating any thing to us; and may lay us under difficulties" (Lonsdale Papers, *Hist. MSS. Comm.*, Report XIII, App. Part VII [London, 1893], pp. 124-125). Sir Thomas Robinson wrote to Lord Carlisle, Dec. 10, O. S., 1734: "They concluded the neutrality with the French without our consent or even knowledge" (Carlisle Papers, *Hist. MSS. Comm.*, Report XV, App. Part VI, p. 142). Newcastle's letter shows that the British government knew that the neutrality was being mooted, even though they were not consulted; they simply were unable to think of any means to prevent it.

[18] Dec. 24, O. S., 1733 (Coxe: *Memoirs of . . . Sir Robert Walpole*, III, pp. 147-148.

[19] Aretin: *Chronologisches Verzeichniss der bayerischen Staats-Verträge*, pp. 374-378. For the protest of the Electors of Bavaria, Cologne and the Palatinate against declaring war, see Rousset: *Recueil historique*, IX, p. 328-337. The French were

Such were the negotiations and events which accompanied the outbreak of the War of the Polish Succession. What, meanwhile, was the attitude of Cardinal Fleury? Historians have been largely content to take their cue from the remark of Frederick the Great, that

The courtiers at Versailles said that Chauvelin had juggled the cardinal into war, but that the cardinal had juggled him into peace.[20]

Authority for this point of view may also be found in the entries of Villars' *Mémoires* for the years 1731, 1732 and 1733. For the Marshal was as convinced as was Elisabeth Farnese that the Cardinal would not go to war under any provocation. By assuming the accuracy of this point of view, many historians have been led to dilate upon the presumed weakness and feebleness of Fleury during this crisis.[21]

It must be confessed that speculation as to Fleury's attitude towards the War of the Polish Succession is not susceptible of absolute proof. Nevertheless, it may reasonably be argued that the views just mentioned do the Cardinal less than justice. In the first place, it is difficult to accept as adequate the motive which is assigned as the cause of Fleury's lukewarmness. This motive, according to the proponents of this point of view, was simply a love for peace, and a desire to avoid the agitation and the expenditure which a war would inevitably entail. In 1733, events were shaping themselves in a manner which promised to draw France from her diplomatic isolation and to increase her

unable to stir up the Swedes against the Russians during this war (R. Nisbet Bain: *The Pupils of Peter the Great* [London, 1897], pp. 228-229). Nor was an alliance concluded with the Turks; the French would have been glad had the Turks chosen this time to make trouble for their neighbours, but Fleury, as a Churchman, was not eager to sign an overt alliance with them. They requested such an alliance (Villeneuve to Chauvelin, Oct. 15, 1733 [Vandal: *Une ambassade française*, p. 201]); it was apparently the renegade Frenchman, Bonneval, who taught them to do nothing for France unless they were rewarded by a French alliance (*ibid.*, pp. 204-208); Chauvelin wrote to Villeneuve on Jan. 26, 1734, as to an alliance: "C'est matière extrêmement difficile à traiter" (*ibid.*, p. 224).

[20] Frederick II: "History of my own Times." *Posthumous Works*, I, part i, p. 14.

[21] Cf. Driault: "Chauvelin, 1733-1737." *Revue d'histoire diplomatique*, VII, pp. 36-38; Boyé: *Stanislas Leszczynski et le troisième traité de Vienne*, chapter iii; Baudrillart: *Philippe V et la cour de France*, IV, pp. 155 and *passim;* Sautai: *Les préliminaires de la guerre de la Succession d'Autriche*, pp. 42-43.

prestige; it does not seem reasonable to affirm that Fleury, who was above all else a diplomat, with a diplomat's love of prestige and appreciation for its value, permitted monetary considerations and an abstract love of peace and quiet to prevent him from taking advantage of an extremely favourable conjuncture of affairs.

There certainly is no doubt that Fleury, in the early months of 1733, showed a marked lack of enthusiasm at the prospect of beginning a war against the Emperor; no less is it true that the military aid sent to Leszczynski at Dantzig in 1734 was very insufficient. This being true, Fleury's critics can find no motive for such conduct other than sheer pusillanimity. But quite to the contrary, there were extremely cogent, although rather subtle, reasons for Fleury's action in both instances. In 1733 he had to restrain his over-eager Council of State from precipitately declaring war in such a fashion that France would appear to be the aggressor. Villars' *Mémoires* show conclusively that the Marshal wanted a war against the Emperor as soon as a coalition could be formed. To a harangue delivered on July 15, 1731, in which Villars had urged such a course, Chauvelin had objected: "But you declare yourselves the aggressors." The Marshal had replied: "Show me any other way."[22] It was just some other way which Fleury and Chauvelin were trying to find in the summer of 1733. This was done by giving the Emperor ample opportunity of putting himself completely in the wrong concerning the liberty of the Polish election: thus, what was nothing but a bare-faced attack on the Emperor's dominions in Italy was palmed off as being merely the effects of the reasonable and justifiable resentment of the King of France at the Emperor's action in Poland. This policy was extremely effective:

France, perhaps for the first Time for a Hundred Years before, was allowed of all Hands to have carried on a just War against the Emperor, for his Adherence to Russia and Saxony in Support of an unfair Election of a King forced upon a free Nation.[23]

[22] Villars: *Mémoires*, V, p. 336.
[23] *The Conduct of the Late Administration* (1742), p. 58.

When one considers how extremely jealous the Maritime Powers were of any increase in the possessions or power of France, it may readily be seen that the French utilization of the Polish crisis to justify their attack on the Emperor was a very clever piece of diplomacy. War could not safely be declared until the Emperor had put himself in the wrong, nor until it was certain that the Dutch would be content to remain neutral. By waiting until the first had occurred, the French statesmen made it appear that the Emperor had no right to demand assistance of the Maritime Powers, whose treaty obligations with him were only of a defensive nature. Thus the war bade fair to remain localized, and not until then was it declared; but these refinements were too subtle for the blunt Marshal and, much more surprisingly, for the French historians of these events.[24]

A similar explanation of Fleury's action can be made in defense of his undoubted neglect of Stanislas Leszczynski, who was immured in Dantzig during the winter of 1733-1734. In August 1733, a squadron of thirteen vessels left Brest for Copenhagen, carrying with them a French nobleman who impersonated Leszczynski, while at the same time the real Stanislas was travelling in disguise to Warsaw by land. This squadron was recalled from Copenhagen in October without having shown itself at Dantzig. The Russians began the siege of that city on February 20, 1734. For its relief the French sent only six thousand men and five war-ships; on May 11 this force was disembarked at the mouth of the Vistula, but the odds against its being of any utility were so great that it was re-embarked before any fighting took place, on May 15, and returned to Copenhagen. Thereupon, the French ambassador at Copenhagen, Plélo, took command of the squadron and troops, on his own authority, and returned to the mouth of the Vistula. On May 23, his force was defeated in a land engagement and he himself was killed; on June 13, Dantzig was blockaded by the Russian fleet, under the command of the

---

[24] So extraneous, in reality, was the Polish issue with reference to the Italian war that Chauvelin had to remind the Spanish sovereigns to include a reference to it in their declaration of war (Baudrillart: *Philippe V et la cour de France*, IV, p. 201).

Scottish Jacobite, Admiral Gordon. On June 22, the remainder of Plélo's force surrendered. Leszczynski fled from Dantzig on the night of June 27, and the city capitulated to the Russians on July 7, 1734.[25] Much ado has been made by French nationalist historians about this betrayal of Leszczynski by Fleury, which they can explain only as the result of his degraded and criminal truckling to the susceptibilities of the British. However, one should steel oneself to endure the thought that this may not be the ultimate explanation. It is certainly true that the British were jealous of France's enterprises in the Baltic. As an apologist for Sir Robert Walpole wrote, in defense of the measures of his administration:

The French durst not venture to the Baltick to relieve Dantzick, whilst our Navy rid in the Downs; . . . [26]

Since such was the state of British feelings, the most rudimentary statecraft exacted as a matter of course that no action should be taken which would irritate the British to the point of active intervention, provided that the general aims of French policy were furthered by preventing the war from becoming general. Obviously this was the case, and the French statesmen had to take care, for in 1734 there was a very real war scare.[27] It was

[25] A florid account of these events is given by Boyé: *Stanislas Leszczynski et le troisième traité de Vienne*, pp. 181, 214, 228, 231, 241-242; see also C. P. V. Pajol: *Les guerres sous Louis XV* (Paris, 1881-1891, seven vols.), I, pp. 168-181; Anderson: *Naval Wars in the Baltic*, pp. 213-214; Pierre Margry: "Une famille dans la marine au XVIIIᵉ siècle (1692-1789)." *Revue maritime et coloniale*, LXII, pp. 664-673; *ibid.*, LXIII, pp. 205-228. Some interesting letters of Admiral Gordon relating to the siege of Dantzig may be found in the Gordon Papers, *Hist. MSS. Comm., Report* X, App. Part I (London, 1885), pp. 191-196.

[26] *The Conduct of the Late Administration*, p. 63. Chauvelin wrote to Plélo on Dec. 3, 1733, that he was afraid that the presence of a French squadron in the Baltic would lead the British to send one there, too (Pierre Margry: "Une famille dans la marine au XVIIIᵉ siècle." *Revue maritime et coloniale*, LXIII, p. 228).

[27] French merchants of Nantes were fully persuaded that war between France and Great Britain would occur in 1734 (Gaston-Martin: *Nantes au XVIIIᵉ siècle: L'ère des négriers (1714-1774), d'après des documents inédits* [Paris, 1931], pp. 213-215). Cf. the letter of Rowland and Samuel Frye to Abraham Redwood, London, Feb. 12, O. S., 1733/4 (*Commerce of Rhode Island*, I [1726-1774]. [*Collections of the Massachusetts Historical Society*, Seventh Series, IX (Boston, 1914)], p. 42). In 1734 Governor Belcher asked the home government for a small naval force to protect Boston from an incursion from Cape Breton (*ibid.*, note). Charles Howard wrote to Lord Carlisle on March 29, O. S., 1734, telling of a debate in the House

of supreme importance to keep the British from intervening in a contest in which France's secret aim was the acquisition of a piece of territory so important as was the duchy of Lorraine. If this were successfully accomplished, it would materially alter the balance of power in Europe, a fact to which the British would have some difficulty in reconciling themselves.

That the acquisition of Lorraine was the secret aim of the French statesmen may reasonably be inferred. For although Fleury had said on several occasions that France would prefer losing three battles to guaranteeing the Pragmatic Sanction, he had nevertheless shown on two occasions, during discussions in the Council of State, that he was willing to guarantee it for a price.[28] Since, then, it is a demonstrable fact that France was willing to be bought off, the next step is to ascertain whether Fleury and Chauvelin had Lorraine in mind as the price which they chose to exact. This, too, may be answered in the affirmative. It is known that the French statesmen were aware of the special importance of the status of Lorraine, in view of the probable marriage between its Duke and the elder Archduchess. Although their betrothal had not been officially announced, it was momentarily expected, and Duke Francis had been loaded with such honours at the court of Vienna as to make it quite clear that Charles VI regarded him as his future son-in-law. This meant that the Austrian influence would be exerted for his election as King of the Romans; but from the French point of view, it was manifestly dangerous to have a Duke of Lorraine elected Emperor, because of the geographical location of the duchy. Chauvelin downrightly said in one of his despatches to Chavigny, written before the death of Augustus II: "We will never tolerate Lorraine and the Imperial Crown in the same House."[29]

Not only, then, is it a known fact that the French were per-

which turned on the argument that the French fleet, ostensibly arming for Dantzig, might in reality be preparing for a descent on the British coast. "I find most agree a war is unavoidable . . ." (Carlisle Papers, *Hist. MSS. Comm.*, *Report* XV, App. Part VI, pp. 134-135).

[28] Villars: *Mémoires*, V, pp. 300, 314, 320, 334, 338. In 1731 and 1732 it had been a question of ceding Luxemburg to the French in payment for their guarantee.

[29] January 28, 1733 (A. É., *Corr. Pol.*, *Angleterre*, vol. 379, f. 75 [Vaucher: *Robert Walpole et la politique de Fleury*, pp. 78-79]).

suaded that some arrangement with reference to the duchy of Lorraine would have to be come to, in the event that the Emperor carried out his plans for marrying Maria Theresa to Duke Francis, but it is also known that the possibility of an accommodation in this respect had been suggested to them *by the British* in 1732. The French had let these suggestions pass without comment, doubtless for the reason that it would be bad policy to forewarn the court of Vienna as to French desires on a point to which Austrian opposition was certain. To this effect Chauvelin wrote to Chavigny on April 24, 1732:

I do not see what advantages the British ministry can secure for us from the Court of Vienna. We can not imagine any to which that Court would wish to consent.[30]

Although the French did not choose to follow up the British insinuations with reference to Lorraine in 1732, it is nevertheless a known fact, as has been shown, that they were aware of the problem and of a possible solution for it; that they made the reversion of Lorraine to France a basis for the negotiation of the Preliminaries of Peace in 1735 is a final and certain indication that Lorraine had been the secret pivot of their policy for some years.

Such being the case, it became extremely important that, in a war fought ostensibly in vindication of the Polish claims of Stanislas Leszczynski and, in reality, for the purpose of securing the reversion of Lorraine to France, Leszczynski's cause in Poland should *not* prosper. The more soundly he was beaten in Poland, the more reason the French would have for demanding compensation for him elsewhere, as a reasonable satisfaction for the injured honour of Louis XV, and under cover of this fine show of altruism and disinterestedness could be disguised a very real accretion of French power and territorial possessions. This was exactly the policy which was followed. The necessity for compensating Leszczynski was made the grounds for demanding Lorraine in the negotiation with the Austrians; for justifying to

[30] For the British suggestion and Chauvelin's reply, see Vaucher: *Robert Walpole et la politique de Fleury*, p. 78, and note.

France's allies the conclusion of a separate peace; and for asserting, to the Maritime Powers, the reasonableness of a solution
which, in reality, altered materially the European balance. So
skilfully did the French present the matter in this light that a
reading of their state papers would almost convince one that out
of the settlement of the War of the Polish Succession France secured no advantage for herself at all.

The foregoing considerations indicate that Fleury's hesitancy
about beginning the war in 1733 and his insufficient support of
Leszczynski in Poland in 1734 ought not be attributed to pusillanimity. On still another point, however, his policy is attacked,
and upon this point, too, it is susceptible of a similar explanation.
The allegation is this: that Fleury showed so much weakness in
his negotiations with the Austrians in 1735 and 1736 that the
final settlement was needlessly delayed, and that his desire to
oblige the Austrians was taken advantage of to such a degree
that France almost lost the fruits of her victory, which were
retrieved only by the energy and competency of Chauvelin. But
it should be remembered that an element of craft played its part
in this pose, when

the victors, loaded with laurels, and apparently fatigued by conquest, made
offers of peace to their vanquished foe, the emperor.[31]

In the period which extended from the conclusion of the preliminaries in October 1735, to the conclusion of the final peace
in November 1738, there was never any danger of the Emperor's
being able to escape the consequences of his defeat so long as the
French retained possession of Philippsburg and Kehl, which, in
spite of all his negotiations, Fleury never relinquished. The real
danger for France during that period was not that the negotiation would be protracted but, on the contrary, that war would
break out once more, whether on the initiative of France's recent
allies, whether on that of the Emperor supported by the Maritime Powers. By maintaining an attitude of sweet reasonable-

[31] Frederick II: "Considerations on the Present State of the Body-Politic in
Europe." *Posthumous Works of Frederic II. King of Prussia* (London, 1789,
thirteen vols.), IV, p. 348. This was written in April 1738.

ness, which manifested itself concretely in an apparent willingness to negotiate endlessly, Fleury kept the European temperature below boiling point, and by sheer weight of reiteration, made the reversion of Lorraine to France seem natural and ineluctable.

Fleury's policy in the negotiations leading up to the peace has here been alluded to because, taken in conjunction with his policy concerning the outbreak of the war and the supplying of Leszczynski with aid in Poland, it furnishes a plausible and comprehensive explanation of his actions throughout the whole period of the crisis of the Polish succession. Such an explanation is not only perfectly consonant with what are known to have been Fleury's general characteristics and diplomatic methods but is also consistent with the documentary evidence. Such a view affords some reasonable connection between cause and effect, whereas the contrary one, which argues that Fleury repeatedly exhibited an aimless pusillanimity almost unparalleled, is more difficult to believe, simply because it is so seldom that a minister's pusillanimity results in his country's becoming the arbiter of Europe, as was indubitably the case with France following the third Treaty of Vienna (1738).

This analysis of the attitude of Fleury toward the whole problem of the War of the Polish Succession has been made at this place for the reason that it clarifies his attitude with reference to the several subordinate subjects of negotiation which were treated during the course of the war, the most important being the British attempts at mediation. These became more pressing in proportion as the military success of the allies, which may be briefly summarized, increased. On the Rhine, on October 29, 1733, the French captured Kehl; in 1734 they took Philippsburg and occupied Worms; in 1735 a desultory war was concluded by a listless campaign chiefly made up of countermarches and foraging expeditions.[32] In Italy, the combined forces of France and Sardinia drove the Austrians out of the Milanese in November

---

[32] Lord Hervey states that the war was intentionally conducted in a listless manner on the Rhine, so as not to provoke the intervention of the Maritime Powers (Hervey: *Some Materials towards Memoirs*, pp. 333, 338).

and December of 1733. From that moment on until the end of the war, the King of Sardinia showed small interest in the active prosecution of campaign plans, because of his growing suspicion of the designs of the Spaniards. The year 1734 was mainly devoted by the allies to defensive operations, in the course of which two severe engagements were fought, one at Parma on June 29, and the other at Guastalla on September 19. In this year the Spanish forces accomplished the conquest of Naples, but left their allies to bear the weight of the Austrian attack in the north. In 1735 the Spanish troops moved to the northern scene, but the whole year was wasted in unseemly bickerings concerning the chief command, precedence and other minutiae of etiquette. The real issue involved was the question of Mantua; the Spaniards ardently desired to capture it, but the King of Sardinia, not wishing to see it in Spanish hands, managed to prevent its fall by refusing to furnish siege artillery. In this year the jealousy between Charles Emmanuel and the Spaniards was so intense that it was obvious that the fall of Mantua would be a signal for a war between the victors which would speedily undo all the military successes previously gained. On this account, the French themselves really hung back during the siege of Mantua, and seemed to be as glad as Charles Emmanuel that the fortress escaped capture. The Preliminaries of Peace of October 5, 1735, for which the disunion of the allies lent some excuse, put an end to the inconclusive Italian campaign of 1735.[33]

Throughout these events, the British remained in an uneasy state of indecision. Although they did not *desire* to intervene actively in the war, they frequently had the uncomfortable feel-

[33] The best account of the military events of this war is to be found in Pajol: *Les guerres sous Louis XV*, I, chapters v-xii. Fleury declared in a letter to Charles VI, written Nov. 18, 1735, that the French had prevented the fall of Mantua: "Votre Majesté ne peut ignorer aussi que les difficultés que nous avons fait naître sur le siège de Mantoue m'ont été réprochées par l'Espagne, [et des gens même de ce pays-ci. (Insertion in Fleury's own hand)]. Ils ont prétendu que si on avoit voulu simplement bloquer cette place elle seroit tombée d'elle-même et les apparences du moins s'y prestent. Si cela fut arrivé la paix devenoit presque impossible et mon unique rève a toujours été d'écarter tous les obstacles qui pouvoient s'y opposer" (A. É., *Corr. Pol., Autriche*, vol. 182, f. 166). Cf. Waldegrave to Newcastle, Sept. 21, 1735 (Coxe: *Memoirs of . . . Sir Robert Walpole*, III, pp. 276-280); also Baudrillart: *Philippe V et la cour de France*, IV, p. 299.

ing that perhaps they should. At least they hoped to conceal their state of chronic indecision from the French, who, however, were well informed of it.[34] Various distractions had afflicted the British ministers. In 1733 there had been the session of Parliament, "which has been but a sower untowardly one," in which Walpole's excise plan had had to be given up; in 1734 there were Parliamentary elections.[35] The consensus of opinion, both Opposition and Ministerial, approved a policy of non-intervention, although with many waverings and misgivings.[36] In accordance

[34] Bolingbroke was the source of the French information that the British would not intervene actively. Bolingbroke probably left England in 1735 because of his apprehension that some of this correspondence had fallen into the hands of the government (Paul Vaucher: *La crise du ministère Walpole en 1733-1734* [Paris, 1924], p. 64 and note).

[35] Delafaye to Waldegrave, June 18, O. S., 1733 (Coxe: *Memoirs of . . . Sir Robert Walpole*, III, p. 134). The debates in the House on the excise plan are summarized in the letters of Sir Thomas Robinson and Col. Charles Howard to Lord Carlisle (Carlisle Papers, *Hist. MSS. Comm., Report* XV, Appendix Part VI, pp. 101-111). An excellent account of the excise plan is given by F. S. Oliver: *The Endless Adventure*, II, pp. 234-273; see also, Norris Arthur Brisco: *The Economic Policy of Robert Walpole* (New York, 1907), pp. 100-122.

[36] The indecision of the Opposition is shown by Pulteney's pamphlet: *The Politicks on Both Sides with Regard to Foreign Affairs* (London, 1734), in which he bitterly attacked the past policy of the administration but carefully refrained from advising a policy for the year in which he wrote. This was hinted at in the pamphlet which was written in reply: *A Series of Wisdom and Policy* (London, 1735), pp. 70-72. Horatio Walpole inquired why "the *Craftsmen* were so silent upon this great Occasion?" ([Horatio Walpole]: *A Letter to the Craftsmen, upon the Change of Affairs in Europe* [London, 1734], p. 4). Sir Thomas Robinson wrote to Lord Carlisle on Dec. 8, O. S., 1733: "Both sides have hitherto been quite silent in their writings, and neither care[s] to begin the battle" (Carlisle Papers, *Hist. MSS. Comm., Report* XV, App. Part VI, p. 125). William Pulteney wrote to Lord Grange from London, Dec. 17, O. S., 1733: "This nation never was in a more extraordinary situation. The ministers themselves are, I believe, even at this time as undetermined what part to take as they are fearful of taking any. . . . They want mightily to know what are the sentiments of their opposers, and for this reason, as well as from the difficulty of saying what is right to be done everybody is mute and observes strict silence" (*Report on the Manuscripts of the Earl of Mar and Kellie,* [*Historical Manuscripts Commission*], [London, 1904], p. 529). French writers on this period frequently seem to assume that the British would not have intervened in the war under any circumstances; however, Pulteney wrote to Lord Grange on Nov. 12, O. S., 1734: "Whether we shall have war or peace is still extreemly uncertain" (*ibid.*, p. 540). By 1741 the Parliamentary Opposition had made up their minds what British policy ought to have been in 1734; they then attempted to bring about an "enquiry of our conduct in not going into the war against France in support of the Emperor in 1733" (H. Walpole to Trevor, Jan. 9 and 23, O. S., 1740/1 [Trevor Papers, *Hist. MSS. Comm., Report* XIV, App. Part IX, pp. 66-67]).

with that policy, Walpole managed to restrain the bellicose ardour of King George and Queen Caroline at the same time that he refused the Emperor's appeals for assistance. Nevertheless, the British could not help feeling that the sudden turn of European affairs was leaving them in an invidiously isolated position. So, while the merchants were enjoying the increased trade which the European war was bringing to them, the government sent Horatio Walpole to The Hague in an endeavour to re-establish a concerted policy with the Dutch.[37] As a result of Dutch insistence, the Maritime Powers gingerly offered their "good offices" to France and the Emperor in February 1734. The Emperor rejected them with a great show of indignation, while Fleury blandly remarked that the impartiality of the Maritime Powers was not equal to that which one had a right to expect in the persons of those who desired to be mediators.[38]

The victory of Walpole in the elections, the fear of British intervention in the Baltic and the news of the activity of the English emissaries at the courts of Copenhagen and Stockholm disposed Fleury, later in the year of 1734, to accept the British mediation.[39] His intentions were not in the least serious; he desired merely to amuse the British and to temporize, which he accomplished for the space of time from August 1734, to February 1735. The negotiations were indeed most extraordinary. Fleury's secret emissary, Jeannel, met the representatives of the United Provinces and Great Britain at The Hague without Fénelon's being aware of it; at the same time, Fleury carried on

[37] "We have yet felt no Effects of this War, but what have proved very beneficial to Trade; and a great Encrease of our Wealth" (*What's to be Expected from a New Parliament* [London, 1735], p. 5). Harrington's and Walpole's correspondence in 1734-1735 reflects the embarrassment caused to the British by the signing of the neutrality by the Dutch (Weston Papers, *Hist. MSS. Comm., Report* X, App. Part I, pp. 251-264); cf. Coxe: *Memoirs of Horatio, Lord Walpole,* I, pp. 320-330.

[38] Newcastle to Waldegrave, Feb. 5 and March (no date), O. S., 1733/4 (*British Diplomatic Instructions: France, 1727-1744,* pp. 124-125, 127-129); Vaucher: *Robert Walpole et la politique de Fleury,* pp. 87-88.

[39] Vaucher: *Robert Walpole et la politique de Fleury,* pp. 91-99. For Harrington's despatches to Finch, British ambassador to Sweden, during this period, see *British Diplomatic Instructions: Sweden, 1727-1789,* pp. 33-42. Count Horn's influence kept Sweden neutral. An Anglo-Danish subsidy treaty was signed at Copenhagen on September 30, 1734 (*ibid.,* p. ix).

a secret correspondence with Horatio Walpole of which Jeannel was not aware, although Fleury conceded more in his correspondence with Walpole than he had authorized Jeannel to concede, which naturally involved the latter in hopeless confusion. Moreover, Chauvelin, from whom Fleury had promised to keep the negotiation secret, knew of Jeannel's mission from the very beginning and knew about Fleury's correspondence with Walpole at least by January 1735. There was not much dignity in Fleury's little expedients for gaining time, but they served their purpose. Perhaps the only serious element in the negotiation, from the French point of view, was the fact that an opportunity was thus given to the British of suggesting the reversion of Lorraine as a basis for peace, which the French, for obvious reasons, did not want to mention of their own initiative. Unfortunately for French hopes, the British did not oblige.[40]

The breakdown of these *pourparlers* showed that no pacification could be reached by private negotiation, and threw the British back upon a scheme for a public and open negotiation of peace. This project was communicated to Fleury on March 9, 1735. Don Carlos was to have Naples and Sicily (which he had already conquered); the possessions of the King of Sardinia were to be extended to the Ticino (which territory had already been conquered by the allies); Charles VI was to have Parma, Piacenza and Tuscany; Leghorn was to become a free port; France was to guarantee the Pragmatic Sanction; and Lorraine was not mentioned.[41] It can readily be seen that small inducement was offered to France by this project, nor was any compensation for

---

[40] This negotiation may be followed in the letters of Harrington and Newcastle to Horatio Walpole and Waldegrave (*British Diplomatic Instructions: France, 1727-1744*, pp. xxiv-xxvi, 137-163); also, see Vaucher: *Robert Walpole et la politique de Fleury*, pp. 99-123. Fleury inaugurated his private correspondence with Horatio Walpole in letters dated Sept. 4 and 22 and Oct. 20, 1734 (A. É., *Corr. Pol., Hollande*, vol. 404, ff. 43, 83, 236). The French undertook these private negotiations because they feared Spain was considering a separate peace with Charles VI, through British mediation (Vaucher: *op. cit.*, p. 104).

[41] This scheme was submitted in the names of the Maritime Powers. Printed in Hervey: *Some Materials towards Memoirs*, pp. 460-464. Consult also Baudrillart: *Philippe V et la cour de France*, IV, p. 276; Vaucher: *Robert Walpole et la politique de Fleury*, p. 124; the peace project may also be found in Massuet: *Histoire de la guerre présente*, pp. 434-442.

Leszczynski mentioned: already the British had made up their minds to agree to France's having the reversion of Lorraine, but they desired to avoid the odium of being the first to suggest such a solution.[42] In order to persuade the Cardinal to accept some such plan as this, Horatio Walpole made a secret and unannounced journey to Versailles; in two interviews, on April 1 and 4, he found, to his chagrined surprise, that the Cardinal was quite unmanageable, which he attributed solely to the machinations of Chauvelin.[43] On May 6, the French rejected the British plans for a general pacification; in reply, the Maritime Powers issued a resolution, dated June 7, in which they expressed the hope that the belligerents would conclude an armistice.[44] Thus the British, whether by private or public negotiation, were totally unsuccessful in bringing the conflict to a close; yet they flattered themselves that the war could not be concluded without their figuring as mediators in a peace congress.

On February 22, 1735, an incident had occurred which raised the hopes of the Emperor that the British might finally be drawn into the war. On that day the Portuguese embassy at Madrid had been raided by the Spanish police and some of the staff had been arrested. As a result of this breach of privilege, Portugal nearly declared war, in which, as her ally, Great Britain would have had to participate. The British did, indeed, send a fleet to the Tagus, which infuriated Chauvelin; but since neither France nor Great Britain was desirous of war, the affair was settled by their joint mediation, greatly to the Emperor's discomfiture.[45]

[42] In discussing the general plan of pacification, Lord Hervey refers to "the cession of Lorraine to France, which Holland and England told Cardinal Fleury they would readily consent to as an engraftment on their plan of pacification, but which it was impossible they could insert in the original draught" (Hervey: *Some Materials towards Memoirs*, pp. 464-465).

[43] This was also Hervey's interpretation (*Some Materials towards Memoirs*, p. 466). The Cardinal alleged that he could not desert his allies (*ibid.*, p. 465). Since he did that very thing a few weeks later, it is probable that his real motive was to avoid permitting the Maritime Powers to be guarantors of the peace.

[44] Vaucher: *Robert Walpole et la politique de Fleury*, pp. 134, 137.

[45] Vaucher: *Robert Walpole et la politique de Fleury*, pp. 136-137; William Coxe: *History of the House of Austria* (Second edition, London, 1820, five vols.), IV, pp. 301-303; Baudrillart: *Philippe V et la cour de France*, IV, pp. 284-287; Boyé: *Stanislas Leszczynski et le troisième traité de Vienne*, pp. 317-318. The incident is

The vanishing of this last hope of securing the active assistance of Great Britain disposed Charles VI to put an end to the war. His armies had distinguished themselves by a lack of success uncommon even in the annals of the House of Hapsburg; to general despondency was added the knowledge that it would be extremely difficult to finance further campaigns. It was obvious that Austria would have to pay heavily for having engaged in the war, but, with some hopes that an abatement in the demands of Spain and Sardinia might be achieved as the result of a separate and secret negotiation, the Emperor acquiesced in treating directly with France.

On the French side, the discord between her allies made it certain that no more successes in a military way would accrue from a further prosecution of the war; France herself was beginning to feel the financial strain, and Fleury wrote in the summer of 1735:

> The necessity for peace is unquestionable, for twenty essential and well known reasons; I shall insist on only one: the war is morally unsustainable for another campaign unless such favourable events should occur that they would change our situation entirely, and on which it would not be prudent to count. . . . Besides, Spain is exhausted, as well as the King of Sardinia, and the whole weight of the war, which is already only too onerous, would fall entirely upon us, which would expose us to misfortunes, the very idea of which makes one tremble.[46]

In reality, conditions were not so unfavourable as Fleury chose to paint them, but his remarks do reveal a real will for peace. Nor was Chauvelin opposed to the idea of concluding a separate peace, if statements which he made in a memorial dated October 19, 1736, may be believed.[47]

---

recounted in great detail by Pierre Massuet: *Histoire de la dernière guerre et des négociations pour la paix* (Amsterdam, 1736, two parts in three vols.), part I, pp. 1-53.

[46] *Mémoire par lequel on prouve la nécessité de travailler à la paix* (A. É., *Corr. Pol., Autriche*, vol. 184, ff. 14 sqq.). This piece is undated; directly following it is the draught of a separate article, enclosed by La Baune in his letter from Vienna, August 22, 1735.

[47] ". . . nous avons sçu profiter d'un seul moment, qui n'auroit pû se retrouver si nous l'avions laisser échaper. . . . Nous estions à la veille, par les caprices de l'Espagne, d'essuyer un changement de fortune, qui nous mettant à la discretion de l'Emp^r, nous auroit obligé à quitter les armes avec tous les désavantages aux-

Inspired by a common irritation with the Maritime Powers and a mutual desire for peace, Fleury and the Imperial ministers began a secret correspondence in 1735, in which the initiative, according to M. Vaucher, was taken by the Cardinal. Early in August, La Baune, who had been *chargé d'affaires* at The Hague during the time that Fénelon had been one of the French plenipotentiaries at the Congress of Soissons, was sent secretly to Vienna, where he had several secret interviews with Sinzendorff and Bartenstein.[48]

The Austrians had insisted that, as one of the conditions upon which this negotiation was based, the whole matter should be kept secret from Chauvelin.[49] To this Fleury submitted, under protest.[50] But it is certain that if the negotiation was kept a secret from him at all, it was not for long; for the second packet sent by La Baune from Vienna to Versailles contained a letter from him addressed to Chauvelin, in which he assumed that Chauvelin knew the contents of his previous despatch to Fleury, and requested Chauvelin to deign to send him positive and peremptory orders with reference to obtaining certain districts from Charles VI for the King of Sardinia.[51] It is safe to infer that

quels nous aurions esté exposés" (*Veues sur les affaires générales* [A. É., *Mém. et Doc., France*, vol. 418, f. 220]). A notation in red ink on the first page of the memorial states: "Par Mr. de Chauvelin, ministre des Affaires Étrangères"; also, that it was approved by the King in his Council, Oct. 19, 1736.

[48] Vaucher: *Robert Walpole et la politique de Fleury*, pp. 145-149. The first communication from the Austrians, dated June 16, 1735, was received by Fleury on July 13 (Fleury to Charles VI, July 16, 1735 [A. É., *Corr. Pol., Autriche*, vol. 181, f. 3]); Fleury's instructions to La Baune, dated "July, 1735," declared that he expected little to come of this negotiation, but that he desired to neglect nothing which might lead to the conclusion of peace (A. É., *Corr. Pol., Autriche*, vol. 181, ff. 24-32). La Baune arrived in Vienna on August 13 and had his first interview with Sinzendorff and Bartenstein on August 15, in a convent of the Trinitarians, on the outskirts of Vienna (La Baune to Fleury, August 16, 1735 [A. É., *Corr. Pol., Autriche*, vol. 181, ff. 93-101]).

[49] This demand was made in an unsigned letter dated June 16, 1735, addressed to Fleury and written by Sinzendorff, according to the statement of its bearer, the Swedish Baron Nierodt (A. É., *Corr. Pol., Autriche*, vol. 180, ff. 344-346). This letter was accompanied by one signed by the Imperial Count Wied, dated Vienna, June 10, 1735, and addressed to Nierodt, which also mentioned the Imperial ministers' distrust of Chauvelin (*ibid.*, ff. 340-341).

[50] Fleury to the Emperor, July 16, 1735 (A. É., *Corr. Pol., Autriche*, vol. 181, ff. 3-8): see Appendices, *infra*.

[51] La Baune to Chauvelin, August 26, 1735 (A. É., *Corr. Pol., Autriche*, vol. 181, ff. 137-138).

La Baune would not have addressed Chauvelin without orders to that effect; probably Chauvelin knew of the negotiation in August, by the very latest, for Fleury would scarcely permit him to learn of it merely by means of La Baune's letter. On the other hand, there is some evidence that Chauvelin did not know of the negotiation at the very beginning. It was Fleury who wrote La Baune's instructions, which would ordinarily have been composed by *commis* in the Foreign Office and would then have been signed by Chauvelin. Moreover, La Baune would probably not have been selected for the mission at all had Chauvelin known about it, for the terms in which Chauvelin replied to La Baune's letter of August 26 do not reveal very great confidence in his ability.[52] On the whole, the most reasonable interpretation seems to be that Chauvelin was not opposed to the idea of a separate negotiation with the Emperor; but that Fleury, who was afraid the Austrians would break off the negotiation if they suspected Chauvelin knew of it, did keep it secret from him until after La Baune was on his way to Vienna. The Cardinal's action was not very loyal, and Chauvelin probably resented it; but at the same time, it can hardly be said that Chauvelin was forced to be the spectator of a policy which he did not approve.[53]

In August 1735, the British learned of the secret negotiations

[52] "Vous jugez bien, Monsieur, que je n'en ai rien à ajouter à ce que *Son Eminence* vous écrit si au long sur l'affaire remise à vos soins et dans laquelle je suis persuadé que vous acheverez de remplir ce qu'Elle pouvoit attendre de vous . . . J'ai pour vous, Monsieur, tous les sentimens que vous meritez" (Sept. 10, 1735 [A. É., *Corr. Pol., Autriche*, vol. 181, ff. 157-158]). In the course of a retrospective memorial written in self-justification by Chavigny in 1738, he remarked: "Il eut été à souhaiter que l'on eut choisi un sujet plus sage et plus étendu que M. de la Beaune . . ." (A. É., *Mém. et Doc., France*, vol. 457, f. 65).

[53] Fleury wrote to Charles VI, July 16, 1735: ". . . . je puis asseurer Votre Majesté qu'il [Chauvelin] pense entièrement comme moi et que dans nos fréquens entretiens il est convenu que l'unique moyen de finir la guerre étoit que tout se passoit directement entr' Elle [His Imperial Majesty] et nous" (A. É., *Corr. Pol., Autriche*, vol. 181, f. 7). In his memorial of Oct. 19, 1736 (cited *supra*, note 47), Chauvelin said: "Trois campagnes, quoyque soutenues par les moyens les moins onéreux, dont il y ait jamais eu d'exemple, nous ont prouvé qu'une plus longue guerre estoit impratiquable sans augmenter les dettes déjà exhorbitantes de l'État" (A. É., *Mém. et Doc., France*, vol. 418, f. 223). The opinion that MM. Driault and Boyé have exaggerated the opposition in the views of Fleury and Chauvelin with reference to this negotiation has been expressed by Baudrillart: *Philippe V et la cour de France*, IV, p. 301, note; and by Vaucher: *Robert Walpole et la politique de Fleury*, p. 152.

with the Emperor, but Fleury was able to persuade them that no peace would be concluded without their participation. The news of the Preliminaries, signed on October 3, 1735, came to them as a complete surprise. Fleury had excluded them from interfering in the peace, as he had prevented them from interfering in the war.[54]

The Preliminaries stipulated that Leszczynski should renounce the Polish throne but retain the title of king; that the duchy of Bar should immediately be turned over to him by the Duke of Lorraine, and the duchy of Lorraine as well, as soon as the death of the reigning Grand Duke of Tuscany would permit Duke Francis III of Lorraine to become Grand Duke at Florence; that Lorraine and Bar should pass to Maria Leszczynska and her children upon the death of Stanislas; that France should guarantee the Pragmatic Sanction; that Don Carlos should possess the Two Sicilies and the Tuscan Presidial States, in exchange for Parma, Piacenza and Tuscany; and that the King of Sardinia should have two cities of the Milanese, with their surrounding territory: Tortona and either Novara or Vigevano.[55]

The Preliminaries were not entirely satisfactory to France because they did not provide for Leszczynski's being put into immediate possession of the duchy of Lorraine: the Grand Duke of Tuscany might outlive him, and thus Leszczynski would never receive the compensation by which France set such store. There is no doubt that La Baune revealed himself to be but an indifferent negotiator. Fleury had warned him in two letters, dated September 11, 1735, to accept nothing less than all of Lorraine, without restrictions.[56] The interminable negotiations of 1736

---

[54] Vaucher: *Robert Walpole et la politique de Fleury*, pp. 144-145, 151-157. By October 12, 1735, Harrington at Hanover had not yet learned of the conclusion of the Preliminaries, nor had Horatio Walpole by October 14, at The Hague (Harrington to H. Walpole, and H. Walpole to Harrington [Weston Papers, *Hist. MSS. Comm., Report* X, App. Part I, pp. 262-263]).

[55] Text in Rousset: *Recueil historique*, X, pp. 519-523; also in Pajol: *Les guerres sous Louis XV*, I, p. 623; cf. Baudrillart: *Philippe V et la cour de France*, IV, pp. 300-303.

[56] A. É., *Corr. Pol., Autriche*, vol. 181, ff. 160-164, 173-174. Fleury wrote to Charles VI on Nov. 18, 1735: "Mr. de la Beaune avait passé ses pouvoirs" (*ibid.*, vol. 182, f. 165); the same to the same, (private), Dec. 2, 1735: "Mr. de la Beaune passa ses pouvoirs en signant et il crut pouvoir le faire *sub sperati*" (*ibid.*, f. 279).

and 1737 were almost wholly concerned with attempts on the part of the French to remedy the mistake which La Baune had committed.

Nevertheless, great things had been accomplished. France, who had been isolated by the action of the British in 1731, had now completely turned the tables. She had fought a very successful war and had established her reversionary rights to a notable acquisition of territory which enhanced her prestige and her strength. This same settlement outlined a *modus vivendi* for Italy which at last promised some stability in the affairs of that peninsula, and the whole had been arranged to the practical exclusion of the Maritime Powers. How greatly had the complexion of European affairs changed since the time when, in 1726, Great Britain had held France in diplomatic vassalage. So notably had the balance of power altered that it was now entirely compatible with the security of France to make that guarantee of the Emperor's succession which had for so many years been the object of the fondest desires of Charles VI. Indeed, it now became the safest policy for a conservative power which preferred tranquillity to turmoil (and such a power was France under the administration of Cardinal Fleury) to seek a *rapprochement* with the Emperor. The years to come were to see an effort on Fleury's part to put such a policy into action. Meanwhile, in October 1735, the more immediate problem was to convert the Preliminaries into a definitive peace while continuing to check the influence of the British in the determination of European affairs.

Also, Chauvelin to L'Estang, Dec. 1, 1735: "A l'égard du Congrès, je vous avoue ma surprise sur ce qui vous a été raporté que M. de la Baune avoit dit. Il me paroît que non seulement sur ce fait mais sur plusieurs autres il a beaucoup parlé et s'est bien avancé de son chef" (*ibid.*, f. 232).

CHAPTER IX

FROM THE PRELIMINARIES OF PEACE, OCTOBER 3, 1735,
TO THE OUTBREAK OF WAR BETWEEN GREAT
BRITAIN AND SPAIN, OCTOBER 1739

THE War of the Polish Succession was brought to a close by Preliminaries of Peace which were in gratifying congruence with the secret aims of Cardinal Fleury. By establishing the principle of the reversion of Lorraine to France, the Preliminaries, in spite of their defects in form, marked a signal victory in diplomacy which matched the French success in arms. Moreover, the acquisition of Lorraine altered the balance of power in France's favour to such a degree that it rendered feasible a reorientation of French policy for which the Cardinal had shown some predilection as early as 1728.[1] The guarantee of the Emperor's succession and a *rapprochement* with the Hapsburg monarchy seemed to have become, according to the ideas of Fleury, not merely compatible with the interests of France, but even desirable as a safeguard for the tranquillity of Europe.[2] Consequently, in the "close Correspondence by Letters, wherein he believed himself to have a great Superiority over most People," Fleury lavished on the Emperor his sentiments for establishing the relations of Austria and France on the basis of a firm and indissoluble union.[3] These letters, beneath their crust of rhetoric, do seem to point to the conclusion that Fleury would gladly have accepted a close connection with the Hapsburg monarchy; the Cardinal was envisaging an alliance which was not finally established, however, until 1756.[4]

[1] Cf. *supra*, p. 196.
[2] In the course of Fleury's instructions to La Baune (July, 1735), it was mentioned "que le véritable interest réciproque et l'avantage de la Réligion semblent démander une union et une confiance qui n'a point encore été entre les Puissances Catholiques" (A. É., *Corr. Pol., Autriche*, vol. 181, ff. 24-32).
[3] The quotation is from the anonymous pamphlet *Memoirs of the Life and Administration of the late Andrew-Hercules de Fleury*, p. 32.
[4] Some of these letters may be found in the Appendices, *infra*.

The first care of the French after the conclusion of the Pre-liminaries of Peace was to palliate to their allies the separate negotiations in which France had engaged with the Emperor. This they did with some assurance in the case of the King of Sardinia, but with very considerable misgivings as to the effect such intelligence would have on the court of Spain.[5] But Elisa-beth Farnese exercised admirable self-restraint, even in spite of Fleury's provocative letter which, beneath the formulae of polite-ness, hinted at the various occasions when Spain had shown her-self to be a difficult and disobliging ally.[6] It is true that the Spanish court made overtures to the British in December 1735, the very thing of which the French were the most apprehensive; but the British were so well persuaded that they would partici-pate in the final peace settlement that they rejected the Spanish advances.[7] Consequently, on February 18, 1736, the Spanish sovereigns accepted the October Preliminaries.[8] For the rest of the year, the French endeavoured to keep them in good humour by persistently inclining towards their side in the mediation of the Hispano-Portuguese dispute which had arisen in 1735.[9]

The two principal preoccupations of Fleury and Chauvelin in 1736 were to exclude the British from participation in the final peace settlement, and to force the Austrians to agree to the im-mediate cession of Bar and Lorraine. On the whole, the British were willing to consent to the compensation stipulated for King

[5] For Fleury's letters of Oct. 27 and Nov. 5, 1735, to the King of Sardinia, see Gay: *Négociations relatives à l'établissement de la maison de Bourbon sur le trône des Deux-Siciles*, pp. 306-311, 312-316. They are chiefly filled with recriminations against Spain. On informing Spain, see Baudrillart: *Philippe V et la cour de France*, IV, pp. 305-317. An armistice (Franco-Austrian) was concluded at Mantua, Dec. 1, 1735 (Pajol: *Les guerres sous Louis XV*, I, pp. 610-611).

[6] Fleury to Their Catholic Majesties, November 29, 1735 (Baudrillart: *Philippe V et la cour de France*, IV, pp. 318-319, note).

[7] See Newcastle's account in his letter to Waldegrave, Dec. 5, O. S., 1735 (*British Diplomatic Instructions: France, 1727-1744*, pp. 176-177).

[8] Baudrillart: *Philippe V et la cour de France*, IV, p. 338,

[9] Vaucher: *Robert Walpole et la politique de Fleury*, pp. 178-184. Cf. the letters of Newcastle to Waldegrave, Jan. 22, Feb. 27, April 30, May 21, Aug. 17, (all Old Style), 1736 (*British Diplomatic Instructions: France, 1727-1744*, pp. 178, 178-179, 180, 181-182, 183-184).

Stanislas.[10] Nevertheless, they were uneasy at the thought of France's separate and secret negotiation with the Emperor, in which they both desired and expected to be associated.[11] For a moment, they conceived it possible to bribe Chauvelin; later, in December 1735, Sir Robert Walpole entered into private correspondence with him, apparently on Chauvelin's invitation.[12] Although the British were informed by the traitorous Bussy of what was going on day by day in the French Foreign Office, they nevertheless found it impossible to hit upon any expedient which could bring them into the negotiation.[13] Just after the conclusion of the Preliminaries, Fleury himself had been in favour of calling a general peace congress, but this idea receded further and further into the background.[14] In June and July, Horatio Walpole instructed Waldegrave to hint at Great Britain's desire to participate in the peace settlement.[15] The result was that Fleury

[10] Harrington and Horatio Walpole approved of the exchange in letters which they wrote to each other in 1735 (H. Walpole to Harrington, The Hague, July 18, 1735 [Weston Papers, *Hist. MSS. Comm., Report* X, App. Part I, pp. 256-257]; Harrington to H. Walpole, Hanover, July 27, 1735 [*ibid.*, p. 257]; H. Walpole to Harrington, The Hague, Sept. 30, 1735 [*ibid.*, pp. 260-261]; the same to the same, The Hague, Oct. 2, 1735 [*ibid.*, p. 261]; Harrington to H. Walpole, Oct. 9, 1735 [*ibid.*, pp. 261-262]).

[11] Newcastle to Waldegrave, Sept. 8 and October 3, O. S., 1735 (*British Diplomatic Instructions: France, 1727-1744*, pp. 172-173, 174-176).

[12] Coxe: *Memoirs of . . . Sir Robert Walpole*, I, p. 487; III, pp. 262-265, 317-318. Chauvelin seems to have intimated to Waldegrave in November 1735, that he would be willing to enter into direct correspondence with Sir Robert; the latter signified his willingness in letters dated Dec. 4/15 (two), 1735, Dec. 24, 1735/Jan. 4, 1736 (two) and Jan. 1/12, 1735/6 (Coxe: *op. cit.*, III, pp. 308-311, 312-314, 316-317). But nothing came of this hopeful beginning; the correspondence seems merely to have been a device for averting the intervention of the British in the Austrian negotiation. Walpole wrote Waldegrave on March 21, O. S., 1735/6: "The private correspondence with our friend seeming to be at an end, or at least wholly uselesse, I have not for some time troubled your lordship about it; altho' I cannot but say there is something in it that appears a little mysterious, that so great hopes should be conceived in the beginning, and the whole drop at once as if no such thing had ever been thought of. It is a great opportunity lost, if ever it could have been had" (Coxe: *op. cit.*, III, p. 317).

[13] Bussy was temporarily *premier commis*, during the absence of La Porte du Theil at Vienna.

[14] Fleury to Charles VI, Nov. 18, 1735 (A. É., *Corr. Pol., Autriche*, vol. 182, ff. 163-164); Fleury to Sinzendorff, Dec. 21, 1735 (*ibid.*, vol. 183, f. 51).

[15] June 18, O. S., and July 9, O. S., 1736 (*British Diplomatic Instructions: France, 1727-1744*, pp. 182-183).

suddenly proposed, not British participation in the peace negotiations, but the revival of the alliance between France and
Great Britain, which he promised to keep secret from Chauvelin.[16] These tactics once more disorganized the policy of the
British; while they were inclined to suspect that the Cardinal
was not sincere, they dared not antagonize him by a refusal. So,
while the British were feeling their way, Chauvelin was left free
to pursue his negotiations with Vienna. After the difficulties
which the Austrians raised had been settled by the Convention
of August 28, 1736, then Fleury showed himself to be entirely
unwilling to discuss further an alliance with the British. The
upshot of all these events was that British policy, as far as the
Austro-French negotiation was concerned, was entirely ineffec-
tive throughout the year 1736.

The negotiation with Austria, the object of which was to secure
the immediate cession of Bar and Lorraine without waiting for
the death of the Grand Duke of Tuscany, was made difficult for
the French by the temporizing and chicanery of the Austrian
ministers. La Baune had returned to Versailles after the signing
of the Preliminaries and in his place was sent a diplomatist
named L'Estang, whose purpose was to alter that agreement in
reference to the Lorraine stipulation. But Fleury made the mistake of letting the Emperor know that L'Estang had orders to
exchange ratifications.[17] The result was that the Austrians not
only refused to alter the Preliminaries in the sense desired by
France, but also made difficulties about the performance of the
obligations to which they had already agreed.[18] Consequently,
both Fleury and Chauvelin ordered L'Estang to exchange ratifi-

---

[16] *British Diplomatic Instructions: France, 1727-1744*, p. xxxi; also, Newcastle
to Waldegrave, Aug. 27, O. S., 1736 (*ibid.*, pp. 184-185). Horatio Walpole to
Waldegrave, August 8, O. S., 1736 (Coxe: *Memoirs of . . . Sir Robert Walpole*,
III, pp. 352-356); Vaucher: *Robert Walpole et la politique de Fleury*, pp. 171-174.

[17] Fleury to Charles VI, Oct. 25, 1735 (A. É., *Corr. Pol., Autriche*, vol. 182, ff.
95-96); the same to the same, Nov. 18, 1735 (*ibid.*, ff. 162-166); Fleury to Sinzendorff, Oct. 25, 1735 (*ibid.*, f. 102).

[18] L'Estang wrote to Chauvelin on Nov. 17, 1735: "Il eut été fort à désirer,
Monseigneur, comme Mr. Bartenstein l'a dit à M. le Comte de Wiedt, que S[on]
Em[inence] n'eut pas promis que j'échangerais les ratifications quelque fut la ré-
ponse de l'Empereur" (A. É., *Corr. Pol., Autriche*, vol. 182, f. 188).

cations immediately.[19] After this was accomplished, L'Estang's place at Vienna was taken by La Porte du Theil, one of the *premiers commis* of the Ministry of Foreign Affairs. The correspondence with Du Theil was handled by Chauvelin and not by Fleury, a fact which has tempted MM. Driault and Boyé to assert that Fleury voluntarily relinquished his share in the negotiation in tacit recognition of his own inability to pursue it with profit.[20] In treating with the Austrian ministers, Chauvelin had an extremely compelling bargaining point in that France refused to surrender Philippsburg and Kehl until satisfaction had been received in the matter of Lorraine. Chauvelin began the negotiation by assurances of the French desire to live on good terms with Charles VI:

> Because in fact (and on this point leave no doubt), the King and His Ministry are very determined to establish with the Emperor and his Council the closest and most sincere harmony.[21]

Nevertheless, Du Theil did not manifest any undue complacence toward the Austrian ministers. Chauvelin encouraged his emissary in this, reminding him on April 8, 1736, that at all times bad temper on the part of the Imperial ministers had been the signal of the court of Vienna that it was on the point of yielding.[22] On April 11, 1736, the Austrian ministers signed a convention "for the Execution of the Preliminaries," which provided that Leszczynski should be put in possession of Lorraine immediately following the conclusion and ratification of a convention to that

[19] Chauvelin and Pecquet to L'Estang, Dec. 1, 1735 (A. É., *Corr. Pol.*, *Autriche*, vol. 182, ff. 229-230, 234).

[20] Driault: "Chauvelin, 1733-1737." *Revue d'histoire diplomatique*, VII, pp. 48-49; Boyé: *Stanislas Leszczynski et le troisième traité de Vienne*, pp. 398-401; also J. O. B. de Cléron, comte d'Haussonville: *Histoire de la réunion de la Lorraine à la France* (Second edition, Paris, 1860, four vols.), IV, p. 266. It is more reasonable to suppose that, the principle having been laid down, Fleury turned over the details of its elaboration to his subordinate (Baudrillart: *Philippe V et la cour de France*, IV, p. 340).

[21] Chauvelin to Du Theil, Jan. 7, 1736 (A. É., *Corr. Pol.*, *Autriche*, vol. 183, f. 177).

[22] Chauvelin to Du Theil, April 8, 1736; cited by Driault: "Chauvelin, 1733-1737." *Revue d'histoire diplomatique*, VII, p. 55.

effect between Louis XV and the Duke of Lorraine.[23] Chauvelin regarded this as a hopeful beginning, but meanwhile France retained possession of Philippsburg and Kehl.[24] In July 1736, Chauvelin affected to be in no hurry about the immediate cession of Lorraine; however, France would henceforth regard the duchy of Bar as conquered territory, subject to direct annexation and not to treaty bargaining. As a result of this threat, the Austrians signed the convention of August 28, 1736, which stipulated the cession of both duchies as soon as the Imperial garrisons should be admitted to Tuscany, and Don Carlos and Elisabeth Farnese should sign their renunciations to claims on the Tuscan inheritance.[25] On September 24, 1736, Duke Francis agreed to the cession of Bar, although the Emperor subsequently delayed validating the cession. This temporizing exhausted Chauvelin's patience, and on November 24, 1736, he threatened Schmerling, the Emperor's representative at the French court, with war. Schmerling thereupon presented him, on November 29, 1736, with the Emperor's ratification of the cession of Bar.[26] On January 5, 1737, the Spaniards and Austrians exchanged their respective cessions of Parma, Piacenza and Tuscany, for the one; and of the Two Sicilies, for the other.[27] On February 13, 1737, Duke Francis finally and reluctantly acceded to the convention of August 28, 1736, thereby permitting the immediate cession of Lor-

---

[23] Printed by Massuet: *Histoire de la dernière guerre et des négociations pour la paix*, part II, vol. ii, pp. 329-339; and by Wenck: *Codex juris gentium*, I, pp. 16-23. Cf. Boyé: *Stanislas Leszczynski et le troisième traité de Vienne*, p. 412.

[24] The importance of France's utilizing her occupation of these strongholds as a lever to prize concessions from the Emperor has been emphasized by Driault: "Chauvelin, 1733-1737." *Revue d'histoire diplomatique*, VII, pp. 53-55, 62.

[25] This meant that the Austrians gave up the stipulation made in the Preliminaries of October 3, 1735, that the exchange should not be effected before the death of the Grand Duke of Tuscany. The Spaniards claimed that Elisabeth Farnese and Don Carlos ought not to be required to surrender the allodial rights (i.e., rights which amounted to extraterritoriality) on extensive estates which belonged to Elisabeth Farnese in Tuscany. This pretension was finally given up (Baudrillart: *Philippe V et la cour de France*, IV, pp. 350-351). For the convention of August 28, 1736, see Rousset: *Recueil historique*, XIII, pp. 441-452; and Wenck: *Codex juris gentium*, I, pp. 51-61. Cf. Boyé: *Stanislas Leszczynski et le troisième traité de Vienne*, pp. 423-424.

[26] Boyé: *Stanislas Leszczynski et le troisième traité de Vienne*, pp. 428-429.

[27] Baudrillart: *Philippe V et la cour de France*, IV, pp. 373-374.

raine to the French.[28] This was the conclusive act of the whole negotiation; what may be said to have been the final and definitive treaty of peace between Austria and France followed as a matter of course on May 2, 1737.[29] This act of May 2, 1737, although it was the treaty which really established peace between the Emperor and Louis XV, was referred to by French and Austrian diplomats as being mere "preliminaries." In part, this was true, because it was simply a bilateral agreement, to which Spain and Sardinia had not acceded; in part, this was disingenuous, because neither the French nor the Austrians desired to flaunt the fact that they had settled the peace without the participation of other European powers. In due time this agreement became the third Treaty of Vienna, signed on November 18, 1738. The King of Sardinia acceded to it on February 3, 1739; Spain on April 21; the Elector-King of Saxony-Poland and the Czarina on May 26 of that year.[30] Thus was concluded the War of the Polish Succession.

In the meantime, by the Declaration of Meudon, dated September 30, 1736, Louis XV and Stanislas Leszczynski settled the terms on which the latter would be permitted to enter upon the possession of his new principality.[31] On February 8, 1737, French officials took over the administration of Bar, in the name of the "King of Poland," and on March 21 they did the same for Lorraine. On April 3, Stanislas Leszczynski took up his residence at Lunéville.[32]

Inasmuch as Chauvelin had been entrusted with the direction of the difficult negotiations with Austria, it was unwise to change that direction as long as the Austrians had not consented to the immediate cession of Lorraine. Exactly seven days after that

[28] Since February 12, 1736, Duke Francis had been married to Maria Theresa.
[29] Boyé: *Stanislas Leszczynski et le troisième traité de Vienne*, p. 430; Vaucher: *Robert Walpole et la politique de Fleury*, p. 219.
[30] Boyé: *Stanislas Leszczynski et le troisième traité de Vienne*, pp. 430-431.
[31] Boyé: *Stanislas Leszczynski et le troisième traité de Vienne*, pp. 456-462. Both financially and administratively, Lorraine really became an integral part of France; Leszczynski was very much more of a pensioner than a sovereign. See also Robert Parisot: *Histoire de Lorraine* (Paris, 1919-1924, three vols.), II, p. 118.
[32] Boyé: *Stanislas Leszczynski et le troisième traité de Vienne*, pp. 476-477, 486, 494.

point had been settled on February 13, 1737, however, Chauvelin was deprived of his offices and exiled, first to his estate at Grosbois, and then to Bourges.[33] Although his disgrace was an event which had been foreseen for some time, its exact cause was the subject of the wildest conjecture.[34] He was supposed to have been guilty of a misuse of funds, an accusation in answer to which he inspired a reply.[35] He was also supposed to have formed a group in the diplomatic service more faithful to him than to the Cardinal, and to have carried on a secret correspondence with these individuals. In this allegation there is probably some truth, for Pecquet, Vaulgrenant (the French ambassador to Spain at the time of Chauvelin's disgrace), Fénelon and Chavigny represented, in their views, the traditional anti-Hapsburg school of which Chauvelin was the leader. According to the anonymous but seemingly well-informed author of the *Memoirs of the Life and Administration of the late Andrew-Hercules de Fleury* (1743), it was the Spanish minister, Patiño, intriguing in collusion with Vaulgrenant, who found means of bringing Chauvelin's perfidy

[33] The order to give up the seals was supposed to have been accompanied by a letter from Fleury to Chauvelin in which appeared the severe phrase: "Vous avez manqué au roi, au peuple et à vous-même." This letter may be found in Flassan: *Histoire . . . de la diplomatie française*, V, pp. 75-76. Philip V, however, declared the letter to be a forgery (Baudrillart: *Philippe V et la cour de France*, IV, pp. 376-377). The best contemporary account of the circumstances of Chauvelin's disgrace is given by Luynes: *Mémoires*, I, pp. 182-185; see also D'Argenson: *Journal et mémoires*, I, pp. 234-239; and Barbier: *Journal*, II, pp. 134, 137.

[34] The Duke of Luynes wrote on January 3, 1737, over six weeks before the disgrace of Chauvelin: "Je n'ai point parlé jusqu'à présent des bruits qui se sont répandus depuis deux mois à Paris, et depuis quinze jours ici, par rapport à M. le garde des sceaux" (Luynes: *Mémoires*, I, pp. 159-160); similar rumours of Chauvelin's disgrace, circulating in January 1737, are noted by D'Argenson: *Journal et mémoires*, I, p. 227; and Barbier: *Journal*, II, pp. 125, 126. Waldegrave wrote Newcastle on Jan. 3, 1737, that the Cardinal treated Chauvelin "as a meer clark, stopping him at once when he offered to put in a word, even to make the thing clearer, and this the Cardinal did with an air of superiority I never saw in him before" (*British Diplomatic Instructions: France, 1727-1744*, p. xxxii); cf. Waldegrave to Sir Robert Walpole, Feb. 6, 1737 (Coxe: *Memoirs of . . . Sir Robert Walpole*, III, p. 450).

[35] *The Defence of Monsieur Chauvelin, late Keeper of the Seals in France, in Answer to the Accusations brought against him before the King in Relation to his Conduct in the Administration of His Affairs* (London, 1737), esp. p. 18. Fleury's comment upon this pamphlet was that it was "too ill-writ to be Chauvelin's own" (Waldegrave to Newcastle, June 26, 1737 [Coxe: *Memoirs of . . . Sir Robert Walpole*, III, p. 481]).

to the Cardinal's notice. Thereupon the Cardinal made no scruple of disgracing Chauvelin, once he was assured that the Spanish court was not particularly desirous of his retention.[36]

Chauvelin's disgrace has also been plausibly explained by Fleury's jealousy of him. There is no doubt that Chauvelin expected to be First Minister after Fleury's resignation or death, nor that he was impatient for that time to come.[37] On this point, Fleury was very sensitive; as he wrote to the daughter of Torcy, with reference to Chauvelin's disgrace:

He grew weary of my living too long; that is a fault of which I have no desire to correct myself for some time to come.[38]

Added to these reasons were the effects of court intrigue; Chauvelin was supported by the Bourbons and the Contis, which had the effect of drawing upon him the enmity of the "Rambouillet Party," whose leaders were the Count of Toulouse and the Noailles family.[39] Besides, Chauvelin was not on good terms

[36] *Op. cit.*, pp. 45-50. This pamphlet was written by a well-informed person, perhaps Horatio Walpole (Vaucher: *Robert Walpole et la politique de Fleury*, pp. 198-199). This intrigue is supposed to have occurred just before Patiño's death, Nov. 3, 1736; there may be some truth in it, for Vaulgrenant did not lose favour with the Cardinal after Chauvelin's fall. The Spanish court was not much concerned about Chauvelin's disgrace (Baudrillart: *Philippe V et la cour de France*, IV, p. 377). For Chauvelin's private correspondence with French diplomats behind the back of Fleury, see Baudrillart: *op. cit.*, IV, pp. 129, 375; *Recueil des instructions . . . Espagne*, III, pp. 121 footnote, 182; Vaucher: *Robert Walpole et la politique de Fleury*, p. 207. Waldegrave wrote to Newcastle, Aug. 16, 1735: "In the course of my conversation my friend [Bussy] told me there had been of late a considerable coldness between the cardinal and his adjunct; his eminency having of late discovered several of the other's practices to make himself master of all the foreign ministers, and consequently of the negociations, by the secret correspondence he has with the ministers" (Coxe: *Memoirs of . . . Sir Robert Walpole*, III, p. 275).

[37] Luynes: *Mémoires*, III, p. 373; D'Argenson: *Journal et mémoires*, I, pp. 235, 238-239; Hénault: *Mémoires*, pp. 153-154.

[38] Luynes: *Mémoires*, II, p. 283.

[39] Toussaint: *Anecdotes curieuses*, pp. 71, 79; Barbier: *Journal*, II, p. 78. Chauvelin's position was weakened, too, by the death of his friend D'Antin on Nov. 2, 1736 (Hénault: *Mémoires*, p. 155). Hénault also wrote that Chauvelin asked him early in 1737 to draw up and submit to the Cardinal a memorial in Chauvelin's defense (*ibid.*, p. 154). Chavigny wrote in 1738 that he had observed the decline in Chauvelin's influence in 1735: ". . . . le crédit et la confiance de M. Chauvelin [était] sur le déclin, car je n'aperçus que trop sa décadence dès le premier abord. M. le Cardinal ne me laissa pas lieu d'en douter dans quelques propos qu'il me tint. . ." (A. É., *Mém. et Doc., France*, vol. 457, f. 63).

with Barjac, the *premier valet* of the Cardinal, who was said to have used his considerable influence to blacken Chauvelin's character in the eyes of the Cardinal.[40]

But these reasons for Chauvelin's disgrace are mere backstairs gossip. On the higher plane of statecraft, Fleury may well have conceived that he was justified in preventing from succeeding him a man who would hasten to put into effect a policy which the Cardinal regarded as wrong. For Fleury regarded a *rapprochement* of France with Austria as the policy which had now become the most practical one for maintaining the European balance and tranquillity. Fleury's policy was not pre-eminently a Bourbon family one; he sought for France broader diplomatic connections than merely those with Spain, and he favoured permitting Austria to play the part in the French diplomatic programme which Great Britain had filled until 1731. Inasmuch as France was about to secure reversionary rights over Lorraine, it was a plan both feasible and statesmanlike; yet it is amazing that a man of Fleury's age should have exhibited such adaptability and such a realistic grasp of the European situation when the majority of his colleagues were still held in bondage by the tradition of hostility to the Hapsburg monarchy. This is not to say that Fleury was by any means prepared to deliver French policy into the hands of the Austrian ministers, to do with it as they would. The Cardinal did not propose surrendering the diplomatic independence of France. The instructions to La Noue, for example, written in 1738 at a time when Fleury was hoping to establish this new departure in French policy, emphasized that, in spite of the recent friendship between Louis XV and the Emperor, La Noue was not to forget that France was a guarantor of the Treaties of Westphalia; his function was to assist France in maintaining a *"juste milieu"* in German affairs.[41] Although the half-measures which the Cardinal adopted during the actual crisis of the Austrian succession belied the asseverations which he made in 1735 and 1736, there is no doubt that in this earlier

---

[40] Luynes: *Mémoires*, I, p. 189; VIII, pp. 378-380. Hénault: *Mémoires*, p. 153.
[41] Auerbach: *La France et le Saint Empire romain germanique*, p. 307.

period he did really desire a "firm and indissoluble union" with the Emperor. Besides the assertions to that effect which appear in his letters to Charles VI, his letters to the Emperor's ministers likewise reveal this disposition. Such was the spirit in which the instructions to La Baune were drawn up; and Fleury wrote to Sinzendorff on October 25, 1735, with reference to L'Estang's ratification of the Preliminaries:

[Your Excellency] will see by the promptness with which the King has lent himself to the consummation of this important treaty how much His Majesty is inclined to unite himself closely with His Imperial Majesty. I have always regarded this union as very important for the tranquillity of Europe. . . . [42]

A letter to Bartenstein of the same date likewise spoke in this vein; and to this Bartenstein replied, on November 17, 1735, in a letter in which he mentioned

the extreme desire which I have to co-operate, feeble instrument though I am, in the great work of the so desirable union between His Imperial Majesty and His Most Christian Majesty, since it has always appeared to me the sure means of confirming the tranquillity of Europe and the general welfare of Christianity. The sentiments of our Court thus correspond perfectly with those of your Eminence.[43]

On December 2, 1735, Fleury wrote to Charles VI of the desire of the King "to establish with Your Imperial Majesty a sincere and perfect union" and of his own

ardent and constant desire which I have always had of being the means of bringing about between the King and Your Imperial Majesty an indissoluble union.[44]

[42] Fleury to Sinzendorff, Oct. 25, 1735 (A. É., *Corr. Pol., Autriche*, vol. 182, f. 102); Fleury's instructions to La Baune, July 1735 (*ibid.*, vol. 181, ff. 24-32).
[43] Bartenstein to Fleury, Nov. 17, 1735 (A. É., *Corr. Pol., Autriche*, vol. 182, ff. 192-193). A copy of Fleury's letter to Bartenstein, Oct. 25, 1735 (*ibid.*, vol. 182, ff. 103-104). Bartenstein, who had been influential in determining the policy which resulted in the War of the Polish Succession and in the Austrian intervention in the Turkish war, was sympathetic to a *rapprochement* with France (Alfred Arneth: "Johann Christoph Bartenstein und seine Zeit." *Archiv für österreichische Geschichte*, XLVI [1871], pp. 30-31, 35-36).
[44] Fleury to Charles VI (private), Dec. 2, 1735 (A. É., *Corr. Pol., Autriche*, vol. 182, ff. 279, 282).

To Sinzendorff he wrote the same day of "the union which I should like to establish between the Emperor and the King," and a letter to Bartenstein, also of that date, reiterated these views. On December 21, 1735, Fleury wrote to Sinzendorff:

That which I am taking the liberty of representing here is inspired merely by the sincere desire of the King to unite himself intimately with His Imperial Majesty, and if this project has been so long deferred, I am able to assure Your Excellency that it has not been my fault, and that if I had been seconded as I flattered myself that I would be, this would have been accomplished long ago, because of my conviction that this union between the two greatest Princes of Europe is not only expedient [*convenable*], but that it is still more so for establishing solidly the public tranquillity.[45]

These views of the Cardinal, Chauvelin never adopted. His memorial *Veues sur les affaires générales*, which was "approved by the King in his Council, October 19, 1736," was worded so as to have the appearance of conforming with Fleury's ideas; nevertheless it betrayed a hostility to Austria and a desire to take advantage of the question of the Austrian succession when Charles VI should die. Fleury, at this moment, contemplated preserving European tranquillity by permitting the undisturbed succession of Maria Theresa, in consonance with France's guarantee of the Pragmatic Sanction; Chauvelin looked forward to the death of the Emperor as providing an opportunity for dismembering the Hapsburg monarchy. Thus Chauvelin remarked:

If we have not been able to diminish the Imperial power substantially, we have at least enfeebled it for a time.

He declared that France had guaranteed the Pragmatic Sanction "only with repugnance" and discreetly criticized Fleury's Austrian policy by remarking:

We can not yet know whether in reality this peace shall have gained for us the friendship of the Court of Vienna. . . . and perhaps it will continue to regard itself as our rival.

[45] Fleury to Sinzendorff, Dec. 2, 1735 (A. É., *Corr. Pol., Autriche*, vol. 182, f. 294); Fleury to Bartenstein, Dec. 2, 1735 (*ibid.*, vol. 182, f. 295); Fleury to Sinzendorff, Dec. 21, 1735 (*ibid.*, vol. 183, f. 52). With these assertions should be compared the instructions to Mirepoix, French ambassador to the Emperor, under date of Dec. 11, 1737: "Elle [Sa Majesté] le [Mirepoix] destine à être l'instrument de ce qui se peut opérer de plus intéressant pour l'Europe entière, c'est-à-dire l'établissement d'une intelligence et d'une union aussi durables qu'intimes entre le Roi et l'Empereur" (*Recueil des instructions . . . Autriche* [Edited by Albert Sorel; Paris, 1884], p. 245).

Finally, Chauvelin's views on the Pragmatic Sanction Fleury may well have considered alarming, although it is known that the Cardinal himself accepted the guarantee of the Pragmatic Sanction with the understanding that it was not to injure the legal claims of third parties.[46] For Chauvelin declared that

> The object of our greatest attention is the fate of the Austrian Power if the Emperor should die without male heirs. . . . The engagement which we have taken to guarantee the Pragmatic does not engage us to co-operate in the election of a King of the Romans. . . . The guiding principle appears to be to put oneself in a situation to profit from all events. . . . Whatsoever arrangement the Emperor may make during his lifetime, there is good cause for believing that at his death, especially if the Archduchess has no male children, the affair of the Pragmatic will be the occasion for many changes; . . . it will be then that it will be necessary to examine well the strength of the different parties, both while especially avoiding being involved in a long war, and in seeking to make one's appearance only when it shall be a question of striking a decisive last blow which shall finish the question.[47]

As M. Vaucher has characterized this memorial, "it was preparation for war which dissembled itself behind a eulogy of peace"; and it may reasonably be argued that it was this fundamental divergence of policy which persuaded Fleury that it would be dangerous to leave Chauvelin in a position of power.[48] It is ironical that, when the crisis of the Austrian succession arose, Fleury ultimately drifted into the adoption of the very policy for which Chauvelin had contended.

[46] See Broglie: "Le cardinal de Fleury et la *Pragmatique Sanction.*" *Revue historique*, XX (Sept.-Dec., 1882), pp. 257-281. Fleury wrote to La Baune on Sept. 11, 1735: "Je crois que vous pouriés en conversation toucher quelquechose comme de vous-même de ces droits de la maison de Bavière, en faisant entendre que pour prévenir tout ce qui pouroit troubler la tranquilité, il seroit bon d'éclaircir les droits de cette maison" (A. É., *Corr. Pol., Autriche,* vol. 181, f. 230).

[47] A. É., *Mém. et Doc., France,* vol. 418, ff. 218-234. Chavigny, writing in 1738, anticipated trouble when the question of the Austrian succession would have to be settled, consequent to the death of Charles VI (*Mémoire de M. Chavigny contenant quelques observations sur les anecdotes les plus importantes qu'il a recueillies dans les différentes négociations qui lui ont été confiées depuis 1712 jusques au mois de May 1738* [A. É., *Mém. et Doc., France,* vol. 457, f. 74]); he recommended supporting the claims of the Elector of Bavaria (*ibid.,* f. 76) and declared that France had not undertaken to guarantee the Pragmatic Sanction to the prejudice of the rights of a third party (*ibid.,* f. 75).

[48] Vaucher: *Robert Walpole et la politique de Fleury,* p. 203. In this connection may be mentioned an interesting anonymous memorial, bearing the date of August 1, 1738 and the notation that it was translated from the English, which severely criticized Fleury's policy of *rapprochement* with Austria (*Considérations sur l'union de la France avec l'Empereur d'Allemagne [pour servir d'apologie au ministère de M. le garde des sceaux Chauvelin]* [A. É., *Mém. et Doc., Autriche,* vol. 8, ff. 56-80]).

The British, it may well be supposed, were delighted with Chauvelin's disgrace, especially since they had recently detected him in correspondence with the Pretender.[49] They naturally were eager to learn what would henceforth be the Cardinal's policy towards themselves. True to his usual course of diverting the attention of the British from Continental affairs by holding out hopes to them of renewed alliance with France, Fleury talked cordially, although vaguely, of his desire for a British alliance. This attitude greatly puzzled the British ministers, but they did not see fit to discourage the Cardinal's advances.[50] However, it was not until January 1738, that he could be persuaded to put his thoughts into writing. And so the year 1737 went by, as the preceding ones had done, without Great Britain's playing any active diplomatic part on the Continent.

On the whole, the years 1737 and 1738 constituted another period of *détente* in European affairs, just as the year 1732 had done. It was a time when the representatives of France were engaged in widespread but inconspicuous negotiations which bore fruit and arrested the attention of Europe in 1739. In Sweden, the French lent their support to the anti-British party, and particularly endeavoured to undermine the power of Count Horn.[51]

[49] The Pretender's letter to Chauvelin was given by him, through mistake, to Waldegrave on Oct. 9, 1736. The British ministers were disposed to be very upset about this, although Horatio Walpole pointed out to his brother, in a letter dated Oct. 28, 1736, that all European courts received letters from the Pretender (Coxe: *Memoirs of . . . Sir Robert Walpole*, III, pp. 420-429). For expressions of British delight at Chauvelin's disgrace, see Coxe: *op. cit.*, III, pp. 448-452, 457-458; also Newcastle's letter to Waldegrave, March 8, O. S., 1736/7 (*British Diplomatic Instructions: France, 1727-1744*, pp. 187-188).

[50] The *pourparlers* for a renewed Anglo-French alliance may be followed in the letters of Sir Robert Walpole to Waldegrave, March 7, O. S., 1736/7, and May —, 1737 (Coxe: *Memoirs of . . . Sir Robert Walpole*, III, pp. 458-459, 469-470); and of Waldegrave to Sir Robert Walpole and the Duke of Newcastle, March 30, April 3 and 13, May 22 and 24, 1737 (Coxe: *op. cit.*, III, pp. 459-460, 461, 462-465, 471-475, 476-477).

[51] See Horatio Walpole's letter to Queen Caroline, Sept. 27, 1737, based on information received from Gedda, Swedish ambassador at Paris (Coxe: *Memoirs of . . . Sir Robert Walpole*, III, pp. 488-494). Cf. Harrington's letters to Finch, Aug. 30, O. S., 1737 (*British Diplomatic Instructions: Sweden, 1727-1789*, pp. 63-64); the same to the same, Feb. 21, O. S., 1737/8 (*ibid.*, pp. 66-67); the same to the same, March 17, O. S., 1737/8, containing the news of Chavigny's attempts at Copenhagen to secure a Swedish-Danish-French alliance (*ibid.*, pp. 67-69); the same to the same, May 19, O. S., 1738 (*ibid.*, pp. 70-71).

at Geneva, and took the first steps which were to lead her ultimately to the acquisition of Corsica.[59]

But to the British the Cardinal remained as gently intractable
and as bafflingly inscrutable as ever. Significantly enough, a dispute concerning the rights of British ships to "seek shelter" or
to "take in water" in the French West Indies dragged its course
throughout these years until it was entirely lost sight of in the
larger excitements of the Wars of Jenkins' Ear and the Austrian
Succession.[60] To the astonishment of the British, relations with
the French did not improve following the disgrace of Chauvelin,
and Horatio Walpole wrote to Queen Caroline of

[59] For the settlement of the Portuguese dispute, see Baudrillart: *Philippe V
et la cour de France*, IV, pp. 431-434; Vaucher: *Robert Walpole et la politique de
Fleury*, p. 216. The Geneva dispute was one of a type familiar to the history of
Switzerland in the eighteenth century; the middle burgher class was discontented
with the partisan and exclusive rule of the aristocratic few. Trouble first broke
out in 1734 and, more seriously, in 1737. Louis XV offered his mediation in
September, and terms of settlement were agreed to on April 7, 1738. A history
of this dispute, together with documents, is given by the Baron of Zur-Lauben:
Histoire militaire des Suisses au service de la France (Paris, 1751-1753, eight vols.),
VIII, pp. 20-43; see, also, Flassan: *Histoire . . . . de la diplomatie française*, V,
pp. 78-79. With reference to the Corsican affair, revolt had broken out there in
1729; the Genoese secured the assistance of the Emperor, who occupied the island
with eleven thousand soldiers from the Milanese. These evacuated Corsica in
1733, after the Genoese had made some concessions to the Corsicans under Imperial guarantee. In 1734 the Corsicans revolted again, declared their independence in 1735, and elected Baron Neuhof as King [Theodore I] in 1736. In a letter
from Chauvelin to Campredon, April 26, 1735, the French policy towards the
Corsican trouble was set forth. In Corsica a party was to be formed desirous of
French protection, while in Genoa Campredon was to seek to form a party desirous of selling the island to the French (*Recueil des instructions . . . Florence,
Modène, Gênes*, pp. 282-283). In 1737 a Genoese-French agreement was signed
whereby the Genoese paid for eight thousand French troops, who occupied Bastia
and St. Florent while taking good care not to antagonize the Corsicans. All but
one regiment were withdrawn in 1741 (*ibid.*, pp. lxxxiv, 283-286, 291-298).

[60] Vaucher: *Robert Walpole et la politique de Fleury*, pp. 262-264; also, see Paul
Vaucher: "Une convention franco-anglaise pour régler le commerce et la navigation dans les Indes Occidentales, 1737-1740." *Mélanges d'histoire offerts à M.
Charles Bémont* (Paris, 1913), pp. 611-617. References to this dispute in the
British papers may be found in the instructions to Waldegrave, April 10, O. S.,
1738 (*British Diplomatic Instructions: France, 1727-1744*, pp. 196-198); Newcastle
to Waldegrave, Nov. 13, O. S., 1738 and Jan. 5, O. S., 1738/9 (*ibid.*, pp. 210-213);
also, *ibid.*, p. xxxv. Waldegrave to Newcastle, Feb. 22, 1737 (Coxe: *Memoirs of
. . . Sir Robert Walpole*, III, p. 452). References to British and French ships
captured during the course of this dispute may be found in *Acts of the Privy Council
of England, Colonial Series*, III, pp. 542-546.

the old gentleman's weakness and tricks, which he has derived from Chauvelin, as if he had been bitt by him; retaining the venom, altho' he has dis-
carded the beast; . . . [61]

Early in 1738 Fleury became quite ill, and his retirement or
death was anticipated; but he recovered remarkably and was of
better colour than ever.[62] The British augured ill from the ad-
mittance of Maurepas to the Council of State, yet they themselves gave the French government reason for resentment by
permitting the Irish Parliament to pass a bill forbidding Irishmen
under penalty of death to enter the service of a foreign power.
It seems strange that the British were not forewarned of French
touchiness on that subject by a recollection of a similar difficulty
which had occurred in 1730.[63] Moreover, the British policy is
particularly hard to explain because at that moment Great Britain was very eager to secure the support of France, or at the
very least, a promise of her neutrality, in view of the crisis in
Anglo-Spanish affairs. Waldegrave was instructed to secure a
treaty which provided for mutual guarantees of possessions and
for "good offices" if the other contracting power should be attacked.[64] This projected treaty was the British answer to the
vague suggestions which the Cardinal had been throwing out
ever since the disgrace of Chauvelin, but now they found that
Fleury took no further interest in the matter. In reality, beginning in June 1738, a Franco-Spanish treaty was being mooted,
and as its negotiation progressed Fleury took what was for him

[61] Sept. 27, 1737 (Coxe: *Memoirs of . . . Sir Robert Walpole*, III, p. 491).
For further evidence of Walpole's disenchantment with the Cardinal, see his
letters to Trevor, Oct. 24, O. S., 1738, March 16, O. S., 1738/9 and April 17, O. S.,
1739 (Trevor Papers, *Hist. MSS. Comm., Report* XIV, App. Part IX, pp. 24,
27, 28).

[62] Vaucher: *Robert Walpole et la politique de Fleury*, pp. 258-259. The Cardinal
made a gossiper, who had said that Fleury was using rouge, rub his cheeks to
prove that it was not so.

[63] Cf. *supra*, p. 226. Newcastle to Waldegrave, May 11, O. S., 1738 (*British
Diplomatic Instructions: France, 1727-1744*, p. 206). Fleury raked up this old
irritation again in 1739 (Newcastle to Waldegrave, May 8, O. S., 1739 [*ibid.*,
p. 218]); also, see *ibid.*, pp. xxxiv-xxxv, and Vaucher: *Robert Walpole et la politique
de Fleury*, pp. 254-257.

[64] April 10, O. S., 1738 (*British Diplomatic Instructions: France, 1727-1744*,
pp. xxxiii-xxxiv, 200-203); Vaucher: *Robert Walpole et la politique de Fleury*, pp.
260-261.

an unusually decisive step by definitely breaking off the *pour-parlers* for an alliance with the British.[65] The attitude of the French made all the difference between Spanish resistance to, or compliance with, the demands of the British, and it is not too much to say that the Irish Enlistment Act was one of the indirect causes of the War of Jenkins' Ear.

The Anglo-Spanish war of 1739 was brought about by the agitation of an unscrupulous Parliamentary Opposition, and is an illustration of the hypothesis that nations periodically crave a blood-letting, just as dogs sometimes eat grass. Walpole's government was becoming more and more unpopular, as may be seen by the fate of the Excise Scheme, the opposition to the Gin Act of 1736, and the effects of the Porteous riots of 1737. More-over, his insistence on submissive obedience was driving more and more men of talent into the Opposition. But as he became more unpopular, he also became more vulnerable. By becoming the head of the Opposition in 1737, the Prince of Wales robbed Walpole of the argument which he had used for twenty years, that the Opposition were Jacobites and enemies of the Hanoverian dynasty; and the death of Queen Caroline in November 1737 deprived Walpole of his most influential support. But, although patriotic pamphleteers inveighed against Parliamentary corruption, Walpole's control of his majority was so absolute that little could be gained by agitation on such an issue.[66] Accordingly, the "Patriots" fell upon Walpole's foreign policy. Their success along these lines was encouraging, for, as one pamphleteer explained the matter:

[65] Baudrillart: *Philippe V et la cour de France*, IV, pp. 469-470. Newcastle to Waldegrave, May 11, June 2, July 31, (all Old Style), 1738 (*British Diplomatic Instructions: France, 1727-1744*, pp. 206-209).

[66] Good examples of the arguments with reference to Walpole's alleged corrupt methods may be found in [Hugh Hume, Third Earl of Marchmont]: *A Serious Exhortation to the Electors of Great Britain* (London, 1740); [Benjamin Robins]: *An Address to the Electors, and other free Subjects of Great Britain; occasion'd by the Late Secession* (London, 1739), esp. pp. 40-45; the Ministry answered these arguments by accusing the Opposition of being corrupted: "Corruption from Want of Place! . . . . Corruption from disappointed Ambition, ..." ([Thomas Gordon]: *An Appeal to the Unprejudiced, concerning the present Discontents occasioned by the late Convention with Spain* [London, 1739], p. 17).

I am sorry to say it, but true it is, that no People in Europe are more easily wrought into Prejudice than our Countrymen, nor any got out of it with more Difficulty. They too suddenly take Fire, but cool too slowly. And, as if they thought it a Reflection to own being in Error and reform, even Experience has not always had that Weight with them, which might be expected from a wise and prudent People.[67]

Stripped of verbiage, what the Opposition taught the people of England to desire was all the profits of the illegal Spanish trade in the Indies without any of the risks. This elemental hankering was made respectable by meretricious declamation about manifest destiny and territorial disinterestedness, which was completely beside the point:

The War we are at present engaged in I take to be perfectly just. We are a trading People, in which we follow Nature. We are placed in the midst of Seas, which shews that Providence invites us to traffick. Our Neighbours on the Continent therefore can have no reason to fear, but on the contrary many to love us. We form no Pretensions on their Dominions. We do not affect Conquests; and whenever we do meddle with the Affairs of those about us, 'tis to prevent Force from becoming Law, the weaker from being swallowed up by the more potent, and to support that Equality of Power, which is as beneficial to others in its Effects, as in the Maintenance thereof 'tis honourable to ourselves.[68]

As a matter of fact, trouble between British contraband traders and Spanish *guarda costas* was endemic in the Indies; the Opposition had tried to exploit that issue before the Treaty of Seville. As a result of that treaty, however, and of the ultimate introduction of the Spanish garrisons into the Italian duchies, the official Spanish attitude had become more obliging. A royal *cedula* of February 8, 1732, had instructed Spanish governors to require bonds of those who sought *guarda costa* commissions, and, although it was true that this *cedula* did not improve conditions very much, still the question slumbered until the Opposition began to make capital of it.

Among the issues which were involved were the British right

[67] *National Prejudice, Opposed to the National Interest* (London, 1748), pp. 29-30.
[68] *A Proposal for Humbling Spain* (London, 1739), p. 44. Indicative of the British state of mind at that time is the publication of a wretched Grub-Street piece of hack work, *Spanish Insolence Corrected by English Bravery. . . . By Captain Jinkins* (Second edition, London, 1739).

to colonize Georgia; the pretended right to cut logwood on the Campeche coast; and the interpretation of the Anglo-Spanish treaty of 1667.[69] The Spaniards, for their part, maintained that any vessel was subject to confiscation which had logwood, cacao or pieces of eight on board. This was an unreasonable pretension, for those articles were the common media of exchange throughout that whole region. On their side, the British claimed that they should be allowed to come within a league of the Spanish coasts, because the difficulties of navigation frequently required sailing close to Spanish shores, and to this pretension they added the further one that all British ships should be free from the right of search.[70]

Walpole's government was not at first inclined to take the Spanish depredations too seriously. Rear Admiral Stewart, commander-in-chief on the Jamaica station, wrote to the Admiralty in a letter received January 22, O. S., 1731/2:

We have fifty trading ships to one of the Spaniards in those seas; so in this way of making reprisals we must in the end be losers. We are the aggressors;

[69] The Duke of Newcastle made the ineffable mistake of grounding British rights in the Indies on the Anglo-Spanish treaty of 1670, which referred only to Continental Spain. Horatio Walpole wrote to Trevor, March 14, O. S., 1737/8: "We have been a good deal embarrassed in having laid, altho' we don't care to own it, the foundation of our arguments upon a wrong treaty. We scramble out of it as well as we can, ..." (Trevor Papers, *Hist. MSS. Comm., Report* XIV, App. Part IX, p. 14). Also, the same to the same, Feb. 28, O. S., 1737/8 (*ibid.*, p. 13). Cf. Coxe: *Memoirs of . . . Sir Robert Walpole*, I, p. 583. For the logwood dispute, see Arthur M. Wilson: "The Logwood Trade in the Seventeenth and Eighteenth Centuries." *Essays in the History of Modern Europe* (Edited by Donald C. McKay; New York, 1936), pp. 3-11.

[70] The Opposition endeavoured to prove that the Spaniards had never claimed the right of search until 1726, and that it was the fault of Walpole's government that such a dangerous pretension had been allowed ([Hugh Hume, Third Earl of Marchmont]: *A State of the Rise and Progress of our Disputes with Spain, and of the Conduct of our Ministers relating thereto* [London, 1739], p. 6). George Lyttelton advanced the extraordinary argument that since all trade with the Spaniards was prohibited, consequently it must be non-existent, and *ergo* the Spaniards had no right to search British ships (*Considerations upon the present State of our Affairs, at Home and Abroad*, p. 12). He was fittingly answered in *Popular Prejudices against the Convention and Treaty with Spain, Examin'd and Answer'd* (London, 1739), p. 22. Bishop Francis Hare wrote to his son, March 14, O. S., 1738/9: "Nothing can be more unreasonable than to say that Spain has a right to prohibit all trade with her subjects in the American seas, but has not a right to the necessary means to make this prohibition effectual" (Hare Manuscripts, *Historical Manuscripts Commission, Report* XIV, Appendix Part IX [London, 1895], p. 244).

by our illicit trade, carried on by armed sloops or with convoy, in defiance of law . . . Villany is inherent to that climate. The traders of Jamaica [are] as great rogues as the Spaniards.[71]

On October 12, O.S., 1731, he wrote to Newcastle: "It is, I think, a little unreasonable for us to do injuries and not know how to bear them."[72] Such, too, was the attitude of the Government until, in 1738, the Opposition made the Spanish disputes the issue in a Parliamentary session distinguished by the violence of its speeches and the examination of Captain Robert Jenkins.[73] Walpole had to exert all his influence, both as a debater and a party manager, to prevent the Commons from forcing him into war, and one of his arguments to which people were still willing to listen was that a war with Spain would probably involve a war with France as well.[74] Although the session of Parliament came to a close without Walpole's having been forced to declare war, the growing dissension in the Cabinet was becoming dangerous.[75] As a result, Walpole practically took the management of Spanish affairs out of the hands of Newcastle and, through

---

[71] R. G. Marsden, editor: *Documents relating to Law and Custom of the Sea*, II (*Publications of the Navy Records Society*, L [1896]), pp. 278-279.

[72] J. K. Laughton: "Jenkins's Ear." *English Historical Review*, IV (1889), pp. 742-743. In this letter Stewart also wrote: "I was a little surprised to hear of the usage Captain Jenkins met with off the Havana"; see Stewart's letter to the Governor of Havana, Sept. 12, 1731 (*ibid.*). A list of British ships taken and plundered between 1734 and 1738 may be found in the Townshend Papers, *Hist. MSS. Comm.*, *Report* XI, App. Part IV, pp. 148-149.

[73] An excellent account of the agitation in 1738 and 1739 may be found in the letters of Francis Hare, Bishop of Chichester, to his son (Hare MSS., *Hist. MSS. Comm.*, *Report* XIV, App. Part IX, pp. 242-257). For a good modern account, see Basil Williams: *The Life of William Pitt, Earl of Chatham* (London, 1913, two vols.), I, pp. 71-78. British cupidity played its part in this war-fever, for it was a long-standing notion that Spanish plunder would make war very profitable: "England may gain by a War with France, but never loses by a War with Spain" (*The Evident Advantages to Great Britain and its Allies from the Approaching War: Especially in Matters of Trade* [London, 1727], p. 13; also, see *The Observations on the Treaty of Seville Examined* [1730], p. 19).

[74] Speech of March 30, 1738 (*History and Proceedings of the House of Commons*, X, pp. 222, 226). Horatio Walpole also used this argument (*The Grand Question, whether War, or no War, with Spain, Impartially Consider'd*, pp. 10, 11, 12).

[75] Vaucher: *Robert Walpole et la politique de Fleury*, pp. 264-267; H. W. V. Temperley: "The Causes of the War of Jenkins' Ear (1739)." *Transactions of the Royal Historical Society*, Third Series, III, p. 201.

Keene, negotiated the Convention of the Pardo, which was presented to Parliament in January 1739.[76]

The Convention received a turbulent welcome, both in Parliament and in the press.[77] Nevertheless, Walpole's majority held firm, and William Wyndham, followed by the bulk of the Opposition, "seceded" from the House on March 20, thus committing a tactical error as a result of which Walpole was left in peace for the rest of the session.[78] It is evident that the Spaniards did not desire war any more than did Walpole; throughout the negotiations the attitude of La Quadra had been that of a man sincerely desirous of reaching an accommodation. At the same

[76] Signed Jan. 14, 1739; printed in *Gentleman's Magazine*, IX (1739), pp. 68-71; also in *The Political State of Great Britain*, LVII (Jan.-June, 1739), pp. 199-206. Spain was to pay British merchants £95,000, but this was contingent upon the South Sea Company's paying the King of Spain £68,000. By the Asiento treaty of 1713, the Company was to pay the King of Spain thirty-three and one-third pieces of eight for each of the 4,800 slaves which they had a right to import annually. The Company had not imported their full annual quota, but the King of Spain claimed this amount anyway; the Company had never paid it and by 1739 was in considerable arrears. This constituted the chief item of the £68,000; the Company disputed the justice of this claim, and were consequently much opposed to the Convention, which they tried hard to have defeated (G. B. Hertz: *British Imperialism in the Eighteenth Century* [London, 1908], pp. 12, 21-23).

[77] Cf. *The Political State of Great Britain*, LVII, pp. 142-150, 155-158, 185-187, 206-217; *Gentleman's Magazine*, IX (1739), pp. 32-34, 86-89, 104-105. In defense of the Convention, one pamphleteer wrote: "What it is that reasonable Men upon this Head, can desire more, I can't conceive: I say reasonable Men, for some are always upon their Prancing Horse" ([Horatio Walpole]: *The Convention Vindicated from the Misrepresentations of the Enemies of our Peace* [London, 1739], p. 17). Opposed to the Convention were *A Reply to a Pamphlet intitled, Popular Prejudices against the Convention and Treaty with Spain, Examin'd and Answered* (London, 1739), which stoutly refused to be intimidated by the prospect of France's joining with Spain (p. 9); [Benjamin Robins]: *Observations on the Present Convention with Spain* (London, 1739), a skilful pamphlet which attacked *seriatim* the Spanish contentions and the articles of the Convention; [William Pulteney]: *A Review of all that hath pass'd between the Courts of Great Britain and Spain, Relating to Our Trade and Navigation from the Year 1721, to the Present Convention; with some Particular Observations upon it* (London, 1739). Bishop Hare wrote to his son, on March 14, O. S., 1738/9: "We have had here on occasion of the late Convention, the greatest party struggle there has been since the Revolution. The Patriots were resolved to damn it, before they knew a word of it, and to inflame the people against it, which they have done with great success" (Hare MSS., *Hist. MSS. Comm.*, Report XIV, App. Part IX, p. 243).

[78] Cf. Bishop Hare to his son, June 14, O. S., 1739 (*Hist. MSS. Comm.*, Report XIV, App. Part IX, p. 248); Vaucher: *Robert Walpole et la politique de Fleury*, pp. 281-283.

time, the Spaniards had the assurance of Louis XV that he would be the ally of Spain even though the conditions of his assistance were not yet determined by a treaty.[79] Moreover, the marriage of Don Philip and the eldest daughter of Louis XV took place this year, with the result that relations between the courts of Spain and France were more cordial than they had been for some time.[80] Yet, although Newcastle presumed that an alliance had been concluded between the Bourbon powers, he had nevertheless taken action which hurried on the war.[81] Apparently on his own initiative he sent orders, dated March 10/21, 1738/9, to Admiral Haddock to remain on the Gibraltar station.[82] But the recall of Haddock had been one of the stipulations of the Convention of January 14, 1739. The Spanish court thereupon demanded payment of their claim on the South Sea Company, under penalty of the suspension of the Asiento; and when Keene, in May, pressed for the payment of the ninety-five thousand pounds for which the Convention had provided, the Spanish court refused, and issued a manifesto in self-justification in-

[79] Amelot, Chauvelin's successor as Minister of Foreign Affairs, told La Mina, Spanish ambassador to France, on August 14, 1738, that France would back up Spain (Baudrillart: *Philippe V et la cour de France*, IV, p. 470). La Marck's instructions, dated Sept. 14, 1738, said in part: "Sa Majesté n'a point hésité à déclarer à l'Espagne qu'Elle prendra sa défense, si elle est attaquée dans ses droits et possessions" (*Recueil des instructions . . . Espagne*, III, p. 201).

[80] The marriage was agreed upon on Sept. 4, 1738. The contract was signed May 12, 1739, and the marriage ceremony took place August 26, 1739 (Baudrillart: *Philippe V et la cour de France*, IV, pp. 487, 490, 501, 505; Casimir Stryienski: *Le gendre de Louis XV; Don Philippe, Infant d'Espagne et duc de Parme* [Paris, 1904], pp. 8-30).

[81] Newcastle to Waldegrave (most private), May 8, O. S., 1739 (*British Diplomatic Instructions: France, 1727-1744*, p. 217); the same to the same, same date (private and particular): "His Majesty has reason to think that there is an offensive alliance carrying on between France and Spain, the terms and conditions of which seem to be agreed, tho' the treaty may not yet be sign'd" (*ibid.*, p. 219). Horatio Walpole also supposed that an alliance had been concluded between France and Spain (H. Walpole to Robert Trevor, April 17, May 1, May 8, June 1 and June 8, (all Old Style), 1739 [Trevor Papers, *Hist. MSS. Comm., Report* XIV, App. Part IX, pp. 28, 29, 30, 32, 34]).

[82] Vaucher: *Robert Walpole et la politique de Fleury*, p. 285; H. W. V. Temperley: "The Causes of the War of Jenkins' Ear (1739)." *Transactions of the Royal Historical Society*, Third Series, III, p. 228. Cf. L. G. Wickham Legg: "Newcastle and the Counter Orders to Admiral Haddock, March 1739." *English Historical Review*, XLVI (1931), pp. 272-274.

stead.[83] By the time Parliament rose in June, war had been fully determined upon and measures in preparation for it were being taken. On July 10, the King of Great Britain determined to issue letters of marque and reprisal.[84] On August 14, 1739, Newcastle ordered Keene to ask for his passports, and Geraldino, the Spanish ambassador, left London in September. In October, the British declared war.[85]

[83] This piece was circulated in London in pamphlet form in 1739: *His Catholick Majesty's Manifesto, Justifying his Conduct in relation to the late Convention. With his Reasons for not paying the Ninety-Five Thousand Pounds* (London, 1739).

[84] *Acts of the Privy Council of England, Colonial Series*, III, p. 636.

[85] See Vaucher: *Robert Walpole et la politique de Fleury*, p. 289.

CHAPTER X

THE COMMERCIAL EXPANSION OF FRANCE DURING THE ADMINISTRATION OF CARDINAL FLEURY

THE British declaration of war against Spain (October 1739) was made in spite of the supposition that France would ultimately intervene in the war on the side of Spain. In June of that year Newcastle had instructed Waldegrave to secure, if he could, a declaration of neutrality from the Cardinal, but this the latter scrupulously avoided.[1] He did indeed tell Waldegrave that he was so sorry that this trouble had broken out that he would have given a hundred louis from his own pocket to have prevented it: the smallness of the sum mentioned made Waldegrave think that he was sincere.[2] In August Waldegrave warned his court that France would certainly join Spain if the British attacked that power; but, in spite of this, Newcastle hurried on the war and seemed to have become desirous of nothing more than to avoid Fleury's offers of mediation.[3]

When one considers that Sir Robert Walpole had found the argument that the French would help the Spaniards an effective one for preventing war in 1738, it seems strange that in 1739 war should be declared in face of the fact that French intervention seemed almost certain. The explanation of this inconsistency

[1] June 7, O. S., 1739 (*British Diplomatic Instructions: France, 1727-1744*, pp. 222-227); "Is there anything His Majesty so much desires as that France should not take part with Spain?" (Newcastle to Waldegrave, July 27, O. S., 1739 [*ibid.*, p. 229]).
[2] Waldegrave to Newcastle, June 26, 1739, cited by Vaucher: *Robert Walpole et la politique de Fleury*, p. 294.
[3] On June 7 and July 27, O. S., 1739, Newcastle instructed Waldegrave to avoid, and, if necessary, to reject Fleury's offers of mediation (*British Diplomatic Instructions: France, 1727-1744*, pp. 224, 229). In August 1739, Fleury suggested that France would guarantee to Great Britain the ninety-five thousand pounds if Great Britain would recall Haddock's fleet; this was refused (Vaucher: *Robert Walpole et la politique de Fleury*, p. 295).

is to be found in the growing conviction of the British public that France was outstripping the English in trade, and that to permit her to strengthen her position by continuing the peace was positively dangerous. Therefore the British would take care of themselves by strengthening their privileged position in the Spanish Indies, and, if France took issue with them over this dispute, that was scarcely to be deplored.[4]

The fact was that British foreign trade was not so prosperous between 1735 and 1739 as it had been during the years of the War of the Polish Succession. This was reflected in the arguments of the pamphleteers; Sir Matthew Decker's *Essay on the Causes of the Decline of the Foreign Trade* first appeared in 1740, and these years saw the appearance of divers pamphlets which discussed the parlous state of British woollen manufactures, the problem of "owling" (clandestine exportation of wool), and the growth of competition from the French. It was just in these years that the British became agitated about the flourishing condition of the French fisheries at Cape Breton, the capture of Great Britain's foreign sugar market by the French, and the increasing prosperity of the French slave trade. Other causes for alarm were the development of the French East India trade, the supplanting of the British by the French in the Levant and the growth of the French fur trade. The British were getting into a peculiar frame of mind with reference to the fancied condition of their foreign trade:

Look round about you, my Countrymen, and consider the Decay of your Manufactures, the Increase of your Poor, the many other Symptoms which every one's Observation must suggest to him of a declining State.[5]

---

[4] This point has been very well brought out by Vaucher: *Robert Walpole et la politique de Fleury*, pp. 296-302.

[5] [Hugh Hume, Earl of Marchmont]: *A Serious Exhortation to the Electors of Great Britain* (1740), p. 34; cf. pp. 37-38: [France] "who, after a most ruinous War, flourishes by its Commerce and Manufactures, and the Discharge of her Debts; while we, after the most successful and glorious one, have every Day more and more languish'd in the Decay of one, and under the Burthen of the other; . . ." A modern author has remarked that "all the evidence which we are gradually accumulating points to the years about 1740 as a period of remarkable commercial activity" (Henri Hauser: "The Characteristic Features of French Economic History from the Middle of the XVI to the Middle of the XVIII Century." *Economic History Review*, IV [1932-1934], p. 268). Statistics indicate that

Silhouette, who was in London in 1739 studying the economic condition of the country, reported that Pulteney and Wyndham were full of admiration for the Cardinal: "The augmentation of our maritime trade is what strikes them most." The *Craftsman*, on December 26, 1739, commented at length on Dutot's striking phrase: "To utilize peace in order to procure for ourselves all the advantages of a large trade is to wage war on our enemies." The *Craftsman* concluded, characteristically, that the Emperor had been the first victim sacrificed to the House of Bourbon, and the Maritime Powers would be the second.[6]

It was because of the political importance of the indisputable economic revival in France that the English writers of the period were filled with such lively concern. That fiercely competitive age was obsessed by the idea that a rival nation's gains in foreign trade constituted a double loss for one's own. In an atmosphere of jealous monopoly and exclusivism, merchants drove a thriving business while remaining more apprehensive of their neighbours' profits than thankful for their own:

For no Thing, Person or Nation is Considerable but by Comparison; and the French at present seem to be the People who are laying a Foundation for the Employment of Multitudes of their People, in a more profitable Way than ever was known before to them; . . . [7]

the period from 1730 to 1750 was one of relative stagnation in the growth of the British merchant marine (Abbott Payson Usher: "The Growth of English Shipping, 1572-1922." *Quarterly Journal of Economics*, XLII [1927-1928], pp. 472-474).

[6] For Silhouette's report to Amelot, Nov. 26, 1739, and the article in the *Craftsman*, see Vaucher: *Robert Walpole et la politique de Fleury*, p. 302.

[7] *The Importance of the British Plantations in America to this Kingdom* (London, 1731), p. 39. On this same point, Thomas Baston wrote: "And nothing is greater, or lesser, but by Comparison" ([Thomas Baston]: *Thoughts on Trade, and a Publick Spirit* [Second edition, London, 1728], p. 36). Otis Little declared: "As Trade enables the Subject to support the Administration of Government, the lessening or destroying that of a Rival, has the same effect, as if this Kingdom had enlarged the Sources of its own Wealth" (Otis Little: *The State of Trade in the Northern Colonies Considered* [London, 1748], p. 11). The prevalence of this idea, which was "based on a *static* conception of economic life," has been emphasized by Heckscher: *Mercantilism*, II, pp. 22-27. Robert Auchmuty wrote: "From the Peace of Utrecht to the Commencement of the present War, Cardinal Fleury having had for the far greater Part of the Time the Administration of the Affairs of France in His Hands, he, I think, may be said to have made War upon this Kingdom by all the Arts of Peace, especially by his continual Care and politick Advancement of their Commerce, and which was thereby enlarged within this last Period of Time to a Degree astonishing even to Persons well skill'd in Trade; . . ." ([Robert Auchmuty]: *The Importance of Cape Breton Consider'd* [London, 1746], p. 14).

The fear of France and the desire to curb her commercial expansion was a growing one:

As to our trade with France, it would be well for us that we had no trade with them, since the balance of our trade with them is greatly against us, and every year growing worse. As we are so much superior by sea to both these nations, it would be happy for us that France would join in this war with the Spaniards, since it would give us a very proper occasion to destroy those great branches of trade which they have got into since the last war, and do so much outdo us.[8]

Lyttelton wrote in 1739:

If the Power of that Crown in former Times had equalled its Ambition, Europe had been lost; if its Ambition now shall equal its Power, it will probably accomplish what it then designed. And bad is our Condition, when our Fate is to depend on a Spirit of Conquest not prevailing in that Court.[9]

Apprehensions like these made popular the idea of a preventive war, and Sir Matthew Decker wrote in 1740:

But because the Incumbrances on our Trade at present have given the French so much the Start of us in times of Peace, that War seemes absolutely necessary to obstruct their growing Power: . . . [10]

William Perrin, also writing in 1740, summed up the burden of his jeremiad in the following words:

On the whole, there seems to be nothing left to hinder the growing Power of France, and the ill Consequences that must thereby accrue to every State in Europe, unless by a formidable and natural Alliance we should engage in a successful War against them; . . . [11]

An anonymous writer, whose pamphlet appeared in 1740, inveighed against those who

imagine, that we ought to put up with the most notorious Insults and Violations of Treaties, rather than resent them in such a Manner, as may give us

---

[8] Sir H. W. Richmond, editor: "The Land Forces of France—June 1738." *Publications of the Navy Records Society*, LXIII, pp. 76-77.

[9] [George Lyttelton]: *Considerations upon the present State of our Affairs, at Home and Abroad*, pp. 19-20.

[10] [Sir Matthew Decker]: *An Essay on the Causes of the Decline of the Foreign Trade* (Second edition, London 1750), p. 155.

[11] William Perrin: *The Present State of the British and French Sugar Colonies, and our own Northern Colonies, considered. Together with some Remarks on the Decay of Our Trade, and the Improvements made of late Years by the French in Theirs* (London, 1740), p. 53; see also *ibid.*, pp. 20, 42, 48.

an Opportunity of retrieving some of the most valuable Branches of Commerce which the French have invaded, and which their late ruinous Neutrality gave them an Opportunity of engrossing. . . . If we suffer France to continue twenty Years longer in Peace, they will unavoidably, in the same Manner, steal into the greatest part of the Trade which the English are now in possession of; but if France, from an Apprehension of losing those valuable Branches of Trade which they have insensibly slipt into during the long Peace, shou'd avoid joining with the Spaniards against us, we shall more easily conquer the Spaniards, and be in readiness to call France to account in a proper Time.[12]

Inspired by sentiments similar to these, Newcastle pushed his willing country and his unwilling colleagues into a war, the first (and almost the last) fruits of which were the capture of Portobelo by that outspoken admiral in whose honour Mount Vernon was named.

French trade did in truth revive and expand remarkably during Fleury's administration, and an examination of the several branches of it will demonstrate that such was the case. In the Levant, the French, besides enjoying high diplomatic prestige consequent upon Villeneuve's embassy to the Porte and his successful mediation in the negotiations which led to the Peace of Belgrade (1739), definitively won the supremacy from their English and Dutch rivals. The average importations from the Levant for the years from 1723 to 1729 inclusive, were about 13,500,000 livres; trade declined somewhat in the following eight years, but from 1737 to 1743 the average importation was 15,177,000 livres. At the same time, exportations to the Levant increased to such a degree that sometimes the balance was in favour of France, a novel phenomenon in that branch of commerce. From 1739 to 1743, exportations averaged 21,550,000 livres annually, and throughout this period the trade employed an average of 270 ships.[13] In 1715 the English had twenty trading houses at Smyrna; in 1735 they had only three. The Aleppo and Cairo trade likewise decayed; M. Paul Masson's researches confirm

[12] *The Present State of the Revenues and Forces, by Sea and Land, of France and Spain. Compar'd with Those of Great Britain* (London, 1740), pp. vi, 40-41.
[13] Masson: *Histoire du commerce français dans le Levant au XVIIIe siècle*, pp. 411-412, 506.

the grounds for the complaints of the British pamphleteers.[14]
The secret of French success in the Levant was the popularity
of Languedoc cloth.[15] French woollens began to compete with
British in both quality and price. In 1726 the complaint was
that the English had lost the French market, which was being
supplied with native cloth.[16] By the middle of the century,
pamphleteers were declaring that the French were invading England's other foreign markets:

> Since that Time [1713] the French have imitated the greatest Part of our
> Woollens, and invented others to which our Artisans are yet Strangers; as I
> saw proved by a Collection of all their Stuffs, which a Gentleman had curi-
> ously made in the Year 1734. . . . he had nicely examined into the Cost of
> every Sort, and we as exactly compared them with our own, and found them
> to be considerably under the Price of the same here; and what added to
> their Value, they were generally more substantial than our's, though for less
> Money. . . . This Perfection and Cheapness of their Manufactures, has
> . . . enabled them to supplant us in the Spanish, Italian and Turkish
> markets; . . . [17]

[14] Masson: *op. cit.*, pp. 367-369. *Some Considerations on the National Debts,
the Sinking Fund, and the State of Publick Credit* (London, 1729), p. 95; [—— Prior]:
*A List of the Absentees of Ireland, and the Yearly Value of their Estates and Incomes
spent abroad. With Observations on the Present Trade and Condition of that Kingdom* (Dublin, 1729), reprinted in *A Collection of Tracts and Treatises Illustrative
of the Natural History, Antiquities, and the Political and Social State of Ireland, at
various Periods prior to the Present Century* (Dublin, 1860-1861, two vols.) II, p.
283; Sir H. W. Richmond, editor: "The Land Forces of France—June 1738."
Publications of the Navy Records Society, LXIII, pp. 76-77; *The Present State of
the Revenues and Forces, by Sea and Land, of France and Spain* (1740), p. 40; *A
Short Essay upon Trade in general, but more Enlarged on that Branch relating to
the Woollen Manufactures of Great Britain and Ireland* (London, 1741), p. 51; *An
Inquiry into the Revenue, Credit, and Commerce of France* (London, 1742), p. 36;
*The Great Importance of Cape Breton, Demonstrated and Exemplified by Extracts
from the best Writers, French and English, who have treated of that Colony* (London,
1746), pp. 55-56.
[15] From 1726 to 1729 inclusive, an average of 41,150 pieces of Languedoc cloth
was sold in the Levant annually; from 1730 to 1736, an annual average of 53,057;
from 1737 to 1743, an annual average of 57,014 ([Pierre d'André O'Héguerty]:
Remarques sur plusieurs branches de commerce et de navigation [n.p., 1757, two
parts], part ii, pp. 29-31). For French competition in the Turkey market, see also
Anderson: *Origin of Commerce*, III, pp. 516-518; Macpherson: *Annals of Commerce*,
III, pp. 240-241; E. Lipson: *The Economic History of England* (London, 1915-1931,
three vols.), II, p. 347.
[16] Erasmus Philips: *The State of the Nation, in Respect to her Commerce, Debts,
and Money* (London, 1726), p. 8.
[17] Wyndham Beawes: *Lex Mercatoria Rediviva* (Fourth edition, London, 1783),
p. 640.

Similar testimony was made by Joshua Gee, William Perrin and Sir Matthew Decker.[18] It was alleged in 1729 that French strouds (blankets) were underselling the British in the North American Indian trade, and it is known that British woollens met similar French competition in the Portuguese market and finally succumbed to it.[19] In the light of such evidence, Defoe's puff of British woollens, with its implicit admission of the severity of French competition, is rather lame:

The French Cloth, with all its superficial French Gloss upon it, is fine, but thin and spungy, and will do the Wearer neither Credit or Service, while the English Cloth wears to the last like a Board, firm and strong, and has a kind of Beauty even in its Rags.[20]

Bitter were the complaints that the French woollen manufactures were being built up on the ruins of the British because English and Irish wool was being "owled" (clandestinely exported) in enormous quantities into France.[21] Although the

---

[18] Joshua Gee: *The Trade and Navigation of Great-Britain Considered* (London, 1729), p. 10; Perrin: *The Present State of the British and French Sugar Colonies* (1740), pp. 41, 45-46; Decker: *An Essay on the Causes of the Decline of the Foreign Trade*, p. 124: the French were underselling the British ten to twelve *per cent*.

[19] *Acts of the Privy Council of England, Colonial Series*, III, pp. 212-213; VI, p. 207. For the Portuguese market, see L. S. Sutherland: *A London Merchant, 1695-1774* (London, 1933), pp. 18, 137.

[20] [Daniel Defoe]: *A Plan of the English Commerce* (London, 1728), p. 178.

[21] [Thomas Baston]: *Thoughts on Trade, and a Publick Spirit* (1728), pp. 31-35; *The Interest of England Consider'd with Respect to the Woollen Manufactures* (London, 1731), pp. 14-15; *Seasonable Observations on the Present Fatal Declension of the General Commerce of England. In which the Genuine Cause of the Decay of our Woollen Manufactures is Particularly Considered* (London, 1737); *The Golden Fleece: Or the Trade, Interest, and Well-Being of Great Britain Considered. With Remarks on the Rise, Progress, and present Decay of our Woollen Manufactures. Also an Estimate of this Valuable Trade, fairly and clearly stated, and the great Proportion given up Yearly to Foreigners, by Suffering (or Conniving at) the illegal Exportation of British and Irish Wool, and Woollen Goods throughly Manufactured in Ireland, to Foreign Parts* (n.p., 173-?), p. 5; Samuel Webber: *An Account of a Scheme for Preventing the Exportation of our Wool* (London, 1740), esp. pp. 21-22; Samuel Webber: *A Short Account of the State of our Woollen Manufacturies, from the Peace of Ryswick to This Time, Shewing, their Former Flourishing, and their Present Ruinous Condition; and that they always flourished when France could not get our Wool, but declined in Proportion to the Quantities of Wool Exported to Them* (Second edition, London, 1741), esp. pp. 7-8; Anthony Sympson: *A Short, Easy and Effectual Method to prevent the Running of Wool, &c., from Great-Britain and Ireland to Foreign Parts* (London, 1741); *The Consequences of Trade, as to the Wealth and Strength of any Nation; of the Woollen Trade in particular, and the*

government and the public were usually in a state of alarm over the illegal exportation of British wool during the seventeenth and eighteenth centuries, extraordinary perturbation was evinced in the years just preceding the War of the Austrian Succession.[22] But the profitable practice continued, in spite of attempts by Parliament to suppress it. The wool thus exported was paid for with smuggled brandies, silks, fine cambrics and "such trumpery stuff," in the production of which the French in this period continued to outrival the British. The French luxury trade was always anathema to the British mercantilists; Joshua Gee entitled a chapter: "French Fashions Pernicious to England."[23] But "An Act for prohibiting the Wearing and Importation of Cambricks and French Lawns" (18 George II, cap. xxxvi) had the usual success of sumptuary laws. Moreover, British ladies were unpatriotic: "Nothing that is mere English goes

---

great Superiority of it over all other Branches of Trade. . . . The Danger we are in of becoming a Province to France, unless an Effectual and Immediate Stop be put to the Exportation of our Wool (London, 1740), pp. 6, 14-15, 18, 21; *A Short Essay upon Trade in general, but more Enlarged on that Branch relating to the Woollen Manufactures of Great Britain and Ireland* (London, 1741), esp. p. 48.

[22] French competition was particularly feared because French labour costs were lower than the British (*An Essay Presented; . . . by an English Woollen Manufacturer* [London, 1744], pp. 1, 16; *Some Thoughts on the Woollen Manufactures of England* [London, 1731], p. 7). One pamphleteer freely admitted the prevalence of "owling," but claimed that it was no worse than it had been in the time of William and Mary, and Queen Anne (*Remarks upon Mr. Webber's Scheme and the Draper's Pamphlet* [London, 1741], pp. 37-38; cf. Cunningham: *The Growth of English Industry and Commerce in Modern Times; Part I. The Mercantile System*, pp. 504-505; Friedrich Lohmann: "Die staatliche Regelung der englischen Wollindustrie vom XV. bis zum XVIII. Jahrhundert." *Staats- und socialwissenschaftliche Forschungen*, XVIII, Heft 1 [Leipzig, 1900], pp. 73-77). It was the fashion to accuse the Irish of being the greatest "owlers," rather than the British, but this was denied, with appropriate *tu quoque* arguments, by Prior (*A List of the Absentees of Ireland*, reprinted in *A Collection of Tracts and Treatises*, II, pp. 280-281). Allusions to the exportation of Irish wool to France may be found in the *Calendar of Treasury Books and Papers, 1735-1738* (London, 1900), pp. 342-343, 356, 511-512; and very numerously in the *Journal of the Commissioners for Trade and Plantations, January 1728-9 to December 1734*, see under index: *Wool* and *Ireland*, and esp. pp. 78-79; also *Journal of the Commissioners for Trade and Plantations, January 1734-5 to December 1741*, *passim*, see index. An Act "for the more effectual Preventing the Exportation of Wool from Great Britain, and of Wool, and Wool manufactured, from Ireland, to Foreign Parts" (12 George II, cap. xxi) was passed in 1739.

[23] Gee: *Trade and Navigation of Great-Britain Considered*, cap. xxii; cf. *The Golden Fleece*, p. 12.

down with our modern ladies. . . . They must be equipped from dear Paris."[24]

No less than the Levant trade and the woollen manufactures, the French fisheries revived astonishingly between 1713 and the outbreak of the War of the Austrian Succession. In what appears to be an official and trustworthy report, dated October 3, 1730, Maurepas, Secretary of State for the Navy and Colonies, stated that in 1715 only two or three ships had sailed from St. Jean de Luz, the home port of the French whaling industry, but that in 1729 there had been thirty-seven, and as many in 1730.[25] The mackerel and herring fisheries in waters contiguous to France enjoyed sufficient prosperity in these years to cause the mercantilist writer, Malachy Postlethwayt, to complain of it.[26] But the value of the local fisheries was feeble in comparison with that which the French developed off the Grand Banks and in Cape Breton waters. Englishmen on both sides of the water became alarmed at its extent. For fisheries were universally regarded as the "nursery of seamen," "that branch of commerce more valuable to the State than all the gold in Peru, since the latter can not train a single sailor, while the former trains several

---

[24] Campbell: The London Tradesman (London, 1747), cited by Lipson: The Economic History of England, II, p. 101.

[25] État des affaires du département de la marine sous M. le comte de Maurepas en 1730: Compte que ce ministre a rendu dans le conseil royal du commerce, tenu le 3 octobre, 1730, de la situation du commerce extérieur du royaume, et de la marine de la France (Maurepas: Mémoires, III, p. 105). The anonymous author of the Mémoire de la situation présente du commerce général [1728] remarked upon the revival of the French whaling industry and stated that "nous sommes en état non seulement de nous passer des huiles et savons des Hollandais, mais encore d'en fournir à l'étranger" (Henri Sée and Léon Vignols: "Mémoires sur le commerce rédigés en vue du congrès de Soissons (1728)." [Ministère de l'instruction publique et des beaux arts: Comité des travaux historiques et scientifiques, section d'histoire moderne (depuis 1715) et contemporaine]: Notices, inventaires & documents, XII: Études et documents divers [Paris, 1926], p. 18). From 1724 to 1732 the British South Sea Company attempted to carry on a monopoly of whale fishing; its net loss was £177,782 (Donald L. Cherry: "The South Sea Company, 1711-1855." Dalhousie Review, XIII [1933-1934], p. 66; Brisco: The Economic Policy of Robert Walpole, p. 197). The monopoly having been surrendered, Parliament placed a bounty of twenty shillings on every ton of shipping engaged in whaling (6 George II, cap. xxxiii [1733]); nevertheless, British tonnage remained small until after 1750.

[26] Postlethwayt: A Short State of the Progress of the French Trade and Navigation, pp. 81-82.

thousand each year."[27] It followed that the French deep-sea fisheries contributed to the growth of France's naval power, at the same time that competition reduced the number of men in Britain's nursery.[28] The British begrudged the French not only the fish they caught, but also the supplying of the considerable amount of woollens and tackle consumed by the fishermen, which encouraged French manufactures.[29] As for the English colonists, Louisburg injured their fisheries to a degree which overbalanced the gain procured from illicit traffic there.[30] In 1747 Marblehead's fleet of fishing schooners, which had numbered 120 in 1732, had dropped to seventy.[31] Governor Shirley himself made a calculation of the extent of the French cod fishery, whereby it appeared that the total value of the catch was £949,192-10-0, that an average of 1,149,000 quintals was caught annually, and that the industry employed 564 ships (exclusive of shallops, brigs and sloops), and 27,500 sailors, including Cape Breton open-boat fishers.[32] Such a calculation, though perhaps an overestimate,

[27] The Chamber of Commerce of Saint-Malo to Choiseul and Berryer, July 8, 1761 ("Les Chambres de Commerce de France et la cession du Canada." *Rapport de l'archiviste de la province de Quebec pour 1924-1925*, pp. 201-202; cf. *ibid.*, pp. 212, 226).

[28] Auchmuty: *Importance of Cape Breton Consider'd*, pp. 4, 10, 27-29.

[29] *An Accurate Journal and Account of the Proceedings of the New England Land-Forces, during the late Expedition against the French Settlements on Cape Breton, to the Time of the Surrender of Louisbourg. . . . With a Computation of the French Fishery . . . as it was carried on before the present War. . . . All sent over, by General Pepperell himself, to his Friend Capt. Hen. Stafford, at Exmouth, Devon* (Exon. [Exeter], 1746), p. 37; *The Great Importance of Cape Breton, Demonstrated and Exemplified*, p. 71; [William Bollan]: *The Importance and Advantage of Cape Breton, Truly Stated and Impartially Considered* (London, 1746), pp. 91-94.

[30] An extensive illicit commerce had sprung up between Cape Breton and New England by 1721 (Charles Blechynden to the Council of Trade and Plantations, April 5, 1721: [*Calendar of State Papers, Colonial Series: America and West Indies, 1720-1721* (London, 1933), p. 283]).

[31] William Douglass: *A Summary . . . of the British Settlements in North America*, I, pp. 302, 537.

[32] *A Computation of the French Fishery, as it was managed before the War in 1744, from the Gut of Canso to Louisburgh, and thence to the North-east Part of Cape Breton. Transmitted by Gov. Shirley in July, 1745. Paper Office, New England*, No. 3 (n.p., one printed folio page, broadside). The same figures for the number of ships and sailors employed are given in *The Great Importance of Cape Breton, Demonstrated and Exemplified*, pp. 46-49, and *An Accurate Journal and Account of the Proceedings of the New England Land-Forces*, pp. 32-36; the former estimates the value of the catch at £981,992-10-0, and the latter at £981,692-10-0. Bollan: *The Importance and Advantage of Cape Breton*, pp. 90-91: "Their Fishery amounted

accounts for the enthusiasm in Massachusetts for the expedition
against Louisburg in 1745:

The French had already the better of us in the Fishery Trade, and in a few
Years more would have supplied all the Markets in Europe, and by underselling, entirely excluded us from the COD-FISHERY, *which is more beneficial and easier wrought than the* Spanish *Mines of* Mexico *and* Peru.[33]

Besides the fact that open-boat fishing was eminently feasible
in Cape Breton waters, and that Louisburg was nearer to the
Grand Banks than any English port in Acadia or New England,
its central position and excellent harbour made Louisburg the
entrepôt for a large traffic.[34] Since merchants and ship captains
disliked sailing from France in ballast, ships were frequently
loaded with supplies for Canada, to be transferred from Louisburg.[35] West Indies ships were accustomed to make Louisburg
their destination, instead of Quebec, for by such an arrangement
they could make two round trips a year and avoid being delayed
by the freezing of the Saint Lawrence.[36] The consequence was
that Louisburg came to be of importance as a center of distribution. Dried cod of the first quality was shipped chiefly to Marseilles, whence it was taken by coasting vessels to Cadiz and the
Italian ports, and to Bordeaux, La Rochelle, Nantes, Le Havre
and Saint-Malo.[37] Inferior qualities were sent to the French

(within a Trifle) to a Million, Sterling: Our's not to one Third of that Sum. They
employed 27,500 Men; We, at most 14 or 15,000. They, 564 Sail of Ships: We
about 300, great and small." Compare also Postlethwayt: *The Universal Dictionary of Trade and Commerce,* I, pp. 376, 784, 825; Anderson: *Origin of Commerce,*
III, pp. 523-529; Macpherson: *Annals of Commerce,* III, pp. 246-250.

[33] Douglass: *A Summary . . . . of the British Settlements in North America,*
I, p. 6.

[34] See table of comparative distances given by J. S. McLennan: *Louisbourg
from its Foundation to its Fall, 1713-1758* (London, 1918), p. 221.

[35] In 1728 forty-one ships touched at Quebec; four from France, three from
Martinique, two from San Domingo and thirty-two from Cape Breton (Maurepas:
Mémoires, III, p. 109).

[36] Louis-Philippe May: *Histoire économique de la Martinique (1635-1763)* (Paris,
1930), pp. 152-153. See also Auchmuty: *Importance of Cape Breton Consider'd,*
p. 2; H. A. Innis: *Select Documents in Canadian Economic History, 1497-1783*
(Toronto, 1929), pp. 78-79, 117.

[37] O'Héguerty: *Remarques sur plusieurs branches de commerce,* part i, p. 170;
Innis: *Documents,* p. 78. Governor Lee of Newfoundland reported in 1736 that
the French were underselling the British in the Italian market by about a dollar
a quintal (Ralph Greenlee Lounsbury: *The British Fishery at Newfoundland, 1634-
1763* [New Haven, 1934], p. 318).

Antilles, together with timber received in illicit traffic with the English colonists.[38] In return, Louisburg was one of the sources of supply of molasses for the New England distilleries.[39] Export and import tables indicate how extensive and valuable the Louisburg trade became; yet its prosperity was entirely the growth of the years following the Utrecht settlement.[40]

The colony of Canada grew slowly, though surely, during this period. In 1715 its population had been about twenty-five thousand and in 1730 it was thought to have attained a number of about thirty-four thousand.[41] Although the economic well-being of Canada may have been sacrificed in the long run to the disproportionate exploitation of the fur trade, during this period the British were unmindful of this possibility, and conscious only that the French were outstripping them in bringing valuable peltries to market:

It is computed they import into France from Canada only to the Value of 135,000 l. Sterling *per annum*, in Beaver] and other Furs, including Dearskins; and the English from all our Northern Colonies not above 90,000 l. Sterling.[42]

Although the French East India Company enjoyed exclusively the right of purchasing beaver skins in Canada and abused their

[38] Bollan: *The Importance and Advantage of Cape Breton*, pp. 118-121. A large traffic was carried on with the English colonists, frequently by the collusion of the governor on the plea of the difficulty of otherwise provisioning the island (Innis: *Documents*, pp. 105-106, 107-113, 128-129, 129-130). A large illicit traffic was also carried on at the Strait of Canso, principally between the Acadians and the French of Cape Breton (Innis: *Documents*, pp. 125-126, 129-132, 143-144, 240).

[39] Bollan: *The Importance and Advantage of Cape Breton*, pp. 118-119. Cape Breton officials wrote Maurepas in 1743 that the sale of New England ships to Cape Breton purchasers was necessary for the good of the colony (Innis: *Documents*, p. 133).

[40] McLennan: *Louisbourg, 1713-1758*, Appendix V.

[41] Maurepas: *Mémoires*, III, p. 109. A modern author states that the population was about twenty thousand in 1713, twenty-five thousand in 1721 and fifty-four thousand in 1744 (James A. Williamson: *A Short History of British Expansion* [London, 1922], p. 359). According to Joannès Tramond: "Le Canada après le traité d'Utrecht." *Histoire des colonies françaises et de l'expansion de la France dans le monde* (Gabriel Hanotaux and Alfred Martineau, editors; Paris, 1929-1933, six vols.), I, p. 109, the population of Canada was 37,716 in 1734.

[42] *The Present State of the British and French Trade to Africa and America Considered and Compared* (London, 1745), quoted by *Two Letters, Concerning some farther Advantages and Improvements that may seem necessary to be made on the taking and keeping of Cape Breton* (London, 1746), p. 5.

privilege in the customary manner of monopolists, nevertheless
the exercise of their monopoly did not seem to discourage supply.[43] Cadwallader Colden wrote on November 10, 1724, that
"the French almost entirely engrossed the Fur Trade of America."[44] Not least perturbing to British mercantilists of the time
was the fact that many New York traders preferred to sell Indian
supplies to the French (who came to Albany for the purpose),
rather than to trade directly with the Indians; for this traffic
was regarded as facilitating the French trade and increasing its
profits: it was tantamount to "building the French forts with
English strouds."[45] Moreover, as a result of the large supply of
beaver, French hat makers found a ready market for their wares
in Spain and Spanish America, where French hats were considered superior to the British product, a fact which furnished
another occasion for pamphleteer repining.[46]

[43] This privilege was granted to the *Compagnie d'Occident* in August 1717 (*Édits,
ordonnances royaux, déclarations et arrêts du conseil d'état du Roi, concernant le
Canada* [Quebec, 1854-1856, three vols.], I, pp. 377-387); and confirmed to the
Compagnie des Indes in June 1725 (Moreau de Saint-Méry: *Loix et constitutions,*
III, pp. 142-145).

[44] George Louis Beer: *The Commercial Policy of England toward the American
Colonies* (New York, 1893), p. 61.

[45] *Acts of the Privy Council of England, Colonial Series,* VI, p. 151; also *ibid.,*
p. 207: complaints in 1729 that the French were underselling the British in foreign
markets and were using their own manufactures in the Indian Trade, inasmuch
as a New York act of 1720 forbade them to trade at Albany; see also *ibid.,* III,
pp. 68, 209-214. The Albany trade and Governor Burnet's attempt to regulate
it are analyzed in detail by C. H. McIlwain: *An Abridgment of the Indian Affairs
. . . . transacted in the Colony of New York, from the Year 1678 to the Year 1751.
By Peter Wraxall. (Harvard Historical Studies,* vol. XXI), (Cambridge [Mass.],
1915), pp. lxv-lxxxv. The thriving character of this trade continued up to the
outbreak of the French and Indian War ([Archibald Kennedy]: *Serious Considerations on the Present State of the Affairs of the Northern Colonies* [New York, 1754],
pp. 18-19.) See also H. A. Innis: *The Fur Trade in Canada* (New Haven, 1930),
pp. 85, 87, 119; *Calendar of State Papers, Colonial Series: America and West Indies,
1720-1721,* pp. 125, 140-141, 202-207; *idem, 1722-1723* (London, 1934), pp. 188,
289-291; *Journal of the Commissioners for Trade and Plantations, January 1722-3
to December 1728,* pp. 163-166, 168-177, 177-178; and Cadwallader Colden's report,
dated Nov. 10, 1724 (E. B. O'Callaghan, editor: *Documents relative to the Colonial
History of the State of New York* [Albany, 1856-1861, eleven vols.], V, pp. 726-733).

[46] [Pierre d'André O'Héguerty]: *Essai sur les intérets du commerce maritime*
(The Hague, 1754), pp. 155-158; *Two Letters, Concerning some farther Advantages*
(London, 1746), p. 6; Postlethwayt: *Great Britain's True System,* p. 264; *Acts of
the Privy Council of England, Colonial Series,* III, p. 212: "That the French have
Established a Manufactory of Hatts at Marseilles, and Supply Spain and Italy
with them, cheaper than they can be Supplyed from England . . ." (1729).

Canadian trade, small as it was, nevertheless prospered during this period. Some effort was made to increase the self-sufficiency of the colony by encouraging the cultivation and manufacture of products which would have a ready sale in European markets, such as ginseng, hemp, tobacco, tar and glue.[47] In 1741 Canadian exports outvalued the imports, "a unique experience in the history of the colony."[48]

Dearer to the hearts of the French than Canada were the islands of the West Indies. Canada, "those fifteen hundred leagues of which three-quarters are frozen deserts," was not to be compared with Martinique, "the best and richest colony of France."[49] In the period following the Utrecht settlement, these islands enjoyed an economic development hitherto undreamed of. The growth of population in Martinique, Guadeloupe and San Domingo attested their prosperity, and the provisioning of these large communities constituted a considerable portion of France's growing trade.[50] For an edict of 1727, confirming and

[47] Innis: *Documents*, pp. 368-374. Perennial difficulty was experienced, even during this period, in providing for an adequate food reserve (Innis: *Documents*, pp. 352-367).

[48] Adam Shortt: *Documents Relating to Canadian Currency, Exchange and Finance during the French Period* (Ottawa, 1925-1926, two vols.), I, p. lxxvii; II, pp. 690-692. For tables indicating the value of beaver exported from Canada during this period (Harold A. Innis: *The Fur Trade of Canada* [Toronto, 1927], pp. 149-152).

[49] Such were the notions of Voltaire: *Précis du siècle de Louis XV*, cap. xxxv. Cf. *Candide*, chapter xxiii: "Vous savez que ces deux nations sont en guerre pour quelques arpents de neige vers le Canada, et qu'elles dépensent pour cette belle guerre beaucoup plus que tout le Canada ne vaut"; O'Héguerty: *Essai sur les intérets du commerce maritime*, p. 96; Saint-Pierre: *Annales politiques (1658-1740)* (ed. Drouet), p. 330.

[50] The population of Martinique was 58,548 in 1731, 66,595 in 1734, 69,909 in 1736 and 74,042 in 1738 (Dessalles: *Histoire générale des Antilles*, IV, pp. 574, 575, 576, 578). Compare May: *Histoire économique de la Martinique*, p. 147.
In 1738 the population of Guadeloupe was 42,653, of whom 32,878 were slaves (Dessalles: *Histoire générale des Antilles*, IV, 580). In 1701 there had been 4,028 whites, 457 free negroes and 7,143 slaves (Jules Ballet: *La Guadeloupe* [Basse-Terre, 1890-1899, three vols.], I, part iii, p. 332).
In 1726 San Domingo had a population of 30,000 free and 100,000 slave (Pierre François Xavier de Charlevoix: *Histoire de l'Isle Espagnole ou de S. Domingue* [Paris, 1730-1731, two vols.], II, p. 482). In 1739 the population was 131,433, of whom 117,411 were slaves (Joannès Tramond: "Les Antilles après le traité d'Utrecht." *Histoire des colonies françaises et de l'expansion de la France dans le monde* [Gabriel Hanotaux and Alfred Martineau, editors], I, p. 455). The total population of the French Antilles in 1700 was 25,000 whites and 70,000 slaves; in

extending similar ones of 1698 and 1717, excluded all foreign commerce from the islands in an effort to make not only their production but also their consumption a monopoly of the metropolis.[51] The demand was so large that French production of some commodities was outstripped, and supplementary regulations were required to mitigate the rigours of an extreme mercantilist exploitation.[52] Irish salt beef and foreign lard, butter, tallow, candles and salted salmon were permitted free entry to the colonies if carried in French ships.[53]

So whole-hearted and yet one-sided was the exploitation of the land in the sugar colonies that the food supply remained precarious in spite of these breaches in the wall of a strict mercantile system. Moreover, the colonists were in constant need of more timber and live stock than could be supplied from Canada or Louisiana.[54] In consequence, a very considerable illicit traffic

1740 it was 60,000 whites and 250,000 slaves (Tramond: *Manuel d'histoire maritime de la France*, p. 376).

[51] Moreau de Saint-Méry: *Loix et constitutions*, I, pp. 599-603; II, pp. 557-565; III, pp. 224-236.

[52] Cf. Henri Sée: "Le commerce du beurre et des salaisons en Bretagne au XVIIIe siècle." *Mémoires et documents pour servir à l'histoire du commerce et de l'industrie en France*, X (1926), pp. 175-185. Similar difficulties in provisioning the sugar islands had been experienced in the seventeenth century (S. L. Mims: *Colbert's West India Policy* [New Haven, 1912], pp. 310-331). The food supply was a problem for the British planters also (Frank Wesley Pitman: "The West Indian Absentee Planter as a British Colonial Type." *Proceedings of the Pacific Coast Branch of the American Historical Association, 1927*, p. 122).

[53] The entry of Irish beef into the colonies was permitted by the Edict of 1727 and confirmed by subsequent decrees of the Council of State throughout this period (Lawrence C. Wroth and Gertrude L. Annan: *Acts of French Royal Administration concerning Canada, Guiana, the West Indies and Louisiana, Prior to 1791* [New York, 1930], decrees numbered 1160, 1191, 1215, 1228, 1250, 1274, 1285, 1290, 1310, 1325. Decrees permitting the importation of salmon (*ibid.*, entries numbered 1077, 1106, 1127, 1150, 1183, 1201, 1260). When the imminence of war threatened the supply of Irish beef, free importation from Denmark and the Cape Verde Islands was permitted (*ibid.*, decrees numbered 1365, 1368, 1370). See also Léon Vignols: "L'importation en France au XVIIIe siècle du boeuf salé d'Irlande." *Revue historique*, CLIX (Sept.-Dec., 1928), pp. 79-95. British mercantilists would have been happy to prohibit to Ireland even this trade (Perrin: *The Present State of the British and French Sugar Colonies* [London, 1740], pp. 20-22).

[54] The French government endeavoured, but with only partial success, to encourage the production of timber in Louisiana for the use of the sugar islands (N. M. Miller Surrey: *The Commerce of Louisiana during the French Régime, 1699-1763* [New York, 1916], pp. 194, 372-381). Witnesses testified before the Board of Trade on December 7, 1731, that Canada and Louisiana could not supply enough lumber to the French islands to satisfy the demand (*Journal of*

with the British American colonists sprang up, which deserves to be considered as one of the causes of the prosperity of the French Antilles, however repugnant it was to mercantilist consistency, or to the interests of the British planters who desired a monopoly of the supply of molasses.[55] For by this intercourse, the existence and extent of which were freely admitted by the pamphleteers opposed to the passage of the Molasses Act (1733), the French planters exchanged the essentials of life for a byproduct which an inflexible mercantile system, by restricting the competition of colonial rum with French brandies, made difficult to market.[56] In spite of the advice of French governors and intendants to legalize this trade, the home government refused during this period to modify the rigidity of the system.[57] Con-

the Commissioners for Trade and Plantations, January 1728-9 to December 1734, pp. 253-254). If a captain carried horses to Martinique, "he was admitted to trade without paying the Governor for his licence, which commonly amounted to about fifty pistoles" (ibid., p. 254).

[55] French mercantile opinion (O'Héguerty: Essai sur les intérets du commerce maritime, pp. 105-106; Henri Sée: "Le commerce de Saint-Malo au XVIIIᵉ siècle, d'après les papiers des Magon." Mémoires et documents pour servir à l'histoire du commerce et de l'industrie en France, IX [1925], pp. 29-30). Complaints of British planters (The Present State of the British Sugar Colonies Consider'd [London, 1731], pp. 6-7, 19-21, 26; this "pernicious trade" was deplored in a representation made to the Board of Trade by the General Assembly of Barbados, and copied [pp. 2-9] in The British Empire in America Consider'd [London, 1732]; The Importance of the Sugar Colonies to Great-Britain Stated, and some Objections against the Sugar Colony Bill answer'd [London, 1731], pp. 9, 25-26; A Comparison between the British Sugar Colonies and New England, as they relate to the Interest of Great Britain [London, 1732], p. 29: "But nothing less will satisfy this unnatural Daughter, than the supplanting her Mother-Country in Navigation and Trade; and subverting her Sister Colonies, by a Trade with our natural Enemies, the French"). The bulk of this trade was of course carried on in the ships of the English colonists, yet there is evidence that the French sold East Indies goods, as well as molasses and sugar, and bought ships with the proceeds, at Boston (Journal of the Commissioners for Trade and Plantations, January 1728-9 to December 1734, p. 172); a Massachusetts Act passed in 1730 laid a tariff to prevent trade in Massachusetts by foreigners (Pitman: The Development of the British West Indies, p. 216).

[56] Supplies "being now purchased chiefly with Molasses, which before this late Intercourse between the Foreign Colonies and the Northern British Colonies were flung away as of no Value" (The Present State of the British Sugar Colonies Consider'd, p. 6; see also p. 19). For a defense of the practice, while admitting its extent, see A True State of the Case between the British Northern-Colonies and the Sugar Islands in America, Impartially Considered (London, 1732), pp. 34, 36, 40.

[57] Cf. the remarks of M. de Valincourt ("Mémoire sur la marine de France" [1725]. [Villette: Mémoires, p. lxi]). Guadeloupe authorities during this period experienced difficulty in securing adequate food supplies without the aid of the illicit trade (Ballet: La Guadeloupe, II, pp. 112, 116, 117, 223, 225, 230-232, 233)

sequently, the authorities "closed their eyes," as one of them, Feuquières, wrote, "in order not to compromise the authority of the King."[58]

Illicit trade with the Spanish colonies, however, was officially encouraged in the early years of Fleury's administration, although it never rivalled the extent of British contraband activity there because British ships in Spanish waters might be able to plead some legal justification for their being there, by virtue of the Asiento, while, on the other hand, French vessels traded under the handicap that the very fact of their presence in Spanish American ports or coastal waters made them *ipso facto* subject to confiscation.[59] Nevertheless, the French government gladly connived at illicit trade with the Spanish possessions, although it steadfastly refused to lend official protection to its nationals

---

[58] May: *Histoire économique de la Martinique*, p. 145. Blondel, intendant at Martinique, wrote on November 24, 1723: "Il faut souffrir ce qu'on ne peut empêcher" (*ibid.*). Champigny was made Governor of the Windward Isles for the purpose of enforcing more strictly the regulations against trade with foreigners, since Feuquières, his predecessor, was accused of having permitted entry of 118 British ships between 1723 and 1726 (J. Saintoyant: *La colonisation française sous l'ancien régime* [Paris, 1929, two vols.], II, p. 125). But even Champigny soon became convinced of the necessity of this trade. His memorial "on the necessity of modifying article iii of the edict of October, 1727, concerning the traffic of foreigners in the French Islands of America" was debated in the Council of Commerce on October 22, November 12 and 25, 1728; on December 16, 1728, a draft of a Declaration was drawn up, permitting the inhabitants of the Windward Isles to trade "with the English of New England for horses and mules, planks, timber, clapboards and fresh meats, on condition of giving in payment only syrups and tafias coming from the sugar mills of the Islands" (Bonnassieux: *Conseil de commerce et bureau du commerce (1700-1791). Inventaire analytique des procès verbaux*, pp. 166, 167). Blondel suggested the same thing to Maurepas in the same year, 1728 (May: *Histoire économique de la Martinique*, p. 162). But the project did not become law.

[59] All of the French possessions except Guiana traded with the Spaniards (Maurepas: *Mémoires*, III, p. 112). The traffic amounted to between three and four million livres a year, and returned a profit of from eighty to ninety *per cent*. (Raynal: *A Philosophical and Political History of the Settlements and Trade of the Europeans in the East and West Indies*, IV, p. 161). The traffic was particularly profitable after the outbreak of war between Great Britain and Spain (1739) until the beginning of war between France and Great Britain in 1744 (O'Héguerty: *Essai sur les intérets du commerce maritime*, p. 160). With engaging ingenuousness, British pamphleteers complained of this traffic (Perrin: *The Present State of the British and French Sugar Colonies*, p. 24; *The Wisdom and Policy of the French in the Construction of their Great Offices* [1755], p. 76).

engaged in that highly profitable, although illegal, traffic.[60]
It was the supply of sugar to the continent of Europe which
made the West Indies islands so valuable to France, and enabled
her to surpass the British in foreign markets.[61] The fresher soils
of Martinique, Guadeloupe and San Domingo produced more
cheaply than the British islands, "Jamaica, Barbados, and the
Leeward Islands being almost worn out and in great decay."[62]
The high cost of British production was likewise charged to the
luxurious habits of the planters, the exploitation of whose estates
also suffered from absenteeism.[63] As a result, the production of
French sugar increased enormously, both absolutely and com-

[60] Benjamin Keene wrote to Delafaye, Newcastle's secretary, on August 19,
1732: "But France, you see by Mr. Stewart's letter, can hold its tongue as long as
she finds a trade which overbalances the ships she loses by the *guarda-costas*, . . ."
(Armstrong: *Elisabeth Farnese*, p. 286). See also Keene and Castres to Newcastle,
October 2, O. S., 1738 (H. W. V. Temperley: "The Causes of the War of Jenkins'
Ear (1739)." *Transactions of the Royal Historical Society*, Third Series, III, p. 205).
Although the French government encouraged its settlers in Louisiana to trade
with the Spanish (Surrey: *Commerce of Louisiana*, pp. 397, 402, 422), the traffic
depended upon Spanish initiative rather than French, and consequently remained
small (*ibid.*, pp. 394-395, 399-400, 414, 436-437). The inference is that French
traders could not count on official support if their goods were confiscated. For
official encouragement of clandestine trade, see the letter of the King to La
Rochalard and Duclos, Governor and Intendant of San Domingo, October 28,
1727 (Moreau de Saint-Méry: *Loix et constitutions*, III, pp. 236-237).
[61] Perrin: *The Present State of the British and French Sugar Colonies*, pp. 43-44.
Contemporary French evidence (1737) quoted by Garnault: *Le commerce rochelais*,
III, p. 63.
[62] Sir H. W. Richmond, editor: "The Land Forces of France—June 1738."
Publications of the Navy Records Society, LXIII, p. 79. Barbados suffered the most
from exhaustion (Gee: *Trade and Navigation of Great-Britain Considered*, p. 45;
Raynal; *A Philosophical and Political History of the Settlements and Trade of the
Europeans in the East and West Indies*, IV, p. 392; *The Importance of the British
Plantations in America to this Kingdom* [London, 1731], pp. 29, 113). Indubitably,
there was distress among the British planters during the decade 1730-1740 (Frank
Wesley Pitman: "The Settlement and Financing of British West India Planta-
tions in the Eighteenth Century." *Essays in Colonial History Presented to Charles
McLean Andrews by his Students* [New Haven, 1931], pp. 256, 274-275, 280; Pitman:
The Development of the British West Indies, pp. 92-94).
[63] *Acts of the Privy Council of England, Colonial Series*, VI, pp. 253-254, 262;
Gee: *Trade and Navigation of Great-Britain Considered*, p. 45; *Some Considerations
humbly offer'd upon the Bill now depending in the House of Lords, relating to the
Trade between the Northern Colonies and the Sugar-Islands* (n.p., 1732), pp. 4-5, 11;
*Considerations on the Bill now depending in Parliament, Concerning the British
Sugar-Colonies in America* (London, 1731), p. 21; John Ellis: *An Historical Account
of Coffee* (London, 1774), p. 56.

paratively.[64] Sugar refining in France became a major industry, while the agitation in Parliament for legislation, which finally issued in the Molasses Act, shows how severely the British planters felt the pinch of French competition.[65] By 1740, the French sugars had captured the bulk of the market in Spain, the Baltic, Germany and the Netherlands.[66] The British product had henceforth to rely on home consumption.

In the production of other West Indian commodities the French prospered as well. Only a small amount of cacao was produced, it is true, partly because most of the trees had been destroyed in the earthquake and hurricane of 1727, partly be-

---

[64] In 1720 the English produced about 45,000 hogsheads of sugar, the French about 30,000 (Postlethwayt: *Great Britain's True System*, p. 262). In 1734 the British produced 85,000 (Macpherson: *Annals of Commerce*, III, p. 200). In 1742 the British produced 65,950 and the French 122,500 (Macpherson, *op. cit.*, III, pp. 262-263).

[65] P.-M. Bondois: "Les centres sucriers français au XVIIIe siècle." *Revue d'histoire économique et sociale*, XIX (1931), pp. 27-77; 456 sugar refineries worked night and day in Martinique in 1742 (May: *Histoire économique de la Martinique*, p. 135). The arguments for and against the Molasses Act summarized (Macpherson: *Annals of Commerce*, III, pp. 171-177). For the effect of French competition on British sugar prices, see table (Pitman: *The Development of the British West Indies*, p. 134). For arguments before the Board of Trade in favour of the Molasses Bill (*Journal of the Commissioners for Trade and Plantations, January 1728-9 to December 1734*, pp. 246, 250, 253-254, 257, 274, 275-276). For Parliamentary debates on the Molasses Bill (*History and Proceedings of the House of Commons*, VII, pp. 81, 84, 133-136, 209-219, 279-284, 309-315).

[66] Gee: *Trade and Navigation of Great-Britain Considered*, p. 44; Postlethwayt: *Great Britain's True System*, pp. 262-263; John Bennet: *The National Merchant: or Discourses on Commerce and Colonies* (London, 1736), pp. 105-106; Burke: *An Account of the European Settlements in America*, p. 181; Lord Chesterfield to his son, London, Nov. 19, O. S., 1750 (Chesterfield: *Letters* [ed. Dobrée], IV, p. 1619; Otis Little: *The State of Trade in the Northern Colonies Considered* (London, 1748), pp. 24, 26. France exported 80,000 hogsheads in 1740, exclusive of what was shipped directly from the islands to Spain (Joannès Tramond: "Les Antilles après le traité d'Utrecht." *Histoire des colonies françaises et de l'expansion de la France dans le monde*, I, p. 460). By edict of Jan. 27, 1726, French merchants were permitted to ship West Indies products, except raw sugar, directly to Spain (Moreau de Saint-Méry: *Loix et constitutions*, III, p. 155). The consequent saving in freight, storage charges and harbour dues, added to their cheaper production costs, enabled the French to undersell the British in Spain thirty *per cent*. (*The Present State of the British Sugar Colonies Consider'd* [London, 1731], pp. 11-13; John Ashley: *The Sugar Trade, with the Incumbrances thereon, Laid Open* [London, 1734], p. i of preface; [John Ashley]: *Some Observations on a Direct Exportation of Sugar, from the British Islands* [London, 1735], p. 4). The British adopted a similar system in 1739 (12 George II, cap. xxx).

cause of the competition of the Spanish Caracas company.[67] Moreover, the culture of tobacco might have been much more valuable had it not been for the anomalous fact that the farmers-general preferred to contract for all their needs from England, and consequently discouraged the introduction of French-grown tobacco into the kingdom.[68] But in this period the production of coffee, which had been introduced to the islands as late as 1723, became of great importance, and in the raising of indigo the French practically enjoyed a monopoly until the British discovered that the plant could be raised profitably in the Carolinas, and subsidized its production by "An Act for Encouraging the Making of Indico in the British Plantations of America" (1748).[69]

The commercial importance of Louisiana remained small during this period. Before the cultivation of sugar cane was introduced in 1745, tobacco had been the colony's most promising crop, but its profitable disposal was hampered, as already mentioned, by the policy of the farmers-general.[70] The Crown,

[67] May: *Histoire économique de la Martinique*, p. 95; F. d'Arcy: "Les débuts du cacao des Isles." *Revue historique des Antilles*, No. 5 (Jan.-March, 1930), pp. 11-16.

[68] The farmers-general (who were opposed to the introduction of French-grown tobacco into France because it would make the exercise of their monopoly more difficult) even continued to import British tobacco, under special license from the Privy Council of Great Britain, during the War of the Austrian Succession (*Acts of the Privy Council of England, Colonial Series*, III, pp. 796-798). Tobacco culture was discontinued at San Domingo after the establishment of the tobacco tax-farm (Maurepas: *Mémoires*, III, p. 104).

[69] May: *Histoire économique de la Martinique*, pp. 101-103, 323; Ballet: *La Guadeloupe*, II, pp. 128-130; Arthur Girault: *The Colonial Tariff Policy of France* (Oxford, 1916), pp. 23-24. For the production of indigo by the French (*The Assiento Contract Consider'd, as also, the Advantages and Decay of the Trade of Jamaica and the Plantations, with the Causes and Consequences thereof* [London, 1714], p. 3; *The Importance of the British Plantations in America to this Kingdom* [London, 1731], p. 38; Gee: *Trade and Navigation of Great-Britain Considered*, p. 47; *Two Letters, Concerning some farther Advantages* [London, 1746], p. 6; Postlethwayt: *Great Britain's True System*, p. 262; Perrin: *The Present State of the British and French Sugar Colonies*, p. 44; Malachy Postlethwayt: *The African Trade, the Great Pillar and Support of the British Plantation Trade in America: Shewing, that our Loss, by being beat out of all the Foreign Markets for Sugar and Indigo by the French, has been owing to the Neglect of our African Trade* [London, 1745], pp. 10, 12-13; Charlevoix: *Histoire de l'Isle Espagnole ou de S. Domingue*, II, p. 489; Joannès Tramond: "Aperçu de l'histoire de Saint-Domingue au XVIIIᵉ siècle." *Revue historique des Antilles*, No. 1 [Oct., 1928], p. 26).

[70] O'Héguerty: *Essai sur les intérets du commerce maritime*, pp. 134-154.

which had taken over the administration of the colony in 1731, endeavoured to encourage its development by subsidies and tax exemptions, by interesting merchants in the colony and by providing for the supply of slaves.[71] Although the population remained very small and the colony was of scant economic significance during these years, Cardinal Fleury was aware of its potential value and strategical importance, as is evidenced by the instructions he gave for its defense in 1740.[72]

At that time, the progressive prosperity of colonies in the Antilles depended upon an adequate supply of slave labor:

The Commerce of Guinea has such Relation to that of the French Islands in the West-Indies, that the one can not subsist without the other.[73]

It was the fact, as logic would lead one to suspect, that as the French West Indies waxed in importance, the French Guinea trade increased in proportion. For French planters were supplied not only by the Dutch at St. Eustatius and clandestinely by the English at Santa Lucia, but also were furnished by French slavers directly from the coast of Africa.[74] Moreover, the French dealt almost exclusively in Gold Coast negroes, considered superior to those of other African tribes:[75]

[71] Surrey: *Commerce of Louisiana*, pp. 169-170, 175-177, 184-185, 194-195, 236-237, 372-381; Garnault: *Le commerce rochelais*, III, p. 46.

[72] Vaucher: *Robert Walpole et la politique de Fleury*, p. 340. The population of Louisiana, according to a census taken in 1745, is said to have been only five thousand, of whom eight hundred were soldiers and two thousand slaves (Maurice Besson: *Histoire des colonies françaises* [Paris, 1931], p. 163). For trade relations, such as they were, between the Spaniards in Texas and the French in Louisiana at this time, see H. E. Bolton: *Texas in the Middle Eighteenth Century* (Berkeley, 1915), pp. 32-39.

[73] "A Memorial Presented by the Council of Trade in France to the Royal Council in 1701" (Postlethwayt: *The African Trade, the Great Pillar and Support*, pp. 4-5).

[74] Pitman: *The Development of the British West Indies*, pp. 87-88. For the procuring of slaves by the French at Santa Lucia, see the letter of Governor William Hart to the Board of Trade, St. Christopher's, Feb. 15, O. S., 1726/7 (Elizabeth Donnan: *Documents illustrative of the History of the Slave Trade to America*. Volume II: *The Eighteenth Century* [Carnegie Institution of Washington, Publication No. 409; Washington (D. C.), 1931], pp. xxvi, 336-337).

[75] *Considerations on the Present Peace, as far as it is relative to the Colonies, and the African Trade* (London, 1763), pp. 17-18; John Atkins: *A Voyage to Guinea, Brasil, and the West-Indies* (London, 1735), p. 179; Frank W. Pitman: "Slavery on the British West India Plantations in the Eighteenth Century." *Journal of Negro History*, XI (October, 1926), pp. 589-591.

The French, from the year 1729 to the end of the year 1738, carried from the Gold Coast, Popo and Whydah *fifteen* or *seventeen thousand* of those valuable people annually; when *four thousand* in any one year during that period, were not carried to the British plantations,[76]

The change in the conditions of competition on the African coast is seen in a comparison of the accounts which James Houstoun gave of the trade there: in 1725 "the Dutch are the only formidable Antagonists we have to deal with."[77] But in 1747 he wrote: "Now the French are more dangerous to us than the Dutch."[78] The growth of the French slave trade is graphically portrayed by the letter of a Rhode Island sea captain writing from the coast of Africa in 1736:

but am like to have a long and trublesom Voyge of it, for there never was so much Rum on the Coast at one time before, Nor the Like of the french shipen—never seen before for no. for the hole Coast is full of them.[79]

British pamphleteers sounded the alarm throughout this period, and it is clear that an expanding and profitable slave trade was one of the foundations on which were built the flourishing fortunes of Nantes.[80]

[76] *Considerations on the Present Peace*, p. 17. That most of the slaves procured by the French were from the Gold Coast is confirmed by Gaston-Martin: *Nantes au XVIIIe siècle*, pp. 218-219. However, the figures mentioned by the pamphleteer are much too high (cf. Gaston-Martin: *op. cit.*, pp. 115, 116, 202).

[77] James Houstoun: *Some New and Accurate Observations, Geographical, Natural and Historical, Containing a true and impartial Account of the Situation, Product, and Natural History of the Coast of Guinea, so far as relates to the Improvement of that Trade, for the Advantage of Great Britain in general, and the Royal African Company in Particular* (London, 1725), p. 44. Atkins, whose observations were based on a voyage made in 1722, also speaks of the Dutch as the principal rivals of the British (Atkins: *Voyage to Guinea*, p. 156).

[78] *Memoirs of the Life and Travels of James Houstoun, M. D.*, p. 149, note.

[79] *Commerce of Rhode Island*, I (*1726-1774*), (*Collections of the Massachusetts Historical Society*, Seventh Series, IX [Boston, 1914]), p. 46. A Captain Wyndham, commanding a war vessel on the African coast, wrote on August 30, 1742: "and as to the Dutch factories, they, as far as I can learn, make no great hand of their trade any more than the English; the French who has [sic] ten ships on the coast to our one, seem to flourish and carry all before them" (*Considerations on the Present Peace*, p. 58).

[80] A—r Z—h: *Considerations on the Dispute now depending before the Honourable House of Commons, between the British, Southern, and Northern Plantations in America* (London, 1731), p. 9; *An Inquiry into the Revenue, Credit and Commerce of France*, p. 36; Sir H. W. Richmond, editor: "The Land Forces of France—June 1738." *Publications of the Navy Records Society*, LXIII, pp. 76-77; Postle-

Even the trade of the East India Company, which had been refounded in 1723 on the débris of Law's Company of the Occident, grew during this period. Although the Crown sustained the stock by artificial means, so that the high price of shares was no reliable criterion of the actual state of the Company's affairs, nevertheless authorities are agreed that the decade between 1730 and 1740 was a prosperous one.[81] Sufficient it was to alarm the British:

In the month of August 1740, the sale of the French East-India company's merchandize at Port L'Orient amounted to twenty-two millions of livres, or about one million sterling; which sufficiently demonstrates the vast increase of that company's commerce to East-India, in the space of a few years past.[82]

This increased commercial activity encouraged navigation in the Indian Ocean. From 1725 to 1744 the sailings from Lorient

thwayt: *A Short State of the Progress of the French Trade and Navigation*, pp. 60-61, 83; Postlethwayt: *Great Britain's True System*, p. 257. Cf. the entry for the year 1737 in Macpherson: *Annals of Commerce*, III, p. 213: "They [the French] monopolized the gum trade at the river Senegal; they had also encroached on the English settlement at the River Gambia, and had largely encreased their slave-trade on that coast for the encouragement of their West India sugar islands. . . ."; also Gaston-Martin: *Nantes au XVIIIᵉ siècle*, pp. 22-23, 158-159, 173-174, 201. "A partir de 1735, la prospérité de la traite s'accusera dans les chiffres de l'armement et des transports. En 8 ans, 180 navires ont traité 55.015 nègres et en ont vendu 45.336 aux Iles, ce qui donne une moyenne annuelle de 7.000 environ, double de celle qui fut précédemment atteinte" (*ibid.*, p. 215).

[81] Joseph Chailley-Bert: *Les compagnies de colonisation sous l'ancien régime* (Paris, 1898), 170-171. Dividends of 148 livres on each share were declared in 1725; 136 in 1736 and 135 in 1743 (*ibid.*). The par value of the stock was a thousand livres; the total capitalization included approximately fifty-six thousand shares. Shares were quoted at 711 on January 1, 1726; at 1776 in 1732; the war scare of 1734 reduced quotations to a point below 1200, but on January 1, 1736 quotations reached 2085 (Wilbert Harold Dalgliesh: *The Company of the Indies in the Days of Dupleix* [Easton (Pa.), 1933], p. 47, note 10). Similar figures given by Raynal (*A Philosophical and Political History of the Settlements and Trade of the Europeans in the East and West Indies*, II, pp. 70-71, 119-125). From 1723 to 1743 the Company purchased merchandise to the value of 136,104,522 livres and sold merchandise to the value of 262,517,805 livres (Dalgliesh: *op. cit.*, pp. 90-91). "La période de 1730 à 1740 fut très prospère" (Alfred Martineau: *Dupleix et l'Inde française* [Paris, 1920-1928, four vols.], I, p. 31).

[82] Macpherson: *Annals of Commerce*, III, p. 226; see also *ibid.*, p. 214; *An Inquiry into the Revenue, Credit, and Commerce of France*, p. 36. Until 1733 Nantes was the staple for the sale of the goods of the East India Company; after that date the sales were held at Lorient (Gaston-Martin: "Nantes et la Compagnie des Indes (1664-1769)." *Revue d'histoire économique et sociale*, XV [1927], pp. 44, 46).

averaged twenty a year, and in 1740 the Company owned forty vessels, of which ten carried from sixty to seventy cannon each.[83] Between 1728 and 1740 there were built in the shipyards at Lorient seventeen vessels, ten frigates and four small boats.[84] Moreover, the Company's increasing trade and navigation on the Indian Ocean was protected by the wise foresight of La Bourdonnais, appointed governor of the Île de France and the Île de Bourbon in 1735, who took advantage of the windward position of those islands in relation to India, by making Port Louis into a respectable naval base.[85]

In consonance with the general development of trade during the administration of Cardinal Fleury was the traffic with Spain, the most important single market for the French at that time.[86] Besides the trade with Spain proper, French merchants despatched large consignments of goods to the Spanish Indies in the galleons and flotillas which put out from Cadiz; their share in this trade was estimated to be two-thirds of the whole.[87]

Finally, the French did not neglect commercial opportunities at the other end of Europe. An extensive trade was carried on with the Austrian Netherlands.[88] The German cities consumed large quantities of French sugars and the Dutch distributed French manufactures and colonial products throughout northern Europe. In the later years of Fleury's administration, some attempts were made to conclude a commercial treaty with Russia

[83] Dalgliesh: *The Company of the Indies*, pp. 129, 130; Horatio Walpole to Robert Trevor, October 3, O. S., 1740 (Trevor Manuscripts, *Hist. MSS. Comm., Report* XIV, Appendix Part IX, p. 57). Even after the War of the Austrian Succession, the Company possessed twenty-six vessels and frigates, besides renting several vessels from the Crown (Dalgliesh: *op. cit.*, p. 129).

[84] Dalgliesh: *The Company of the Indies*, p. 130.

[85] Admiral G. A. Ballard: *Rulers of the Indian Ocean* (London, 1927), p. 249; Raynal: *A Philosophical and Political History of the Settlements and Trade of the Europeans in the East and West Indies*, II, pp. 73-77.

[86] Émile Levasseur: *Histoire du commerce de la France.* I: *Avant 1789* (Paris, 1911), p. 511; *National Prejudice, Opposed to the National Interest* (London, 1748), p. 43.

[87] So thought Horatio Walpole (H. W. V. Temperley: "The Relations of England with Spanish America, 1720-1744." *Annual Report of the American Historical Association for the Year 1911*, I, p. 235). Cf. Maurepas: *Mémoires*, III, p. 99; Saint-Pierre: *Annales politiques (1658-1740)* (ed. Drouet), p. 373.

[88] Patrice-François, comte de Nény: *Mémoires historiques et politiques sur les Pays-Bas autrichiens* (Paris, 1784, two vols.), II, pp. 4-5.

and to inaugurate direct trade with that country.[89] At the same time, an extensive exchange of timber and ores for colonial products and articles *de luxe* was carried on between France and the Baltic, a lucrative traffic in which the Dutch figured as the principal carriers, although the growth of this branch of French navigation was sufficient to alarm Malachy Postlethwayt, whose cacklings were intended to warn the British that the citadel of foreign trade was being surprised by the Gauls.[90]

[89] S. Rojdestvensky and Inna Lubimenko: "Contribution à l'histoire des relations commerciales franco-russes au XVIIIᵉ siècle." *Revue d'histoire économique et sociale,* XVII (1929), pp. 389, 401.

[90] Postlethwayt: *A Short State of the Progress of the French Trade and Navigation,* p. 18. See also, Louis-Philippe May: "La France, puissance des Antilles." *Revue d'histoire économique et sociale,* XVIII (1930), p. 468; Henri Sée: "Les relations commerciales et maritimes entre la France et les pays du Nord au XVIIIᵉ siècle." *Revue maritime,* Nouvelle Série, No. 71 (November 1925), p. 599; O'Héguerty: *Essai sur les intérets du commerce maritime,* p. 182. French navigation to Norway also remained small during this century (Oscar Albert Johnsen: "Le commerce entre la France méridionale et les pays du Nord sous l'ancien régime." *Revue d'histoire moderne,* II [1927], pp. 88-89). In the eighteenth century, Dutch navigation to the Baltic increased absolutely, although the British navigation finally surpassed it (Max Gideonse: *Dutch Baltic Trade in the Eighteenth Century* [Harvard College Library, manuscript thesis, 1932], pp. 63-64). The catalogue of French vessels passing through the Sound during this period is a small one. The following table is compiled from the volume by Nina Ellinger Bang and Knud Korst: *Tabeller over Skibsfart og Varetransport gennem Øresund, 1661-1783, og gennem Storebælt, 1701-1746. Første Del: Tabeller over Skibsfarten* (Copenhagen, 1930), pp. 56-84:

Year	French Ships East Bound	French Ships West Bound
1715	25	22
1716	7	5
1717	6	7
1718	8	6
1719	8	12
1720	19	17
1721	10	10
1722	11	11
1723	28	27
1724	16	18
1725	11	11
1726	8	10
1727	9	9
1728	3	3
1729	7	7
1730	5	5
1731	7	8
1732	13	13

It is obvious that the years of the administration of Cardinal Fleury saw a notable increase in the magnitude of France's foreign trade. Various estimates of the value of French imports and exports during these years have been made, and, although their results must be accepted with caution, it is incontestable that this was an era of prosperity for France.[91] Naturally, the corollary of the increased sale of French manufactures abroad was the development of French industry within the country:

Nevertheless, great industrial progress was made during the period from 1715 to 1750, especially beginning with 1730.[92]

In every branch of foreign trade, save in that of the Baltic, the growth of French commerce was accompanied by the growth of French navigation. Voltaire stated that in 1718 the French

Year	French Ships East Bound	French Ships West Bound
1733	6	5
1734	0	1
1735	5	5
1736	4	4
1737	6	5
1738	3	2
1739	5	6
1740	17	15
1741	6	7
1742	11	11
1743	9	9

Only one French ship passed by the Grand Belt in this whole period (1717): (*ibid.*, p. 442).

[91] Levasseur: *Histoire des classes ouvrières et de l'industrie en France avant 1789*, prints a table (vol. ii, p. 546) of France's exports and imports during this period, based upon calculations by Ambroise-Marie Arnould (1791), an employé of the French *bureau de la balance du commerce*:

(Annual average stated in millions of livres)

	IMPORTS		EXPORTS	
	From Europe	From Other Countries	To Europe	To Other Countries
1716-20	65.1	27.2	106.2	16.3
1721-32	80.2	35.6	116.7	31.7
1733-35	76.6	46.7	124.4	29.8
1736-39	102.0	65.6	143.4	51.0
1740-48	112.8	69.8	192.3	46.2

[92] Henri Sée: *Economic and Social Conditions in France during the Eighteenth Century* (New York, 1927), p. 159. Cf. Levasseur: *Histoire des classes ouvrières et de l'industrie en France avant 1789*, II, pp. 545-548.

merchant marine was reduced to three hundred vessels, excluding small coasting and fishing ships.[93] The report made by Maurepas to the Royal Council of Commerce in October 1730, gave a total of 3,060 ships of all sizes and 37,976 mariners; and in 1738, Voltaire estimated the number of large merchant vessels to be 1,800.[94] An English estimate of the year 1744 declared that the French employed a thousand ships and twenty thousand sailors in the European commerce, six hundred ships and twenty-seven thousand men in the fisheries and seven hundred ships and fourteen thousand men in the navigation to the French West Indies, a total of two thousand three hundred ships and sixty-one thousand sailors.[95] Finally, a list in the *Archives nationales*, dated September 1743, the year in which Fleury died and the year before war was formally declared between France and Great Britain, gives a total of 5,308 ships with a tonnage of 269,909, of which 3,365, averaging about forty-five tons each, were engaged in the coasting trade; the high seas fleet was numbered at 1,934, with a total tonnage of 185,784.[96]

[93] "Observations sur MM. Jean Lass, Melon, et Dutot; sur le commerce, le luxe, les monnaies et les impôts." *Oeuvres de Voltaire*, XXXVII, p. 529.

[94] *Oeuvres de Voltaire, ibid.;* Maurepas: *Mémoires*, III, pp. 95-112. Maurepas explained that the figure which he gave of 3,707 ships and 19,472 sailors in the coasting trade should be divided by three, as each coaster averaged three clearances a year. This correction has been made in the table below. Maurepas did not include the navigation of the East India Company.

Trade	Ships	Sailors	Tonnage
Herring	124	2523	2990
Portugal	43	393	3006
Coasting	1236	6490	....
Spain	160	2293	14423
Levant	726	9330	57362
Dutch	50	475	3977
English	35	286	1205
Baltic	25	276	1591
Cod	296	7489	26007
Antilles	316	8421	39806
Canada	4	....	....
Netherlands	8	....	....
Whaling	37	....	....

[95] Estimate made by Massie in his *Historical Account of the Naval Power of France* (Sinclair: *Thoughts on the Naval Strength of the British Empire*, p. 19, note).

[96] Louis-Philippe May: "La France, puissance des Antilles." *Revue d'histoire économique et sociale*, XVIII (1930), p. 466.

These estimates of the growth and extent of French navigation ought not to be accepted as absolutely trustworthy, but it is reasonably safe to conclude that a notable expansion did occur. Moreover, this development re-enforced France's pretensions to consideration as a power of naval importance, especially in that day of privateering and in an era when sailors of the merchant marine were equally efficient when put to serve on men-of-war. No less, the increase of national wealth as a result of the prosperous colonial and foreign trade of this epoch had high political significance. As Dutot had remarked, if money is the sinews of war, the balance of power must follow that of commerce. Indubitably, foreign estimation of France increased during Fleury's administration because the state was flourishing and prosperous. But trade and diplomacy are intimately related; as F. S. Oliver observed in *The Endless Adventure:*

It would be hard to prove, but still harder not to believe, that the rapid growth of French prosperity owed a great deal to the prestige which Fleury had lately won for his country among the nations of Europe.

CHAPTER XI

THE ISOLATION OF GREAT BRITAIN ACCOMPLISHED

EXCEPT for the crisis in the Spanish and British relations, which constituted a danger for French tranquillity, the year 1739 was a very prosperous one for French diplomacy. In the first place, steps were taken to prevent the succession in Jülich and Berg from becoming a European crisis. On February 10, 1738, as a result of negotiations at The Hague, Austria, France, Great Britain and the United Provinces had presented identical notes at Berlin and Mannheim, suggesting that the succession should be mediated but that the Sulzbach heir should provisionally occupy the duchies after the death of the Elector Palatine, until such time as the mediators should arrive at a settlement. This suggestion was rejected at Berlin with something approaching contumely, and its only concrete result was to increase the distrust between Frederick William I and Charles VI, which it is not to be supposed that France decried. On January 13, 1739, France and Austria concluded a secret treaty, which France subsequently refused to ratify, providing that the Sulzbach heir should occupy the disputed duchies for two years following the death of the Elector Palatine. But at the same time, Fénelon and Luiscius, respectively French ambassador and Prussian envoy to the States General of the United Provinces, were carrying on negotiations at The Hague which ended in the treaty of April 5, 1739.[1] France guaranteed all of Ravenstein and a carefully stipulated portion of the duchy of Berg to Prussia, and agreed to persuade the Elector Palatine to consent to this arrangement.[2]

---

[1] See *Recueil des instructions. . . . Prusse*, pp. lxxvii-lxxviii, 350, 356. For these several treaties, see Loewe: *Preussens Staatsverträge*, pp. 478, 480-487.

[2] Valory's instructions stated that these *negotiations* with Prussia were undertaken with the knowledge and consent of the Elector Palatine, although they were contrary to the Treaty of Marly, Feb. 15, 1733. Of the Franco-Prussian *treaty* the Elector Palatine knew nothing, and did not welcome the insinuations made by France in accordance with it (*Recueil des instructions. . . . Prusse*, pp. 357-359).

This treaty opened the way for a French *rapprochement* with Prussia. The instructions to Valory, who went to Berlin as ambassador in 1739, show that this was an object of French desires; as a result of it, France would not only be on good terms with the two leading powers in Germany but would also, by using the Swedes in conjunction with the Prussians, be able to restrain the ambitions of Russia.[3]

The resignation of Horn and the appointment of Gyllenborg as his successor in the office of President of the Chancery were a victory for the French influence in Sweden. Significantly enough, the Marquis d'Antin cruised with a small squadron in the Baltic in 1739, and that autumn Chavigny began negotiations for a triple alliance of France, Sweden and Denmark, the object of which was to guarantee the Swedish succession to a Danish prince and thus prevent the recognition of Russia's candidate, Frederick of Holstein-Gottorp, as heir to the throne.[4] Finally, through the guidance of Villeneuve, the French ambassador at Constantinople, the Swedes and the Turks concluded a treaty of defensive alliance, which afforded them mutual protection against the designs of Russia and by doing so no less served the interests of France.[5]

Most striking of all the negotiations in that *annus mirabilis* of French diplomacy was Villeneuve's negotiation at Belgrade. The military operations which Charles VI had undertaken against the Turks as a result of his engagements with Russia had not turned out happily.[6] Since July 1737, the Turks had requested

---

[3] *Recueil des instructions. . . . Prusse*, pp. 359-360. The instructions mention French appreciation of the Prussian attitude in the Polish war (*ibid.*, pp. 352-354).

[4] Francis Hare wrote to his son, May 31, O. S., 1739: "France is encouraging the Swedes to attack the Czarine, and is sending a squadron into the Baltic, which may oblige us to do so too" (Hare MSS., *Hist. MSS. Comm., Report* XIV, App. Part IX, pp. 245-246). For Chavigny's negotiation, see *Recueil des instructions . . . Danemark*, p. li; the Count of Stolberg wrote to his sovereign, the King of Denmark, on Jan. 9, 1740, that the Hanoverian ministers were "in no small Disquiet and Apprehension touching an Alliance said to be upon the Carpet between Yr Majty and the Crown of France" (Weston Papers, *Hist. MSS. Comm., Report* X, App. Part I, p. 436).

[5] Treaty dated Dec. 22, 1739 (Gabriel Noradounghian: *Recueil d'actes internationaux de l'Empire Ottoman* [Paris, 1897-1903, four vols.], I, pp. 267-269).

[6] For the Austro-Russian convention of Jan. 9, 1737, stipulating mutual assistance against the Turks, see Martens: *Recueil des traités et conventions conclus par*

the sole mediation of the French, and early in 1738 Villeneuve received the authorization of Charles VI to mediate for him as well.[7] Thus the negotiation was centered in the hands of the French ambassador, who utilized his opportunity with the skill and *sang froid* of a Stratford Canning. Moreover, the French government took the important step of guaranteeing the eventual treaty of peace, the first time that the French had ever done this where the Ottoman Empire was concerned.[8] In April, Villeneuve received from Russia full powers to negotiate a peace, and consequently, when he journeyed to the Turkish camp at Belgrade in August 1739, he was complete master of the negotiation.[9] The fact which was so striking about his mediation was that he made haste to accept the preliminaries of September 1, 1739, which the ineptitude of the Emperor's representative, Count Neipperg, had allowed, and attached the guarantee of France to them.[10] Not only had Neipperg consented to the surrender of Belgrade, but he also had permitted the Turks to gain by negotiation what it was apparent they could not win by arms. The French guarantee prevented the Emperor from repudiating the preliminaries, and the Austrian ratification of the prelimi-

---

la Russie, I, pp. 69-80; for the declaration of March 18, 1737, concerting the military measures to be taken, see *ibid.*, pp. 80-84. An account of the part played in this war by Austria may be found in Coxe: *History of the House of Austria*, IV, pp. 320-364; a very good account of the 1739 campaign and the Peace of Belgrade has been written by Theodor Tupetz: "Der Türkenfeldzug von 1739 und der Friede zu Belgrad." *Historische Zeitschrift*, XL (1878), pp. 1-52.

[7] For the letter of the Grand-Vizier Mehemet to Fleury, asking for French mediation, July 17, 1737, see Wenck: *Codex juris gentium*, I, pp. 398-401. For Louis XV's full powers to Villeneuve, see *ibid.*, I, pp. 403-406. Charles VI's full powers to Villeneuve, Oct. 15, 1738 (*ibid.*, I, pp. 407-409). Cf. Vandal: *Une ambassade française*, p. 322. The British and Dutch had also offered to mediate, but their offers were rejected (Sir Richard Lodge: "The First Anglo-Russian Treaty, 1739-42." *English Historical Review*, XLIII [1928], p. 356; A. C. Wood: "The English Embassy at Constantinople, 1660-1762." *English Historical Review*, XL [1925], pp. 554-555). Villeneuve was instructed to attempt to divide Austria and Russia by concluding separate peace treaties with the Turks, instead of one general one (Lodge: *art. cit.*, E. H. R., XLIII, p. 361).

[8] Amelot to Villeneuve, April 12, 1738 (Vandal: *Une ambassade française*, p. 327).

[9] For the Czarina's full powers to Villeneuve, April 9, 1739, see Wenck: *Codex juris gentium*, I, pp. 411-413.

[10] Neipperg unwisely cut himself off from communication with the Austrians; consequently, he did not know that the Austrian military situation had improved. For the preliminaries, see Wenck: *Codex juris gentium*, I, pp. 316-322.

naries, in turn, forced the Russian withdrawal from the war, although, on August 28, 1739, they had won a victory. Consequently, the preliminaries were converted into a final peace at Belgrade on September 18, 1739; Russia and Austria remained allies in name but hardly in spirit, so that Villeneuve's action was another step in the French policy of isolating Russia.[11] At the same time the Turks, who were delighted at their extrication from a difficult military situation on such favourable terms, made no difficulty about renewing and extending the privileges of the French in the Ottoman Empire. The Capitulations of May 28, 1740, carried French prestige and privileges to the highest point ever attained there.[12]

As a result of these several negotiations, it became very unlikely that a war would break out on the Continent. This fact explains Fleury's rather casual attitude towards the war between Spain and Great Britain. To the latter, he contented himself with hinting that France would not permit Great Britain to occupy any new territory in the West Indies.[13] But, far from hastening to conclude a new treaty with the Spaniards, he insisted that a commercial treaty would have to be the price paid for political alliance. What the French wanted was a preferential

---

[11] For the Austro-Turkish treaty, see Wenck: *Codex juris gentium*, I, pp. 326-359; Villeneuve's guarantee (*ibid.*, I, pp. 360-361); the Russo-Turkish Treaty of Belgrade, Sept. 18, 1739 (*ibid.*, I, pp. 368-387); cf. Noradounghian: *Recueil d'actes*, I, pp. 243-255, 257-265. For the part played by Russia in the negotiations leading to the Peace of Belgrade, see Hans Uebersberger: *Russlands Orientpolitik in den letzten zwei Jahrhunderten.* I: *Bis zum Frieden von Jassy* (Stuttgart, 1913), pp. 210, 223-224, 233-240. The continuous French hostility to Russia is shown by the character of La Chétardie's instructions (1740). Russia in respect to the balance of power in the North is too powerful, and the Russian union with the Hapsburg monarchy is extremely dangerous. The instructions go on to comment upon the appearance of Russian troops in Germany during the War of the Polish Succession (R. Nisbet Bain: *The Pupils of Peter the Great* [London, 1897], p. 308).

[12] Noradounghian: *Recueil d'actes*, I, pp. 277-306; Wenck: *Codex juris gentium*, I, pp. 538-584. M. Émile Bourgeois remarked of this period of the reign of Louis XV, particularly with regard to the renewing of the Capitulations: "Ce fut, par la vertu d'un bon conseiller, le moment le plus brillant de son règne: . . ." (É. Bourgeois: *Manuel historique de politique étrangère*, I, p. 488). Frederick II said of France at the time of his own accession to the throne that "This kingdom had not found itself in a more prosperous situation since the year 1672" (Frederick II: "History of my own Times." *Posthumous Works*, I, part i, p. 12).

[13] For a summary of Waldegrave's despatches upon this point, see *British Diplomatic Instructions: France, 1727-1744*, pp. xxxvii-xxxviii.

tariff for their colonial products, as well as fixed and certain customs regulations; they had suffered quite enough from arbitrary indults.[14] For two years, from September 1738 until August 1740, the negotiations made no progress, because Spain refused to grant a commercial treaty and France refused to lend aid unless it was granted.[15] In August of 1740, the Spaniards at last gave in, but in September of that year Fleury took the surprising step of breaking off the negotiations for both the political alliance and the commercial treaty, on the ostensible grounds that their conclusion would alarm Europe and might lead to a general war.[16]

At the moment at which he took this surprising step, Fleury was expecting a British declaration of war on France. On September 11, 1740, he had an interview with Waldegrave in which he said that

It was incumbent upon him to protect his own commerce and prevent as much as in him lay to our making ourselves masters of all the West Indian trade,

which he claimed was obviously the British intention. Moreover, he stated that it was his duty as a French minister

to hinder as much as he could our becoming more powerfull than we were already.[17]

Two French squadrons had in fact already put to sea, one of eighteen vessels from Brest and another of fifteen from Toulon.[18] In his interview with Waldegrave, Fleury had not spoken of war with Great Britain, but nevertheless he expected it. This is certain, because, owing to a period of indisposition, Fleury transacted business with his ministers by correspondence; and in a

[14] Amelot to La Marck, July 6, 1739 (Baudrillart: *Philippe V et la cour de France*, IV, p. 527, note).

[15] References to French despatches of this period which show French refusal to conclude a political alliance without a commercial treaty may be found in Baudrillart: *Philippe V et la cour de France*, IV, pp. 467-471, 474-475, 477, 492, 525-529, 531, 535, 537-539, 548, 557-558.

[16] Baudrillart: *Philippe V et la cour de France*, IV, p. 560.

[17] Waldegrave to Newcastle, Sept. 11, 1740 (*British Diplomatic Instructions: France, 1727-1744*, p. xxxix).

[18] Vaucher: *Robert Walpole et la politique de Fleury*, p. 338.

letter which he wrote to Amelot on August 20, 1740, after he had decided upon sending out the squadrons, he said:

After a resolution similar to that of the expedition of M. d'Antin . . . one can not reasonably doubt that the English will declare war in due form.

Therefore nothing should be done, he continued, which might provoke a diversion in favour of Great Britain on the Continent. The negotiations begun with Denmark should be pressed forward, as well as those at Berlin, "in order that Sweden may profit from the scene which is going to unfold."[19] France must take care to present herself to the Emperor and to the United Provinces in the guise of a defender of the Treaties of Utrecht: "the one and the other being contracting parties, we should ask their assistance in our favour, not for the purpose of securing it, but in order to assure ourselves of their neutrality, which will suffice." In order the more readily to secure Dutch neutrality, he recommended abstaining from undertaking any restoration or improvement of the works at Dunkirk or Mardyck; moreover, France should assure the Dutch that she did not propose taking steps to change the dynasty in Great Britain. In America, Louisiana should be put in a state of defense, and an attack on Acadia ought to be considered. "As we have no land war to fear, it seems to me we can transfer a certain augmentation of expenses in favour of the navy." Decision should be made as to the things to do in order to encourage privateers; also, we should

[19] Accordingly, Valory suggested to Podewils the conclusion of a close alliance, to which Sweden and Denmark should accede. Frederick II refused it (Frederick II to Podewils, Magdeburg, Sept. 22, 1740 [*Politische Correspondenz Friedrich's des Grossen*, I, pp. 49-50]). The negotiations with Denmark which Fleury referred to involved taking six thousand Danish troops into French employ by virtue of a subsidy treaty, as soon as the Anglo-Danish treaty, then valid, should expire in December 1741: see the minutes of the Cabinet Council, May 5, O.S., 1740 (Hervey: *Some Materials towards Memoirs*, pp. 929-930). It should be mentioned that there was even some talk of Fleury's being elected Pope during the summer of 1740. Clement XII died on February 6, and his successor, Benedict XIV, was elected on August 17, 1740. Prince Frederick wrote to Voltaire, March 18, 1740: "On dit que votre cardinal éternel deviendra pape" (*Correspondance de Voltaire* [*Oeuvres complètes de Voltaire* (Paris, 1883-1885), XXXV, p. 398]). In discussing the papal election, Charles de Brosses spoke of the very high credit of Cardinal Fleury in Italy; he was regarded as "l'oracle de l'Europe" (Charles de Brosses: *Lettres familières sur l'Italie* [Edited by Yvonne Bezard; Paris, 1931, two vols.], II, p. 490; see, also, *ibid.*, II, p. 511).

"augment our navy with as many vessels as we can from now until next spring, whether by building or by buying them." All these things were to be done with the view of carrying on an active campaign in 1741.[20]

These observations of the Cardinal show that the motive he alleged for suspending the negotiations with Spain was the true one. He could count upon keeping the British diplomatically isolated, so long as the power of France did not alarm the rest of Europe; this might occur if French policy took the appearance of being pre-eminently a Bourbon family one. As it was, France could count upon the assistance of the Spanish navy without the necessity of signing a treaty. On the other hand, there had come to be great advantages in not signing a treaty with Spain. By not doing so, France avoided having to undertake obligations for the establishment of Don Philip in Italy; also, a Bourbon Family Compact would obviously seem aimed at the overturn of the Utrecht settlement: the Cardinal proposed to keep Europe quiet by avoiding the suspicion of any such thing.

So completely had Fleury isolated the British that it actually became discreet for him to challenge them in their own element. It was a policy coolly considered, and it was by no means foolhardy. One might expect to find that the British welcomed a decisive conflict in a branch of warfare wherein they were so vastly superior. Instead of that, the French action threw the English ministers into abject panic. The reason was that they had no prospect of being able to create the usual European diversion which hitherto had always distracted France from devoting all her energies to maritime affairs during Anglo-French wars. "Nothing but a diversion upon the Continent can save us," wrote Horatio Walpole to Trevor on September 23, O. S., 1740.[21] Great

[20] A. É., *Corr. Pol., Angleterre*, vol. 408, ff. 29 sqq., cited by Vaucher: *Robert Walpole et la politique de Fleury*, pp. 338-341.
[21] Trevor Papers, *Hist. MSS. Comm., Report* XIV, App. Part IX, p. 54. A week later (Sept. 30), Walpole wrote to Trevor: ". . . if there is no diversion by a land war upon the Continent, and we have no security against an invasion from France besides our own strength, . . I am afraid that by next spring or summer, the seat of the war will be in this island . . ." (*ibid.*, p. 56); on October 3, O. S., 1740, Horatio Walpole wrote to Trevor: "I must freely own that without a special partiality of Providence on our side I do not see how we can cope with

Britain was beginning, to her sorrow, to reap the fruits of her neutrality during the War of the Polish Succession.

Throughout the year 1740, British councils were divided on two issues. In the first place, Newcastle had desired to send as many troops as were available to the West Indies; Walpole, however, desired to retain them for home defense.[22] In the second place, Newcastle had desired to sound out Austria with reference to a political alliance, while in opposition to that, the Walpoles had insisted on endeavouring to conclude a treaty with the new King of Prussia.[23] The divided councils of the British had led to indecisive measures, which were crowned by the failure of the attacks on Carthagena and Santiago de Cuba.[24] The diplomatic situation of Great Britain was so bad that it seems likely that Fleury could have waged his maritime war with success. At that moment, the posture of affairs, so far as France was concerned, was almost ideal. An intricate balance of power was being maintained in Italy and Germany, under such circumstances that no one state in either of these geographical divisions monopolized

that nation, even by a maritime war only . . ." (*ibid.*, p. 57); in a letter to the same, dated Oct. 7, O. S., 1740, Horatio Walpole deplored the prospect of a war "without our being able to give them a diversion by land" (*ibid.*, p. 59). Bishop Francis Hare wrote to his son, March 14, O. S., 1738/9, in disapproval of engaging upon a war "without one ally to assist us" (Hare MSS., *Hist. MSS. Comm., Report XIV*, App. Part IX, p. 243).

[22] For example, see the minutes of the Cabinet Councils for May 6 and 22, O. S., 1740, reported by Lord Hervey: *Some Materials towards Memoirs*, pp. 933-941. Cf., also, Vaucher: *Robert Walpole et la politique de Fleury*, pp. 323-327, 334-335.

[23] Vaucher: *Robert Walpole et la politique de Fleury*, pp. 345-352. Horatio Walpole discussed the advantages of a Prussian alliance in a series of letters to Robert Trevor, June 7, June 21, Sept. 16, Sept. 23, and Sept. 30, (all Old Style) 1740 (Trevor Papers, *Hist. MSS. Comm., Report XIV*, App. Part IX, pp. 49-51, 51-52, 54, 54, 55-56). The King, who spent the summer at Hanover, was opposed to a Prussian alliance, and Harrington, who was with him, seconded him and foiled the designs and plans of his colleagues at London. The lack of co-ordination in British plans upon this issue is reflected in Frederick II's letters to his special envoy to George II at Hanover, Truchsess. The new King of Prussia was not attracted by vague and general protestations of friendship; see, especially, Frederick II to Truchsess, Oct. 13, 1740 (*Politische Correspondenz Friedrich's des Grossen*, I, p. 61).

[24] Admiral Sir H. W. Richmond: *The Navy in the War of 1739-48* (Cambridge [England], 1920, three vols.), I, pp. 101-138; Fortescue: *History of the British Army*, II, pp. 60-79. Cf. Smollett: *An Account of the Expedition against Carthagena*, and *Roderick Random*, caps. xxxi-xxxiv. See also Sir H. W. Richmond's remarks upon Admiral Vernon and General Wentworth in *History*, XX (1935-1936), pp. 47-48.

political power to the extent of being a danger to France. In eastern Europe the malevolence of Russia was held in check by France's protégés, Sweden and the Porte. The policy of holding Europe in diplomatic equilibrium by promoting measures which tended to keep Germany and Italy in a state of political disunion, on the one hand, while maintaining close relations with client powers in eastern Europe, on the other, was thoroughly in accordance with traditional, one might almost say, with classic, French policy. But rarely has it been applied to such purpose or with such good fortune as it was by the Cardinal in the year 1740. As a result, Europe was diplomatically immobilized and Great Britain was isolated: consequently, French policy was enabled to co-ordinate imperial and colonial considerations with her Continental diplomatic programme. The Cardinal was on the eve of waging a maritime war with the British under extremely propitious circumstances. For the latter, accordingly, the sudden death of Charles VI, on October 20, 1740, was a godsend: for Fleury it meant the collapse of his plans for maintaining the isolation of Great Britain.

CHAPTER XII

THE LAST YEARS OF THE ADMINISTRATION OF CARDINAL
FLEURY. CONCLUSION

THE death of the Emperor necessitated the suspension of Fleury's plans for undertaking a maritime war with the British. The squadrons, which had sailed from Brest and Toulon in August, were recalled, and the attention of French statesmen was diverted from the conflict in the Caribbean to a consideration of the posture of affairs in Germany. The policy which Fleury adopted in this crisis was one which, characteristically, required only the ordinary resources of diplomacy. To secure the election as Emperor of Charles Albert of Bavaria while at the same time respecting the succession of Maria Theresa to the undivided dominions of her father was a policy which at the same time offered positive advantages and permitted France to cut a becoming figure in the disposition of German affairs while not endangering the tranquillity of Europe.

The consummation of this pacific policy, however, presupposed that other powers would manifest an equal reliance on the efficacy of negotiation. Recourse to arms on the part of any power in Germany would break the spell which Fleury's diplomacy had cast, and would probably precipitate a general conflict in central Europe. In such a situation it would be argued with overwhelming effect, just as Belle-Isle did, that France ought to substitute arms for diplomacy, under pain of being excluded from the settlement of affairs.

Accordingly, the policy which Fleury adopted in this crisis was an extremely safe and reasonable one. He discouraged the wild schemes of the court of Spain for dividing the Hapsburg inheritance, and evaded pouring out further subsidies to the Elector of Bavaria, the pretext in each case being the straitened circumstances of France because of the floods and poor harvest of that year.[1] But, on the other hand, he freely recognized the succession of Maria Theresa and declared that France, as a result of her treaty obligations, would respect the Pragmatic Sanction.[2] This was the policy which was advised by the two Frenchmen who, of all their compatriots, probably had most knowledge of German affairs, and it was favoured by the apparent collapse of the Bavarian pretensions to the Hapsburg inheritance.[3]

[1] Baudrillart: *Philippe V et la cour de France*, V, pp. 2-7. For Fleury's reply, dated Nov. 24, 1740, to the schemes of Philip V, see Sautai: *Les préliminaires de la guerre de la Succession d'Autriche*, pp. 487-491; Charles Albert's letter to Louis XV, Oct. 29, 1740 (*ibid.*, pp. 117-118); Fleury's letter in reply, Dec. 17, 1740 (*ibid.*, pp. 491-496). The bad harvests of 1740 are mentioned in a letter from Salley, secretary of Maurepas, to Caylus, Fontainebleau, Oct. 31, 1740 (*Report on the Manuscripts of Lady Du Cane*, [*Historical Manuscripts Commission*], [London, 1905], p. 277).

[2] Fleury to Liechtenstein, Austrian ambassador to Louis XV, Fontainebleau, Nov. 1, 1740 (Alfred Arneth: *Maria Theresia's erste Regierungsjahre* [Vienna, 1863-1865, three vols.], I, p. 371.) Chambrier reported to Frederick II on Nov. 25, 1740, that France intended to respect the Pragmatic Sanction (Sautai: *Les préliminaires de la guerre de la Succession d'Autriche*, pp. 124-125). Louis XV said to Liechtenstein on Nov. 10, 1740: "Vous lui [Maria Theresa] manderez que je ne manquerai en rien à mes engagements" (Luynes: *Mémoires*, III, p. 269). See also Fleury's letter to the Grand Duke of Tuscany [Francis, the husband of Maria Theresa], Nov. 13, 1740 (Sautai: *op. cit.*, p. 133).

[3] Blondel, French representative at the court of the Elector Palatine, drew up two memorials for Fleury, the first dated in mid-November 1740, and analyzed by Sautai: *Les préliminaires de la guerre de la Succession d'Autriche*, pp. 125-126; the second dated Dec. 8, 1740, a part of which was published by Sautai: *op. cit.*, pp. 478-480. Advice similar to that of Blondel was given by Chavigny, then French ambassador to Portugal, in a memorial sent to Fleury in January 1741 (Sautai: *op. cit.*, pp. 481-486). As to the Bavarian pretensions, Charles Albert claimed the Austrian dominions by virtue of the will of Ferdinand I. On December 4, 1740, the Bavarian copy was compared with the original and discovered to be a forgery. Fleury wrote to Philip V on Nov. 24, 1740: "If the pretensions of the Elector of Bavaria had had any foundation, we would have supported them, and one would have been able to find in the dismemberment of the Emperor's succession some opening for taking advantage of it in favour of the Most Serene Infant, but Your Majesties will have learned what has taken place at Vienna on that point, and that it is clear, by the will of Ferdinand I, that the House of Bavaria has no claim to the Austrian Succession" (Sautai: *Les préliminaires de la guerre de la Succession d'Autriche*, p. 487). Fleury's attitude, as revealed in this letter, indicates the consistency of the French contention that their guarantee of the Pragmatic Sanction could not be construed to nullify the prior rights of third parties; cf. Broglie: "Le cardinal de Fleury et la *Pragmatique Sanction*." *Revue historique*, XX (Sept.-Dec., 1882), pp. 257-281. However, by subsequently seeking to dismember the succession of Charles VI, *after* the pretended rights of Bavaria had been examined and pronounced false, France did violate the guarantee which she had made in the third Treaty of Vienna in 1738. This point, too, is discussed by the Duke of Broglie

Although Fleury made no difficulty, at first, about recognizing the succession of Maria Theresa to the dominions of Charles VI, from the very beginning he was opposed to the election of her husband as Emperor. This attitude was entirely compatible with France's treaty obligations: in guaranteeing the Pragmatic Sanction, Fleury had undertaken no agreement with reference to the choice of a King of the Romans or a future Emperor. For a short period following the death of Charles VI, Fleury was able to maintain the distinction between the two issues of Maria Theresa's succession and the election of an Emperor. It was because of the influence of Belle-Isle that they were disastrously linked together.

From the moment that the death of Charles VI was known, Fleury made apparent his intention of assisting Charles Albert of Bavaria in his candidacy for election to the dignity of Emperor.[4] At first view, it seems strange that the Cardinal should have considered the matter of great enough moment to become a major objective of French policy. Was it not apparent that that dignity had become of little real importance, and that the power of an Emperor depended, not upon the dignity of his office, but upon the strength he derived from the possession of hereditary lands? On the contrary, Fleury had cogent reasons for favouring the election of the Bavarian Elector. In the first place, if the influence of France carried him to that dignity, this fact would constitute a satisfaction of the French obligations to Bavaria which had been contracted by the treaties of 1714, 1727, 1733 and 1738. In the second place, the French were afraid that if the husband of Maria Theresa became Emperor he would be tempted to utilize his position in order to regain his former duchy of Lorraine. Considering the fact that Francis had not relinquished his patrimony willingly, that he was known to be hostile to France and, finally, that the Diet of the Empire had never

in his *Frédéric II et Marie-Thérèse, 1740-1742* (Paris, 1883, two vols.), I, pp. 367-401. See also documents published by Sautai: *Les préliminaires de la guerre de la Succession d'Autriche*, pp. 453-464.

[4] Cf. Fleury's letter to Philip V, Nov. 24, 1740 (Sautai: *Les préliminaires de la guerre de la Succession d'Autriche*, p. 487); Fleury's letter to Charles Albert of Bavaria, Dec. 17, 1740 (*ibid.*, p. 492).

ratified the third Treaty of Vienna, by virtue of which France enjoyed the reversion of Lorraine, it is evident that this apprehension was not manufactured out of utterly ridiculous and ungrounded fears.[5] Moreover, the policy of favouring the election of Charles Albert had the advantage of requiring no immediate initiative on the part of France. Fleury could play a waiting game, as it is known he desired to do.[6] The sole thing which had to be done out of hand was the appointment of a French ambassador-at-large whose function would be to influence the choice of the other Electors in favour of the Elector of Bavaria, and this was taken care of on December 12, 1740, by the appointment of the Count of Belle-Isle, a choice which was dictated by the consummate knowledge which the Count seemed to possess of German affairs, joined to the fact that his connections with the Bavarian court and his rank and prominence in France assured his being able to co-operate with the Elector of Bavaria as well as to impress the other German potentates.[7]

In most respects, this appointment was an admirable one; yet it was the beginning of all of Fleury's subsequent troubles. For the first time, he had admitted into affairs a minister whom he dared not dismiss and whose views he could not repudiate. Step by step, he was led far from the position which he had originally held, until, less than a year later, France had practically repudiated the Pragmatic Sanction and a large French army was campaigning in Bohemia.

From the beginning of his administration until December 1740,

[5] This point was emphasized in Blondel's memorial, which was presented to Fleury in November 1740 (Sautai: *Les préliminaires de la guerre de la Succession d'Autriche*, p. 126). Frederick II surmised the same thing; see his letter to Camas and Chambrier, Berlin, Oct. 29, 1740 (*Politische Correspondenz Friedrich's des Grossen*, I, pp. 78-79). This consideration has also been given its due importance by Droysen: *Geschichte der preussischen Politik*, V, vol. i, p. 276; also, see Sir Richard Lodge: *Great Britain and Prussia in the Eighteenth Century*, p. 31.

[6] Cf. Fleury's letter to Philip V, Nov. 24, 1740 (Sautai: *Les préliminaires de la guerre de la Succession d'Autriche*, p. 488).

[7] For a very good description of Belle-Isle and of his previous career, see Broglie: *Frédéric II et Marie-Thérèse*, I, pp. 167-174; also, Sautai: *Les préliminaires de la guerre de la Succession d'Autriche*, pp. 133-152. Blondel claimed that he had so primed the Count with knowledge of German affairs that he was able to impress the Cardinal very much (*ibid.*, pp. 496-497). On Belle-Isle's Bavarian connections, see *ibid.*, pp. 157-160.

Fleury had enjoyed and had jealously guarded the sole administration of affairs. That administration had been almost constantly accompanied by success in ever-increasing degree. By 1740 a great diplomatic system had been built up through which France drew into her orbit the courts of Vienna and Berlin, of Stockholm and Copenhagen; put the Turks in her debt; made harmless the ill will of Russia; and isolated Great Britain. So successful had been French policy that Fleury intended waging a maritime war with Great Britain, when the unexpected death of the Emperor necessitated his waiting to see what would be the resultant events. His own policy, though temporarily confounded by this accident, was clearly defined and logical. It was to respect the Pragmatic Sanction and to secure the election of the Elector of Bavaria as the successor of Charles VI. Quite impeccably, he appointed as ambassador at Frankfort the Frenchman who was probably best qualified to fulfill his mission with success; the appointment once made, Belle-Isle, for his part, did nothing which would justify his dismissal, and Fleury was carried along a course which he did not care to pursue, simply because his favourite methods of seeking for expedients and adaptations were overwhelmed by the positive and enthusiastic schemes of a man who knew that he spoke with the authority of public approval. The disastrous era of half-measures had arrived. Perhaps Fleury might nevertheless have triumphed had not the sudden invasion of Silesia by Frederick II in December 1740, played directly into the hands of the war party in France. Henceforth it became practically certain that the question of the Austrian succession would be the cause of a general war.

The intentions of the King of Prussia, from his accession in May 1740 until his invasion of Silesia in December of that year, were a mystery to the rest of Europe. In the summer he had augmented his army and had thereby raised wide-spread apprehensions that he intended to settle the question of the Prussian claims to Berg and Ravenstein by wresting them forcibly from the Elector Palatine.[8] Following the death of Charles VI, Fred-

---

[8] Vaucher: *Robert Walpole et la politique de Fleury*, pp. 348-351; Sautai: *Les préliminaires de la guerre de la Succession d'Autriche*, pp. 174-176. For Frederick

erick II concentrated his troops upon the frontiers of Silesia, but whether for an attack or merely for a collusory occupation, no one knew. Fleury wrote to the Elector of Bavaria on December 17, 1740:

The character of the king of Prussia appears to me so extraordinary and so indecipherable that I can not divine either what he wishes to do or what he thinks. He marches into Silesia and one can no longer doubt it. Whether he has in view seizing it or whether he does it in concert with the Archduchess is an impenetrable enigma for us and I can only inform you of my conjectures on that point.[9]

On the eve of the invasion of Silesia, Frederick II suggested to the French ambassador the desirability of concluding an alliance. The project, which was accordingly sent to him by way of reply in January 1741, was an indication that the French considered a Prussian alliance of value; but, at the same time, its terms betrayed the Cardinal's desire to confine his action to diplomatic and defensive measures.[10] Had the King of Prussia been willing to accept France as a quiescent ally instead of an active one, the Cardinal might have been able to resist the enthusiasms of Belle-Isle. But, once having enticed the French into *pourparlers* for an alliance, Frederick II insisted on active French military assistance as a *sine qua non*.[11] The French court, by instructions to Valory dated February 22, 1741, consented to these demands, but when they arrived, Frederick II had not yet completed his shopping for alliances on the bargain counters of Europe, and the French alliance was left in suspense until June.[12]

Meanwhile, Belle-Isle had launched his attack on the Cardinal

II's quarrel with the Bishop of Liége over the barony of Herstal and the summary way in which he settled it, see *Preussische Staatsschriften aus der Regierungszeit König Friedrichs II*. (Edited by Reinhold Koser; Berlin, 1877-1892, three vols.), I, pp. 5-39.

[9] Sautai: *Les préliminaires de la guerre de la Succession d'Autriche*, p. 493.

[10] Valory to Amelot, Dec. 13, 1740 (Broglie: *Frédéric II et Marie Thérèse*, I, pp. 136-139); for the French project of January 1741, see *ibid.*, I, pp. 188-189.

[11] Broglie: *Frédéric II et Marie Thérèse*, I, pp. 199-204. Valory to Amelot, Jan. 31, 1741 (Sautai: *Les préliminaires de la guerre de la Succession d'Autriche*, pp. 205-206).

[12] Amelot to Valory, Feb. 22, 1741 (Sautai: *Les préliminaires de la guerre de la Succession d'Autriche*, pp. 210-212).

for the purpose of securing the military intervention of France in German affairs. Two memorials which he presented in January 1741 outlined an extensive military programme which he insisted must be set in motion by May 1, and for which preparations should be made from that moment.[13] His fundamental assumption was that the Elector of Bavaria was a prince "with no resources of his own"; consequently, that it was absurd to think that subsidies and diplomatic support alone would be sufficient to secure his election. This argument was directly opposed to the intentions of Fleury, who counted upon being able to secure the election of Charles Albert merely by the manipulation of the Electors. Fleury's attitude in January 1741 was rather hostilely described by Belle-Isle:

He did not know what part to take, and saw no other means of extricating himself from the affair than to remain quiet while waiting for what resources time and events might furnish him. . . . [14]

Belle-Isle made the mistake of supposing that the Cardinal's policy of playing a waiting game was tantamount to having no policy at all. It was an erroneous assumption which had frequently been made throughout the course of Fleury's administration, and one which he had traded upon. But his method of patient and intelligent obstruction ended in disaster when the moment came, as happened at that time, when he lost control over his subordinates. Belle-Isle had written that "it would be much better to do nothing at all than to do it late and by half" and that

Kingdoms are not conquered and an empire is not obtained without fighting battles, and to think and to act on other principles is to wish to risk all and even to lose all.[15]

Yet Fleury, as though he tacitly approved such fiery principles, permitted Belle-Isle to start out on his German mission.[16]

[13] These are published *in extenso* by Sautai: *Les préliminaires de la guerre de la Succession d'Autriche*, pp. 501-521.

[14] Sautai: *Les préliminaires de la guerre de la Succession d'Autriche*, pp. 196-197.

[15] Sautai: *Les préliminaires de la guerre de la Succession d'Autriche*, pp. 516, 518.

[16] In 1740 and 1741, Fleury lost his control over the King, which explains his inability to restrain Belle-Isle (É. Bourgeois: *Manuel historique de politique étran-*

Belle-Isle, in the course of his travels in Germany, visited the courts of the Electors of Cologne, Treves, Mainz and Saxony, and early in May conferred with Frederick II in Silesia. The victor of Mollwitz, covered with flour and glory, had emerged from the mill in which he had taken refuge the night of the battle, to find that all Europe was rushing to the aid of the conqueror. Belle-Isle's own negotiations with him were inconclusive, but after his departure the treaty of June 5, 1741 was signed, which committed France to military intervention in Germany, besides guaranteeing to the King of Prussia Lower Silesia, including Breslau. Frederick II, in return, gave up his claims to the succession in Berg and Ravenstein and agreed to cast his Electoral vote for Charles Albert of Bavaria.[17] In the meantime, Belle-Isle was at the court of the Elector of Bavaria, where he supervised the conclusion of a subsidy treaty between Bavaria and Spain, and employed his spare time in finding the answers to thirty-one questions on the condition of Bavaria which the court of France, inspired by the desire to temporize, had asked on March 15, 1741.[18]

gère, I, p. 490). Various entries made by D'Argenson, beginning in 1738, record his knowledge that the King was maintaining a secret and indirect correspondence with Chauvelin, who was in exile (D'Argenson: *Journal et mémoires*, I, p. 300; II, pp. 2-9, 30, 64, 173, 248, 301, 354, 388; III, pp. 264-266, 294-295).

[17] For Belle-Isle's negotiations in Germany, see Broglie: *Frédéric II et Marie Thérèse*, I, pp. 273-332; the treaty of June 5, 1741 (*ibid.*, I, pp. 407-413). France was also to persuade the Swedes to declare war on Russia. Droysen pointed out (*Geschichte der preussischen Politik*, V, vol. i, pp. 277-278) that in this treaty Frederick II's obligations were in the future, while those of France were immediate. Frederick's determination to close with France followed the failure of Lord Hyndford's attempted mediation between Prussia and Austria (Droysen: *op. cit.*, V, vol. i, pp. 262-263, 267, 272-273 and note; Leopold von Ranke: *Zwölf Bücher preussischer Geschichte*, vol. II, book viii, pp. 427-429). The British policy of reconciling Prussia and Austria and uniting those powers against France may be followed in the letters of Horatio Walpole to Trevor, Dec. 19, O. S., 1740; March 17, March 20, March 31, April 24, May 12, June 10, and June 24, (all Old Style) 1741 (Trevor Papers, *Hist. MSS. Comm.*, *Report* XIV, App. Part IX, pp. 62-63, 68-74).

[18] For the Treaty of Nymphenburg, May 28, 1741, see Aretin: *Chronologisches Verzeichniss der bayerischen Staats-Verträge*, pp. 390-396; Cantillo: *Tratados*, pp. 346-349; Baudrillart: *Philippe V et la cour de France*, V, p. 38. It was long supposed that France was a signatory to this or a similar treaty signed at Nymphenburg; this point was discussed by D. J. Hill: *A History of Diplomacy in the International Development of Europe* (New York, 1905-1914, three vols.), III, p. 459 note. For the thirty-one questions and answers, see Sautai: *Les préliminaires de la guerre de la Succession d'Autriche*, pp. 290-292, 560-605.

As late as the middle of July, hardly a step had been taken in preparation for the campaign which Belle-Isle had urged should be begun not later than the first of May. There is no doubt that this was because of the obstructive tactics of the Cardinal, who persisted in his course even though Frederick II was urging France to begin the campaign, in letters which made no attempt to conceal his ill humour.[19] Belle-Isle, for his part, was convinced that it would require more than ill-tempered letters from the King of Prussia to triumph over the Cardinal's immobility. For Fleury wrote to the Marshal on June 17, 1741:

It is unfortunate that he [the Elector of Bavaria] is not more rich nor more powerful, and when I reflect that we have almost no other allies than princes in very embarrassed circumstances, I do not cease to be dismayed by the war which we are going to undertake. I confess that the king of Prussia, who is not in this situation, disquiets me more than any other. He has no order in his disposition: he listens to no counsel and takes his resolutions thoughtlessly, without having previously prepared measures suitable for success. Good faith and sincerity are not his favourite virtues and he is false in everything, even in his caresses. I even doubt whether he is sure in his alliances, because he has for guiding principle only his own interest. He will wish to govern and to have his own way without any concert with us, and he is detested throughout Europe.[20]

The fact was that Fleury could not conquer his dislike of a policy which, as the Duke of Broglie has remarked, "had the singular fortune of uniting every possible error with every possible risk, and imprudence with disloyalty."[21] Yet he either did not have the courage or the authority to assert his own policy; the result was that he spent his days in untimely and unedifying vacillation. He permitted Belle-Isle and the war party to upset his schemes for securing the election of Charles Albert through negotiation, but he, in turn, upset and delayed theirs by his temporizing. At the moment when the Cardinal recommended the appoint-

---

[19] *Politische Correspondenz Friedrich's des Grossen*, I, pp. 258, 263-265, 267, 270-271, 276-277. D'Argenson also noted during this time the obstructive tactics of the Cardinal, whom he called "un vieux singe"; Orry, he thought, was provoking bankruptcies in order to show the impossibility of waging war (D'Argenson: *Journal et mémoires*, III, pp. 338, 341, 346-347, 352-353).

[20] Sautai: *Les préliminaires de la guerre de la Succession d'Autriche*, p. 271.

[21] Broglie: *Frédéric II et Marie-Thérèse*, I, p. 150.

ment of Belle-Isle, his troubles had begun. On January 10, 1741, he said to Wasner, the Austrian *chargé d'affaires:*

If you knew how harassed I am and what my situation is, you would pity me; I am, as the Scripture says, *in medio pravae et perversae nationis.*[22]

In the early months of 1741, Fleury was able to deceive Maria Theresa into thinking that France did not intend to declare war, for the simple reason that he was deceiving himself on the very same point. Although a note of equivocation crept into his letters to the Queen of Hungary, and although Thompson, the British *chargé d'affaires*, reported in April that the Cardinal had declared that he did not consider France bound by the Pragmatic Sanction, nevertheless Fleury assured Wasner on May 31 that "he could swear that such [a strengthening of the French army] was most certainly done in no way with the view of undertaking a war."[23] Because he would not violate the Pragmatic Sanction, Fleury refused to conclude a treaty with the King of Sardinia, and this attitude prevented any action at all in Italy in 1741, a fact which greatly incensed the Spaniards.[24] Not only is it clear that the Cardinal was profoundly dubious about the wisdom of Belle-Isle's forward policy in Germany, but also, from what is known of Fleury's plans for carrying on a maritime war in 1741, it must have occurred to him that Belle-Isle's expensive and adventuresome schemes were conceived with an absolute disregard of France's maritime interests, as a perusal of the memorials

[22] Arneth: *Maria Theresia's erste Regierungsjahre*, I, p. 389.

[23] For Fleury's letters to Maria Theresa, see Broglie: *Frédéric II et Marie-Thérèse*, I, pp. 209-211. For Thompson's letter to Newcastle, April 14, 1741, see Richmond: *The Navy in the War of 1739-48*, I, p. 143. For Wasner's despatch to Maria Theresa, May 31, 1741, see Arneth: *Maria Theresia's erste Regierungsjahre*, I, p. 390.

[24] The French insisted that the Spaniards must conclude an alliance with Sardinia (Baudrillart: *Philippe V et la cour de France*, V, pp. 18-19); Charles Emmanuel, for his part, insisted that France should also be a member of that alliance (*ibid.*, V, pp. 23, 25, 32, 35, 53); the French finally consented to this, on condition of receiving Savoy, but this was refused (*ibid.*, V, pp. 53-56). The French did promise the Spaniards that the Toulon fleet would protect the Spanish transports (Amelot to Vauréal, Sept. 21 and Oct. 9, 1741 [*ibid.*, V, p. 65]). For these negotiations, see also Sautai: *Les préliminaires de la guerre de la Succession d'Autriche*, pp. 388-404.

which Belle-Isle composed in January 1741, abundantly shows.[25]
The indecision which resulted from this complex of conflicting
considerations did not escape the public notice, and Chambrier
reported to Frederick II on May 22, 1741:

It has been the entry of Your Majesty into Silesia which has made the
Cardinal quit the pacific policy which he had designed. He hoped to arrange
everything by negotiation and to do what he pleased with the court of
Vienna by engaging it to throw itself into the arms of France, but, although
he is obliged by the conduct of Your Majesty to change his system at
present, his great repugnance for war and his excessive economy will always
induce him to do tardily and feebly what shall be absolutely necessary for
him to do at all.[26]

It became apparent to Belle-Isle that the Cardinal did not
contemplate beginning the war in 1741; the lateness of the season
was the point argued by Amelot in a letter dated June 21.[27]
But Belle-Isle's idea was that the war in Germany should be
fought at once and in great force, which was certainly the best
advice provided that a war was to be fought at all. Accordingly,
he received permission to return to Versailles in order to confer
with the ministers there. From July 10 until his return to Frankfort on July 25, he had daily consultations with the ministers, in
which Fleury did not directly participate "in order to avoid the
bother and dullness of details, in consideration of the weakness
of his head," a confession of physical debility probably intended
to disguise the loss of his control over events.[28] D'Argenson remarked that Belle-Isle's arrival was a triumph, and that he intimidated the ministers and governed everything.[29] At all events,

[25] Cf. Sautai: *Les préliminaires de la guerre de la Succession d'Autriche*, pp.
501-521. Dr. Wm. Douglass remarked on this: "In this present War, the *French*
Court seem to neglect their Colonies, Trade and Navigation, the principal Care
of their late good and great Minister Cardinal *de Fleury;* and do run into their
former Romantick Humour of Land-Conquests" (Douglass: *A Summary . . . of
the British Settlements in North America*, I, p. 2).

[26] Sautai: *Les préliminaires de la guerre de la Succession d'Autriche*, pp. 255-256.

[27] Sautai: *Les préliminaires de la guerre de la Succession d'Autriche*, pp. 329-330.

[28] The quotation is from the entry of July 11 in Belle-Isle's journal (Sautai:
Les préliminaires de la guerre de la Succession d'Autriche, pp. 605-606).

[29] D'Argenson: *Journal et mémoires*, III, pp. 334-336, 350-351. A secretary of
Maurepas, Toussaint Remond, wrote to Caylus on July 29, 1741: "M. le Maréchal
de Belleisle règne ici, et travaille seul avec les ministres, soit ensemble, soit
séparément" (*Report on the Manuscripts of Lady Du Cane* [*Historical Manuscripts*

the decision was made to enter immediately upon the campaign, which, in conjunction with the fact that at the same time the Swedes declared war on Russia, very much mollified Frederick the Great.[30] In August a French corps, which figured as the auxiliaries of the Elector of Bavaria, entered Germany, while another French army, under the command of Maillebois, was posted on the Moselle.[31]

The months of August and September 1741 threatened the direst disaster for the Austrians. By the first of September, Belle-Isle at Frankfort had secured the disposition of the votes of the Electors of Cologne, Treves and Mainz.[32] On September 19, through the good offices of Belle-Isle, the Elector of Saxony forsook the cause of Maria Theresa and allied himself with the Elector of Bavaria.[33] In September, George II and Harrington, both of whom were in a panic for the safety of Hanover, which was threatened by the army which Maillebois commanded, authorized a convention which guaranteed the neutrality of the Electorate, in return for which George II agreed to abstain from voting in the election for an Emperor.[34] This decision, which was taken independently of the Ministry in London, quite paralyzed the British plans for lending assistance to the Queen of Hungary, and, coming as it did on top of the news of the dis-

Commission], p. 294). On July 21, 1741, Belle-Isle wrote to Valory, French ambassador to Frederick II, that the business was settled: "The difficulty has been to persuade His Eminence" (Sautai: *Les préliminaires de la guerre de la Succession d'Autriche*, p. 352). On the same day Belle-Isle wrote to his brother: "If I had not come here, nothing at all would have been done" (*ibid.*, p. 355).

[30] See Frederick's letters to Cardinal Fleury, to Valory and to Belle-Isle, all under date of July 30, 1741 (*Politische Correspondenz Friedrich's des Grossen*, I, pp. 289-290). The French had offered subsidies of two million livres for 1741 and an equal sum for 1742 if the Swedes would declare war on Russia (Amelot to Saint-Séverin, March 16 and July 16, 1741 [Sautai: *Les préliminaires de la guerre de la Succession d'Autriche*, pp. 383-386]).

[31] Broglie: *Frédéric II et Marie-Thérèse*, II, pp. 27-32.

[32] Maurice Sautai: *Les débuts de la guerre de la Succession d'Autriche* (Paris, 1909), pp. 276-280.

[33] For the negotiations leading up to this treaty, see Sautai: *Les débuts de la guerre de la Succession d'Autriche*, pp. 307-327; the treaty is printed by Aretin: *Chronologisches Verzeichniss der bayerischen Staats-Verträge*, pp. 396-401. This treaty was supplemented by a Spanish-Saxon treaty, signed Sept. 20, 1741 (Cantillo: *Tratados*, pp. 359-360).

[34] Vaucher: *Robert Walpole et la politique de Fleury*, pp. 394-406; Sautai: *Les débuts de la guerre de la Succession d'Autriche*, pp. 285-306.

astrous failures at Carthagena and Santiago, utterly demoralized the British government at the same time that it antagonized the Dutch.[35] As a consequence of being threatened by so many enemies and of having been forsaken by so many allies, Maria Theresa attempted to detach France from the coalition arrayed against her by offering Luxemburg to France and either portions of the Milanese to Sardinia or portions of the Netherlands to Spain.[36] The refusal of Fleury, who pleaded the sacredness of his engagements with his allies, gave her no recourse but to buy off the arch-enemy, the King of Prussia. While the Franco-Bavarian army, instead of striking directly at Vienna as Frederick II had advised, was pursuing its leisurely way towards Prague, Maria Theresa offered to recognize, until a definitive treaty could be made, the Prussian possession of all of Lower Silesia, including Neisse, which was to surrender after a mock siege lasting fifteen days. On these terms, Frederick II was really to withdraw from the war, although ostensibly he was to remain an active combatant. This offer, which was presented by Lord Hyndford, was accepted on October 9, 1741. The Convention of Klein-Schnellendorf, although it was only an informal agreement with no binding legal validity, was a boon to the Austrians, for it relieved the pressure in Silesia and permitted Marshal Neipperg to withdraw his troops for the protection of Prague.[37]

[35] Vaucher: *Robert Walpole et la politique de Fleury*, pp. 406-413. For British endeavours to soothe the Dutch, see Horatio Walpole's letters to Trevor, Sept. 12, 16 and 19, O. S., 1741 (Coxe: *Memoirs of Horatio, Lord Walpole*, II, pp. 28-43). In a letter dated Oct. 6, O. S., 1741, Horatio Walpole expressed to Trevor the dissatisfaction of the British ministers at London concerning Harrington's action at Hanover (Trevor Papers, *Hist. MSS. Comm., Report* XIV, App. Part IX, pp. 78-79). Cf. P. Geyl: "Holland and England during the War of the Austrian Succession." *History*, X (1925-1926), pp. 47-48.

[36] Broglie: *Frédéric II et Marie-Thérèse*, II, pp. 74-79.

[37] The Convention is printed in *Politische Correspondenz Friedrich's des Grossen*, I, pp. 371-372. See, also, Droysen: *Geschichte der preussischen Politik*, V, vol. i, pp. 348-350; Ranke: *Zwölf Bücher preussischer Geschichte*, vol. II, book viii, pp. 470-472. Frederick II's apology for treating his allies so cavalierly was that "It was requisite therefore to manoeuvre adroitly; and especially not to be outwitted by an old politician, who in the last war had sported with more than one crowned head" ("History of my own Times." *Posthumous Works*, I, part i, p. 160). In a circular rescript sent to Prussian diplomats abroad, Nov. 4, 1741, Frederick II categorically denied that he had made his peace with Vienna (*Preussische Staatsschriften*, I, pp. 316-317). The march on Prague, instead of Vienna, was a bad

The Convention of Klein-Schnellendorf gave Maria Theresa some respite, while the enthusiasm with which she had been greeted by the Hungarians on the occasion of her coronation raised her prestige and afforded her the surety of valuable military assistance.[38] The Hungarian levies could not immediately be put into the field, however, and in the meantime Prague was taken by the French in a surprise attack on November 25, 1741. The capture of Prague was the decisive event which determined the outcome of the election of an Emperor. On January 24, 1742, Charles Albert of Bavaria received the unanimous vote of the ballots cast in the Electoral College, and his coronation took place at Frankfort on February 21, 1742.

These events were the high water mark of French fortune. Henceforth, both diplomatic and military affairs began to set against them. In the north of Europe, the Swedes were fighting the Russians listlessly, while in Russia itself the new Czarina, Elizabeth, was organizing her resources energetically in order to repel the invaders and, after having utilized the assistance of the French ambassador in the *coup d'état* of December 6, 1741, was adopting a policy not in consonance with the desires of France.[39] On February 1, 1742, the King of Sardinia concluded a "provisional treaty" with Austria; although this document gave him

mistake, yet Charles Albert of Bavaria and Belle-Isle had so planned it from the beginning of the campaign (Sautai: *Les préliminaires de la guerre de la Succession d'Autriche*, pp. 414-416, 609-613; Sautai: *Les débuts de la guerre de la Succession d'Autriche*, pp. 199-203; Broglie: *Frédéric II et Marie-Thérèse*, II, pp. 351-355).

[38] Coxe: *History of the House of Austria*, IV, pp. 437-443.

[39] On October 28, 1740 Czarina Anna died, leaving her favourite, Biren, as Regent for the infant Czar Ivan VI. On Nov. 18, 1740 a *coup d'état* took the Regency from Biren and gave it to Ivan's mother, niece of the late Czarina. The final *coup d'état* of December 6, 1741, gave the power to Elizabeth, daughter of Peter the Great and Catherine I. See *Recueil des instructions. . . . Russie*, I, pp. 363-373. The French ambassador, La Chétardie, took a prominent part in favouring the seizure of power by Elizabeth; the real motive was to weaken that country in her contest with Sweden. Likewise, the French urged the Turks to declare war on Russia in order to relieve pressure on the Swedes (Sir Richard Lodge: "The Treaty of Abo and the Swedish Succession." *English Historical Review*, XLIII [1928], p. 541). This attitude of the French toward Russia was shortly discovered; La Chétardie left Russia, almost in disgrace, on Sept. 1, 1742. An Anglo-Russian defensive alliance was concluded on Dec. 22, 1742; see Martens: *Recueil des traités et conventions conclus par la Russie*, IX, pp. 91 sqq.; Sir Richard Lodge: "The First Anglo-Russian Treaty, 1739-42." *English Historical Review*, XLIII (1928), pp. 354-375.

the right to reverse his alliances on a month's notice, for the year 1742 it rendered Austrian Italy safe from the attacks of the Spaniards.[40] The French were unable to obtain a guarantee of Dutch neutrality in return for an undertaking to respect the territorial integrity of the Austrian Netherlands, a device which had been of such great assistance to the French during the War of the Polish Succession.[41] In Great Britain, the fall of Walpole on February 13, 1742, and the resultant influence of Lord Carteret in foreign affairs paved the way for the adoption of more aggressive measures and for British intervention on the Continent. For this purpose, Lord Stair, who was to command the "Pragmatic Army," went to The Hague to arouse the Dutch. This was no easy matter, however, and since, as usual, the British were inclined to make their active intervention in Continental broils dependent upon the co-operation of the United Provinces, nothing was done in 1742 save for the forming of a military camp in Flanders.[42] Nevertheless, the attitude of the British was a source of great anxiety to the French, who resigned themselves to suffering indignities if only they could postpone a British declaration of war. Fleury wrote to the French ambassador to Spain, on July 5, 1742:

The insults which she [England] has already inflicted on us, and which she continues to do, are indeed humiliating, but it is necessary to endure them when one can not avenge oneself.[43]

[40] For an excellent account of the negotiations affecting Sardinia in 1741-1742, see Sir Richard Lodge: "The Treaty of Worms." *English Historical Review*, XLIV (1929), pp. 225-239; cf. Baudrillart: *Philippe V et la cour de France*, V, pp. 78-79. Montemar, commander of the Spanish expeditionary force in Italy, was able to do little in 1742, especially as the British fleet forced Don Carlos, King of the Two Sicilies, to declare, on August 18, 1742, his neutrality for the course of the war, under penalty of the immediate bombardment of Naples (*ibid.*, V, p. 106). Don Philip and his Spanish army were able only to occupy Savoy (*ibid.*, V, pp. 112-120).

[41] For French efforts to secure Dutch neutrality, see *supra*, p. 134; Adolf Beer: "Holland und der österreichische Erbfolge-Krieg." *Archiv für österreichische Geschichte*, XLVI (1871), pp. 308-311, 315-316; *Preussische Staatsschriften*, I, pp. 322-323; *Lettres et négociations de Monsieur van Hoey*, pp. 134-139.

[42] Fortescue: *History of the British Army*, II, pp. 83-87.

[43] Baudrillart: *Philippe V et la cour de France*, V, p. 100. Amelot wrote to Vauréal, May 23, 1742, that the British must not be provoked, so that the Dutch could also be kept neutral (*ibid.*, V, p. 93). In June 1742, the British burned six Spanish galleys in the French port of Saint-Tropez, but the French did not dare to express their resentment (*ibid.*, V, p. 98).

Aside from engaging in some half-hearted negotiations with the Jacobites, Fleury's policy with reference to the British remained a purely passive one.[44]

On January 28, 1742, Amelot wrote to Belle-Isle:

It is now necessary to work for peace and to endeavour that France, after so many difficulties, risks and expenses, should draw some advantage from them.[45]

But, at that very moment, the military successes of the Austrians made it apparent that they would have something to say on that point. On January 23, Ségur, the commander of the French forces at Linz, had been forced to surrender; thus the Danube line of communications with France was cut off, and the Austrian army under Khevenhüller was able to enter Munich at the very same time that its sovereign was being crowned Emperor at Frankfort.[46] The loss of Linz, however, did not imperil the safety of the French army in Prague, so long as the French could count on the assistance of Frederick II. But on June 11 the King of Prussia concluded the Preliminaries of Breslau, which on July 28 became the definitive Peace of Berlin, as a result of which he enjoyed the Austrian cession of all of Silesia and left his French allies completely in the lurch.[47] Words can scarcely

---

[44] Jean Colin: *Louis XV et les Jacobites; le projet de débarquement en Angleterre de 1743-1744* (Paris, 1901), pp. 6-12. These negotiations are alluded to in the Jacobite papers found in the Weston Papers, *Hist. MSS. Comm., Report* X, App. Part I, pp. 225-227.

[45] Broglie: *Frédéric II et Marie-Thérèse*, II, p. 167.

[46] Arneth: *Maria Theresia's erste Regierungsjahre*, II, pp. 10-13.

[47] The capture of Prague had encouraged Frederick II to re-enter the war. He defied Austrians and French alike to prove that he had signed a neutrality agreement; in January he captured Iglau, but in February his attack on Brünn failed. On March 22 he ordered Podewils to begin negotiating for an Austrian peace, through the medium of Lord Hyndford (*Politische Correspondenz Friedrich's des Grossen*, II, pp. 84-85). The Austrians were unwilling to accept the terms which Frederick offered in March; but, inasmuch as he offered the same terms after winning the battle of Czaslau or Chotusitz on May 17, 1742, the Austrians then accepted (Arneth: *Maria Theresia's erste Regierungsjahre*, II, pp. 51-55, 75-77). "Thus ended an alliance in which each party endeavoured to outwit the other; . . ." (Frederick II: "History of my own Times." *Posthumous Works*, I, part i, p. 230). Achilles was more clever than Nestor, according to Voltaire's view of the affair. A specious defense of his conduct was written by Frederick, but not published at that time; it is printed in *Preussische Staatsschriften*, I, pp. 335-337: "Lettre de M. le comte de — à un ami." The anti-Prussian policy of La Ché-

describe the consternation of the French or the lamentations of the Cardinal. The two Austrian armies under Lobkowitz and Prince Charles of Lorraine effected a junction and shut up the French forces in Prague; on August 13, the siege of Prague commenced, and the French army was reduced to extremities.

Under these circumstances, Fleury rather naturally endeavoured to be a peace maker; with a total lack of dignity, he wrote to the Austrian Marshal, Königsegg, on July 11, 1742, in terms which threw all the blame on Belle-Isle:

Many people know how opposed I have been to the resolutions which we have taken, and that I have been to a certain extent obliged to consent to them by the pressing reasons which have been pleaded to me, and Your Excellency is too well informed of what has taken place not to guess easily who was the one who set to work to determine the King to enter into a path which was so contrary to my tastes and my principles.[48]

This letter Maria Theresa had the malice to publish, and the distress of France and the weakness of the Cardinal were exposed to the gaze of Europe.[49] Partly because of this check, and partly because of a desire to retain his control over affairs at a time when his physical powers were failing him, Fleury introduced two of his henchmen into the Council of State in August 1742. These were Cardinal Tencin and Count d'Argenson, who served as ministers without portfolio.[50] In the meantime, the army

tardie, French ambassador at St. Petersburg, contributed to deciding Frederick to conclude the Treaty of Breslau (*Politische Correspondenz Friedrich's des Grossen*, II, p. 263; Sir Richard Lodge: "Russia, Prussia, and Great Britain, 1742-4." *English Historical Review*, XLV [1930], p. 580).

[48] Luynes: *Mémoires*, IV, p. 322. See also *ibid.*, IV, p. 209; Arneth: *Maria Theresia's erste Regierungsjahre*, II, pp. 108-109. Fleury's letters to Königsegg are also to be found in Flassan: *Histoire . . . . de la diplomatie française*, V, pp. 160-164.

[49] The letter was published in a Dutch gazette; the Austrian government asserted that it was published without its authorization. Opinion now seems to be that it was published by Austrian authority (*Preussische Staatsschriften*, I, pp. 331-332); but cf. Arneth: *Maria Theresia's erste Regierungsjahre*, II, p. 490. The publication of his letter provoked Fleury to write another to Königsegg, August 13, 1742 (Luynes: *Mémoires*, IV, pp. 336-337).

[50] D'Argenson: *Journal et mémoires*, IV, pp. 21-23; Luynes: *Mémoires*, IV, pp. 212-213. The recall of Chauvelin was also rumoured at that time (Albert, duc de Broglie: *Frédéric II et Louis XV, 1742-1744* [Paris, 1885, two vols.], I, pp. 53-57). Cardinal Bernis stated that the appointment of Tencin was made in order to prevent the return of Chauvelin (Bernis: *Mémoires . . . . du cardinal de Bernis*, I, p. 56).

which Maillebois commanded was ordered to the relief of Prague, which it was unable to effect. In December 1742, Belle-Isle evacuated Prague and marched the remnants of his army through the defiles of the Bohemian mountains, thus managing, after a very difficult retreat, to make good his escape. The French had had quite enough of German adventures, and on January 12, 1743, Amelot instructed Belle-Isle to break the news to the phantom Emperor that the French were withdrawing from him their military support.[51] In the course of the year 1743 the battle of Dettingen was fought, the French evacuated Bavaria, and the seat of war was transferred from Germany to Alsace, Italy and the Netherlands. In 1744, France and Great Britain mutually declared war; the French found compensation for the ignominy of Prague in the glory of Fontenoy and Lauffeldt, while the stipulations of an undeservedly favourable peace made atonement to the British for the checks and reverses of an indecisive war.

While Maillebois was marching to the relief of Prague and Belle-Isle was retreating painfully from the city which the French had so pridefully occupied just one short year before, Fleury's life was slowly drawing to a close. Even in September 1742, his sight and hearing were failing badly, and from November until his death on January 29, 1743, he was incapable of carrying on business. Yet he clung to power with a tenacious grasp, and what he was himself unable to do he prevented others from doing. Affairs were at a stand during those weeks, while the court intrigued furiously. On January 29 he died at last, and Louis XV announced, to the delight of his subjects, his intention to rule by himself.

It is impossible to disagree with Ranke's remark that it would have been better for Fleury's reputation had he died several years earlier.[52] Whether one adopts Ranke's view that the Cardinal sought to utilize the crisis of the Austrian succession to

---

[51] Broglie: *Frédéric II et Louis XV, 1742-1744,* I, pp. 389-393.

[52] Leopold von Ranke: *Französische Geschichte vornehmlich im sechzehnten und siebzehnten Jahrhundert* (Leipzig, 1876-1877, six vols.), IV, pp. 370-371. Bernis remarked that Fleury "vécut trop longtemps pour sa gloire" (Bernis: *Mémoires . . . . du cardinal de Bernis,* I, p. 44).

attain to universal dominion or whether one believes, on the other hand, that he accepted the struggle "*à son corps défendant,*" as Chambrier said, in either case the conclusion is valid that Fleury very much compromised his reputation by connivance at or participation in a policy which turned out disastrously. So much, at least, can be said, without attempting to appraise the Cardinal's policy by moral criteria. If there was guilt in the attack which was made on the Hapsburg dominions, it was guilt shared equally by Frederick II and Cardinal Fleury. Yet the former has found many apologists, the latter none; for Frederick II, as Fleury uneasily anticipated, made the Cardinal his dupe, and that ungrateful rôle can never be sustained with credit.

The demonstrable fact is that France in 1743 had waged for almost two years an expensive war in which she had secured neither honour nor advantage. Had Belle-Isle been permitted to exercise the sole direction of affairs, a large French army might have been ready by May 1, 1741, as he had urged, and the war might have been waged with all the profit which he anticipated. Had Fleury, on the other hand, not admitted Belle-Isle to a position of influence, he might very readily have negotiated the election of Charles Albert of Bavaria while respecting the Pragmatic Sanction, and have maintained peace with honour. Neither had his way, and the result of their uneasy compromise was a policy which has redounded to the lasting discredit of each.

The jealous care with which Fleury guarded his exclusive authority came to be resented by a restive nation which confused aggressiveness with ability, and assumed that the Cardinal's policy of patient adaptation was really no policy at all. Yet, save for the fact that he did not permit even his own sovereign to accustom himself to the cares and responsibilities of his position, Fleury's absolute power was exerted for the good of his country, and the only grievous mistake of his administration lay precisely in the fact that he unwittingly surrendered to Belle-Isle a share in determining the policy of France.

The events preceding Fleury's death were an anti-climax whose bathos has obscured the solid virtues of his rule; in reality his administration revealed diplomatic ability of a high order. Recognizing as he did the necessity of keeping France at peace, he skilfully evaded war in the difficult and unsettled first years of his administration, while he slowly regained that diplomatic equality which the precipitate policy of his predecessor had forfeited to Great Britain. When Great Britain, by recognizing the Pragmatic Sanction in 1731, isolated France, the progress which Fleury had made can readily be judged by the fact that such isolation was not of that dangerous character which had menaced the security of France as a result of the repudiation of the Infanta in 1725. The Cardinal could afford to wait, therefore, for a turn of the wheel of fortune, which came in 1733 with the opening of the question of the Polish succession. By making what was really an act of Bourbon aggression seem to be merely a defense of the interests of the father-in-law of the King of France, Fleury was able to prevent the ensuing war from becoming a general one; and by acquiring, in the peace which followed, the reversion to France of Lorraine, he secured the largest and most valuable territorial enlargement which France made in the eighteenth century.

Just as Fleury had managed to prevent the intervention of the British in the War of the Polish Succession, so he continued to forestall their participation in the conclusion of the peace which followed. The third Treaty of Vienna (1738) and Villeneuve's consummate mediation in the Turkish war carried French prestige to such a point that it is no exaggeration to say that in those years France enjoyed the diplomatic hegemony of Europe. This hegemony was exerted for the purpose of accomplishing the diplomatic isolation of Great Britain, and was so successfully utilized that in September of 1740 Fleury wilfully gave Great Britain ample provocation for declaring war, which the latter, significantly enough, avoided doing. But the unexpected death of Charles VI necessitated the jettisoning of these plans, the French squadrons were recalled, and France carefully abstained from providing the Maritime Powers with further provocation. Instead of remaining neutral in the war which followed the Emperor's death, the Cardinal permitted himself to be cajoled into undertaking a war in Germany, the disastrous results of which have already been related.

Yet the war was not irretrievably lost, simply because a French army had failed in its German adventure. The resources which the pacific and economical administration of Fleury had permitted the French nation to store up stood France in good stead in the years before 1748. Exhausted as France was in that year, she was nevertheless the victor, and only the boon of a timely and unexpectedly favourable peace permitted the British to forget the failures and deficiencies which had characterized their waging of that war which they had begun in 1739 with such bravado. For the notable commercial and economic expansion which France experienced during Fleury's administration directly contributed to the economic vitality which enabled the country to fight with honour a long and exhausting war. This expansion had not been the result of beneficent governmental absent-mindedness, but rather was, as has been shown, the object of the solicitous care of Fleury and his ministers, both with reference to domestic and to foreign policy. The government maintained a fixed monetary value at the same time that it utilized the resources of its diplomacy to conclude commercial treaties and to encourage trade and navigation. It preserved and improved the navy during a time when it also regained diplomatic prestige. In short, to the alarm and concern of the British, in an age when it was generally conceived that the balance of trade had become the balance of power, the policy of Fleury manifested itself to be in consonance with the axiom which Dutot had laid down:

To utilize peace in order to procure for ourselves all the advantages of a large trade is to wage war on our enemies.

APPENDICES

I.

The Notification to French Diplomatic Representatives of Chauvelin's Appointment as Adjunct to Cardinal Fleury.

Il y a déjà longtems, Monsieur, que je suplioit le Roy de vouloir bien me permettre de me faire soulager dans le grand detail d'affaires dont je suis charge, et d'y appeller quelqu'un qui pust même se former de plus en plus sous mes yeux aux principes que Sa M.^te veut continuer de suivre dans l'administration de ses affaires. Sa Maj^te a enfin consenti et agréé que j'appellasse quand je le desirerois M. le garde des sceaux au travail que j'ai l'honneur de faire avec Sa Maj^te et que dans les tems d'absence ou de maladie il fût destiné à remplir le même travail que moi. Vous aurès soin de faire part en mon nom à la Cour où vous êtes de cette disposition que Sa Maj^te vient de déclarer, et vous ferez connoitre en même temps que loin que cet arrangement apporte aucun changement dans les principes et les maximes sur lesquelles les affaires se conduisent, il ne fera qu'en asseurer la continuation la plus fidèle et la plus exacte. Je suis, etc.

A. É., *Mém. et Doc., France*, vol. 1275, fo. 21: "Aux Ministres du Roy dans les Pays etrangers, le 1er avril, 1732, à Versailles."

II.

Fleury's First Letter to the Emperor, July 16, 1735.

Sire,

M. le Baron de Nierost attaché à M. le Comte de Wied arriva ici il y a trois jours et démanda à me parler en particulier. Il étoit conduit par un françois que j'ai toujours regardé comme honneste homme et dont je n'ai aucun sujet de me defier. Ce Baron me montra une manière d'instruction qu'il m'assura avoir été dictée par M. le Comte de Sinzendorff par laquelle je vois que Votre Majeste Imperiale concourroit avec plaisir avec le Roy mon maître à un traité de paix sous des conditions equitables et solides.

Cette Instruction est accompagné d'un Mémoire plus ample dans lequel on s'explique encore plus au long et d'une lettre de M. le Comte de Wied audit Baron qui confirme la verité de toutes les pièces et qu'il agit avec ordre. Je ne les detaille point parceque j'ai lieu de supposer par tout ce qui y est énoncé que Votre Maj^te en a connaissance et [illegible] je vais avoir l'honneur d'y répondre dans la confiance où je dois être que tout s'est fait par Ses Ordres.

L'instruction commence par le doute où on est que je sois porté à la paix et j'ose asseurer que celui qui l'a dressé ne me rend pas justice et on oublie qu'on étoit si persuadé du contraire il y a deux ans qu'on repandoit partout que je la désiroit à un tel point que je ne me resoudroit jamais à conseiller la guerre au Roy, quelque sujet qu'il eut de s'y déterminer. On veut aujourd'hui m'imputer de ne vouloir plus la paix et on ne se trompe pas moins sur l'un que sur l'autre de ces faits.

J'ai cru que l'honneur du Roy et de la France si ouvertement blessé dans l'affaire de Pologne devoit l'engager à prendre les armes, mais quoique cette resolution ait été suivie de succès, je puis protester avec serment à Votre Majesté que je n'ai jamais perdu la paix de veue, pourvu qu'elle soit solide et honorable. Ce sentiment est gravé dans mon coeur et d'autant plus encore qu'en mon particulier c'est avec une très-grande repugnance que j'ai veu que le Roy ne pouvoit se dispenser d'entrer en guerre avec V^re Maj^te pour laquelle je conserverai toute ma vie le plus profond respect et la plus vive reconnoissance des bontés dont Elle a daigné m'honorer.

Je sais que nos ennemis ne cessent de m'imputer des sentiments bien opposés pour éloigner de moi V^re Maj^te et lui faire croire que je voudrois s'il étoit possible la dépouiller de tous ses Etats. Ces sortes d'artifices sont ordinaires à de certains gens, mais ce que je ne puis leur pardonner est de recourir à des calomnies qui n'ont pas la plus legère apparence de fondement. Je ne puis m'empêcher d'en rapporter une qui aura fait impression sur V^tre Maj^te, et qui lui aura fait perdre la bonne opinion qu'Elle avait bien voulu avoir jusqu'ici de ma probité.

Il m'est revenu qu'on m'avoit accusé auprès d'Elle d'avoir revelé au Roy d'Angleterre le projet d'une ligue que Votre Majesté offroit de faire avec la France pour le detrôner, que ce Prince en avait eu connaissance par moi, que par l'ancienne et aveugle confiance que j'avois aux Anglois, je leur avois fait part des avances que Votre Majesté m'avoit faites et que le Roy de la Grande Bretagne lui en avoit fait porter les plaintes les plus amères. Quoique ce soit la plus noire des impostures, j'avoue qu'elle n'a pas laissé de me toucher sensiblement et j'ai même quelque honte d'être obligé de m'en justifier, n'ayant pas cru de me voir jamais exposé à une pareille accusation.

Votre Majesté sait s'il y a jamais été question d'une semblable ligue et il faudroit que je fûsse le plus scélérat des hommes, sans foy ni Religion pour avoir inventé une si fausse supposition. Je ne ferai d'aucun récrimination contre les auteurs de cette calomnie et je me contente de declarer à Votre Majesté qu'elle est fausse de tous points et je défie qui que ce soit dans le monde d'oser la soutenir. Dès qu'on a recours à des mensonges si denués de toute vraisemblance on ne peut marcher en seureté et il est triste de s'y voir exposé. Je reviens, Sire, à l'objet principal de cette lettre.

L'Instruction et le mémoire portent que si je consens à traiter de la paix avec Votre Majesté il faut y observer un secret inviolable et que le moyen le plus court, le plus prompt et le plus sur d'y réussir est que j'envoye un homme au plustost à Vienne qui s'y rendra avec le Baron de Nierost sans avoir besoin d'aucun passeport. J'accepte avec respect toutes ces propositions et je commence par declarer à Votre Majesté que quelque puisse être le succès de notre negotiation je n'en decouvrirai jamais rien, ni devant ni après à personne du monde. C'est au nom du Roy que je fais cette déclaration en conséquence de celle d'une pareille que Votre Maj^te a bien voulu faire.

Votre Majesté exige une autre condition qui me fait une vrai peine parcequ'elle n'est pas fondée mais à laquelle je ne laisse pas de me soumettre pour ne pas retarder un ouvrage si important qui doit décider de la tranquillité de l'Europe. Votre Majesté exige donc que je ne confie cette negotiation à aucun autre du Conseil du Roy et qu'elle ne passe que par moi seul, parcequ'Elle a pour suspect un ministre qu'il est facile de deviner. Je crains fort, Sire, que les auteurs de la calomnie dont je me suis plaint cydessus, ne les soient aussi des preventions qu'on lui a données contre ce ministre.

Je n'entrerai pas dans un plus long detail de sa justification mais je puis asseurer Votre Majesté qu'il pense entièrement comme moi et que dans nos frequens entretiens il est convenu que l'unique moyen de finir la guerre étoit que tout se passoit directement entr'Elle et nous. Je ne puis croire qu'il ait jamais manqué au profond respect qu'il lui doit, et s'il lui est echapé dans quelque depesche, dont je doute pourtant, quelqu'expression que ait pu la blesser, ça étoit seurement contre son intention et contre ce qu'il pense.

Cependant je me soumets à la volonté de Votre Majesté quoique je ne laisserai pas d'être embarrassé pour le choix de l'homme que j'envoyerai à Vienne sans sa participation et pour des details de la negotiation. J'espère que dans la suite Votre Majesté voudra bien lui rendre plus de justice, et je puis lui repondre par avance que tous ses sentimens et sa manière de penser sont entièrement conformes aux miens.

Comme la choix de l'homme que j'enverrai retardera peut être de deux ou trois jours son depart, et qu'il faudra que je travaille à ses instructions j'ai cru que je devois le faire preceder par cette lettre afin que Votre Majesté soit asseurée par avance des dispositions sincères du Roy mon maître et des miennes par consequent. Je prens d'autant plus volontiers ce parti, que l'Instruction et le mémoire portent qu'on souhaiteroit voir un acquièscement de moi par écrit à ce qui y est contenu. Je n'ai aucun soupçon que tout ne soit avec la participation de Votre Majesté et quoique je n'en aye aucune Sureté—Elle connoitra par là toute l'étendue de ma confiance.

J'ay l'honneur d'être avec le plus profond respect, etc.,

A. É., *Corr. Pol.*, *Autriche*, vol. 181, fols. 3-8. (Copy).

III.

A Portion of Fleury's Letter to the Emperor, August 28, 1735.

.   .   .   .

Je ne prendrois pas la liberté de Luy repeter ce que j'ay déjà eu celuy de Luy protester dans ma lettre précédente et je suplie V[otre] M[ajesté] d'être persuadée que la chose du monde que je désire le plus est une parfaite union du Roy mon maître avec V[otre] M[ajesté], qu'il y est porté lui-même par son inclination et pour Moi, en particulier, Sire, je mourrois content si je pouvais être l'instrument d'une intelligence que je crois non seulement utile pour les deux couronnes mais encore avantageuse à la

Religion et la tranquillité de l'Europe. Ce sont mes véritables sentiments remplis du plus profond respect avec lequel je serai toute ma vie,

Sire, de Votre Majesté,

Le tres humble et tres obéissant

serviteur le Card. de Fleury.

A. É., *Corr. Pol., Autriche*, vol. 181, fols. 74-78. (Copy).

IV.

Sire,

Fleury's Letter to the Emperor, September 11, 1735.

J'ay receu avec la plus vive et la plus respectueuse reconnoissance par le Courrier de M. de la Baune la lettre dont Votre Majesté Imp^le a bien voulu m'honorer du 21 du mois dernier. C'est ici la 4e que j'ay l'honneur de luy écrire. La p^re quand le Baron de Nierodt me porta deux mémoires non signés qu'il me dit avoir été dictés par M. le Comte de Sinzendorff et qu'il se chargea de faire tenir à V[otre] M[ajesté]. La Séconde au départ du Sr de la Baune et la 3e sur une ouverture que M. le Nonce de Flandres avait faite à M. le Cte de la Marck. Ce n'est que pour plus grande regularité et affin [*sic*] de constater les faits que je prends la liberté de faire mention de ces différentes lettres.

Je commence par assurer V[otre] M[ajesté] au nom du Roy mon maître du desir sincère qu'il a de parvenir à une véritable reconciliation avec Elle et j'ose la suplier [*sic*] de ne point regarder la mémoire que M. de la Baune aura l'honneur de lui presenter comme venant d'aucun esprit de difficulté ou de pretentions trop fortes, mais plustost comme un effet des engagements que nous avons avec nos alliés et auxquels nous ne pourrions manquer jusqu'à un certain point sans nous déshonorer, ou même sans laisser des semences de division et de discorde capables de rallumer bientost une nouvelle guerre.

Il s'agit, Sire, de rétablir dans l'Europe une parfaite tranquillité et de prévenir autant que la prudence humaine peut le prevoir, tout ce qui pourroit la troubler. Pour y parvenir, il faut que si nos alliés n'obtiennent pas tout ce qu'ils souhaiteroient il leur soit du moins donné un partage dont ils ne puissent raissonnablement se plaindre et que les autres puissances impartiales de l'Europe ayent sujet de leur imputer le blame du refus qu'ils feroient de l'accepter.

Je voudrais, s'il m'est permis de le dire, que V[otre] M[ajesté] pust se mettre un moment à ma place et qu'Elle pust connoître toute l'étendue de l'embarras où je me trouve pour concilier les pretentions de nos alliés avec l'envie sincère que le Roy a dans le coeur de faire cesser les malheurs de la guerre et de voir renaître avec V[otre] M[ajesté] une amitié qui seule peut asseurer la gloire de nôtre Ste Religion et fixer la tranquillité constante de l'Europe. Si nous manquons un aussy heureuse occasion de ramener la paix on ne pourra plus repondre des suites ni envisager de terme à une guerre qui n'a déjà couté que trop de sang.

Je conçois que V[otre] M[ajesté] doit avoir quelque peine de ceder au Roy de Sardaigne ce que le Roy propose, mais qu'Elle me permette s'il luy plaît de luy representer qu'il est en possession de tout le Milanès, qu'il a fait des depenses immenses pour s'en rendre maître et le peu qu'on luy cède en le comparant à ce qu'il possède actuellement.

Je suplie [sic] V[otre] M[ajesté] de vouloir bien considerer d'un autre costé l'obligation que nous avons à ce Prince d'estre entré dans notre querelle, la fidelité avec laquelle il a rempli ses engagemens, et les justes reproches qu'il auroit à nous faire si nous l'abandonnerions jusqu'à un certain point. Sa puissance peut-elle jamais faire ombrage à celle de V[otre] M[ajesté], dès que nous serons surtout garants de tous les engagements qu'il contractera?

V[otre] M[ajesté] I[mpériale] est un si grand Prince qu'un très petit Pays de plus ou de moins ne peut rien diminuer de sa puissance, et je voudrois estre à portée de me jetter à ses pieds pour Le conjurer de peser d'un costé ce qu'on luy demande et de l'autre la seureté qu'Elle obtiendra pour la succession de ses Etats aussy bien que la gloire du sacrifice qu'Elle voudra bien faire pour éteindre une guerre aussy funeste à la Religion qu'au Bonheur et au repos de toute l'Europe.

S'il estoit libre au Roy mon maître de prendre plus qu'il ne fait sur ses Alliés il ne s'y refuseroit certainement pas, et le plus grand avantage qu'il se propose, si on est assez heureux pour y parvenir, est l'esperance qu'elle servira à établir une union indissoluble de la France avec V[otre] M[ajesté]. En mon particulier je puis luy protester que ç'a toujours été mon objet principal et il me seroit aisé de luy en donner des preuves demonstratives. V[otre] M[ajesté] m'a honoré de tant de marques de ses precieuses bontés et même de sa confiance qu'elles ne s'effaceront jamais de mon coeur.

Je suis infiniment flaté [sic] de celle qu'Elle veut bien avoir encore en moy, en me laissant le choix des moyens et des personnes qui doivent concourir à la consommation d'un ouvrage si important et je tacheray de me conformer sans reserve à ses vuees.

Il n'est pas étonnant qu'il y ait de la ressemblance entre les propositions faites par M. de la Baune et celles de M. Robinson. V[otre] M[ajesté] peut croire aisément qu'après beaucoup de tentatives réiterées de l'Angleterre pour nous faire accepter son plan, Elle n'a rien oublié depuis pour penétrer du moins quels pourroient estre nos principes sur une pacification.

Son Ministre en notre Cour m'a tenu differents propos sur la satisfaction que nous pourrions désirer pour le Beau-Père du Roy, et il a esté question aussy en général en plus d'une occasion de ce que nous croyions qu'on pourroit accorder à l'Espagne et au Roy de Sardaigne. Il est même en dernier lieu entré plus avant en matière, toujours comme de luy mesme, et il n'est pas surprenant que les idées qui luy sont venues soient à peu près les mesmes que celles que M. de la Baune a presenté aux ministres de V[otre] M[ajesté].

Je ne serois pas étonné qu'Elles luy fussent communiquées, mais j'ose l'asseurer avec serment qu'il ne m'est rien échapé [sic] et ne m'échapera certainement pas, sur l'envoy de M. de la Beaune à Vienne ni surtout ce qu'il y pourra traiter. Le secret que V[otre] M[ajesté] a la bonté de me promettre dans tous les cas et auquel je me confie sans reserve sera inviolablement gardé de ma part et je la suplie [*sic*] de n'en avoir pas le plus leger doute.

Le Ministère d'Angleterre paroist désirer sincèrement la pacification de l'Europe, et nous ne la desirons pas moins sans aucune acception des personnes qui pourront y contribuer. Si V[otre] M[ajesté] I[mpériale] juge que nous convinsions des articles essentiels ou les communiquassions à l'Angleterre comme un simple projet non arresté ni signé c'est à Elle à nous conduire car nous ne voulons aller qu'au bien par les voyes qui paroissent les plus propres à V[otre] M[ajesté] pour le procurer. Si c'estoit son avis on pourroit en ce cas ne faire qu'une signature commune entre nous et l'Angleterre, sans pourtant donner aucune atteinte à ce que nous aurions déjà signé en secret.

Je souhaite ardament, Sire, que la reponse à ce que j'ay l'honneur de proposer à V[otre] M[ajesté] soit la signature des preliminaires de la pais, et je prens la liberté de la conjurer de ne consulter dans ce grand ouvrage que la noblesse et la generosité de son coeur aussy bien que son amour pour la Religion. Tels sont les motifs qui animent aussi le Roy, et j'y ajouterois avec verité que celuy de s'unir avec V[otre] M[ajesté] I[mpériale] par des liens indissolubles n'est pas un des moindres.

C'est une sensible satisfaction pour moy d'apprendre par V[otre] M[ajesté] qu'Elle daigne approuver le choix que j'ay fait de M. de la Baune, et j'espère que son conduite justifiera le glorieux temoignage dont V[otre] M[ajesté] veut bien l'honorer.

J'ay l'honneur d'estre avec le plus profond respect,

A. É., *Corr. Pol.*, *Autriche*, vol. 181, fols. 242-245. (Copy).

V.

A Portion of Fleury's Letter to the Emperor, October 19, 1735.

. . . .

J'ay l'honneur de raporter tous les faits à V[otre] M[ajesté] dans la plus exacte verité et je proteste que je n'ai revelé notre secret à personne du monde sans exception. . . .

Je declare Devant Dieu et je l'en prends à temoin que le Roy désire sincèrement la paix et que je ne la désire pas moins, non seulement par ce que je dois être soumis à toutes ses volontés mais encore par mon inclination particulière. Je declare de plus avec le même serment que dans les motifs que le Roy mon Maître a de désirer la paix celuy de former une union intime entre luy et V[otre] M[ajesté] est un des plus réels et que ç'a été toujours ma principale vue. Si j'avois l'honeur d'être à ses pieds, il ne me seroit pas difficile de l'en convaincre, et je defie qui que ce soit dans le Monde d'oser dire que j'aye jamais parlé de V[otre] M[ajesté] quand il en a été question que dans les termes les plus remplis de respect, de vénération qui luy sont dues, et même d'un attachement personnel fondé sur la haute opinion que j'ay de ses grandes qualités aussi bien que sur ma reconnoissance.

. . . J'ay Dieu Mercy la religion et la justice dans le coeur et j'espère que V[otre] M[ajesté] voudra bien ne pas se livrer à la mauvaise opinion qu'on cherche à luy donner de mes intentions. Je prends donc la liberté de la suplier de juger plustost de moy par son équité naturelle et par ses lumières que par les impressions de ceux qui par quelque interêt secret ou par des préventions injustes travaillent à luy donner une idée de moy bien opposée.

J'ajouterai, Sire, que si dans les suites j'aurois une conduite contraire à ce que je prends la liberté de dire à V[otre] M[ajesté] il luy sera libre de me faire passer dans l'Europe pour un homme de la plus mauvaise foy et cette lettre lui en servira de preuve. L'honneur du Roy mon Maître passera toujours devant tout, et je serois indigne de ses bontés et de sa confiance si j'étois capable de ne pas les preferer à ma propre vie mais je suis fortement persuadé que l'avantage de la religion, la tranquillité de l'Europe et l'interêt de V[otre] M[ajesté] aussi bien que celuy de la France demandent une union intime entre les deux Couronnes dés qu'elles n'ont point envie d'envahir les Etats l'une et l'autre et je proteste que le Roy de son Côté est bien éloigné d'avoir cette pensée comme je suis persuadé que V[otre] M[ajesté] est dans le même esprit.

. . . .

Je vois avec une vraie douleur que nous sommes encores assès éloignés d'une parfaite conciliation, mais je ne desespère pas que nous ne puissions y parvenir si V[otre] M[ajesté] veut bien avoir la bonté de se raprocher de ceque le Roy desireroit. Notre negotiation doit être l'ouvrage d'une entière confiance, et du désir reciproque que V[otre] M[ajesté] et le Roy mon Maître sont suposés avoir de cimenter pour l'avenir une intime union. Si nous sommes assès heureux pour y parvenir il me semble qu'on pouroit commencer par convenir d'abord d'un armistice par la voye des Puissances mediatrices, et je crois pouvoir assurer que nos alliés ne s'en éloigneront pas. . . .

. . . .

A. É., *Corr. Pol., Autriche*, vol. 182: Fleury to Charles VI, (private) October 19, 1735. (Copy).

VI.

A Portion of Fleury's Letter to the Emperor, October 25, 1735.

Pour S[a] M[ajesté] I[mpériale] seule, s'il luy plaist.

Sire,

Je demande très humblement pardon à V[otre] M[ajesté] I[mpériale] si je prends la liberté de la fatiguer de cette seconde lettre, mais j'ay des raisons personnelles si fortes de luy réiterer mes plus respectueuses instances sur l'article de la Lorraine, que, comptant comme Elle m'a permis de le fair [sic] sur ses precieuses bontés, j'ay l'honneur de luy ouvrir mon coeur sur les circonstances où je me trouve. Je ne dissimulerai point à V[otre] M[ajesté] que toutes les personnes qui composent le conseil du Roy ne pensent pas tout à fait sur la paix comme M. le Garde des Sceaux et moi. J'ay tout lieu de craindre que quand les articles Preliminaires y seront rapportés, je ne trouve de l'opposition dans quelqu'uns d'eux et quoique leur opposition ne changera certainement rien à tout ce que nous aurons signés il seroit très désagreable pour moi que le projet de pacification ne fût pas unanimement approuvé et que je fusse obligé à des justifications toujours facheuses et qui iroient à diminuer un peu du credit dont j'ay tant de besoin dans une conjoncture si delicate.

Je ne crains point que cela altère en aucune facon la confiance entière dont S[a] M[ajesté] veut bien m'honorer mais ceux qui voudront se faire l'honneur d'avoir pensé plus noblement et plus conformément au génie et aux dispositions présentes de notre nation ne garderont peut être pas un secret bien parfait et me feront un démérite d'avoir trop cedé par le désir de la pais et un pareil bruit ne pouroit que produire un effet très désagréable pour moy.

Il seroit encore augmenté par les reproches du peu de fidelité que nous aurons observés envers nos alliés et il seroit assez triste d'avoir à soutenir en même temps leurs clameurs et celles des françois qui sans rien examiner, ny même estre en état de le faire, se soucient peu de la tranquillité publique et ne songent qu'à censurer le ministère sous le faux pretexte qu'il n'a pas profité des avantages que nous paroissions avoir et de sacrifier l'interest et l'honneur de la nation à mon inclination pacifique.

Ces accusations tourneroient principalement contre moi mais si elles ne faisoient que me nuire personnellement je m'en consolerois par ce que Dieu connoît les motifs qui m'ont fait agir et la pureté de mes intentions, mais, Sire, dans celle que j'ay toujours eu, et que je n'ay jamais perdue de veu— d'établir une union intime entre le Roy et V[otre] M[ajesté], j'aurois lieu d'apréhender que ces accusations ne traversassent la facilité ou du moins n'affoiblissent les moyens d'y parvenir.

Je conjure donc V[otre] M[ajesté] autant qu'il m'est possible d'avoir la bonté d'écouter mes très humbles représentations et si Elle a des raisons essentielles de se refuser à la cession de la Lorraine dès à present ainsy que M. de la Beaune nous l'avoit fait esperer dans sa première depesche, je la supplie très respecteusement de vouloir bien se rendre à l'expedient de fixer cette cession au moment du mariage de la sérenissime archiduchesse avec M. le Duc de Lorraine; si j'avois l'avantage d'estre à ses pieds je me flaterois de toucher et persuader V[otre] M[ajesté]. Si je n'aurois craint de l'embarrasser, le Roy en auroit écrit pour le luy demander.

Au cas que V[otre] M[ajesté] voulût bien se prester à cet expédient, j'ay fait dresser d'avance un projet d'article que M. de Lestang est autorisé à signer et qui seroit ratiffié ensuite sans que cela retarde pour le présent l'échange des ratiffications des articles signés à Vienne.

Quelque soit la decision de V[otre] M[ajesté], M. de Lestang a ordres de changer contre les ratiffications de V[otre] M[ajesté] celles du Roy dont il est chargé. Je ne puis donner à V[otre] M[ajesté] une plus grande marque de la confiance que je lui dois et avec laquelle j'en agiray dans tout le cours de cette affaire.

A. É., *Corr. Pol., Autriche*, vol. 182, ff. 95-96. (Copy).

BIBLIOGRAPHY

I. UNPUBLISHED MATERIALS

THE unpublished documents which were utilized in the preparation of this study are to be found among the *Newcastle Papers (Additional Manuscripts)* in the British Museum and in the *Archives du Ministère des Affaires Étrangères* at Paris. Of the former I have studied volumes 32751-32755. Particularly important among the papers consulted in the *Archives du Ministère des Affaires Étrangères* were found to be the *Correspondance politique: Autriche*, vols. 175-176, 180-186 and *Supplément*, vol. 12, which cover the negotiations leading up to the conclusion of the Preliminaries of Peace of October 3, 1735, and to the ultimate acquisition of the reversion of Lorraine. These volumes give evidence of Cardinal Fleury's inclination to bring about a *rapprochement* with the Hapsburg monarchy; some of his letters to that effect are published in the Appendices (*supra*, pp. 351-358). Also of great interest are the *Mémoires et Documents: France*, vols. 418, 457, 493, 494, 501, 503, 1275-1276. The divers summaries, memorials and *avis sur les partis à prendre*, of various authorship, which comprise these volumes are frequently of notable assistance in comprehending the secret springs and hidden perplexities of French policy. The writer has also consulted at the *Archives du Ministère des Affaires Étrangères: Correspondance politique: Espagne*, vols. 350, 387, 405; *Correspondance politique: Hollande*, vols. 391, 404, 406; *Mémoires et Documents: Autriche*, vol. 8.

II. PUBLISHED MATERIALS

1. *Bibliographical Aids*

The following titles have been of assistance in assembling the materials used for this study; the writer, however, relied by no means exclusively upon the more formal bibliographies for his knowledge of extant material. Of equal value and frequently of greater critical worth are those bibliographies given in monographs which deal with phases of the period here under consideration. The following finding list consequently makes no pretensions to being exhaustive. Titles of general works which touch upon this period will be found usually to have been omitted from this bibliography, on the presumption that they may readily be discovered by consulting the works mentioned under *Bibliographical Aids*.

Abbott, Wilbur C. *An Introduction to the Documents Relating to the International Status of Gibraltar, 1704-1934*. New York, 1934. 112 pp.

Allison, W. H., Fay, S. B., Shearer, A. H., and Shipman, H. R., editors. *A Guide to Historical Literature*. New York, 1931. 1222 pp.

Brackmann, Albert, and Hartung, Fritz, editors. *Jahresberichte für deutsche Geschichte.* Leipzig, 1927-   . Vol. I (1927) for the year 1925, and later volumes.

Cambridge Modern History, The. Vol. VI: *The Eighteenth Century.* Cambridge [England], 1909. Contains useful and extensive, although uncritical, bibliographical lists.

Caron, Pierre, and Stein, Henri. *Répertoire bibliographique de l'histoire de France.* Paris, 1923-   . Tome I (1923) for years 1920-1921, and later volumes.

Dahlmann-Waitz. *Quellenkunde der deutschen Geschichte.* Ninth edition, edited by Hermann Haering. Leipzig, 1931. 992 pp.

Du Péloux, Charles, vicomte. *Répertoire général des ouvrages modernes relatifs au XVIIIe siècle français (1715-1789).* Paris, 1926. 308 pp.

———. *Supplément au Répertoire des ouvrages modernes relatifs au XVIIIe siècle français (1715-1789).* Paris, 1927. 62 pp. The titles listed in these two works are arranged alphabetically by authors; no attempt is made to arrange them topically. Comprehensive but uncritical.

International Committee of Historical Sciences, The. *International Bibliography of Historical Sciences.* Washington [D. C.], 1930-   . Vol. I (1930) for the year 1926, and later volumes.

Myers, Denys Peter. *Manual of Collections of Treaties and of Collections Relating to Treaties.* Cambridge [Mass.], 1922. 685 pp.

Saulnier, E., and Martin, A. *Bibliographie des travaux publiés de 1866 à 1897 sur l'histoire de la France de 1500 à 1789.* Vol. I. Paris, 1932. 411 pp.

2. Treaty Collections

Aretin, Carl Maria, Freiherr von. *Chronologisches Verzeichniss der bayerischen Staats-Verträge, vom Tode Herzog Georgs des Reichen (1503), bis zum Frankfurter Territorial-Recess (1819). Nebst einer Sammlung von 94 bisher ungedruckten Recessen, Conventionen, Protokollen, und andern in gleiche Kategorie gehörenden Urkunden.* Passau, 1838. 514 pp.

Bittner, Ludwig. *Chronologisches Verzeichnis der österreichischen Staatsverträge: Die österreichischen Staatsverträge von 1526 bis 1763.* Vienna, 1903. 228 pp. This volume constitutes vol. I of the *Veröffentlichungen der Kommission für neuere Geschichte Österreichs.*

Cantillo, Alejandro del. *Tratados, convenios, y declaraciones de paz y de comercio que han hecho con las potencias estranjeras los monarcas españoles de la casa de Borbon. Desde el año de 1700 hasta el dia.* Madrid, 1843. xxxix, 908 pp. This valuable collection published for the first time many of the secret Spanish treaties.

Clercq, Alexandre Jehan Henry de, and Clercq, Étienne François Jules de. *Recueil des traités de la France, publié sous les auspices du ministre des affaires étrangères.* Paris, 1880-1917. 23 vols. Vol. I (1880. 623 pp.) covers the period from 1713 to 1802. This collection is useful for the nineteenth century, but most unsatisfactory for the eighteenth. Some treaties are not listed at all, and frequently treaties are merely mentioned, with a reference to some other collection, usually that by Koch (*q.v.*, *infra*), itself not an entirely satisfactory work. Cf. Myers: *Manual of Collections of Treaties*, p. 153.

Davenport, Frances Gardiner. *European Treaties bearing on the History of the United States and its Dependencies.* Volume III: (*1698-1715*). [Carnegie Institution of Washington, Publication No. 254], Washington [D. C.], 1934. 269 pp.

Dumont, Jean, baron de Carelscroon. *Corps universel diplomatique du droit des gens; contenant un recueil des traitez d'alliance.* . . . Amsterdam and The Hague, 1726-1731. 8 vols. Vol. VIII, part ii, together with a supplement and addition, cover the period from 1719 to the second Treaty of Vienna (1731); vol. VIII, part i, covers the period from 1701 to 1718. For a description of this excellent collection, see Myers: *Manual of Collections of Treaties*, pp. 22-23.

General Collection of Treatys of Peace and Commerce, Renunciations, Manifestos and other Publick Papers, relating to Peace and War, A. London, 1732. 4 vols. Vol. III covers the period from 1642 to 1713; vol. IV "from the end of the reign of Queen Anne to the year 1731." See Myers: *Manual of Collections of Treaties*, p. 190.

Koch, Christophe Guillaume de: see Schoell, *infra.*

Lamberty, Guillaume de. *Mémoires pour servir à l'histoire du XVIII siècle, contenant les négociations, traitez, resolutions, et autres documens authentiques concernant les affaires d'état;* . . . The Hague and Amsterdam, 1724-1740. 14 vols. The supplement to vol. X, paginated separately, contains many treaties up to and including the Treaty of Vienna, March 16, 1731.

Loewe, Viktor. *Preussens Staatsverträge aus der Regierungszeit König Friedrich Wilhelms I.* (*Königlich-Preussischen Publikationen.* Band LXXXVII). Leipzig, 1913. xiv, 499 pp.

Martens, Feodor Fedorovich. *Recueil des traités et conventions conclus par la Russie avec les puissances étrangères, publié d'ordre du Ministère des Affaires Étrangères.* St. Petersburg, 1874-1909. 15 vols. Vol. I includes the treaties concluded with Austria between 1648 and 1762; V, treaties with "Germany" from 1656 to 1762; IX (X), treaties with Great Britain from 1710 to 1801; XIII, treaties with France from 1717 to 1807. See Myers: *Manual of Collections of Treaties*, pp. 301-302.

Noradounghian, Gabriel. *Recueil d'actes internationaux de l'Empire Ottoman.* Paris, 1897-1903. 4 vols. Volume I covers the years from 1300 to 1789.

Pribram, Alfred Francis. *Österreichische Staatsverträge: England bis 1748.* Innsbruck, 1907. 813 pp. This work constitutes vol. III of the *Veröffentlichungen der Kommission für neuere Geschichte Österreichs.*

Rousset de Missy, Jean. *Recueil historique d'actes, négociations, mémoires, et traitez, depuis la paix d'Utrecht.* . . . The Hague, 1728-1748. 19 vols. A first-rate source, containing all manner of public papers of this period, arranged in approximately chronological order. It is particularly complete on affairs appertaining to the United Provinces and Germany.

Schmauss, Johann Jacob. *Corpus juris gentium academicum, enthaltend die vornehmsten Grund-Gesetze, Friedens- und Commercien-Tractate, Bündnüsse und andere Pacta der Königreiche, Republiquen, und Staaten von*

*Europa, welche seither zweyen Seculis biss auf den gegenwärtigen Congress
zu Soissons errichtet worden.* Leipzig, 1730. 2 vols., paged continuously.
The documents in vol. II fall in the period between 1696 and 1731.

Schoell, Friedrich. *Histoire abrégée des traités de paix entre les puissances
de l'Europe, depuis la paix de Westphalie; par feu M. de Koch. Ouvrage
entièrement refondu, augmenté, et continué jusqu'au congrès de Vienne et
aux traités de Paris de 1815; par F. Schoell.* Paris, 1817-1818. 15 vols.
Material touching upon the period of Fleury's ministry may be found
in vols. II and XIII. This work is more of a diplomatic history, with
quotations from important articles of treaties, than it is a treaty collection. Useful for an *aperçu.* See Myers: *Manual of Collections of
Treaties,* p. 39.

Srbik, Heinrich, Ritter von. *Österreichische Staatsverträge: Niederlande bis
1722.* Vienna, 1912. 648 pp. Volume X of the *Veröffentlichungen der
Kommission für neuere Geschichte Österreichs.*

Wenck, Friedrich August Wilhelm. *Codex juris gentium recentissimi, e
tabulariorum exemplorumque fide dignorum monumentis compositus.*
Leipzig, 1781-1795. 3 vols. Volume I covers the years from 1735
to 1743.

3. Published Sources, other than Treaty Collections

Acts of the Privy Council of England, Colonial Series. Hereford [England]
and London, 1908-1912. 6 vols. Vol. III (Hereford, 1910. xiii, 903
pp.) includes the summaries of documents for the years 1720-1745;
vol. VI, "The Unbound Papers" (London, 1912. xlix, 686 pp.). Some
of the papers summarized in this work give evidence of France's commercial expansion during this period.

Bang, Nina Ellinger, and Korst, Knud. *Tabeller over Skibsfart og Varetransport gennem Øresund, 1661-1783, og gennem Storebælt, 1701-1748.
Første Del: Tabeller over Skibsfarten.* Copenhagen, 1930. xviii, 478 pp.

Boislisle, A. M. de, editor. *Correspondance des Contrôleurs généraux des
finances avec les intendants des provinces (1683-1715).* Paris, 1874, 1883,
1897. 3 vols. This work prints (vol. II, pp. 482-499) the *Mémoire du
sieur des Casaux du Hallay, député de Nantes, sur l'état du commerce en
général,* cited *supra,* p. 66.

Bonnassieux, Pierre. *Conseil de commerce et bureau du commerce (1700-1791).
Inventaire analytique des procès verbaux.* Paris, 1900. lxxii, 699 pp.
The useful introduction to this work was contributed by Eugène Lelong.

British Diplomatic Instructions, 1689-1789. London, edited for the Royal
Historical Society.

    I. *Sweden, 1689-1727.* J. F. Chance, editor; Camden Third Series, vol.
    XXXII (1922). xxxviii, 250 pp.

    II. *France, 1689-1721.* L. G. Wickham Legg, editor; Camden Third
    Series, vol. XXXV (1925). xxxviii, 212 pp.

    III. *Denmark, 1689-1789.* J. F. Chance, editor; Camden Third Series,
    vol. XXXVI (1926). xli, 229 pp.

    IV. *France, 1721-1727.* L. G. Wickham Legg, editor; Camden Third
    Series, vol. XXXVIII (1927). xl, 253 pp.

V. *Sweden, 1727-1789.* J. F. Chance, editor; Camden Third Series, vol. XXXIX (1928). xxvi, 268 pp.

VI. *France, 1727-1744.* L. G. Wickham Legg, editor; Camden Third Series, vol. XLIII (1930). xl, 255 pp.
This well-edited series contains not only the instructions given at the beginning of a mission but also the additional instructions given in the ordinary course of despatches sent by the minister to his diplomatic agents.

Bussemaker, C. H. T., editor. "Een Memorie over de Republiek uit 1728." *Bijdragen en Mededeelingen van het Historisch Genootschap,* XXX (1909), pp. 96-197. This "Memorie" was the summary of Dutch politics and of French policy in the United Provinces which Fénelon composed for the use of his successor, La Baune; it has now been published also in the *Recueil des instructions . . . Hollande,* II (1924), pp. 471-540, but does not include the valuable notes contributed by Bussemaker to this earlier publication of it.

Calendar of State Papers, Colonial Series: America and West Indies, March, 1720 to December, 1721. London, 1933. lxiii, 588 pp Contains some information on the French trade at Cape Breton and at Albany; see Index.

Idem, 1722-1723. London, 1934. lxi, 496 pp. Contains papers on the Albany trade and the Santa Lucia dispute.

Calendar of Treasury Books and Papers, 1735-1738. London, 1900. lxxx, 761 pp. Contains references to the prevalence of wool "owling" to France; see Index.

"Les Chambres de Commerce de France et la cession du Canada." *Rapport de l'archiviste de la province de Quebec pour 1924-1925,* pp. 199-228. This report publishes the several letters of protest written in 1761 in the name of the French Chambers of Commerce, setting forth commercial reasons against the cession of Canada.

Commerce of Rhode Island, I (1726-1774). [*Collections of the Massachusetts Historical Society,* Seventh Series, vol. IX]. Boston, 1914. 525 pp. Gives evidence of French activity in the slave trade.

Dickson, William Kirk. *The Jacobite Attempt of 1719: Letters of James Butler, Second Duke of Ormonde, Relating to Cardinal Alberoni's Project for the Invasion of Great Britain on Behalf of the Stuarts, and to the Landing of a Spanish Expedition in Scotland.* [*Publications of the Scottish History Society,* vol. XIX]. Edinburgh, 1895. lix, 306 pp.

Donnan, Elizabeth. *Documents illustrative of the History of the Slave Trade to America.* Volume II: *The Eighteenth Century.* [Carnegie Institution of Washington, Publication No. 409]. Washington [D. C.], 1931. lxii, 731 pp.

Édits, ordonnances royaux, déclarations et arrêts du conseil d'état du Roi, concernant le Canada. Quebec, 1854-1856. 3 vols.

Frederick II of Prussia. *Politische Correspondenz Friedrich's des Grossen.* Edited by J. G. Droysen, Max Duncker, Heinrich von Sybel and G. B. Volz; Berlin and Leipzig, 1879- . 44 vols.

I. (Berlin, 1879). 472 pp. Correspondence from June 3, 1740 to December 31, 1741.

II. (Berlin, 1879). 530 pp. Correspondence from January 1, 1742 to December 31, 1743.

Gachard, Louis Prosper. *Collection de documents inédits concernant l'histoire de la Belgique.* Brussels, 1833-1835. 3 vols. Vol. III contains "documents concerning the establishment of the Austrian domination, 1706-1725."

Geyl, P., editor. "Engelsche Correspondentie van Prins Willem IV en Prinses Anna (1734-1743)." *Bijdragen en Mededeelingen van het Historisch Genootschap*, XLV (1924), pp. 89-140.

His Catholick Majesty's Manifesto, Justifying his Conduct in relation to the late Convention. With his Reasons for not paying the Ninety-Five Thousand Pounds. Printed for Robert Amey; London, 1739. 53 pp.

Historical Manuscripts Commission (London):

Report II, Appendix (1871): The Granard Manuscripts, pp. 210-217. Papers concerning the entrance of Admiral Forbes into the service of the Emperor for the purpose of improving the Austrian navy.

Report X, Appendix Part I (1885): The Charles Stirling-Home-Drummond Moray Manuscripts contain (pp. 191-196) letters of Admiral Thomas Gordon relating to the siege of Dantzig and the War of the Polish Succession.

Ibid., pp. 199-520: The Weston Papers. Weston was an under-secretary of state for the Southern Department of foreign affairs. This collection contains a great many letters on diplomatic topics, a number of them written by Horatio Walpole.

Report XI, Appendix Part IV (1887): The Townshend Papers. 467 pp.

Report XIII, Appendix Part VII (1893): The Lonsdale Papers. Contains (pp. 124-125) an important letter from the Duke of Newcastle which reveals the attitude of the British government toward the crisis of the Polish succession.

Report XIV, Appendix Part IX (1895), pp. 1-154: The Trevor Papers. This collection contains some very valuable letters. Trevor was British envoy at The Hague from 1739 to 1747; see Horn: *British Diplomatic Representatives, 1689-1789*, p. 164.

Ibid., pp. 200-266: The Hare Manuscripts. These papers, which include the letters written by Francis Hare, Bishop of Chichester, to his son in 1738 and 1739, give a vivid picture of the Parliamentary agitations at the time of the outbreak of war with Spain.

Ibid., pp. 458-520: The Onslow Papers. Interesting character sketches of the leading British politicians during this time, written by the Speaker of the House of Commons.

Report XV, Appendix Part VI (1897): The Carlisle Papers. Contains excellent accounts of Parliamentary debates. Pp. 52-199 deal with the years of particular interest to this study.

Report on the Manuscripts of Lady Du Cane. London, 1905. xxxv, 393 pp. This report includes (pp. 241-350) the Caylus Papers, which consist of letters written to Caylus, a French naval officer who in

1745 was appointed governor of Martinique, by Maurepas and his secretaries. These papers, however, contain disappointingly little on the policies and organization of the French navy during this period.

Report on the Manuscripts of the Earl of Mar and Kellie. London, 1904. xxviii, 608 pp. Of little interest; it contains, however, (pp. 529, 540) two important letters from William Pulteney to Lord Grange, December 17, 1733 and November 12, 1734, which indicate the indecision of the Parliamentary Opposition during the crisis of the Polish succession.

Report on the Manuscripts of Lord Polwarth. London, 1911-1931. 3 vols. Lord Polwarth was British ambassador to Denmark from 1716 to 1721 and plenipotentiary to the Congress of Cambrai; see Horn: *British Diplomatic Representatives, 1689-1789,* p. 3. Voluminous papers, but for the period just before that considered in this study.

Historical Register, Containing an Impartial Relation of all Transactions, Foreign and Domestick, The. London, 1717-1738. 23 vols. This publication was compiled primarily for the use of the policyholders of the Sun Fire Assurance Company; it is extraordinarily complete, and did for its time what Burke's *Annual Register* later did.

History and Proceedings of the House of Commons from the Restoration to the Present Time, The. Printed for Richard Chandler; London, 1742-1744. 14 vols. A useful source for the Commons' debates during this period.

Höfler, C. *Der Congress von Soissons, nach den Instructionen des kaiserlichen Cabinetes und den Berichten des kaiserl. Botschafters Stefan Grafen Kinsky.* [*Fontes rerum Austriacarum: Oesterreichische Geschichtsquellen, herausgegeben von der historischen Commission der kaiserlichen Akademie der Wissenschaften in Wien.* Zweite Abtheilung: *Diplomataria et acta,* vols. XXXII, XXXVIII].
    I. *Die Instructionen und Berichte des Jahres 1729 enthaltend.* Vienna, 1871. xlvii, 439 pp.
    II. *Die Instructionen und Berichte der kaiserlichen Botschafter in Paris vom 2. Jänner 1730, bis zum 6. März 1732.* Vienna, 1876. xxviii, 437 pp.

Horn, D. B. *British Diplomatic Representatives, 1689-1789.* London; edited for the Royal Historical Society, Camden Third Series, vol. XLVI (1932). 178 pp.

Innis, H. A. *Select Documents in Canadian Economic History, 1497-1783.* Toronto, 1929. xxxiv, 581 pp.

Isambert, F. A., Decrusy, M., and Jourdan, A. J. L., editors. *Recueil général des anciennes lois françaises.* Paris, 1823(?)-1833. 29 vols. Arranged chronologically; volumes XXI-XXII (*1715-1737; 1737-1744*) are the most useful for the period of this study.

Journal of the Commissioners for Trade and Plantations
    From November 1718 to December 1722. London, 1925. 435 pp.
    From January 1722-3 to December 1728. London, 1928. 481 pp.
    From January 1728-9 to December 1734. London, 1928. 464 pp.

From January 1734-5 to December 1741. London, 1930. 447 pp.
From January 1741-2 to December 1749. London, 1931. 510 pp.

La Chesnaye-Desbois, François Alexandre Aubert de, and Badier, M. *Dictionnaire de la noblesse*. Third edition; Paris, 1863-1876. 19 vols. Gives the genealogies and a chronological account of the noble families of France. Alphabetical arrangement.

Marsden, R. G., editor. *Documents relating to Law and Custom of the Sea*, II (*Publications of the Navy Records Society*, vol. L), London, 1896. xxxiii, 457 pp.

Mémoire sur les négociations entre la France et le Czar de la Grande Russie Pierre I, fait en 1726 par m-r Le-Dran, premier commis des affaires étrangères. See *Sbornik, infra*.

Moreau de Saint-Méry, Médéric Louis Élie. *Loix et constitutions des colonies françoises de l'Amérique sous le Vent*. Paris, 1784-1790. 6 vols. Arranged chronologically.

Neuville, D., editor. *État sommaire des Archives de la Marine antérieures à la Révolution*. Paris, 1898. lxii, 694 pp. Cites some documentary evidence on the expenditures for the French navy during this period.

O'Callaghan, E. B., editor. *Documents relative to the Colonial History of the State of New York*. Albany, 1856-1861. 11 vols. Information concerning the French fur trade during this period may be found in vol. V; see Index.

Preussische Staatsschriften aus der Regierungszeit König Friedrichs II. Berlin, 1877-1892. 3 vols. Volume I (1877; edited by Reinhold Koser. liv, 726 pp.), which deals with this period, 1740-1745, gives an excellent account of the periodical publications in Europe at that time (pp. xxxiii-l); this publication demonstrates how much attention Frederick II paid to influencing public opinion.

Recueil des instructions données aux ambassadeurs et ministres de France depuis les traités de Westphalie jusqu'à la Révolution française. Paris, 1884- . This valuable series is not yet completely published; the volumes for *Angleterre* covering this period have yet to appear, as well as any of the volumes of instructions to French ambassadors to the Porte. Unlike the similar British series now in process of publication, this series undertakes to print only the initial instructions. In some cases, the editors include supplementary correspondence, which is extremely useful. Some of the volumes, in particular those on *Autriche*, *Russie* and *Prusse*, contain extended and very valuable editorial comment; others, such as *Diète germanique* and *Danemark*, have been edited very perfunctorily. Volumes in this series which deal with the years of Fleury's administration are:

I. *Autriche*. Albert Sorel, editor; 1884. 552 pp.

II. *Suède*. Auguste Geffroy, editor; 1885. cii, 517 pp.

III. *Portugal*. Le vicomte de Caix de Saint-Aymour, editor; 1886. lix, 426 pp.

IV, V. *Pologne*. Louis Farges, editor; 1888. lxxxii, 344; 371 pp.

VII. *Bavière, Palatinat, Deux-Ponts*. Andr. Lebon, editor; 1889. xxxv, 616 pp.

VIII. *Russie*, I (*Des origines jusqu'à 1748*). Alfred Rambaud, editor; 1890. lviii, 500 pp.

X. *Naples et Parme*. Joseph Reinach, editor; 1893. clxxxvi, 252 pp.

XII, XII *bis*. *Espagne*. A. Morel-Fatio and H. Léonardon, editors; 1898, 1899. xl, 434; 498 pp.

XIII. *Danemark*. Auguste Geffroy, editor; 1895. lxxii, 240 pp.

XIV. *Savoie-Sardaigne et Mantoue*. Le comte Horric de Beaucaire, editor; 1898. c, 432 pp.

XVI. *Prusse*. Albert Waddington, editor; 1901. ciii, 628 pp.

XVIII. *Diète germanique*. Bertrand Auerbach, editor; 1912. xcviii, 400 pp.

XIX. *Florence, Modène, Gênes*. Édouard Driault, editor; 1912. cvi, 416 pp.

XXII, XXIII. *Hollande*. Louis André and Émile Bourgeois, editors; 1923, 1924. 547; 514 pp.

Registres de l'Académie françoise, 1672-1793, Les. Paris, 1895-1906. 4 vols.

Ruffhead, Owen, and Runnington, Charles. *The Statutes at Large, from Magna Charta, to . . . the Forty-first Year of the Reign of King George the Third.* London, 1786-1800. 14 vols.

Saint-Philippe, Vincent Bacallar y Sanna, marquis de. *Mémoires pour servir à l'histoire d'Espagne sous le règne de Philippe V.* Amsterdam, 1756. 4 vols. These memoirs, written in a most impersonal fashion, contain many useful *pièces justificatives*. The memoirs do not go beyond the year 1725.

Sbornik Imperatorskago Russkago Istoricheskago Obshchestva, [Collection of the Imperial Russian Historical Society]. St. Petersburg, 1867-1916. 148 vols.

V (1870). Contains (pp. 295-479) the reports of Le Fort, Polish-Saxon envoy, to Augustus II and Augustus III from 1727 to 1734.

XL (1884). Contains the French diplomatic correspondence for 1719, 1720 and 1721, and the first part (pp. i-lxxxii) of Le Dran's summary, written in 1726, of French negotiations with Peter the Great.

XLIX (1885). Continues Le Dran's summary (pp. i-lxix) and publishes the French diplomatic correspondence for 1722 and 1723.

LII (1886). Concludes Le Dran's summary (pp. i-xlvi) and publishes the French despatches for the period 1723-1725.

LVIII (1887). Correspondence of Campredon and Morville in the latter part of 1725.

LXIV (1888). Correspondence from October 9, 1725 until June 12, 1727, between Campredon and Magnan in Russia and Morville and Chauvelin at Versailles.

LXXV (1891). French diplomatic correspondence for the years 1727-1730.

LXXXI (1892). Despatches exchanged between Magnan and Chauvelin until the former's departure from Russia in July, 1733; contains the correspondence relative to Münnich's negotiation for a French alliance in 1732.

Shortt, Adam. *Documents Relating to Canadian Currency, Exchange and Finance during the French Period.* Ottawa, 1925-1926. 2 vols.

Statutes at Large, The: see Ruffhead, *supra.*

Turba, Gustav. *Die pragmatische Sanktion. Authentische Texte samt Erlaüterungen und Übersetzungen.* Vienna, 1913. 200 pp.

Villette, Philippe le Valois, marquis de. *Mémoires du marquis de Villette.* L. J. N. Monmerqué, editor; Paris, 1844. lxviii, 362 pp. The introduction contains (pp. lxiii-lxviii) the memorial on the state of the French navy, written in 1724 by the Count of Toulouse.

Whitworth, Charles. *A Collection of the Supplies, and Ways and Means, from the Revolution to the Present Time.* London, 1764. 183 pp.

Wroth, Lawrence C., and Annan, Gertrude L. *Acts of French Royal Administration concerning Canada, Guiana, the West Indies and Louisiana, Prior to 1791.* New York, 1930. 151 pp. Lists titles chronologically.

4. Memoirs, Pamphlets and Miscellaneous Works

Anonymous pamphlets are listed alphabetically under the first word, not an article, of each title. Brackets enclosing a personal name indicate that the work or pamphlet was published anonymously, but was written by the individual named. The authority for such attribution is given by the following abbreviations:

Att. B. M.: Catalogue of the British Museum.

Att. B. P. L.: Catalogue of the Boston Public Library.

Att. D. N. B.: *Dictionary of National Biography* [British].

Att. H. C. L.: Catalogue of the Harvard College Library.

Att. L. C.: Catalogue of the Library of Congress.

The political complexion of British pamphlets during this period is often betrayed by the names of their publishers, although scarcely a pamphlet was printed during this time which did not bear in its title a claim to being impartial. In particular, pamphlets published by J. Roberts were either semi-official or at least sympathetic to the point of view of Walpole's government; some pieces published by him were obviously officially inspired. On the other hand, Richard Francklin was the printer for the *Craftsman* and the Pulteney-Bolingbroke party; the "impartial" pamphlets which issued from his press were very partial indeed.

An Accurate Journal and Account of the Proceedings of the New England Land-Forces, during the late Expedition against the French Settlements on Cape Breton, to the Time of the Surrender of Louisbourg. . . . Dated Louisbourg, Oct. 20, 1745; and in Form attested by Lieut. General Pepperell. . . . With a Computation of the French Fishery . . . as it was carried on before the present War: The Whole of which did then depend, in a great Manner, on the Port of Louisbourg, as a Cover and Protection to it, etc., All sent over by General Pepperell himself, to his Friend Capt. Hen. Stafford, at Exmouth, Devon. Printed by A. and S. Brice; Exon. [Exeter], 1746. 40 pp.

Alembert, Jean Baptiste le Rond d'. *Oeuvres.* J.-F. Bastien, editor; Paris,

1805. 18 vols. Volume XI of this edition contains some of the *éloges* delivered by D'Alembert in his capacity of perpetual secretary of the Academy; the *Éloge de l'abbé de Saint-Pierre* (*loc. cit.*, pp. 101-182) includes a discussion of the part played by Fleury in the expulsion of Saint-Pierre from the Academy.

[Amhurst, Nicholas]. *A Letter to Caleb d'Anvers, Esq.: Occasioned by the Depredations committed by the Spaniards in the West Indies. With some Observations on the Trade carried on from Jamaica to the Spanish Coast.* Printed for H. Whitridge; London, 1729. 32 pp. Att. B. P. L. Anti-ministerial; on this author, see *Dictionary of National Biography, sub nomine.*

[Anderson, Adam]. *An Historical and Chronological Deduction of the Origin of Commerce, from the Earliest Accounts.* Dublin, 1790. 6 vols. A mine of useful information; the author was a clerk at South Sea House for over forty years; see *Dictionary of National Biography, sub nomine.*

Argenson, René Louis de Voyer de Paulmy, marquis d'. *Journal et mémoires du marquis d'Argenson.* E. J. B. Rathery, editor; Paris, 1859-1867. 9 vols. [La Société de l'histoire de France. *Publications*, No. 34]. Volumes I-IV deal with this period. A first-rate source, written by a man who was later Secretary of State for Foreign Affairs. D'Argenson was a chronic grumbler, and allowance needs always to be made on that account in accepting his testimony.

[Ashley, John]. *Some Observations on a Direct Exportation of Sugar, from the British Islands. In a Letter from a Gentleman in Barbados, to his Friend in London.* No printer named; London, 1735. 23 pp. Att. L. C. Ashley was a Barbados planter; his writings are temperate and reliable.

———. *The Sugar Trade, with the Incumbrances thereon, Laid Open.* Printed for J. Peele; London, 1734. 22 pp.

The Assiento Contract Consider'd, as also, the Advantages and Decay of the Trade of Jamaica and the Plantations, with the Causes and Consequences thereof. Printed for Ferd. Burleigh; London, 1714. 50 pp. Argues against the Asiento contract.

Atkins, John. *A Voyage to Guinea, Brasil, and the West-Indies, in His Majesty's Ships, the Swallow and Weymouth; . . . with Remarks on the Gold, Ivory, and Slave-Trade.* Printed for C. Ward and R. Chandler; London, 1735. 265 pp. The voyage occurred in 1722.

[Auchmuty, Robert]. *The Importance of Cape Breton Consider'd; in a Letter to a Member of Parliament from an Inhabitant of New England.* Printed for R. Dodsley; London, 1746. 61 pp. Attribution of authorship made by *The Great Importance of Cape Breton, Demonstrated and Exemplified*, p. 46. For this author, see *Dictionary of American Biography, sub nomine.*

Barbier, Edmond Jean François. *Journal historique et anecdotique du règne de Louis XV.* A. de la Villegille, editor; Paris, 1847-1856. 4 vols. [La Société de l'histoire de France. *Publications*, No. 21]. An extremely valuable and reliable diary, of which vols. I and II were used in the preparation of this study. Barbier was a lawyer, with the typical point of view of a Parisian *bourgeois*. His account of court affairs is well-informed gossip; his knowledge of affairs pertaining to the *Parlement* of Paris is first-hand.

[Baston, Thomas]. *Thoughts on Trade, and a Publick Spirit.* Printed for the author; second edition. London, 1728. 212 pp. Att. L. C.

Beatson, Robert. *Naval and Military Memoirs of Great Britain from 1727 to 1783.* London, 1804. 6 vols. Prints many valuable documents relating to naval affairs.

Beawes, Wyndham. *Lex Mercatoria Rediviva: or, the Merchant's Directory . . . 4th edition, considerably improved, enlarged and altered to render it suitable to the present Time.* Printed for J. Rivington and Sons; London, 1783. 944 pp. This work has been used sparingly, because it is difficult to determine exactly to what date information refers.

Bennet, John. *The National Merchant: or Discourses on Commerce and Colonies; Being an Essay for Regulating and Improving the Trade and Plantations of Great Britain. . . .* Printed for J. Walthoe; London, 1736. 143 pp.

Bernis, François-Joachim de Pierre, cardinal de. *Mémoires et lettres de François-Joachim de Pierre, cardinal de Bernis (1715-1758).* Frédéric Masson, editor; Paris, 1903. 2 vols. Contains some interesting information on the personality of Cardinal Fleury.

[Blois, Théodore de]. *Histoire de Rochefort.* Paris, 1757. 281 pp. Att. H. C. L.; B. M.

[Bolingbroke, Henry St. John, Viscount]. *The Case of Dunkirk Faithfully Stated and Impartially Considered.* Printed for A. Moore; London, 1730. 32 pp. This piece was designed to discomfit the Government by showing that Dunkirk was being restored in spite of treaty stipulations to the contrary. The attribution of authorship is made by Sichel: *Bolingbroke and his Times,* II, pp. 276, 523-524.

[Bollan, William]. *The Importance and Advantage of Cape Breton, Truly Stated and Impartially Considered.* Printed for Paul and John Knapton; London, 1746. 156 pp. Att. L. C.

The British Empire in America, Consider'd. In a Second Letter, from a Gentleman of Barbadoes, to his Friend in London. Printed for J. Wilford; London, 1732. 29 pp. In favour of the Molasses Act; probably written by John Ashley.

The British Sailor's Discovery: Or the Spanish Pretensions confuted. . . . Proving that the Sovereign Sole Dominion claimed by the Crown of Spain to the West Indies, is founded upon an unjustifiable Possession; whilst the Rights and Possessions of the British Subjects in those Parts are both agreeable to the Law of Nations and Principles of Christianity. . . . The Whole concluding with Reflections on their former and late Conduct, and plain Reasons why a Certainty of Peace is not to be relied on from that Nation, any longer than they are kept in Awe by the Maritime Forces of Great-Britain. Printed for T. Cooper; London, 1739. 72 pp. Published after the declaration of war in that year.

Brosses, Charles de. *Lettres familières sur l'Italie.* Yvonne Bezard, editor; Paris, 1931. 2 vols.

Buffon, G. L. Leclerc, comte de. "Mémoire sur la conservation et le rétablissement des forests." *Mémoires de l'Académie royale des sciences pour l'année 1739* (Paris, 1741), pp. 140-156.

――――. "Mémoire sur la culture des forests." *Mémoires de l'Académie royale des sciences pour l'année 1742* (Paris, 1745), pp. 233-246.

――――. "Moyen facile d'augmenter la solidité, la force et la durée du bois." *Mémoires de l'Académie royale des sciences pour l'année 1738* (Paris, 1740), pp. 169-184.

[Burke, Edmund]. *An Account of the European Settlements in America.* Boston, 1835. 335 pp. This work was first published in 1757. Att. D. N. B., as reviser, not author.

Burrish, Onslow. *Batavia Illustrata; Or, a View of the Policy, and Commerce, of the United Provinces: Particularly of Holland. With an Enquiry into the Alliances of the States-General, with the Emperor, France, Spain and Great Britain.* Printed for William Innys; London, 1728. 580 pp. A well-informed work.

Buvat, Jean. *Journal de la Régence (1715-1723).* Émile Campardon, editor; Paris, 1865. 2 vols.

Cantillon, Richard. *Essai sur la nature du commerce en général.* Henry Higgs, editor; London, 1931. 394 pp.

The Case of the Hessian Forces, in the Pay of Great-Britain, Impartially and Freely Examin'd; With some Reflections on the present Conjuncture of Affairs. In Answer to a late Pamphlet, intitled, Considerations on the present State of Affairs, &c. Printed for R. Francklin; London, no date. 36 pp. A clever anti-Ministerial attack. Internal evidence shows it to have been written between November 9, 1729 and March 16, 1731.

Charlevoix, Pierre François Xavier de. *Histoire de l'Isle Espagnole ou de S. Domingue.* Paris, 1730-1731, 2 vols. Books xi and xii deal with this period. The author was a well-informed Jesuit missionary.

Chesterfield, Philip Dormer Stanhope, Fourth Earl of. *The Letters of Philip Dormer Stanhope, Fourth Earl of Chesterfield.* Bonamy Dobrée, editor; London, 1932. 6 vols., paged continuously.

Chesterfield, Philip Dormer Stanhope, Fourth Earl of, and Waller, Edmund. *The Case of the Hanover Forces in the Pay of Great Britain, impartially and freely examined: With some seasonable Reflections on the present Conjuncture of Affairs.* Printed for T. Cooper; London, 1742. 35 pp. Att. D. N. B. Chesterfield made capital throughout his political career of the alleged disadvantages of the Hanoverian connection. Horatio Walpole wrote to Robert Trevor, April 25/May 6, 1743: "The pamphlet of the *Case of the Hanover Forces* made a great noise, and had a bad influence upon the minds of all sorts of people" (Trevor Papers, *Hist. MSS. Comm., Report* XIV, Appendix Part IX, p. 87).

"Chronique du règne de Louis XV, 1742-1743." *Revue retrospective*, First Series, vols. IV, V (Paris, 1834-1835). The compilation of street gossip by a police spy.

Clerk, John. *An Essay on Naval Tactics, Systematical and Historical.* Third edition, Edinburgh, 1827. xlvi, 331 pp.

A Collection of Tracts and Treatises Illustrative of the Natural History, Antiquities, and the Political and Social State of Ireland, at various Periods prior to the Present Century. Dublin, 1860-1861. 2 vols.

A Comparison between the British Sugar Colonies and New England, as they relate to the Interest of Great Britain. With some Observations on the State of the Case of New England. Printed for James Roberts; London, 1732. 43 pp. Very hostile to the northern colonies.

A Computation of the French Fishery, as it was managed before the War in 1744, from the Gut of Canso to Louisburgh, and thence to the North-east Part of Cape Breton. Transmitted by Gov. Shirley in July, 1745. Paper Office, New England, No. 3. N.p., one printed folio page, broadside.

The Conduct of Queen Elizabeth, Towards the Neighbouring Nations; and particularly Spain; Compared with that of James I. In View of the late and present Behaviour of Great Britain. By Palæophilus Anglicanus. Printed for J. Robinson; London, 1729. 62 pp. Rather poorly written; favourable to the measures of Walpole's government.

The Conduct of the Late Administration, with regard to Foreign Affairs from 1722 to 1742, wherein that of the Right Honble the Earl of Orford (late Sir Robert Walpole) is Particularly Vindicated. In a Letter to a certain Right Honourable Gentleman, Member of the present Parliament. Printed for T. Cooper; London, 1742. 80 pp. An able defense, full of commonsense views picturesquely expressed.

The Consequences of Trade, as to the Wealth and Strength of any Nation; of the Woollen Trade in particular, and the great Superiority of it over all other Branches of Trade. The present State of it in England and France, with an Account of our Loss, and their Gains. The Danger we are in of becoming a Province to France, unless an Effectual and Immediate Stop be put to the Exportation of our Wool. By a Draper of London. Fourth edition, printed for T. Cooper. London, 1740. 35 pp.

Considerations on the American Trade, Before and Since the Establishment of the South-Sea Company. Printed for J. Roberts; London, 1739. 31 pp. Argues that the activities of the Company have decreased the British trade to the Spanish colonies.

Considerations on the Bill now depending in Parliament, Concerning the British Sugar-Colonies in America. Wherein all the Arguments for the Support of the said Bill are considered. In a Letter to a Member of Parliament. Printed for J. Peele; London, 1731. 24 pp. Against the West Indian planters, and opposed to the passage of the Molasses Bill.

Considerations on the Present Peace, as far as it is relative to the Colonies, and the African Trade. Printed for W. Bristow; London, 1763. iv, 68 pp. Gives evidence of the French activity in the slave trade.

Considerations on the Present State of Affairs in Europe, and particularly with Regard to the Number of Forces in the Pay of Great-Britain. Printed for J. Roberts; London, 1730. 53 pp. A clever pamphlet, officially inspired.

Courtivron, Marquis de. "Discours sur la nécessité de perfectionner la métallurgie des forges, pour diminuer la consommation des bois." *Mémoires de l'Académie royale des sciences pour l'année 1747* (Paris, 1752), pp. 287-304.

The Craftsman. Collected edition; printed for R. Francklin. London, 1731-1737. 14 vols. The *Craftsman* was the leading Opposition paper; it was edited by Nicholas Amhurst; Pulteney and Bolingbroke supported it and frequently were contributors.

The Craftsman Extraordinary, Wednesday, November 18, 1730. This number was devoted to attempts to alarm the public concerning the French enlistment of Irish soldiers.

Dangeau, Philippe de Courcillon, marquis de. *Journal du marquis de Dangeau.* L. Dussieux and E. Soulié, editors; Paris, 1854-1860. 19 vols. A source for the reign of Louis XIV rather than for that of Louis XV, but contains references to personages dealt with in this study.

The Danverian History of the Affairs of Europe, for the Memorable Year 1731. With the present State of Gibraltar, and an Exact Description of it, and of the Spanish Works before it. Also of Dunkirk, and the late Transactions there. With curious Plans of both those Places. Printed for J. Roberts; London, 1732. 94 pp. A skilful pro-Ministry pamphlet.

[Decker, Sir Matthew]. *An Essay on the Causes of the Decline of the Foreign Trade, Consequently of the Value of the Lands of Britain, and on the Means to restore both.* Second edition; printed for John Brotherton. London, 1750. 183 pp. Decker is mentioned as "the reputed author" of this work by the *Dictionary of National Biography, sub nomine.* This work was begun in 1739.

The Defence of Monsieur Chauvelin, late Keeper of the Seals in France, in Answer to the Accusations brought against him before the King in Relation to his Conduct in the Administration of His Affairs. Printed for J. Roberts; London, 1737. Thought by Fleury to have been inspired, but not written, by Chauvelin; see *Memoirs of . . . . Sir Robert Walpole,* III, p. 481.

A Defence of the Measures of the Present Administration. Being an impartial Answer to what has been objected against it. Printed for J. Peele; London, 1731. 32 pp. Well-informed, but somewhat general.

[Defoe, Daniel]. *A Plan of the English Commerce. Being a Compleat Prospect of the Trade of this Nation, as well the Home Trade as the Foreign. Part I. Containing a View of the present Magnitude of the English Trade. . . . Part II. Containing an Answer to that great and important Question, now depending, Whether our Trade, and Especially our Manufactures, are in a declining Condition, or no? Part III. Containing several Proposals entirely New, for Extending and Improving our Trade.* Printed for C. Rivington; London, 1728. 368 pp. Att. D. N. B. Argues most interestingly that the hard times from which England was suffering at that time were because of over-production.

Dorsanne, Abbé Antoine. *Journal qui contient tout ce qui s'est passé à Rome et en France au sujet de la bulle Unigenitus, depuis 1711 jusqu'en octobre, 1728.* Second edition; Rome, 1753. 2 vols. Trustworthy memoirs, written by an ecclesiastic of Jansenist leanings. Deals only with church affairs.

Douglass, William, [M.D.]. *A Summary, Historical and Political, of the first Planting, progressive Improvements, and present State of the British Set-*

tlements in North America. Boston, 1749, 1753. 2 vols. An excellent work, written in a delightfully crabbed and pungent style.

————. *A Discourse concerning the Currencies of the British Plantations in America.* Boston, 1740. This piece, now become rare, was edited by Charles J. Bullock and published in the *Economic Studies of the American Economic Association,* II (New York, 1897), pp. 265-375.

Duclos, Charles Pineau. *Mémoires secrets sur les règnes de Louis XIV et de Louis XV.* Paris, 1791. 2 vols. Duclos discontinued his account with the year 1726, just after the accession of Fleury to power, and resumed the story with the events of the Diplomatic Revolution in 1756. The earlier account resembles that to be found in the *Mémoires* of Saint-Simon, to a manuscript of which he probably had access. Useful for the period of the Regency and the administration of the Duke of Bourbon. Duclos was royal historiographer of France.

[Dutot, C. de F.]. *Réflexions politiques sur les finances et le commerce.* The Hague, 1738. 2 vols. Principally concerned with defending the "System" of John Law. Att. B. M.

Egmont, John, Viscount Percival, afterwards First Earl of. *Diary of Viscount Percival, afterwards first Earl of Egmont.* [*Historical Manuscripts Commission*]. London, 1920-1923. 3 vols. Full of detailed information about Parliamentary affairs.

Ellis, John. *An Historical Account of Coffee.* Printed for Edward and Charles Dilly; London, 1774. 71 pp.

Encyclopédie méthodique. Paris, 1782-1832. 155 vols. The sections devoted to *Commerce* (vols. LVI-LVIII, 1783-1784) are useful.

English, Thomas. *The Crisis; or, Impartial Judgment upon Publick Affairs.* Second edition; printed for J. Roberts. London, 1731. 24 pp. Sympathetic to the policy of Walpole's Ministry; not very well-informed.

An Essay Presented; or a Method Humbly Proposed, to the Consideration of the Honourable the Members of both Houses of Parliament: by an English Woolen Manufacturer, to Pay the National Debts, without a new Tax, to inlarge Trade in general, by Reviving and Securing for Time to come, the British Woolen Exportation Trade, and preventing the Running of Brandy, Tea, &c., in; And to improve all waste uncultivated Lands, within his Majesty's British Dominions. Printed for J. Robinson; London, 1744. 45 pp.

The Evident Advantages to Great Britain and its Allies from the Approaching War: Especially in Matters of Trade. Printed for J. Roberts; London, 1727. 44 pp. This was published in February 1727; see Chance: *Alliance of Hanover,* p. 616. It is frequently attributed to Daniel Defoe.

Firth, Sir Charles, editor. *Naval Songs and Ballads.* [*Publications of the Navy Records Society,* XXXIII]. London, 1908. cxxiii, 387 pp.

Forman, Charles. *Mr. Forman's Letter to the Right Honourable William Pulteney, Esq.: Shewing how Pernicious, the Imperial Company of Commerce and Navigation, lately established in the Austrian Netherlands, is likely to prove to Great Britain, as well as to Holland.* Printed for S. Bussey; London, 1725. 71 pp.

Frederick II of Prussia. "Considerations on the Present State of the Body-

Politic in Europe." *Posthumous Works of Frederic II. King of Prussia.* (Translated by Thomas Holcroft and printed for G. G. J. and J. Robinson; London, 1789. 13 vols.), IV, pp. 339-386. Interesting for its views on the prestige of Fleury's government; the statements in this fugitive piece, however, must be accepted with great caution. It was written in early 1738, and was intended for publication in anonymous pamphlet form, with the purpose of alarming the Maritime Powers at the growing power of France. Because the relations between Prussia and France suddenly improved, the *Considerations* were not sent to the press, and were published only posthumously. See M. W. Duncker: *Aus der Zeit Friedrichs des Grossen und Friedrich Wilhelms III.* (Leipzig, 1876), pp. 3-46: "Eine Flugschrift des Kronprinzen Friedrich."

————. "The History of my own Times." *Posthumous Works of Frederic II. King of Prussia,* vol. I. The first pages of this work describe the state of Europe in 1740, and frequently repeat the views previously expressed in the *Considerations.* These memoirs are interesting because of their verve and authorship; reasonably reliable in the passages in which Frederick's own conduct is not involved.

Fréret, ————. "Éloge de M. le cardinal de Fleury." *Histoire de l'Académie royale des inscriptions et belles-lettres,* XVI (Paris, 1751), pp. 356-366. The eulogy was pronounced on April 23, 1743.

Gee, Joshua. *The Trade and Navigation of Great-Britain Considered.* Printed for Sam. Buckley; London, 1729. 145 pp. Gee was a die-hard mercantilist, who was convinced that Great Britain was losing her foreign trade. David Hume remarked in his essay *Of the Balance of Trade* that "the writings of Mr. Gee struck the nation with an universal panic."

Gentleman's Magazine. The issues which comprise vol. IX (1739) give one an excellently vivid impression of the war fever in Great Britain during that year.

Gibraltar a Bulwark of Great Britain. In a Letter to a Member of Parliament . . . By a Gentleman of the Navy. Printed for J. Peele; London, 1725. 59 pp.

The Golden Fleece; Or the Trade, Interest, and Well-Being of Great Britain Considered. With Remarks on the Rise, Progress and present Decay of our Woollen Manufactures. Also an Estimate of this Valuable Trade, fairly and clearly stated, and the great Proportion given up Yearly to Foreigners, by Suffering (or Conniving at) the illegal Exportation of British and Irish Wool, and Woollen Goods throughly Manufactured in Ireland, to Foreign Parts. No printer named; n.p., 173-? 26 pp.

[Gordon, Thomas]. *An Appeal to the Unprejudiced, concerning the present Discontents occasioned by the late Convention with Spain.* Printed for T. Cooper; London, 1739. 32 pp. Att. L. C. Pro-Ministerial; very fine argumentation.

[————]. *Considerations Offered upon the Approaching Peace, and upon the Importance of Gibraltar to the British Empire.* Fourth edition; printed for J. Roberts. London, 1720. 31 pp. Att. D. N. B. Inspired by the Townshend-Walpole group of the Whigs.

376 FRENCH FOREIGN POLICY

The Great Importance of Cape Breton, Demonstrated and Exemplified by Extracts from the best Writers, French and English, who have treated of that Colony. Printed for John Brindley; London, 1746. 72 pp.

[Hare, Francis, Bishop of Chichester]. *The Barrier Treaty Vindicated.* Third edition; printed for A. Baldwin. London, 1713. 200 pp. Defends Townshend's Barrier Treaty of 1709; a very superior piece of argument. Included in Hare's works, but probably written by S. Poyntz.

Hénault, Charles Jean François. *Mémoires du président Hénault.* François Rousseau, editor; Paris, 1911. 457 pp. Hénault was an Academician, well connected at the court, and a member of the *coterie* of Queen Maria Leszczinska. Consequently he was very hostile to Fleury; his testimony is mostly first-hand. A reliable source.

[Hervey, John Hervey, Baron]. *A Letter to the Craftsman, on the Game of Chess.* Printed for J. Peele; London, 1733. 29 pp. Att. H. C. L.

[――――]. *Observations on the Writings of the Craftsman.* Printed for J. Roberts; London, 1730. 31 pp. Att. D. N. B.

――――. *Some Materials towards Memoirs of the Reign of King George II by John, Lord Hervey.* Romney Sedgwick, editor; London, 1931. 3 vols., paged continuously. Lord Hervey was a man of great talent, an able pamphleteer and a good speaker. He became Lord Privy Seal in Walpole's Government, as well as being Chamberlain at the court of George II. He was a particular friend of Queen Caroline; his memoirs are extraordinarily informative concerning British policies and backstairs political intrigue from about 1730 to the death of Queen Caroline in 1737.

Histoire générale de la marine. Paris, 1744-1748. 3 vols. Volume I deals with ancient and mediaeval naval history; volume II carries the naval history of France to the year 1690 and that of some of the other European countries to the date of publication. Volume III continues the history of the French navy to the year 1715 and also contains a collection of edicts with reference to the French navy for the period from 1647 to 1689.

[Hoadly, Benjamin, Bishop of Salisbury]. *A Defence of the Enquiry into the Reasons of the Conduct of Great Britain, &c., Occasioned by the Paper published in the Country-Journal or Craftsman on Saturday, Jan. 4, 1728/9. By the Author of the "Enquiry."* Printed for J. Roberts; London, 1729. 40 pp. Att. H. C. L.

[――――]. *An Enquiry into the Reasons of the Conduct of Great Britain, with Relation to the Present State of Affairs in Europe.* Printed for James Roberts; London, 1727. 112 pp. Att. H. C. L. Pro-Ministerial; one of the very important political pamphlets of the period. It was published just before the Parliamentary session, on January 10, 1727; see Chance: *Alliance of Hanover,* p. 616.

Houstoun, James. *Memoirs of the Life and Travels of James Houstoun, M.D., (Formerly Physician and Surgeon-General to the Royal African Company's Settlements in Africa, and late Surgeon to the Royal Assiento Company's Factories in America).* Sold by J. Robinson; London, 1747. 435 pp.

―――. *Some New and Accurate Observations, Geographical, Natural and Historical, Containing a true and impartial Account of the Situation, Product, and Natural History of the Coast of Guinea, so far as relates to the Improvement of that Trade, for the Advantage of Great Britain in general, and the Royal African Company in particular.* Printed for J. Peele; London, 1725. 62 pp.

The Importance of the British Plantations in America to this Kingdom; with the State of their Trade and Methods for improving it; as also a Description of the Several Colonies there. Printed for J. Peele; London, 1731. 114 pp. An extremely well-informed pamphlet.

The Importance of the Ostend-Company Consider'd. Printed for J. Roberts; London, 1726. 55 pp. Hostile to the Ostend Company.

The Importance of the Sugar Colonies to Great-Britain Stated, and some Objections against the Sugar Colony Bill answer'd. Printed for J. Roberts; London, 1731. 40 pp.

An Inquiry into the Revenue, Credit and Commerce of France. Second edition, printed for J. Roberts. London, 1742. 64 pp. Designed to enhearten the British at the prospect of a war with France by underestimating French financial and naval resources. What it says is useful as "reluctant testimony."

The Interest of England Consider'd with Respect to the Woollen Manufactures; or, Remarks on a late Pamphlet Intitled, Some Thoughts on the Woollen Manufactures of England. Printed for T. Cox; London, 1731. 24 pp.

Janiçon, François-Michel. *État présent de la République des Provinces-Unies, et des païs qui en dépendent.* The Hague, 1729-1730. 2 vols. An extremely factual and detailed work; Janiçon was a political agent of the Landgrave of Hesse-Cassel.

[Kennedy, Archibald]. *Serious Considerations on the Present State of the Affairs of the Northern Colonies.* Printed for the author; New York, 1754. 24 pp. Att. B. P. L.

Ker, John. *The Memoirs of John Ker, of Kersland, in North Britain, Esq.; Relating to Politicks, Trade, and History. . . . Containing his secret Transactions and Negotiations in Scotland, England, the Courts of Vienna, Hanover and other Foreign Parts. With an Account of the Rise and Progress of the Ostend Company in the Austrian Netherlands.* Printed for the author; London, 1726. 2 vols. A busybody; see *sub nomine, Dictionary of National Biography.*

King, Lord. "Notes of Domestic and Foreign Affairs, during the last Years of the Reign of George I and the early Part of the Reign of George II." These notes (132 pp., separate pagination) are published as a sort of appendix to vol. II of Lord King's *Life of John Locke* (London, 1830. 2 vols.). King was Lord Chancellor; his fragmentary notes give as excellent a view of the inner workings of the British Cabinet as do Villar's *Mémoires* for the French Council of State.

The King of France's Declaration of War against Spain, Dated January 9, N.S., With a Manifesto, containing the Reasons; and a Postscript of an Intercepted Letter from Cardinal Alberoni to the Prince de Cellamare.

Printed by His Majesty's Order at Paris. Printed for A. Bell and J. Osborn; London, 1719. 43 pp.

Lassay, Armand-Léon de Madaillan de Lesparre, marquis de. *Recueil de différentes choses.* Lausanne, 1756. 4 vols. Useful for the "Mémoire sur l'état de la France depuis la mort de Louis XIV jusqu'en 1726" (vol. IV, pp. 101-128), which gives information and judgments on the Duke of Bourbon and Fleury.

Lediard, Thomas. *The Naval History of England in all its Branches, from the Norman Conquest in the Year 1066 to the Conclusion of 1734.* London, 1735. 2 vols.

Lemau de la Jaisse, ———. *Carte générale de la monarchie françoise.* Paris, 1733. 20 pp. Enumerates the French army, by regiments and arms.

Lettres et négociations de Monsieur van Hoey, ambassadeur à la cour de France. Pour servir à l'histoire de la vie du cardinal de Fleury. Chez John Nourse; London, 1743. 168 pp. Abraham van Hoey, a notorious Francophil, was Dutch ambassador to France from 1727 to 1746. These letters are the despatches sent by Hoey to the States-General for the years 1741-1743; they are very interesting, although they contribute little to the history of the life of Cardinal Fleury, as they purport. Their publication caused a sensation, and constituted an example of how difficult it was to keep state papers secret in the United Provinces at that time; see *Preussische Staatsschriften aus der Regierungszeit König Friedrichs II.*, I, pp. xxxviii, 353.

Little, Otis. *The State of Trade in the Northern Colonies Considered; With an Account of their Produce, and a particular Description of Nova Scotia.* Printed by G. Woodfall; London, 1748. 84 pp.

Luynes, Charles-Philippe d'Albert, duc de. *Mémoires du duc de Luynes sur la cour de Louis XV (1735-1758).* L. Dussieux and E. Soulié, editors; Paris, 1860-1865. 17 vols. Especially vols. I-III. Luynes was a member of the Queen's *coterie.* His memoirs are made up of detailed information of the day by day occurrences of the court, set down with a surprising freedom from generalization or *parti pris.*

[Lyttelton, George]. *Considerations upon the present State of our Affairs, at Home and Abroad, In a Letter to a Member of Parliament from a Friend in the Country.* Printed for T. Cooper; London, 1739. 67 pp. An Opposition pamphlet. Lyttelton was one of the "Young Patriots." Att. B. M.

———. *The Works of George Lord Lyttelton.* George Edward Ayscough, editor; third edition. London, 1776. 3 vols. Lyttelton was one of the secretaries of Stephen Poyntz at the Congress of Soissons. Vol. III contains some interesting letters from Lyttelton to his father.

Macpherson, David. *Annals of Commerce, Manufactures, Fisheries and Navigation, with brief Notices of the Arts and Sciences connected with them.* London, 1805. 4 vols. Vol. III, pp. 1-326, concerns this period. This work is arranged chronologically, and is an avowed reproduction of Adam Anderson's *Historical and Chronological Deduction of the Origin of Commerce,* for the period prior to 1762.

Mairan, ——. "Éloge de M. le cardinal de Fleury." *Histoire de l'Académie royale des sciences pour l'année 1743* (Paris, 1746), pp. 175-184.

Marais, Mathieu. *Journal et mémoires de Mathieu Marais, avocat au Parlement de Paris, sur la Régence et le règne de Louis XV (1715-1737)*. M. de Lescure, editor; Paris, 1863-1868. 4 vols. Marais belonged to a slightly higher stratum of society than did Barbier. Like the latter, his diary is that of an intelligent man who reproduces the *on-dits* of court gossip but is authoritative on Parlementary affairs. Covers only the early part of Fleury's administration.

[Marchmont, Hugh Hume, Third Earl of]. *A Serious Exhortation to the Electors of Great Britain, Wherein the Importance of the approaching Elections is particularly proved from our Present Situation both at Home and Abroad*. Printed for T. Cooper; London, 1740. 50 pp. Marchmont, who as Lord Polwarth had been a leader of the "Patriot" opposition in the House of Commons before he succeeded to his title in 1740, was a very skilful speaker and pamphleteer. Att. L. C.

[——]. *A State of the Rise and Progress of our Disputes with Spain, and of the Conduct of our Ministers relating thereto*. Printed for T. Cooper; London, 1739. 76 pp. Att. L. C. The best presentation of the facts from the "Patriot" point of view.

Massuet, Pierre. *Histoire de la guerre présente; contenant tout ce qui s'est passé de plus important en Italie, sur le Rhin, en Pologne, & dans la plupart des cours de l'Europe*. Amsterdam, 1735. xxvi, 447 pp. A detailed chronicle of events, which also publishes some relevant State Papers. Contains practically nothing concerning the diplomacy of the war.

——. *Histoire de la dernière guerre et des négociations pour la paix. . . . Avec la vie du prince Eugène de Savoye*. Amsterdam, 1736. Two parts in three vols. This work concludes with the Convention of April 11, 1736. It contains an account of the public events of the war and publishes the relevant papers concerning the attempted mediation of the Maritime Powers, but gives no inkling, of course, of the secret springs of European policy of the time.

Maurepas, Jean Frédéric Phelippeaux, comte de. *Mémoires du comte de Maurepas*. J. L. G. Soulavie, editor; second edition. Paris, 1792. 4 vols. Soulavie had access to the authentic Maurepas papers, and it is probable that the papers of an official complexion printed in this collection are trustworthy. On the whole, the editor's use of these papers was most unscrupulous and unreliable; M. de Boislisle, in discussing these pretended memoirs, remarks: "tout y est de seconde main et fort douteux, sauf quelques pièces sans importance soustraites aux archives administratives du ministre" (*Mémoires authentiques du maréchal de Richelieu*, p. xxviii, note). This study cites from this compilation the *État des affaires du département de la marine sous M. le comte de Maurepas en 1730: Compte que ce ministre a rendu dans le conseil royal du commerce, tenu le 3 octobre, 1730, de la situation du commerce extérieur du royaume, et de la marine de la France* (vol. III, pp. 95-119).

McCulloch, J. R. *A Select Collection of Scarce and Valuable Tracts on Commerce.* London, 1859. xvi, 623 pp. Contains (pp. 426-480) the *Proposals Made by his late Highness the Prince of Orange (v. infra,* p. 382). [Melon, Jean François]. *Essai politique sur le commerce.* N.p., 1736. 399 pp. Att. B. M.

———. *A Political Essay upon Commerce.* Translated by David Bindon; printed for Philip Crampton, Dublin, 1738. xxxii, 352 pp. Att. B. M.

Memoirs of the Duke de Ripperda. Printed for John Stagg and Daniel Browne; London, 1740. xv, 344 pp. A wretched piece of hack-work.

Memoirs of the Life and Administration of the late Andrew-Hercules de Fleury, ... in which are likewise contain'd some remarkable Circumstances relating to the Fall of M. Chauvelin, Keeper of the Seals; and the Rise of Cardinal Tencin, by an Impartial Hand. Printed for J. Roberts; London, 1743. 101 pp. An extremely well-informed work, rather hostile in tone. Perhaps it was written by Horatio Walpole; see Vaucher: *Robert Walpole et la politique de Fleury,* p. 198.

A Miscellaneous Essay concerning the Courses pursued by Great Britain in the Affairs of her Colonies: With some Observations on the Great Importance of our Settlements in America, and the Trade thereof. Printed for R. Baldwin; London, 1755. 134 pp.

Montagu, Lady Mary Wortley. *The Letters and Works of Lady Mary Wortley Montagu.* W. Moy Thomas, editor; third edition. London, 1861. 2 vols. Gives a striking comparison of the state of France during the Regency and in 1739 (II, pp. 42-43).

Montgon, Charles Alexandre de. *Mémoires de Monsieur l'abbé de Montgon, publiez par lui-même. Contenant les différentes négociations dont il a été chargé dans les cours de France, d'Espagne, & de Portugal; & divers événemens qui sont arrivés depuis l'année 1725 jusques à présent . . . .* Lausanne, 1748-1753. 8 vols. Montgon was sent secretly to Paris in 1727 by Philip V for the purpose of securing French support for Philip V in case that Louis XV should die.

[Mouffle d'Angerville]. *Vie privée de Louis XV; ou principaux événemens, particularités et anecdotes de son règne.* London, 1781. 4 vols. The attribution of authorship is made by *La grande encyclopédie, vide sub nomine.* Well-informed court gossip.

National Prejudice, Opposed to the National Interest, Candidly Considered in the Detention or Yielding up Gibraltar and Cape-Briton by the Ensuing Treaty of Peace: With some Observations on the Natural Jealousy of the Spanish Nation, and how far it may Operate to the Prejudice of the British Commerce if not removed at this Crisis. Printed for W. Owen and J. Swan; London, 1748. 50 pp.

The Natural Probability of a Lasting Peace in Europe; Shewn from the Circumstances of the Great Powers, as they are now situated; Compared with the State of Affairs when the Treaties of Ryswick and Utrecht were severally concluded. Printed for J. Peele; London, 1732. 22 pp.

Nény, Patrice-François, comte de. *Mémoires historiques et politiques sur les Pays-Bas autrichiens.* Paris, 1784. 2 vols. Originally written for the instruction of the children of Maria Theresa and Francis I.

Observations on the Conduct of Great-Britain, with Regard to the Negociations and other Transactions Abroad. Printed for J. Roberts; London, 1729. 61 pp. A very skilful pamphlet; pro-Ministerial.

The Observations on the Treaty of Seville Examined. Printed for R. Francklin; London, 1730. 34 pp. Anti-Ministry.

[O'Héguerty, Pierre d'André]. *Essai sur les intérets du commerce maritime.* The Hague, 1754. 258 pp. Att. L. C.

[———]. *Remarques sur plusieurs branches de commerce et de navigation.* N.p., 1757. Two parts, pp. 206, 168. Att. H. C. L.

Perrin, William. *The Present State of the British and French Sugar Colonies, and our own Northern Colonies, considered. Together with some Remarks on the Decay of Our Trade, and the Improvements made of late Years by the French in Theirs.* Printed for T. Cooper; London, 1740. 63 pp.

Philips, Erasmus. *The State of the Nation, in Respect to her Commerce, Debts, and Money.* Second edition, printed for J. Woodman and D. Lyon. London, 1726. 114 pp.

The Political State of Great Britain. Edited by Abel Boyer; London, 1711-1740. 60 vols.

Poncet de la Grave, Guillaume. *Précis historique de la marine royale de France.* Paris, 1780. 2 vols.

Popular Prejudices against the Convention and Treaty with Spain, Examin'd and Answer'd. With Remarks on a Pamphlet, Entitled, Considerations upon the Present State of our Affairs at Home and Abroad. Printed for T. Cooper; London, 1739. 30 pp.

Postlethwayt, Malachy. *The African Trade, the Great Pillar and Support of the British Plantation Trade in America: Shewing, that our Loss, by being beat out of all the Foreign Markets for Sugar and Indigo by the French, has been owing to the Neglect of our African Trade. . . .* Printed for J. Robinson; London, 1745. 44 pp.

———. *Great Britain's True System.* Printed for A. Millar; London, 1757. cl, 363 pp. This is a sort of introduction to Postlethwayt's translation and adaptation of Savary des Bruslon's commercial dictionary.

———. *A Short State of the Progress of the French Trade and Navigation: Wherein is shewn, the great Foundation that France has laid, by dint of Commerce, to increase her maritime Strength to a Pitch equal, if not superior, to that of Great Britain, unless somehow checked by the Wisdom of His Majesty's Councils.* Printed for J. Knapton; London, 1756. 86 pp.

———. *The Universal Dictionary of Trade and Commerce, Translated from the French of the Celebrated Monsieur Savary . . . . with large Additions and Improvements incorporated throughout the whole Work. . . .* Second edition, printed for John Knapton. London, 1757. 2 vols.

The Present State of the British Sugar Colonies Consider'd; In a Letter from a Gentleman of Barbadoes to his Friend in London. No printer named; London, 1731. 28 pp.

The Present State of the Revenues and Forces, by Sea and Land, of France and Spain. Compar'd with Those of Great Britain, Being an Essay to demonstrate the Disadvantages under which France must enter into the present

War, if the natural Force of Britain is vigorously exerted. Printed for Tho. Cooper; London, 1740. 62 pp. Almost identical with *The Land Forces of France—June 1738;* see below, under Richmond, Admiral Sir Herbert W.

The Pretensions of Don Carlos Considered: With a View to the Treaty of Seville, and the Nature of Feudal Tenures. Printed for J. Roberts; London, 1730. 31 pp. Argues juridically that the British Government was justified in undertaking to assist Don Carlos in Italy. Very able and very dull.

[Prior, ——]. *A List of the Absentees of Ireland, and the Yearly Value of their Estates and Incomes spent abroad. With Observations on the Present Trade and Condition of that Kingdom.* Second edition, printed for R. Gunne. Dublin, 1729. Reprinted in *A Collection of Tracts and Treatises Illustrative of . . . . the Political and Social State of Ireland,* II, pp. 225-304.

A Proposal for Humbling Spain. Written in 1711 by a Person of Distinction. And now first printed from the Manuscript. To which are added, Some Considerations on the Means of Indemnifying Great Britain from the Expences of the Present War. Printed for J. Roberts; London, 1739. 72 pp. The proposal, originated by one John Pullen, was to capture Buenos Aires.

Proposals made by His late Highness the Prince of Orange, to their High Mightinesses the States General . . . . for Redressing and Amending the Trade of the Republick. Printed for H. Kent; London, 1751. Reprinted by McCulloch: *A Select Collection of Scarce and Valuable Tracts on Commerce,* pp. 426-480.

[Pulteney, William, Earl of Bath]. *The Politicks on Both Sides with Regard to Foreign Affairs, stated from their own Writings, and examined by the Course of Events, with some Observations on the Present State of Affairs in Great Britain, and the Effects of our Negotiations, for several Years past.* Printed for R. Francklin; London, 1734. 75 pp. Att. H. C. L.

[——]. *A Short View of the State of Affairs, with Relation to Great Britain, for four Years past; with some Remarks on the Treaty lately Published and a Pamphlet intitled, Observations upon it.* Printed for R. Francklin; London, 1730. 36 pp. Att. H. C. L.

[——]. *A Review of all that hath pass'd between the Courts of Great Britain and Spain, Relating to Our Trade and Navigation from the Year 1721, to the Present Convention; with some Particular Observations upon it.* Printed for H. Goreham; London, 1739. Att. B. P. L. and H. C. L.

Raunié, Émile. *Chansonnier historique du XVIIIe siècle.* Paris, 1879-1884. 10 vols.

Raynal, Guillaume Thomas François. *A Philosophical and Political History of the Settlements and Trade of the Europeans in the East and West Indies.* Second edition, printed for T. Cadell. London, 1776. 5 vols. Translated by J. Justamond.

Réaumur, René Antoine Ferchault de. "Réflexions sur l'état des bois du royaume; et sur les précautions qu'on pourroit prendre pour en empêcher le dépérissement, & les mettre en valeur." *Mémoires de l'Aca-*

démie royale des sciences pour l'année 1721 (Paris, 1723), pp. 284-301.
Remarks upon Mr. Webber's Scheme and the Draper's Pamphlet. Printed for J. Roberts; London, 1741. 40 pp. Another pamphlet concerned with the problem of "owling."

A Reply to a Pamphlet intitled, Popular Prejudices against the Convention and Treaty with Spain, Examin'd and Answered. Printed for T. Cooper; London, 1739. 31 pp.

Richelieu, Armand Jean du Plessis, le cardinal, duc de. *Mémoires du cardinal de Richelieu.* Count Horric de Beaucaire and Fr. Bruel, editors; Paris, 1907-1929. 9 vols. [La Société de l'histoire de France. *Publications*, No. 104]. Cited for his harangue as representative of the First Estate, February 23, 1615 (vol. I, pp. 340-365).

Richelieu, Louis François Armand du Plessis, le maréchal, duc de. *Mémoires authentiques du maréchal de Richelieu (1725-1757).* A. de Boislisle, editor; Paris, 1918. [La Société de l'histoire de France. *Publications*, No. 120]. xcvi, 260 pp.

Richmond, Admiral Sir Herbert W., editor. "The Land Forces of France—June 1738." *The Naval Miscellany*, vol. III, [*Publications of the Navy Records Society*, LXIII], (London, 1928), pp. 51-84. This document was discovered in vol. 200 of the *Miscellaneous State Papers* in the Public Record Office; *The Present State of the Revenues and Forces, by Sea and Land, of France and Spain* (see above, p. 381) is very similar.

Robe, Thomas. *Ways and Means to Man the Navy with not less than Fifteen Thousand able Sailors, upon any Emergency with less Expence to the Government; and no wise Inconvenient to the Merchants, Traders, &c.* Third edition; London, 1740. 30 pp.

[Robins, Benjamin]. *An Address to the Electors, and other free Subjects of Great Britain; occasion'd by the late Secession.* Printed for H. Goreham; London, 1739. 63 pp. Att. D. N. B. An attack upon the Convention and an apology for the secession.

[———]. *Observations on the Present Convention with Spain.* Printed for T. Cooper; London, 1739. 60 pp. Att. D. N. B. Against the Convention of 1739.

Rose, Sir George Henry. *A Selection from the Papers of the Earls of Marchmont in the Possession of the Right Honble Sir George Henry Rose, Illustrative of Events from 1685 to 1750.* London, 1831. 3 vols.

Saint-Pierre, Charles Irenée Castel, l'abbé de. *Annales politiques (1658-1740).* Joseph Drouet, editor; Paris, 1912. xxxvi, 399 pp.

———. *Annales politiques de feu Monsieur Charles Irenée Castel, abbé de St. Pierre, de l'Académie françoise.* Geneva, 1767. 2 vols. This edition contains (pp. vii-xvi) the speech delivered by Fleury demanding the expulsion of Saint-Pierre from the French Academy.

———. *A Discourse of the Danger of Governing by One Minister. In which is demonstrated, that the most advantageous Administration, both for the King and the People, consists in an Establishment of Many Councils; or, a Poly synody.* Printed for T. Warner; London, 1728. xvi, 140 pp.

———. *Les rêves d'un homme de bien, qui peuvent être réalisés; ou les vues utiles et pratiquables de M. l'abbé de Saint-Pierre, choisies dans ce grand nombre de projets singuliers, dont le bien public étoit le principe.* Paris, 1775. 502 pp.

Saint-Simon, Louis de Rouvroy, duc de. *Mémoires de Saint-Simon.* A. de Boislisle, editor; Paris, 1879-1928. 41 vols. It is necessary to rely on the index in consulting these famous memoirs, because Saint-Simon had no regard for strict chronological treatment. He was harsh in his judgment of Fleury, for reasons ascribable chiefly to snobbishness.

Seasonable Observations on the Present Fatal Declension of the General Commerce of England. In which the Genuine Cause of the Decay of our Woollen Manufactures is Particularly Considered, and Plain and Parcticable [sic] Methods are Proposed for Retrieving the National Trade before it be past Recovery. Printed for J. Huggonson; London, 1737. Another pamphlet concerned with the prevalence of wool "owling."

A Series of Wisdom and Policy, Manifested in a Review of our Foreign Negotiations and Transactions for several Years past. Being a complete Answer to Politicks on both Sides, with Regard to Foreign Affairs. Printed for J. Roberts; London, 1735. 73 pp.

A Short Account of the Late Application to Parliament Made by the Merchants of London upon the Neglect of their Trade: With the Substance of the Evidence thereupon as sum'd up by Mr. Glover. Fourth edition, printed by A. Reilly. Dublin, 1742. 47 pp. Gives evidence concerning the severe British losses from privateers.

A Short Essay upon Trade in general, but more Enlarged on that Branch relating to the Woollen Manufactures of Great Britain and Ireland; wherein is detected the scandalous Exaggerations and Calculations of Mess. Webber, London, and the Draper; and Also a Method propos'd to prevent the Owling of unmanufactur'd Wool, by a Publick Registry, at such Expence, that the Crown may not suffer, or the Grower of Wool be oppress'd. Humbly address'd to the Lords Commissioners of Trade and Plantations, by a Lover of his Country, and the Constitution of Great-Britain. Printed for J. Huggonson; London, 1741. 69 pp.

Sinclair, John. *Thoughts on the Naval Strength of the British Empire.* Printed for T. Cadell; London, 1782. 58 pp.

Smith, Adam. *The Wealth of Nations.* Eighth edition; London, 1796. 3 vols.

Some Considerations humbly offer'd upon the Bill now depending in the House of Lords, relating to the Trade between the Northern Colonies and the Sugar-Islands, in a Letter to a Noble Peer. No printer named; n.p., 1732. 19 pp. Against the point of view of the West Indian sugar planters.

Some Considerations on the National Debts, the Sinking Fund, and the State of Publick Credit. Printed for R. Francklin; London, 1729. 99 pp. Anti-administration.

Some Farther Remarks on a late Pamphlet, intitled, Observations on the Conduct of Great Britain; particularly with Relation to the Spanish Depredations and Letters of Reprisal. . . . Printed for R. Francklin; London, 1729. 38 pp. An early attempt to distress the Ministry by exploiting the Spanish "depredations."

Some Observations on the Assiento Trade, As it has been exercised by the

South-Sea Company; Proving the Damage, which will accrue thereby to the British Commerce and Plantations in America, and Particularly to Jamaica. Printed for H. Whitridge; London, 1728. 38 pp.

Some Observations on the Present State of Affairs, in a Letter to a Member of the House of Commons. By a Member of Parliament. Printed for J. Roberts; London, 1731. 34 pp. A defense of the policy of the Ministry.

Some Thoughts on the Woollen Manufactures of England. Printed for J. Roberts; London, 1731. 19 pp.

Spanish Insolence Corrected by English Bravery; being, an Historical Account of the many Signal Naval Atchievements Obtained by the English over the Spaniards from the Year 1350 to the present Time. . . . By Captain Jinkins. Second edition, printed for R. Thomas. London, 1739. 116 pages. A piece of hack-work; that it found a market indicates to what a pitch the British war fever must have risen.

The Squire and the Cardinal: An Excellent New Ballad. Printed for A. Moore; London, 1730. 5 pp. Doggerel which ridicules Horatio Walpole's boasted influence over Fleury.

The State of the Nation Consider'd, in a Letter to a Member of Parliament. Third edition, printed for W. Webb. London, 1748. 58 pp. Opposed to a conclusion of the war; very critical of the manner in which it had been conducted.

The State of the Nation, with a General Balance of the Publick Accounts. Second edition, printed for M. Cooper. London, 1748. 55 pp. Very hostile to the Peace of Aix-la-Chapelle; likewise contemptuous of the way in which the British ministers had carried on the war.

Steele, Sir Richard. *The Importance of Dunkirk Consider'd.* Printed for A. Baldwin; London, 1713. 63 pp.

Strenuous Motives for an Immediate War against Spain. With a Short Account of the vigorous War made by King Edward I for the Depredations upon his Subjects. Printed for G. Spavan; London, 1738. 35 pp. General and diffuse.

Swift, Jonathan. "The Conduct of the Allies; and of the late Ministry, in beginning and carrying on the present War." *The Works of Jonathan Swift* (Second edition; Edinburgh, 1824. 19 vols.), vol. IV, pp. 300-381.

Sympson, Anthony. *A Short, Easy and Effectual Method to prevent the Running of Wool, &c. from Great-Britain and Ireland to Foreign Parts; humbly submitted to the Consideration of Parliament.* Printed for the author; London, 1741. viii, 15 pp.

Torcy, Jean-Baptiste Colbert, marquis de. *Memoirs of the Marquis of Torcy, Secretary of State to Lewis XIV. Containing the History of the Negotiations from the Treaty of Ryswic to the Peace of Utrecht.* Printed for P. Vaillant; London, 1757. 2 vols.

Toussaint, François-Vincent. *Anecdotes curieuses de la cour de France sous le règne de Louis XV.* Paul Fould, editor; Paris, 1908. cxxxi, 351 pp. Admirably edited; itself a reliable court chronicle.

The Treaty of Seville, and the Measures that have been taken for the Four Last Years, Impartially Considered. Printed for J. Roberts; London, 1730. 32 pp. Pro-Ministerial.

A True State of the Case between the British Northern-Colonies and the Sugar Islands in America, Impartially Considered. No printer named; London, dated April 5, 1732. 46 pp. Opposed to the passage of the Molasses Act.

Two Letters, Concerning some farther Advantages and Improvements that may seem necessary to be made on the taking and keeping of Cape Breton, Humbly offer'd to Public Consideration. No printer named; London, 1746. 12 pp. This anonymous author was extremely alarmed about the growth of French trade.

Ulloa, Don Bernardo de. *Rétablissement des manufactures et du commerce d'Espagne.* Amsterdam, 1753. Two parts, 139, 235 pp. This work and that by Uztariz, cited in the next entry, give abundant evidence of how highly the eighteenth century was impressed with the value of trade; for these works, written for a public which had long been prone to regard gold and silver mines as the only source of real wealth, systematically endeavoured to demonstrate that manufactures and an increased domestic and foreign trade were the sole means of restoring Spain to economic health. This work was originally published in 1740.

Uztariz, Jerónimo. *The Theory and Practice of Commerce and Maritime Affairs.* Printed for John and James Rivington; London, 1751. 2 vols. This work was first published in 1724, but was suppressed at that time. It was republished in 1742.

Vauban, Maréchal Sebastien Le Prestre de. *Projet d'une dixme royale.* N.p., 1707. 268 pp.

Veitia Linaje, José de. *The Spanish Rule of Trade to the West-Indies: . . . . Written in Spanish by D. Joseph de Veitia Linage, Knight of the Order of Santiago, and Treasurer and Commissioner of the India House. Made English by Capt. John Stevens.* Printed for Samuel Crouch; London, 1702. 367 pp. The original Spanish edition was printed in 1671. A mine of authoritative information.

A View of the Depredations and Ravages Committed by the Spaniards on the British Trade and Navigation, Most humbly offered to the Consideration of the Parliament of Great Britain. Printed for W. Hinchcliffe; London, 1731. 44, ix pp.

Villars, Claude Louis Hector, le maréchal, duc de. *Mémoires du maréchal de Villars.* Charles Pierre Melchior, le marquis de Vogüé, editor; Paris, 1884-1904. 6 vols. [La Société de l'histoire de France. *Publications,* No. 72]. Vols. IV-VI are of particular importance for this period. From 1725 to 1733, when Villars left for Italy to take command of the French army, he was a member of the French Council of State; consequently his journal gives an opportunity for discovering what were the subjects of discussion there. His judgments were superficial and his journal entries betray a rather childish conceit and sense of self-importance; moreover, his journal shows most strikingly how many of the real aims of the policy of Fleury and Chauvelin were never presented for discussion to the Council at all. Nevertheless, this is a first-rate source.

Voltaire, François Marie Arouet. "Observations sur MM. Jean Lass, Melon et Dutot; sur le commerce, le luxe, les monnaies et les impôts." *Oeuvres de Voltaire*, [A. J. Q. Beuchot, editor; Paris, 1826-1840. 72 vols.], XXXVII, pp. 527-544.

————. *Précis du siècle de Louis XV*. Various editions: caps. iii, xxxv.

————. *Correspondance*, II (*1736-1738*), and III (*1738-1740*). (*Oeuvres complètes de Voltaire* [Paris, 1883-1885. 52 vols.], XXXIV, XXXV). This edition contains the complete exchange of letters between Voltaire and Frederick of Prussia; vol. II includes the letters exchanged while Frederick was still Crown Prince, and a few exchanged after his accession to the throne.

[Walpole, Horatio]. *The Convention Vindicated from the Misrepresentations of the Enemies of our Peace*. Printed for J. Roberts; London, 1739. 29 pp. Att. L. C.

[————]. *The Grand Question, whether War, or no War, with Spain, Impartially Consider'd: In Defence of the present Measures against those that delight in War*. Printed for J. Roberts; London, 1739. 32 pp. Att. B. P. L.

[————]. *A Letter to the Craftsmen, upon the Change of Affairs in Europe by the War that is begun against the Emperour*. Printed for J. Roberts; London, 1734. 64 pp. Attribution of authorship made by Vaucher: *Robert Walpole et la politique de Fleury*, p. 81.

[Walpole, Sir Robert]. *Observations upon the Treaty between the Crowns of Great-Britain, France, and Spain, Concluded at Seville on the Ninth of November, 1729, N.S.*, Printed for J. Roberts; London, 1729. 29 pp. Att. H. C. L.; also by Vaucher: *Robert Walpole et la politique de Fleury*, p. 32.

Webber, Samuel. *An Account of a Scheme for Preventing the Exportation of our Wool*. Printed for T. Cooper; London, 1740. 37 pp.

————. *A Short Account of the State of our Woollen Manufacturies, from the Peace of Ryswick to This Time, Shewing, their Former Flourishing, and their Present Ruinous Condition; and that they always flourished when France could not get our Wool, but declined in Proportion to the Quantities of Wool Exported to Them*. Second edition, printed for T. Cooper. London, 1741. 26 pp.

What's to be Expected from a New Parliament: Or, a Seasonable Application to the Publick; Previous to the Meeting of the Parliament. By a Friend to the People. Printed for T. Wait; London, 1735. 16 pp. Likewise by a friend to Walpole's government.

The Wisdom and Policy of the French in the Construction of their Great Offices, so as best to answer the Purposes of extending their Trade and Commerce, and enlarging their Foreign Settlements. With some Observations in relation to the Disputes now subsisting between the English and French Colonies in America. Printed for R. Baldwin; London, 1755. 133 pp. The author of this pamphlet was alarmed about the increase of French trade, which he attributed largely to the French Chambers of Commerce and central *bureau de commerce*.

[Yonge, Sir William]. *Sedition and Defamation Display'd; in a Letter to the Author of the Craftsman*. Printed by J. Roberts; London, 1731. 48, viii pp. A fierce attack upon Pulteney, Bolingbroke and the group whom they led. This pamphlet occasioned a duel between Pulteney and Lord Hervey. Att. H. C. L.

Z—h, A—r. *Considerations on the Dispute now depending before the Honourable House of Commons, between the British, Southern, and Northern Plantations in America.* Printed for J. Roberts; London, 1731. 30 pp. Favours the point of view of the sugar planters.

Zur-Lauben, Baron of. *Histoire militaire des Suisses au service de la France.* Paris, 1751-1753. 8 vols. Vol. VIII contains documents with reference to Fleury's mediation in the Geneva dispute of 1737.

5. Secondary Works and Periodical Articles

The following list naturally does not pretend to include all the books consulted, nor even all of the titles used. Usually it will be found that titles of general works have been omitted, as have also those of monographs or articles dealing only incidentally or indirectly with the period or subject matter under treatment; in cases where such material is used, full citation will be found in the notes.

Aiton, A. S. "The Asiento Treaty as Reflected in the Papers of Lord Shelburne." *Hispanic-American Historical Review*, VIII (1928), pp. 167-177. A summary of the papers of the South-Sea Company included in the Shelburne Papers preserved in the Clements Library at the University of Michigan.

Albion, R. G. *Forests and Sea Power; the Timber Problem of the Royal Navy, 1652-1862.* (*Harvard Economic Studies*, vol. XXIX). Cambridge [Mass.], 1926. xv, 485 pp. This excellent monograph studies the British problem only. It contains little on the period between 1713 and 1763.

Anderson, R. C. *Naval Wars in the Baltic during the Sailing-Ship Epoch, 1522-1850.* London, 1910. 423 pp. A catalogue of ships.

Andrews, C. M. "Anglo-French Commercial Rivalry, 1700-1750: the Western Phase." *American Historical Review*, XX (1914-1915), pp. 539-556, 761-780. A remarkably good review of the British pamphlet literature of this period.

Aragon, Marcel. "La Compagnie d'Ostende et le grand commerce en Belgique au début du XVIIIe siècle." *Annales des sciences politiques*, XVI (1901), pp. 216-247.

Arcy, F. d'. "Les débuts du cacao des Isles." *Revue historique des Antilles*, No. 5 (Jan.-March, 1930), pp. 11-16.

Armstrong, Edward. *Elisabeth Farnese.* London, 1892. xxiv, 415 pp. A reliable work, based on Spanish and British sources.

Arneth, Alfred. *Maria Theresia's erste Regierungsjahre.* Vienna, 1863-1865. 3 vols. This title comprises the first three volumes of Arneth's *Geschichte Maria Theresia's* (Vienna, 1863-1879. 10 vols.), the definitive study of this reign.

———. *Prinz Eugen von Savoyen.* Vienna, 1858. 3 vols. The standard biography, based on Austrian sources.

Atkinson, C. T. *A History of Germany, 1715-1815*. London, 1908. xx, 732 pp.

Aubertin, Charles. *L'esprit public au XVIIIe siècle*. Paris, 1873. 499 pp.

Auerbach, Bertrand. *La France et le Saint Empire romain germanique depuis la paix de Westphalie jusqu'à la Révolution française*. Paris, 1912. lxxiii, 485 pp. An excellent study, based on French sources.

Baillon, Charles, comte de. *Lord Walpole à la cour de France, 1723-1730, d'après ses mémoires et sa correspondance*. Paris, 1868. xviii, xxv, 389 pp. A diluted version of Coxe's *Memoirs of Horatio, Lord Walpole*.

Ballard, Admiral George Alexander. *Rulers of the Indian Ocean*. London, 1927. xv, 319 pp.

Ballet, Jules. *La Guadeloupe*. Basse-Terre, 1890-1899. 3 vols., of which the first is in three parts. Volume II covers the period from 1715 to 1774.

Barnes, Donald G. "The Duke of Newcastle, Ecclesiastical Minister, 1724-54." *Pacific Historical Review*, III (1934), pp. 164-191.

Baschet, Armand. *Histoire du dépôt des Archives des Affaires Étrangères*. Paris, 1875. xxviii, 590 pp. Provides considerable information concerning some of the *personnel* of the French Foreign Office.

Baudrillart, Alfred. "Examen des droits de Philippe V et de ses descendants au trône de France, *en dehors des revendications d'Utrecht*." *Revue d'histoire diplomatique*, III (1889), pp. 161-191, 354-384. These important articles prove that the public law of the French monarchy did permit a prospective heir to the throne to renounce his claims; this was a most controversial question until the birth of the Dauphin in 1729.

———. "L'influence française en Espagne au temps de Louis Ier. Mission du maréchal de Tessé, 1724." *Revue des questions historiques*, LX (1896), pp. 485-561.

———. *Philippe V et la cour de France*. Paris, 1890-[1901]. 5 vols. This work is a very monument of scholarship. It discusses in great detail, with lengthy quotations from the French and Spanish archives, the Hispano-French relations from the time that Louis XIV accepted the will of Charles II until the death of Philip V.

———. "Les prétentions de Philippe V à la couronne de France." *Séances et travaux de l'Académie des sciences morales et politiques*, CXXVII (1887), pp. 723-743, 851-897.

Becher, Ernst. *Die oesterreichische Seeverwaltung, 1850-1875*. Trieste, 1875. 282 pp. The introductory chapter gives some information about Trieste as a free port in the time of Charles VI.

Beer, Adolf. "Holland und der österreichische Erbfolge-Krieg." *Archiv für österreichische Geschichte*, XLVI (1871), pp. 297-419. Discusses the French efforts to secure Dutch neutrality during this war.

———. "Zur Geschichte der Politik Karl's VI." *Historische Zeitschrift*, Neue Folge, Band XIX (1886), pp. 1-70. An important contribution, based on Austrian sources.

Beer, George Louis. *The Commercial Policy of England toward the American Colonies*. (*Studies in History, Economics and Public Laws, edited by the University Faculty of Political Science of Columbia College*, vol. III,

No. 2). New York, 1893. 167 pp. The other books by the late Mr. Beer do not particularly deal with the period of interest to this study.

Beyrich, Rudolf. *Kursachsen und die polnische Thronfolge, 1733-1736.* (*Leipziger historische Abhandlungen,* Heft XXXVI). Leipzig, 1913. xvi, 174 pp. A monograph, the material for which was drawn from the Dresden archives.

Bolton, Herbert Eugene. *Texas in the Middle Eighteenth Century.* (*University of California Publications in History,* III). Berkeley [Cal.], 1915. 501 pp. Contains some information on the trade relations between Louisiana and the Spanish dominions during this period.

Bondois, P.-M. "Les centres sucriers français au XVIIIᵉ siècle." *Revue d'histoire économique et sociale,* XIX (1931), pp. 27-76.

Boullée, Auguste. *Histoire de la vie et des ouvrages du chancelier d'Aguesseau.* Paris, 1835. 2 vols. A good biography of the man who was Chancellor of France at the same time that Fleury was at the head of affairs. This work gives information in detail about Parlementary affairs of the time.

Bourgeois, Émile. *Manuel historique de politique étrangère.* Paris, 1892-1926. 4 vols. Volume I deals with the events of this period; this is an extremely useful reference book, although it contains several inaccuracies in dates.

———. *La diplomatie secrète au XVIIIᵉ siècle.* II. *Le secret des Farnèse. Philippe V et la politique d'Alberoni.* Paris, [1909].

Bourgois, Vice-Admiral. "La guerre de course; la grande guerre et les torpilles." *Nouvelle revue,* XLI (July-August, 1886), pp. 273-307. Contains an interesting criticism of the policy of Pontchartrain and demonstrates, too, that the problems of naval strategy are ever the same.

Boyé, Pierre. *Un roi de Pologne et la couronne ducale de Lorraine: Stanislas Leszczynski et le troisième traité de Vienne.* Paris, 1898. xx, 568 pp. This work is based on research in the Austrian and French sources; it is, however, deeply biased against Fleury and consequently tends to attribute too much importance to Chauvelin. The author too frequently indulges a disposition to become rhetorical.

Brandt, Otto. "Das Problem der 'Ruhe des Nordens' im 18. Jahrhundert." *Historische Zeitschrift,* Band CXL (1929), pp. 550-564.

Briavoinne, Natalis. "Mémoire sur l'état de la population, des fabriques, des manufactures et du commerce dans les provinces des Pays-Bas, depuis Albert et Isabelle jusqu'à la fin du siècle dernier." *Mémoires couronnés par l'Académie royale des sciences et belles-lettres de Bruxelles* [in-4°], XIV, part II (1841).

Brisco, Norris Arthur. *The Economic Policy of Robert Walpole.* (*Studies in History, Economics and Public Law, edited by the Faculty of Political Science of Columbia University,* vol. XXVII, No. 1). New York, 1907. 222 pp.

Broglie, Albert, duc de. "Le cardinal de Fleury et la *Pragmatique Sanction.*" *Revue historique,* XX (Sept.-Dec., 1882), pp. 257-281. This important article discusses the fact that France guaranteed the Pragmatic Sanction saving the prior rights of third parties, and that the conduct of Charles VI was such as tacitly to admit the validity of the reservation.

———. *Frédéric II et Louis XV, 1742-1744.* Paris, 1885. 2 vols.

———. *Frédéric II et Marie Thérèse, 1740-1742.* Paris, 1883. 2 vols.

Brown, Vera Lee. "Contraband Trade: A Factor in the Decline of Spain's Empire in America." *Hispanic-American Historical Review,* VIII (1928), pp. 178-189.

———. "The South Sea Company and Contraband Trade." *American Historical Review,* XXXI (1925-1926), pp. 662-678.

Brun, V. *Guerres maritimes de la France: Port de Toulon, ses armements, son administration, depuis son origine jusqu'à nos jours.* Paris, 1861. 2 vols. A very useful work.

Cambridge History of British Foreign Policy, The. Sir A. W. Ward and G. P. Gooch, editors; Cambridge [England], 1922-1923. 3 vols. The introductory chapter, contributed by Sir A. W. Ward, provides a useful analysis of this period.

Carré, H. *Le règne de Louis XV (1715-1774).* Paris, 1911. 428 pp. This constitutes vol. VIII, part II of the *Histoire de France depuis les origines jusqu'à la Révolution* (Ernest Lavisse, editor; Paris, 1903-1911. 9 vols. in 18 parts). The best account of this reign.

Castex, Raoul. *Les idées militaires de la marine du XVIIIᵉ siècle: De Ruyter à Suffren.* Paris, [1911]. 371 pp. This admirable work points out the faulty conceptions of strategy which dominated the thinking of French naval experts during the eighteenth century.

Chabannes La Palice, E. de. "Au seuil de la guerre de Succession d'Autriche, 1741-1744." *Revue maritime,* Nouvelle Série, No. 151 (July, 1932), pp. 29-47; No. 152 (August, 1932), pp. 187-204; No. 153 (September, 1932), pp. 342-363. Prints several documents which show the state of the finances of the French navy at this time.

Chabaud-Arnault, Ch. "Études historiques sur la marine militaire de la France, XII: La marine française sous la Régence et sous le ministère de Maurepas." *Revue maritime et coloniale,* CX (1891), pp. 49-85.

———. "Études historiques sur la marine militaire de la France, XIII: La marine française pendant la guerre de la Succession d'Autriche." *Revue maritime et coloniale,* CX (1891), pp. 365-393.

Chailley-Bert, Joseph. *Les compagnies de colonisation sous l'ancien régime.* Paris, 1898. 192 pp.

Chance, J. F. *The Alliance of Hanover.* London, 1923. xvi, 775 pp. A detailed and authoritative study, based throughout on documentary sources; it treats exhaustively the period between the beginning of 1725 and May 31, 1727.

———. *George I and the Northern War.* London, 1909. xviii, 516 pp. An equally detailed and authoritative study.

Charles-Roux, François. "Les Échelles de Syrie et de Palestine au dix-huitième siècle." *Revue d'histoire diplomatique,* XX (1906), pp. 559-594; XXI (1907), pp. 134-151, 236-267, 427-456, 508-530. The first article in this series contains material of general interest; the other articles deal with the local history of the several *Échelles, seriatim.*

———. *France et Afrique du Nord avant 1830: Les précurseurs de la conquête.*

Paris, 1932. 749 pp. Devotes a chapter to the policy of France toward North Africa during the administration of Cardinal Fleury.

Clamageran, J.-J. *Histoire de l'impôt en France.* Paris, 1867-1876. 3 vols. Vol. III deals with the eighteenth century. The best account of French financial history during the *ancien régime,* prior to that written by M. Marion.

Clark, G. N. "War Trade and Trade War, 1701-1713." *Economic History Review,* I (1927-1928), pp. 262-280.

Colin, Jean. *Louis XV et les Jacobites; le projet de débarquement en Angleterre de 1743-1744.* Paris, 1901. 189 pp. Discusses Fleury's relations with the Jacobites.

Costa, Ethbin Heinrich von. *Der Freihafen von Triest.* Vienna, 1838. 228 pp.

Coxe, William. *History of the House of Austria, from the Foundation of the Monarchy by Rhodolph of Hapsburgh, to the Death of Leopold the Second: 1218 . . . to . . . 1792.* Second edition; London, 1820. 5 vols. Vol. IV deals with this period. Reliable and very readable, although of course somewhat antiquated.

————. *Memoirs of Horatio, Lord Walpole, Selected from his Correspondence and Papers, and Connected with the History of the Times, from 1678 to 1757.* Third edition; London, 1820. 2 vols. This work contains valuable correspondence, supplementary to that which is published in the same author's *Memoirs of . . . Sir Robert Walpole.*

————. *Memoirs of the Kings of Spain of the House of Bourbon.* London, 1815. 5 vols. This history gives an interesting and readable account, principally from the point of view of diplomatic history. It is based in large part on the despatches of Harrington and Keene, for this period.

————. *Memoirs of the Life and Administration of Sir Robert Walpole, Earl of Orford.* London, 1798. 3 vols. Volume I of this work contains the author's account of his hero's life; it is an interesting and substantial biography, inspired by sturdy Whig prejudices. The other two volumes are composed of correspondence which is on the whole faithfully transcribed, and constitutes a very important source.

Crisenoy, J. de. "Les écoles navales et les officiers de vaisseau depuis Richelieu jusqu'à nos jours." *Revue maritime et coloniale,* X (1864), pp. 759-791.

Cunningham, William. *The Growth of English Industry and Commerce in Modern Times; Part I. The Mercantile System.* Cambridge [England], 1903. xxxviii, 608 pp.

Dahlgren, E. W. "L'expedition de Martinet et la fin du commerce français dans la mer du Sud." *Revue de l'histoire des colonies françaises,* I (1913), pp. 257-332.

————. *Les relations commerciales et maritimes entre la France et les côtes de l'océan Pacifique (Commencement du XVIIIᵉ siècle): I. Le commerce de la mer du Sud jusqu'à la paix d'Utrecht.* Paris, 1909. 740 pp. Contains an exposition of the manner in which Spanish trade with the Indies was conducted.

————. "Voyages français à destination de la mer du Sud avant Bougainville (1695-1749)." *Nouvelles archives des missions scientifiques*, XIV (1907), pp. 423-554.

Dalgliesh, Wilbert Harold. *The Company of the Indies in the Days of Dupleix*. Easton [Pa.], 1933. 238 pp. This recent monograph discusses, *inter alia*, the extent of French trade to the Orient during the administration of Fleury.

Descamps, Éd. "La constitution internationale de la Belgique." *Bulletin de la classe des lettres et des sciences morales et politiques et de la classe des beaux-arts: Académie royale de Belgique, 1901*, pp. 81-213. Contains a discussion of the international status of the Austrian Netherlands in the eighteenth century.

Dessalles, Adrien. *Histoire générale des Antilles*. Paris, 1847-1848. 5 vols. Volume IV deals with this period; it contains statistics of the population of the French islands.

Dollot, René. *Les origines de la neutralité de la Belgique et le système de la Barrière (1609-1830)*. Paris, 1902. 570 pp.

Doneaud, Alfred. "La marine française et ses arsenaux." *Revue maritime et coloniale*, XXVIII (1870), pp. 384-432, 682-694.

———. "La marine française du XVIIIe siècle au point de vue de l'administration et des progrès scientifiques." *Revue maritime et coloniale*, XXI (1867), pp. 465-493, 580-599.

Doniol, H. "Le Ministère des Affaires Étrangères de France sous le comte de Vergennes." *Revue d'histoire diplomatique*, VII (1893), pp. 528-560. M. Doniol brought to light in this contribution the *mémoire* written in 1784 by Hennin at the request of Catherine the Great, in which the manner of organization of the Foreign Office was set forth.

Donnan, Elizabeth. "The Early Days of the South Sea Company, 1711-1718." *Journal of Economic and Business History*, II (1929-1930), pp. 419-451.

Driault, Édouard. "Chauvelin, 1733-1737: Son rôle dans l'histoire de la réunion de la Lorraine à la France." *Revue d'histoire diplomatique*, VII (1893), pp. 31-74. This valuable article is somewhat inclined to overstate the contrast between the policies of Fleury and Chauvelin, and consequently to appraise too highly the part Chauvelin played in the reversion of Lorraine.

Drouet, Joseph. *L'abbé de Saint-Pierre: L'homme et l'oeuvre*. Paris, 1912. viii, 397 pp. The best biography of Saint-Pierre, whose relations with Fleury with reference to Saint-Pierre's expulsion from the Academy in 1717 and the suppression of the *Entresol* club in 1730 serve to illustrate aspects of the Cardinal's character.

Droysen, J. G. *Geschichte der preussischen Politik*. Leipzig, 1868-1886. Five parts in 14 vols. Of use in this study were Part IV, vols. 2-4; Part V, vol. 1 and the first section of vol. 2. A well-known study, thoroughly grounded on the documents, many of which are published in the course of the work.

Dullinger, Josef. "Die Handelskompagnien Oesterreichs nach dem Oriente und nach Ostindien in der ersten Hälfte des 18. Jahrhunderts." *Zeitschrift für Social- und Wirtschaftsgeschichte*, VII (1900), pp. 44-83.

Duncker, M. W. *Aus der Zeit Friedrichs des Grossen und Friedrich Wilhelms III.* Leipzig, 1876. Pp. 3-46 include Duncker's study, with documents, on the history of Frederick's famous essay, *Considerations on the Present State of the Body Politic in Europe:* "Eine Flugschrift des Kronprinzen Friedrich."

Dureng, Jean. *Le duc de Bourbon et l'Angleterre (1723-1726).* Paris, [1912]. 544 pp. Utilizes French and British archival material. A reliable and useful monograph.

————. *Mission de Théodore Chevignard de Chavigny en Allemagne, septembre 1726-octobre 1731.* Paris, [1912]. 133 pp. Based on the French sources; good for French policy in Germany for the period mentioned.

Erdmannsdörffer, Bernhard. *Deutsche Geschichte vom westfälischen Frieden bis zum Regierungsantritt Friedrich's des Grossen, 1648-1740.* Berlin, 1892-1893. 2 vols. The best account which is both brief and comprehensive.

Fayle, C. Ernest. "Economic Pressure in the War of 1739-48." *Journal of the Royal United Service Institution,* LXVIII (Feb.-Nov., 1923), pp. 434-446.

Flammermont, Jules. *Les correspondances des agents diplomatiques étrangers en France avant la Révolution.* Paris, 1896. 628 pp. This volume publishes some useful documents.

Flassan, Jean Baptiste Gaëtan de Raxis de. *Histoire générale et raisonnée de la diplomatie française.* Paris, 1809. 6 vols. Useful for a *coup d'oeil* but has many omissions. Volumes IV and V.

Fortescue, Sir John W. *A History of the British Army.* London, 1910-1930. 13 vols. The standard work on this topic. Volume II.

————. "A Side Show of the Eighteenth Century." *Blackwood's Magazine,* CCXXXIII (Jan.-June, 1933), pp. 330-345.

Fournier, August. "Zur Entstehungsgeschichte der pragmatischen Sanktion Kaiser Karl's VI." *Historische Zeitschrift,* XXXVIII (1877), pp. 16-47.

Fournier, Joseph. *La Chambre de Commerce de Marseille et ses réprésentants permanents à Paris (1599-1875).* Marseilles, 1920. 334 pp.

Frankowski, Félix. "La dynastie de Saxe sur le trône de Pologne (1697-1815)." *Revue d'histoire diplomatique,* XLV (1931), pp. 119-140. Undocumented and general in character.

Gachard, L.-P. *Études et notices historiques concernant l'histoire des Pays-Bas.* Brussels, 1890. 3 vols. Cited here for the study entitled "Acceptation et publication aux Pays-Bas de la Pragmatique Sanction de l'Empereur Charles VI" (II, pp. 1-26).

————. *Histoire de la Belgique au commencement du XVIIIe siècle.* Brussels, 1880. 607 pp. Very good on the Barrier treaties; does not discuss the Ostend Company.

Garnault, Émile. *Le commerce rochelais au XVIIIe siècle, d'après les documents composant les anciennes archives de la Chambre de Commerce de La Rochelle.* La Rochelle, 1888-1900. 5 vols. Volume III discusses the period from 1718 to 1748.

Gassier, Émile. *Les cinq cents Immortels: Histoire de l'Académie française, 1634-1906.* Paris, 1906. 491 pp.

Gaston-Martin. *Nantes au XVIIIe siècle: L'ère des négriers (1714-1774), d'après des documents inédits.* Paris, 1931. 452 pp. Includes much useful information on the French slave trade in the eighteenth century.

———. "Nantes et la Compagnie des Indes (1664-1769)." *Revue d'histoire économique et sociale,* XV (1927), pp. 25-65, 231-253.

Gay, Charles. *Négociations relatives à l'établissement de la maison de Bourbon sur le trône des Deux-Siciles.* Paris, 1853. 335 pp. This production includes many documents from the archives of the French Ministry of War; the text itself is valueless.

Germiny, Count Marc de. "Les brigandages maritimes de l'Angleterre sous le règne de Louis XV, d'après les Archives nationales et des documents inédits." *Revue des questions historiques,* LXXXIII (1908), pp. 476-491; LXXXIV (1908), pp. 85-112, 472-508. The first article of this series gives some information relating to this period.

Geikie, Roderick, and Montgomery, Isabel A. *The Dutch Barrier, 1705-1719.* Cambridge [England], 1930. xxi, 418 pp. A sober and scholarly work.

Geyl, P. "Holland and England during the War of the Austrian Succession." *History,* X (1925-1926), pp. 47-51.

Gideonse, Max. *Dutch Baltic Trade in the Eighteenth Century.* Harvard College Library, manuscript thesis. 391 pp. The author's summary of his thesis may be found in *Summaries of Theses Accepted in Partial Fulfilment of the Requirements for the Degree of Doctor of Philosophy, 1932 (Harvard University: Graduate School of Arts and Sciences),* pp. 103-105.

Girard, Albert. *Le commerce français à Séville et Cadix au temps des Habsbourg: Contribution à l'étude du commerce étranger en Espagne aux XVIe et XVIIe siècles.* Paris, 1932. xxiii, 604 pp.

———. *La rivalité commerciale et maritime entre Séville et Cadix jusqu'à la fin du XVIIIe siècle.* Paris, 1932. xvi, 119 pp.

Goslinga, A. *Slingelandt's Efforts towards European Peace.* The Hague, 1915. 388, xxiv pp. An excellent but rather prolix study of diplomatic events from July 1727, until the Treaty of Seville, November 9, 1729. The contemplated second part of this work has not yet appeared.

Goumy, Édouard. *Étude sur la vie et les écrits de l'abbé de Saint-Pierre.* Paris, 1859. 332 pp.

Hannay, R. H. "Gibraltar in 1727." *Scottish Historical Review,* XVI (1918-1919), pp. 325-334. Contains the "Journal of a Voyage from Leith to Newfoundland, Barcelona, etc., in 1726-1727," by Edward Burd, Jun., supercargo of the ship *Christian* of Leith.

Hanotaux, Gabriel, and Martineau, Alfred, editors. *Histoire des colonies françaises et de l'expansion de la France dans le monde.* Paris, 1929-1933. 6 vols. An ambitious work which would have been vastly improved by a display of documentation. Noteworthy are the sections in volume I contributed by Joannès Tramond: "Les Antilles après le traité d'Utrecht," and "Le Canada après le traité d'Utrecht," esp. pp. 433-503, 99-153.

Hardy, Georges. *Le cardinal de Fleury et le mouvement janséniste.* Paris, 1925. 360 pp. An excellent investigation of the religious aspects of Fleury's administration.

Haring, C. H. *Trade and Navigation between Spain and the Indies in the*

Time of the Hapsburgs. (*Harvard Economic Studies*, vol. XIX). Cambridge [Mass.], 1918. xxviii, 371 pp.

Harsin, Paul. "Une oeuvre inédite de l'économiste Dutot." *Annales de la Société scientifique de Bruxelles, Série D: Sciences économiques et techniques*, XLVII (Louvain, 1927), pp. 151-165.

Haussonville, J. O. B. de Cléron, comte d'. *Histoire de la réunion de la Lorraine à la France.* Second edition; Paris, 1860. 4 vols. This history, which deals sympathetically with Chauvelin, publishes many useful documents. Volume IV.

Heckscher, Eli F. *Mercantilism.* London, 1935. 2 vols. Intentionally deals lightly with the period after 1713.

Hertz, G. B. *British Imperialism in the Eighteenth Century.* London, 1908. 247 pp. Particularly useful for the essay "The War Fever of 1739" (pp. 7-60), which is based on pamphlet material.

———. "England and the Ostend Company." *English Historical Review*, XXII (1907), pp. 255-279. An excellent article.

Hill, David Jayne. *A History of Diplomacy in the International Development of Europe.* New York, 1905-1914. 3 vols. On the whole, this history gives a just view of the broad outlines of diplomatic history; the account of this period, however, swarms with minor inaccuracies. Volume III.

Hubert, Eugène. "Les garnisons de la Barrière dans les Pays-Bas autrichiens (1715-1782)." *Mémoires couronnés et mémoires des savants étrangers publiés par l'Académie royale des sciences, des lettres et des beaux-arts de Belgique*, LIX (1901-1903), fasc. iv. 399 pp. Interesting and detailed information concerning the relations of the Dutch garrisons with the inhabitants of the Austrian Netherlands.

Huisman, Michel. *La Belgique commerciale sous l'empereur Charles VI: La Compagnie d'Ostende.* Brussels, 1902. xii, 556 pp. An excellent work; the limitation of the subject has unfortunately, although perhaps unavoidably, caused the author to attribute too much international diplomatic importance to the Ostend Company.

Hussey, Roland Dennis. *The Caracas Company, 1728-1784: A Study in the History of Spanish Monopolistic Trade.* (*Harvard Historical Studies*, vol. XXXVII). Cambridge [Mass.], 1934. xii, 358 pp.

Immich, Max. *Geschichte des europäischen Staatensystems von 1660 bis 1789.* Munich, 1905. xiii, 462 pp. The best short treatment of this period of diplomatic history.

Innis, H. A. *The Fur Trade in Canada.* New Haven, 1930. 444 pp.

———. *The Fur Trade of Canada.* Toronto, 1927. 172 pp. This work is principally concerned with the history of the fur trade in recent times.

Janet, Paul. "Une académie politique sous le cardinal de Fleury de 1724 à 1731." *Séances et travaux de l'Académie des sciences morales et politiques*, LXXIV (1865), pp. 107-126.

Johnsen, Oscar Albert. "Le commerce entre la France méridionale et les pays du Nord sous l'ancien régime." *Revue d'histoire moderne*, II (1927), pp. 81-98.

Jorissen, Theod. *Historische Studien, V: Lord Chesterfield en de Republiek der Vereenigde Nederlanden.* Haarlem, 1894. 300 pp. The extensive notes include some of Slingelandt's memorials and diplomatic correspondence.

Lacour-Gayet, Georges. *La marine militaire de la France sous le règne de Louis XV.* Paris, 1902. 571 pp. A useful history, although it imparts little information about the organization or cost of the navy.

Lambert de Sainte Croix, [Alexandre]. *Essai sur l'histoire de l'administration de la marine de France, 1689-1792.* Paris, 1892. 457 pp. A superficial and disappointing work.

Lanier, L. "Le club de l'Entresol (1723-1731)." *Mémoires de l'Académie des sciences, des lettres et des arts d'Amiens,* Troisième Série, VI (1880). pp. 1-56.

Laughton, J. K. "Jenkins's Ear." *English Historical Review,* IV (1889), pp. 741-749.

————. *Studies in Naval History.* London, 1887. 469 pp.

Lavisse, Ernest, editor. *Histoire de France depuis les origines jusqu'à la Révolution.* See Carré, H., (*supra* p. 391).

Lavisse, Ernest. *La jeunesse du Grand Frédéric.* Paris, 1891. 451 pp.

Legg, L. G. Wickham. "Newcastle and the Counter Orders to Admiral Haddock, March 1739." *English Historical Review,* XLVI (1931), pp. 272-274.

Lerer, David. *La politique française en Pologne sous Louis XV (1733-1772).* Toulouse, [1929]. 207 pp. This thesis is based on some Polish and French secondary authorities. It does not contribute to the general knowledge on this subject; the part devoted to the years of Fleury's administration are pp. 35-68.

Levae, Ad. "Recherches historiques sur le commerce des belges aux Indes pendant le XVIIᵉ et le XVIIIᵉ siècle." *Trésor national,* Première Série, II (Brussels, 1842), pp. 179-269; III (Brussels, 1842), pp. 55-161. Contains some useful points concerning the Ostend Company.

Levasseur, Émile. *Histoire des classes ouvrières et de l'industrie en France avant 1789.* Second edition; Paris, 1900-1901. 2 vols. Volume II.

————. *Histoire du commerce de la France.* I: *Avant 1789.* Paris, 1911. xxxiii, 611 pp.

Levot, P. *Histoire de la ville et du port de Brest.* Brest and Paris, 1864-1866. 3 vols. Of use in a study of this period were vol. II, cap. ii; vol. III, cap. ii.

Lippert, Gustav. "Die Entwicklung der österreichischen Handelsmarine." *Zeitschrift für Volkswirtschaft, Socialpolitik und Verwaltung,* X (1901), pp. 347-405.

Lipson, E. *The Economic History of England.* London, 1915-1931. 3 vols. Vol. II.

Lodge, Sir Richard. "The Continental Policy of Great Britain, 1740-60." *History,* XVI (1931-1932), pp. 298-305. A valuable generalization of recent findings and judgments upon this topic.

————. "English Neutrality in the War of the Polish Succession." *Trans-*

actions of the Royal Historical Society, Fourth Series, XIV (1931), pp. 141-174. Argues most convincingly that Great Britain was mistaken in not intervening in the War of the Polish Succession.

——. "The First Anglo-Russian Treaty, 1739-42." *English Historical Review*, XLIII (1928), pp. 354-375.

——. *Great Britain and Prussia in the Eighteenth Century*. Oxford, 1923. 221 pp.

——. "The Maritime Powers in the Eighteenth Century." *History*, XV (1930-1931), pp. 246-252. Traces the growing attitude of independence taken by the United Provinces with reference to their diplomatic relations with Great Britain.

——. "Russia, Prussia, and Great Britain, 1742-4." *English Historical Review*, LXV (1930), pp. 579-611.

——. "The Treaty of Abo and the Swedish Succession." *English Historical Review*, XLIII (1928), pp. 540-571.

——. "The Treaty of Seville (1729)." *Transactions of the Royal Historical Society*, Fourth Series, XVI (1933), pp. 1-45. This excellent paper admirably analyzes the diplomatic situation of Europe at the time of the Congress of Soissons.

——. "The Treaty of Worms." *English Historical Review*, XLIV (1929), pp. 220-255. An excellent analysis of the negotiations involving the Kingdom of Sardinia in 1741-1743.

Loevenbruck, Pierre. "La flotte française à Copenhague, en 1733." *Revue maritime*, Nouvelle Série, (July-Dec., 1926), pp. 156-171. Contains the anonymous diary of a French naval officer.

Lohmann, Friedrich. "Die staatliche Regelung der englischen Wollindustrie vom XV. bis zum XVIII. Jahrhundert." *Staats- und socialwissenschaftliche Forschungen*, XVIII, Heft 1 (Leipzig, 1900), pp. 1-100.

Lord, Robert Howard. *The Second Partition of Poland*. (*Harvard Historical Studies*, vol. XXIII). Cambridge [Mass.], 1915. xxx, 586 pp. Gives an excellent analysis of the Polish constitution.

Luçay, Comte Hélion de. *Des origines du pouvoir ministériel en France: Les secrétaires d'État depuis leur institution jusqu'à la mort de Louis XV*. Paris, 1881. 647 pp. Contains some very useful miscellaneous information concerning the several Secretaries of State during Fleury's administration.

Mahan, A. T. *The Influence of Sea Power upon History, 1660-1783*. Boston, 1890. 557 pp.

——. *Types of Naval Officers, Drawn from the History of the British Navy*. Boston, 1901. 500 pp.

Mahon, Philip Henry Stanhope, Lord. *History of England from the Peace of Utrecht to the Peace of Versailles, 1713-1783*. Fifth edition; London, 1858. 7 vols. The appendices contain documents from the Stanhope and Stuart papers.

Margry, Pierre. "Une famille dans la marine au XVIIIᵉ siècle (1692-1789)." *Revue maritime et coloniale*, LXII (1879), pp. 395-410, 640-673; LXIII (1879), pp. 205-236; LXVIII (1881), pp. 92-118.

Marion, Marcel. *Histoire financière de la France depuis 1715.* Paris, 1914-1931. 6 vols. Volume I. The best treatment of this subject.

Martineau, Alfred. *Dupleix et l'Inde française.* Paris, 1920-1928. 4 vols. Volume I.

Masson, Frédéric. *Le département des Affaires Étrangères pendant la Révolution, 1787-1804.* Paris, 1877. xvi, 570 pp. The introductory pages impart very valuable information about the organization of the Foreign Office during the *ancien régime.*

Masson, Paul. *Histoire du commerce français dans le Levant au XVIIIe siècle.* Paris, 1911. 678 pp. Comprehensive and exhaustive.

May, Louis-Philippe. "La France, puissance des Antilles." *Revue d'histoire économique et sociale,* XVIII (1930), pp. 451-481.

――――. *Histoire économique de la Martinique (1635-1763).* Paris, 1930. 334 pp. The author utilizes all available statistics; a valuable work.

Mayer, Franz Martin. "Zur Geschichte der österreichischen Handelspolitik unter Kaiser Karl VI." *Mittheilungen des Instituts für oesterreichische Geschichtsforschung,* XVIII (1897), pp. 129-145.

McIlwain, C. H., editor. *An Abridgment of the Indian Affairs . . . . transacted in the Colony of New York, from the Year 1678 to the Year 1751. By Peter Wraxall. (Harvard Historical Studies,* vol. XXI). Cambridge [Mass.], 1915. cxviii, 251 pp. The introduction contains an excellent account of the illicit Albany trade between colonial merchants and French fur traders.

McLennan, J. S. *Louisbourg from its Foundation to its Fall, 1713-1758.* London, 1918. 454 pp. A reliable work, containing useful tabulations and charts.

Mémoires et documents pour servir à l'histoire du commerce et de l'industrie en France. Julien Hayem, editor; Paris, 1911-1929. 12 vols. Articles cited from this publication are listed under their authors' names.

Mertens, Louis. "La Compagnie d'Ostende." *Bulletin de la Société de géographie d'Anvers,* VI (1881-1882), pp. 381-419.

Michael, Wolfgang. *Englische Geschichte im achtzehnten Jahrhundert.*
Erster Band. *Die Anfänge des Hauses Hannover.* Second edition; Berlin, 1921. 866 pp.
Zweiter Band. *Das Zeitalter Walpoles.* Erster Teil: *Die Krisis des hannöverschen Königtums.* Berlin, 1920. 640 pp.
Dritter Band. *Das Zeitalter Walpoles.* Zweiter Teil: *Walpole als Premierminister.* Berlin, 1934. 598 pp.
A full-length presentation, characterized by great erudition; a definitive work.

Mims, Stewart Lea. *Colbert's West India Policy.* New Haven, 1912. 385 pp. Useful for purposes of comparison, when studying the condition of the French West Indies in the eighteenth century.

Nettels, Curtis. "England and the Spanish-American Trade, 1680-1715." *Journal of Modern History,* III (1931), pp. 1-33.

Nolhac, Pierre de. *Études sur la cour de France. Louis XV et Marie Leczinska, d'après de nouveaux documents.* Paris, [1928]. 345 pp.

Oliver, F. S. *The Endless Adventure*. New York, 1931-1934. 3 vols. An example of fine writing in the best sense. Well-informed and pellucid; see, for example, the remarkable explanation of Walpole's excise scheme. The book is unfortunately not provided with the apparatus of documentation, which has caused reviewers to underestimate its worth.

Olszewicz, V. "L'évolution de la constitution polonaise." *Revue des sciences politiques*, XXVI (1911), pp. 610-619; XXVII (1912), pp. 456-469; XXVIII (1912), pp. 58-68.

Oncken, Wilhelm. "Sir Charles Hotham und Friedrich Wilhelm I. im Jahre 1730." *Forschungen zur brandenburgischen und preussischen Geschichte*, VII (1894), pp. 377-407; VIII (1895), pp. 487-522; IX (1896), pp. 23-53.

Pajol, C. P. V. *Les guerres sous Louis XV*. Paris, 1881-1891. 7 vols. The standard military history of the reign. This work publishes many documents from the archives of the Ministry of War; it is accurate enough on matters purely military, but makes many lamentable slips in its account of diplomatic and domestic events. Volume I.

Parisot, Robert. *Histoire de Lorraine*. Paris, 1919-1924. 3 vols. Volume II deals with this period.

Philipp, Albrecht. *August der Starke und die pragmatische Sanktion*. (*Leipziger historische Abhandlungen*, Heft IV). Leipzig, 1908. 139 pp.

Picavet, C.-G. *La diplomatie française au temps de Louis XIV (1661-1715): Institutions, moeurs et coutumes*. Paris, 1930. 339 pp. An excellent study of the organization and mechanics of the French diplomatic system, the broad features of which remained unchanged throughout the *ancien régime*.

Piccioni, Camille. *Les premiers commis des Affaires Étrangères au XVIIᵉ et au XVIIIᵉ siècles*. Paris, 1928. 282 pp. A very useful work, which gives biographical notices of those important officials, the *premiers commis*, and considerable incidental information concerning the mechanics of the French Ministry for Foreign Affairs, as well.

Pichon, Jérôme. *La vie de Charles-Henry, comte de Hoym, ambassadeur de Saxe-Pologne en France et célèbre amateur de livres, 1694-1736*. Paris, 1880. 2 vols. The appendix publishes several of Hoym's despatches. The text is of little value.

Pitman, Frank Wesley. *The Development of the British West Indies, 1700-1763*. New Haven, 1917. xiv, 495 pp. This useful work confines itself almost entirely to a study of the sugar trade.

———. "The Settlement and Financing of British West India Plantations in the Eighteenth Century." *Essays in Colonial History Presented to Charles McLean Andrews by his Students* (New Haven, 1931), pp. 252-283.

———. "The West Indian Absentee Planter as a British Colonial Type." *Proceedings of the Pacific Coast Branch of the American Historical Association, 1927*, pp. 113-127.

Pribram, A. F. *Die böhmische Commerzcollegium und seine Thätigkeit*. (*Beiträge zur Geschichte der deutschen Industrie in Böhmen*, VI). Prague, 1898. 278 pp.

Quarré de Verneuil, R. *L'armée en France depuis Charles VII jusqu'à la Révolution (1439-1789)*. Paris, 1880. 368 pp.

Ranke, Leopold von. *Französische Geschichte vornehmlich im sechzehnten und siebzehnten Jahrhundert*. Leipzig, 1876-1877. 6 vols. Volume IV, book xvii; volume V, pp. 322-332. A brief but brilliant analysis of Fleury's administration.

———. *Zwölf Bücher preussischer Geschichte*. Leipzig, 1874. 3 vols. Books v and vi. A classic work.

Raynal, Paul de. *Le mariage d'un roi, 1721-1725*. Paris, 1887. 352 pp. This volume studies the diplomatic setting of the marriage of Louis XV; a commendable work.

Richmond, Admiral Sir Herbert W. *The Navy in the War of 1739-48*. Cambridge [England], 1920. 3 vols. A very detailed account by the leading authority on this topic. Volume I, especially.

Rocquain, Félix. *L'esprit révolutionnaire avant la Révolution, 1715-1789*. Paris, 1878. 541 pp. Develops the interesting thesis that revolutionary discontent existed in France throughout the eighteenth century; his conclusions for the first half of the century are vitiated by a too exclusive reliance on the testimony of D'Argenson.

Rojdestvensky, S., and Lubimenko, Inna. "Contribution à l'histoire des relations commerciales franco-russes au XVIIIᵉ siècle." *Revue d'histoire économique et sociale*, XVII (1929), pp. 363-402.

Rosenlehner, August. *Kurfürst Karl Philipp von der Pfalz und die jülichsche Frage, 1725-1729*. Munich, 1906. 488 pp. Based on unpublished sources at Munich and Mannheim. An extraordinarily thorough work.

Rouxel, Albert. *Chronique des élections à l'Académie française (1634-1841)*. Paris, 1886. xvi, 295 pp.

St. John, James Hamilton. *Anglo-Spanish Commercial Relations, 1700-1750*. State University of Iowa Library, manuscript thesis, 1927. 511 pp. This excellent dissertation is based on a study of the treaties and British pamphlet material; very useful for bibliographical suggestions.

Saintoyant, J. *La colonisation française sous l'ancien régime*. Paris, 1929. 2 vols. A useful manual.

Saint-Priest, François Emmanuel Guignard, comte de. *Mémoires sur l'ambassade de France en Turquie et sur le commerce des français dans le Levant*. (*Publications de l'École des langues orientales vivantes*, Première Série, VI). Charles Schefer, editor; Paris, 1877. 542 pp. Publishes documents concerning Bonnac's mediation in 1724 and Villeneuve's in 1739.

Salandra, Dominic. "Porto Bello, Puerto Bello, or Portobelo?" *Hispanic-American Historical Review*, XIV (1934), pp. 93-95.

Sautai, Maurice. *Les préliminaires de la guerre de la Succession d'Autriche*. Paris, 1907. 633 pp. A work of considerable utility, which endeavours to combine diplomatic and military considerations. It is based on French sources, and includes lengthy appendices of unpublished documents. This volume concludes with the entrance of the French armies into German territory in September, 1741.

————. *Les débuts de la guerre de la Succession d'Autriche.* Paris, 1909. 413 pp. This volume discusses diplomatic and military events up to the French capture of Prague.

Scelle, Georges. "The Slave Trade in the Spanish Colonies of America: The Assiento." *American Journal of International Law,* IV (1910), pp. 612-662.

————. *La traite négrière aux Indes de Castille.* Paris, 1906. 2 vols. Volume II. An excellent study, which, regrettably, does not extend beyond the year 1715.

Schefer, Charles. *Mémoire historique sur l'ambassade de France à Constantinople par le marquis de Bonnac, publié avec un précis de ses négociations à la Porte Ottomane.* Paris, 1894. lxviii, 287 pp. Publishes many documents referring to Bonnac's mediation in 1724.

Schilling, Heinrich. *Der Zwist Preussens und Hannovers, 1729-1730.* Halle, 1912. 164 pp. A doctoral dissertation.

Sée, Henri. "Les armateurs de Saint-Malo au XVIIIᵉ siècle." *Revue d'histoire économique et sociale,* XVII (1929), pp. 29-35.

————. "Le commerce de Morlaix dans la première moitié du XVIIIᵉ siècle, d'après les papiers de Guillotou de Keréver." *Mémoires et documents pour servir à l'histoire du commerce et de l'industrie en France,* IX (1925), pp. 168-210.

————. "Le commerce de Saint-Malo au XVIIIᵉ siècle, d'après les papiers des Magon." *Mémoires et documents pour servir à l'histoire du commerce et de l'industrie en France,* IX (1925), pp. 1-130.

————. "Le commerce du beurre et des salaisons en Bretagne au XVIIIᵉ siècle." *Mémoires et documents pour servir à l'histoire du commerce et de l'industrie en France,* X (1926), pp. 175-185.

————. "Esquisse de l'histoire du commerce français à Cadix et dans l'Amérique espagnole au XVIIIᵉ siècle." *Revue d'histoire moderne,* III (1928), pp. 13-31.

————. "Les relations commerciales et maritimes entre la France et les pays du Nord au XVIIIᵉ siècle." *Revue maritime,* Nouvelle Série, No. 71 (Nov., 1925), pp. 595-609.

————. "Les spéculations d'un officier de finance à Cadix et dans l'Amérique espagnole (1734-1739)." *Mémoires et documents pour servir à l'histoire du commerce et de l'industrie en France,* XII (1929), pp. 338-360.

Sée, Henri, and Vignols, Léon. "L'envers de la diplomatie officielle de 1715 à 1730: La rivalité commerciale des puissances maritimes et les doléances des négociants français." *Revue belge de philologie et d'histoire,* V (1926), pp. 471-491.

————. "La fin du commerce interlope dans l'Amérique espagnole." *Revue d'histoire économique et sociale,* XIII (1925), pp. 300-313.

————. "Mémoires sur le commerce rédigés en vue du congrès de Soissons (1728)." [Ministère de l'instruction publique et des beaux-arts: Comité des travaux historiques et scientifiques, section d'histoire moderne (depuis 1715) et contemporaine]: *Notices, inventaires & documents,* XII: *Études et documents divers* (Paris, 1926), pp. 1-33.

Seeley, Sir J. R. "The House of Bourbon." *English Historical Review,* I

(1886), pp. 86-104. Emphasizes and somewhat overstates the bearing of the First Family Compact (1733) on European diplomacy.

Sichel, Walter. *Bolingbroke and his Times.* London, 1901-1902. 2 vols. Publishes a considerable amount of Bolingbroke's correspondence. Volume II.

Siégler-Pascal, S. *Un contemporain égaré au XVIIIe siècle: Les projets de l'abbé de Saint-Pierre, 1658-1743.* Paris, 1900. 288 pp.

Srbik, Heinrich, Ritter von. *Der staatliche Exporthandel Österreichs von Leopold I. bis Maria Theresia.* Vienna, 1907. xxxii, 432 pp. Contains incidental information concerning the economic development of the Hapsburg monarchy under Charles VI.

Steur, Charles. "Précis historique de l'état politique, administratif et judiciaire, civil, religieux et militaire des Pays-Bas autrichiens, sous le règne de Charles VI." *Mémoires couronnés en 1828 par l'Académie royale des sciences et belles-lettres de Bruxelles* [in-4], VII (1829). 411 pp.

Stryienski, Casimir. *The Eighteenth Century.* New York, [1916]. 345 pp. This work constitutes volume IV of the series entitled *The National History of France,* edited by Fr. Funck-Brentano. It rests heavily upon memoir sources, is reasonably good while discussing domestic affairs, but is weakest in the domain of international events. H. N. Dickinson, translator.

———. *Le gendre de Louis XV: Don Philippe, Infant d'Espagne et duc de Parme.* Paris, 1904. 493 pp.

———. *Mesdames de France, filles de Louis XV.* Fifth edition; Paris, 1911. 454 pp.

Surrey, N. M. Miller. *The Commerce of Louisiana during the French Régime, 1699-1763.* (*Studies in History, Economics and Public Law, edited by the Faculty of Political Science of Columbia University,* vol. LXXI, No. 1). New York, 1916. 476 pp.

Sutherland, Lucy Stuart. *A London Merchant, 1695-1774.* London, 1933. 164 pp.

Syveton, Gabriel. *Une cour et un aventurier au XVIIIe siècle: Le baron de Ripperda.* Paris, 1896. 309 pp. An excellent study, based on Austrian sources. It should be supplemented by the full-length review of it contributed by Edward Armstrong to the *English Historical Review,* XII (1897), pp. 796-800.

———. "Un traité secret de mariage et d'alliance entre les cours de Vienne et de Madrid en 1725." *Revue historique,* LIV (1894), pp. 77-97.

Teissier, Octave. *La Chambre de Commerce de Marseille.* Marseilles, 1892. 411 pp.

Temperley, H. W. V. "The Causes of the War of Jenkins' Ear (1739)." *Transactions of the Royal Historical Society,* Third Series, III (1909), pp. 197-236. An excellent contribution, drawn from the British diplomatic correspondence.

———. "The Relations of England with Spanish America, 1720-1744." *Annual Report of the American Historical Association for the Year 1911,* I, pp. 231-238.

Tramond, Joannès. "Aperçu de l'histoire de Saint-Domingue au XVIIIe siècle." *Revue historique des Antilles*, No. 1 (Oct., 1928), pp. 17-34.

———. *Manuel d'histoire maritime de la France*. Paris, 1916. 911 pp. A useful book for handy reference.

Tschierschky, Siegfried. *Die Wirtschaftspolitik des schlesischen Kommerz-kollegs, 1716-1740*. Gotha, 1902. 132 pp.

Tupetz, Theodor. "Der Türkenfeldzug von 1739 und der Friede zu Belgrad." *Historische Zeitschrift*, XL (1878), pp. 1-52.

Turba, Gustav. *Die pragmatische Sanktion, mit besonderer Rücksicht auf die Länder der Stephanskrone*. Vienna, 1906. 199 pp.

Uebersberger, Hans. *Russlands Orientpolitik in den letzten zwei Jahrhunderten*. I: *Bis zum Frieden von Jassy*. Stuttgart, 1913. 380 pp.

Vandal, Albert. *Une ambassade française en Orient sous Louis XV: La mission du marquis de Villeneuve, 1728-1741*. Paris, 1887. xv, 461 pp. A reliable and excellently written work.

———. *Louis XV et Elisabeth de Russie*. Paris, 1882. xv, 446 pp. Very good, although a trifle rhetorical.

Vaucher, Paul. "Une convention franco-anglaise pour régler le commerce et la navigation dans les Indes Occidentales, 1737-1740." *Mélanges d'histoire offerts à M. Charles Bémont* (Paris, 1913), pp. 611-617.

———. *La crise du ministère Walpole en 1733-1734*. Paris, 1924. 70 pp. An excellent study of the Excise scheme and the political crisis which it caused.

———. *Robert Walpole et la politique de Fleury (1731-1742)*. Paris, 1924. xi, 473 pp. This excellent work handles all the categories of sources, published and unpublished, in a masterly manner.

Verlaque, V. *Histoire du cardinal de Fleury et de son administration*. Paris, 1878. 319 pp. This pretentious title is attached to a book which is worthless. The author betrays an extremely casual and superficial knowledge of the period.

Vignols, Léon. "L'ancien concept monopole et la contrebande universelle: Le 'commerce interlope' français à la mer du Sud, au début du XVIIIe siècle, type de cette contrebande." *Revue d'histoire économique et sociale*, XIII (1925), pp. 239-299.

———. "*L'asiento* français (1701-1713) et anglais (1713-1750) et le commerce franco-espagnol vers 1700 à 1730." *Revue d'histoire économique et sociale*, XVII (1929), pp. 403-436.

———. "L'importation en France au XVIIIe siècle du boeuf salé d'Irlande." *Revue historique*, CLIX (Sept.-Dec., 1928), pp. 79-95.

Vignon, E. J. M. *Études historiques sur l'administration des voies publiques en France aux dix-septième et dix-huitième siècles*. Paris, 1862-1880. 4 vols. Gives information concerning the inauguration of the system of *grandes corvées*.

Ward, Sir Adolphus William. *Great Britain and Hanover*. Oxford, 1899. 218 pp.

Wiarda, Tileman Dothias. *Ostfriesische Geschichte*. Aurich, 1791-1798. 9 vols. Volumes VII and VIII deal exhaustively with East-Frisian history in the first half of the eighteenth century.

Wiesener, Louis. *Le Régent, l'abbé Dubois et les anglais.* Paris, 1891-1899. 3 vols. The author strongly approves of the policy of Dubois and of the Anglo-French alliance. Based on unpublished French and British sources.

Willequet, Edmond. "Histoire du système de la Barrière dans les négociations antérieures à la paix d'Utrecht." *Annales des Universités de Belgique,* VI-VII (*1847-1848*), (Brussels, 1850), pp. 188-363.

Williams, Basil. "The Duke of Newcastle and the Election of 1734." *English Historical Review,* XII (1897), pp. 448-488.

———. "The Foreign Office of the first two Georges." *Blackwood's Magazine,* CLXXXI (Jan.-June, 1907), pp. 92-105.

———. "The Foreign Policy of England under Walpole." *English Historical Review,* XV (1900), pp. 251-276, 479-494, 665-698; XVI (1901), pp. 67-83, 308-327, 439-451. A brilliant study of European diplomatic history from about 1721 to the second Treaty of Vienna (March 16, 1731).

———. *The Life of William Pitt, Earl of Chatham.* London, 1913. 2 vols. Volume I gives an excellent account of the war fever in 1738-1739.

———. *Stanhope.* Oxford, 1932. 478 pp. An excellent biography; not the least of this book's merits is that it shows the relation between the affairs of northern and southern Europe during Stanhope's ministry.

Wilson, Arthur M. "The Logwood Trade in the Seventeenth and Eighteenth Centuries." *Essays in the History of Modern Europe* (Donald C. McKay, editor; New York, 1936), pp. 1-15.

Wood, A. C. "The English Embassy at Constantinople, 1660-1762." *English Historical Review,* XL (1925), pp. 533-561.

Wright, Thomas. *England under the House of Hanover; Its History and Condition during the Reigns of the Three Georges, Illustrated from the Caricatures and Satires of the Day.* London, 1848-1849. 2 vols.

Yorke, Philip C. *The Life and Correspondence of Philip Yorke, Earl of Hardwicke, Lord High Chancellor of Great Britain.* Cambridge [England], 1913. 3 vols.

Zeller, Gaston. "La monarchie d'ancien régime et les frontières naturelles." *Revue d'histoire moderne,* VIII (1933), pp. 305-333.

Zwiedineck-Südenhorst, Hans von. "Die Anerkennung der pragmatischen Sanction Karls VI. durch das deutsche Reich." *Mittheilungen des Instituts für oesterreichische Geschichtsforschung,* XVI (1895), pp. 276-341.

INDEX

INDEX

Acadia, 43, 300, 323.

Act of Settlement (1700), 50.

Adelaide of Savoy, mother of Louis XV, 23.

Aguesseau, Henri-François d', chancellor of France (1717-51), 178-9.

Ahmed III, sultan of Turkey (1703-30), 148.

Aix-la-Chapelle, 165; treaty of (1748), 89, 136 *n.*, 347.

Albany, trade with French at, 302.

Alberoni, Giulio, Cardinal, prime minister of Spain (1716-19), 9, 10, 11, 13 *and n.*

Aldobrandini, Alessandro, papal nuncio at Madrid (1717-27), 160, 173 *n.*

Aleppo, 294.

Algiers, 75, 76.

Alliance of Hanover, *see* Hanover, Alliance of.

Alliance of Vienna, *see* Vienna, Alliance of.

Almanza, battle of (1707), 44 *n.*

Alsace, 344.

Amelia of Saxony (1724-60), wife of Don Carlos, 280.

Amelot de Chaillou, Jean-Jacques, French secretary of state for foreign affairs (1737-44), 134 *n.*, 288 *n.*, 323, 337, 342, 344.

Amhurst, Nicholas, British political writer, 210 *n.*

Amsterdam, treaty of (1717), 139.

Andalusia, 44.

Anderson, Adam (*d.* 1765), British writer on trade, 117 *n.*, 119.

Andrezel, Vicomte d', French minister at Constantinople (1724-7), 147, 148.

Anfossy, Sieur d', French secret envoy to the king of Sardinia (1726), 148, 152.

Angervilliers, Nicolas-Prosper Bauyn d', French minister of war (1728-40), 93 *n.*

Anna (1709-1759), eldest daughter of George II, 115 *n.*, 137 *n.*

Anna Ivanovna, czarina (1730-40), 235, 241 *n.*, 271, 340 *n.*; *see also* Russia.

Anna Petrovna, dau. of Peter the Great, wife of Charles Frederick of Holstein-Gottorp, 140 *n.*

Anne, wife of Philip Lewis of Neuburg, 154.

Anne, queen of England (1702-7) and of Great Britain (1707-14), 44 *n.*

Anthony Farnese, duke of Parma (1727-31), 12 *n.*, 228.

Antin, Antoine-François de Pardaillan de Gondrin, marquis d' (*d.* 1741), vice admiral of France, 76, 319, 323.

Antin, Louis-Antoine de Pardaillan de Gondrin, duc d' (*d.* 1736), 273 *n.*

Antwerp, congress of, 136 *n.*, 228 *n.*; treaty of (1715), 44 *n.*, 128 *n.*; *see also* Barrier.

Appel comme d'abus, 237 *and n.*

Argenson, Marc-Pierre de Voyer de Paulmy, comte d', French minister of war (1742-57), 343.

Argenson, René-Louis de Voyer de Paulmy, marquis d', French secretary of state for foreign affairs (1744-7), 62 *n.*, 98 *n.*, 185 *n.*, 337; quoted, 66, 97.

Armenonville, Joseph - Jean - Baptiste Fleuriau d', keeper of the seals (1722-7), 178-9.

Armstrong, Colonel (later Brigadier-General) John (*d.* 1742), British military expert, 158, 182 *n.*

Asiento, Portuguese, 46; French, 43, 46 *and n.*; British, 43 *and n.*, 53, 117-21,

409

early life of, 22-4; preceptor of Louis XV, 23, 25-6; influence of, upon, 21; and the Duke of Bourbon, 21, 27-8, 31, 34-6, 40; during the Regency, 26-7; and Marshal Villeroy, 23, 26-7; member of the *conseil de conscience*, 26; devoutness of, 103 *and n.*; opposition of, to the Jansenists, 23-4, 26, 177-8 *and n.*; and Maria Leszczynska, 34-5; and the Abbé of Saint-Pierre, 24-5, 97; diplomatic task of, upon assuming office, 29, 40-1, 91, 101-3, 149-50; condition of France improved under, 3-4, 42, 63, 67 *n.*, 88-90, 290-317, 345-7; pacific policy of, 54-5, 225-6; economical policy of, 55, 68-9; interest of, in French trade, 55-68, 197-8, 292 *n.*, 317; naval policy of, 71-88, 323-4; awareness of, of the disadvantages of the British alliance, 99, 124, 166, 197; maintains stability of the currency, 63; and fiscal reform, 68-71; leisurely negotiations of, 189-90; ministerial changes made by, 92-3; character of, 93-101; secretiveness of, 98; jealous spirit of, 74, 95-7; skill of, in governing the court, 96-7; policy of, misunderstood by contemporaries, 94-100; becomes a cardinal, 93; regards France as a "satiated" power, 105-6; and Austria, 104-13, 162-5, 168, 196, 200-2, 215-7, 241-2, 251, 261-4, 274-6, 279-80, 319-21, 323, 327-30, 336, 343; and the Pragmatic Sanction, 104-7, 229-30, 232, 277, 328, 331, 336; and the Ostend Company, 129, 162-6; and Denmark, 144, 323; and Great Britain, 41, 58, 76, 86-7, 113-6, 132-4, 138, 143, 144, 149-50, 151-2, 158-9, 166-7, 168, 174-5, 180-4, 190, 196-7, 202-3, 204, 207-9, 213-4, 217, 219, 221-227, 230, 250-1, 255-9, 262-3, 266-8, 278, 281-3, 290, 322-6, 341-2, 346; German policy of, 110-2, 147, 224, 274; and the "Electoral Union," 193-4, 202, 208; and Poland, 144-6; and Prussia, 139, 280 *n.*, 318-9, 323, 332, 334-5; and Russia, 140-1, 319-21;

and Spain, 103-4, 149, 159-62, 172, 282-3, 321-2; and Sardinia, 148-9; and Sweden, 142-4; and Turkey, 147-8, 247 *n.*, 319-21; and the United Provinces, 129-38, 245-6, 257-9, 323, 341; and the Preliminaries of Paris (1727), 152-67; increasingly independent of Great Britain, 175-6, 210-1, 213-4; and Chauvelin, 176-84, 247, 253, 258, 261-2, 269; marks of confidence in, 179; makes Chauvelin his adjunct, 236-7; co-operation with, 183-4; disagreement with, 272-4, 276-7; and the Convention of the Pardo (1728), 188-191; and the Congress of Soissons (1728-9), 192-206; attempts of, to play the mediator, 182, 197, 199, 211, 213-4; and the treaty of Seville, 210; policy of, following that treaty, 214, 215-9, 221-2; isolated by Great Britain, 227-9; adopts in consequence a waiting policy, 229-32, 238-9; failure of, to foresee British change of policy, 224-7; domestic difficulties of, 177-8, 237-8; subtle policy of, during the War of the Polish Succession, 54, 76, 242 *and n.*, 247-54; accused of pusillanimity, 247-8, 254; secretly desires to secure Lorraine, 251-4; secures Dutch neutrality, 132-4, 245-6; prevents British intervention, 250-1, 255-9; excludes the British from peace negotiations, 262-3, 264, 266-8, 278; engages in secret peace negotiations, 260-4; really alters the balance of power, 248-9, 252-3, 264-265; desire of, for *rapprochement* with Austria, 196, 264, 265, 274-6, 277 *n.*, 279-80, 351-8; mediation of, in the Turkish war, 279 *and n.*, 319-21; contemplates intervention therein, 60-1, 76-7, 282-3, 288, 290, 321-4; isolates Great Britain, 322-6; policy of, and the Austrian succession (1740), 327-30; frustrated by the schemes of Belle-Isle, 330-1, 332-3, 335-8; and Belle-Isle, 330-1, 332-8, 343; half-measures taken by, 329-31, 337; distress of,